EAST CENTRAL EUROPE
AND COMMUNISM

The communists of East Central Europe came to power promising to bring about genuine equality, paying special attention to achieving gender equality, to build up industry and create prosperous societies, and to use music, art, and literature to promote socialist ideals. Instead, they never succeeded in filling more than a third of their legislatures with women and were unable to make significant headway against entrenched patriarchal views; they considered it necessary (with the sole exception of Albania) to rely heavily on credits to build up their economies, eventually driving them into bankruptcy; and the effort to instrumentalize the arts ran aground in most of the region already by 1956, and, in Yugoslavia, by 1949.

Communism was all about planning, control, and politicization. Except for Yugoslavia after 1949, the communists sought to plan and control not only politics and the economy, but also the media and information, religious organizations, culture, and the promotion of women, which they understood in the first place as involving putting women to work. Inspired by the groundbreaking work of Robert K. Merton on functionalist theory, this book shows how communist policies were repeatedly undermined by unintended consequences and outright dysfunctions.

Sabrina P. Ramet is a Professor Emerita at the Norwegian University of Science & Technology (NTNU). She earned her Ph.D. in Political Science at UCLA in 1981. She is the author of 15 previous scholarly books, including *Alternatives to Democracy in Twentieth-Century Europe: Collectivist Visions of Modernity* (Central European University Press, 2019).

Routledge Open History

Routledge Open History provides a platform for the open access publication of monographs and edited collections across the full breadth of the discipline from Medieval History until the present day. Books in the series are available for free download and re-use according to the terms of Creative Commons licence via the Routledge and Taylor & Francis website, as well as third party discovery sites such as the Directory of OAPEN Library, Open Access Books, PMC Bookshelf, and Google Books.

Publication will be arranged via a Gold Open Access model. If you have a book proposal for the series, please contact Rob Langham at robert.langham@tandf. co.uk Note that the series is not the only platform for publishing open access at Routledge but the aim is for it to be front and central in our open access publishing in History.

Islam and the Trajectory of Globalization
Rational Idealism and the Structure of World History
Louay M. Safi

Public and Private Welfare in Modern Europe
Productive Entanglements
Edited by Fabio Giomi, Célia Keren, and Morgane Labbé

East Central Europe and Communism
Politics, Culture, and Society, 1943–1991
Sabrina P. Ramet

EAST CENTRAL EUROPE AND COMMUNISM

Politics, Culture, and Society, 1943–1991

Sabrina P. Ramet

Routledge
Taylor & Francis Group

LONDON AND NEW YORK

Designed cover image: © Alamy

First published 2023
by Routledge
4 Park Square, Milton Park, Abingdon, Oxon OX14 4RN

and by Routledge
605 Third Avenue, New York, NY 10158

Routledge is an imprint of the Taylor & Francis Group, an informa business

British Library Cataloguing-in-Publication Data
A catalogue record for this book is available from the British Library

ISBN: 978-1-032-31818-9 (hbk)
ISBN: 978-1-032-31820-2 (pbk)
ISBN: 978-1-003-31151-5 (ebk)

DOI: 10.4324/9781003311515

Typeset in Bembo
by Apex CoVantage, LLC

Hope paints a picture of a possible future. The more we struggle to make that hope a reality, the more committed we become to our dream of how the future should look and the more our collective identity is bound up with that dream. And when our efforts fail of their purpose or, worse, lead us into a future different from that to which we aspired, it is understandable that we may feel betrayed by those who sketched the dream for us.

In memory of Robert K. Merton

CONTENTS

PREFACE

There have been a number of undertakings to recount the history of East Central Europe either focusing exclusively on the years of communist rule or covering both the years of communist rule and years of post-communist rule. Inevitably, some of these books have been better than others. But what has struck me about all of those which I have read is that their attention is largely focused on politics and economics, typically with some limited discussion of religious organizations and, where culture is concerned, taking account only of the Czechoslovak rock group, Plastic People of the Universe, because members of that group were put on trial in 1976. However good some of these accounts have been, I have felt that, by omitting any serious discussion of the communists' policies regarding literature, orchestral music, and pictorial art, reducing discussion of policies declared to have been developed to promote gender equality, and offering at best circumscribed accounts of the fortunes of the religious communities of the region, these accounts have omitted important parts of the history of communism in East Central Europe. I am convinced that these sectors are of fundamental importance in any society and have seen that the communists assigned a certain priority to policies in these sectors.

Yet, even though the communists worked out not only economic plans (the famous "five-year plan" among them), but also plans for the cultural sector, for gender policies, and for religious policy, their policies repeatedly had unintended consequences which worked against the objectives of those policies, whether directly or indirectly. This book is an effort both to offer a more complete history of East Central Europe under communism and also to show how the unintended consequences of policies in all of these sectors, especially in the economic sector, contributed in important ways to the eventual unravelling of communism. It is vital to keep in view the fact that a one-party system (de facto one-party system in certain states in the region) excluded political competition, except between factions within each communist party. Thus, at its base, the communist system was fundamentally illegitimate in the eyes of many of its citizens. All of these factors fed into the decay of the communist system, which began immediately after its establishment, as shown by the anti-communist upheavals in East Germany in 1953 and Hungary in 1956. When the Soviet invasion of Czechoslovakia in 1968 ended any hope of using the local communist party to promote a more liberal system, those opposed to communism looked for new ways to find ways to live in truth, as Václav Havel put it, and to press for communist recognition of certain rights. The rise of the Solidarity trade union in Poland in 1980 was an expression of the demand for recognition of the right to found independent trade unions responsive to their members. Although the Polish communist party retracted its legal recognition of Solidarity just over a year after the union's legal registration, that short period of legality had changed the thinking of Poles and also provided a model noticed elsewhere in the bloc. Ultimately, it was seriously flawed economic policies especially but not only in East Germany and Poland that drove all of the countries of the Soviet bloc deep into debt, making the communist systems in those countries unsustainable; but it was independent activists (dissidents) and religious organizations that provided visions for an alternative future.

Yugoslavia and Albania shared some of the features and problems of the bloc but chartered their own courses – in both countries from the very beginning but breaking with the Soviet Union only in 1948 where Yugoslavia was concerned, and in 1960–61 where Albania was concerned. The Yugoslav communists presided over a multiethnic federation in which the branch parties in the constituent republics quarrelled over the structure of the system, over the extent of powers to be allowed to the republics, over policies, and, for a while, also over the ethnic identity of the Muslim inhabitants of Bosnia-Herzegovina – today usually called Bosniaks. The collapse of communism in Yugoslavia coincided with the country's breakup, while in Albania the collapse came about as a consequence of the increasingly obvious untenability of a left-wing one-party system.

Some readers may associate the communist era in East Central Europe with the years 1945–89. However, I have chosen a slightly longer time-frame for this book, starting the story with the proclamation by the communist-led Anti-Fascist Council for the People's Liberation of Yugoslavia of a provisional government for Yugoslavia in November 1943, followed by the proclamation of a (communist) provisional government for Poland in July 1944. I end the story in 1991 with the outbreak of the War of Yugoslav Succession in June of that year and with the holding of the first multiparty elections held in Albania since 1923 (in April) and the first multi-party elections held under the post-communist constitution in Bulgaria (in October).

I am deeply grateful to Rob Langham, publisher at Routledge, for having commissioned me to write this book. I also wish to thank Lucian Leustean for checking all the chapters, Lavinia Stan for helpful feedback on chapters 1 and 5, Peter Sohlberg for helpful feedback on chapter 1, Gordana P. Crnković, Daša Duhaček, Bernd Fischer, Jože Pirjevec, Zdenko Radelić, and Gregor Tomc for helpful suggestions for chapter 5, and Tatjana Aleksić, Nikica Barić, Agnes Barla-Szabo,

Frank Cibulka, Gordana P. Crnković, Zachary T. Irwin, Branko Milanović, Ines Murzaku, Irena Pavlović, Neal Pease, Isabel Ströhle, Radina Vučetić, and Milan Vukomanović for their generosity in sending me useful books. I am grateful too to Daniela Kalkandjeva for sending me some of her papers dealing with the Bulgarian Orthodox Church. I am also grateful to Vladimir Đorđević for tracking down certain information about the representation of women in Czechoslovak institutions and translating it from Czech for me. A special thanks also to librarians Magnus Rom Jensen, Jenny Bakken Aslaksen, Inger Marie Gran, Joost Hegle, Jan Larsen, Astrid Dalåmo Letnes, Mildred Moen, and Maylen Valsø for their assistance with this project. I also benefited greatly from access for a full year (January 2021 to January 2022) to the online holdings of the University of Illinois Library at Urbana-Champaign and am grateful to John Randolph, Joseph Lenkart, Stephanie Porter, Maureen Elizabeth Marshall, James Fleener, and Rachel Stauffer of the Russian, East European, and Eurasian Center for making this possible. I am also grateful to Neva Hahn, who read some State Department reports about Poland, Bulgaria, and Albania for me and also tracked down a microfilm of *Borba* and translated certain articles from that paper for me. I am also grateful to Palgrave Macmillan (Springer) for permission to reprint in chapter 2 an abridged version of the chapter dealing with the Soviet occupation zone in Germany from my book, *Nonconformity, Dissent, Opposition, and Resistance in Germany, 1933–1990: The Freedom to Conform* (2020). As ever, I am also deeply appreciative of the interest my partner, Chris, has taken in my work and for her moral support of this endeavor.

Finally, looking to the future, Lavinia Stan, Professor of Political Science at St. Francis Xavier University, and I are already at work on a volume devoted to East Central Europe during the years from 1989 to the present.

Sabrina P. Ramet
Saksvik, Norway

GLOSSARY

Brezhnev Doctrine The doctrine that, whenever a socialist system is endangered and eroded, it is the *duty* of other socialist states to intervene and restore socialism.

Central Committee an executive body typically consisting of between 40 and 200 members, with additional numbers of candidate members, the Central Committee was nominally the highest executive body of the communist party, between Congresses but in practice it served primarily to discuss policy options and remained subordinate to the Politburo.

COMECON The Council of Mutual Economic Relations, consisting of the Soviet Union and member states of the Soviet bloc. COMECON was established in January 1949 and renamed the Organization for International Economic Cooperation in 1991.

Cominform Abbreviation for the Communist Information Bureau, which was founded in September 1947 with nine members (the communist parties of the Soviet Union, Bulgaria, Czechoslovakia, Hungary, Poland, Romania, Yugoslavia, France, and Italy). Initially headquartered in Belgrade, the Cominform moved its seat to Bucharest after Yugoslavia was expelled from this organization. The Cominform's main function was to generate and disseminate propaganda in the interests of the Soviet Union. It was shut down on 17 April 1956 as a concession to Belgrade, after the Soviets and Yugoslavs reconciled.

Communism (a) the political creed that, in practice, involved establishment of a one-party state, the nationalization of the means of production, central planning, a dream of changing people's thinking and values to the point that one could speak of a "New Socialist Man" and "New Socialist Woman", and an undertaking to variously limit, control, and marginalize religion or instrumentalize it to advance the objectives of the ruling party and, in the long term, to

eradicate at least religious institutions, if not also religious beliefs altogether;
(b) the final stage of post-revolutionary development, in which the state, law,
and all institutions of coercion (above all the police) will cease to exist, and
hence references in Marxism-Leninism to the "withering away of the state".

Comrade   a form of address reserved for members of the party in good standing,
for example "Comrade Honecker".

Cosmopolitanism   In communist parlance, an unhealthy receptivity to ideas,
culture, and politics from countries not ruled by communist parties.

Formalism   Art for art's sake, art or music in which the creator places stress on
the form and structure of the work of art or music; non-political art.

Ideology   an interrelated set of assumptions about and interpretations of social
and political phenomena, values, and lessons drawn from the political past,
codified into doctrine, identifying enemies and communicated through specific jargon making use of value-laden language.

Marxism–Leninism   the ideology derived from the writings of Karl Marx
(1818–1883) and Vladimir Ilyich Lenin (1870–1924); the same as communism.

Politburo (or Presidium)   the highest executive body of the communist party,
consisting typically of between 8 and 15 (full) members and between 5 and 8
candidate members, the locus of strategic decision-making.

Purge   removal from office, sometimes to include also removal from membership
in the party; some purges were bloodless, while some involved the execution
of the persons being purged.

Self-criticism   a ritual prescribed in most communist states and used either as a
means to a partial rehabilitation of the person engaging in this ritual (typically
entailing demotion) or as a way of delegitimating that person as a preliminary
to his or her removal from office.

Self-management   The system introduced in Yugoslavia between 1950 and 1952
through which workers' councils were organized and given some responsibility in their respective enterprises.

Socialism (in communist jargon)   an intermediary stage preceding the
achievement of full communism, in which norms of equality are promulgated;
a one-party state functions on the basis of socialist law, and with the promotion of gender equality, control of culture and the media, promotion of literacy
(where literacy levels were low), and control of organized religion.

Socialist realism   An officially sanctioned style imposed in East Central Europe
after World War Two until 1956 in some countries, and longer in others, for all
branches of culture, including painting, literature, concert music (orchestral,
chamber, opera), sculpture, and film. The doctrine of socialist realism required
that socialism (and the construction of communism) be portrayed in heroic
terms and that communist leaders be shown as strong and wise. Workers in all
fields were portrayed as positive heroes, including engineers, scientists, bricklayers, and farmers.

UNRRA   The United Nations Relief and Rehabilitation Administration, founded
in November 1943 and disbanded in September 1948.

The Warsaw Pact   the military alliance of the Soviet bloc, consisting of the Soviet Union, the German Democratic Republic, Poland, Czechoslovakia, Hungary, Romania, and Bulgaria, and, until 1961 in actual terms and until 1968 nominally, Albania. Officially known as the Warsaw Treaty Organization, the Soviet-led alliance was formed in May 1955 and dissolved in February 1991.

ACRONYMS

Rather than deriving all acronyms from local languages or, alternatively, all acronyms from English, I have decided on a mixed system, opting for those acronyms which are most common in the literature. Thus, for example, for the Socialist Unity Party of Germany, I use the acronym SED, derived from the German original, Sozialistische Einheitspartei Deutschlands, while, for the Bulgarian Communist Party, I use the acronym BCP, derived from the English. I trust that readers of this book will find this system user-friendly.

ACP	Albanian Communist Party
APL	Albanian Party of Labor
AUW	Albanian Union of Women
B	Belgrade
BCP	Bulgarian Communist Party
C	confidential
CC	Central Committee
CDU	Christlich Demokratische Union (Christian Democratic Union – Germany, East or West)
CIA	Central Intelligence Agency
COMECON	Council for Mutual Economic Relations
CPSU	Communist Party of the Soviet Union
CPY	Communist Party of Yugoslavia
CSCE	Commission on Security and Cooperation in Europe
CzCP	Czechoslovak Communist Party
D	Dispatch
DBD	Demokratische Bauernpartei Deutschlands (Democratic Peasant Party of Germany)
decl.	declassified
FIA	Freedom of Information Act
FM	Foreign Minister

GDR	German Democratic Republic
HCP	Hungarian Communist Party
HSWP	Hungarian Socialist Workers' Party
HWP	Hungarian Workers' Party
KOK	Committee for the Defense of the Country (Poland)
KOS	Committee for Social Resistance (Poland)
KPN	Confederation for an Independent Poland
LCY	League of Communists of Yugoslavia
LDPD	Liberal-Demokratische Partei Deutschlands (Liberal-Democratic Party of Germany)
NA	National Archive (Maryland, USA)
NATO	North Atlantic Treaty Organization
NDH	Nezavisna Država Hrvatska (Independent State of Croatia)
NDPD	National-Demokratische Partei Deutschlands (National-Democratic Party of Germany)
NPP	National Peasant Party (Hungary)
OPEC	Organization of Petroleum Exporting Countries
PM	Prime Minister
PPR	Polish Workers' Party
PPS	Polish Socialist Party
PSL	Polish Peasant Party
PZPR	Polska Zjednoczona Partia Robotnicza (Polish United Workers' Party)
RCP	Romanian Communist Party
S	secret
SAWPY	Socialist Alliance of Working People of Yugoslavia
SBZ	Sowjetische Besatzungszone (Soviet Occupation Zone)
SD	Stronnictwo Demokratyczne (Democratic Party – Poland)
SDP	Social Democratic Party
SED	Sozialistische Einheitspartei Deutschlands (Socialist Unity Party of Germany)
SHP	Smallholders' Party (Hungary)
SL	Suzzallo Library, University of Washington
SMAD	Sowjetische Militäradministration in Deutschland (Soviet Military Administration in Germany)
SPD	Sozialdemokratische Partei Deutschlands (Social Democratic Party of Germany)
T	Telegram
TKK	Interim Coordinating Committee (Poland)
TM	Transcendental Meditation
WSN	Freedom-Justice-Independence (Poland)
WTO	Warsaw Treaty Organization, i.e., the Warsaw Pact
Z	Zagreb
ZSL	Zjednoczone Stronnictwo Ludowe (United Peasant Party – Poland)

FOREWORD: AN INVITATION TO IDEALISTIC REALISM

Vladimir Tismaneanu

Sabrina Ramet is one of the finest, most insightful analysts of East-Central European politics, societies, and cultures. Her historical knowledge matches the keen understanding of the intimate relations between ideas, institutions, and human behaviors. This book bears testimony to her comprehensive understanding of the often-uncanny interplay of traditions, memories, nostalgias, and symbols in the making and unmaking of modern national communities and state entities in a region still haunted by the shadows of past heroes, victories, defeats, illusions, and disappointments. This book belongs to a tradition which includes the works of distinguished scholars such as Ivo Banac, Daniel Chirot, Jan T. Gross, Andrew Janos, Barbara and Charles Jelavich, Ken Jowitt, Mark Kramer, Joseph Rothschild, Gale Stokes, Peter Sugar, and from the younger generation Maria Bucur, John Connelly, Grzegorz Ekiert, Padraic Kenney, Charles King, Jan Kubik, Nicholas J. Miller, Marci Shore, Timothy Snyder, and Lavinia Stan. Professor Ramet's methodology is sophisticated and rigorous. She respects facts, shares information with the reader, but does it in a compelling conceptual framework which combiners historical interpretation, sociological perspective, and psychological acumen. What we have here is a thrilling panorama of the emergence, dynamics, crises, and final breakdown of what used be called the Soviet Bloc. With a sure hand, Sabrina Ramet highlights the dialectics of exogenous and endogenous factors in the establishment of Leninist regimes. This explains her special discussion of the two "eccentric" cases: Yugoslavia and Albania. Both Titoism (from Josip Broz Tito) and Enverism (from Enver Hoxha) belong to a tradition that political historians regard as Balkan Communism. In both cases, the cult of the leader was a strong ingredient for a politics of defiance to foreign intervention. The difference was however decisive: Tito's challenge to Stalin led to a critique of the Stalinist despotic model whereas Hoxha's stubborn Stalinism led to anti-Titoism, anti-Khrushchevism, and a romance with Maoism.

Professor Ramet writes vividly about human passions and does not pretend to be dispassionate. For her objectivity does not exclude empathy with the oppressed. She knows the enthusing power of ideas and invites the reader to a fascinating journey through some of the most dramatic moments of the second half of what historian Eric Hobsbawm called "the age of extremes"; the Cold War, the emergence of "people's democracies" in East Central Europe, Yugoslav leader Josip Broz Tito's defiance of Stalin's imperialism, post-Stalin disenchantment, Nikita Khrushchev's onslaught on Stalin's "cult of personality", the Polish October, the Hungarian Revolution, the Prague Spring, Romania's "national Stalinism", the rise of alternative forms of social activism, countercultural challenges to the monopolistic Communist ideology are all there. I write this text a week after I came back to Washington, DC, from a conference at Colby College in Waterville, Maine, titled "Havel and the Crisis of Our Times." Among the participants, a former dissident and Charter 77 spokesman, the ambassadors to the US, Israel, and UK, author of the seminal Havel biography Michael Zantovsky, Canadian writer, cultural critic and main translator of Havel's writings into English, Paul Wilson, French political scientist Jacques Rupnik, and Yale historian Marci Shore were all in attendance. Also from Yale, historian Timothy Snyder delivered an engrossing keynote address linking Havel's political and moral worldview and the values cherished by Ukrainian president Volodymyr Zelensky. The themes we explored converged with Ramet's theoretical, historical, cultural, and moral concerns: The crisis of truth, the crisis of values, the crisis of language, and the crisis of kindness. Having experienced the totalitarian regimentation, coercion, and surveillance, the denizens of the countries analyzed by Sabrina Ramet know what Putinism is about. Even those who were not born in 1968 when the USSR invaded Czechoslovakia and crushed the experiment in socialism with a human face, know the fundamental difference between legitimate and illegitimate political regimes, between Lie and Truth. This is Havel's idealism, the conviction that human beings are born to be free, that Ramet shares and explains masterfully.

This is a book about the revolutionary tradition and its forgotten treasure, to paraphrase the title of a famous essay by Hannah Arendt. Ramet's book is a marvelous exercise in excavating the enduring values and ideals which inspired the men and the women of East Central Europe's successive upheavals. Is this idealism? I proudly admit it, without succumbing to inchoate and groundless reveries. Havel and the members of Charter 77 were not some sectarian utopians. Sabrina Ramet documents persuasively how these civil society initiatives, the quintessential antisystemic movement from below, articulated responses to increasingly inept official policies. In my own writings, generously cited in the book, I tried to formulate the main characteristics of the anti-political politics developed within the unofficial "niches". In some countries, civil society initiatives developed more broadly than in others. The explanation is linked to the nature of the communist political cultures, the existence of what the late historian Tony Judt called "the usable past" which emerging democratic forces could invoke and revive. Ramet is at her best when exploring these efforts to resist ideological impositions and the role of critical intellectuals in debunking the official mendacious narratives. A political and philo-sophical essay such as Havel's "The Power of the Powerless" had tremendous awak-ening, mobilizing, and liberating effects. It contained a realistic understanding of how non-conformity comes into being, the phenomenology of self-assertion, the recognition of the corrosive impact of truth on a system built on self-reproducing, mechanically repeated, hollow slogans.

Sabrina Ramet discusses the immense gap between the ideological pretense of the communist elites (the professed goals) and their failure to deliver even a modicum of the promised Utopia. It was precisely this ideological decline, the obsolescence of the original egalitarian pledge, the rampant corruption, the self-destructive cynicism that led to the terminal crisis. Ramet is right in considering the birth of the independent, self-governing workers' union Solidarity and its legal recognition by the dwindling authoritarian regime as having signaled the imminent breakdown. An intensifying political and moral crisis, radicalized by favorable fac-tors such as Pope John Paul II's appeals to living without fear, generated a revolu-tionary situation first in Poland, then in the whole region. This was a peculiar type of revolution: Non-violent, conscious of its limitations, suspicious of any utopian hubris. They combined reform and revolution in one unprecedented exploit. To use British historian Timothy Garton Ash's concept, they were "refolutions".

As I write these pages, war devastates Ukraine. It is impossible not to notice that Vladimir Putin's kleptocratic tyranny, a self-styled fascism mixed with national-ist mystique and imperial delusions, reminds one of the East German militaristic dictatorship. Professor Ramet's book offers significant elements for grasping what kind of socialism existed in the country where Angela Merkel grew up and where Vladimir Putin lived for five years. Established on October 7, 1949 in the post-WW II Soviet zone of occupation, the so-called German Democratic Republic claimed to be "the first German state of workers and peasants." It was in fact an anti-proletarian police state. Its main institutions were the SED (the "Socialist Unity Party") and the Stasi (State Security). Dissent (political, cultural, religious) was harshly punished. For its entire existence, the regime leaders (Walter Ulbricht, Erich Honecker, Egon Krenz) were hard-core Stalinists. As Ramet points out, here was no real reformist faction in the SED leading bodies. I met the former head of the East German intelligence service Markus (Mischa) Wolf at a conference on "Open Wounds" organized by the Einstein Forum in Potsdam in the Spring of 2005. Among the participants: Tony Judt, Jan T. Gross, Susan Neiman, Eric Hobsbawm, Norbert Frei, Timothy Snyder, Omer Bartov, and Dariusz Stola. Wolf was sun-tanned, wearing Ray-Ban glasses, smiling, and unrepentant. He reiterated all the hackneyed self-exculpatory platitudes about the "original noble principles," etc. Yet, in spite of terror, there were niches, often under Evangelical and Catholic Church shelter, in which civil society was alive. There were conscientious objec-tors who resisted socialist militarism. There were poets and balladeers who defied the asphyxiating drabness of everyday life. Then came glasnost, the gerontocrats at the top were increasingly nervous. On November 9, 1989, the Berlin Wall fell. The East German civic revolution was non-violent. The GDR vanished in

October 1990. Among those who mourned its extinction was a KGB lieutenant-colonel stationed in Dresden. He is now the President of the Russian Federation and the butcher of Ukraine. Retired Stasi General Markus Wolf passed away on November 9, 2006.

Superbly documented, engagingly written, combining persuasively comparative theoretical analysis with political, social, and intellectual history, as well as an interest in ideas and values rather than ideological fallacies, Sabrina Ramet's new book is an outstanding scholarly achievement.

Washington, DC
October 11, 2022

1

COMMUNISM'S UNINTENDED CONSEQUENCES

An introduction[1]

What was communism all about or, more specifically, what was East Central European communism all about? A cautious observer will immediately point out that there were some rather important differences across the communist world and that one needs to be wary of forgetting, for example, that the megalomanic Romanian dictator Ceaușescu, who managed to eke out a measure of independence in domestic policy and even in foreign policy, ought not to be equated with the more self-effacing Husák of Czechoslovakia and Hungary's Kádár, who had to clear policies with the Kremlin before implementing them. And then there were the differences in the status of the Churches across the region (completely suppressed in Albania vs. enjoying some form of support in East Germany, for example) or in agriculture or even in the degree of flexibility in the cultural sector. Even so, the question does not go away. What was communism all about anyway?

Some one-word or two-word answers suggest themselves as pointers in one or another direction. Two seem as useful as any – *organizational monopoly*, pointing to the fact that no independent organizations were allowed to exist, other than the Churches in East Germany, Poland, and Yugoslavia (partially independent in Hungary, thoroughly or largely penetrated in Romania, Bulgaria, and Czechoslovakia); and *planned society*, with the planned economy as the centerpiece, though planning and control were also reflected in communist-sponsored women's organizations and organizations for young people, in efforts to organize people's leisure, and in the control of the media. Yet, for convinced communists, other terms might come to mind: *opportunity*, for the first post-war generation, who were able to rise in newly created hierarchies; *social equality* or *social justice*, for those hoping that communism would bring about a new and better world; and *new man/new woman*, reflecting the communists' ambition to change the way people thought and behaved (never entirely successful but nowhere without some impact at least in the public sphere).

DOI: 10.4324/9781003311515-1

Building socialism and building communism – the terms employed by the communists to refer to the process of constructing and developing a new society –
entailed programs and policies. How well did these work? As the great sociologist
Robert K. Merton pointed out, programs and policies have three kinds of results:
those which are intended and perceived (he called them "manifest functions"); those
which are not intended but are perceived (he called them "side effects"); and those
which are not intended and not perceived at the time or not understood to be connected with the policies which produced them (he called these "latent functions").[2]
Unintended consequences can, in theory, be functional for a specific policy sector
or, conceivably, for the system as a whole, although this seems to imply that policy
planners are so ineffective in their jobs that their results are better only due to consequences they did not intend. In any event, unintended but functional consequences
are not my concern in this book. Merton was, of course, fully aware that, alternatively, unintended consequences can be *dysfunctional*, by which he meant that they
tended to lead "to instability and ultimately change"[3] whether in a specific policy
sector (such as happened with the abandonment of agricultural collectivization in
Poland in 1956) or for the system as a whole. The unintended, dysfunctional consequences of communist policies will be one of my central concerns in this book.

It is a simple matter to identify some of the programs and policies adopted in at
least some of the countries of the region. These would include: economic planning; agricultural collectivization; the suppression of alternative political parties
and independent secular organizations; and the effort to instrumentalize religious
organizations as far as possible and to wean the young generations from religion,
among other means by restricting their access to religious instruction. Although
the manifest functions were not necessarily as useful for the regimes as the communists had hoped, it was the unintended consequences, whether perceived at the
time or not, which produced the major trouble for these regimes. The staggering
debts accumulated by the 1980s by seven of the eight countries in the region and
paid off, at the cost of huge self-inflicted harm only by Romania, were clearly
unintended and just as obviously dysfunctional, even if the elites were aware of
their rising indebtedness to foreign banks. These debts were one of the major
contributors to the collapse of communism in the region but were an unintended
cost of the programs and ambitions of these regimes. Nor did economic planning
ever work as intended, among other reasons because of the difficulty in creating a
mechanism able to respond to supply and demand in the absence of a competitive
market and because of the limits to the information that could be made available
to the planners. Unintended consequences of economic planning included product standardization (only one kind of male doll and two kinds of female doll were
available in Hungarian souvenir shops in 1982, for example), shortages (a perennial
problem), bottle-necks, undertakings by some enterprise manages to go around the
system and ignore regulations (in order to make things work), and even the falsifi-
cation, at least in Albania, of economic data (so that the plan would be realized at
least on paper). Agricultural collectivization had the unintended consequence in

the short run of provoking stiff peasant resistance and, in the long run, of having a negative impact on production. The suppression of alternative political parties and independent secular organizations seemed to be working, more or less, until the summer of 1980, when the rise of the Independent Trade Union Solidarity in Poland and its legalization in November of that year sent tremors throughout the Soviet bloc. Coincidentally, Yugoslavia's President Tito died in May 1980, opening a new chapter in that country's history at the same time that pressures for repluralization were growing in the bloc countries. As for weaning the young from religion, this worked up to a point at one level but backfired at another level: specifically, although belief in God and the saints, in heaven and hell, declined with each passing generation, young people especially in East Germany and Poland gathered around their Churches as their best protectors of human rights including the right to independent culture. The communist hostility to religion, thus, strengthened the legitimacy of the main Churches in those two countries, demonstrating that their policies as regards religion were dysfunctional from the communists' point of view. Yet the communists were pursuing a vision of a historically new civilization – an alternative future.

Communism, as is well known, bore a certain relationship to utopianism – the dream of a better world. Utopia is sometimes thought of as a "perfect" society, frozen in its perfection, changeless. It is immediately obvious that it would be completely impossible to combine perfect freedom, whatever that might mean, with perfect civil order or, again, perfect freedom of the press – however that might be defined – with protection against defamation and libel. Or again, can we actually imagine perfect equality without, at the same time, imagining the homogenization of the population and the crushing of individual creativity? An alternative way to think of utopia is to see it as a project to maximize one or a few values, at the expense of and potentially also to the detriment of others. If we embrace this second understanding of utopia, then one can plausibly argue that, in establishing their control in countries of East Central Europe in the second half of the 1940s, the communists sought to maximize two values – *equality* (even though not to the exclusion of privileges for high-ranking communists or of the political dominance of the Politburo and Central Committee of the communist party) and *control* of political life, the economy, the arts, and social life in general, as well as, in those countries where it was possible, the religious organizations. The communists viewed control as the means to achieve equality and to construct a communist system. Their focus on equality reflected not only their awareness of the profound social, economic, and political inequality prevailing in the region (and, for that matter, in the world at large), but also the sociological/ideological[4] framework they inherited from the writings of Karl Marx and Friedrich Engels. They saw economic inequality between classes and between men and women, inequality at the level of politics (with exploitation at the heart of capitalist politics), and inequality in the family, with women subservient to men. In addition to equality, the communists also sought to maximize control, *their* control of society, of politics, of the means of production since, in their view, no other party could be trusted to construct the eventual communist paradise of equality and leisure where

> each can become accomplished in any branch he wishes, society regulates the general production and thus makes it possible for me to do one thing today and another tomorrow, to hunt in the morning, fish in the afternoon, rear cattle in the evening, criticise after dinner, just as I have a mind, without ever becoming [a] hunter, fisherman, shepherd or critic.[5]

Marx's flight of fancy, written when he was no more than 26 years old, should not be taken literally. What this passage reveals is not a program or even a dream, but rather Marx's hope for a better future in which people would cease to be defined and controlled by their roles in production.

The communists pushed forward with their programs at the expense of the free press, since they understood that not everyone agreed with their plans and at the expense of having an informed, as opposed to a misled, public. Indeed, in all of the communist states of East Central Europe, they established controls over the secular press and, in varying degrees, also over the religious press, relying either on post-publication censorship, as in East Germany and Yugoslavia, or pre-publication censorship everywhere else. The communist press functioned as propaganda. Thus, to take an East German example, the main party newspaper, *Neues Deutschland*, pointed to local successes, such as a successful wheat harvest, while emphasizing problems in the West, such as unemployment in West Germany while ignoring major developments in the outside world, as I saw for myself when I visited four East German cities in 1988. The cost was that locals typically found the official news too boring to bother with or simply refused to believe what they read. The unintended consequence of communist handling of the media was that many people in the region turned to Radio Free Europe, broadcasting out of Munich, for news about their own countries while, in East Germany, most people were able to tune in to West German television.

In agriculture, the communists herded peasants onto collective farms and made them surrender their private farms and livestock to these collectives – to the detriment of agricultural productivity. They established their control over school and university curricula, textbooks, and teaching staff, driving some professors (for example, in East Germany) to flee to the West. Schoolbooks to learn English offered English-language texts with topics such as racial inequality in the United States or America's unpopular war in Vietnam. Or again, in the religious sphere, the communists wanted control, hoping (as already mentioned) to instrumentalize the religious organizations for their own purposes in the short run and to promote the extinction of religion in the long run. Throughout the Soviet bloc states (East Germany, Poland, Czechoslovakia, Hungary, Romania, and Bulgaria) high-ranking communists repeated the formula, "Religion is the private affair of the individual," which in practice meant that religious organizations had no right to engage in the public sphere or to address issues of the day. Among the reasons for communist hostility to religion were the fact that religious organizations promoted rival value systems to the value system of communism and the historical record of religion figuring as a factor for inequality. The communists were able to gain control of episcopal appointments in Romania and Bulgaria and enjoyed partial control of such appointments in Czechoslovakia, where the Catholic Church still exercised its prerogative to veto appointments favored by the communists, but not the right to appoint bishops of whom the communists did not approve. The communists also took control of the Church press in these three countries – which explains why the Romanian Church press was brimming with praise for Romanian dictator Nicolae Ceauşescu. Albania adopted the harshest policies in the religious sphere, imprisoning or encouraging the murder of clergy and eventually, in May 1967, closing or demolishing all 2,169 places of worship and also officially declaring the country an atheistic state.[6] In the German Democratic Republic, Poland, and to a certain extent also Hungary, religious organizations enjoyed more favorable situations after 1956 (and, in Yugoslavia, already beginning in 1952). The unintended consequence of the anti-religious policies was that, after almost half a century of communism, religiosity remained high in most of the region,[7] especially in the countryside, though not in East Germany, even while it had declined steadily in Western Europe.

The communist desire for control extended inevitably to the arts, where the doctrine of socialist realism – hegemonic in the region from the late 1940s until the mid-1950s, and in Romania even longer – was perfectly attuned to the utopianism of the communists. In painting, socialist realism figured "above all [as] a means of replacing reality with an idealised projection of society, conceived to resemble a Communist utopia."[8] According to this formula, the idealized picture of reality was to consist in the first place of construction sites, machine-building, and harvests. Since the communist concept of equality as represented in art involved the reduction of people to typical roles in typical settings, "typicality" was highly prized by those overseeing the cultural sphere. Paintings produced in Slovakia in the hey-day of socialist realism were characterized by a "fetishization of tools and machines" and a "typicalisation of characters according to their class belonging, [with] the same eloquent gestures, the same outfits, and the same exaggerations of expression that resemble the deceptively lifelike quality of wax figures."[9] Among the titles of Slovak paintings from this era we find Mária Medvecká's "The Construction of the Orava Dam" and her "Delivery of the Quota in Upper Orava", as well as Ladislav Guderna's "Construction of a Machinery Station in Galanta". While homogenizing the aesthetic landscape may have succeeded in banishing paintings expressive of personal feelings and individual tastes, it also reduced art to politics and, over time, painters throughout the bloc got fed up with socialist realism and simply abandoned it. That was true also in music and literature.

For citizens of communist states there were some very real benefits, among them: universal and free medical care, guaranteed pensions, generally low crime (although statistics were not always accessible), heavily subsidized prices for basic foods and public transportation, and, for intellectuals, good earnings and financial security as long as they did not write things that offended the authorities. Composers and artists were likewise financially secure as long as the authorities were pleased with their output. And then there was the promise of guaranteed employment (not fully realized in practice[10]). Communist control of the economy produced an interesting side-effect, viz., that workers, for instance in Poland, who objected to increases in food prices could compel the authorities to withdraw the price hikes by going on strike or, in some cases, rioting. In a pluralist system, by contrast, where there is no central authority controlling all the food prices in the country, ordinary people can, at most, apply pressure on specific stores by organizing boycotts.

Communist rule did make some headway with promoting equality, whether by raising levels of literacy significantly or by a partial leveling of wages including between women and men[11] or by introducing extensive welfare benefits ranging from generous maternity leave to childcare nurseries to free medical care. But, as will be seen in chapters 4 and 5, the utopic welfare states, funded by loans and credits contracted from Western banks, proved to be economically unsustainable throughout the region (with a curious exception for Albania which, unlike the other seven states in the region, avoided taking out loans in Western banks). But there is a difference between utopia and utopianism. Utopia is supposed to be an achieved state, a stable order of things in which one can measure the benefits against the costs and unintended consequences (such as huge debts to Western banks) of policy choices. The countries of East Central Europe may have aspired to utopia, but they never achieved it. Moreover, by definition, a utopia does not need to be reformed and yet, in the wake of the change of leadership in Poland in October 1956, the party allowed the collective farms to be dismantled with a return to private farming, in the process retreating on a central component of the communist party's aspiration to the control of society. In addition, in the course of the 1960s, East Germany, Poland,[12] Czechoslovakia, Hungary, Bulgaria,[13] and Yugoslavia all undertook meaningful economic reforms, and, of course, the utopian aspiration was confuted by the realization which gripped communist leaders in 1989 that their formulae were not working and, worse yet, that it was impossible to devise workable formulae within the framework of a one-party system prioritizing economic equality and seeking to maximize control of society whether by arresting "trouble-makers" or bugging their apartments or forcing them into exile, the tapping of private telephones, surveillance by "informal collaborators" with the secret police, the promotion of Marxism-Leninism in the schools, the discrimination against religious believers in education and employment, or collective farms, or the Five-Year Plans for the economy.

I have alluded above to the problem of unintended consequences of communist programs and policies. This will be a recurrent theme throughout the book, with the argument advanced that unintended consequences created complications for communist authorities. This aspect was made more complicated by the facts that social and political change can be driven by intra-elite conflicts and rivalries, as well as by mass discontent, that literature, painting, and music were able to play political roles, with authorities, in response, seeking to control the cultural sphere, and that policy spheres are interconnected and interactive. As Gerald Allen Cohen observed in 1978, in reference to Marxist-Leninist societies, "All elements of social life are interconnected. They strongly influence one another and in aggregate form one inseparable whole."[14]

Marx – himself a utopian[15] – whose ideas, filtered through the writings and speeches of Soviet leaders Lenin and Stalin, figured as a kind of map for East Central European communist leaders, not only felt that the free market was a seedbed for exploitation but also despised what he called "the anarchy of the market". Marx believed that rational planning was the answer and, if planning and control were good for the economy, they were good for all of society, whether for education, the arts, religion, the status of women, or, most obviously, the media. The factory, under the firm hand of the factory director, was Lenin's model for his failed utopia. As Andrzej Walicki observed more than two decades ago, socialism was intended to "transform the whole of society into 'one big factory'. The invisible hand of the market would give way to the visible hand of the creators and executors of the plan . . ..Thus the ideal of the complete elimination of the market and the organization of the whole of society in the likeness of a single big factory was not some kind of 'original sin of Bolshevism', but the very heart of the communist utopia of the founders of Marxism."[16] Josef Stalin, who ruled the Soviet Union unopposed from 1928 to 1953, dictated the politics of the six Soviet bloc states from the consolidation of communist control in those states until his death in 1953. He was determined to realize his own vision of communist utopia in both his own country and the countries of the bloc. There were problems along the way, for example with Polish First Secretary Edward Gierek complaining in 1971 of "specific dogmatic and sectarian errors," a need for "the restoration of respect for socialist law, . . . [and] compromises with revisionism and other tendencies alien to the ideology of our Party."[17] But in spite of such complications, let alone the temporary breakdown of communist control in East Germany in 1953 and Hungary in 1956, and, for that matter, the Czechoslovak Communist Party's launching in early 1968 of a program which the Soviets viewed as nothing less than "counterrevolution",[18] the communist leaders in East Central Europe never lost sight of the importance they attached to programmatic ("ideological" in their language) unity and control or of the desirability of shaping how people thought.

As already noted, when policies have unintended consequences, this can be a force for change; moreover, policy spheres are interconnected so that a liberal phase in terms of rehabilitating innocent victims of terror is likely, for example, to be associated with liberalization in economics (as the Nagy era in Hungary illustrates); and finally, discontent, conflict, and the failure of the system to deliver on its promises can all energize and drive change. The subtitle of this book identifies three central themes: politics, culture, and society. Under politics I understand not just the endless contest over power, policy, and patronage, but also the contest over programs and values. Parliamentary pluralism and communism are not just alternative systems, they are also rival ideologies, offering rival narratives, heroes, and villains. Values are embedded in any political system, but the values espoused by the elites of a system may be challenged by dissidents of various stripes, for example by the members of the independent peace movement in communist East Germany or by novelists writing politically subversive texts, as happened in Hungary in the 1950s. Under culture I focus on pictorial art, music, and literature, although I discuss the more important films produced in Poland, Czechoslovakia, and Yugoslavia in passing. But challenges to the system were found in pictorial art, music, and literature, while film directors who might have thought of producing films challenging the central principles of the system in which they were working, would have taken into account the ease with which their products could be suppressed, even after huge investments. Finally, in looking at society, I have chosen to focus on three spheres: the economy, religion, and gender relations. These three spheres are pivotal for the legitimacy of any system. A system which cannot assure a reasonable standard of living or which attacks the established and traditional religions of the community or violates customary notions of decency in relations between the genders risks losing legitimacy and, potentially, the possibility to continue in operation.

In crediting *functionalism* (not structural-functionalism, which is a special subset of the methodology), I have in mind that it is the proper business of a historian or political scientist or sociologist to investigate not only what governments say their policies are doing, but also what unintended consequences (whether what functionalists have called "latent functions" or side effects) are associated with the policies. Thus, when the communists launched programs of agricultural collectivization in the 1950s, they did not intend that production would be negatively impacted, let alone that resistance would be as strong throughout the region as it was, indeed forcing a permanent retreat from collectivization in Poland and a temporary retreat in Hungary. Or again, when, at the height of Stalinism, purge trials were organized in which various leading communists including László Rajk in Hungary, Traicho Kostov in Bulgaria, and Rudolf Slánský in Czechoslovakia, were executed, the communists carrying out these trials did not intend to see the posthumous rehabilitation of any of them or to witness the opening of investigations into the purge trials. To be interested in history one must be interested in not only intended results but also unintended consequences, and, in the course of things, the responses by elites and populations to these unintended consequences.

As already suggested, policies evolve in interaction with each other and reflect underlying objectives of the regime. Thus, for example, looking at the Soviet bloc especially in the era of Stalinism, one finds that the communist authorities wanted to establish a high degree of control over all aspects of social and political life. The result was that, in the years until 1955 or 1956 in most of the Soviet bloc countries, the communists pursued a hard line in politics (purging rivals, incarcerating those deemed hostile to communism), in economics, in culture, and in the religious sphere, among other policy spheres. When the communists relaxed in one sphere, they usually relaxed in other spheres as well; this was due to the fact that the relaxation of the mid-1950s reflected weakness, but it also reflected the interaction between policy spheres. Both relaxations and rehardenings of policy in the communist era came in response to the realization that existing policies were not working. But these adjustments and policy reversals were made under what Merton called the "imperious immediacy of interest," rather than long-term calculations and therefore having potentially unforeseen and even undesirable consequences over the long term.[19] Thus, as Peter Sohlberg has written, "Functional tensions . . . constitute a strong driving force for change"[20] both at the governmental level and in terms of responses from nongovernmental actors

Functionalism has sometimes been declared to be passé. Some people may find the word embarrassing. But no one could doubt the utility of examining the effects, both manifest and latent, both intended and unintended, of policies or the short-term and long-term ramifications of policies.

Notes

1 I am grateful to Lucian Leustean, Lavinia Stan, and Peter Sohlberg for helpful comments on an earlier draft of this chapter.
2 Robert K. Merton, *Social Theory and Social Structure*, enlarged ed. (New York: Free Press, 1968).
3 Frank W. Elwell, "Merton on Structural Functionalism", in *Socio-Cultural Systems*, at www.faculty.rsu.edu/users/f/felwell/www/Theorists/Essays/Merton1.htm#:~:text=Merton%20insisted%20that%20social%20structures,component%20elements%20of%20sociocultural%20systems [accessed on 30 January 2022].
4 See Henri Lefebvré, *The Sociology of Marx* (New York: Pantheon Books, 2015).
5 Karl Marx and Friedrich Engels, *The German Ideology*, 3rd rev. ed. (Moscow: Progress Publishers, 1976), p. 53.
6 Bernhard Tönnes, "Religious Persecution in Albania", in *Religion in Communist Lands*, Vol. 10, No. 3 (1982), pp. 250–252.
7 See "Religious Belief and National Belonging in Central and Eastern Europe", in *Pew Research Center* (10 May 2017), at www.pewforum.org/2017/05/10/religious-belief-and-national-belonging-in-central-and-eastern-europe/ [accessed on 13 September 2021].
8 Zora Rusinová, "The Embodiment of Communist Utopia: Socialist Realism in Slovakia, 1948–1956", in *The Courtauld* (2015), p. 2 of 13, at https://courtauld.ac.uk/research/research-resources/publications/courtauld-books-online/a-reader-in-east-central-european-modernism-1918-1956/the-embodiment-of-communist-utopia-socialist-realism-in-slovakia-1948-1956/ [accessed on 12 September 2021].
9 *Ibid.*, pp. 4–5 of 13.
10 See, for example: Janina Miedzinska, "Bezrobocie w Polsce", in *Kultura* (Paris), No. 9/215 (195), trans. into German under the title "Fragen der Arbeitslosigkeit in Polen", in *Ost-Probleme*, 20/2965, pp. 622–627; Janez Malačič and Aleš Vahčič, "Yugoslav Economists on Unemployment in Yugoslavia", in *Eastern European Economics*, Vol. 15, No. 4 (Summer 1977), pp. 60–72.
11 See Sharon L. Wolchik, "Ideology and Equality: The Status of Women in Eastern and Western Europe", in *Comparative Political Studies*, Vol. 13, No. 4 (January 1981), pp. 445–476.
12 Adam Bromke, "Poland's Political Crisis", in *The World Today*, Vol. 25, No. 3 (March 1969), p. 119.
13 Re. Bulgaria, see Apostol Pashev, "The New System of Management: An Important Stage in the Development of the Bulgarian Economy", in *Eastern European Economics*, Vol. 5, No. 3 (Spring 1963), pp. 3–8.
14 Gerald Allen Cohen, *Karl Marx's Theory of History: A Defence* (Oxford: Clarendon Press, 1978), p. 283, as quoted in Peter Sohlberg, *Functionalist Construction Work in Social Science: The Lost Heritage* (London and New York: Routledge, 2021), p. 40.

15 See Scott L. Montgomery and Daniel Chirot, *The Shape of the New: Four Big Ideas and How They Made the Modern World* (Princeton, NJ: Princeton University Press, 2015), p. 99.

16 A. Walicki, "The Communist Utopia and the Fate of the Socialist Experiment in Russia", in *Russian Studies in Philosophy*, Vol. 39, No. 4 (Spring 2001), pp. 11, 13.

17 *Party's Tasks in the Further Socialist Development of the Polish People's Republic: Programme Report of the Political Bureau for the 6th PUWP Congress*, Delivered by First Secretary of the Central Committee Edward Gierek (6 December 1971), trans. and published by the Polish Interpress Agency, p. 5.

18 See Kieran Williams, *The Prague Spring and Its Aftermath: Czechoslovak Politics 1968–1970* (Cambridge: Cambridge University Press, 1997).

19 Robert K. Merton, "The Unanticipated Consequences of Purposive Social Action", in *The American Sociological Review*, Vol. 1, No. 6 (December 1936), p. 901.

20 Sohlberg, *Functionalist Construction Work in Social Science*, p. 209.

2

THE SOVIET BLOC, PART ONE

1944–1956[1]

The record of the communist era in East Central Europe fully bears out the four central arguments being advanced in this volume – first, that diverse policy spheres are interconnected and even interactive, so that, for example, a phase of liberalization in the cultural sphere should be expected to be associated with liberalization in the religious sphere as well as in politics (Imre Nagy's term as prime minister in Hungary during 1953–1955 may serve as an example); second, that policies may have not just intended effects (manifest functions, to use the language of the functionalist tradition[2]) but also unintended consequences whether perceived (side effects) or overlooked or ignored (latent functions); third, that just as politics may influence and affect the cultural sector, so too may cultural actors and developments impact and influence the political sphere; and fourth, that change can be driven by conflicts between different opinion groups both at the elite level and, at times, also among the politicized sector of the general population as well as by mass discontent, when it reaches a critical threshold.

Unintended consequences are typically the bane of politicians anywhere. In the Soviet bloc, they compromised regime strategies and subverted the policies, programs, and strategies in play. For example, the programs of agricultural collectivization initiated throughout the bloc which were abandoned temporarily in Hungary and permanently only in Poland were supposed to increase efficiency and production and, ideally, build morale among collectivized farmers, while extending communist control in the agricultural sector. In practice, however, collective farms were never as efficient or productive as private farms, morale could scarcely be described as high, and control of an inefficient sector could not be portrayed as a triumph for communism. Again, the policies adopted in the religious sphere were intended to exploit the Churches and other religious communities in the short run (whether for purposes of foreign policy, as in Bulgaria, or to meet domestic needs, as in East Germany), to bring them under control as soon as possible (achieved

DOI: 10.4324/9781003311515-2

most dramatically in Romania and Bulgaria), and, over the long term, to whittle down the clergy and persuade believers of the falsity of their faith, thereby leading people to abandon their Churches, causing them to implode. In actual practice, the anti-religious policies that were supposed to weaken the faith of believers induced them, in many cases, to hold onto their Churches all the more strongly, viewing them, among other things, as their best defense against the communist regimes (this, most obviously in Poland). And further, while communists dreamt of refashioning human nature on the model of the New Soviet Man and New Soviet Woman, among other means by imposing controls in the cultural sector and on intellectual activity (the former by enforcing the socialist realist formula under which an optimistic vision of the socialist future would be promoted), the unintended consequences were to energize dissent (as per Robert Havemann in East Germany and Václav Havel in Czechoslovakia, for example), giving it a weight it only rarely achieves in pluralist societies and to convince the more talented writers, musicians, film-makers, and artists of the necessity to defy the regime's controls and produce works of integrity and authenticity (as, for example, Czesław Miłosz and film-maker Andrzej Wajda achieved in Poland). Finally, the undertaking to regiment society and to suppress all forms of pluralism (except for the Catholic and Protestant Churches in Poland and East Germany) failed to build a solid foundation for mass conformity, instead producing variously widespread apathy (inducing communist leader János Kádár to say, famously, "He who is not against us is with us") or often quiet hostility to the regime or, at "best", self-centered opportunism.

The nature of communism

Communism was born out of outrage at economic injustice, including child labor, long working hours, low pay, outright exploitation, and the absence of provisions for either universal medical care at government expense or pensions. Inspired by the writings of Karl Marx (1818–1883) and Friedrich Engels (1820–1895), as well as by the often polemical writings of V. I. Lenin (1870–1924), communists dreamt of a better world – a world in which people not only were paid wages on which they could live decently but also would have the leisure to devote time to rewarding or pleasurable activities.[3] They dreamt of a world without alienation, without exploitation, and most definitely without slavery. They dreamt of a world in which everyone would be treated equally on the basis of merit or need. And yet, in practice, communism looked very different from the image sketched in *The Communist Manifesto* or *The German Ideology*. The ruthless rule of Soviet leader Josef Vissarionovich Stalin (1878–1953), whose role in shaping the politics in East Central Europe after 1945 was decisive, may afford part of the explanation– which is not to excuse Vladimir Ilyich Lenin (1870–1924), founder of the Bolshevik Party, from culpability. Other relevant factors would include: the relative backwardness (including widespread illiteracy) of the East European societies in which a version of the communist project was undertaken; and the regimentation of these societies, with controlled media, controlled youth organizations, and a distrust of bourgeois parties that reinforced the decision to impose one-party rule. With some variation in policies across the eight East Central European countries to be ruled by communist parties, the general assumption was that, insofar as religion offered a rival value system to that of communism, the religious associations presented a three-fold challenge: first, by espousing values different from and independent of the values of Marxism-Leninism; second, by looking to God – rather than the General Secretary of the party – as the highest authority in moral, and thus also political, choices; and third, by maintaining hierarchies independent (in some cases) of communist control. The communists were able, in many cases, to infiltrate, compromise, or subvert local hierarchies – in some cases by sending uncooperative bishops to labor camps[4] – but they were never able to resolve the challenges presented by the religious associations' rival value systems and worship of God.

Economics lay at the heart of the communist promise of a better life. Looking at the experiences of nineteenth-century Western Europe (and, for that matter, the United States), communists did not nurture any illusions that competition between economic enterprises would redound to the benefit of all. On the contrary, since free enterprise – capitalism – was driven by the desire to maximize profits, the natural tendency of capitalist society could only be for enterprises to make use of every means to aggrandize their wealth and to squeeze out their competition whenever possible. The solution, they concluded, was to regulate the economy in the equal interest of everyone and, moreover, to entrust a central party or government body with the responsibility and authority to plan investments and control prices and wages. Since neither the party nor the government had a vested interest in profit-making, the result would be – so they hoped – an economy driven by a commitment to social justice. For this to work, the planning system, GOSPLAN in the Soviet Union, would have to have essentially complete information about available supplies, local demand, fluctuations in the socialist market, etc., as well as control over the flows of raw materials, goods, and services. In actual practice, planners not only did not have as much information as they needed, but also faced the challenge, especially in the years up to 1956, that enterprises would submit reports of production which satisfied the expectations of the planners, rather than reports which provided accurate information. Corruption was another problem. And then there were informal channels, by-passing the planners, in which enterprise managers would agree on exchanges of products they needed: this allowed the enterprises to function as well as possible within the planned economy, but left the planners ignorant of some of the most essential economic processes. One of the results was persistent shortages of anything from firewood to bananas to oranges to strawberries to beef to pork, among other products. In a classic example of the problem, a friend of mine saw the complete works of Lenin on display in the window of a prominent bookshop in Budapest. My friend wanted to purchase the set and entered the shop. When he asked to buy the set, however, he was told that it was the shop's only copy of Lenin's complete works, that they needed to have Lenin's writings on display, and that they were therefore not for sale. Cars were also in short supply and, in the 1980s, used cars in East Germany were tangibly more expensive than their new counterparts. The reason? To purchase a new car you had to put your name on a waiting list and wait for six years or more. At the right price, you could purchase a used car immediately.

In communist East Central Europe, societies were controlled and conversations were often guarded. I remember, on visiting Budapest in November 1968, that a friend and I were seated at a downtown restaurant and were joined by a local physician who wanted to tell us what life was like in communist Hungary. His main complaint, albeit among others, was that, as a skilled physician, he was paid only a little more than a bus driver. But he spoke in hushed tones and expressed concern that anyone in the restaurant might be a secret police agent or a paid informant. Again, on visiting Leipzig twenty years later, I decided to take dinner at a popular restaurant. No tables were free; so the waitress seated me at a table with three locals. We got to talking and, in the course of our conversation, I told them that, back in Seattle, I had a *Stammtisch*, where a group of us would meet regularly at a local German restaurant to converse in German and thereby keep up our language skills. My Leipzig conversation partners replied that, in communist East Germany, any planned get-together of a group of friends would have to be reported to the *Stasi* (the state security police) in advance, providing the police with a list of our "members" and a summary of what topics we planned to discuss, even if of the most idle variety.

As World War Two drew to a close, the communists found themselves divided, broadly, into two groups (see Table 2.1). On the one side were those communists who had spent the war years either in their home country or in the West, fighting against the *Wehrmacht*. These home communists (including János Kádár of Hungary) tended to be sensitive to the needs, challenges, resources, and opportunities in their respective homelands. On the other side were those communists who had spent the war years in Moscow (such as Hungarian Imre Nagy), where they had obtained first-hand experience with and knowledge of the Soviet model of development. When the Muscovites returned to their respective home countries, they formed a natural faction and pushed for development along the lines of the Soviet model. The home communists held that they had a better sense of what their countries needed. Since Stalin knew the Muscovites personally, he tended to favor them. East Germany remained under Soviet occupation and did not enjoy any form of sovereignty until 1949. Not surprisingly, in four of the five remaining future-bloc states that emerged from the rubble after World War Two, the Muscovites emerged triumphant; the exception was Romania, where Gheorghe Gheorgiu-Dej, a communist activist who had spent more than a decade in prison for his role in Grivița railway strike in 1933, skillfully succeeded in marginalizing and purging his 'Muscovite' rivals. Although the dust seemed to have settled on most of these intramural rivalries by 1952, with the Muscovites dominant everywhere except in Romania, home communists Gomułka and Husák rose to the leadership positions in their respective countries by 1956 and 1969 respectively. It is worth noting that both of these men spent some time in prison during their years in the political wilderness and that one of the people who signed a note sending

TABLE 2.1 Home communists vs. 'Muscovites' in Soviet bloc countries

Country	Home communists	'Muscovites'	When resolved
Bulgaria	Anton Yugov Todor Zhivkov Traicho Kostov	Georgi Dimitrov Vulko Chervenkov Vasil Kolarov	1950
Czechoslovakia	Gustáv Husak Laco Novomeský Vladimír Clementis#	Klement Gottwald Rudolf Slánský	1950/1968
German Democratic Republic	Franz Dahlem Erich Honecker Otto Grotewohl Karl Schirdewan	Walter Ulbricht Wilhelm Pieck Anton Ackermann Wilhelm Zaisser Rudolf Herrnstadt	1953/1958
Hungary	László Rajk János Kádár Antal Apró István Kossa	Mátyás Rákosi Ernő Gerő Mihály Farkas Imre Nagy	1956
Poland	Władysław Gomułka Edward Gierek## Zenon Kliszko Marian Spychalski Jakub Berman	Bolesław Bierut Edward Ochab Hilary Minc	1948/1956
Romania	Gheorghe Gheorghiu-Dej Emil Bodnăraș Lucrețiu Pătrășcanu Gheorghe Apostol	Ana Pauker Vasile Luca	1952

\# Clementis spent the war years first in prison in Paris, and subsequently, upon his release, in London.
\## Gierek spent the war years in the Belgian resistance.
Note: I have placed Clementis and Gierek in the column with the home communists because they were not under the direct and immediate influence of Moscow.

János Kádár to prison in 1951 was none other than Imre Nagy (1896–1958), in whose removal from power Kádár would play a part.

The Soviet bloc in operation

Communism may be understood as a system based on organizational monopoly and planning in which a single party (the communist party) is hegemonic and exercises control over the media, religious life, and also aspects of the social life of citizens. At its peak in East Cemtral Europe in the 1950s, 1960s, and 1970s, the communist party's organizational monopoly meant that there was no room for any independent organizations of any kind. Young people's associations, sporting clubs, or anything else had to be founded by and controlled by the communist party or its affiliate youth organization. The sole exception until the 1980s – in the GDR, Poland, and Yugoslavia – was the Churches and other religious communities, which were able to make space available for activities for young people not connected with the communist party (CP). In fact, beginning in 1978, there was an active and independent peace movement in the GDR (described in chapter 4), operating under the protection of the Protestant (Lutheran and Reformed) Church.

In Albania, religion became illegal in 1967, and in 1976 a new constitution declared that Albania was the first atheist state in the world. In Romania and Bulgaria the Orthodox Church functioned as a branch of the political establishment. In Czechoslovakia, the Catholic Church was under especially close surveillance and the newspaper *Katolícke noviný* was prepared under the supervision of communist officials. In Hungary, the three major Churches – the Roman Catholic, Lutheran, and Reformed (Calvinist) Churches – developed a "theology of diakonia", meaning service within the system. And, in all the countries in which the secret police archives have been opened, it has been revealed that higher clergy (archbishops, bishops, metropolitans, et al.) collaborated with the local secret police; this applies to Poland, the Czech Republic, Slovakia, Hungary, Slovenia, Croatia, Bosnia-Herzegovina, Romania, and Bulgaria.[5]

Planning was an all-embracing term, which meant that not only economic production but also urban planning (atheist cities, constructed without churches) and cultural policy came under the control of the party. Planning presumed, of course, the long-term presence and dominance of a planner and in turn justified the political monopoly of the communist party. The communists also sought to maintain an ideological monopoly. Where religious associations were concerned, the communists fought back by confiscating Church-owned properties (including in Poland and Yugoslavia), by censoring or controlling Church publications, and, in Czechoslovakia, by vetoing candidates for bishop whom the communists considered undesirable. As early as 1946–47, communist authorities seized Church printing presses in Poland and shut down various Catholic periodicals; the same process unfolded elsewhere in the bloc. The communists also seized 375,000 hectares of land from the Roman Catholic Church in Poland,[6] also confiscating lands owned by rural parishes in Hungary (albeit providing temporary subsidies for the salaries of lower clergy in compensation).[7] Land reform also affected Protestant Churches in Hungary, as well as Orthodox Churches in Albania, Bulgaria, and Romania, while the Eastern-Rite Catholic Church in Romania was despoiled of its lands and facilities, which were turned over to the Romanian Orthodox Church.[8] Some priests in Czechoslovakia were incarcerated in forced labor camps,[9] while Orthodox priests in Bulgaria and Romania were variously murdered or imprisoned.[10]

The CP also created "patriotic priests' associations" in order to draw clergy into a cooperative relationship. Marriage between a Communist Party-member and a believer was strictly forbidden. József Révai, Minister of Culture and Education in Hungary, explained, in the early 1950s, that true love must include having shared values and ideals, which was not possible between a communist and a religious believer.[11]

The desire to maintain an ideological monopoly extended also to the field of history, where entire subjects could be suppressed (as in Czechoslovakia, where one could not study the Middle Ages). The premise of the system was that the communists were leading the way in the construction of a better world, founded on social justice and economic equality. In fact, what developed was a curious caste system in which wage disparities were on the whole not as great as in capitalist countries, but with various privileges and perks for the upper echelons in the system, and in which the disparity between the wages of women and those of men was roughly comparable to the disparity in Western Europe. As an example of the privileges of the upper echelon, one may note that in the late 1940s Mihály Farkas (1904–1965), Hungarian Minister of Defense and chief of the army, "refused to accept a villa until its swimming pool had been equipped with underwater illumination."[12] There were special shops for party cadres in several countries, and also hard currency shops, where the national currency was not accepted; here one could buy higher-quality stereos, televisions, and other appliances, Western clothing and Western chocolates (such as Suchard, now called Milka), among other things. In the German Democratic Republic, there was even a three-currency system: (1) the national currency (nonconvertible); (2) dollars, West German Marks, and other Western currencies (hard currency); and (3) special script issued to party elites (also a hard currency).

For such a system to work, censorship was critical. There were two kinds of censorship: pre-publication censorship (Poland most of the time, Czechoslovakia, Hungary, Romania, Bulgaria, and Albania) and post-publication censorship (the GDR and Yugoslavia by the 1980s). In the case of pre-publication censorship, party officials would review the texts for articles prior to their appearance in print.[13] In the case of post-publication censorship, the published newspaper would be delivered to the censor's office early in the morning; if there was a problem, the entire issue could be confiscated. Censors paid the most attention to the daily newspapers and to the publications of religious associations, and much less attention to philatelic magazines or to magazines oriented to other special interests, such as the East German magazines *Der Hund* and *Sowjetische Frau*. Some topics were explicitly forbidden. For example, in Poland, it was forbidden at one time to mention Zbigniew Brzezinski, who served as President Carter's National Security Adviser.[14]

Supportive participation

The regimes understood that some believers might be prepared to cooperate within the system, even though they would not join the explicitly atheist communist party. The regimes therefore typically adopted one of two strategies to bring believers into supportive participation. The first involved the presence of noncommunist parties, such as the Christian Democratic Party in East Germany, and their conversion into obedient transmission belts; by the late 1970s, such parties could be found only in the GDR, Poland, Czechoslovakia, and Bulgaria. The second strategy involved the conversion of wartime anti-fascist fronts into supportive mobilization organizations; examples included the Socialist Alliance of Working People of Yugoslavia, the Patriotic People's Front (founded in 1954 in Hungary), and the

National Front (in Czechoslovakia). The noncommunist parties were allocated a certain number of seats in the parliament, diplomatic posts, and posts in the government, including middle-level positions. This provided a less competitive route to middle-level positions than was afforded via the dominant party. But these noncommunist parties typically held joint meetings with the communist party (though not in Poland during 1980–81) and would adopt decisions jointly.

Where the local CP was concerned, one needs to differentiate among three categories of parties as regards the degree to which they were controlled by the Communist Party of the Soviet Union: (1) parties independent of Soviet control (Yugoslavia and Albania); (2) a party operating autonomously but needing to take Soviet interests and wishes into account (Romania); and (3) parties under direct Soviet control (the rest of the countries, which is to say the German Democratic Republic, Poland, Czechoslovakia, Hungary, and Bulgaria). This chapter, and the two that follow, discuss only countries in the last two categories.

In the case of Czechoslovakia, the Presidium of the Central Committee of the Communist Party never concerned itself with analyzing the international situation or with the government's foreign policy, but simply made use of the evaluations of Soviet institutions. A key figure for communists in category 3 countries was the local Soviet ambassador, who would routinely provide "guidance" concerning what was permitted and what was not permitted. More particularly, the local general secretary could stay in power (or perhaps better said, in privilege) only as long as he enjoyed the support of the Kremlin.[15] But when Czechoslovak leader Antonín Novotný lost Moscow's support in early 1968, he was removed from the office of General Secretary and replaced by Alexander Dubček. Similarly, when Walter Ulbricht (1893–1973), General Secretary of the East German Socialist Unity Party (SED[16]), proved to be an obstacle to Soviet-West German reconciliation, he was kicked upstairs in May 1971 and replaced by Erich Honecker (1912–1994), a native of Saarbrücken (in West Germany).

Phases

The communist era may be divided into five broad phases, although with variations where Yugoslavia, Albania, and Romania are concerned:

1. 1943/44–1948/49: the establishment of the communist regimes
2. 1948–1956: Stalinism (ending with the crushing of the Hungarian Revolution in November 1956, and with elite turnover in Poland and Bulgaria during that year)
3. 1956–1971: until August 1968, the reformist option appeared to be open (this was put to the test in Czechoslovakia); the anti-Semitic purge in Poland that same year marked a definite end to any notion of liberalization in Poland; in East Germany, Walter Ulbricht still seemed firmly in control in 1968 but was out of power by May 1971. Thus, between April 1969 and May 1971 the leadership in each of the three northern tier countries was changed, with Gustáv

Husák replacing Alexander Dubček in April 1969, Edward Gierek replacing Władysław Gomułka in December 1970, and Erich Honecker replacing Walter Ulbricht in May 1971

4. 1971–1980: failure of the reformist option and rising discontent (culminating in the workers' strikes in Poland and the formation of the Independent Trade Union 'Solidarity' in that country)

5. 1980–1989/91: the awakening of independent activism (dissidents and dissident circles), with communism in decline, culminating in the collapse of communism in the countries of the Soviet bloc.

The first phase, 1943/44–1948/49 (the conquest of power)

This phase began with the proclamation of the communist-led government of Yugoslavia (AVNOJ, at Jajce, 29 November 1943) and, where the Soviet bloc is concerned, with the establishment of a communist provisional government for Poland in Lublin in summer 1944 (recognized by the Soviets at the end of December 1944). During this phase, there were some mixed systems, e.g., in Bulgaria and Romania, which briefly allowed King Simeon II and King Michael to return to their respective countries as ceremonial monarchs. The former was sent into exile in September 1946 but would return much later to serve as prime minister of post-socialist Bulgaria from 2001 to 2005; the latter abdicated under duress in December 1947, living first in England and subsequently in Switzerland, until he was allowed to return to Romania in 1992. In the immediate post-war years, there was armed resistance to communism in Poland (until 1946), Bulgaria (until 1951), and Romania (until 1962) (see Table 2.2).

In Poland, Hungary, Czechoslovakia, and, in its own way, also Yugoslavia, there were efforts after the end of World War Two, to restore multiparty systems. In some countries, the communists agreed to participate in coalition governments, but they prioritized gaining control of the ministries of interior and justice, and placing a "fellow traveler" (a noncommunist who would collaborate with the communists), such as Zveno's Kimon Georgiev in Bulgaria or Zdeněk Fierlinger in Czechoslovakia in office. In the communist playbook for political takeover, other crucial tactics included the forced merger of Social Democratic parties with the communist party (see Table 2.3), gaining control of the countryside through forced collectivization, the establishment of secret police and networks of informants (and the politicization of the courts), the establishment of a system of surveillance of all correspondence as well as the tapping of telephones, confessionals, and even some homes, the incarceration of persons deemed hostile to the communist party, and closure of the borders.

What the communists achieved in the period beginning even before World War Two had come to an end was a *revolutionary breakthrough*. As Ken Jowitt has explained, crediting Franz Schurmann, what defines a revolutionary breakthrough is that it made "a return to the *status quo ante* impossible."[17] And while "[t]here was

TABLE 2.2 Resistance, uprisings, protests, and local revolts in the Soviet bloc, 1949–1989

1944–1946: armed resistance to communism in Poland

Late 1940s until 1951: armed resistance to communism in Bulgaria

Mass demonstrations 1949–1950 against collectivization and cooperatives in Poland and 1949–1953 against the plowing of new farmland, as well as 650 incidents of political terror in the Polish countryside in 1950

Various years between 1949 and 1970: mass demonstrations and protests against collectivization in Hungary

Beginning in 1949, violent revolts against collectivization across 10 counties in Romania; Securitate and Militia troops shot a number of protesting peasants

Beginning on 3 July 1950: chaos and resistance in Bulgaria, starting in the village of Burdarski Geran and spreading quickly to the villages of Stavertzi, Kozloguy, and three villages on the plain of Vratza, etc.

31 May-2 June 1953: the Pilsen (Plzeň) uprising in Czechoslovakia, involving mainly workers protesting currency reform

16–17 June 1953: anti-communist uprising across all of East Germany

28–30 June 1956: protests by workers in Poznań, Poland, to demand better work conditions

23 October-10 November 1956: the Hungarian Revolution

22 August 1968: Czechs gather on the streets of Prague to protest the invasion of their country

24–30 June 1976: protests in Płock, the Warsaw suburb of Ursus, Radom, and elsewhere against announced increases in food prices

1–3 August 1977: the Jiu Valley Miners' Strike in Romania, initiated by work stoppage on the part of 35,000 miners

7–31 August 1980: the formation of the Independent Trade Union Solidarity in Poland, accompanied by strike action at the Gdańsk shipyard

Beginning in 1981: local revolts in multiple locations across Romania

15 November 1987: the Brașov rebellion, involving about 20,000 workers from the Brașov Tractor Plant, protesting reduced salaries and a proposal to cut roughly 15,000 jobs

27 June 1988: between 30,000 and 50,000 Hungarians marched to the Romanian Embassy in Budapest, to protests Ceaușescu's plans to destroy more than half of the country's villages, many of them inhabited by Hungarians

4 September-late December 1989: protests/demonstrations/uprising across East Germany, Czechoslovakia, and Romania, leading to the collapse of communism in these countries

Select sources: The following chapters from Constantin Iordachi and Arnd Bauerkämper (eds.), *The Collectivization of Agriculture in Communist Eastern Europe* (Budapest & New York: Central European University Press, 2014): Dariusz Jarosz, "The Collectivization of Agriculture in Poland: Causes of Defeat", p. 129; József Ö. Kovács, "The Forced Collectivization of Agriculture in Hungary, 1948–1961", pp. 231, 233; Constantin Iordachi and Dorin Dobrincu, "The Collectivization of Agriculture in Romania, 1949–1962", pp. 270–273; and Mihail Gruev, "Collectivization and Social Change in Bulgaria, 1940s-1950s", p. 353. Also: "Czechs protest against Soviet invasion", *History* (22 August 1968), at www. history.com/this-day-in-history/czechs-protest-against-soviet-invasion#:~:text=On%20August%20 22%2C%20thousands%20of,in%20the%20days%20to%20come. [accessed on 30 January 2021]; Ilko-Sascha Kowalczuk, "Von der Freiheit, Ich zu sagen. Widerständiges Verhalten in der DDR", in Ulrike Poppe, Rainer Eckert, and Ilko-Sascha Kowalczuk (eds.), *Zwischen Selbstbehauptungund Anpassung. Formen des Widerstandes und der Opposition in der DDR* (Berlin: Ch. Links Verlag, 1995), p. 105; and Anneli Ute Gabanyi, *Die unvollendete Revolution. Rumänien zwischen Diktatur und Demokratie* (Munich: Piper Verlag GmbH, 1990), pp. 49, 82.

TABLE 2.3 Forced party mergers after 1945

21 April 1946: the Social Democratic Party of Germany (SPD) was forced to merge with the Communist Party of Germany (KPD) to form the Socialist Unity Party (SED)

February 1948: the Social Democratic Party of Romania was forced to merge with the Romanian Communist Party to form the Romanian Workers' Party; in 1965, it was renamed the Romanian Communist Party

1948: the Czech Social Democratic Party was forced to merge into the Czechoslovak Communist Party

June 1948: the Social Democratic Party was forced to merge with the Hungarian Communist Party to become the Hungarian Workers' Party; at the end of October 1956, the party was reconstituted as the Hungarian Socialist Workers' Party (MSzMP)

December 1948: the Bulgarian Social Democratic Party was forced to merge into the Bulgarian Communist Party

15–21 December 1948: the Polish Socialist Party was forced to merge with the Polish Workers' Party to form the Polish United Workers' Party (PZPR)

27 November 1949: Mikołayczyk's Peasant Party was forced to merge with the communist-controlled party of the same name to form the United Peasant Party

no master plan" to guide the East-Central European states toward socialism and eventually, in theory, communism, there *was*, according to Vladimir Tismaneanu, "a fanatic, preestablished idea of how society should be."[18]

Poland

At the end of the war, Poland lay in ruins. Two-thirds of its industrial stock had been destroyed, national income stood at not much above one-third of what it had been in 1938, and the population now stood at 24 million, as opposed to 35 million within a somewhat larger pre-war territory. More than 5 million citizens of Poland lost their lives during World War Two, accounting for about approximately 17% of the population; this figure includes as many as 3 million Polish Jews liquidated by the Nazis.[19] There were also huge losses in clerical ranks, with an estimated 2,517 religious dying in Nazi concentration camps.[20] At that time, there were two groups of politicians claiming to constitute the legitimate government of Poland. On the one hand, there was the Polish government-in-exile in London, headed since the death of Władysław Sikorski in July 1943 by Stanisław Mikołajczyk (1901–1966), head of the Polish Peasant Party (PSL[21]); on the other hand, there was the communist-dominated Committee of National Liberation, which had been set up in Lublin behind Red Army lines in 1944. This rivalry was resolved when Mikołajczyk returned to Poland in June 1945 together with other émigré politicians and agreed to serve as one of two deputy prime ministers in a coalition government of national unity headed by Prime Minister Edward Osóbka-Morawski (1909–1997), the leader of the Polish Socialist Party (PPS[22]). Władysław Gomułka (1905–1982), General Secretary of the Polish Workers' Party (PPR[23]), as the communists now called their party, took office as the second deputy prime minister. Of the 21 ministerial portfolios, the communists and their allies held 17, including security, defense, foreign policy, justice, and information.

Parliamentary elections were held on 19 January 1947, with six parties offering candidates: the PPR, PPS, Democratic Party (PD[24]), and the Peasant Party – these four in a pre-election coalition with an agreement on the distribution of seats; Mikołajczyk's PSL, which with 600,000 members in January 1946 was the largest political grouping in the country, and the Labor Party were in opposition. But the communists arrested 1,000 PSL activists, closed a number of PSL branch offices by force, and resorted to violence, including raids on PSL headquarters during the election campaign, leading up the January 1947 elections. The elections were neither fair nor free, and resulted in the communists and the socialists taking 119 seats each in the Polish Sejm (parliament), with 103 seats for the Peasant Party, and 43 seats for the PD, with 43 seats divided between PSL and the Labor Party, and the remaining seats scattered among some small groupings.[25] The communists now installed themselves in power; Mikołajczyk fled the country that same year. Osóbka-Morawski's term as prime minister ended on 5 February 1947, when fellow-socialist Józef Cyrankiewicz (1911–1989) succeeded him, serving as prime minister, with a two-year hiatus between 1952 and 1954, until December 1970. Bolesław Bierut (1892–1956), the leading figure among Muscovite Poles, became President of Poland, serving in that office until passage in 1952 of a new constitution, which abolish the presidency.

Gomułka, Zenon Kliszko, and Marian Spychalski had spent the war years in Poland and they were convinced that, in constructing a socialist system, it would be necessary to take Polish specificities into account. Thus, at a Central Committee meeting on 3 June 1948, Gomułka criticized the pre-war Communist Party of Poland (KPP[26]), for having underestimated the importance of national independence; he also underlined that the Polish Workers' Party should follow its own model and need not copy other countries or parties. "Socialism is not," Gomułka told the CC members, "and cannot be the same in different historical situations."[27]

Bierut, together with Jakub Berman (1901–1984) and Hilary Minc (1905–1974), had spent the war years in Moscow and, much more than Gomułka, these were Stalin's creatures. They were also more impressed with the Soviet example than Gomułka and his allies were. On 15 August 1948, Bierut visited Moscow in order to inform Stalin about the situation in Poland and to gain his support to remove Gomułka from power. Bierut told Stalin that his rival was leading a rightist-deviationist faction and claimed that the Politburo was agreed that Gomułka should not continue as party General Secretary.[28] Stalin considered Gomułka's autonomism unacceptable and agreed that he had to be removed as General Secretary of the PPR.

Soon after Bierut's return to Warsaw, the PPR Politburo met for "stormy sessions" on 18 and 19 August, at which Bierut led the charge against the doomed General Secretary. His detractors objected precisely to his autonomist thinking, which is to say his belief that one could not just copy the Soviet model in Poland.

Bierut and his Muscovites, who dominated the Politburo 5 to 3 brought their case against Gomułka to a plenary session of the CC held on 31 August-3 September 1948, charging him with being "a 'nationalist deviationist' with dictatorial tendencies and a 'rightist' opponent of the program of a socialist revolutionary change."[29] Gomułka was dismissed as General Secretary and removed from the Politburo and the Secretariat. Bierut now inherited the leadership post. Addressing an assembly of party *aktiv* soon after the CC session had ended, Bierut summarized Gomułka's various alleged failings. According to Bierut, the erstwhile General Secretary had failed to "immediately understand the resolutions and directives of the July Central Committee Plenary Session," had failed to take a firm stand against the policies of the Communist Party of Yugoslavia (for more information on Yugoslavia, see chapter 5), had expressed "doubts and reservations" during the founding conference of the Cominform (in September 1947), and had a tendency to deny that the Polish path to socialism cannot be and is "not something qualitatively different, but is a vari[ation on] the general path of development towards socialism [charted by] . . . the USSR."[30] Before being dismissed from his positions, Gomułka had been forced to engage in the well-established Soviet ritual of self-criticism, although he did not yield on the most fundamental points.[31]

In the wake of these events, the formal merger of the PPR and the PPS to form the Polish United Workers' Party (PZPR[32]) took place at a Congress held 15–21 December 1948. The Congress brought together 995,990 communists and 531,350 socialists. The new Politburo, the decision-making body in the communist system, included 11 members – eight from the PPR and three from the PPS. The ex-PPR members were Bolesław Bierut, Jakub Berman, Hilary Minc, Franciszek Jozwiak, Stanisław Radkiewicz, Roman Zambrowski, Aleksander Zawadzki, and Marian Spychalski. The ex-PPS members were Józef Cyrankiewicz, Adam Rapacki, and Henryk Swiatkowski. A little less than a year later, the leading "home communists" – Gomułka, Kliszko, and Spychalski – were purged from the ranks of the PZPR, with Spychalski being removed at the same time from the Politburo. Yet the purges in Poland were mild compared to what unfolded in the other bloc states. Indeed, in Czechoslovakia, Hungary, Romania, and Bulgaria, there were show trials and executions.

The Catholic Church

The early post-war years were years of hardship for all of Poland and not only because of the war. The Kraków Curia launched the weekly news organ *Tygodnik Powszechny* already in March 1945, even before the war had ended. Cardinal-Primate August Hlond (1881–1948) returned to Poland on 29 July 1945. On 15 August, just over two weeks after his return, Hlond divided the "recovered territories" (formerly German lands) into five dioceses and approved apostolic administrators for these jurisdictions. The seminaries reopened in 1946 and, on 12 May 1946, Cardinal Hlond consecrated 10 new bishops; among them was Stefan Wyszyński (1901–1981), his eventual successor as Primate.[33]

Things were not going to be easy for the Church. To begin with, the communists viewed religion as superstition and hoped to be rid of it in due course. On
12 September 1945, the communist-dominated government declared the Concordat of 1925 null and void; the reason given was that there were German bishops
still in charge of dioceses in the "recovered territories". Bierut, in his capacity as
state president, declared that "Respect for religious feelings and religious practices is the Polish people's immutable, steadfast principle, to which they will most
firmly adhere."[34] But in the years 1946–47, the regime confiscated Church printing
presses, suppressed Catholic periodicals, and removed Catholic books from public
libraries. The authorities also nationalized 375,000 hectares of land hitherto in the
Church's possession.[35] The regime harassed the clergy in various ways, attacked
the Church in the mass media, organized a so-called "patriotic priests" association which as of 1955 would attract an estimated 1,700 of the Church's 11,000
priests to its conferences, and promoted the Pax Association, a regime-friendly
quasi-Catholic splinter group headed by Bolesław Piasecki (1915–1979), a former
fascist.[36] In other moves, the regime introduced civil marriage and civil divorce – a
decision not welcomed by the Church –and shortened the time made available for
religious instruction in the schools. On 22 October 1948, Cardinal Hlond died at
the age of 67. On his deathbed, he dictated a letter to the Holy See, suggesting that
Bishop Wyszyński be named his successor as Primate. The Vatican granted his wish
and, on 12 November 1948, Wyszyński assumed the office of Archbishop Metropolitan of Gniezno and Warsaw and thus also Primate of Poland.

Demographic and economic transformation, to 1950

Among the priorities of the incoming regime were the transformation of Poland
into an ethnically homogeneous community and the country's economic transformation into an industrialized, socialist economy. With the Soviet Union annexing
a large swathe of what had been eastern Poland and the country being assigned
territories in the west, at Germany's expense, Poland was shifted westward. About
1.5 million Poles who had lived in what now became Soviet territory crossed the
new Polish borders, joining the approximately 300,000 Poles who had fled during
the war from what had been southeastern Poland. These "eastern Poles" constituted the majority of settlers moving into homes being abandoned by Germans in
Poland's "recovered territories". Between late 1944 and early 1945, about 6 million Germans fled from lands being taken by Poland or were forcibly deported.[37]
The expulsions of Germans were often brutal, with Polish soldiers taking revenge
for the sufferings inflicted by the Third Reich during the war. However, it would
have been economically disastrous if all Germans with important skills had been
expelled. Accordingly, Polish authorities drew up a hierarchy of skills, expelling the
unskilled and those with less valued skills and holding onto those whose skills were
needed until they could be replaced by Poles. By the end of 1949, there were just
300,000 Germans still living in Poland.[38]

On the economic front, real earnings sank to less than 10% of their 1938 levels by April 1945 and there were serious food shortages in urban centers. In the closing months of World War Two, there were short strikes, problems with absenteeism in industry, and violence in the countryside. The economy started to stabilize in 1946, but a severe winter, followed by floods in spring 1947 and a summer drought resulted in serious inflation.[39] The climate extremes hit agriculture very hard, but matters were not much better in industry where, as of April 1947, production stood at 19% of its 1937 level. Partly to address this situation and partly to show fealty to Stalin, the Polish authorities introduced a norm-busting program known as *współzawodnictwo* in 1947. Modeled on the Soviet Stakhanovite movement,[40] the Polish Stakhanovites distributed a report that one Wincenty Pstrowski, a coal miner in Silesia, had exceeded his work norm by 270%: others were supposed to emulate this "hero worker", though, in practice, most industrial workers were angered at the sudden pressure to quicken their pace of work and there were violent strikes in some locales, such as in Łódź. In the event, Pstrowski was not an ideal choice for promotion as a hero worker since he died in April 1948.[41] Yet, by 1948, overall production at least had recovered and, in some sectors, exceeded pre-war production levels, even as large-scale migration from the countryside to urban centers assured industry of adequate numbers of unskilled laborers.

The communists sought to transform the agriculture sector. They did this in two stages. *In the first stage*, beginning in September 1944, estates 50 hectares in size or more were seized, parceled, and distributed to landless peasants. Subsequently, Polish settlers arriving in the "recovered territories" took possession of farms averaging 6.9 hectares each. About a million peasants benefited from this land distribution. In total, about 6 million hectares obtained new owners.[42]

In the second phase, initiated in 1948, peasants were first encouraged, later coerced to join cooperatives or collective farms. In a farm cooperative, peasants retained ownership of their land and usually there was little to distinguish cooperative farming from private farming aside from the sharing of farm implements and pooling of labor. In a collective farm, the peasants ceded their land to the collective. While they were, at least in theory, allowed to withdraw from the collective, they enjoyed a right, not to reclaim their original land, but to obtain an equivalent parcel of land on the outer fringe of the collective.[43]

*In **Hungary***, as the Red Army advanced into Hungary, a provisional government was established in Debrecen, in which non-communists were granted positions of nominal authority, while communists were installed in politically more important positions. This government declared war on Nazi Germany on 28 December 1944 and sent a delegation to Moscow, signing an armistice on 20 January 1945, in which the Hungarians renounced the Vienna Accords under which German Führer Adolf Hitler (1889–1945) had augmented the territory of Hungary at the expense of Czechoslovakia and Romania. The provisional government also agreed to pay $200 million in reparations to the USSR and $100 million to be split between Czechoslovakia and Yugoslavia (from which Hungary had annexed territories in the north and northwest of the country in April 1941). Meanwhile, as the Red Army moved through Hungary, its troops pillaged and raped. About 600,000 Hungarians were rounded up and transported to the Soviet Union to perform forced labor. It has been estimated that one out of every three Hungarians sent to the Soviet Union never returned to Hungary.[44]

Already in January 1945, the Central Committee of the communist party, still based in Debrecen, announced the start of a land reform, expropriating larger estates and distributing land parcels to all peasants seeking land. By late June, more than a third of all arable land had been distributed, benefiting 642,342 peasants. In the meantime, Mátyás Rákosi (1892–1971), who had spent the war years in Moscow, arrived in Budapest on 21 February 1945 and was named General Secretary of the Hungarian Communist Party (HCP) two days later. The nearly 200 Hungarian communists who had been with Rákosi in Moscow were commonly called Muscovites, to distinguish them from the home communists, such as János Kádár (1912–1989), who had stayed in Hungary during the war.

The communists actively sought to recruit persons who had participated in the anti-fascist resistance, but also welcomed former members of the fascist Arrow Cross into their ranks. In fact, the party abandoned strict vetting in February 1945, allowing its membership to grow from 30,000 to 500,000 by August.[45] In the meantime, the provisional government was able to transfer to Budapest on 12 April 1945. For the time being, the communists did not reveal their long-term intentions and claimed to respect private property, even assuring the Social Democrats on 21 February that they hoped to collaborate with them "for long years to come."[46] Other political parties at the time included the popular Smallholders' Party, which favored a pluralist democracy with a mixed economy, and the National Peasant Party, among whose prominent members István Bibó (1911–1979) sketched a vision of a third path between Western and Soviet political models. On 16 October 1945, Soviet Marshal Klement Voroshilov (1881–1969) met with leaders of the main political parties and pressed them to agree to a single list, with the distribution of seats in the National Assembly determined in advance. He suggested that the Smallholders be allocated 40% of the seats and, when they rejected that proposal, offered them 47.5%, which they likewise refused. The elections for the Assembly were duly held on 4 November 1945. The Smallholders (SHP), thanks in part to the strong endorsement from the Catholic Church, emerged as the clear winner, clearing 57% of the vote. The Social Democrats collected 17.4% of the vote, with the communists close behind at 17%. The National Peasant Party attracted just 6.9% of the vote.[47] Zoltán Tildy (1889–1961), a Reformed minister and a leading figure in the SHP, became prime minister.

Under normal parliamentary rules, the Smallholders should have been able to form a government on their own. However, even before the elections were held, the Soviets informed the Hungarians that the communist party (HCP) should be invited to join a government coalition, regardless of the outcome of the elections. Tildy agreed that the Smallholders would be assigned seven of the 14 cabinet portfolios. Of the remaining portfolios, the SDP and HCP would receive three each, and the National Peasant Party (NPP) was granted one.[48] Tildy had wanted to install Béla Kovács (1908–1959), a fellow member of the SHP, to head the Ministry of the Interior. But this was a critical post and the Soviets were determined to see a communist occupying it. Thus, under pressure from Voroshilov, Tildy yielded the interior ministry to communist Imre Nagy (1896–1958), who served in that capacity from 15 November 1945 until 20 March 1946, when he was succeeded by László Rajk (1909–1949), a home communist who had been incarcerated by the Arrow Cross for a few months beginning in December 1944. The unfortunate Béla Kovács was allowed to serve as Minister of Agriculture for three months, ending on 23 February 1946.

The communists were bent on whittling down the Smallholders' Party and, following Rákosi's "salami tactics", sliced off a portion of that party, forcing it to expel 21 of its deputies, whom the communists characterized as "reactionaries", in March 1946.[49] (That same month, Ferenc Szálasi, leader of the fascist Arrow Cross movement, and several of his associates were executed.) Under communist pressure, the Smallholders expelled additional members from their ranks in the months that followed. By then, Tildy was moving (on 1 February 1946) from the office of the prime minister to the presidency of the republic. The SHP proposed to install Dezsö Sulyok to succeed him as prime minister, but the communists blocked his appointment and, instead, another SHP member, Ferenc Nagy (1903–1979) became prime minister. Sulyok was dismissed from the SHP in March 1946 but, with authorization from the Allied Control Council, set up another political organization, the Freedom Party, under his leadership. A fresh round of elections for the Assembly was held on 31 August 1947. In addition to the four coalition parties (the HCP, SHP, SDP, and NPP), the Allied Control Council had approved an additional six parties to contest the 1947 elections. Given communist tactics, the share of the vote that went to the Smallholders shrank from 57% to 15.4%, while the communists picked up some votes to capture 22.27%, rather than the 17% they had won two years earlier (though some of this gain has been attributed to fraud). But the second strongest party was the (Catholic) Democratic People's Party, which took 16.41% of the vote. The other results were: 14.9% for the Social Democrats, 13.42% for the Hungarian Independence Party (as the Freedom Party was now called), 8.31% for the NPP, 5.21% for the Independent Democratic Party, 1.68% for the Radical Party, 1.39% for the Christian Women's League, and 1.01% for the Civic Democratic Party.[50] Soon after the elections, the communists attacked the Hungarian Independence Party as fascistic and orchestrated the removal of that party's deputies from the Assembly. Later, in the context of communist maneuvers, the Democratic People's Party dissolved itself and its erstwhile leader, István Barankovics, fled the country in February 1948.

On 14 May 1947, Ferenc Nagy departed for Switzerland, intending a short holiday. In his absence, Rákosi assumed the duties of acting prime minister and called a cabinet meeting on 28 May to discuss "evidence" passed along by the Soviet purporting to document Ferenc Nagy's complicity in a treasonous conspiracy. Rákosi demanded that Nagy return to Hungary to stand trial. Instead, after securing safe passage for his five-year-old son out of Hungary, Nagy tendered his resignation effective the end of the month. The liquidation of the parliamentary system was completed with the forced merger of the SDP with the HCP on 8 March 1948 and the forced resignation of Tildy as president on 30 July that same year. His successor as president was Arpád Szakasits, a pro-communist Socialist.

In *Czechoslovakia*, Edvard Beneš returned as president in April 1945, following negotiations between communist and noncommunist politicians in Moscow the previous month. At those negotiations, Klement Gottwald (1896–1953), chair of the communist party, presented the non-communists with a 32-page draft program to which they were expected to propose only minor changes. A coalition government was formed, with communists in charge of the ministries of the interior, defense, agriculture, education, and information. Gottwald became deputy prime minister, serving under noncommunist fellow traveler Zdeněk Fierlinger (1891–1976). Jan Masaryk (1886–1948), the son of Czechoslovakia's first president, Tomáš Masaryk (1850–1937), and a non-communist, was named foreign minister, but a communist was installed as his deputy. One of the first acts of the government was to order the expulsion of almost all German-speakers from Sudetenland. Their property was seized without compensation, and the area was now settled by Czechs. Between 1945 and 1948, all but 170,000 of the three million Germans who had lived in Czechoslovakia before the end of the war were expelled from the country – driven out by "state-induced violence".[51] There were 6,500 officially recognized anti-fascists among the country's Germans and untold numbers who were unable to document their anti-fascist credentials. But even those officially recognized as anti-fascists encountered pervasive hatred of Germans among Czechs and many of them eventually left for Germany.[52] Elections were held in May 1946. The communists secured the largest share of the vote: 38% overall (40% in the Czech lands, 30% in Slovakia). As a result of the elections, Gottwald became prime minister; nine of the 26 members of the cabinet were communists. But the Slovak Democratic Party had won an impressive 62% of the vote in Slovakia. Moreover, a public opinion poll conducted in January 1948 showed that support for the communists had fallen to just 25%.[53]

On 13 February 1948, Minister of Justice Prokop Drtina presented a report to the cabinet concerning communist penetration of the secret police. According to the report, eight non-communist police in Prague had been dismissed and replaced.[54] The police were under the supervision of the Minister of Internal Affairs (Václav Nosek) – a communist, as already noted. When this report came out, a decision was taken, in the absence of Nosek, to halt any further changes of personnel in the security police and to investigate communist influence. Late on 16 February, leaders of the (Czechoslovak) National Socialist Party (no connection with the German Nazi party) pressed for an agreement that non-communist members of the cabinet should resign as a bloc if the communists failed to cooperate on these measures. The communists refused to cooperate and cabinet members representing the National Socialists, the People's Party, and the Slovak Democratic Party now agreed to resign, in order to provoke a governmental crisis, presumably leading to fresh elections. In response, the Presidium of the Central Committee (CC) of the communist party accused the non-communists of planning to install a nonparliamentary government and to hold undemocratic elections. The party's General Secretary – Rudolf Slánský (1901–1952) – called on industrial workers to be prepared to defend the government from a potential non-communist coup. That very night meetings were held at various factories and orders went out to mobilize the factory militia.[55]

At this point, the Communists approached the Social Democrats with a proposal to form a government consisting of their two parties alone. The Social Democrats rejected this overture on 19 February, and the next day, 12 of the 17 non-communist ministers resigned. The nine communist and non-communist members who did not resign still constituted a quorum and, under the terms of the 1920 constitution, the government was authorized to continue to function. At 4 p.m., Gottwald, Nosek, and Ludvík Svoboda (1895–1979) visited President Beneš, asking him to accept the resignations and to authorize their replacement. A proclamation drawn up by the Communists was broadcast on the radio and a mass meeting on the Old Town Square was announced for the following day. By the following morning, workers were heading to the square in large numbers. On Sunday, 8,000 industrial workers assembled in Prague's Exhibition Hall. Meanwhile, the non-communist parties remained passive and postponed any countermeasures. While communist action committees were being set up in various towns and villages, including in factories and even in government offices, an arrest warrant was issued for Jan Ursíny, the leader of the Slovak Democratic Party, "for having allegedly transmitted military and state secrets to a spy acting for the Slovak émigré, Durčiansky."[56] On 25 February, Beneš accepted the resignations of the 12 non-communist ministers and told Gottwald that he could propose replacements for those who had resigned. The workers' militia staged a parade through the streets of Prague that evening, signaling the left-wing triumph. In the new cabinet, there were 12 communist ministers alongside 12 non-communist ministers, most of them pro-communist. As H. Gordon Skilling noted, while the transfer of power was superficially legal, ". . . the forms of constitutionalism had been given a revolutionary content. Not only were the action committees themselves illegal, but so were their seizure of party headquarters and newspaper presses, and their purge of public and private institutions."[57]

The communists now rushed through a new constitution by 9 May 1948,[58] under which private ownership of enterprises employing up to 50 workers was guaranteed. In addition to individual rights, the constitution also guaranteed social rights, including the right to an education, the right to work, gender equality, and the right to healthcare. On the day the new constitution was promulgated, Klement Gottwald addressed the communist party's Central Committee with the following words: "We have here a massive Communist Party, which is generally recognized as the leading force. It is the political brain, the political motor which drives our whole life."[59]

At the end of May, scarcely three weeks after the issuance of the constitution, elections for the newly established National Assembly were held. A single list of candidates was presented to voters, with fixed proportions of representatives assigned to the various political parties. According to the official report, 89.2% of valid votes endorsed the single list. The seats in the Assembly were then allocated as follows. Of the 300 seats comprising the Assembly, 183 were assigned to the Communist Party of Czechoslovakia and a further 54 seats to the Communist Party of Slovakia. The Czech People's Party and Czech Socialists (formerly called National Socialists) were allocated 23 seats each, with 12 for the Party of Slovak Rebirth, four for the Slovak Party of Freedom, and one for a delegate with no party affiliation.[60]

The National Assembly soon proved to serve merely a ceremonial function, always voting unanimously and celebrating each speech and each vote with "stormy applause". Gottwald explained the functions of the Assembly by asserting, "We are building a democratic regime of a new type . . . Our regime is not one of formal parliamentary democracy but a regime of popular democracy."[61] By March 1948, thus, there were only two "problems" left for Stalin in Eastern Europe: Yugoslavia, where Yugoslav leader Josip Broz Tito (1892–1980) and his coterie refused to follow orders, and the Soviet occupation zone in eastern Germany.

In *Bulgaria*, local communists and their allies, organized into the Fatherland Front, seized control of the government and various key installations during the night of 8–9 September 1944. Among the installations over which the communists took control now were the Ministry of War, the main post office, the National Bank, Radio Sofia, and the telephone exchange. At 6:25 a.m. on 9 September, Kimon Georgiev (1882–1969), a member of Zveno and designated prime minister, took to the radio to announce that the Front was now in charge. In early September, between 25,000 and 30,000 persons were murdered or disappeared. Their number included police and army officers, civil servants such as mayors, and also lawyers, teachers, journalists, and clergy.[62] The terror, which was not limited to fascists and fascist sympathizers, continued into October, making use of a list of "enemies" provided by the special services unit of the Red Army. The end of the extrajudicial terror did not mean, however, an end to the persecution of those viewed as problematic from the communist point of view. On the contrary, a People's Court was set up and, between November 1944 and April 1945, tried and convicted various defendants of war crimes, including "Regents and the Tsar's advisors, cabinet ministers of all governments and all members of the parliament from the years 1941–44, [and] senior state and military officials. The People's Court tried 135 cases against 11,122 defendants, of whom 2,730 were sentenced to death, 1,516 were pronounced not guilty, and the rest were given different prison terms . . . [P]roportiona[tely] to the population these numbers were unprecedented in European practice."[63] Ekaterina Nikova underlines that very few of those convicted were actually guilty of war crimes. In addition, about 1,100 officers, allegedly having nurtured sympathies for Germany, were purged from the ranks of the military by the end of 1944.[64]

In the waning years of World War Two, Bulgaria had sustained damage from Allied air raids. Added to the burden of economic reconstruction was the fact that, under the terms of the 1947 peace treaty, Bulgaria was obliged to pay $25 million in reparations to Yugoslavia and $50 million in reparations to Greece.[65] In the meantime and before setting in motion a plan for reconstruction, the three leading figures in the Bulgarian Communist Party (BCP) – Georgi Dimitrov (1882–1949), Vasil Kolarov (1877–1950), and Traicho Kostov (1897–1949) – traveled to Moscow for consultations with Stalin and Molotov. Among the subjects they discussed was "the pace at which the revolutionary transformations would come about and measures to strengthen the people's democratic power in Bulgaria."[66]

Two economic measures adopted in 1946–47 inflicted heavy blows on ordinary Bulgarians. The first of these was a new tax law, passed in 1946, imposing a requirement that unpaid taxes since 1942 be paid off against a short deadline. The second was the currency reform passed in March 1947 requiring that people convert their savings to the new currency being introduced at an unfavorable rate. In addition, a special tax was levied on people's savings.[67] That same year, authorities launched a two-year plan for reconstruction and large-scale industrialization. Under the plan, industrial output was supposed to increase by 67% over the level achieved on the eve of World War Two, while agricultural production was to increase by 34%.[68]

Already by the end of 1944, the establishment of a communist dictatorship was well underway. This may be seen from the fact that, as of the end of 1944, 63 of the country's 84 town mayors were communists, as were 879 of the country's 1,058 village mayors.[69] But, until late August 1947, the communists faced a vocal challenge from the reestablished Bulgarian Agrarian National Union (BANU), led since January 1945 by the outspoken Nikola Petkov (1893–1947). The BANU newspaper *Narodno Zemedelsko Zname* and the Social Democratic newspaper *Svoboden Narod* both adopted stances critical of the communists. In the course of spring 1945, Petkov moved to take the BANU out of the communist-led Fatherland Front coalition and operate independently. Alexander Obbov, a fellow member of BANU, urged Petkov to keep the party within the Fatherland Front. When Petkov refused, the BANU leadership council met in May and expelled Petkov from the party, installing Obbov to succeed him as General Secretary of BANU. The Agrarian fraction led by Alexander Obbov would show itself to be more compliant with communist wishes than Petkov's group, which continued to hoist the banner of BANU. Meanwhile, the Social Democratic Party also split when Georgi Popov led a smaller portion of that party to remain within the Fatherland Front while the mainstream of the party, led by Kosta Lulchev, withdrew from the coalition.[70] Parliamentary elections were held on 18 November 1945, resulting in the BCP and the BANU winning 94 seats each. Zveno placed third with 45 seats. A referendum was held on 8 September 1946 concerning whether to adopt a republican model or retain the monarchy. According to the official tally, 93% of ballots were cast in favor of establishing a republic, with 4% favoring retention of the monarchy; 3% of the ballots were deemed invalid.[71] Fresh parliamentary elections were held the following month: the results showed that the communists won 53.1% of the vote (capturing 278 out of 465 seats in the Constitutional Assembly), followed by the opposition bloc with 28.0% and Obbov's BANU with 13.2%. No other party crossed the 2% threshold. In the wake of these elections, Georgi Dimitrov, the most senior Bulgarian communist and, together with Traicho Kostov, and Vasil Kolarov, one of the dominant troika in the Bulgarian Communist Party, became Prime Minister; Kimon Georgiev, his predecessor in that office, now took office as Foreign Minister. In the wake of the elections, Obbov gravitated toward opposition; in response, the communists orchestrated an internal party coup and replaced Obbov with Georgi Traikov, who immediately conducted a purge of party ranks.

Petkov continued to speak his mind and was warned that he should stop criticizing the communists. He ignored the warning and, speaking at a session of the Grand National Assembly, called for a restoration of the Turnovo constitution of 1879. In June 1947, he was arrested on the floor of the Assembly and put on trial, charged with having organized a military clique to recruit reactionary and pro-fascist army officers to stage a coup d'état.[72] It was further alleged that Petkov had been acting at the behest of certain foreign powers – the USA and Great Britain were intended – in order to secure capitalism in Bulgaria.[73] Although the charges were fabricated, Petkov was found guilty after a lengthy trial and hanged in September 1947. Elections for the Grand Subranie (Assembly) were held the month after Petkov's execution. Noncommunist parties were still allowed to contest the election and, in spite of widespread terror, still managed to attract almost 30% of the vote. After the election, the only noncommunist party allowed to exist was what was left of BANU but it was by no means independent. Beginning in December 1947, the communists asserted control over trade unions, youth organizations, women's associations, and professional societies, asserted a monopoly over foreign trade, and imported the Stalinist model of prioritizing the development of heavy industry. The communist vision of economic planning, the creation of a New Socialist Man and New Socialist Woman with new and different values from past generations, and the undertaking to remake the society as a whole all required control. By the time of its Fifth Congress in 1948, the Bulgarian Communist Party, operating according to explicit Soviet prescription,[74] had put in place the structures of control it needed for the transformations it intended to realize.

The abortive union with Yugoslavia

It was during these years that there were active discussions between the Bulgarians and the Yugoslavs concerning the establishment of a federative union of their two countries. Stalin raised the issue with Tito in September 1944 and, according to Edvard Kardelj's memoirs, Georgi Dimitrov readily endorsed this proposal at the time.[75] Yugoslav communists drew up a proposal for union in early November 1944 and referred it to the BCP Central Committee for review. The Bulgarians, however, had their own ideas and replied with a proposal of their own on 13 November. At that time, both sides imagined that their union could be announced as early as the new year. Proposals and counterproposals were drafted in rapid succession and, by January, the Yugoslavs had presented the 8th draft plan, under which Bulgaria would enter Yugoslavia as the country's seventh republic.[76] The Bulgarians had thought in terms of their country enjoying equal weight with Yugoslavia in a union of equals. In giving his support to the Bulgarian position, Stalin even recalled the Austro-Hungarian Dual Monarchy of 1867–1918 as a possible model.[77]

Eventually, in the course of face-to-face talks in Bled in July 1947, Dimitrov and Yugoslav leader Tito agreed "in principle" on the unification of their two states. However, the agreement signed on 1 August said nothing about the Yugoslav idea of annexing the Pirin region in western Bulgaria to its Macedonian Republic, let alone stipulating which of the two rival formulae for union would be adopted.[78] Yugoslav hopes for the union were encouraged when Bulgaria announced that schools would open in Pirin Macedonia with Macedonian as the language of instruction and when a Macedonian National Theater was opened in Bulgaria on 7 November 1947.[79] Shortly after this, Stalin called on the Yugoslavs and Bulgarians to send delegations to Moscow for the purpose of ironing out their differences and reaching a binding agreement. High-ranking delegations from the two countries arrived in Moscow in early January 1948 but negotiations were getting nowhere. Then, on 10 February 1948, Stalin turned their meeting into an occasion "to browbeat the Yugoslavs and Bulgarians into submission, repeatedly insisting that all decisions be cleared with him in advance. The Yugoslavs, seeing how servile the Bulgarian communists were becoming vis-à-vis the Kremlin, now backed away from the planned unification."[80]

Religion

As early as Autumn 1944, the communists launched a frontal attack on the Bulgarian Orthodox Church, arresting and murdering between 500 and 600 Orthodox clerics n the years 1944–49; among these were Fr. Atanas Yanev from Kableshkovo, Brother Paladii (Dimitar Danov), and Fr. Petar Ruskov.[81] Metropolitan Kiril of Plovdiv (1901–1971) and Metropolitan Paisii of Vratsa were incarcerated from October 1944 to March 1945. During their time in prison, they were tortured and humiliated. When they were finally released, they had been tamed – Kiril more successfully than Paisii. In the meantime, Metropolitan Stefan of Sofia (1878–1957) had been elected Exarch of Bulgaria on 21 January 1945. In 1946, the regime banned religious instruction in the state schools, introducing civil marriage about the same time. Between 1946 and 1948, the regime confiscated most of the Church's land and, in 1947, adopted a new constitution which declared the separation of Church and state.

In the meantime, Exarch Stefan had shown that he was not inclined to automatic obedience to either the Bulgarian communists or the Kremlin and, on 9 July 1948, Dimitar Iliev, chief of the Office for Religious Affairs, met with a group of metropolitans who had their own disagreements with Stefan and told them that the Exarch had collaborated with British intelligence.[82] Exarch Stefan had expressed a critical point of view in a 1948 book and was further accused of damaging Bulgaria's relations with the Soviet Union. In September of that year, he was dismissed both as Exarch and as Metropolitan of Sofia. On 24 November 1948, he was taken into custody by the militia and driven to the village of Banya near Plovdiv, where he would spend the rest of his life.

Romania

In August 1944, King Michael (1921–2017) had the Axis collaborator Marshal Ion Antonescu (1882–1946) arrested and broke with the Third Reich. At the time, the Soviet news organ *Pravda* commented favorably on this *volte face*, although, until 1961, the royal coup was not mentioned in Soviet histories. Meanwhile, on 24 August, Romania was attacked by both the Wehrmacht and the Red Army. At the King's order, the Romanian army offered no resistance to the Red Army. As they took control of Transylvania, Dobruja, and Banat, the Soviets quickly replaced mayors and other local officials. In the peace treaty between Romania and the Soviet Union, Romania had to accept Soviet annexation of Bessarabia and northern Bukovina; in compensation, Romania regained northern Transylvania, which German *Führer* Hitler had awarded to Hungary. Romania had to pay for the costs of the Soviet occupation, grant the Soviets use of certain industrial and transport enterprises, and pay the Soviet Union $300 million in goods as reparations.[83] The Soviets also established Soviet-Romanian joint companies called SOVROMs. All dividends from these companies were paid to the Soviet Union. At peak, there were 13 major SOVROMs in fields such as banking, trade, metals, air transport, and river transport.[84] As elsewhere, the communist elite was divided between Muscovites, who had spent the war years in Moscow, and home communists, who had spent the war years in the home country – in this case, Romania. Among the Muscovites were Ana Pauker (1893–1960) and Vasile Luca (1898–1963), who returned to Romania in September 1944; the most important home communists were Gheorghe Gheorghiu-Dej (1901–1965), Emil Bodnăraș (1904–1976), Lucrețiu Pătrășcanu (1900–1954), and Gheorghe Apostol (1913–2010).

Initially, the communists entered into a coalition with other political parties. In this government, Petru Groza (1884–1958) of the Ploughman's Front became prime minister; the communists controlled the ministries of justice (Pătrășcanu), communications (Gheorghiu-Dej), internal affairs (Teohari Georgescu), and propaganda (Petre Constantinescu-Iași).[85] In June 1947, Ion Mihalache (1882–1963) and Iuliu Maniu (1873–1953), the leaders of the National Peasant Party, which been prominent in the interwar years, were arrested and sentenced to life imprisonment. In August, the National Peasant Party and the National Liberal Party were forced to disband. The communists waged a war of terror against leaders and members of the National Peasant Party, executing an estimated 60,000 of their number.[86] In the meantime (March 1947), the communists had established a youth organization, followed, in May, by a National Union of Romanian Students. In December 1947, King Michael, who had been allowed at first to play a role in Romanian politics, was forced to abdicate and sent into exile.

In February 1948, the Social Democratic Party of Romania was pressed into a forced marriage with the Romanian Communist Party (RCP). The resulting party was to be known as the Romanian Workers' Party (RWP). The Securitate (secret police) was set up that same year, replacing the Siguranţa. On 4 August 1948, a Law on Religious Cults established state control in the religious sector and reduced the number of legally recognized religious bodies from 60 to 14.[87] In accordance with this law, the regime nationalized all properties and funds of the Orthodox Church, taking direct control of Church finances. Article 32 of the law declared that "ministers of religious cults who express anti-democratic attitudes may be deprived temporarily or permanently of their salar[ies], which [are] provided by the state."[88] Another law gave the government a role in the appointment of bishops. The Greek (or Eastern Rite) Catholic Church was suppressed; its properties were turned over to the Orthodox Church with which it was said to be reuniting. Four of the five Greek Catholic bishops who were arrested "died in prison, and four hundred priests were executed with another two hundred imprisoned."[89] In the meantime, on 17 July 1948, Bucharest unilaterally abrogated the 10 May 1927 Concordat with the Holy See. On 3 August 1948, after passage of an education reform bill, Catholic schools and seminaries were shuttered. Subsequently, on 29 July 1949, a decree was issued, ordering the closure of all Catholic religious orders. The Orthodox Church fared no better in education when the regime nationalized or closed all 2,300 elementary schools, 24 secondary schools, and 13 seminaries hitherto operated by that body.[90]

In forced fidelity to Stalin's playbook, the communist-dominated government pushed forward with the development of heavy industry. Economic planning was introduced and small businesses were suppressed. An agrarian reform adopted in March 1945 resulted in the breakup of large estates and the distribution of 1,057,674 hectares to 796,129 peasant families.[91] This generosity would soon be reversed, when collectivization became the order of the day. In art and literature, fascist-era restrictions were lifted and, in the years 1944–1947, *avant garde* art and literature enjoyed substantial freedom. Subsequently, the doctrine of socialist realism was imposed in the arts; writers who refused to abide by this formula could be imprisoned.[92]

The Soviet Military Administration in (East) Germany

The Soviet Red Army entered Berlin the night of 21 April 1945.[93] On 6 June, the Soviets set up the Soviet Military Administration in Germany *(Sowjetische Militärad-ministration in Deutschland,* SMAD), establishing their authority over the provinces of Brandenburg, Mecklenburg-West Pomerania, Saxony, Saxony-Anhalt, and, after the withdrawal of American troops from that province, Thuringia. Some 273,000 Red Army troops would now occupy the eastern zone, supported by 29,000 air force and 2,700 naval personnel.[94] The Soviets' priorities in their zone were: exacting reparations (among other things through the wholesale expropriation of industrial plants), denazification (even if not carried through to the end), reeducating the Germans living in their zone, and settling the fate of Germany – probably in that order of priority. In the short term, within about 10 days of Germany's surrender, the Soviets arranged for a functioning food distribution system within their sector; they also began work repairing houses and fixing utilities. At war's end, most of Germany's cities lay in ruins and many of their residents had fled. For example, Berlin, which had had a population of 4,325,000 at the start of the war, had just 2,560,000 residents as of May 1945.[95]

At war's end, across the Soviet Occupation Zone (SBZ[96]) as a whole, approximately 80% of judges and public prosecutors were members of the Nazi party.[97] On 4 September 1945, SMAD issued Order No. 49, regulating the denazification of the justice system. Overall, as Helga Welsh reports, "[t]he denazification of judges and public prosecutors in the Soviet Occupation Zone was carried out more thoroughly than [for persons] in other professions."[98] But replacing former Nazis took time. Thus, in Brandenburg in late 1945, more than 50% of all jurists were still former members of the NSDAP; even in 1949, about 20% of public prosecutors were former Nazis.[99] Following SMAD Order No. 35 in February 1948, some ex-Nazis were brought into the judicial system.[100]

Reparations

The Soviets extracted reparations in three forms: wholesale removal of factories to the Soviet Union, levies on output at remaining factories, and recruitment of German workers for forced labor in the Soviet Union. The Soviets claimed that physical damage caused by the Nazis in the USSR totaled 128 billion dollars (in 1945 prices).[101] Accordingly, the Soviets dismantled and transported back to their country an estimated 3,400 factories.[102] An additional 200 enterprises that remained on German territory were converted into Soviet limited companies, with their output confiscated by Soviet authorities. It has been estimated that these Soviet-controlled companies accounted for roughly 25% of total East German production in the immediate years after war's end.[103] However, the dismantling and shipment to the Soviet Union of entire industrial plants hit the economy hard and actual industrial production in the SBZ in 1948 stood at just 60% of the level attained in 1936.[104]

At the beginning of 1946, all of the important industrial concerns in the zone were nationalized and a central planning system was introduced.[105] In 1946, reparations payments to the Soviet Union consumed almost half of the country's GDP, and reparations continued until 1953, albeit involving gradually declining exactions. In addition to the wholesale dismantling and removal of factories, the Soviets also confiscated various supplies and miscellaneous equipment and imposed a levy on East German output. The Soviets also compelled the East Germans to invest in industries that could produce goods for export to the USSR; this included the prioritization of automotive and heavy engineering industries and the construction of an ocean-going ship-building industry.[106]

As early as October 1945, SMAD had ordered the expropriation of all estates larger than 100 hectares (approximately 250 acres), along with government property and the property previously held by Nazi leaders. This land went into a central pool, out of which parcels of land were distributed among approximately half a million people. Nonetheless, the eventual introduction of a system of collective farming would be taken up only several years after the establishment of the German Democratic Republic.

Finally, in what might be seen as reparations in human form, the Soviets apprehended a number of German scientists, taking them to work in Russia. Reports soon spread that the German scientists (and technicians) were being treated with respect, given the best housing available, and provided with generous rations. As a result, additional numbers of scientists and technicians volunteered to move to the Soviet Union.[107]

Noncommunist parties

In summer 1945, two middle-class parties applied to Soviet authorities for permission to organize in the SBZ. The two parties – the Christian Democratic Union (CDU[108]) and the Liberal Democratic Party of Germany (LDPD[109]) – were quickly granted permission. The CDU, built on traditions of the (Catholic) Center Party, had not existed before 1933 (or before 1945, for that matter) and was intended to bring together non-socialists who would support the democratic reconstruction of Germany on the basis of Christian teachings. The LDPD figured as a revival of the Weimar-era liberal German Democratic Party.[110] Thus, as of the end of 1945, there were four parties operating in the SBZ: the KPD, the Social Democratic Party of Germany (SPD[111]), the CDU, and the LDPD. Both the CDU and the LDPD were committed to the defense of private property.[112] Subsequently, two further parties were formed in response to the express wish of the Soviet Military Administration[113]: the German Peasants' Party (Bauernpartei or DBD[114]), with its leadership drawn mostly from officials of the Farmers' Cooperative; and the National Democratic Party of Germany (NDPD[115]), which was "specifically designed to embrace former Nazis and nationalists . . . [and which] was dominated by Communists who had not previously appeared in the public eye."[116] These two parties were established specifically in the hope of diluting the support for the CDU and the LDPD, and the leaders of the Bauerpartei and the NDPD were installed by the communists.[117]

The establishment of the SED[118]

Meanwhile, plans were afoot to snuff out the SPD, by forcing its members to "merge" into a renamed communist party. The SPD had rebuilt its structure by the end of 1945, with already some 400,000 members, and was clearly more popular than the KPD. But the KPD was applying increasing pressure on the SPD to agree to a merger of the two parties. This pressure was felt at all levels, from the leadership down to local branches. The Central Committee of the SPD registered its opposition to merger for the last time in January 1946. Meanwhile, SMAD police intensified surveillance of SPD leaders and members and even resorted to "terrorist" measures to intimidate the party. As opposition to the merger on the part of Social Democrats continued, police rounded up the recalcitrant and, between December 1945 and April 1946, at least 20,000 Social Democrats were incarcerated, some serving long sentences; others were killed.[119] Finally, on 21 April 1946, thus on the first anniversary of the entry of the Red Army into Berlin, the SPD was forced to amalgamate with the KPD, forming the new Socialist Unity Party of Germany (SED). In the end, 1,298,415 members of the SPD joined the newly formed SED, accounting for 52.3% of the merged party's membership.[120] Wilhelm Pieck (1876–1960), who had spent the war years in Moscow before returning to German territory to reestablish the KPD, and Otto Grotewohl (1894–1964), erstwhile head of the SPD, became co-chairs of the new party. Walter Ulbricht became General Secretary of the SED on 25 July 1950, the same day that Pieck and Grotewohl resigned as co-chairmen of the party; Ulbricht, thereby, became head of the party.[121]

In spite of the forced merger, there continued to be forms of organized opposition on the part of former Social Democrats in the first years after the creation of the SED. Some Social Democrats simply resigned from the SED, while many fled the SBZ. Among those who fled was Erich W. Griffke, who originally had supported the merger and was even a member of the Central Committee of the SED. He fled to the West in October 1948, after having joined Max Fechner and other former Social Democrats in the first half of 1948 in trying to open a discussion among Social Democrats about the future of cooperation with the communists "under existing conditions".[122] Opposition on the part of the majority of former SPD members reached its peak in 1948. They were specifically opposed to the obvious Leninization of the SED, which now described itself as a "party of a new type". At the time, the incarceration of former Social Democrats was still underway and, in the late 1940s, they constituted the largest group among those sent to forced labor camps. Meanwhile, former Social Democrats continued to be purged from the upper echelons of the SED.[123]

Denazification

Just as in the Western zones of occupation, so too in the Soviet Occupation Zone efforts at denazification encountered misunderstanding on the part of local officials and bureaucratic obstacles. Moreover, Soviet officials and East German communists were not always on the same page, and deadlines were repeatedly missed. In fact, SMAD granted local German commissions considerable authority in effecting denazification; as a result, Soviet authorities "had little direct influence over the day-to-day operations of the purge" of Nazis from positions of responsibility.[124] Altogether, some 30,000 persons were reviewed by these commissions, mostly men 30–60 years of age; about one-fourth of them were dismissed from their places of employment. But physicians and others considered essential were treated more leniently.

As early as 30 April 1945, the Soviets banned the Nazi Party together with its subordinate organizations, such as the Gestapo and the Hitler Youth. The Soviets

quickly arrested Nazi mayors and other Nazi functionaries, although often innocent civilians were also rounded up. The Third Reich's police force was dismantled
and a new "anti-fascist" militia was set up in its place.[125] On 14 July 1945, a meeting
of anti-fascist parties was convened, only to reveal differences of opinion concerning the criteria for distinguishing between "active" Nazis and "nominal" Nazis.[126]

As of 1 October 1945, 15,466 former NSDAP members were still teaching in
the schools of the SBZ,[127] accounting for more than 90% of local teachers.[128] At
that time, 72% of the teaching staff in the SBZ's *Volksschulen* were former Nazis;
in Thuringia, the figure was 90%. To address this challenge, the Soviets launched
teacher-training classes in August 1945 for persons with anti-fascist records, including industrial workers and farmers.[129] In Thuringia, as of 12 April 1945, 78% of
employees at the Ministry of Education were Nazis; five months later, the number
of former Nazis at the ministry had been reduced to 28%.[130] University professors
who were compromised were arrested.

The official denazification commissions were reinforced by anti-fascist committees, which sprang up spontaneously and, in some areas such as Leipzig, helped to
topple what was left of the Nazi apparatus. Some of these committees were headed
by communists, others by Social Democrats, and still others by anti-Nazi bourgeois
groups. In addition to the "antifas", there were also spontaneous workers' committees under the leadership of communists and socialists, that seized control of
factories across Germany; in some cases, the workers wreaked vengeance on petty
Nazis, in the process removing skilled personnel from the operations of the factories.[131] The KPD was dismayed at seeing the antifas deciding independently on the
standards by which to assess individual complicity in the Nazi system and criticized
the anti-fascists for "ideological confusion".[132]

The denazification program lasted from May 1945 to March 1948 in the Soviet
occupation zone. In the period May 1945-December 1946, 390,478 persons
were dismissed from their positions for reasons of past Nazi affiliation and did
not receive fresh appointments. Between January and June 1947, a further 64,578
persons were dismissed without being appointed to new positions. Finally, in the
period July 1947-March 1948, 11,167 persons were dismissed and 10,482 were
transferred to new positions. A total of 44,025 applications for employment in
new positions were denied. All told, denazification in the SBZ affected 520,730
persons.[133]

Yet denazification was not restricted to former Nazis and war criminals; from
the beginning the SED wanted reliable cadres who could follow orders and had no
use for independent-minded persons. Thus, even before the prospect of a unified
neutral Germany in which communists would be prominently represented in the
higher echelons of power was confirmed to be a dead letter, the Soviet occupation authorities and the German communists committed to building a new system,
culminating in the avowal by the SED in January 1949 that it considered itself "a
party of a new type."[134] At the end of July 1948, the SED Party Executive (Vor-
stand) decided that it was necessary to cleanse party ranks of "hostile and decadent
elements"; the campaign would target former Social Democrats in the first place.

Thus, starting in 1949 and running into 1952, the SED reviewed the records of approximately 1.5 million members, expelling roughly 10% of those reviewed.[135]

At the same time, SMAD Order No. 43 opened the way for even incriminated ex-Nazis to find a way to inclusion in the emerging system. In a word, ex-Nazis willing to conform to the new order being constructed in the SBZ, who offered relevant skills, could be rehabilitated. Accordingly, as Olaf Kappelt has pointed out, "even Nazi mass murderers were won over to collaboration with the communist state."[136] Allied Control Council Directive No. 24 (12 January 1946) had set forth some guidelines for denazification. But, on 17 February 1947, the antifascist bloc parties spoke out against Directive 24 and demanded that most of those considered to have been merely nominal Nazis be allowed to retain their posts.[137] Not only were nominal Nazis often allowed to keep their jobs, but over time 44,025 former Nazis would be appointed to new positions in the SED bureaucracy.[138]

Denazification was therefore employed both against Nazis not deemed "valuable" and against irreconcilable nonconformists. "Fascist" was operationalized to cover not only former Nazis but also anti-communists and potential troublemakers.[139] Even communists who offered views dissenting from the KPD/SED line could find themselves arrested and incarcerated. Altogether between 160,000 and 250,000 Nazis and non-Nazis were sent to SBZ prison camps, while approximately 25,000 Germans were deported to the Soviet Union.[140] The prison camps continued to function until 1950.

The educational sector

From 1946 onward, admissions committees at universities in the SBZ were expected to give preferential treatment to applicants from working-class and peasant families.[141] Shortly after Germany's surrender, the East German SPD and the KPD asserted their control in higher education, working closely with Soviet authorities. As noted above, more than 80% of teaching faculty in the zone's six universities were dismissed, although overaged anti-Nazi teachers who had been teaching before 1933 were rehired. The Soviets also set about training a new teaching force[142] and Sovietizing social science. University rectors in Rostok, Leipzig, and Greifswald were dismissed and replaced with new appointees who were prepared to cooperate with the occupation regime. Private schools were ordered to shut down, and the Churches were informed that henceforth religious instruction would not be permitted in the state schools. The CDU and LDPD, which had not yet been brought into line, opposed the 1946 law, with the CDU in particular mounting a defense of confessional and private schooling. As battle lines were drawn, the Protestants joined the Catholics in opposition to the SED program of secularization of the schools. Many members of the LDPD as well as Social Democrats supported the CDU's plea for the continuation of confessional schools.

Although SED members increasingly dominated the ranks of teaching faculties, there continued to be rumblings of dissent in the ranks of German educators in the SBZ, who developed their own vision of the 'new school', resulting in sometimes uneasy relations with SMAD authorities.[143] Not surprisingly, opposition to *Gleich-schaltung* was even stiffer among students at East German universities, and a large number of students were arrested on orders from SMAD and the SED.

Religion and the Churches

Soviet plans entailed not just secularization but also the active promotion of atheism. The CDU, as already mentioned, wanted to see religious instruction retained in the curriculum. Eventually, in spring 1946, a compromise was reached: religion would not figure as part of the regular curriculum, but the Churches would be permitted to organize and teach religion in the school buildings after normal school hours.

Where the confessional schools were concerned, Soviet occupation authorities had them shut down, prompting Bishop Konrad von Preysing of Berlin (later elevated to the College of Cardinals) to protest that "the areligious school necessarily provides an education antithetical to faith."[144] In some respects, however, the Soviets' policy as regards the Churches was initially quite similar to that of the three Western Allies. Thus, "a large number of Church witnesses from 1945 testified to the benevolent attitude of Soviet occupation authorities vis-à-vis the Churches."[145] The Soviets also agreed that the Churches could denazify their own ranks.[146] All in all, as Robert Goeckel has suggested, the policy adopted by the Soviet occupation authorities toward the Churches was "relatively mild".[147] There were at least four reasons for the milder course taken in the religious sphere compared to that adopted elsewhere in Eastern Europe at that time. First, there was the bond formed between local communists and pastors during the time they spent together in Nazi concentration camps. Second, there was the fact that, at the time, the Protestants maintained a single organizational structure for all of Germany, maintaining active contact across the four zones. Third, East Berlin, which the Soviets controlled, had not yet been sealed off from West Berlin, which was under the control of the Western Allies. And fourth, Soviet General Secretary Stalin hoped to bring about the reunification of Germany as a demilitarized and neutral state. Indeed, Stalin would pass along a proposal to this effect to the USA, Great Britain, and France on 10 March 1952, two-and-a-half years after the establishment of the two separate German states![148]

The status of women

In time, Soviet authorities would offer some support for gender equality in the SBZ and take steps to improve women's situation. In the short term, however, poorly disciplined Russian troops exacted their idea of vengeance on Germans by perpetrating a rash of rapes. Security for women actually worsened in 1946, but improved in early 1947. In garrison towns such as Frankfurt-an-der-Oder, the problem continued into 1947; women were afraid to go out of their homes after dark and simply stayed indoors.[149] Railroad stations were especially dangerous for women and, when railroad officials tried to intervene to protect the women, they were beaten up.

Official communist policy regarding what the communists called "the woman question" emphasized gender equality and efforts to improve women's situation. Through films and periodicals, Soviet occupation authorities and their East German collaborators worked hard to undermine the traditional understanding of women's role, summed up in the *Kaiserreich*-era slogan, *Kinder, Küche, Kirche* (Children, Kitchen, Church), which limited women to the domestic and religious spheres.[150] Soon after its founding in 1946, the SED set up a Central Women's Section, promising to promote equal rights and equal pay for East German women.[151]

Art and music

The effort to reshape identities and promote the idea that Germans in the SBZ were fashioning an antifascist nation was manifested not only in the religious sphere and the sphere of gender equality – albeit contested in both cases – but also in the cultural sphere. In the first three years after the war, however, there was a degree of liberal toleration in culture, with the journal *Bildende Kunst*, edited by Karl Hofer and Oskar Nerlinger, publishing favorable articles about the works of Pablo Picasso, the Dadaist painter Max Ernst, the post-impressionist painter Georges-Pierre Seurat, the Cubist painter Juan Gris, the expressionist painter Lyonel Feininger, and other free spirits. But toward the end of 1948, Lt. Col. Alexander Dymschitz took over as head of SMAD's cultural department; with that, the artistic freedom enjoyed since 1945 came to an abrupt end.[152]

From the standpoint of the Soviet authorities and their SED acolytes, there were progressive cultural products which moved society upwards along the socialist path as well as reactionary cultural products which obstructed the social transformation of society. Small art exhibitions came under fire in the Soviet-zone press, with the works on display condemned for lack of social engagement – "formalism" in the Soviet jargon. The *Deutsche Volkszeitung* likewise served as a vehicle for rebuking artists, excoriating them in August 1945 for not expressing optimism about the future, while insisting two months later, "We have no use for surrealism or any other kind of ism; we need an art representing life in a fashion that renders all its hidden interconnections more profoundly and in a thoroughly understandable fashion to the viewer, not less so or entirely incomprehensible."[153]

In fact, in the sphere of culture, there was only one "ism" which the Soviet authorities enthusiastically endorsed – socialist realism, which required that artistic creations, whether paintings or scupture or music, represent everyone and everything associated with socialism as heroic and triumphant, while linking capitalism with exploitation, injustice, imperialism, war, and suffering. SMAD Order No. 51 (1945) was devoted to setting the course in the cultural sector, demanding in particular the "active utilization of artistic means in the struggle against fascism and for the reeducation of the German people."[154] Art societies which had existed before 1945 were suppressed, the staging of art exhibits in the Soviet zone required prior permission from occupation authorities, and, with the passage of time, there were attacks on Picasso, Paul Klee, and expressionist painter Karl Schmidt-Rottluff.

Nor were the new cultural tsars shy about sharing their views about music and theater. Thus, in 1948, Colonel Dymschitz criticized the musical giant Paul Hindemith, alleging "that Hindemith's opposition to fascism was 'not revolutionary' and that the hero of his opera *Mathis der Maler*, the sixteenth-century artist [Matthias] Grünewald, embodied the kind of opposition to the forces of reaction destined to fail because of its 'individualism'."[155] Needless to say, there was no room either for Arnold Schoenberg's 12-tone music in the new socialist cultural space being constructed.

The Berlin Airlift

In early 1948, the Soviets found out that Great Britain, the United States, and France were working in secret to lay the foundation for a West German state. In response, the Soviets stopped meeting with its three erstwhile Allies to coordinate their policies in occupied Germany. Then, on 20 June, the three Western occupation powers introduced a new currency, the Deutschmark, for use in their sectors as well as in West Berlin. Four days later, the Soviets closed off Western access to West Berlin by road, rail, and canals. What the Soviets hoped to achieve was to force the West to cede West Berlin to Soviet control. Soviet military strength exceeded the combined military strength of the three Western states at this point; thus, a Western military response was out of the question.[156] But the Western Allies were not prepared to pull out of Berlin. So, on 26 June 1948, just two days after the Soviets closed off all surface routes to West Berlin, the Allies launched Operation VITLLES, better known as the Berlin Airlift.

The Allies began deliverng 5,000 tons of supplies each day, later increasing this to 8,000 tons of supplies every day. The Allies had originally expected the Soviets to lift the blockade soon after they saw Western determination to supply the needs of West Berliners. Instead, the Soviets continued the blockade, hoping to break Western resolve. But the Western Allies continued the airlift, sending almost 300,000 flights to West Berlin, until the Soviets finally lifted their blockade on 12 May 1949. In the course of the nine months of the blockade, the Western Allies had delivered 2.3 million tons of cargo to West Berlin.[157] The long-term effect of the Soviet blockade ran counter to Soviet interests since it provided a stimulus to the creation of the North Atlantic Treaty Organization − NATO − with the United States, Canada, and 10 West European states signing on to the alliance in April 1949.[158] The Soviets' blockade and the Berlin Airlift also put a definite end to any lingering notions of German reunification (which had been premised, on the Soviet side, on a neutral, disarmed Germany).

The second phase, 1948/49–1956 (Stalinism)

In the first phase, there were those who expected the communists to fail rather quickly; there were, accordingly, anti-communist guerrillas who held out in the woods of Poland and Yugoslavia for a few years.[159] In addition, in July 1949, Pope Pius XII (1876–1958; reigned 1939–1958) pronounced an anathema on anyone who would cooperate with the communists and announced the automatic excommunication of all who did so. But communism did not crumble and, on the contrary, the communist regimes proved ready to resort to extralegal and outright illegal methods to suppress any opposition to their rule.

The period of "high Stalinism" began as early as 1946 or 1947 in some countries but, for purposes of this book, I date the inception of this phase from the communist coup in Czechoslovakia in February 1948 and the completion of the communist takeover of Hungary in June 1948 (with the forced merger of the SDP into the HCP), while noting that the German Democratic Republic was not established until October 1949. In spite of Stalin's death on 5 March 1953, the era of high Stalinism lasted until 1956. In that latter year, Carl J. Friedrich and Zbigniew K. Brzezinski published a book in which they outlined a syndrome consisting of six features which they had identified in the Soviet bloc: (1) an official, chiliastic ideology; (2) a single political party monopolizing power; (3) a centrally directed economy; (4) party control of the media and mass communications; (5) party control of the military; and (6) a terroristic secret police.[160] While Friedrich and Brzezinski described this syndrome as "totalitarian" rather than "Stalinist", they were looking at the East European states and the USSR in drawing up this list. There were, however, several other features which were typical of the East European communist states and for that matter also the USSR: (7) a cult of the leader; (8) an aspiration to transform human nature (in the USSR, to create "the new Soviet man" and "the new Soviet woman"); (9) an anti-religious campaign, intended to control, instrumentalize, and marginalize religious life in the short run, and to promote its extinction in the long run; (10) agricultural collectivization (soon abandoned in Yugoslavia and Poland, and temporarily abandoned in Hungary in 1956); (11) a prescribed formula called *socialist realism* in art, music, literature, and architecture, emphasizing achievement and conveying a sense of optimism about the socialist project, or art for the sake of politics; and (12) an emphasis on heavy industry, especially machine-building.

It was Italian dictator Benito Mussolini (1883–1945) who first popularized the term "totalitarian", applying the term to describe his own rule. Since then, the term has lost much of its original meaning and is sometimes misunderstood to mean that a government or regime might have a total control over people's lives right down to when they do their laundry. The term is, therefore, unusable. Rather than trying to put a controversial and sometimes misunderstood term to use, I prefer to accept Jürgen Kocka's understanding of Stalinist society as a *durchherrschte Gesellschaft*[161] (a penetrated society) as appropriate in looking at the Soviet bloc countries. The regimes' penetration of their respective societies was marked by the following features: the regimes of the Soviet bloc sought to mold people's thoughts about religion and politics and extirpate religion over the long term, creating the New Communist Man and New Communist Woman; upon coming to power, they banned the boy scouts and girl scouts, the YMCA and YWCA, and any organizations which they did not control, and even the Churches were penetrated to a greater or lesser extent, depending on the country; any group of friends in East Germany meeting on a regular basis even if only to have coffee and talk about their families, had to report their meeting in advance, provide a list of "members" to the police, and even provide a list of topics they would discuss – and, in any case, they were supposed to obtain permission to meet; members of the communist party were not allowed to attend religious ceremonies of any kind; certain academic disciplines could be suppressed, as happened in Stalin's Russia with genetics and sociology or subverted, as happened in Stalin's Russia with psychology, geography, physics, and history[162]; certain subjects could not be studied at the university level, for example, as already mentioned, the Middle Ages in Czechoslovakia; the children of persons designated as "class enemies" could be denied access to higher education; the party regimes took a political interest in art, literature, and music, wanting these cultural genres to serve communist objectives and suppressed those cultural artifacts of which they did not approve; those who articulated alternative political visions ("dissidents") could be deported, as happened to Rudolf Bahro in the German Democratic Republic, or imprisoned, as happened on several occasions including from 1979 to 1983 to Václav Havel in Czechoslovakia; in Romania, after a presidential decree was issued in December 1985, conversation with a foreigner was considered a criminal infraction;[163] and travel outside the Soviet bloc was severely restricted for ordinary citizens most of the time. But two qualifications should immediately be made. First, the degree of penetration of the East Central European societies by their respective regimes was greatest, with some variation, in the years 1948–1956, diminishing over time as these regimes relaxed in one or another policy sphere (albeit, in some cases, only temporarily). Moreover, by 1988 citizens not only of Poland but also of Czechoslovakia and Hungary were increasingly organizing independent groups, in defiance of the regimes. Second, there were variations from one country to the next so that, for example, while the Czechoslovak Catholic newspaper *Katolické noviny* was directly controlled and scripted by the Czechoslovak secret police, East German Protestant newspapers such as *Die Kirche* were written by the staff of those newspapers and faced, at most, post-publication suppression (which was, of course, costly to the given newspaper). The regimes, thus, encroached on aspects of people's lives which are normally considered sacrosanct in democratic countries to the point of being intrusive.

The cult of the leader was a prominent feature in all of the Soviet bloc states but, unlike Yugoslavia and Albania, which glorified only the leaders of their respective communist parties, Tito and Hoxha, the states of the Soviet bloc rotated around two suns: the local leader and, until he was posthumously dethroned, Soviet leader Josef Stalin. This veneration was the direct result of Stalin's determinative power in the region. It was Stalin who decided on the economic plans in the Soviet bloc states, dictated when they should launch agricultural collectivization, and determined who should be promoted or demoted or purged. He was, in effect, something approaching a god in the bloc. He was adulated, as a Romanian source expressed it, as "the great genius of working mankind, the leader of the working people around the world, the liberator and friend of our nation"[164] and, of course, "the coryphaeus of science".[165] Not surprisingly, Stalin's 70th birthday was treated as an enormously important event throughout the bloc.[166] Romanian composers, to take just one example, produced more than 100 musical works to mark the occasion; among these, the best known were the *Cantata Dedicated to Comrade Stalin* by Zeno Vancea, the *Cantata Dedicated to Comrade Stalin* by Mihail Andricu, the *Ode to Stalin's Law* by Hilda Jerea, and *Cantata Dedicated to Comrade Stalin* by Alfred Mendelsohn.[167]

Whatever else it was, Stalinism was a project to construct an alternative modernity – a "socialist modernity".[168] Stalinist modernity, as Stephen Kotkin and Anna Krylova have noted,[169] was both anti-capitalist and anti-individualist. Stalinism stressed development (economic and social) and control. Under *development*, Stalinism understood not only the spread of literacy but also industrialization, emphasizing heavy industry. Among future members of the Soviet bloc, illiteracy was highest in Bulgaria and in the Romanian countryside and lowest in Czecho-slovakia and Hungary (see Table 2.4).

Under heavy industry, the Stalinists understood metalworks, machine-building, and mining. After the devastation of World War Two and, more especially, given that most of these states were largely agrarian, it was possible to achieve double-digit annual rates of growth of industrial production through 1954 (see Table 2.5). In the four northern tier countries, rates of growth remaining respectable, for the most part, through 1963, although the Hungarian Revolution of 1956 had a severe

TABLE 2.4 Illiteracy before 1945

	Year	% illiterate
Bulgaria	1934	31.4% of persons age 10 or older
Czechoslovakia	1930	5% of persons age 6 or older
Hungary	1941	7.1–7.4% of persons age 6 or older
Poland	1939	18% (age range not specified)
Romania (rural areas)	1930	70–75% of persons age 7 or older
Romania (urban areas)	1930	15–20% of persons age 7 or older

Source: For Romania, *România – un Secol de Istorie* (Bucureşti, 2018), p. 72; other data from Sabrina P. Ramet, "Interwar East Central Europe, 1918–1941: The failure of democracy-building, the fate of minorities – an Introduction", in Sabrina P. Ramet (ed.), *Interwar East Central Europe, 1918–1941: The Failure of Democracy-building, the Fate of Minorities* (London and New York: Routledge, 2020), p. 8.

Note: The Romanian census of 1930 was the last reliable census before the communists took power. The Czechoslovak census of 1930 was the last census undertaken prior to the communist takeover; the 1940 census was conducted only in Bohemia and Moravia, under Nazi auspices. The Bulgarian census of 1934 was the last census conducted before the end of World War Two; the next census was conducted in 1946.

TABLE 2.5 Annual Rates of Growth of Industrial Production, 1950–1956 in per cent

	1950	1951	1952	1953	1954	1955	1956
Bulgaria	15	19	16	15	11	8	15
Czechoslovakia	15	14	18	9	4	11	9
German Democratic Republic	26	23	16	12	10	8	6
Hungary	29	24	21	12	10	9	−10
Poland	28	22	19	17	11	11	9
Romania	—	24	17	15	6	14	11

Source: Z. M. Fallenbuchl, "The Communist Pattern of Industrialization", in *Soviet Studies*, Vol. 21, No. 4 (April 1970), p. 468.

TABLE 2.6 Rate of Growth of Industrial Output in the Four Northern Tier States, 1950–1963 annual increments, in %

	East Germany	Poland	Czechoslovakia	Hungary
1950	28.5	28.3	14.5	28.8
1951	22.4	22.1	14.7	25.8
1952	15.6	18.0	16.7	23.3
1953	12.4	19.0	8.7	11.1
1954	11.0	11.1	4.0	5.0
1955	8.1	10.2	11.5	9.4
1956	6.0	8.8	9.5	−9.2
1957	7.9	10.0	9.4	11.6
1958	11.0	9.4	10.3	10.9
1959	12.0	8.6	10.8	11.9
1960	8.4	10.7	11.9	12.6
1961	6.6	9.8	8.9	11.1
1962	5.5	8.2	6.2	7.9
1963	5.0	5.0	0.4	7.0

Source: Josef Goldmann, "Fluctuations and Trend in the Rate of Economic Growth in Some Socialist Countries", in *Eastern European Economics*, Vol. 4, No. 1 (Autumn 1965), p. 15.

impact on industrial production in Hungary that year, and Czechoslovakia actually experienced negative growth in 1963 (see Table 2.6).

Stalinism was also concerned with *control*. For example, while the collective farms were significantly less productive than private farms, except for Poland after October 1956, all the political elites in the bloc states demanded the collectivization of agriculture. This was, in the first place, because Stalin demanded it. But what it achieved, if not an increase in productivity, was control, with the collective farms having to realize goals set by the communist party and being dependent upon authorities for the use of agricultural machinery.

The religious sphere

The communists were aware that religious organizations propounded alternative value systems to communism, thus challenging communist hegemony. Accordingly, the communist regimes sought to control and weaken the Churches and other religious faiths. Between 1948 and 1953, the following mainly Catholic hierarchs in Soviet bloc countries were either consigned to house arrest or imprisoned: Catholic Cardinal József Mindszenty of Esztergom and Lutheran Bishop Lajos Ordass of Hungary in 1948; Archbishop Josef Beran of Prague and Archbishop Alexandru Cisar of Bucharest in 1949; Bishop Aron Marton of Alba Julia (Romania) and his colleague Bishop Anton Durcovici of Iaşi in 1950; Archbishop József Groesz of Kalocsa in 1951; several bishops in Poland in 1951–52; and Cardinal Stefan Wyszyński, Primate of Poland, in 1953.[170] Convents and monasteries were closed and, except in the case of the German Democratic Republic, Church-operated nursing homes and orphanages were seized by the authorities. Most elementary and secondary schools operated by the Churches were shut down, and limits were imposed on the number of young men to be admitted to seminaries. Religious instruction in the public schools was restricted – typically limited to after-school hours. Everywhere in the bloc, state offices for religious affairs were established to regulate and control religious life. The Czechoslovak communist news organ explained: "every religion, with its faith in eternal life, with its preaching of humility, resignation to fate, love even to the enemy, with its rejection of the active fight of the workers for true happiness on earth is [in] absolute and sharp contradiction to the communist world view."[171] Accordingly, from the Stalinist point of view prevalent at the time, religion needed to be eradicated. In the short term, of course, the communists were prepared to harness one or another Church or clergyman for their purposes. But in the long term, there could be no place for religion in communist society.

The cultural sphere

Nor did the cultural sphere escape the communists' desire for control. The "engineers of the human soul" (as Stalin called writers, composers, and artists) were expected to accept socialist realism as their guiding principle. This formula, or doctrine, was first imposed on Soviet writers at the First Congress of the Writers' Union of the USSR in 1934 and quickly extended also to composers, being spelled out in an article published in the journal *Sovetskaya Muzyka* that same year.[172] In an address to that Congress, Andrey Zhdanov (1896–1948), Second Secretary of the CPSU and the Soviet Union's cultural "tsar", outlined what was to be understood under *socialist realism*. Following Zhdanov's address, the Writers' Union adopted a resolution calling on writers to present Soviet reality in a positive light. Optimism about the Soviet future was mandatory. Literature in the spirit of art-for-the-sake-of-art ("formalism") and experimental forms of writing ("decadence") were to be avoided. The doctrine was subsequently imposed on pictorial artists and composers alike.[173] Simplicity and easy comprehensibility were the order of the day. Hence, composers were expected to create "simple and uncomplicated music, using musical language based on the traditional major-minor rules, and referring as frequently as possible to national folklore."[174] The Soviets convened a Congress of Composers and Musicologists from the Soviet bloc states in Prague in May 1948. The Congress adopted a resolution calling on composers "to renounce 'extreme subjectivism' in favor of expressing the 'aspirations of the popular masses and progressive ideals of contemporary life.'"[175] In fact, in the Soviet bloc states, the party endeavored to assert firm control of culture beginning in 1947; this control began to come undone after the death of Stalin in March 1953.[176] Referring to the Polish case, Bogdan Gierzaczyński wrote that "Formalism, in the view of the communist bureaucrats, was a synonym for subversion . . . [I]t was a particularly serious and dangerous accusation against an artist, and it was not at all difficult to deserve it. All one had to do was to follow the traditions and progressive trends in European music!"[177]

Collectivization

Initially, communists in all the socialist countries of Eastern Europe favored the collectivization of agriculture. Albania's Enver Hoxha spoke for the communist mainstream in 1966, when he declared that "Any other road leads only to the restoration of capitalism in the countryside."[178] Even Władysław Gomułka, First Secretary of the Polish United Workers' Party (i.e., communist party), talked at first of the importance of collectivization, telling the Second Plenum of the party's Central Committee (in June 1959) that the communist party "believes in the socialist transformation of agriculture and realizes that such a transformation can be implemented only through setting up large collective peasant farms."[179] But Gomułka was talking malarkey as he had already allowed most of Poland's arable land to return to private hands.

But in the early years, collectivization was pushed forward across the region through a combination of devices including forced deliveries in large quantities, heavy taxes, violence, and of course active encouragement by local communist zealots. Collectivization was not achieved all at once but the percentage of land in the socialist sector increased gradually over time (see Table 2.7). Indeed, as Zbigniew Brzezinski has noted, except in Bulgaria and Czechoslovakia, agricultural collectivization proceeded at a slower pace than it had in the Soviet Union in 1930–38.[180] The communist regime of Poland, like that of Yugoslavia, would abandon its collectivization drives in the 1950s, leaving only a small proportion of arable land in collective farms. In Hungary, the communists aped Soviet policies by organizing a violent campaign against "kulaks" (*kulak* being the Russian word for a successful peasant). The Hungarian kulaks responded as their Russian namesakes had – by slaughtering their livestock. By 1954, the Hungarian communist party called for "the strengthening of the class war against the kulak" and even "the liquidation of the kulak".[181] Coerced onto collective farms, most peasants responded by working less than they had on their own private farms. In spite of that, total agricultural production in Eastern Europe as a whole grew at an average annual rate of 3.9% between 1950 and 1963.[182]

TABLE 2.7 Percentage of arable land in the socialist sector (1950–1960)

	1950	1953	1956	1958
Poland	12	17	24	15
GDR		11.6	23.2	37.0
Czechoslovakia	25	48	45	77
Hungary	19	37	33	85[#]
Romania	12	21	35	51
Bulgaria	44	62	77	92

\# 1960 for Hungary, rather than 1958.

Sources: Bulgaria 1956 from Marin Pundeff, "Bulgaria", in Joseph Held (ed.), *The Columbia History of Eastern Europe in the Twentieth Century* (New York: Columbia University Press), p. 10; Hungary 1960 from Paul Katona, "Collectivization of Agriculture in Central Europe", in *The World Today*, Vol. 16, No. 9 (September 1960), p. 409; GDR figures from Hermann Weber, Geschichte der DDR, 2nd ed. (Munich: Deutscher Taschenburh Verlag, 2000), p.. 215; 1960; all other figures from Zbigniew K. Brzezinski, *The Soviet Bloc: Unity and Conflict*, Revised & enlarged ed. (Cambridge, Mass.: Harvard University Press, 1967), p. 99.

Czechoslovakia, 1948–1957

Even before the first elections were conducted under the 9 May constitution, the communists staged the first major show trial, bringing leading officials of the Slovak Democratic Party before the court; all of the accused were convicted. In the period October 1948-December 1952, 178 persons were executed for political reasons. In the years up to 1957, no fewer than 35,770 persons were imprisoned for serious crimes, with an additional 50,000–60,000 being incarcerated for lesser crimes. An estimated 22,000 people were sentenced to forced labor camps during these years. According to *Rudé právo* (15 March 1968), there were at least 107 labor camps in operation in 1952.[183]

In an effort to centralize communist hegemony over the entire country, the Central Committee of the Slovak Communist Party (KSS) used its plenary session of 27 September 1948 to define the KSS as (merely) "a territorial organization" of the Communist Party of Czechoslovakia "in Slovakia".[184] Meanwhile, trials continued. Twelve politicians, all but one from non-communist parties, were put on trial on trumped-up charges of anti-state activities. The trial ran from 31 May to 8 June 1950, ending with all 12 found guilty and death sentences handed down for four of the accused. In the wake of this trial, there were another 35 trials across the country, resulting in the conviction of 639 politicians, the execution of 10, and sentences to life imprisonment for 48 of them.[185]

In 1950, authorities in Prague went after three of the most prominent Slovak communists – Dr. Vladimír Clementis (1902–1952), foreign minister since 1948; poet Laco Novomeský (1904–1976); and Gustáv Husák (1913–1991), at the time a member of the Czechoslovak Communist Party (KSČ) Central Committee. Clementis was taken to task for having criticized the Nazi-Soviet Pact of August 1939 and accused of bourgeois nationalism and espionage for Western countries. Presumably under the influence of torture, he confessed to the charges and was executed on 3 December 1952.[186] Novomeský confessed to the concocted charges but may have cooperated with the interrogators by allegedly making statements which were used against Rudolf Slánský. Novomeský was sent to prison but was released at the end of 1955. Husák, although subjected to sustained torture, refused to confess to the charges brought against him; instead of execution, Husák was given a life sentence but was released from prison in 1960.[187] He was readmitted to the party in 1964.

The most spectacular trial of the years during which Gottwald was at the helm involved the erstwhile General Secretary of the KSČ, Rudolf Slánský (1901–1952), who was arrested in November 1951 together with 13 of his cohorts, all long-time party members. Under torture Slánský confessed to the crimes of which he was accused (all fabricated). Together with ten of the other defendants, he was sentenced to death on 27 November 1952; he was executed on 3 December 1952, the same day as Clementis. The remaining three defendants in the trial of Slánský et al. received life sentences.[188] The purges of communist party ranks, which were pursued throughout the bloc, served two purposes: first, to resolve intra-elite rivalries, for example between the home communists and the Muscovites; and second, by inculcating feelings of uncertainty and inchoate fear, to establish patterns of automatic obedience and discipline. The number of those purged in the Soviet bloc was highest in Czechoslovakia, as shown in Table 2.8.

Purges and executions declined in number after the death of Stalin on 5 March 1953. Meanwhile, President Gottwald caught a serious cold in Moscow while attending Stalin's funeral. By 14 March, Gottwald was dead.

Following the death of Stalin, there was an attack by 3,000 locals in April 1953 on municipal headquarters in Prostějov to protest the demolition of a statue of Tomáš Masaryk, while, in early June, thousands of workers in Plzeň rose up in protest of harsh economic conditions and inadequate supplies of food and lack of freedom.[189] Students at universities in Prague, Brno, Ostrava, Košice, Nitra, Plzeň, and Banská Bystrica drew up resolutions in May 1953 demanding change.

Gottwald's successor as First Secretary of the KSČ was Antonín Novotný (1904–1975), who had been admitted to the Politburo in 1951. Following the demise of Antonín Zápotocký on 13 November 1957, he assumed the post of President of the Republic. Seven important trials were staged after Stalin and Gottwald had

TABLE 2.8 The number of communists purged in the years 1948–53

Bulgaria	90,000
Czechoslovakia	550,000
German Democratic Republic	300,000
Hungary	200,000
Poland	370,000
Romania	200,000

Source: Zbigniew K. Brzezinski, *The Soviet Bloc: Unity and Conflict,* Rev. & enlarged ed. (Cambridge, Mass.: Harvard University Press, 1967), p. 97.

died, which to say on Novotný's watch. Ignoring the protests and calls for change, Novotný had a giant statue of Stalin erected on Letná plain on 1 May 1955.[190]

After Khrushchev's secret speech at the Twentieth CPSU Congress on 25 February 1956, pressure grew on Novotný and his clique to embrace de-Stalinization (which is to say, some measure of political and cultural liberalization) and to reexamine the purge trials in the preceding years and to rehabilitate, even if only posthumously, those who had been unfairly convicted – which is to say everyone. Novotný understood that rehabilitations could threaten his position and, for that matter, also the positions of other leading members of the party. Indeed, Interior Minister Rudolf Barák uncovered evidence in 1955–57 of the role of the ruling elite in staging the show trials and planned to use this evidence to drive Novotný out of office and seize power for himself. Novotný caught wind of Barák's plan and had him removed from the Presidium, expelled from the party, and given a 15-year prison term – allegedly because of embezzlement.[191]

The Catholic Church

Gottwald wanted the local Catholic Church to sever its links with the Holy See and enter into a collaborative relationship with the communist state. In the early months of 1949, representatives of Church and state met for ultimately unsuccessful negotiations.[192] In the meantime, the communists began recruiting "progressive priests" who were prepared to work with the regime and support its programs. The best known of these priests was Fr. Josef Plojhar, who subscribed to Marxist-Leninist doctrines and was named Minister of Health.[193] The communists also had the episcopal conference bugged. When the bishops discovered this on 22 March 1949, Archbishop Josef Beran (1888–1969) protested, telling Gottwald that, under given conditions, "the Church could not declare its loyalty to the government."[194] With this, the negotiations came to a decided end. The following Sunday, Beran was taken into custody and placed under house arrest. After he smuggled out a pastoral letter on 26 June 1949, condemning the regime, the regime in turn banned all pastoral letters and stipulated that any gathering of believers must be approved in advance by the government. The following month, the Holy See excommunicated all members of the Communist Party, as well as communist sympathizers. In October 1949, Law No. 217 provided for the creation of the Office for Religious Affairs, under the rubric of the Ministry of Culture. This office approved and censored pastoral letters, monitored the activities of clergy, "and, through state-appointed commissars ('Church secretaries'), controll[ed] the day-to-day administration of the dioceses."[195]

The Catholic Church embraces seven rites, of which the largest is the Roman (or Latin). The other rites are: the Greek (also called the Byzantine or Eastern-Rite), Alexandrian, Syriac, Armenian, Maronite, and Chaldean.[196] Although most Czechoslovak Catholics adhered (as Czech and Slovak Catholics do today) to the Roman rite, there were also approximately 300,000 Greek Catholics in

Czechoslovakia in 1948. The communists outlawed the Greek Catholic Church on 29 April 1950, giving its clergy a choice: either join the Orthodox Church or go to prison. Many Greek Catholic clergy refused to convert to Orthodoxy and were arrested, including Bishops Gojdic and Hopko.[197]

The regime also took steps to whittle the Church down, seizing approximately 500 monasteries and convents, converting them to other uses.[198] Many clergy were drafted into the army. Other priests were incarcerated in forced-labor camps or imprisoned; by October 1950, roughly 2,000 Catholic clergy had been consigned to prison or labor camps.[199] Among the features that made up the regime's strategy vis-à-vis the Catholic Church were measures to nationalize the Church's elementary schools, high schools, and vocational schools, to dissolve Catholic Action (albeit replacing it with a regime-controlled organization with the same name), to shut down most of the Church's publications, and to close most of its seminaries and schools of theology.[200]

Culture

Following the communist coup of February 1948, avant-garde art was removed from museums,[201] the communists banned jazz, and some better known jazz musicians such as Rudolf Antonín Dvorský were put in prison.[202] It was not possible for local artists to maintain any official contact with artists in the West. Gottwald, in a speech delivered soon after the coup, declared that artists were obliged to make their creations comprehensible to ordinary Czechoslovaks. In the same speech, he promised that his regime would use "an iron broom" to "sweep away the heritage" of the past.[203] As elsewhere in the bloc, socialist realism was to serve as the measure of what was useful in art, music, and literature; in a word, communists were convinced that these media communicated messages and values, whether consciously intended or not. In accord with this guideline, the League of Czechoslovak Composers convened a conference in September 1948, attacking "formalistic" music and calling for music to be characterized by "joyful, melodious" and, of course, triumphant strains.[204] It was much the same in literature, where, at a working session of the Association of Czechoslovak Writers on 22 January 1950, Ladislav Štoll, who would supervise the cultural sector in Czechoslovakia, urged those in attendance to view themselves as "engineers of the soul", employing Stalin's expression, which is to say as bearing a serious social responsibility.[205] Politics infiltrated poetry in the most explicit way. Thus, among those poets who received state prizes at this time were: Vítězslav Nezval for his poem "Stalin"; Marie Pujmanova for a love song for Stalin; Jan Kostka for his poem "For Stalin"; and Stanislav Neumann for his poem "Song about Stalin".[206]

To keep the members of the cultural elite in line, the authorities maintained constant pressure, reiterating what was desired and what was taboo. Writing in the journal *Výtvarné umění* (The Visual Arts) in 1950, Vladimír Šolta insisted that Impressionism, Cubism, and Surrealism worked to "construct an art outside reality, to deprive it of its effect as an instrument for enhancing knowledge and transforming reality."[207] Autonomous art groups were suppressed and did not reemerge until after the deaths of Stalin and Gottwald. Where the classics of orchestral music were concerned, the communists preferred the "patriotic" Smetana to the "cosmopolitan" Dvořák.[208] For new musical compositions, of course, socialist realism was prescribed. The writers were the most difficult to discipline and, in Slovakia, communist authorities carried out a general purge in literature, even sending a group associated with the literary magazine *DAV* to prison.[209] On 14 March 1956, *Rudé právo* quoted Zdeněk Nejedlý to demand, "We need a culture that speaks to millions, not to a specific small group of people."[210]

But within a couple of years after Stalin's passing, Czechoslovak cultural figures who had earlier endorsed socialist realism, now turned against it, and complained that it promoted sameness in the local cultural sector. Indeed, Czechoslovak artists came to view the entire socialist realist genre as boring.[211] The official Art Union was soon constrained to admit that artists should enjoy a certain amount of artistic freedom. Then came Khrushchev's anti-Stalin speech in February 1956 (described in more detail below). In the wake of this speech, cultural policies were relaxed throughout the Soviet bloc. In Czechoslovakia, this allowed the publication of fictional works by Josef Škvorecký, Ivan Klíma, Ladislav Fuks, Ludvík Vaculík, Vladimír Paral, and the surrealist writer Bohumil Hrabal.[212]

Women

After the end of World War Two, authorities in Czechoslovakia were concerned about a population deficit and demanded that people marry and bear children. František Pachner, an obstetrician involved in high-level discussions concerning the fertility rate, wanted couples raising only one or two children to pay a higher rate of tax than couples raising three or more children.[213] As elsewhere in the Soviet bloc, Czechoslovak communists held up the ideal of the "New Socialist Woman", who would raise a family, hold down a full-time job, keep pace with political developments, and, of course, give her full support to the ruling party. Added to these duties were the household chores which, by tradition, were assumed to be largely the responsibility of the women. Where employment was concerned, women's representation in the work force rose from 37.8% in 1948 to 42.8% in 1960 and 45.5% in 1970. The proportion of women in the work force increased from 53.1% in 1950 to 61.8% in 1961 and 72.4% in 1970.[214] At the same time, the average level of education of women increased steadily through the 1950s and 1960s.

However, there were limits to the realization in the professional or political worlds of the guarantees in the constitution, where women's equality with men was loudly proclaimed. First, women tended to be excluded from top-level and managerial positions, even when fully qualified. Second, even among women who did attain managerial positions, there were fewer, the higher up the scale of ranks one looked. Third, women often worked in jobs not related to their training. And fourth, "a considerable number of female specialists with university and secondary-school education . . . [worked in] jobs which require[d] a lower educational level" than what they had attained.[215] In addition, in the years between 1948 and the end of the 1950s, women played only a small role in the nation's politics; to the extent that they were involved at all, it was largely at the local level. In the National Assembly, in the years 1948–54, women made up only 12% of the deputies.[216] The first woman to hold a ministerial post in the Czechoslovak government was Ludmila Jankovcová, a social democrat who had supported the merger of her party with the communist party in 1948 and was named Minister of Nutrition/Food Industry in Antonín Zápotocký's government; she was the only female government minister until 1954, when Božena Machačová-Dostálová joined the government as Minister of Purchasing.[217]

In 1945, the National Front of Women and the Council of Czech Women were formed. As Sharon Wolchik notes, these commissions were involved in "mobilizing women to participate in the reconstruction efforts and join the labor force. They also served . . . to defend women's interests and bring women's needs to the attention of political decisionmakers."[218] After a brief period, the National Front was shut down, leaving the Council of Czech Women as the only organization functioning specifically to advocate for women in early communist Czechoslovakia. Then, in 1952, communist authorities declared that the "woman question", as they called the issue of gender inequality, was "solved". With this argument as justification, the authorities shut down the Council of Czech Women.

Poland

During the era of Stalinism, 1948–52, the Muscovite Poles now in control of the PZPR sought to press the country into a socialist mold. It was comparable, as a popular witticism from that era put it, to trying to put a saddle on a cow. There were numerous signs of Stalinization, ranging from the restructuring of local and regional administration along Soviet lines to passage in July 1952 of a new constitution on the Soviet model (eliminating the office of President of the Republic) to the prioritization of heavy industry under the provisions of the Six-Year Plan launched in 1950. Agricultural collectivization figured prominently in the Muscovite Poles' plans to transform Poland and Polish thinking. The decision to initiate collectivization was taken at CC plenary sessions in July-September 1948[219] – the latter session thus taking place after Gomułka's removal from power. Peasants initially offered resistance to collectivization, and complained that the program would destroy their traditional way of life – which was, in fact, part of the purpose of collectivization in the first place.

To apply pressure on peasants to join the collectives, the authorities established huge delivery quotas and then penalized those who could not meet the delivery targets. When neither persuasion nor financial pressure sufficed to induce peasants to join collectives "voluntarily", the militia and security forces, and sometimes even army units, were employed to force peasants to give up their land to collective farms.[220] Mass protests escalated during 1949 and 1950, and in 1950 alone there were 650 reports of political terror, mostly in the countryside.[221] Disgusted and outraged by this new policy, many peasants who had previously joined the PZPR or the pro-regime United Peasant Party now dropped out of these organizations. Between 1948 and 1955, peasant enrollment in the PZPR dropped from 244,000 to 175,000, while peasant membership in the United Peasant Party declined from 240,000 to 156,000 in the same period.[222] Even so, the number of cooperatives grew from 2,199 in late 1950 to 9,790 in 1955.[223] On 11 August 1955, the PZPR Central Committee called for a five-year moratorium on collectivization,[224] little knowing that the project to collectivize agriculture in Poland was effectively dead.

As elsewhere in the bloc, economic policy prioritized heavy industry, machine tools, metallurgy, and mining, together with the nationalization of economic enterprises. The structural changes effected in the Polish economy were, as Jan Boguszewski and Michel Vale put it, "almost revolutionary".[225] Actually, that is probably an understatement. Writing in the *Polish Sociological Bulletin*, Ewa Kaltenberg-Kwiatowska summarized the post-war Polish economic strategy as follows:

(1) Development and enforced advancement of the heavy and mining industries at the expense of other branches of industry and economy.
(2) Extensive development at an exorbitant cost, with growing employment, low labour productivity and overexploitation of natural resources.
(3) Industrialization carried out at the cost of agriculture, especially until 1952 . . .
(4) Unsteady and unbalanced development of branches of industry and national economy, regions of the country, urban and rural areas.
(5) Industrialization carried out mainly through launching new huge investments which, combined with the overestimated benefits of the large scale . . . , led to transport difficulties, a shortage of expenditure on the modernization of the existing resources and the peculiar detrimental effects resulting from crossing a certain threshold of magnitude . . .
(6) Domination of politics over economics, combined with an insufficient regard for the economic and social costs of decisions . . .[226]

Meanwhile, the proportion of national income derived from the socialist sectors grew from 54.0% in 1950 to 72.8% in 1960.[227] At the same time, the annual rate of growth in industrial production sank for six years in succession between 1950 and 1956 (as the figures in Table 2.5 show). Whatever one makes of the raw economic indices, it was troubling that Polish economic thought stagnated in the years following 1948. As P. J. D. Wiles put it, "what the regime had achieved (by the beginning of 1956) was to impose ignorance and low intellectual standards [in economic thinking]. In a period when French economics has made itself respectable, Polish economics, starting at about the same level, has stood still."[228]

Throughout the years that Bierut stood at the apex of the political pyramid, everything Stalin said or did was to be justified, defended, adulated, and copied. Stalinism prevailed not just in economics but also in cultural policy, religious policy, policy regarding women and gender, cadres policy, even science.[229] In October 1956, Gomułka described how the political system operated in the age of Stalin and Bierut:

> . . . this system consisted in the fact that an individual, hierarchical ladder of cults was created. Each such cult comprised a given area in which it functioned. In the bloc of socialist states, it was Stalin who stood at the top of this hierarchical ladder of cults. All those who stood on the lower rungs of the ladder bowed their heads before him. Those who bowed their heads were not only the other leaders of the Communist Party of the Soviet Union, but all the leaders of communist and workers' parties of the countries of the socialist camp. The latter, that is, the first secretaries of the Central Committees of the parties of the various countries who sat on the second rung of the ladder of the cult of the personality, in turn donned the robes of infallibility and wisdom. But their cult[s] radiated only on the territory of the countries where they stood at the top of the national cult ladder. This cult could be called only a reflected brilliance, a borrowed light. It shone as the moon does. And yet, in the area of its influence it was omnipotent.[230]

In fact, one of the phrases used to flatter Stalin in his lifetime was precisely "sun of the universe".[231]

Once the post of President of the Republic was abolished in 1952, Bierut – the moon to Stalin's sun – took the post of Prime Minister, while remaining party chief. His closest collaborators were Jakub Berman (1901–1984), in charge of political security, and Hilary Minc (1905–1974), in charge of economic transformation. In Poland, as elsewhere in the bloc, the Central Committee was reduced to a mere rubber stamp for policies decided in the Politburo.

In August 1955, an anti-Soviet poem appeared with the line, "there are Polish apples which Polish children cannot reach."[232] Everyone could understand the coded message here, but for the time being the dam still held. Then came the Twentieth Congress of the Communist Party of the Soviet Union, held in Moscow from 14 to 25 February 1956 and the tapestry of lies, fabrications, and obscurantism which had served to dam up resentments and memories of human suffering, while maintaining the system of control, gave way before First Secretary Nikita Khrushchev's blistering attack on the "father of peoples".[233] Although delivered in a closed session in the final two days of the Congress, the speech was quickly leaked.[234] The speech provided many examples of Stalin's tyranny and chastised him for "his intolerance, his brutality and his abuse of power," as well as for his "mania for greatness . . . his suspicion and [his] haughtiness."[235]

Bierut, Osóbka-Morawski, and Cyrankiewicz were among the Polish delegates attending the Congress and were shell-shocked by Khrushchev's revelations.
Bierut was so shocked that he fell ill and remained in Moscow while the rest of
the Polish delegates returned home. While Bierut lay ill in Moscow, the PZPR
Central Committee met for an extraordinary plenum on 3–4 March. Osóbka-
Morawski and Cyrankiewicz addressed the plenum, with the former telling the
assembled CC that the "cult of the individual" still permeated science, art, and
literature in Poland and needed to be rooted out.[236] Bierut died in Moscow on 12
March 1956; Edward Ochab (1906–1989), who had joined the Central Committee of the PPR in 1944, was elected his successor as First Secretary by unanimous
vote in the Central Committee, following the Politburo's "recommendation".
Shortly thereafter, the PZPR Politburo induced Jakub Berman to step down from
his posts.

Even by 1954, the higher echelons of the party were conceding that the security service ("secret police") had operated in disregard for the law. Gomułka was
released from prison in September 1954, according to PAP, although this was not
revealed to the Polish public until 7 April 1956.[237] Censorship weakened in the
course of 1955 and many Poles were in a state of high expectation. The PZPR
leadership became increasingly aware of its fundamental illegitimacy. The challenge
was to find a way to regain (or gain) people's trust and lay a fresh claim to political
legitimacy. As spring 1956 wore on, it became increasingly clear to both conservatives and liberals that there was only one man, at that moment in time, who could
rescue them – and that was Gomułka. His steadfast Marxism, his undeviating belief
that Poland could not simply copy the Soviet example, his refusal to admit any
wrongdoing, and even the time he had spent in prison all put him in good stead. It
is likely that it was in early April 1956 that the Polish Politburo came to this conclusion.[238] The legitimation of Gomułka in the public eye was an unintended latent
function of the persecution to which he had been subjected and, of course, also of
his persistent defiance. Riots in Poznań on 28 June over economic issues made the
question of leadership seem all the more urgent.

On 5 August 1956, *Trybuna ludu*, the party's news organ, announced that
Gomułka's party membership had been restored. Hilary Minc, who had presented
a vicious attack on Gomułka in November 1949, resigned from the Politburo on
9 October. Gomułka's advocates, both conservatives and liberals, grew in number and, by mid-October, almost all the leading communists, including Ochab,
were agreed that Gomułka should return to the party leadership as First Secretary.
Being aware of Gomułka's record of independent thinking, the Soviets watched
developments in Poland with concern and, on 18 October, informed the Poles
that a high-ranking Soviet delegation would arrive shortly.[239] The following day,
Khrushchev, Molotov,[240] Mikoyan,[241] Kaganovich,[242] and Marshal Konev[243] arrived
in Warsaw, accompanied by about a dozen other political and military notables;
that same morning, two Soviet tank divisions based in Poland left their bases and
began moving in the direction of Warsaw.[244] Also on 19 October, Gomułka and

three of his closest supporters – Zenon Kliszko, Marian Spychalski, and Ignacy Loga-Sowiński – were coopted into the Central Committee.

On 20 October, the Poles succeeded in persuading the Soviets that the return of Gomułka to the leadership was the best remedy for the political destabilization in the country and that his return would strengthen the socialist system. Not only did the Soviets accept this argument, but they also promised that the Polish leadership would enjoy "internal independence".[245] That same day, the newly reelected First Secretary presented an address to the nation. Among other things, he noted that collective farms were less efficient than private farms and that state farms were less efficient even than collective farms. He called for collectivization to be reversed and also rejected the hitherto official account that the June riots in Poznań had been the work of "imperialist agents and *agents provocateurs*," stressing that the rioters were protesting real problems, which he traced to "distortions of the basic rules of socialism."[246] He expressed admiration for the Soviets' achievements but immediately added that the Soviet path should not be considered the only path to socialism. Gomułka underlined that, in his view, "There can be different types of socialism. It can be the socialism that was created in the Soviet Union, or it can be formed as we see it now in Yugoslavia, or it can be of some other type still."[247] Konstantin Rokossovsky (1896–1968), the Polish Minister of Defense "on loan" from the Soviet Union, was let go and replaced by Gomułka's friend, Spychalski. Rokossovky returned to Moscow to become a Soviet Deputy Minister of Defense.

The Catholic Church

On 20 March 1949, Msgr. Sigismund Choromański, Secretary of the Episcopate, met with Władysław Wolski, Minister of Public Administration, in order to ascertain the regime's intentions in the religious sphere. Following the meeting, Wolski issued a statement that the government would not interfere in the internal affairs of the Church, "provided that the Church kept out of (anti-regime) politics, and Wolski specifically guaranteed the continuation of religious instruction in the state schools."[248] But the regime broke its promises, nationalizing the Church's hospitals on 21 September 1949. The Polish hierarchy protested this move, but to no avail.[249] Instead of retreating, the regime pressed forward with its assault on the Church, seizing all the property of the Catholic charity organization "Caritas" on 23 January 1950 and confiscating approximately 375,000 acres (152,000 hectares) of Church lands on 20 March 1950.[250] This was a huge loss, "leaving intact only places of worship, office space, living quarters, and those landholdings that provided for the subsistence of certain sectors of the clergy."[251] Also, in 1950, Polish authorities set up the Office for Religious Affairs, the staff of which started offering their opinions regarding whom the bishops should appoint to run the dioceses under their respective jurisdictions. Under pressure, representatives of the Episcopate signed a 19-point agreement with representatives of the state on 14

April 1950, an agreement which Borodziej has characterized as "a clear victory of the party over the Church."[252] Under this agreement, the bishops "distanced themselves from anti-state activities and obliged the clergy to preach obedience to the state."[253] In return, the government agreed to permit religious instruction in the state schools and the continued operation of the Catholic University in Lublin (KUL) as well as some Catholic associations and periodicals.[254] Although the agreement was made public, there was, according to Bishop Choromański, an unpublished annex containing five points.[255] According to Belgian clergy said to be well acquainted with the Polish Episcopate, the Church accepted the agreement only to prevent the state from establishing a rival "national Church" not respecting the authority of the Vatican.[256]

In the wake of this agreement, the authorities' solemn pledges notwithstanding, the regime forced Catholic schools to close, made it difficult for priests to teach in state schools, and obstructed the work of Catholic publishing houses. The regime wanted the Vatican to adjust its diocesan boundaries to Poland's new western borders and, in order to apply pressure on the Holy See to this end, had the Bishop of Kielce, Czesław Kaczmarek (1895–1963), arrested on 20 January 1951 and put on trial, among other charges for "anti-state activities and espionage." His real "offense" was his known hostility to communism and his influence among the clergy in his diocese. He would remain incarcerated until March 1955.[257] Other hierarchs were taken into custody, including Archbishop Eugeniusz Baziak and Suffragan Bishop Stanisław Rozpond, arrested in December 1952 and put on trial for "illicit sales of art and [dealing in] foreign currency, as well as espionage."[258]

On 9 February 1953, in blatant violation of the 1950 Church-state agreement, the authorities issued a decree, claiming jurisdiction over the appointment of clergy to ecclesial posts.[259] The Polish Episcopate rejected this decree and, on 8 May 1953, Wyszyński announced that he preferred to leave episcopal posts vacant, rather than have them filled by the regime's candidates.[260] Relations between the regime and the Primate became even more strained when the former called on Wyszyński to condemn the imprisoned Kaczmarek. When the Cardinal-Primate refused to accommodate the authorities' wish, he was arrested on 25 September 1953. By late 1953, several hundred clergy, including nine bishops, found themselves behind bars. Wyszyński would remain in detention until the return of Gomułka to power. Gomułka set a high priority on achieving better relations with the Catholic Church and invited the Cardinal for a discussion. Gomułka wanted to release Wyszyński immediately, but the Cardinal refused to accept release until several conditions were met – specifically, that the 1953 decree establishing state control over appointments within the Church be withdrawn, that all imprisoned clergy be released, and that religious instruction be once more permitted in state schools. Gomułka agreed to all of Wyszyński's conditions and, on 28 October 1956, the Cardinal-Primate emerged from detention. Commenting on the importance of harmony in Church-state relations, Gomułka declared that it was mistaken to think "that socialism can be constructed by communists alone, [or] only by people with materialistic social views."[261]

Music

Nothing illustrates Stalinism's gargantuan hunger for control as well as the doctrine of socialist realism and the way it was imposed on composers, writers, pictorial artists, and architects throughout the bloc. Among those Polish composers who were the most prominent in the immediate post-war years, two fled to exile – Andrzej Panufnik (1914–1991) and Roman Paleter (1907–1989) – while two remained in Poland – Witold Lutosławski (1913–1994) and Krzysztof Penderecki (1933–2020). In music, the most important event in Poland in the era of Stalinism was the commemoration in 1949 of the 100th anniversary of Frédéric Chopin's birthday. One might think that such a celebration of an internationally renowned composer, whose waltzes are among the most beloved of his works, might have lain outside politics. This was not the case, however. On the contrary, Bierut used the occasion to present a speech in which he offered his advice that "an artist should be an educator, combining socialism with revolutionary Romanticism," adding that Chopin's revolutionary Romanticism should "raise people's spirits, . . . encourage them to new great and heroic acts, . . . [and] help them build happiness."[262] Elaborating on this theme, a 1950 publication affirmed that the task of socialist realist art "was to 'remake and excite a man,' while rejecting 'all passivity, pessimism and apathy.'"[263] As for Chopin, he was recast as a "prophet announcing the advent of the victorious era of revolutionary socialism."[264]

To promote the celebration of Chopin, a state committee was established, chaired by the prime minister. The Third Frédéric Chopin International Piano Competition had been held in 1937; the competition was now revived, in 1949, for its fourth incarnation. In addition, special postage stamps were issued in the composer's honor, and a film and a panegyric novel were also commissioned. A Chopin Exhibition opened in the National Museum on 19 October 1949; Prime Minister Józef Cyrankewicz was on hand for the opening. And throughout 1949, concerts of Chopin's music were organized in villages across Poland, allowing many peasants to hear his music for the first time. Although the communists professed to appreciate all of Chopin's corpus, they were especially keen on Chopin's mazurkas which, because of their simple structure and obvious derivation from folk melodies, struck them as the most "democratic" of Chopin's compositions.[265] As for the contemporary composers, "the artist, who is free from superstitions," should "realize that the basic source of his creativity is the hard work of a [factory] worker and a peasant."[266]

As elsewhere in the bloc, the apparent cultural freedom in the early postwar years gave way soon enough, in this case by 1947, to cultural Stalinism, as the party pressured composers to avoid formalism and embrace socialist realism, and to produce musical works easily understood by factory workers and peasants and with transparent political content. For the latter consideration, mass songs and cantatas with politically positive texts were best. The campaign against formalism received a major impetus at a conference held in the small town of Łagów in August 1949, attended by Deputy Minister for Culture and Art Włodimierz

Sokorski (1908–1999) and 25 prominent composers and musicologists (though not by Panufnik, who chose not to take part). The Poznań Philharmonic was on hand to play examples of both formalist and socialist realist music.[267] Sokorski spoke for the party in urging composers to embrace socialist realism. During the next few years, socialist realism was ascendant and even the most brilliant composers, such as Panufnik and Lutosławski, found themselves attacked by Witfold Rudziński, the abrasive eventual president of the Composers' Union, for allegedly insufficient progress in resisting and fighting formalism in their works.

Various composers hurried to ingratiate themselves with the authorities. Lutosławski, for example, wrote a march celebrating young people "forever in love with steel," while Alfred Gradstein produced a march accompanied with a text ending with the words "Glory, glory, glory to the party. Salute the party!"[268] Then there was Kazimierz Serocki's cantata *Warsaw Bricklayer* (1951). And, of course, there were a number of musical works composed in Stalin's honor, such as Jan Maklakiewicz's two works in this genre, "Song about Stalin" and "Stalin is with us", and Gradstein's cantata *A Word about Stalin* (1951). But after Stalin's death, composers increasingly challenged socialist realism. Finally, at the Eighth Congress of the Polish Composers' Union in June 1955, Sokorski completely reversed his earlier position. He now denied ever having pressed composers to adopt socialist realism as their model and, instead, urged composers to find their own paths.[269] The era of socialist realism in Poland had lasted barely eight years.

Women in a Stalinist context

In 1945, the League of Women was created in order to educate women politically and ideologically, bring women into active involvement in politics, and assist women in general. Much like communist officials elsewhere in the bloc, league functionaries talked of fashioning a "New Socialist Woman", who would be "knowledgeable and devoted to socialism," as the league's president, Alicja Musiolowa put it in 1950.[270] In the early 1950s, the league had about 2 million members, of whom perhaps between 20,000 and 70,000 served as agitators.[271] In that capacity, they were expected to keep female employees informed about matters considered of priority, encourage them to achieve high levels of productivity, educate women about communist policies, and ensure that women generally worked hard. The league brought out two publications for the membership: *Poznajmy prawda (Let's learn the truth)* and *Nasza praca (Our work)*. But in 1952, it became clear that, in some provinces, the league was running out of steam and, that year, *Poznajmy prawde* ceased publication.[272] In September 1952, the PZPR Central Committee entertained the possibility of shutting the league down, on the argument that its focus on "narrow" issues of interest to women was unhelpful. Yet, by 1955, the league was paying more attention to motherhood and women's everyday needs,[273] than to women's socialist consciousness. With the return of Gomułka to the party leadership, the party embraced reforms to the welfare system and pensions.[274]

Hungary

Although the final nail in the coffin of Hungarian pluralism was not hammered in until March 1948, the excessive adulation showered on Rákosi as part of his leadership cult began as early as 1945, when a regional party secretary described the communist leader as the new Messiah.[275] This was no isolated remark, as the 4 March 1945 issue of *Szabad Magyarország* referred to him as "the watchful director of the struggle for the country's democratic reconstruction,"[276] at a time when, although holding the post of General Secretary of the Hungarian Communist Party, he held no post in the government and the communist party was a minority party. The communist press wanted to convince Hungarians that Rákosi cared deeply for their welfare and, thus, in one account claimed that "he pays attention to the smallest things, because he knows that the price of potatoes is often more important for the working little man than the great political problems."[277] And after communist hegemony was secure, the cult of Rákosi knew no bounds, as shown in a comment quoted in *Szabad Nép* on 11 May 1953, which asserted that "The people of a new Hungary, those who [have] realized the most beautiful dreams of the past, have come here to meet the greatest son of the homeland, who has accomplished and continued the work of Rákóczi, Kossuth, and 1919: Comrade Rákosi."[278]

As early as August 1947, the Hungarian Communist Party (HCP) published its electoral platform, spelling out a three-year economic plan, promising to work for lower unemployment and a higher standard of living, and confirming peasants' right to their newly acquired land holdings. On 12 February 1948, the Politburo of the HCP enumerated its economic priorities, among which was the elimination of the private sector. By then, the banks had already been nationalized. Now the right to strike was abolished. Subsequently, after the merger of the SDP with the HCP, to form the Hungarian Workers' Party (HWP), a new Politburo was elected, consisting of nine veteran communists and five former socialists.

As elsewhere in the bloc (Czechoslovakia, Romania, and Bulgaria), intra-elite rivalries were settled by the trial and execution of a leading communist and his associates. Thus, on 30 May 1949, László Rajk, who had served as Minister of the Interior from March 1946 until August 1948 and who was still serving at the time as Foreign Minister since August 1948, was arrested. His trial began on 16 September 1949 after he had been worn down by torture. At the trial, following the absurd script he had been forced to memorize, he confessed to having worked as an informer for Miklós Horthy's secret police in the years before 1944, to have done his best to undermine the legitimate government in the Spanish Civil War of 1936–1939, to have put himself in the employ of Adolf Hitler's Gestapo, to have recruited fascists and criminals after World War Two ended, and to have in due course served as an agent for Yugoslavia's communist dictator, Josip Broz Tito.[279] Convicted of these preposterous charges, he was hanged on 15 October. The absurdity of the charges was conscious and deliberate, being intended to communicate the message that anyone in People's Hungary could be convicted of anything. (Rákosi would later be forced to admit that the entire script of the trial was a complete fabrication.)

Church and state in Hungary

In the early months following the end of the war, the communists undertook measures to assist local Christians, even helping to rebuild churches which had been severely damaged or destroyed in the war. But tensions between the Catholic Church and the communists flared soon after the end of the war. Already on 18 October 1945, Cardinal József Mindszenty, Primate of Hungary (1892–1975), sent around a pastoral letter urging Hungarians to vote for the Smallholders' Party in the upcoming elections. Subsequently, the communists organized a petition campaign to secularize Hungary's primary and secondary schools, confiscating approximately 3,000 schools,[280] and seized seven-eighths of the Church's land holdings (albeit pledging financial support in compensation).[281] The communists allowed the Catholic Church to publish two small weekly newspapers, but subjected them to strict censorship. In July 1946, the government, under pressure from the Soviets, had ordered the dissolution of all organizations for Catholic youth.[282]

Mindszenty was opposed to the communists, not just because they were atheists but also because they refused to recognize the Habsburgs as the legitimate heads of state of Hungary. Indeed, he viewed the entire post-war coalition as illegitimate and decided that, as Archbishop of Esztergom and Primate of Hungary, he was the new Regent for the absent Habsburg heir to the throne.[283] When, in May 1948, it was announced that Church-run schools would be nationalized, there were violent protests across the country. Many of the protesters were arrested and sent to prison. On 16 June 1948, the Primate excommunicated all Catholic deputies who had voted for the school bill. In response, communist-controlled newspapers published attacks on the cardinal.[284] There were mass demonstrations against the communists especially in the villages. The Reformed Church offered no resistance. On the contrary, under the leadership of Bishop Albert Bereczky, the synod of the Reformed Church proclaimed its "social theory" on 30 April 1948. The text of the synod's resolution declared that the "Church offers its whole[hearted] willingness for every service in the new state and social order which can be done in the name of Jesus Christ and the power of the Holy Spirit."[285] By contrast, Bishop Lajos Ordass (1901–1974) of the Lutheran Church would not bow to communist pressure and specifically opposed the nationalization of Lutheran schools. On 7 September 1948, he was ordered to resign as bishop. When he refused, he was taken into custody and put on trial for "foreign currency manipulation" – a violation of Hungarian law. He was convicted in October and sentenced to two years' imprisonment and six years of enforced silence. The Presbyterian bishop, László Ravasz, was likewise put on trial.[286]

Two months later, on 23 December 1948, Cardinal Mindszenty was apprehended and put on trial on trumped up charges of espionage, conspiracy, and currency speculation. In prison, he suffered beatings and was also drugged. Once he was broken down, he signed a confession prepared by the secret police. His trial opened on 3 February 1949, ending with his sentence to life imprisonment; in July 1955, over Rákosi's objections, the aging cardinal was moved to house arrest.[287]

The trial of Cardinal Mindszenty was followed by arrests of Catholic priests and the closure of the Church's monasteries and convents. On 30 August 1950, following two months of negotiations, the Catholic bishops signed a concordat with the communist regime, promising to support the regime's policies, including agricultural collectivization, which had been initiated in summer 1948.[288] The Church also agreed to allow the formation of a Clerical Peace Movement, with membership consisting of pro-regime priests. Finally, in June 1951, Archbishop József Grösz of Kalocsa (1887–1961), the acting Primate, was likewise put on trial and sent to prison, in his case for 15 years for having allegedly conspired to overthrow the government. But the Reformed Church maintained a docile posture and, in March 1952, on the occasion of Rákosi's 60th birthday, issued the following statement:

> Since the liberation we have learned and we are continuously learning a new lesson taught to us by his life, teaching and example [and] we are increasingly aware of the great gift which was and is given to us by his wisdom, humaneness and knowledge. [He is] the great statesman whose wise and strong hand leads the life of our country.[289]

Consolidation of the regime

Approximately 70,000 people, including 14,000 Hungarians of Jewish origin, were deported from their places of residence. According to Jörg Hoensch, citing official data,

> . . . the forced resettlement included 6 ex-princes, 52 counts, 41 barons, 22 ministers and state secretaries of former governments, 85 generals, 324 staff officers, 30 factory owners, 46 bankers and 250 magnates. Like the others, they were forced to earn a living as agricultural labourers, barred from leaving their allotted place of residence.[290]

An additional 141 Hungarians were put on trial for political reasons between 1949 and 1951, resulting in 15 executions, 11 life sentences, and dozens of long terms in prison. Among those put on trial at this time were: János Kádár, arrested in April 1951 and charged with treason and espionage; Colonel Szücs, deputy chief of the AVH (secret police) and a key figure in orchestrating the trial of Rajk et al., arrested together with his brother, with both executed by being thrown into boiling oil; and General Gábor Péter, chief of the AVH, arrested and scheduled to go on trial as part of an anti-Zionist case when the trial was canceled after Soviet General Secretary Stalin died.[291]

Meanwhile, in the May 1949 elections, the single list of candidates was endorsed by 95.5% of voters. In the wake of these elections, Rákosi made his famous declaration: "Those who are not with us are against us."[292] The nationalization of the industrial sector was completed by the end of 1949. Given the regime's push for rapid industrialization (emphasizing heavy industry), 370,000 agricultural workers were drafted to work in heavy industry or mining, or simply abandoned farming for jobs in those sectors of their own accord.

Soviet oversight

Soviet "advisers" stationed in Hungary provided daily input to guide economic planning and the chief of the Hungarian news agency MTI was in regular telephone contact with Moscow to make sure that the agency's press releases were in line with Soviet interests.[293] Mihály Farkas, the Minister of Defense, was actually a Soviet citizen. Then, in May 1953, Rákosi was summoned to the Kremlin and instructed to bring along Farkas, Gerő, Nagy, and István Dobi, the powerless president of Hungary. At the meeting, the Soviets upbraided the Hungarian General Secretary for incompetence in economic affairs. The dressing down of the Hungarians reflected a change in the dynamics of power in Moscow. Specifically, after Stalin's demise, Georgi Malenkov (1902–1988) had become prime minister, serving in that capacity from March 1953 until March 1955, when he would be replaced by Nikolai Bulganin (1895–1975). Nikita Khrushchev (1894–1971) became First Secretary, serving in that capacity until October 1964, and assuming the office of prime minister in March 1958. Each of them had clients in the East European states and, in Hungary, Malenkov wanted to install his Hungarian protégé, Imre Nagy (1896–1958), as prime minister. The Soviets told Rákosi that they were "deeply appalled" by his "high-handed and domineering style" as leader and charged him with having committed "mistakes and crimes".[294] After heated arguments with his Soviet comrades, Rákosi was forced to yield that office but remained General Secretary of the HWP, thus replicating the unstable duality of power recently established in Moscow. A Central Committee session was held 27–28 June 1953 and saw the adoption of resolutions which came to be known as "the June resolutions". These resolutions called for slowing down the pace of industrialization, giving priority to light industry, improving the standard of living, reducing taxes levied on those peasants who continued to operate private farms, cutting mandatory deliveries of agricultural products, and slowing the pace of collectivization. But Rákosi was able to prevent the resolutions from being published and did his best to obstruct the adoption of the measures which the resolutions had called for. On 4 July 1953, the newly minted prime minister addressed the National Assembly and outlined his program for a New Course.

A central problem, as Nagy saw it, was that the countries of the Soviet bloc – the "People's Democracies" – were being pressed into a common mold, ignoring or downplaying differences in conditions, resources, and comparative advantage in these societies. Accordingly, as he wrote after leaving the prime ministership, "the copying of Soviet methods under completely different internal and international [conditions has] resulted in the loss in its essence of the people's democratic character in all People's Democracies."[295] He accused Rákosi of "stupid and harmful political recklessness" and of having made himself "independent of the will and opinion of the Party membership and of the decisions of the Party."[296] In his address to the Assembly, Nagy added that, under Rákosi, the regime had "often disregarded the provisions of the Constitution which safeguard the rights, liberties, [and] securities of the citizen."[297]

Nagy promised to close the internment camps, to extend amnesty to those convicted of minor offenses, and to review the more important political trials, in order to establish who had been wronged in these trials. Nagy demanded the release and exoneration of "all who are not guilty" and demanded that the transgressions of legality in the past should "never be repeated."[298] He declared that nationalization had gone too far and allowed private retail trade and crafts to revive. Significantly, his government also condemned the resort to coercion in relations with Churches and stressed the need to respect legality.[299] Nagy also wanted to strengthen the government apparatus, which he headed, at the cost of the party apparatus which Rákosi headed. But Nagy experienced difficulties in carrying out his policies and, in January 1954, traveled to Moscow to complain about obstruction on the part of Rákosi; the Soviets ordered the latter to be more cooperative.

In spite of the problems created by Rákosi, Nagy was able to close all the internment and labor camps by the end of summer 1953. However, while some of the 150,000 persons who had been incarcerated in them were released, others were merely transferred to ordinary jails.[300] A rehabilitation committee was created, chaired by Nagy, Rákosi, and Gerő (interior minister at the time), to review the purge trials. But, as Bennett Kovrig has written, to have corrected "past perversions of justice, especially against communists, would have amounted to a devastating indictment of the Rákosi clique. [Accordingly,] Rákosi pursued a dilatory tactic, and Nagy finally resigned from the committee."[301] Nonetheless, Rákosi sought to appease those seeking reforms by approving the arrest of former AVH chief Gábor Péter in December 1952. Sentenced to life imprisonment, Péter was nonetheless released from prison in 1959 and took jobs as a tailor and as a librarian.[302] By October 1954, between 100 and 200 communists were released from prison, including Kádár, who was released in July of that year.

Meanwhile, under the New Course, investments in heavy industry were reduced by more than 40% in 1954, while there were corresponding increases in investments in light industry and consumer industry. To Rákosi's mind, this shift in investment strategy was symptomatic of "rightist opportunist deviation".[303] Then, in February 1955, Nagy's Soviet protector was ousted from the prime ministership in the U.S.S.R: Rákosi moved quickly to take advantage of the new situation. Thus, when in early 1955 Nagy was confined to his bed with heart problems, the Central Committee, once more firmly under Rákosi's control, met in Nagy's absence on 2–4 March to pin the label of "rightist opportunist" on the unfortunate Nagy. Rákosi demanded that his rival resign, but Nagy refused. In early April, Mikhail Suslov, member of the Soviet Presidium (Politburo), arrived in Budapest; under his supervision, a text was drafted, accusing Nagy of factionalism and of having attempted to place himself ahead of the party. In mid-April 1955, Nagy was expelled from the CC and stripped of his prime ministership. On the same occasion, Farkas was expelled from the Politburo and also from the Secretariat, apparently for having supported Nagy. With this, there was a renewed emphasis on investments in heavy industry as well as a renewed push for agricultural collectivization. András Hegedüs (1922–1999), a Rákosi loyalist, now became prime minister. But in February 1956, Khrushchev delivered his aforementioned "secret speech" to the CPSU Central Committee, revealing many of Stalin's crimes and denouncing the cult of the leader. Although secret, the full text of the speech soon became public knowledge, being published, inter alia, on the front page of the *New York Times*. As the speech became known throughout Eastern Europe, it pulled the rug from under the feet of East European leaders.

The cultural sphere

As Imre Nagy noted in his political testament, the establishment of communist rule in Hungary brought about a cultural revolution, not only in art, music, and literature, but also in science and this, he mused, was damaging to the moral life of Hungarian society.[304] In concert music, the shadow of socialist realism initially had a darkening effect. The communist superintendents of music wanted happy, melodious music, with triumphant chords, in major keys and ideally music one could whistle. As the émigré Hungarian composer György Ligeti (1923–2006) told Toru Takemitsu in 1991,

> In Communist Hungary, dissonances were forbidden and minor seconds were not allowed because they were anti-socialist. I knew very little Schoenberg, Berg or Webern and practically nothing of Cowell or Ives, but I had heard about clusters. They were forbidden, of course, as was twelve-tone music. As a reaction to this I very naïvely decided to write music which was built on the forbidden music seconds. I was an anti-harmonist because harmony, tonal harmony was permitted in Communist Hungary and chose dissonances and clusters because these were forbidden.[305]

In this context, much of the music of Béla Bartók (1881–1945) was banned in Hungary because his compositions were thought to reflect the influence of Arnold Schoenberg and Igor Stravinsky, both of whom were out of favor throughout the bloc. But 1955 was the tenth anniversary of Bartók's death and this occasioned a revival of many works of his which had not been heard since before 1950. The years of repression gave Bartók's music a political significance they might otherwise not have had. They became "symbols of resistance" to the Rákosi regime[306] and of course symbols of artistic freedom in a society where such freedom was not acknowledged as legitimate by the regime.

Living composers were, of course, expected to embrace the doctrine of socialist realism and, for example, Endre Szervánszky's early works – *Serenade for Strings* (1947) and *Clarinet Serenade* (1950) – reflected his faith in Marxism-Leninism; he was awarded the Kossuth Prize in 1951 and again in 1955. But, after a time, he wanted to stretch his musical limbs. His *Concerto in Memory of József Attíla* (1955) has been said to have anticipated the approaching political storm. He also braved communist displeasure by drawing upon the banned twelve-tone method in composing his *Six Orchestral Pieces* in 1959; this work provoked a strong reaction upon its premiere in 1960.[307] By the 1970s, the musical world was opening up and Hungarian concert music of that decade showed the influence of the American composer John Cage (1912–1992).[308]

In 1952, after some poets and novelists had continued to ignore the guidelines associated with socialist realism, József Révai (1898–1959), Hungary's Minister of Culture, reiterated yet again that poets and writers should adhere to the socialist realist formula.[309] Just as in music, so too in literature: the communists were convinced that cultural artifacts could be the vehicles of dangerous ideas. When it came to the literature of the past, books which had to be removed from public libraries included the works of Louisa May Alcott (author of *Little Women*, 1868), Pearl Buck, Lewis Carroll, Alduous Huxley, Sinclair Lewis (author of *Babbitt*, 1922), Upton Sinclair, and H. G. Wells.[310] As for contemporary Hungarian writers, they were expected to uphold the party line (the content) and accept socialist realism (the form). Tibor Déry (1894–1978), an independent-minded novelist and playwright, who chose to work freely in both content and style, was inevitably excoriated (by Révai in 1952) for "bourgeois moralizing" and "rightist deviation".[311] He had joined the communist party in 1918 and rejoined it after the war, but was expelled from its ranks in 1953 when he undertook to write satirical works about communism. Among others, the first two volumes of his planned tetralogy – *Felelet* (The Answer) – drew sharp attacks from the communists. On 27 June 1956, at a meeting of the free-thinking Petőfi Circle (see below), Déry offered the challenge: "The real trouble [with Hungarian political life] is not the personality cult, dogmatism, or the lack of democracy: it is the lack of freedom."[312] In 1957, after the crushing of the Hungarian Revolution, 63-year-old Déry was arrested, tried for his role in "laying the intellectual groundwork" for the uprising, and sent to prison to serve a nine-year term. He was joined behind bars by poet Zoltán Zelk and playwright Gyula Háy. Thanks to an international campaign, Déry was released from prison in 1961; the following year, he was granted an amnesty.[313] His stories "Szerelem" (Love), "Vidám temetés" (Gay Funeral), and "A téglafal mögält" (Behind the Brick Wall), as also his endearing novella *Niki: the story of a dog*[314] "accurately reflect[ed] the oppressive political climate of Hungary in the mid-fifties."[315] During his time in prison, he wrote a dystopian novel; in the preface, he declared, "Order without freedom will sooner or later blow up. Freedom without order? My novel is a warning, a cry of protest against this particular circle of hell."[316]

The Hungarian revolution

To Rákosi's dismay, his triumph over Imre Nagy in 1955 proved to be a pyrrhic victory; in the years Nagy had been in power, many people had come to know about the communists' illegal behavior in the early years of the republic and to value his integrity. As discontent with Rákosi percolated, the General Secretary tried to defuse tensions by authorizing the formation of a discussion club called the Petőfi Circle. The Circle began meeting in March 1956 but quickly proved to be a sounding board for critical voices. Meanwhile, a group of reform communists –Géza Losonczy, Ferenc Donáth, Miklós Vásárhelyi, Sándor Haraszti, and others – stepped forward in defense of Nagy's program. On 7 June 1956, when Nagy turned 60, a large group of admirers came to his home to show their respect.

The Soviet ambassador at the time was Yuri Andropov (1914–1984), the future CPSU General Secretary. Andropov feared that the proceedings of the 20th CPSU Congress and specifically Khrushchev's anti-Stalin "secret speech" at that Congress were having a strong impact on Hungarians. After Andropov called the Kremlin to update the Soviet leaders about the mood in Hungary, the CPSU Presidium decided to send Mikhail Suslov, a Presidium member, to Budapest. He arrived on 7 June for a week-long visit but, erroneously, reported back to Moscow that opposition to Rákosi was limited to members of the HWP Central Committee. However, on 27 June, a large crowd gathered for an opposition rally at which Losonczy called for Nagy to return to the prime minister's office: he was met with a standing ovation. According to Michael Polanyi, this rally "was the actual beginning of the Hungarian Revolution."[317] Three days later, Rákosi ordered the suspension of the Petőfi Circle. He also proposed to the Politburo on 12 July that Nagy and at least 400 other communists be arrested and put on trial for conspiring against the party. Upon learning of this, Soviet Ambassador Andropov contacted the Kremlin and the next day Soviet Presidium member Anastas Mikoyan flew to Budapest to meet with Rákosi, Gerő, Hegedüs, and Béla Veg. Their talks in the Hungarian capital convinced the Soviets that Rákosi had to resign. Gerő, whose perspectives scarcely differed from Rákosi's, now became First Secretary and Rákosi was flown to the Soviet Union, never to return to Hungary.[318]

In early October, Gerő flew to Moscow. On 6 October, while he was still at the Kremlin, the remains of four high-ranking victims of the purge, among them László Rajk, were ceremoniously reinterred while a few hundred thousand persons watched. Gerő had given his permission for this ceremony but, upon his return to Budapest, regretted that decision as the reburial of Rajk had, in his own words, "dealt a massive blow to the party leadership, whose authority was not all that [great] to begin with."[319] Meanwhile, Gerő wanted to improve relations with Yugoslav President Tito, but Tito had one condition for any improvement before the Hungarian First Secretary could be welcomed in Belgrade: Nagy had to be readmitted to the party. On 13 October, the Politburo accepted this condition and reinstated Nagy. On the same day, Budapest's major daily newspapers reported that Farkas, who had played a central role in the purges, had been arrested.[320] On 20 October, a mass meeting was held at the statue of Polish General József Bem (1794–1850), who had taken part in the Polish revolution of 1830 as well as in the Hungarian revolution of 1848–1849, to demonstrate solidarity with the Poles as they confronted their own crisis of leadership. As crowds gathered at the statue, there were calls for Imre Nagy. That night, insurgents entered Budapest's radio station, buildings of the daily news organ, *Szabad Nép*, and local party and police offices. Tension was rising and, on 22 October, there were public meetings at the universities of Budapest, Szeged, Miskolc, Pécs, and Sopron. Students drafted a program in which they called for a multiparty system, a free press, guarantees of civic rights, the withdrawal of Soviet troops from Hungary, punishment of all those complicitous in the purges in the 1950s, and an end to mandatory classes in Russian.[321] The following day, the Hungarian party Politburo first banned public demonstrations, then retracted the ban, then reinstated it ineffectively. Students became aware of the party's uncertainty and, at 3 p.m., undertook a march involving 50,000 students to the statue of poet Sándor Petőfi (1823–1849) and, from there, once again to the statue of Bem. The crowd expanded until it reached between 150,000 and 200,000 participants. Gathering finally in front of the Hungarian parliament, they called on Imre Nagy to speak to them. After a while, Nagy appeared on one of the parliament's balconies and addressed the crowd. Later, at 8 p.m., Gerő, who was in Yugoslavia at the time, spoke over Radio Budapest, condemning the gathering. Gerő's address angered the crowd and a large group of protesters now headed over to the statue of Stalin on the edge of the city park, toppled it, and chopped it into pieces. Nervous HWP leaders now asked those Soviet military units already stationed in the country to restore order. The Central Committee also met for an emergency session during the night of 23–24 October, electing Nagy to the Politburo and restoring him to the office of prime minister.

Although some shots had been fired the evening of 23 October, the uprising was, at that point, essentially peaceful. That was to change very quickly. On 24 October, Prime Minister Nagy issued a proclamation pledging to pursue a Hungarian road to democratic socialism but, by then, the uprising had taken on clear anti-Soviet characteristics. The following day, Mikoyan and Suslov came once more to Budapest, now demanding that Gerő be replaced by János Kádár – a demand being raised also on the streets.[322] But that same day, Hungarian secret police (ÁVH) agents, perched on rooftops, shot and killed more than one hundred unarmed protesters who had assembled in front of the parliament building. At this point, industrial workers took control of factories and set up workers' councils to run the factories. By the following day, insurgents were declaring the formation of "revolutionary committees" to assume the functions of local government. On 26 October, the Association of Hungarian Writers and Artists issued a set of demands, calling, *inter alia*, for Soviet units to return to their bases, the Hungarian Army to take charge of assuring public order, and the grant of a general amnesty. The Association also called for the formation of a government of people's unity under PM Nagy.[323] The entire country, but especially Budapest, remained in a state of social and political ferment. Indeed, armed groups of Hungarian insurgents could be seen on Budapest's streets and, as of 28 October, Nagy, fearing that the CC was about to call on Soviet forces to move against these revolutionary committees, contemplated resigning. Instead, he announced that Soviet armed forces would be withdrawn from Budapest, that the ÁVH would be disbanded, and that negotiations would start concerning the withdrawal of Soviet forces from Hungary altogether. The Soviet Presidium met on 28 October and agreed that withdrawal of forces from Hungary was out of the question. But two days later, the Soviet Presidium still hoped for a diplomatic solution to the crisis and some Soviet units were, at that point, actually pulling out of Hungary.

On 30 October, emboldened insurgents had attacked party headquarters in Budapest, wounding disarmed ÁVH troops. By the following day, insurgents had taken control of the building. Worse yet from the Soviet perspective, "Hungarian army tanks, which had been sent to help the defenders of the site, ended up defecting to the insurgents."[324] During the night of 31 October-1 November, Soviet troops were brought into Budapest and other key locations but later pulled back, apparently because they lacked clearly defined objectives.[325] These troop movements have come down as the Soviet Union's "first intervention" in Hungary. Kádár, no doubt uncertain as to how this would play out, declared that communists admired "our people's glorious uprising" and promised that the Hungarian Socialist Workers' Party (HSWP), as the HCP/HWP had just been renamed, would support "the government's demand for the complete removal of Soviet forces."[326] That same day, Nagy declared Hungary's withdrawal from the Warsaw Pact and the country's political neutrality. He called on Western powers (the U.S., U.K., and France) to recognize and protect Hungary's newly declared neutrality.

These developments notwithstanding, on 3 November, the cabinet was reconstructed, with Nagy remaining prime minister but also assuming the portfolio for foreign affairs. That same day, Cardinal Mindszenty, who had been released from house arrest three days prior, addressed the people of Hungary in a public address broadcast over the radio. But, rather than giving his blessing to the new government, he highlighted rather the importance, in his mind, of seeing a Christian Democratic party in power.[327] By the following day, the short-lived Hungarian Revolution was essentially over. Soviet tanks had entered Budapest in force, encountering no organized resistance. Nagy and a few of his associates took refuge in the Yugoslav embassy, while Mindszenty was granted asylum in the American embassy.

For a while, there was scattered armed resistance in Budapest as well as in Transdanubia, but after 10 days it was all over and about 200,000 Hungarians fled the country. Kádár invited Nagy and Géza Losonczy to leave the Yugoslav embassy and join him for talks, suggesting that they could collaborate in the new government. Nagy accepted the invitation and, on 22 November, he and a group of his associates boarded a government bus. However, a Soviet military unit swooped in, removed the Yugoslav diplomats who had boarded the bus in order to guarantee the safety of Nagy's group, and took the bus to a nearby military academy. Five days later, Nagy and his associates were put on a plane and flown to Romania. Losonczy died in prison; Nagy was executed on 16 June 1958.

The German Democratic Republic

In the years until Stalin's death on 5 March 1953, nothing could be done without the Soviet dictator's approval or direct order. Even the establishment of the German Democratic Republic (GDR) on 7 October 1949 was proclaimed only after Stalin had given his consent.[328] Although the constitution was adopted on the same day that the GDR was created, two months passed before the provisional *Volkskammer* (People's Chamber) authorized the establishment of the Supreme Court of the GDR and the State Prosecutor's Office. The Ministry for State Security (MfS) – in effect, the secret police, whose members were known colloquially as the Stasi – was formed only on 8 February 1950 and was subordinated only to the Politburo, not to any government body. In 1950, the MfS had a staff of approximately 1,000; by 1957, this would expand to 17,500.[329] There were show trials in 1950, though not of persons as prominent as those put on trial in Hungary, Czechoslovakia, or Bulgaria.[330] Although the KPD and SPD had merged to form the SED on the sup-position of parity, when the ruling party canceled the membership of more than 320,000 erstwhile members on grounds of hostility to the party line, moral defi-ciency, or purely careerist motivation, more than half of these were former Social Democrats.[331] The SED, with its 51-member Central Committee (and 30 candidate members) and seven-member Politburo, exercised complete power in the system, even though four powerless noncommunist parties, listed earlier, continued to exist.

In spite of party discipline, purges, and rewards for conformity, the SED party-state dictatorship was creaky from the beginning. The planning mechanism, cre-ated to maximize party control of the economy, was, with occasional exceptions (in particular after the June 1953 uprising described below), not responsive to the needs and wishes of consumers or, for that matter, to the market, or even to the needs of industrial enterprises, which typically had to resort to informal networks and bartering to obtain the equipment and materials they needed. As Jürgen Kocka has written,

> The GDR was a dictatorship with a command economy, but in everyday practice contradictory aims and unintended consequences of political meas-ures counteracted a clear-cut domination from above. Much in this state-organized economy looked more like a chaotic and inefficient muddling through than like a well-ordered party state.[332]

Long-term stability would have required fundamental reform but, as will be seen in the following chapter, although there were clear-sighted advocates of thorough-going reform, they were drowned out by conservatives who felt that it was enough just to tinker with the system.

For the SED, there were five tasks to be undertaken: The first and, in some ways, the most urgent task was to legitimate the existence of a second German state alongside the economically more successful Federal Republic of Germany. There were two dimensions to this challenge: on the one hand, the SED wanted to distance itself in the most decisive way possible from Hitler's Third Reich; on the other hand, the SED wanted to distinguish itself from the Federal Republic and lay claim to a higher moral authority. The SED addressed both of these by evoking German communists' participation in defending the Spanish Republic during the Spanish Civil War (July 1936-April 1939) and in active resistance to Nazism.[333] On this basis, the SED cast East Germany as an anti-fascist nation, distinct from the "barbarous" West German state.[334]

Second, the party wanted to assert control over agriculture by liquidating private farms and herding peasants onto collective farms. Collectivization was set in motion in 1952 and unfolded in two waves – 1952–53 and 1958–60, with a break during the years 1953–58. Although the party news organ *Neues Deutschland* heralded the launch of collectivization as a purely voluntary affair in which peasants spontaneously decided to form collectives and surrender their land to the collective farms,[335] only the earliest agricultural collectives were formed freely and this typically involved small farms created in 1945 and surviving economically only thanks to generous state subsidies. Successful farmers, on the other hand, resisted pressure to join collectives; in response, the CC decided, at its Tenth Plenum (November 1952) to step up the pressure on private farmers, "punishing, harassing, and [even] jailing" recalcitrants.[336] Pressure was also applied by raising taxes on small farms, increasing the quantities of produce and grain to be delivered to the state at fixed prices, and reducing farmers' access to credits and agricultural machinery. When farmers failed to deliver the quantities stipulated, authorities confiscated their land.[337] These confiscations resulted in a marked decline in agricultural production and had a negative impact on the standard of living. In 1953, 5,681 peasant families left the GDR for the West.[338] After Stalin's death, the SED called a halt to collectivization in May 1953 and, in June 1953, allowed collective farms to be broken up, restoring private farms. The unrest of June 1953 actually began in the countryside as early as 12 June, with farmers demanding a reversal of the collectivization drive.

Third, the SED wanted to socialize the bulk of the economy, emphasize the development of heavy industry, and save money for investments in heavy industry and machine-building by being niggardly when it came to investing in foodstuffs and consumer goods. In 1950, the SED proclaimed that the country was now a people's democracy and that the transition to socialism would be started.[339] In line with this newly declared ambition, authorities called for an acceleration in the expansion of heavy industry and advanced some production targets originally set for 1955 to 1953 or even, in some cases, to late 1952.[340] This came against the backdrop of an increase in November 1951 of targets for the extraction of certain raw materials and in certain branches of heavy industry. At the same time, investments in industrial plants that manufactured agricultural machinery or produced artificial fertilizers and consumer goods were cut back, lowering the general standard of living. As 1953 opened, there were serious shortages of milk, butter, margarine, other fats, sugar, fish, fish oil, and potatoes. These shortages were the direct result of the peasants' refusal to satisfy the high delivery quotas imposed by the government.

Meanwhile, the government realized that the higher targets set in industrial production could be achieved only by demanding more work for the same pay (a "norm increase") in the factories. On 5 May 1953, the Central Committee decided to raise the work norms and on 28 May the government announced that industrial production would have to be increased by 10% – this, without pay incentives, without hiring additional workers, and without improvements in technology or machinery.[341] The anger on the part of industrial workers was so intense that the government backed down, admitted that it had committed "mistakes", and, on 9 June, promised a "New Course". On 16 June, the government retracted its demand for a 10% increase in output. But this came too late to prevent workers from going on strike and taking to the streets. The first workers' strike had actually taken place in Magdeburg in December 1952; this was followed by strikes in multiple locations across the GDR in April 1953, to protest poor food supplies and living conditions in general.[342] Then, on the morning of 16 June 1953, workers at construction block 40 on Berlin's Stalinallee began a protest march. They started with 300 construction workers but, as they marched past other work sites, their number grew to 2,000. By the time the protesters approached the building for the Minister of Industry, their number had swelled to 10,000. Fritz Selbmann, the Minister for Industry, went outside to talk with the marchers. But he did not have the authority to offer them anything and their anger did not subside.

The following day, 20,000 construction workers assembled on Strausberger Platz. Protesters stormed more than 250 police stations and other public buildings, freeing about 1,400 inmates from 12 prisons. The strike had, in fact, ignited an uprising across the entire GDR, *inter alia* with strikes and demonstrations in Brandenburg, Gera, Görlitz, Jena, and once again Magdeburg. Altogether between one million and 1.5 million people took part in protests across more than 700 towns and villages between 16 and 21 June. Work stoppages involved a minimum of half a million workers at between 600 and a thousand plants. As many as 20 officials and security police died in clashes with protesters and between 60 and 100 civilians lost their lives.[343] Soviet authorities declared martial law and employed massive military force to suppress the uprising. After the uprising was put down, at least 20 persons were executed.[344] More than 1,500 persons were tried and sent to prison. Experiencing a workers' uprising in a putative workers' state was difficult for the SED to digest; accordingly, *Neues Deutschland* blamed "fascist and other reactionary elements in West Berlin" for provoking the unrest that started on 16–17 June.[345]

Although the New Course had been announced a few days before the uprising, the SED now confirmed that it would continue with the New Course.
Grotewohl pledged that there would be an improvement in living conditions.
Already in July, wages for low-income earners were increased, effective 1 August,
while those whose wages had been reduced in January were told that their wages
would be restored to pre-January levels. Another concession to the public was
the announcement that the output targets for consumer goods under the plan
ending in 1955 would be increased.[346] In fact, the New Course resulted in a relative improvement in living conditions, with a lowering of prices of foodstuffs,
cooking oil, etc., by 10–25%; the regime also undertook to subsidize the cost of
cars, furniture, radios, and other consumer commodities. Even so, many citizens
continued to find the conditions of life in the GDR unbearable. Thus, in the
course of 1953, more than 331,000 citizens took advantage of the open border in
Berlin to leave East Germany, followed by 184,000 in 1954 and a further 252,000
in 1955.[347]

Nonetheless, it was not all bad news for the SED on the economic front. Between
1950 and 1955, the proportion of industry in the state sector rose from 76.5% to
85.3%, in construction from 38.9% to 52.9%, in transport from 82.4% to 85.5%, in
retail trade from 47.2% to 68.0%, and in wholesale trade from 71.1% to 95.3%.[348]
As for the continued hemorrhaging of the population, the Soviet-controlled daily
newspaper *Tägliche Rundschau* had this to say a year after the uprising:

> The working class plays the leading role in the German Democratic Repub-
> lic, precisely because state power belongs to it and to working peasants. The
> interests of the working class, the interests of the peasants and of the intel-
> ligentsia determine the character and the direction of the whole political
> system and economy in the GDR.[349]

The fourth task that the SED set for itself was to transform society from top to
bottom, as well as people's mental outlook (and thereby, create the New Socialist
Man and New Socialist Woman). To achieve this, surveillance and control in the
cultural sphere, the religious sphere, and even in gender relations were critical.
These policy spheres are examined below.

And the fifth task that the SED undertook was to gain a seat for the GDR in the
United Nations and to open diplomatic relations with as many countries as possible and potentially useful. However, under West Germany's Hallstein Doctrine,
named for Walter Hallstein, West Germany would immediately break off relations
with any country recognizing East Germany. The result was that, until the early
1970s, the GDR had exceedingly few diplomatic contacts outside the Warsaw
Pact. Then, in 1970, the East and West German leaders met for the first time and,
on 21 December 1972, the two Germanys signed a Basic Treaty laying the foundation for mutual diplomatic recognition and for scuttling the Hallstein Doctrine.
Finally, on 18 September, the German Democratic Republic was admitted to the
United Nations, alongside the Federal Republic of Germany.

During the years 1949–56, Ulbricht faced a serious challenge to his leadership. This came in May-June 1953 when Wilhelm Zaisser (1893–1958), then Minister for State Security, and Rudolf Herrnstadt (1903–1966), then editor of *Neues Deutschland*, enjoying the backing of KGB chief Lavrenti Beria (1899–1953), moved to remove him from power. But Beria was arrested by his Kremlin colleagues on 26 June 1953 and the remaining Soviet leaders, trusting Ulbricht, demanded that Zaisser and Herrnstadt be relieved of their positions. Zaisser and Herrnstadt were, thus, not only dismissed from their posts but also expelled from the Central Committee.[350] In 1957, there would be a challenge from Ernst Wollweber (1898–1967), Zaisser's successor as Minister for State Security, and Karl Schirdewan (1907–1998), a member of the SED Politburo. Their challenge will be discussed in chapter 3.

Socialist realism in culture

In 1957, Walter Ulbricht offered his thoughts about culture in a speech to the Thirtieth Plenum of the SED Central Committee. In his view, the arts were not to be isolated from reality and hence, he thought, not cut off from ordinary people. He told his listeners that East German novelists, artists, and scientists, who confronted great assignments, needed to visit factories, machine-tractor stations, and agricultural collectives. What is more, these creative intellectuals needed to identify their interests with the interests of factory workers and collectivized peasants.[351] Or, to put it differently, the SED wanted to control the cultural sphere. Indeed, there was no sector of culture to which the SED was indifferent, whether literature or pictorial art or sculpture or film[352] or architecture[353] or music of all kinds including opera[354] or even children's music education.[355]

The politicization of culture began already during the years of the Soviet Occupation Zone, but gained momentum as Stalin's hopes for a united, neutralized Germany faded. Beginning in 1950, the SED was taking a hard line on modern art, condemning it as "formalistic and destructive".[356] Then, the following year, the SED Central Committee, meeting for its Fifth Plenum (1951), announced that socialist realism would serve as the mandatory doctrine for the arts. The periodical *Musik und Gesellschaft* explained the doctrine for composers: "Socialist realism is not just a new style, some sort of new "-ism", but rather an attitude reflective of a worldview and by that virtue a creative method. It is the essence of this worldview that the composer is filled with loving concern for the welfare of the restless creative workers."[357] Socialist realism was understood to entail the effort to reflect reality faithfully in a politically engaged way and without experimentation. Where newly composed music was concerned, composers were advised to build on the classics without simply repeating their styles.[358] Although there were some guidelines for all the cultural genres, the SED was the ultimate judge of what was progressive and true to socialist realism and what was not. As Johannes R. Becher (1891–1958), who served as Minister of Culture in the years 1954–58, put it, "art and education had never been so connected with power" as in the GDR.[359]

Becher was, in fact, a key figure in the formation of cultural policy first in the Soviet Occupation Zone and subsequently in the GDR. Already in July 1945, Becher organized the Cultural League for the Democratic Renewal of Germany, serving as its first chair. The League was the focal point in the early years for the promotion and organization of culture in the GDR. On 14 August 1945, Becher established Aufbau Verlag, as a publishing house for the Cultural League, and, within a fortnight, Aufbau Verlag brought out the first issue of *Aufbau*, a journal for culture and cultural policy. Becher was committed to the idea that there was a duty "to preserve and transmit the [nation's] cultural heritage."[360] Becher, a poet in his own right, was put under pressure to declare himself against "formalism" (i.e., against art lacking a social or political message, hence art for the sake of art). He was uncomfortable with this and dragged his feet and, when he did make some effort to accommodate the anti-formalist line, he did so only with reservations. He sought to curry favor in 1949 by writing poems celebrating agricultural collectivization. That same year he wrote the text for the GDR's national anthem – Hanns Eisler (1898–1962) wrote the music – and in 1950 he wrote a cantata in honor of the SED's Third Party Congress.[361] Even so, he found himself attacked in *Neues Deutschland* (10 June 1950) for "inadequate support for the anti-formalism campaign of the SED."[362]

Indeed, Becher was conflicted. On the one hand, he firmly held that

> A political system would abandon the most important part of itself if it were to maintain a neutral, indifferent position in matters of culture and permitted chaotic, anarchistic conditions. Those who deny the state the right to influence cultural development . . . either underestimate the enormous importance of culture and art in the people's education, or . . . confuse the state in which we live with the former German political structures.[363]

But note that he defended the right of the state "to *influence* cultural development" and not a right to control it. And hence, on the other hand, in his writings of 1952–57, Becher repeatedly defended the autonomy of poetry and insisted that poetry should not be reduced to serving as the handmaiden of politics.[364] That same principle extended implicitly to all cultural sectors.

There were past composers whom the SED revered, such as Beethoven[365] and Wagner,[366] and those whom it reviled, such as the twelve-tone composer Arnold Schoenberg (1874–1951) and his student Alban Berg (1885–1935).[367] And yet, East Germany's most distinguished composer, Hanns Eisler, presented a lecture at the (East) Berlin Academy of Music in December 1954 praising Schoenberg, suggesting that he was the greatest orchestral composer of the first half of the twentieth century,[368] and, for that matter, it was possible to stage Berg's *Wozzeck* at the (East) Berlin State Opera House in 1955. By the same virtue, there were authors whom the SED viewed as "progressive" and those whose works were criticized. Among German authors, those counted as progressive included (in alphabetical order): Kurt Bartel (Kuba), Johannes Becher, Bertolt Brecht, Stephan Hermlin, Bernhard

Kellermann, Anna Seghers, Erich Weinert, and Arnold Zweig.[369] Among American authors enjoying SED favor was Upton Sinclair (1878–1968), whose many books include *The Jungle* (1906) and *King Coal* (1917).[370] On the other hand, when a dramatization of *The Adventures of Tom Sawyer*, a novel by the American author Mark Twain (1835–1910) was staged in Halle in 1953, a serious discussion ensued as to whether it should have been performed at all.[371]

When, in June 1953, the SED announced its "New Course" in the economy, Becher championed extending it into the cultural sphere. In the new atmosphere associated not only with the announcement of the New Course but also with the death of Stalin months earlier, the Academy of Arts issued a 10-point declaration on 30 June 1953, criticizing cultural policy and demanding that the regime leave the choice of style or method up to the artist or writer, which is to say to cease dictating socialist realism as the mandatory style in the arts. Indeed, the Academy endorsed the idea that there should be a "variety of themes and styles" in all sectors of the arts.[372] Then, on 5 February 1956, *Sonntag*, the weekly periodical of Becher's Cultural League, published an article by Günter Cwojdrak criticizing rigid party control of the arts. The apparent cultural thaw received a boost during the fallout from Khrushchev's secret speech and, in another article in *Sonntag* (2 December 1956), Hans Mayer demanded that Western literature be made available in the GDR.[373] But, by the end of 1956, the thaw was coming to an end and the party now resumed its hard line in culture. Becher, although he had been named the GDR's first Minister of Culture in January 1954, was subjected to attack; moreover, in November 1957, for the first time, the SED espoused a "socialist revolution in the realm of ideology and culture."[374] In January 1958, addressing the Thirtieth Plenum of the CC, Ulbricht singled out Aufbau Verlag and *Sonntag* as having provided the organizational foundation for Harich's dissident group.[375] But when Becher died in October 1958, Ulbricht presented a eulogy, asserting that "the mainstream of modern German poetry leads from Goethe and Hölderlin to Becher, and continues onwards," and praising Becher as "the greatest poet of our time."[376] As for cultural policy, Kurt Hager, the Secretary for Science, Higher Education, and People's Education, put it this way in 1957: "For us art and literature are weapons for socialism."[377]

Religion

There are at least two, over time perhaps three, reasons why the Churches of the German Democratic Republic received a gentler, at times friendly, treatment from the authorities. The first and most often mentioned is that the leading figures of the Protestant (Lutheran and Reformed) Church had proven anti-fascist credentials; indeed, as previously mentioned many of them had been incarcerated in concentration camps alongside communists, who came to know and trust their fellow inmates. The second, equally obvious, reason is that, until 1952, Stalin was keeping open the option of allowing East Germany to merge with West Germany into a united, neutralized state; naturally, the East German communists were opposed to this. The third reason, which emerged over time, is that, with its 52 hospitals, 280 homes for the aged, 112 convalescent homes, more than 550,000 parish welfare centers, and other welfare facilities,[378] the Protestant Church was playing a constructive role in East Germany. Indeed, these activities proved so useful that, with time, the authorities made generous contributions to support the Protestant Church.

The 1949 constitution offered a number of guarantees for religious believers and Churches. To begin with, Article 41 guaranteed "complete freedom of faith and conscience . . . without interference," while Article 42 assured believers that their civil rights and duties were neither compromised nor restricted by their religious affiliation. Article 43 guaranteed that every religious body could regulate and administer its own affairs autonomously, and finally, Article 44 guaranteed "[t]he right of the Church to give religious instruction on school premises."[379] But the regime had four ambitions which came into conflict with these constitutional guarantees. First, the regime wanted the Churches operating in the GDR, and especially the large Protestant Church (with 8 million believers in 1974),[380] to sunder their organizational links with their sister Churches in West Germany (in violation of Article 43). Where the Protestant Church was concerned, this was accomplished only in the course of 1968–69. Second, the regime wanted to remove religious instruction from the state schools (Church-run schools had been shut down already prior to the establishment of the GDR). Although this ambition was in conflict with Article 44, the authorities found a solution in 1958 by requiring that, at the end of the instruction in secular subjects, there would be a two-hour break before religious instruction could be offered.[381] This was enough to serve as a disincentive for most pupils to return to the school building after two hours. In 1960, the Church set up its own system of religious instruction outside the state school system. Third, the SED wanted to keep itself informed about confidential discussions and initiatives on the part of the Church and therefore, in a move not in the spirit of Article 41 (which guaranteed that there would be no interference in Church matters on the part of the authorities), the SED began recruiting informants among the clergy from early on. One example is Oberkirchenrat (Higher Church Counselor) Gerhard Lotz of Eisenach, recruited as a Stasi informant in 1955.[382] Moreover, in violation of Article 42, the SED instituted systematic discrimination against believers in access to higher education and employment. Finally, in contradiction of the spirit of Article 41, the regime decided on a dual-track program to wean young people away from religion.

In chronological terms, the first track involved the establishment in 1945 of the Free German Youth (*Freie Deutsche Jugend*, or FDJ). But this communist-sponsored youth organization soon faced competition from the Protestant Church's youth group, the *Junge Gemeinde* (Youth Community), which had obtained qualified sanction from Soviet authorities in October 1947.[383] Relations between these rival organizations quickly became tense. Thus, on 29 May 1952, Walter Ulbricht declared, at the FDJ's Fourth Congress, that that organization should increase its activity, with the goal of recruiting young people from the *Junge Gemeinde*.[384] But in

June 1953, the SED shifted its stance, deciding to cease obstruction of the Church's work among young people. In any event, membership in the *Junge Gemeinde* grew steadily from 108,417 on 1 June 1952 to 119,855 on 1 June 1954, growing further to 123,025 by 1 June 1955.[385]

The second track of the SED's plan to secularize young people involved its instrumentalization of the *Jugendweihe* (Youth Consecration) as an alternative to the sacrament of confirmation. The *Jugendweihe* had existed in a different form in nineteenth-century Germany and, after years of repression under the Third Reich, reemerged after the war.[386] In November 1954, the SED took control of the *Jugendweihe*, giving it a socialist character. The *Jugendweihe* was controversial among Christians and even the usually pliable Bishop Moritz Mitzenheim (1891–1977) of Thuringia expressed his opposition to the ritual, as recast by the SED. At first, the Protestant Church insisted that participation in the *Jugendweihe* was incompatible with Church confirmation; later, the Church relented and allowed that young people could participate in both. In spring 1955, according to official figures, some 60,000 adolescents, representing about a fifth of those who were eligible, took part in the *Jugendweihe*.[387]

Although the regime allowed six theological faculties to continue to operate within their respective universities, paying the salaries of the theological staff, and also provided assistance in support of church construction, and, in spite of Catholic Bishop Otto Spülbeck's effort to achieve a *modus vivendi* with the SED state,[388] Church-state relations could not be said to have been unaffected by ideological tension and relations of inequality. Hence, in 1956, the same Bishop Spülbeck of Meissen bemoaned that "We are living under the stairs in a house that is not our own."[389]

Women and gender equality

When it comes to gender equality, the constitution of 1949 followed the model adopted throughout the Soviet bloc, guaranteeing women equal rights with men (Article 7), "special protection in employment . . . enabling women to co-ordinate their tasks as citizens and workers with their duties as wives and mothers" (Article 18), and the right to "particular protection and care by the state" during maternity (Article 32). The constitution further placed marriage and family under the protection of the state (Article 30).[390] When it came to maternity, East German women were guaranteed six weeks of paid time off prior to giving birth and 20 weeks after giving birth. Moreover, women enjoyed a constitutional guarantee of equal pay for equal work.[391]

We may say that there are five dimensions of gender equality: (1) equality in education, hiring, and salaries; (2) recognition of women's right to birth control and abortion, and the protection of their right to return to their previous employment after giving birth; (3) equal representation in political offices (in the legislative, executive, and judicial branches, as well as in appointive positions); (4) respectful portrayals of women in the media, films, plays, and fiction; and (5) mutual respect between husband and wife and sharing of housework and other household duties (such as shopping). In the long term, the GDR did comparatively well with assuring equal treatment of women in dimensions 1, 2, and 4, although, Christel Sudau noted in 1978, that, at the time she was writing, only 11% of women in the GDR had either a university degree or a vocational degree.[392] In terms of access to legal abortion, East German women would have to wait until 1972.

In terms of representation in political office (factor 3 in the list above), East German women were clearly unequal, although it should be conceded that they fared much better at that time, in this regard, than women in West Germany or the United States. Be that as it may, in the first *Volkskammer* (the country's highest legislative body), only 111 of the 466 deputies were women (23.8% of the total) and, in the first Council of State, only two of its 16 members were women. Prior to 1956, only one woman attained candidate membership in the SED Politburo – Elli Schmidt, serving in that capacity from 1950 to 1954 – and only two women were entrusted with ministerial portfolios – Elisabeth Zaisser, Minister of Education, 1952–53, and Hilde Benjamin, Minister of Justice, 1953–67.[393] Women were also a distinct minority in the SED Central Committee.

Respect for women (factor 5 in the list above), whether in the family or in society more broadly remained problematic. Even though traditional attitudes waned over time, as late as 1977–78, East German women were handling 37 hours of housework a week, even though more than 70% of women were also holding down full-time jobs[394]; men did on average 5.5 hours of housework each week, with children contributing four hours.[395] And finally, male chauvinism remained a problem, with East German women's magazines providing examples.[396]

Romania

A draft constitution for Romania was published on 6 March 1948 and approved by the Grand National Assembly on 13 April that year. On paper, the rights assured to the country's citizens looked beyond reproach. But there were qualifications attached to these rights. For example, Article 32 declared: "The citizens have the right of association and organization, if the aims pursued are not directed against the democratic order established by the Constitution."[397] Or again, under the Constitution, private ownership of land as well as of industrial and commercial concerns was sanctioned. But on 11 June 1948, the Grand National Assembly authorized the nationalization of the economy, including industrial enterprises, banking, mining, and the transport sector. A week later, the State Planning Commission was set up. A new militia was established on 22 January 1949; even prior to that, the existing police force had been restaffed.

It was now that the terror was stepped up, beginning with the expropriation, ordered on 2 March 1949, of all farmlands greater than 50 hectares. Militia forces took the owners into custody and deported them. The confiscated farmlands were then turned over to state farms. This was followed, on 25 May 1949, by the decision to begin construction of a canal linking the Danube River with the Black

Sea – a project of high interest for Stalin. Prisoners, including erstwhile members of suppressed noncommunist parties, were put to work on the canal, alongside uncooperative intellectuals, despoiled members of the middle class, kulaks, and Orthodox priests. In addition, a 450-man labor brigade consisting wholly of Catholic priests was sent to join the work on the canal; almost half of the Catholic priests, as well as many others, died at the work site.[398]

The nationalization of private housing began in 1950 with the issuance of Decree No. 92. The communists thought that eliminating private property would promote the fashioning of a collectivist, socialist consciousness and, with it, the creation of the New Socialist Man and New Socialist Woman. Interestingly enough, nationalization occurred even while the civil code adopted in 1864, based in part on the Napoleonic Code, was still in place (it remained in force until 2011). Nationalization did not necessarily entail the ejection of the former owners from their housing, however; on the contrary, many were allowed to remain in their now-nationalized homes but forced to share them with new tenants.[399]

Until spring 1952, Petru Groza served as Prime Minister in a coalition government. During these years, his government suppressed nine provincial newspapers. Upon the expiration of his term on 2 June 1952, Groza became President of the Presidium of the Grand National Assembly, holding that post until his death seven-and-a-half years later. Gheorghe Gheorghiu-Dej, General Secretary of the Romanian Workers' Party and erstwhile Deputy Prime Minister, now became Prime Minister of Romania. Groza's Ploughman's Front was dissolved in 1953.

In the years after the seizure of power, there were other prominent Romanian communists, among them: Vasile Luca (1898–1963), who was nominally in charge of economic policy from 1947 until March 1952 (but in actual practice only until January 1951); Ana Pauker (1893–1960), Foreign Minister from December 1947 until July 1952; Emil Bodnăraş (1904–1976), Minister of War from 1947 to 1955 and First Deputy Prime Minister from 1955 to 1967; and Lucretiu Pătrăşcanu (1900–1954), Minister of Justice, 1944–48. Although the communists controlled the pinnacles of power by 1948, there was still resistance in the early years. Specifically, as many as 20,000 armed partisans resisted communist rule until at least 1952 if not even later,[400] while peasants resisted pressure to join the collective farms, even resorting to economic sabotage.[401] The regime executed some peasants and deported others to unknown locations.[402] The decision to collectivize was the result of pressure from the Kremlin and was announced in early March 1949. But while Pauker and her associates had argued for a *gradual* collectivization,[403] she would later be charged with having "committed left-wing deviations from the Party line by permitting the violation of the free consent of the working peasants."[404]

There were two reasons for the purge of some of the leading figures in the party. The first is that, in 1952, Stalin ordered Gheorghiu-Dej to purge "Zionists" from RWP ranks.[405] "Zionist" was Stalin's code for Jewish and Ana Pauker, who had actually recommended Gheorghiu-Dej for the party leadership,[406] found herself on the firing line. The second reason for the purge is that Gheorghiu-Dej wanted to get rid of his rivals, the so-called "Muscovites", by de-fanging them (Pauker was put under house arrest, Luca given a prison sentence for life), while Pătrăşcanu was executed in 1954. Whatever their personal fate, their books were removed from the country's libraries, along with more than 8,000 other books judged to be problematic.[407] Gheorghiu-Dej had been in alliance with Pauker, Luca, Bodnaraş, and Pintilie Bodnarenko; with the removal of the former two, Gheoghiu-Dej, Bodnaraş, and Bodnarenko formed a new working alliance with Petre Borila and Leonte Răutu (1910–1993), serving as head of Agitprop since 1948 – in which position he would remain until 1965.

Soon after Stalin's death in March 1953, Romania's leaders shut down the project to construct the Danube-Black Sea canal. Four months later, on 8 July 1953, a new Constitution was published. As had been the case with the 1948 Constitution, the 1953 document did not include any provisions separating legislative, executive, and judicial powers.[408] The Constitution also confirmed the establishment the previous year of the Hungarian Autonomous Region.[409] Now, having purged the leading figures in the Muscovite faction, Gheorghiu-Dej issued a general amnesty, pardoning more than half a million persons of crimes committed "against public order" and authorized the release from confinement of 15,000 political prisoners.[410] In August 1955, Gheorghiu-Dej requested the withdrawal of Soviet troops from Romania; Khrushchev agreed, although the withdrawal would not be accomplished for another three years.

A few months later came Khrushchev's bombshell at the 20th CPSU Congress in Moscow. Gheorghiu-Dej was dismayed by Khrushchev's revelations and there followed a number of CC sessions designed to control and limit the impact of Khrushchev's speech. As Tismaneanu recalls, at these sessions

> . . . every member of the communist supreme echelon was asked to engage in the notorious Leninist practice of criticism and self-criticism. At the March 23–25 plenum, Gheorghiu-Dej presented a politburo report *(Dare de seamă)* in which he criticized Stalin and especially his personality cult. However, the secret speech was not explicitly mentioned. As for Stalinism in his own party, Gheorghiu-Dej spoke of Romanian Stalinists without mentioning names and insisted that the RWP had expelled them in 1952 . . . and that he, Gheorghiu-Dej, deserved credit for having courageously embarked on de-Stalinization . . . long before the Twentieth Congress.[411]

As for the Romanian public, little was divulged, lest Khrushchev's charges against Stalin excite repercussions on the home front.

Literature and music

Up until 1955, Leonte Răutu was in charge of cultural policy and, in the latter 1940s and into the 1950s, he devoted his time to criticizing traces of "bourgeois decadence" in literature. His reign came to an end in 1955, when Miron

Constantinescu became Deputy Prime Minister with responsibility for culture. With this, the Zhdanovshchina was wound down and intellectuals and literati enjoyed more latitude. After February 1956, one could speak of a cultural thaw, albeit a transient one.[412] But, at the dawn of the communist era, cultural history was rewritten in order to excise any mention of authors now branded as "nationalists", "cosmopolitans", or "objectivists", or simply as "decadent". Writers were expected to produce works inspired by socialist realism; those who refused to abide by this formula could be imprisoned.[413] A collection of a hundred poems by Tudor Arghezi (1880–1967), published on 30 December 1947, did not reflect socialist realist think- ing and was quickly confiscated. Another writer, Lucian Blaga, was unable to pub- lish his work on eighteenth-century Transylvania and Romanian philosophy. In general, the RWP condemned "anti-realism" in literature and art[414] but, in spite of the strict enforcement of socialist realism, there were complaints as late as 1953 that censorship was lax in some places.

Where concert music (orchestral and chamber music alike) was concerned, local composers worked under the shadow of the émigré composer George Enescu (1881–1955), who had fled to Paris in 1946, where he was known as Georges Enesco. As Hugh Wood recorded in 1968, Enescu's "influence [was] everywhere: in statues and memories; in prizes, competitions, festivals; in articles by young composers reinterpreting his work; and in a host of pieces entitled 'Homage to Enesco'."[415] But if Enescu was untouchable, in spite of his occasional use of atonal- ism and quarter-tone progressions, the same was not true in the early 1950s for the new generation of Romanian composers. At that time, authorities wanted to dictate the form, modalities, and spirit of music and were keen on hearing tunes they could hum. Mihai Jora (1891–1971) certainly gratified the cultural overlords with his *Lieder* marked by a "melodious consistency pleasing to the ear."[416] But after 1956, the old prescriptive formulae were considered passé.

Religion

Already in 1947, a law had been enacted establishing a mandatory retirement at age of 70 for all clergy. As a result, Metropolitan Ireneu of Moldavia, Metropoli- tan Nifon of Oltenia, Bishop Lucian, Bishop Cosma of the Lower Danube, and Bishop Gheronte of Constanța all had to retire. This law, thus, actually preceded passage of the Law on Religious Cults mentioned in the previous section. Super- vising the religious sphere was a Ministry of Cults, with broad powers of supervi- sion. The communists banned all charitable and educational work on the part of the Churches and also excluded them from caring for the sick and injured. As of January 1953, between 300 and 500 Orthodox priests were in concentration camps. The Churches were limited to performing religious rituals and the Min- istry controlled admission to the seminaries.[417] The regime also took care to see that the Holy Synod and the National Church Council included hefty contingents of communist party members. Metropolitan Justinian of Moldavia, who became

Patriarch of the Romanian Orthodox Church on 24 May 1948, had won the trust of Gheorghiu-Dej and would lead his Church into a compliant, quiescent, and collaborative relationship with the communist regime.[418]

Women

Decree No. 2218 (issued on 13 July 1946) affirmed the legal equality of men and women. Law No. 560, passed the same year, declared that "women have the right to vote and may be elected in the [Grand National] Assembly . . . under the same conditions as men."[419] This declaration of equality between women and men was reaffirmed in the Constitutions of 1948 and 1952, while the Fundamental Law affirmed that women enjoyed equal rights, *inter alia*, in public and cultural life. As in other bloc states, there were guarantees of state protection for families as well as paid leave for pregnant women. Moreover, the 1954 Family Code prescribed full equality in the family between husband and wife. On the other hand, during 1948–49, independent feminist and women's organizations were suppressed, being replaced by a communist-controlled union for women.[420] Abortion, which had been legal before the communist takeover, was banned in 1948.

The 1948 Constitution contained a number of provisions in regard to women, family, and even the birth rate. The fundamental article in regard to the equality of women was Article III, which promised that the state would assure equal rights for women and men, including equal rights to education, work, and leisure, as well as equal pay for equal work.[421] The Constitution went even further, guaranteeing women special conditions at work in connection with pregnancy and child care, and special care in the event of pregnancy.[422] The Constitution also declared that "marriage and the family enjoy the protection of the State," adding that "the State shall take systematic measures in the interest of the increase of the population within the nation."[423]

Bulgaria

As of the end of 1948, the leadership troika in the Bulgarian Communist Party consisted of Georgi Dimitrov (Prime Minister since 23 November 1946, member of the Politburo, and General Secretary of the communist party from 27 December 1948), Traicho Kostov (Deputy Prime Minister since 1946 and member of the Politburo since 1948), and Vasil Kolarov (Deputy Prime Minister and Minister of Foreign Affairs since 1947). By January 1950, all three of them were dead: Dimitrov died at the Barvikha sanatorium near Moscow on 2 July 1949; Kostov was executed on 16 December 1949 on charges of spreading anti-Soviet views, among other things; and Kolarov, who had succeeded Dimitrov as Prime Minister in July 1949, died on 23 January 1950. Vulko Chervenkov (1900–1980), succeeded Dimitrov as General Secretary of the Bulgarian Communist Party and succeeded Kolarov as Prime Minister. He would hold the post of General Secretary until January 1954 and continue as Prime Minister until April 1956. During the war, he had worked for the Soviet broadcasting service in Moscow. After the Soviet break with Tito on 28 June 1948, Bulgaria moved its Macedonians (officially recorded as numbering 180,000 in the country's 1956 census[424]) far from its border in the West. About the same time, 50,000 Jews were granted permission to emigrate and a large number of Turks were forced out, to resettle in Turkey. Chervenkov talked in terms of allowing 250,000 Turks to move to Turkey; Ankara eventually admitted 162,000 but then closed its border in 1952.[425]

Meanwhile, by 1949, a showdown loomed between the home communists, among whom Traicho Kostov was the leading figure, and the Muscovites, led by Georgi Dimitrov and Vasil Kolarov. In March 1949, Kostov was accused of being a "Bulgaria-firster", i.e., of wanting to give priority to Bulgarians' interests over those of the Soviets. He immediately lost his posts as Deputy Prime Minister and Chair of the Economic and Financial Committee and was dismissed from the Politburo. On 20 June 1949, Kostov was arrested. Six months later, he was put on trial, together with 10 other communists, on charges of espionage and treason. More specifically, he was accused of having collaborated with British and American intelligence services during World War Two and, later, with Tito in an alleged conspiracy to overthrow the Bulgarian regime. Immediately before the start of the trial, a large number of communist party members were arrested, especially officials and teachers.[426] The trial ran from 7 to 14 December. Kostov created a sensation on 7 December when, in a calm voice, he denied the principal charges against him, conceding only that he had made ideological mistakes. At that point, the court went into a short recess, returning after 20 minutes, with an apparently repentant Kostov now admitting to the main charges.[427] Whether he was tortured into repudiating his claim of innocence or simply replaced by a virtual look-alike must remain in the realm of speculation. Whatever the case may be, when his guilty verdict was handed down later, Kostov repudiated his repudiation and courageously told the court,¨

> In my last words before this distinguished court, I consider it a duty to my conscience to tell the court and through it the Bulgarian people, that I never served English intelligence, never participated in the criminal plans of Tito and his clique . . .. I have always held the Soviet Union in devotion and respect . . . Let the Bulgarian people know that I am innocent![428]

Sentences were handed down on 14 December; Kostov was executed on 16 December. In the wake of the trial of Traicho Kostov, at least 100,000 comrades were expelled from the party; many of them were taken to labor camps.[429]

The death of Stalin in March 1953 provided the backdrop to the closure of some labor camps in Bulgaria that year and for a reduction in police terror.[430] That same year, the Five-Year Plan for 1953–57 was launched, calling for significant increases in industrial production, ferrous and nonferrous metallurgy, and food processing. Whereas the ratio of national income derived from agriculture to that from industry had been 75.2% to 24.8% in 1939, by 1956, 67.5% of national income came from industrial production.[431]

After Stalin's death, as already noted, there was pressure on bloc leaders to separate the premiership from leadership of the party, as had been done in the Soviet Union. Chervenkov, like Romania's Gheorghiu-Dej, chose to retain the premiership and gave up the post of General Secretary on 26 January 1954. But whereas Gheorghiu-Dej retook the party leadership in 1955, Chervenkov's surrender of the General Secretaryship initiated his slow political demise which ended in 1962. Todor Zhivkov (1911–1998), who had succeeded Chervenkov as "First" Secretary (with a change of title, thus), did not attend the CPSU's Twentieth Party Congress in February 1956. Nonetheless, it was he who presented the principal report on that Congress and on Khrushchev's anti-Stalin speech to the Bulgarian CC plenum held in April 1956. The CC adopted a resolution on this occasion, criticizing Chervenkov for having glorified himself with a cult of his leadership and for having monopolized power, thus undermining collective leadership in the party.[432] Following the plenum, Chervenkov resigned as Prime Minister on 17 April 1956, but was compensated with appointment as Minister of Education and Culture.

Agricultural collectivization

At war's end, the Bulgarian countryside was still seriously underdeveloped, with many villages lacking electricity and modern plumbing. The communists, no doubt recalling Lenin's famous declaration that "Communism is Soviet power plus the electrification of the whole country,"[433] undertook to correct these deficiencies. By the time the communist era came to an end in 1990, 100% of the population had access to electricity.[434] Moreover, as of 1994, 4,422 of Bulgaria's towns and villages were supplied with water, though the national sewer network had been constructed along only 13% of the country's streets.[435] The communists failed to deal with the problem of pollution and, in 1990, it was reported that "Twenty percent of Bulgaria's rivers are virtual open sewers."[436] In 1946, three-quarters of the Bulgarian population lived in small villages,[437] but the communists had big plans for the peasantry and, as early as autumn 1945, private farmers were encouraged, but not yet forced, to join collective farms. By summer 1947, before the official launch of the collectivization drive, authorities were applying pressure on the peasants to collectivize. Requisitions of foodstuffs were the major form of pressure at the time and provoked strong resistance. One tactic used by farmers was to hide their produce. As the first push for collectivization was officially set in motion in 1948, there was massive resistance on the part of the peasants, especially in northwestern Bulgaria.[438] The communists did not back down and some peasants were sent to "labor educational communities" – in effect, concentration camps.[439]

Peasants withheld cereals by storing as much as they could in secret hiding places and also withheld milk, leaving some urban populations without milk.[440] Some peasants held meetings to protest the requisitions; others distributed anti-government leaflets in the villages, calling for an uprising against the communists; still others engaged in sabotage, for example by destroying threshing machines. There were instances of violence as well.[441] By December 1950, 44.2% of all arable land had been collectivized.[442]

In the months from October 1950 to February 1951, the authorities tried to take peasants' livestock into the collective farms; peasants responded by hiding livestock and fodder and, in some cases, by slaughtering their livestock. In November 1950, Bulgarian authorities took the first step to dispossess the more well-to-do peasants ("kulaks" in Russian parlance) and resettle them by force in other parts of the country. When these peasants offered serious resistance, the Bulgarian communists decided to solicit Stalin's "advice". Accordingly, in January 1951, Chervenkov led a delegation to Moscow to discuss plans to dispossess the kulaks. Meeting with Chervenkov and other Bulgarian leaders, Stalin advised them to hold off the confiscation of kulak land for the time being and not to copy the Soviet example "blindly". Advice from Stalin was as good as an order, since ignoring his input would have signaled disrespect and, in the event, also stupidity. Thus, on 19 March 1951, a decree issued by the BCP Central Committee criticized "outrages" committed against kulaks and signaled a (temporary) halt to collectivization.[443] On 7 April 1951, Chervenkov delivered a speech in which he said that collectivization would be ended and that peasants who had been collectivized against their will would be allowed to leave the collective farms and return to family farming. His speech was published in the press on 12 April and, following this, there was further unrest, spreading to 95 villages. There were reports of peasants organizing secret resistance groups across the border in Yugoslavia in 1951. The State Security arrested many peasants at this time. Some were released after their interrogations were concluded; others were brought to court for show trials; still others were sent to concentration camps. Tens of thousands of peasants submitted applications requesting to be allowed to leave the collectives and return to private farming.[444]

As of March 1956, about half of all farmers were members of collective farms. That year, the communists resumed the collectivization campaign, relying on brute force to bring the process to a conclusion. Peasants responded once more with sabotage, committing 132 acts of sabotage in 1956 and 57 in 1957. In addition, the chairmen of the collective farms in Belotinci and Kǎlnovo were assassinated, and there were attempts on the lives of two others in positions of authority in the collective farms. Disturbances in 1956 affected between 50 and 60 villages and, in some instances, peasants hid entire flocks and herds in remote mountainous areas. There were also 18 cases of arson on collective farms during 1957 and 1958. In spite of this sustained, even desperate resistance, authorities made a final push for collectivization in 1957–58 and, by the end of the first quarter of 1958, the

countryside had been largely pacified and authorities declared that they had completed the collectivization of the countryside.[445]

The cultural scene

1948 marked a caesura in Bulgarian cultural life, with socialist realism proclaimed –
as elsewhere in the bloc – as the only concept that would be allowed in any sector
of cultural life, whether literature, music, art, architecture, or even stage design.[446]
The Committee for Science, Arts, and Culture, the successor to the Chamber of
National Culture, had the task of advancing the communist party's goals in the
arts. Boris Babochkin accepted the task of directing *Leipzig 1933*, a play depicting
the recently deceased Georgi Dimitrov as an anti-fascist hero, which premiered in
November 1951. Babochkin described his approach in undertaking that politically
important assignment:

> [We are] using the method of [an] artist's materialistic view, the method that
> not only judges rightly the objectively existing reality, but also actively inter-
> venes in it, reshaping it to choose what is the new, the progressive, the revo-
> lutionary, fostering the new growth in its development, struggling against
> everything reactionary and antiquated.[447]

Beauty, originality, and creativity were not valued in their own right and could
even lead to a cultural product being classified as "formalistic" – which meant not
allowed. That did not mean that cultural workers should strive for a literal-minded
copying of reality – or, in music, a mimicry of factory sounds. Peter Uvaliev, in
his review of Aleksandr Afinogenov's *Mashenka* for *Literaturen front*, the organ of
the Association of Bulgarian Writers, explained that "Socialist Realism was not a
photographic resemblance to reality, but rather 'a stage translation of its advanced
nature.'"[448]

On the face of it, it might seem that music was less susceptible than literature
to the requirement that it advance socialism. This was not the case. To begin with,
jazz was banned in Bulgaria, while other genres – especially mass songs, orato-
rios with communist texts, and cantatas – were favored. Moreover, as Bulgarian
composers found, at the height of socialist realism, simple music was considered
"best".[449] Finally, explicit political commitment could put a plume in any composer's chapeau. Pancho Vladigerov (1899–1978) and Lyubomir Pipkov (1904–1974)
accommodated the party's wish by composing music dedicated to the Bulgarian
Communist Party.[450] The latter had nurtured sympathies for the communist party
even before the Second World War. But once the communists were in power,
Pipkov found himself under pressure to make his compositions more readily comprehensible by people unschooled in music. He turned to writing mass songs.
By contrast, fellow composers Konstantin Iliev (1924–1988) and Lazar Nikolov
(1922–2005) were drawn to the music of Arnold Schoenberg, Alban Berg, and

Anton Webern and starting writing atonal and twelve-tone music. As we have seen in the case of East Germany, such music was considered highly problematic and both Iliev and Nikolov were attacked for formalism.[451]

Among novelists, Dimitar Dimov (1909–1966) is especially noteworthy. A trained veterinary surgeon who also wrote plays, Dimov came to the attention of the authorities in 1951, when his novel *Tyutyun* (Tobacco) came out. The story revolves around revolutionary tendencies among tobacco workers prior to and during World War Two. In spite of its revolutionary theme, the novel was initially denounced by communists because the main characters were thought to be too complex. What the party critics wanted was clear heroes and obvious villains and no ambiguities. Soon, however, Chervenkov intervened to defend the novel, criticizing its detractors for "dogmatism".[452] With that, the way was cleared for the novel's eventual adaptation as a film released in 1962. Finally, socialist realism in Bulgaria carried over into architecture, with the most famous example being, perhaps, the mausoleum constructed in Sofia for Georgi Dimitrov, who had died in Moscow in July 1949. The mausoleum for Dimitrov was erected on the model of Lenin's tomb in Moscow with columns evocative of neo-classicism.[453]

Religion

On 24 February 1949, a Law on Religious Faiths was promulgated. The Law defined the Bulgarian Orthodox Church as "the traditional Church of the Bulgarian people . . . inseparable from their history," and hinted that the way was open for it to become "in form, substance, and spirit, a People's democratic Church."[454] Communist *apparatchiks* drew up the statutes for the Church; these were approved by the Council of Ministers on 31 December 1950 and ratified by the Holy Synod on 3 January 1951. Article 1 of the statutes declared the restoration of the Patriarchate.[455] A communist-backed "patriotic" Priests' Union, led by Fr. Georgi Georgiev, put together a Committee to Reform the Church, taking the Living Church of early Soviet days as its model. But this initiative figured as little more than an internal pressure group, albeit one that pushed hard to see its members win seats in the May 1951 parish council elections. On 10 May 1953, the National Council of the Church elected Metropolitan Kiril of Plovdiv, who had been proposed by the BCP Politburo on 10 October 1950,[456] to serve as Patriarch of the Church. Kiril was a competent administrator and an eminent scholar. He kept the clergy together so that there was no sign of internal dissent within the Church during his 18 years as Patriarch.[457] In order to whittle the Orthodox Church down, authorities expropriated church buildings, banned missionary work, ended Orthodox religious instruction in the schools, and did their best to limit the Church to the performance of religious rituals and the sale of candles.

The Orthodox Church was, however, not the only religious body affected by communist policies. As was the case with the Orthodox Church, Catholic religious instruction in the schools was terminated and the new statute for the Catholic Church was drawn up by communist officials.[458] Expatriate priests and members of religious orders were expelled from the country, all social and educational institutions were shuttered, and, in 1953, all Church properties were seized by the regime. In 1950, authorities had a number of Catholic clergy and laity arrested, with at least some of them executed without trial. There was one open trial with charges of espionage for the Vatican, hiding weapons, and speaking out against communism brought against Monsignor Evgenii Bosilkov, Bishop of Nikopol, two Catholic editors, and approximately 30 other priests, nuns, and Catholic laity. The trial ended on 3 October 1952, with death penalties handed down for Bosilkov and three others; the remainder were sent to prison for terms of varying lengths.[459] Nonetheless, while the Greek Catholic Church in Czechoslovakia and Romania was liquidated and its clergy ordered to affiliate with the respective Orthodox Church, the Greek Catholic Church in Bulgaria was allowed to continue to function – possibly because its small membership (no more than 15,000 members at the time) was considered insignificant.[460]

Protestantism had only a modest presence in post-war Bulgaria. The largest of these was the Congregationalist Church, with 4,300 members at the time, as well as 22 ministers and 27 church buildings. The other Protestant Churches were the Methodist Church, the Baptists, and the Pentecostals. In 1950, the regime forced these denominations to sever all ties with their co-religionists abroad. As with the Orthodox and Catholic Churches, some Protestant pastors were murdered or sent to labor camps. There were also show trials of Protestant clergy. Jews were included in some of the arrests of Protestant clergy. Finally, the four Protestant denominations were forced to merge into a Union of the Allied Evangelical Churces in Bulgaria, under the supervision of the Ministry of Foreign Affairs and Cults.[461] Finally, where the Islamic community was concerned, Bulgarian authorities closed all Quranic schools in 1949. Suppression of instruction in Turkish had begun with the addition of an article in the law on education in 1946. The suppression of Turkish continued in 1951–52, when all Turkish schools were forced to merge with Bulgarian schools and to adopt Bulgarian as the exclusive language of instruction.[462]

Women and gender equality

In 1944, the newly established People's Government adopted a law guaranteeing equal juridical rights to women and men. As the country put people back to work on postwar reconstruction, women comprised 45% of the labor force in 1946. That same year, women with university education accounted for just 0.4% of the labor force.[463] Subsequently, under the 1947 constitution, women were granted full legal equality with men.

Meanwhile, the Committee of the Bulgarian Women's Movement (hereafter, the Women's Committee) was founded in 1946. Its first priority was to eradicate illiteracy – a greater problem among women than among men. The literacy campaign lasted for four years – from 1946 to 1950 – and made a difference for many women. The Women's Committee had its own periodical, *Zhenata dnes* (Woman Today). Sonia Bakish, a member of the periodical's editorial board from 1958 to 1980 and editor-in-chief for more than 17 years, opened the pages of *Zhenata dnes* to discussions of women's real concerns. This action boosted the popularity and readership of the publication and allowed it to expand.[464]

As of 18 December 1949, 15.0% of representatives in the National Assembly were women – a statistic that compares favorably with women's representation in Western parliaments at the time (and even later). By 1953, this figure would rise to 15.7%.[465] Women would make some gains in subsequent years, although equal representation in decision-making bodies was never achieved in the years that the BCP ruled Bulgaria. Nonetheless, as Kristen Ghodsee has pointed out, the Women's Committee, "although politically constrained, did much to represent women's interests to Bulgaria's communist elites . . . [F]rom 1968 onward the committee was constantly challenging state policies with regard to women and families, and pressuring the Politburo into expanding scarce resources to support women as both workers and mothers."[466]

Conclusion: a record of unintended consequences

Throughout the years 1944–53, communist authorities in the Soviet bloc repeatedly consulted with the Kremlin, to ascertain or confirm Stalin's wishes. Bierut checked with Stalin before removing Gomułka as General Secretary. Gottwald responded to clear instructions from Stalin to remove and execute Slánský. And Chervenkov temporarily slowed down collectivization again in direct response to Stalin's "advice". After Stalin's passed away, the pattern was that communist leaders would check with the local Soviet ambassador, who would act as an intermediary with the Kremlin. What inspired these vassals of Stalin was a vision of a future socialist society (still in construction in these years) in which the memories of presocialist society would fade away, new socialist/collectivist values would become deeply ingrained, and the economy would operate like clockwork according to ambitious but realizable plans. They also envisioned a future in which women would be (approximately or perhaps nearly) equal with men at the workplace but still shouldering the greater part of the housework and in which religious belief would first be emptied of knowledge about the faith and then drained of any fervor, until one day it would be found to have faded away. They also aspired, in the years of Stalinism, to instrumentalize composers, literati, pictorial artists, architects, filmmakers, and other intellectuals and creative artists to buttress and reinforce the socialist system. And they dreamt of a future in which everyone, including the peasantry, would be in the employment of the party-state.

But there were problems from the beginning and the consequences of communist policies were often different from what had been intended. To begin with, the Churches either offered some form of resistance (as in Poland, most obviously) or developed independent initiatives (as the Protestant Church did with its

Jugendgemeinde and, beginning in the late 1970s, its peace initiative in East Germany); even the Orthodox Churches included clergy prepared to disagree with the communists, until a combination of selective murders, torture, and confinement to labor camps of the most recalcitrant convinced the remaining hierarchs and ordinary clergy that collaboration would be essential to their physical survival. The peasants resisted collectivization throughout the region and, in Poland, thanks also to Gomułka's conviction that the policy was wrongheaded for his country, peasants succeeded in getting their farms back. Elsewhere, while the communists had claimed that collectivized agriculture would be more efficient than private farming, the reverse proved to be the case.

Taming creative artists and other intellectuals also encountered problems, generating unintended consequences. Indeed, as in the cases of religious organizations and the peasantry, the results included entirely foreseeable problems. Although some writers and composers, for example, especially those of only mediocre ability, were content to serve up whatever dishes they thought would please the communist satraps who kept a close eye over their work, others and especially those with genuine talent, driven one might say by a private muse, resisted regimentation and, like composer Hanns Eisler in the GDR and novelist Tibor Déry in Hungary, were prepared to assert their independence.

On the surface, until Stalin died, it seemed that the effort to regiment the people of the Soviet bloc was succeeding. But just below the surface, people were increasingly frustrated, as the Plzeň uprising of 31 May to 2 June 1953 and the uprising across East Germany 16–17 June 1953 made clear. The latter uprising, in particular, sent a clear message that there were limits to what the party could expect of its workers (or other citizens, for that matter). And then came Khrushchev's secret speech in February 1956 and the fallout from it. The Hungarian Revolution of 1956 and the Soviet response taught people two lessons: first, that the Stalinist system was not working and not sustainable; and second, that it was not possible, under the conditions given at the time, to remove the communists and reestablish pluralism. Gomułka's Poland seemed, at the time, to offer the prospect of a liberalized form of communism – liberalized in the religious sphere, in the cultural sector, where agriculture was concerned, and even in social life. Over time, it became apparent that there were limits to Gomułka's liberalization: in essence, it proved to be static, rather than growing. But in the context of de-Stalinization, it was clear that a new chapter was opening in East Central Europe.

Notes

1   I am grateful to Neva C. Hahn for taking notes for me from the *Records of the Department of State relating to the Internal Affairs of Bulgaria and Poland,* to Vladimir Đorđević for translating a portion of Jana Kočišková's master's thesis concerning the situation of women in Czechoslovak politics in the communist era, and to the Norwegian University of Science & Technology (NTNU) for providing funding to pay for Hahn's services. I am also grateful to the Russian, East European, and Eurasian Center of the University

of Illinois at Urbana-Champaign for granting me access to the rich online resources of the University of Illinois Library. I also wish to thank Lucian Leustean for his input into an earlier draft of this chapter.

2 See Robert K. Merton, *Social Theory and Social Structure*, Enlarged ed. (New York: Free Press, 1968); Peter Sohlberg, *Functionalist Construction Work in Social Science: The Lost Heritage* (London and New York: Routledge, 2021).

3 Karl Marx and Friedrich Engels, *The German Ideology*, 3rd rev. ed. (Moscow: Progress Publishers, 1976), p. 53.

4 See, for example: Raoul Bossy, "Religious Persecutions in Captive Romania", in *Journal of Central European Affairs*, Vol. 15, No. 2 (July 1955), p. 162; Emil Ciurea, "Religious Life", in Alexandre Cretzianu (eds.), *Captive Rumania* (London: Atlantic Press, 1956), p. 167; Romanian National Committee (Washington D.C.), *Information Bulletin,* no. 46 (January 1953), p. 11; and *Radio Vatican* (6 January 1953), as cited in Ciurea, "Religious Life", p. 173.

5 See Sabrina P. Ramet, "Religious Organizations in Post-Communist Central and Southeastern Europe: An Introduction", in Sabrina P. Ramet (ed.), *Religion and Politics in Central and Southeastern Europe: Challenges since 1989* (Basingstoke: Palgrave, 2014), pp. 9–11; Fr. Tadeusz Isakowicz-Zaleski, *Księża wobec bezpieki*: (Warsaw: Wydnawnictwo Znak, 2007).

6 Jan Siedlarz, *Kirche und Staat im kommunistischen Polen 1945–1989* (Paderborn: Ferdinand Schöningh, 1996), p. 52.

7 Leslie László, "The Catholic Church in Hungary", in Pedro Ramet (ed.), *Catholicism and Politics in Communist Societies* (Durham, NC and London: Duke University Press, 1990), p. 159.

8 Joseph Pungur, "Protestantism in Hungary: The Communist Era", in Sabrina Petra Ramet (ed.), *Protestantism and Politics in Eastern Europe and Russia: The Communist and Postcommunist Eras* (Durham, NC and London: Duke University Press, 1992), p. 114; Pedro Ramet, "The Albanian Orthodox Church", in Pedro Ramet (ed.), *Eastern Christianity and Politics in the Twentieth Century* (Durham, NC and London: Duke University Press, 1988), p. 155; Spas T. Raikin, "The Bulgarian Orthodox Church", in Ramet (ed.), *Eastern Christianity*, p. 172; Lucian N. Leustean, "Constructing Communism in the Romanian People's Republic: Orthodoxy and State, 1948–49", in *Europe-Asia Studies*, Vol. 59, No. 2 (March 2007), pp. 322–323; Lavinia Stan and Lucian Turcescu, *Religion and Politics in Post-Communist Romania* (Oxford and New York: Oxford University Press, 2007), p. 139; Alan Scarfe, "The Romanian Orthodox Church", in Ramet (ed.), *Eastern Christianity*, pp. 218–219.

9 Josef Rabas, *Kirche in Fesseln. Materialen zur Situation der katholischen Kirche in der ČSSR,* Vi (Munich: Sozialwerk der Ackermann-Gemeinde, 1984), p. 3.

10 Subcommittee to Investigate the Administration of the Internal Security Act and other Internal Security Laws, *The Church and State Under Communism*, Vol. 2 (Washington DC: U.S. Printing Office, 1965), p. 29. See also Raikin, "The Bulgarian Orthodox Church", p. 171.

11 R. J. Crampton, *Eastern Europe in the Twentieth Century – and After*, 2nd ed. (London and New York: Routledge, 1997), p. 245.

12 R. J. Crampton, *Eastern Europe in the Twentieth Century* (London and New York: Routledge, 1994), p. 246.

13 See Antony Buzek, *How the Communist Press Works* (London: Pall Mall Press, 1964).

14 Jane Curry, *The Black Book of Polish Censorship* (New York: Vintage Books, 1984), pp. 383–384.

15 Karel Kaplan, *The Communist Party in Power: A Profile of Party Politics in Czechoslovakia,* ed. and trans. by Fred Eidlin (Boulder, CO: Westview Press, 1987).

16 From the German, *Sozialistische Einheitspartei Deutschlands.*

17 Ken Jowitt, "Stalinist Revolutionary Breakthroughs in Eastern Europe", in Vladimir Tismaneanu (ed.), *Stalinism Revisited: The Establishment of Communist Regimes in East-Central*

Europe (Budapest and New York: Central European University Press, 2009), p. 17. See also Kenneth Jowitt, *Revolutionary Breakthroughs and National Development: The Case of Romania, 1944–1965* (Berkeley and Los Angeles: University of California Press, 1971).

18 Vladimir Tismaneanu, "Introduction", in Tismaneanu (ed.), *Stalinism Revisited*, pp. 3, 4.

19 Jaime Reynolds, "Communists, Socialists and Workers: Poland 1944–48", in *Soviet Studies*, Vol. 30, No. 4 (October 1978), p. 518; "Poland Still Counts Losses from WW2 Invasion", in *BBC News* (31 August 2019), at www.bbc.com/news/world-europe-49523932 [accessed on 28 July 2021].

20 *The Roman Catholic Church in People's Poland* (Warsaw: The Central Priests' Committee, Affiliated to the Organization of Fighters for Freedom and Democracy, 1953), p. 105.

21 From the Polish, *Polskie Stronnictwo Ludowe*.

22 From the Polish, *Polka Partia Socjalistyczna*.

23 From the Polish, *Polska Partia Robotnicza*.

24 From the Polish, *Partia Demokratyczna*.

25 Jan B. de Weydenthal, *The Communists of Poland: An Historical Outline*, Rev. ed. (Stanford, CA: Hoover Institution, 1986), p. 51.

26 From the Polish, *Komunistyczna Partia Polska*.

27 As quoted in de Weydenthal, *The Communists of Poland*, p. 55.

28 Krystyna Kersten, *The Establishment of Communist Rule in Poland, 1943–1948*, trans. and annotated by John Micgiel and Michael H. Bernhard (Berkeley and Los Angeles: University of California Press, 1991), p. 450.

29 de Weydenthal, *The Communists of Poland*, p. 55.

30 Bierut, speech to party *aktiv* on 6 September 1948, as summarized and quoted in Telegram from the U.S. Embassy in Warsaw [hereafter, simply Warsaw] to the U.S. Department of State [hereafter, simply State] (9 September 1948), in *Records of the Department of State Relating to the Internal Affairs of Poland* [hereafter, *Records Relating to Poland*] *1945–1949,* Decimal file 860c, Reel 3 (files 00/2–647 to 00/11–1548).

31 Telegram from Warsaw to State (sent on 15 September, received on 17 September 1948), in *Records Relating to Poland 1945–1949*, Decimal file 860c, Reel 3 (files 00/2–647 to 00/11–1548).

32 From the Polish, *Polska Zjednoczona Partia Robotnicza*.

33 Siedlarz, *Kirche und Staat im kommunistischen Polen*, p. 47.

34 As quoted in *The Roman Catholic Church in People's Poland*, p. 5.

35 Sabrina P. Ramet, *The Catholic Church in Polish History: From 966 to the Present* (New York: Palgrave Macmillan, 2017), pp. 157–158, citing Siedlarz, *Kirche und Staat*, p. 52.

36 Vincent C. Chrypinski, "The Catholic Church in Poland, 1944–1989", in Pedro Ramet (ed.), *Catholicism and Politics in Communist Societies* (Durham, NC and London: Duke University Press, 1990), p. 120; Mikołay Stanisław Kunicki, *Between the Brown and the Red: Nationalism, Catholicism, and Communism in 20th-Century Poland – the Politics of Bolesław Piasecki* (Athens, OH: Ohio University Press, 2012).

37 Hugo Service, "Reinterpreting the Expulsion of Germans from Poland, 1945–9", in *Journal of Contemporary History*, Vol. 47, No. 3 (July 2012), pp. 533–535.

38 *Ibid.*, pp. 536, 543–544, 547.

39 Reynolds, "Communists, Socialists", p. 525.

40 See Sabrina P. Ramet, *Alternatives to Democracy in Twentieth-Century Europe: Collectivist Visions of Modernity* (Budapest and New York: Central European University Press, 2019) – chapter 2.

41 Reynolds, "Communists, Socialists", pp. 528, 536.

42 Dariusz Jarosz, "The Collectivization of Agriculture in Poland: Causes of Defeat", in Constantin Iordachi and Arnd Bauerkämper (eds.), *The Collectivization of Agriculture in Communist Eastern Europe: Comparison and Entanglements* (Budapest and New York: Central European University Press, 2014), pp. 114–115.

43 J. C., "The Peasant in Poland Today: Reactions to Land Reform and Collectivization", in *The World Today*, Vol. 8, No. 2 (February 1952), pp. 73–74.

44 Bennett Kovrig, *Communism in Hungary: From Kun to Kádár* (Stanford, CA: Hoover Institution Press, 1979), pp. 161–162.

45 *Ibid.*, p. 168.
46 As quoted in *Ibid.*, p. 174.
47 Jörg K. Hoensch, *A History of Modern Hungary, 1867–1986,* trans. from German by Kim Traynor (London and New York: Longman, 1988; second impression 1989), p. 173. See also Miklós Molnar, *From Béla Kun to János Kádar: Seventy Years of Hungarian Communism,* trans. from French by Arnold J. Pomerans (New York, Oxford and Munich: Berg, 1990), p. 108.
48 Kovrig, *Communism in Hungary,* p. 183; these figures are confirmed in Stephen D. Kertesz, "The Methods of Communist Conquest: Hungary, 1944–1947", in *World Politics,* Vol. 3, No. 1 (October 1950), p. 42.
49 Kertesz, "The Methods of Communist Conquest", p. 43.
50 *Ibid.*, p. 47.
51 Matěj Spurný, "Political Authority and Popular Opinion: Czechoslovakia's German population 1948–60", in *Social History,* Vol. 37, No. 4 (November 2012), pp. 452, 455. See also Eagle Glassheim, "National Mythologies and Ethnic Cleansing: The Expulsion of Czechoslovak Germans in 1945", in *Central European History,* Vol. 33, No. 4 (December 2008), p. 465.
52 Spurný, "Czechoslovakia's German Population", p. 458.
53 Edward Taborsky, *Communism in Czechoslovakia, 1948–1960* (Princeton, NJ: Princeton University Press, 1961), p. 41.
54 H. Gordon Skilling, "The Prague Overturn in 1948", in *Canadian Slavonic Papers,* Vol. 4 (1959), pp. 89–90.
55 *Ibid.*, pp. 91–92.
56 *Ibid.*, p. 100.
57 *Ibid.*, p. 110.
58 The 1948 constitution is posted by Masarykova Universita at http://czecon.law.muni.cz/content/en/ustavy/1948/ [accessed on 12 May 2021].
59 As quoted in H. Gordon Skilling, "The Czechoslovak Constitutional System: The Soviet Impact", in *Political Science Quarterly,* Vol. 67, No. 2 (June 1952), p. 221.
60 H. Gordon Skilling, "Czechoslovakia: Government in Communist Hands", in *The Journal of Politics,* Vol. 17, No. 3 (August 1955), pp. 435–436.
61 As quoted in Paul E. Zinner, "Marxism in Action: The Seizure of Power in Czechoslovakia", in *Foreign Affairs,* Vol. 28, No. 4 (July 1950), p. 650.
62 Ekaterina Nikova, "Bulgarian Stalinism Revisited", in Tismaneanu (ed.), *Stalinism Revisited,* pp. 289–290.
63 *Ibid.*, p. 291.
64 J. F. Brown, *Bulgaria Under Communist Rule* (New York: Praeger Publishers, 1970), p. 85.
65 *Ibid.*, p. 18.
66 Mito Isusov, *Politicheskite partii v Bŭlgarii, 1944–1948* (Sofia, 1978), as quoted in John D. Bell, *The Bulgarian Communist Party from Blagoev to Zhivkov* (Stanford, CA: Hoover Institution Press, 1986), p. 94.
67 R. J. Crampton, *A Concise History of Bulgaria,* 2nd ed. (Cambridge: Cambridge University Press, 2005), pp. 185–186.
68 Bell, *The Bulgarian Communist Party,* p. 110.
69 *Ibid.*, p. 84.
70 Wayne S. Vucinich, "Bulgaria: I. Consolidation of the Fatherland Front", in *Current History,* Vol. 13, No. 75 (November 1947), p. 273.
71 Bell, *The Bulgarian Communist Party,* p. 94.
72 Telegram from the U. S. Embassy in Sofia (hereafter, Sofia) to State, received on 7 June 1947, in *Records Relating to the Internal Affairs of Bulgaria (hereafter, Records Relating to Bulgaria), 1945–1949,* Decimal file 874, at SL, Reel 3 (files .00/1–447 to .00/11–1348); and Telegram from Sofia to State, received on 24 July 1947, in *Records Relating to Bulgaria 1945–1949,* Decimal file 874, at SL, Reel 3 (files .00/1–447 to .00/11–1348).
73 Telegram from the U. S. Embassy in Moscow to State, received on 10 June 1947, in *Records Relating to Bulgaria 1945–1949,* Decimal file 874, at SL, Reel 3 (files .00/1–447 to .00/11–1348).

74 M. P., "Bulgaria as a Communist State", in *The World Today*, Vol. 4, No. 9 (September 1948), pp. 380–381.
75 Živko Avramovski, "Devet projekata ugorova o jugoslovensko-bugarskom savezu i federaciji (1944–1947)", in *Istorija 20. veka*, Vol. 2 (1983), p. 91, citing E. Kardelj, *Sećanja. Borba za priznanje i nezavisnost nove Jugoslavije 1944–1957* (Ljubljana and Belgrade, 1980), Državna založba Slovenije & Radnička štampa, pp. 103, 104.
76 Avramski, "Devet projekata", pp. 93–94.
77 Georgi Dimitrov, *Georgi Dimitrov, Dnevnik 1933–1949*, ed. by Dimitur Sirkov (Sofia: Universitetsko Izdatelstvo "Sv. Kliment Ohridski", 1997), p. 460.
78 Slobodan Nešović, *Bledski sporazumi: Tito-Dimitrov (1947)* (Zagreb: Globus & Školska knjiga, 1979), pp. 52, 57, 64; Dimitrov, *Georgi Dimitrov*, p. 554.
79 Nešović, *Bledski sporazumi*, pp. 126, 132–133.
80 Sabrina P. Ramet, *The Three Yugoslavias: State-Building and Legitimation, 1918–2005* (Washington, DC and Bloomington: Woodrow Wilson Center Press & Indiana University Press, 2006), p. 175. See also Hilde Katrine Haug, *Creating a Socialist Yugoslavia: Tito, Communist Leadership and the National Question* (London and New York: I. B. Tauris, 2012), p. 127.
81 Daniela Kalkandjeva, "Martyrs and Confessors in the Bulgarian Orthodox Church Under Communism", Paper presented at a conference on *Martyrdom and Communion*, at the Monastery of Bose, Italy, 7–10 September 2016, typescript, pp. 3, 5, 6.
82 Daniela Kalkadjeva, "The Bulgarian Orthodox Church", in Lucian Leustean (ed.), *Eastern Christianity and the Cold War, 1945–91* (London and New York: Routledge, 2010), p. 82.
83 Ghita Ionescu, *Communism in Rumania 1944–1962* (London and New York: Oxford University Press, 1964), p. 91.
84 G. I., "Rumania in 1952: A Political Analysis of the Economic Crisis", in *The World Today*, Vol. 8, No. 7 (July 1952), p. 294.
85 Vladimir Tismaneanu, *Stalinism for All Seasons: A Political History of Romanian Communism* (Berkeley and Los Angeles: University of California Press, 2003), p. 90.
86 Ionescu, *Communism in Rumania*, p. 131.
87 Dennis Deletant, *Communist Terror in Romania: Gheorghiu-Dej and the Police State, 1948–1965* (London: Hurst, 1999), pp. 88–89.
88 As quoted in Dennis Deletant, *Ceaușescu and the Securitate: Coercion and Dissent in Romania, 1965–1989* (Armonk, NY: M. E. Sharpe, 1995), p. 10.
89 Scarfe, "The Romanian Orthodox Church", p. 218. Regarding four bishops dying in prison: Vlad Georgescu, *The Romanians: A History*, trans. from Romanian by Alexandra Bley-Vroman (London and New York: I. B. Tauris, 1991), p. 236.
90 Deletant, *Communist Terror in Romania*, pp. 90–91.
91 Tismaneanu, *Stalinism for All Seasons*, p. 108; Constantin Iordachi and Dorin Dobrincu, "The Collectivization of Agriculture in Romania, 1949–1962", in Iordachi and Bauerkämper (eds.), *The Collectivization of Agriculture in Communist Eastern Europe*, p. 254.
92 Anneli Ute Gabanyi, *Partei und Literatur in Rumänien seit 1945* (Munich: R. Oldenbourg Verlag, 1975), p. 12.
93 This section is an abridged version of chapter 5 in Sabrina P. Ramet, *Nonconformity, Dissent, Opposition, and Resistance in Germany, 1933–1990: The Freedom to Conform* (London and New York: Palgrave Macmillan, 2020). I am grateful to Palgrave Macmillan (Springer) for permission to reuse this material.
94 Norman Naimark, *The Russians in Germany: A history of the Soviet Zone of Occupation, 1945–1949* (Cambridge, MA: The Belknap Press of Harvard University Press, 1995), pp. 11, 21.
95 Gregory W. Sandford, *From Hitler to Ulbricht: The Communist Reconstruction of East Germany, 1945–46* (Princeton, NJ: Princeton University Press, 1983), p. 23.
96 From the German, *Sowjetische Besatzungszone*.
97 Helga A. Welsh, *Revolutionär Wandel auf Befehl? Entnazifizierungs- und Personalpolitik in Thüringen und Sachsen (1945–1948)* (Munich: R. Oldenbourg Verlag, 1989), p. 133.

98 *Ibid.*, p. 143.
99 *Ibid.*, p. 145.
100 Damian van Melis, *Entnazifizierung in Mecklenburg-Vorpommern, Herrschaft und Verwaltung 1945–1948* (Munich: R. Oldenbourg Verlag, 1999), p. 237.
101 Franz L. Neumann, "Soviet Policy in Germany", in *Annals of the American Academy of Political and Social Science*, Vol. 263 (May 1949), pp. 173–174.
102 André Steiner, "From the Soviet Occupation Zone to the 'New Eastern States': A survey", in Hartmut Berghoff and Uta Andrea Balbier (eds.), *The East German Economy, 1945–2010: Falling Behind or Catching Up?* (Cambridge: Cambridge University Press, 2020), p. 18. Stefan Doernberg provides a somewhat higher figure, reporting that, "by mid-1948, 3,843 industrial concerns out of a total of 39,919 in the Soviet zone of occupation had been expropriated [by the Soviets]." -- S. Doernberg, *Die Geburt eines neuen Deutschland 1945–1949* (Berlin: Rütten & Loening, 1959), p. 433, as quoted in Karl Wilhelm Fricke, *Selbstbehauptung und Widerstand in der Sowjetischen Besatzungszone Deutschlands* (Bonn and Berlin: Deutscher Bundesverlag, 1964), p. 21.
103 Kurt Sontheimer and Wilhelm Bleck, *The Government and Politics of East Germany,* trans. from German by Ursula Price (London: Hutchinson & Co., 1975), pp. 24–25.
104 Christoph Buchheim, "Kriegsfolgen und Wirtschaftswachstum in der SBZ/DDR", in *Geschichte und Gesellschaft*, Vol. 25, No. 4 (October–December 1999), p. 517. See also Cristiano Andrea Ristuccia and Adam Tooze, "Machine Tools and Mass Production in the Armaments Boom: Germany and the United States, 1929–44", in *The Economic History Review,* Vol. 66, No. 4 (November 2013), pp. 964, 972.
105 Buchheim, "Kriegsfolgen und Wirtschaftswachstum", p. 519.
106 Steiner, "From the Soviet Occupation Zone", p. 24.
107 Naimark, *The Russians in Germany,* p. 219.
108 From the German, *Christlich Demokratische Union.*
109 From the German, *Liberal-Demokratische Partei Deutschlands.*
110 See Ekkehart Krippendorff, "Die Gründung der liberal-demokratischen Partei in der sowjetischen Besatzungszone 1945", in *Vierteljahrshefte für Zeitgeschichte,* Vol. 8, No. 3 (July 1960), pp. 290–309; Gerhard Keiderling, "Scheinpluralismus und Blockparteien. Die KPD und die Gründung der Parteien in Berlin 1945", in *Vierteljahrshefte für Zeitgeschichte*, Vol. 45, No. 2 (April 1997), pp. 257–296.
111 From the German, *Sozialdemokratische Partei Deutschlands.*
112 Martin McCauley, "Liberal Democrats in the Soviet Zone of Germany, 1945–47", in *Journal of Contemporary History,* Vol. 12, No. 4 (October 1977), p. 781.
113 Burkhard Stachelhaus, "Bürgerliche Parteien in der SBZ/DDR: Zur Geschichte von LDP, NDPD und DBD 1945–1953: Gummersbach, 13. bis 15. Dezember 1993", in *Historical Social Research / Historische Sozialforschung,* Vol. 19, No. 2 (70) (1994), p. 143.
114 From the German, *Demokratische Bauernpartei Deutschlands.*
115 From the German, *National-Demokratische Partei Deutschlands.*
116 J. P. Nettl, *The Eastern Zone and Soviet Policy in Germany 1945–50* (London, New York, and Toronto: Oxford University Press, 1951), p. 109. Regarding the CDU in the Soviet Occupation Zone, see Dieter Segert, "The East German CDU: An Historical or a Post-Communist Party?" in *Party Politics*, Vol. 1, No. 4 (1995), pp. 590–591.
117 Damian van Melis, "'Das letzte Jahr der SBZ im Prozess der Staatsgründung der DDR'. Tagung des Instituts für Zeitgeschichte München, Außenstelle Berlin, vom 18. Bis 20. November 1998 im Bundesarchiv Berlin", in *Vierteljahrshefte für Zeitgeschichte,* Vol. 47, No. 2 (April 1999), p. 300.
118 From the German, *Sozialistische Einheitspartei Deutschlands.*
119 Fricke, *Selbstbehauptung und Widerstand*, pp. 23–30.
120 Fricke, *Selbstbehauptung und Widerstand,* p. 30.
121 See Lucio Caracciolo, "Der Untergang der Sozialdemokratie in der sowjetischen Besatzungszone. Otto Grotewohl und die 'Einheit der Arbeiterklasse' 1945/46", in *Vierteljahrshefte für Zeitgeschichte,* Vol. 36, No. 2 (April 1988), pp. 281–318.
122 Fricke, *Selbstbehauptung und Widerstand*, pp. 32–33. The extract appears on p. 33.

123 *Ibid.*, pp. 35–36.
124 Timothy R. Vogt, *Denazification in Soviet-Occupied Germany: Brandenburg, 1945–1948* (Cambridge, MA: Harvard University Press, 2000), p. 132.
125 Manfred Wille, *Entnazifizierung in der Sowjetischen Besatzungszone Deutschlands 1945–48* (Magdeburg: Helmuth-Bloc-Verlag, 1993), p. 24.
126 *Ibid.*, p. 47.
127 Wolfgang Meinicke, "Die Entnazifizierung der sowjetischen Besatzungszone 1945 bis 1948", in *Zeitschrift für Geschichtswissenschaft*, Vol. 32, No. 11 (1948).
128 Wille, *Entnazifizierung in der Sowjetischen Besatzungszone*, p. 86.
129 Naimark, *The Russians in Germany*, p. 455.
130 *Ibid.*, pp. 83–84.
131 Sandford, *From Hitler to Ulbricht*, p. 32.
132 *Ibid.*, p. 32. Regarding the antifas, see Jeannette Michelmann, Aktivisten der ersten Stunde. Die Antifa in der Sowjetischen Besatzungszone (Cologne: Böhlau, 2002).
133 Marcel Boldorf, "Brüche oder Kontinuitäten? Von der Entnazifizierung zur Stalinisierung in der SBZ/DDR (1945–1952)", in *Historische Zeitschrift*, Vol. 289, No. 2 (October 2009), p. 307.
134 Christoph Kleßmann, "Politische Rahmenbedingungen der Bildungspolitik in der SBZ/DDR 1945 bis 1952", in Manfred Heinemann (ed.), *Umerziehung und Wiederaufbau. Die Bildungspolitik der Besatzungsmächte in Deutschland* (Stuffgart: Klett-Cotta, 1981), p. 239.
135 *Ibid.*, pp. 315, 317–318.
136 Olaf Kappelt, *Die Entnazifizierung in der SBZ sowie die Rolle und Einfluß ehemaliger Nationalsozialisten in der DDR als ein soziologisches Phänomen* (Hamburg: Verlag Dr. Kovač, 2010), p. 75.
137 *Ibid.*, pp. 255, 259.
138 Meinicke,"Die Entnazifizierung in der Sowjetischen Besatzungszone 1945 bis 1948", as cited in Kappelt, *Die Entnazifizierung in der SBZ*, p. 253.
139 *Ibid.*, pp. 235, 528; confirmed in Michael Klonovsky and Jan von Flocken, *Stalins Lager in Deutschland 1945–1950* (Berlin and Frankfurt-am-Main: Ullstein, 1991), p. 13; reconfirmed in Christa Hoffmann, *Stunden Null? Vergangenheitsbewältigung in Deutschland 1945 und 1989* (Bonn and Berlin: Bouvier, 1992), p. 216.
140 Kappelt, *Die Entnazifizierung in der SBZ*, p. 242.
141 John Connelly, "East German Higher Education Policies and Student Resistance, 1945–1948", in *Central European History*, Vol. 28, No. 3 (1995), p. 265.
142 John Connelly, *Captive University: The Sovietization of East German, Czech, and Polish Higher Education, 1945–1956* (Chapel Hill, NC and London: University of North Carolina Press, 2000), pp. 4, 29; Helmut Wagner, "The Cultural Sovietization of East Germany", in *Social Research*, Vol. 24, No. 4 (Winter 1957), p. 401.
143 Blessing, *The Antifascist Classroom*, p. 28.
144 As quoted in Robert F. Goeckel, "The Catholic Church in East Germany", in Ramet (ed.), *Catholicism and Politics in Communist Societies*, p. 95.
145 Jörg Thierfelder, "Die Kirchenpolitik der vier Besatzungsmächte und die evangelische Kirche nach der Kapitulation 1945", in *Geschichte und Gesellschaft*, Vol. 18, No. 1 (1992), p. 17.
146 Christoph Kleßmann, "Zur Sozialgeschichte des protestantischen Milieus in der DDR", in *Geschichte und Gesellschaft*, Vol. 19, No. 1 (1993), p. 34.
147 Goeckel, "The Catholic Church", p. 94.
148 See Ronald Bitzer, "Soviet Policy on German Reunification in 1952", in *World Affairs*, Vol. 132, No. 3 (December 1969), pp. 245–256; Gerhard Wettig, "Stalin and German Reunification: Arhival Evidence on Soviet Foreign Policy in Spring 1952", in *The Historical Journal*, Vol. 37, No. 2 (June 1994), pp. 411–419.
149 Naimark, *The Russians in Germany*, pp. 87–88.

150 See Gunilla-Friederike Budde, "'Tüchtige Traktoristinnen' und 'schicke Stenotypistin-nen'", in Konrad Jarausch and Hannes Siegrist (eds.), *Amerikanisierung und Sowjetisierung in Deutschland, 1945–1970* (Frankfurt and New York: Campus Verlag, 1997), p. 243.

151 Donna Harsch, "Approach/Avoidance: Communism and Women in East Germany, 1945–9", in *Social History,* Vol. 25, No. 2 (May 2000), pp. 156–157.

152 Sigrid Hofer, "Dürers Erbe in der DDR: Vom Kanon des sozialistischen Realismus, seinen Unbestimmtheiten und historischen Transformation", in *Marburger Jahrbuch für Kunstwissenschaft,* Vol. 36 (2009), p. 414.

153 As quoted in David Pike, *The Politics of Culture in Soviet-Occupied Germany, 1943–1949* (Stanford, CA: Stanford University Press, 1992), p. 188.

154 SMAD Order No. 51, as quoted in Pike, *The Politics of Culture,* p. 93.

155 Pike, *The Politics of Culture,* p. 468.

156 Katie Lange, "The Berlin Airlift: What It Was, Its Importance in the Cold War", in *Inside DOD* (Historical Collection), at www.defense.gov/News/Inside-DOD/Blog/article/2062719/the-berlin-airlift-what-it-was-its-importance-in-the-cold-war/ [accessed on 25 January 2022], pp. 3–4 of 7.

157 "Berlin Airlift", in *History* (last updated on 3 February 2020), at www.history.com/topics/cold-war/berlin-airlift [accessed on 25 January 2022], pp. 1, 3–4 of 5.

158 See "The Berlin Airlift", in *North Atlantic Treaty Organization,* at www.nato.int/cps/en/natohq/declassified_156163.htm [accessed on 25 January 2022], pp. 4–5 of 8.

159 See Harry Rositzke, *CIA's Secret Operations: Espionage, Counterespionage, and Covert Action* (New York: Reader's Digest, 1977); Ramet, *The Three Yugoslavias.*

160 Carl J. Friedrich and Zbigniew K. Brzezinski, *Totalitarian Dictatorship and Autocracy* (Cambridge, MA: Harvard University Press, 1956).

161 Jürgen Kocka, "Eine durchherrschte Gesellschaft", in Hartmut Kaelble, Jürgen Kocka, and Hartmut Zwahr (eds.), *Sozialgeschichte der DDR* (Stuttgart: Klett-Cotta, 1994), pp. 547–553.

162 See Robert C. Tucker, "Stalin and the Uses of Psychology", in *World Politics,* Vol. 8, No. 4 (July 1956), pp. 455–483; Denis J. B. Shaw and Jonathan D. Oldfield, "Totalitarianism and Geography: L. S. Berg and the Defence of an Academic Discipline in the Age of Stalin", in *Political Geography,* Vol. 27 (2008), pp. 96–112.

163 Dennis Deletant, "Cheating the Censor: Romanian Writers Under Communism", in *Central Europe,* Vol. 6, No. 2 (November 2008), p. 156.

164 Ioan Scurtu, "Impunerea modelului stalinist in România. Revoluția culturală (1948–1953)", in *Historia,* 87, as quoted in Nicolae Gheorghița, "'We Are Chanting to Stalin Too!' Musical Creation in the People's Republic of Romania on the 70th Anniversary of the Geniealissimo Generalissimo (1949)", in *Musicology Today,* No. 2 (38), April–June 2019, p. 90.

165 Ethan Pollock, "Stalin as the Coryphaeus of Science: Ideology and Knowledge in the Post-War Years", in Sarah Davies and James Harris (ed.), *Stalin: A New History* (Cambridge: Cambridge University Press, 2006).

166 See Jan C. Behrends, "Exporting the Leader: The Stalin Cult in Poland and East Germany (1944/45–1956)", in Balázs Apor, Jon C. Behrends, Polly Jones, and E. A. Ross (eds.), *The Leader Cult in Communist Dictatorships: Stalin and the Eastern Bloc* (Basingstoke: Palgrave Macmillan, 2004), pp. 161–178.

167 Gheorghița, "'We Are Chanting to Stalin Too!'", p. 93.

168 See Stephen Kotkin, *Magnetic Mountain: Stalinism as Civilization* (Berkeley and Los Angeles: University of California Press, 1995); Griffin, *Modernism and Fascism*; Ramet, *Alternatives to Democracy.*

169 The latter in her article "Soviet Modernity: Stephen Kotkin and the Bolshevik Predicament", in *Contemporary European History,* Vol. 23, No. 2 (May 2014), p. 168.

170 François Fejtö, *A History of the People's Democracies: Eastern Europe Since Stalin,* trans. from French by Daniel Weissbort (Harmondsworth: Penguin, 1974; reprinted in 1977),

p. 438; Pungur, "Protestantism in Hungary", pp. 124, 139. See also Pedro Ramet, "The Interplay of Religious Policy and Nationalities Policy in the Soviet Union and Eastern Europe", in Pedro Ramet (ed.), *Religion and Nationalism in Soviet and East European Politics,* Rev. and expanded ed. (Durham, NC and London: Duke University Press, 1989), pp. 24–25.

171 *Rudé právo* (Prague, 1953), as quoted in V. Chalupa, *Situation of the Catholic Church in Czechoslovakia* (Chicago: Czechoslovak Foreign Institute in Exile, January 1959), p. 34.

172 Boris Groys, *The Total Art of Stalinism: Avant-Garde, Aesthetic Dictatorship, and Beyond,* originally published in German, trans. by Charles Rougle (Princeton, NJ: Princeton University Press, 2011), p. 36. See also C. Vaughan James, *Soviet Socialist Realism: Origins and Theory* (London and Basingstoke: Palgrave Macmillan, 1973).

173 Matthew Cullerne Brown, *Art Under Stalin* (New York: Holmes & Meier, 1991), p. 90; Groys, *The Total Art of Stalinism,* p. 36.

174 Beata Boleslawska, "Andrzej Panufnik and the Presssures of Stalinism in Post-War Poland", in *Tempo,* New Series, No. 220 (April 2002), p. 16.

175 Steven Stucky, *Lutosławski and His Music* (Cambridge: Cambridge University Press, 1981), p. 35.

176 David G. Tompkin, *Composing the Party Line: Music and Politics in Early Cold War Poland and East Germany* (West Lafayette, IN: Purdue University Press, 2013), pp. 25–27.

177 Bogdan Gieraczyński, "Witold Lutoslavski in Interview", in *Tempo,* New Series, No. 170 (September 1989), p. 5.

178 As quoted in Peter R. Prifti, *Socialist Albania Since 1944: Domestic and Foreign Developments* (Cambridge, MA: MIT Press, 1978), p. 66.

179 Speech of 22 June 1959 at the Second Plenum of the Central Committee of the Polish United Workers' Party, as quoted in Paul Katona, "Collectivization of Agriculture in Central Europe", in *The World Today,* Vol. 16, No. 9 (September 1960), p. 403.

180 Zbigniew K. Brzezinski, *The Soviet Bloc: Unity and Conflict,* Rev. and enlarged ed. (Cambridge, MA: Harvard University Press, 1967), p. 99.

181 Bela A. Balassa, "Collectivization in Hungarian Agriculture", in *Journal of Farm Economics,* Vol. 42, No. 1 (February 1960), p. 42.

182 György Enyedi, "The Changing Face of Agriculture in Eastern Europe", in *Geographical Review,* Vol. 57, No. 3 (July 1967), p. 366.

183 Mary Heimann, *Czechoslovakia: The State that Failed* (New Haven, CT: Yale University Press, 2009; paperback edition 2011), p. 179; Robert K. Evanson, "Political Repression in Czechoslovakia, 1948–1984", in *Canadian Slavonic Papers,* Vol. 28, No. 1 (March 1986), pp. 3–4.

184 Heimann, *Czechoslovakia,* p. 181.

185 *Ibid.,* p. 185.

186 Alexander Dubcek, *Hope Dies Last: The Autobiography of the Leader of the Prague Spring,* trans. by Jiri Hochman (New York: Tokyo-London: Kodansha International, 1993), p. 77.

187 *Ibid.,* p. 93.

188 Igor Lukes, "The Rudolf Slánský Affair: New Evidence", in *Slavic Review,* Vol. 58, No. 1 (Spring 1999), p. 184.

189 Kevin McDermott, "Popular Resistance in Communist Czechoslovakia: The Plzeň Uprising, June 1953", in *Contemporary European History,* Vol. 19, No. 4 (November 2010), pp. 287, 291.

190 Heimann, *Czechoslovakia,* pp. 205, 207.

191 *Ibid.,* p. 218.

192 Bradley Abrams, "Hope Died Last: The Czechoslovak Road to Stalinism", in Tismaneanu (ed.), *Stalinism Revisited,* p. 361.

193 Heimann, *Czechoslovakia,* p. 186.

194 *Ibid.*

195 Sabrina P. Ramet, *Nihil Obstat: Religion, Politics, and Social Change in East-Central Europe and Russia* (Durham, NC and London: Duke University Press, 1998), p. 123.

196 "The Rites of the Catholic Church", in *Catholic News Agency*, at www.catholicnews agency.com/resource/56009/the-rites-of-the-catholic-church [accessed on 16 July 2021].

197 Milan Reban, "The Catholic Church in Czechoslovakia", in Pedro Ramet (ed.), *Catholicism and Politics in Communist Societies* (Durham, NC and London: Duke University Press, 1990), pp. 148–149.

198 V. Chalupa, *Situation of the Catholic Church in Czechoslovakia* (Chicago: Czechoslovak Foreign Institute in Exile, January 1959), pp. 24, 28–29.

199 Josef Rabas, *Kirche in Fesseln*, Materialen zur Situation der Katholischen Kirche in der ČSSR, VI (Munich: Sozialwerk der Ackermann-Gemeinde, 1984), p. 33.

200 Ramet, *Nihil Obstat*, p. 126.

201 Maruška Svašek, "The Politics of Artistic Identity: The Czech Art World in the 1950s and 1960s", in *Contemporary European History*, Vol. 6, No. 3 (November 1997), p. 390.

202 Filip Pospíšil, "Youth Cultures and the Disciplining of Czechoslovak Youth in the 1960s", in *Social History*, Vol. 37, No. 4 (November 2012), p. 4.

203 Gottwald, as quoted in Svašek, "The Politics of Artistic Identity", p. 387.

204 D. E. Viney, "Czech Culture and the 'New Spirit', 1948–52", in *The Slavonic and East European Review*, Vol. 31, No 77 (June 1953), p. 469.

205 Rudolf Urban, "Die literarische Entwicklung in der Tschechoslowakei seit 1945", in *Osteuropa*, Vol. 9, No. 11 (November 1959), p. 702.

206 *Ibid.*

207 As quoted in Svašejm, "The Czech Art World", p. 388.

208 Viney, "Czech Culture", p. 484.

209 Urban, "Die literarische Entwicklung", p. 704.

210 As quoted in *Ibid.*, pp. 706–707.

211 Svašek, "The Czech Art World", pp. 393, 399.

212 Sharon Wolchik, *Czechoslovakia in Transition: Politics, Economics and Society* (London and New York: Pinter Publishers, 1991), p. 287. For an example of Bohumil Hrabal's surrealism, see his *Mr Kafka and Other Tales*, trans. from Czech by Paul Wilson (New York: Vintage, 2015); this book was published in Czech in 1965.

213 Kateřina Lišková, *Sexual Liberation, Socialist Style: Communist Czechoslovakia and the Science of Desire, 1945–1989* (Cambridge: Cambridge University Press, 2018), p. 53.

214 J. L. Porket, "Czechoslovak Women Under Soviet-Type Socialism", in *The Slavonic and East European Review*, Vol. 59, No. 2 (April 1981), p. 243.

215 *Ibid.*, p. 246.

216 Jana Kočišková, *Postaveni žen ve vrcholné politice na koni šedesatých let 20. století a jejech postoje k sovětské okupaci ČSSR*, Master's thesis, Univerzita Karlova v Praze (Prague, 2009), pp. 39–43; Porket, "Czechoslovak Women", p. 257.

217 Kočišková, *Postaveni žen ve vrcholné politice*, pp. 39–43.

218 Sharon L. Wolchik, "Elite Strategy Toward Women in Czechoslovakia: Liberation or Mobilization?" in *Studies in Comparative Communism*, Vol. 14, Nos. 2–3 (Summer/Autumn 1981), p. 128.

219 Jarosz, "The Collectivization of Agriculture in Poland", p. 119.

220 *Ibid.*, pp. 125–126.

221 *Ibid.*, p. 129.

222 Donald E. Pienkos, "Peasant Resposes to Collectivization: A Comparison of Communist Agriculture Politics in the U.S.S.R. and Poland", in *Journal of Baltic Studies*, Vol. 4, No. 3 (Fall 1973), pp. 198–199.

223 Jarosz, "The Collectivization of Agriculture", p. 134.

224 "Agrarpolitischer Richtungsstreit in der Satellitenstaaten", in *Neue Zürcher Zeitung* (19 August 1955), reprinted under the title "Kollektivisierungs-Moratorium in Polen", in *Ost-Probleme*, Vol. 36 (1955), p. 1391. *Ost-Probleme* articles are found in the Central and East European Online Library (CEEOL).

225 Jan Boguszewski and Michel Vale, "Growth and Productivity in Industry and Its Principal Sectors in the FRG, Austria, Poland, and Hungary, 1960–72", in *Eastern European Economics*, Vol. 18, No. 2 (Winter 1979–1980), p. 13.

226 Ewa Kaltenberg-Kwiatowska, "Industrialization and its Effect on the Transformation of Cities in Poland After World War II", in *The Polish Sociological Bulletin,* No. 73/74 (1985), p. 39. I have omitted points 4, 7, and 9 from her list and have renumbered the list accordingly.

227 "Poland", in *Eastern European Economics,* Vol. 2, No. 4 (Summer 1964), p. 42.

228 P. J. D. Wiles, "Changing Economic Thought in Poland", in *Oxford Economic Papers,* New Series, Vol. 9, No. 2 (June 1957), p. 191.

229 See, for example, William Dejong-Lambert, "Lysenkoism in Poland", in *Journal of the History of Biology,* Vol. 45, No. 3 (Fall 2012), pp. 499–524.

230 *Nowe drogi* (October 1956), as quoted in de Weydenthal, *The Communists of Poland,* pp. 39–40.

231 As quoted in William Henry Chamberlin, "Khrushchev's War with Stalin's Ghost", in *The Russian Review,* Vol. 21, No. 1 (January 1962), p. 3.

232 As quoted in Tony Kemp-Welch, "Khrushchev's 'Secret Speech' and Polish Politics: The Spring of 1956", in *Europe-Asia Studies,* Vol. 48, No. 2 (March 1996), p. 181.

233 Another epithet used to refer to Stalin. See *Ibid.*

234 See John Rettie, "How Khrushchev Leaked His Secret Speech to the World", in *History Workshop Journal,* No. 62 (Autumn 2006), pp. 187–193.

235 Extracts from Khrushchev's speech, as quoted in Albert Parry, "The Twentieth Congress: Stalin's 'Second Funeral'", in *The American Slavic and East European Review,* Vol. 15, No. 4 (December 1956), p. 463.

236 Kemp-Welch, "Khrushchev's 'Secret Speech'", p. 183; Włodzimierz Borodziej, *Geschichte Polens im 20. Jahrhundert* (Munich: Verlag C. H. Beck, 2010), pp. 296–297.

237 Nicholas Bethell, *Gomułka, His Poland and His Communism* (London: Longmans, 1969), p. 197.

238 *Ibid.,* p. 206.

239 Borodziej, *Geschichte Polens,* p. 299.

240 Vyacheslav Molotov (1890–1986).

241 Anastas Mikoyan (1895–1978).

242 Lazar Kaganovich (1893–1991)

243 Ivan Konev (1897–1973).

244 Borodziej, *Geschichte Polens,* p. 299.

245 Bethell, *Gomułka,* p. 216.

246 As quoted in *Ibid.,* p. 218.

247 As quoted in *Ibid.,* p. 219.

248 Ramet, *The Catholic Church in Polish History,* p. 158, citing Elizabeth Valkenier, "The Catholic Church in Communist Poland, 1945–1955", in *The Review of Politics,* Vol. 18, No. 3 (July 1956), p. 313.

249 Telegram from the U.S. Embassy in London to State, 3 April 1950, attaching an English translation of a letter from the Polish Episcopate to President Bierut, signed by Cardinals Sapieha and Wyszyński (16 February 1950), in *Records Relating to Poland 1950–1954,* Decimal file 748, at SL, Reel 1 (files 00/1–450 to 00/8–2351.

250 S. L., "Church and State in Poland", in *The World Today,* Vol. 14, No. 10 (October 1958), p. 423. See also Tadeusz N. Cieplak, "Church and State in People's Poland", in *Polish American Studies,* Vol. 26, No. 2 (Autumn 1969), pp. 15–30, especially pp. 19–20.

251 Robert E. Alvis, *White Eagle, Black Madonna: One Thousand Years of the Polish Catholic Tradition* (New York: Fordham University Press, 2016), p. 223; also Valkenier, "The Catholic Church in Communist Poland", p. 314.

252 Borodziej, *Geschichte Polens,* p. 287.

253 *Ibid.,* p. 287.

254 Alvis, *White Eagle, Black Madonna,* p. 224.

255 Telegram from Warsaw to State, 17 April 1950; received 18 April 1950, in *Records Relating to Poland 1950–1954,* Decimal file 848, at SL, Reel 10, files .2422/1–1350 to .413/6–3053.

256 Telegram from Warsaw to State, 22 April 1950, in *Records Relating to Poland 1950–1954*, Decimal file 848, at SL, Reel 10, files .2422/1–1350 to .413/6–3053.

257 Siedlarz, *Kirche und Staat,* pp. 82, 91; Adam Dziurok, "Metody walki dezintegracyjnych służby bezpieczeństwa w latach sześć dziesiątych XX wieku", in Rafała Łatki (ed.), *Stosunki Państwo-Kościół w Polsce 1944–2010: Studia i materiały* (Kraków: Księgarnia Akademika, 2013), p. 67; and *Catholic Herald* (4 March 1955), p. 8.

258 Zygmunt Zieliński, with the cooperation of Sabina Bober, *Kościół w Polsce 1944–2007* (Gdański-Zaspa: Wydawnictwo Poznańskie, 2009), p. 83.

259 Alvis, *White Eagle, Black Madonna,* p. 225.

260 Leonid Luks, *Katholizismus und Politische Macht im Kommunistischen Polen 1945–1989. Die Anatomie einer Befreiung* (Köln, Weimar and Wien: Böhlau Verlag, 1993), p. 27.

261 As quoted in *Ibid.*, p. 31.

262 As quoted in Michał Bruliński, "Chopin on Barricades: About the 100th Anniversay of Chopin's Birth (1949) and Socialist Realism Doctrine in Poland", in *Kwartalnik Młodych Muzykologów UJ,* No. 36 (1/2018), p. 100.

263 *Ibid.*, p. 83.

264 As quoted in *Ibid.*, p. 101.

265 *Ibid.*, p. 93.

266 Bierut, as quoted in *Ibid.*, p. 101.

267 David. G. Tompkins, *Composing the Party Line: Music and Politics in Early Cold War Poland and East Germany* (West Lafayette, IN: Purdue University Press, 2013), p. 27.

268 Both extracts as quoted in *Ibid.*, p. 37.

269 *Ibid.*, p. 45.

270 As quoted in Basia A. Nowak, "Constant Conversations: Agitators in the League of Women in Poland During the Stalinist Period", in *Feminist Studies,* Vol. 31, No. 3 (Fall 2005), p. 499.

271 *Ibid.*, pp. 489, 494.

272 *Ibid.*, pp. 494, 497, 506.

273 *Ibid.*, p. 505.

274 Piotr Perkowski, "Wedded to Welfare? Working Mothers and the Welfare State in Communist Poland", in *Slavic Review,* Vol. 76, No. 2 (Summer 2017), p. 462.

275 Balázs Apor, *The Invisible Shining: The Cult of Mátyás Rákosi in Stalinist Hungary, 1945–1956* (Budapest and New York: Central European University Press, 2017), p. 54.

276 As quoted in *Ibid.*, p. 55.

277 As quoted in *Ibid.*, p. 62.

278 As quoted in *Ibid.*, p. 142.

279 Kovrig, *Communism in Hungary,* p. 244.

280 Hoensch, *Modern Hungary,* p. 196.

281 Peter Kenez, "The Hungarian Communist Party and the Catholic Church, 1945–1948", in *The Journal of Modern History,* Vol. 75, No. 4 (December 2003), p. 868.

282 Stephen Kertesz, "Church and State in Hungary: The Background of the Cardinal Mindszenty Trial", in *The Review of Politics,* Vol. 11, No. 2 (April 1949), p. 215.

283 Kenez, "The Hungarian Communist Party", pp. 872–873.

284 Kertesz, "Church and State in Hungary", pp. 215–217.

285 As quoted in Joseph Pungur, "Protestantism in Hungary: The Communist Era", in Sabrina Petra Ramet (ed.), *Protestantism and Politics in Eastern Europe and Russia: The Communist and Postcommunist Eras* (Durham, NC and London: Duke University Press, 1992), p. 120.

286 *New York Times* (4 February 1950), p. 12; Tibor Fabiny, "Bishop Lajos Ordassy and the Hungarian Lutheran Church", in *Hungarian Studies,* Vol. 10, No. 1 (1995), pp. 75–76; H. David Baer, *The Struggle of Hungarian Lutherans Under Communism* (College Station, Tex.: Texas A&M University Press, 2006), pp. 23–26; Hoensch, *Modern Hungary,* p. 199.

287 Hoensch, *Modern Hungary,* p. 212.

288 Kovrig, *Communism in Hungary*, pp. 257–258. See also József Kovács, "The Forced Collectivization of Agriculture in Hungary, 1948–1961", in Iordachi and Bauerkamper (eds.), *The Collectivization of Agriculture in Communist Eastern Europe*, pp. 211–247.

289 As quoted in Pungur, "Protestantism in Hungary", p. 121.

290 Hoensch, *Modern Hungary*, p. 200.

291 Ivan T. Berend, *Central and Eastern Europe 1944–1993: Detour from the Periphery to the Periphery* (Cambridge: Cambridge University Press, 1998; reprinted 2001), pp. 64–68.

292 As quoted in Kovrig, *Communism in Hungary*, p. 252.

293 *Ibid.*, pp. 263–264.

294 As quoted in Mark Kramer, "The Soviet Union and the 1956 Crises in Hungary and Poland: Reassessments and New Findings", in *Journal of Contemporary History*, Vol. 33, No. 2 (April 1998), p. 175.

295 Imre Nagy, *On Communism: In Defence of the New Course* (London: Thames and Hudson, 1957), p. 8.

296 *Ibid.*, pp. 47, 51.

297 Nagy, as quoted in Kovrig, *Communism in Hungary*, p. 269.

298 As quoted in Molnar, *From Béla Kun to János Kádár*, p. 160.

299 Ivan Behrend, *Central and Eastern Europe, 1944–1993: Detour from the Periphery to the Periphery* (Cambridge: Cambridge University Press, 1996), p. 102.

300 Kovrig, *Communism in Hungary*, p. 279.

301 *Ibid.*

302 *Ibid.*, p. 280; and *New York Times* (12 April 1993), Section D, p. 11.

303 As quoted in Kovrig, *Communism in Hungary*, p. 281.

304 Nagy, *On Communism*, p. 44.

305 As quoted in Danielle Foster-Lussier, "'Multiplication by Negative One': Musical Values in East-West Engagement", in György Péteri (ed.), *Nylon Curtain: Transnational and Transsystemic Tendencies in the Cultural Life of State-Socialist Russia and East-Central Europe* (Trondheim: Trondheim Studies on East European Cultures & Societies, No. 18, August 2006), p. 21.

306 *Ibid.*, p. 17.

307 "Endre Szervánszky", in *Liszt Academy*, at https://lfze.hu/notable-alumni/szervan szky-endre-1713 [accessed on 21 May 2021].

308 György Kroó, "New Hungarian Music", in *Notes*, Second Series, Vol. 39, No. 1 (September 1982), p. 46.

309 Molnar, *From Béla Kun to János Kádár*, p. 151.

310 Ann Demaitre, "The Hungarian Shores of Realism", in *Comparative Literature*, Vol. 1, No. 4 (1964), p. 320.

311 As quoted in Ivan Sanders, "The Ironic Hungarian: Tibor Déry at Eighty", in *Books Abroad*, Vol. 49, No. 1 (Winter 1975), p. 13.

312 As quoted in Kovrig, *Communism in Hungary*, p. 293.

313 Sanders, "The Ironic Hungarian", p. 13; and "Tibor Déry", revised and updated by Maren Goldberg, in *Britannica Online Encyclopedia*, at www.britannica.com/print/arti cle/1459159 [accessed on 11 June 2021], p. 2 of 2.

314 Tibor Déry, *Niki: The Story of a Dog*, trans. from Hungarian by Edward Hyams (New York: New York Review Books, 2009). The book was published in Hungarian in 1956.

315 Sanders, "The Ironic Hungarian", p. 14.

316 As quoted in *Ibid.*, p. 17.

317 Polanyi, as quoted in Behrend, *Central and Eastern Europe*, p. 19.

318 Kramer, "The Soviet Union and the 1956 Crises", p. 179; Charles Gati, "From Liberation to Revolution, 1945–1956", in Peter F. Sugar (general editor), Péter Hanák (associate editor), and Tibor Frank (editorial assistant), *A History of Hungary* (Bloomington and Indianapolis: Indiana University Press, 1990; first paperback edition, 1994), p. 377; Kovrig, *Communism in Hungary*, p. 294.

319 As quoted in Kramer, "The Soviet Union and the 1956 Crises", p. 181.

320 Behrend, *Central and Eastern Europe,* p. 121.
321 Hoensch, *Modern Hungary,* p. 216.
322 *Borba* (Belgrade ed.), 26 October 1956, p. 1.
323 *Borba* (27 October 1956), p. 3.
324 Kramer, "The Soviet Union and the 1956 Crises", p. 189.
325 See the discussion in Ferenc Vali, *Rift and Revolt in Hungary* (Cambridge, MA: Harvard University Press, 1961).
326 As quoted in Gati, "From Liberation to Revolution", pp. 381–382.
327 Kovrig, *Communism in Hungary,* pp. 310–311.
328 Hermann Weber, *Geschichte der DDR,* Rev. & expanded ed. (Munich: Deutsche Taschenbuch Verlag, GmbH, 2000), p. 125.
329 *Ibid.,* p. 130.
330 *Ibid.,* p. 136: and Franz-Joef Kos, "Politische Justiz in der DDR. Der Dessauer Schauprozeß von April 1950", in *Vierteljahrshefte für Zeitgeschichte,* Vol. 44, No. 3 (July 1996), pp. 395–429.
331 Dietrich Staritz, *Die Gründung der DDR. Von der sowjetischen Besatzungsherrschaft zum sozialistischen Staat,* 3rd rev. ed. (Munich: Deutscher Taschenbuch Verlag, 1995), p. 178; Weber, *Geschichte der DDR,* p. 137.
332 Jürgen Kocka, *Civic Society and Dictatorship in Modern German History* (Waltham, MA: Brandeis University Press, 2010), p. 53.
333 See Arnold Krammer, "The Cult of the Spanish Civl War in East Germany", in *Journal of Contemporary History,* Vol. 39, No. 4 (October 2004), pp. 531–560; Josie McLellan, *Antifascism and Memory in East Germany: Remembering the International Brigades, 1945–1989* (Oxford: Clarendon Press, 2004); Catherine Plum, *Antifascism After Hitler: East German Youth and Socialist Memory* (New York and London: Routledge, 2015), esp. p. 5.
334 See Dietrich Orlow, "The GDR's Failed Search for a National Identity, 1945–1989", in *German Studies Review,* Vol. 29, No. 3 (October 2006), p. 547; Sabrina P. Ramet, *Nonconformity, Dissent, Opposition, and Resistance in Germany, 1933–1990* (London and New York: Palgrave Macmillan, 2020), p. 149.
335 Jens Schöne, "Ideology and Asymmetrical Entanglements: Collectivization in the German Democratic Republic", in Iordachi and Bauerkämper (eds.), *The Collectivization of Agriculture in Communist Eastern Europe,* pp. 149–150.
336 *Ibid.,* p. 151.
337 *Ibid.*
338 *Ibid.,* p. 152.
339 Dietrich Staritz, *Sozialismus in einem halben Land. Zur Programmatik und Politik der KPD/SED in der Phase der antifaschistisch-demokratische Umwälzung in der DDR* (Berlin: Verlag Klaus Wagenbach, 1976), p. 182.
340 A. N. P., "Eastern Germany Since the Risings of June 1953", in *The World Today,* Vol. 10, No. 2 (February 1954), p. 60.
341 *Ibid.,* pp. 61–62.
342 Weber, *Geschichte der DDR,* p. 164.
343 Gareth Dale, *Popular Protest in East Germany 1945–1989* (London and New York: Routledge, 2005), pp. 9–10; also Weber, *Geschichte der DDR,* p. 165. Dale writes that more than a thousand factories experienced work stoppages, involving at least 1.5 million workers. Weber writes that about half a million workers went on strike at approximately 600 factories.
344 Weber, *Geschichte der DDR,* p. 166; confirmed in Dale, *Popular Protest,* p. 10.
345 "Bekanntmachungen der Regierung der DDR", in *Neues Deutschland* (18 June 1953), p. 1.
346 A. N. P., "Eastern Germany", pp. 65, 67.
347 Weber, *Geschichte der DDR,* p. 171.
348 Wolfgang Stolper, "The Labor Force and Industrial Production in Soviet Germany", in *The Quarterly Journal of Economics,* Vol. 71, No. 4 (November 1957), p. 521.

349 "Die Lage der Arbeiterklasse in der DDR", in *Tägliche Runschau* (4 June 1954), reprinted under the title "Ulbrichts Arbeiterparadies", in *Ost-Probleme*, 26/1954, p. 1018.

350 Karl Wilhelm Fricke, *Opposition und Widerstand in der DDR. Ein politischer Report* (Cologne: Verlag Wissenschaft und Politik, 1984), pp. 105–106; Silke Schumann, *Parteierziehung in der Geheimpolizei. Zur Rolle der SED im MfS der fünfzige Jahre* (Berlin: Ch. Links Verlag, 1997), pp. 28–31; Weber, *Geschichte der DDR*, p. 172. See also Ramet, *Nonconformity, Dissent*, pp. 153–155.

351 "Zum Kampf zwischen dem Marxismus-Leninismus und dem Ideologien der Bourgeoisie. – Aus der Ulbricht – Rede vor dem 30. Plenum des ZK der SEK, 30.1.-1.2.1957", in *Neues Deutschland* (5 February 1957), reprinted under the title "Ulbricht über Dichter und Denker", in *Ost-Probleme, 9/1957*, p. 322.

352 Weber, *Geschichte in der DDR*, p. 91.

353 "Fragen des Präsidiums der Deutschen Bauakademie", in *Neues Deutschland* (9 June 1955), reprinted under the title "Fassadenarchitektur", in *Ost-Probleme, 37/1955*, pp. 1413–1415.

354 See Joy Haslam Calico, *The Politics of Opera in the German Democratic Republic, 1945–1961,* Ph.D. dissertation (Duke University, 1999).

355 Anicia Chung Timberlake, *The Practice and Politics of Children's Music Education in the German Democratic Republic, 1949–1976,* Ph.D. dissertation (University of California, Berkeley, 2015).

356 Weber, *Geschichte der DDR,* p. 156.

357 "Über den sozialistischen Realismus", in *Musik und Gesellschaft* (Berlin), January 1955, reprinted under the title "Sozialistischer Realismus in der Musik", in *Ost-Probleme,* 37/1955, p. 1419.

358 *Ibid.*, pp. 1419–1420.

359 As quoted in Weber, *Geschichte der DDR,* p. 157.

360 Becher, as quoted in Alexander Stephan, "Johannes R. Becher and the Cultural Development of the GDR", trans. by Sara and Frank Lennox in *New German Critique,* No. 2 (Spring 1974), p. 77.

361 *Ibid.*, p. 81.

362 *Ibid.*

363 Becher, in November 1953, as quoted in *Ibid.*, p. 84.

364 Manfred Jäger, *Kultur und Politik in der DDR. Ein historischer Abriß* (Cologne: Edition Deutschland Archiv, 1982), pp. 71–72.

365 Alan Nothnagle, "From Buchenwald to Bismarck: Historical Myth-Building in the German Democratic Republic, 1945–1989", in *Central European History,* Vol. 26, No. 1 (1993), p. 97.

366 "Für eine deutsche Nationaloper", in *Neues Deutschland* (1 November 1952), reprinted under the title "SED schafft Nationaloper" in *Ost-Probleme,* 47/1952, p. 1582. See also Eckart Kröplin, *Operntheater in der DDR. Zwischen neuer Ästhetik und politische Dogmen* (Leipzig: Henschel Verlag, 2020).

367 Wes Blomster, "The Reception of Arnold Schoenberg in the German Democratic Republic", in *Perspectives of New Music,* Vol. 21, No. 1–2 (Autumn 1982–Summer 1983), pp. 117, 124–126; Laura Silverberg, "Between Dissonance and Dissidence: Socialist Modernism in the German Democratic Republic", in *The Journal of Musicology,* Vol. 26, No. 1 (Winter 2009), pp. 51–52.

368 Blomster, "The Reception of Arnold Schoenberg", *passim.*

369 Weber, *Geschichte der DDR,* p. 157.

370 *Ibid.*

371 Jäger, *Kultur und Politik,* p. 70.

372 Stephan, "Johannes R. Becher", p. 83.

373 *Ibid.*, p. 86.

374 As quoted in *Ibid.*, p. 85.

375 *Ibid.*, p. 87.

376 As quoted in *Ibid.*, p. 73.

377 As quoted in Eric D. Weitz, *Creating German Communism, 1890–1990: From Popular Protests to Socialist State* (Princeton, NJ: Princeton University Press, 1997), p. 370.

378 As of 1977. See Caroline Ward, "Church and State in East Germany", in *Religion in Communist Lands*, Vol. 6, No. 2 (1978), p. 89, citing Irmela Roitsch, "Die Evangelischen Kirchen in der DDR. Ein Überblick", in *Informationsdienst des Katholischen Arbeitskreises für Zeitgeschichtliche Fragen*, No. 83 (Bonn: Bad Godesberg, 1977).

379 Constitution of the German Democratic Republic (7 October 1949), at www.cvce.eu/content/publication/1999/1/1/33cc8de2-3cff-4102-b524-c1648172a838/pub lishable_en.pdf [accessed on 17 August 2021].

380 Ward, "Church and State", p. 89, citing Trevor Beeson, *Discretion and Valour: Religious Conditions in Russia and Eastern Europe* (London: Fontana, 1974), p. 171.

381 Thomas Kothmann, *Religionsunterricht, evangelisch* (Stuttgart: Deutsche Bibel Gesellschaft, 2015), pp. 2–3.

382 Mary Fulbrook, *Anatomy of a Dictatorship: Inside the GDR* (Oxford and New York: Oxford University Press, 1995), p. 98.

383 For details, see Hermann Wentker, " 'Kirchenkampf' in der DDR. Der Konflikt um die Junge Gemeinde 1950–1953", in *Vierteljahrshefte für Zeitgeschichte*, Vol. 42, No. 1 (January 1994), pp. 96–97.

384 *Ibid.*, pp. 102, 104.

385 *Ibid.*, p. 127.

386 Plum, *Antifascism After Hitler*, p. 43.

387 Foreign Service Despatch, from U.S. Mission, Berlin (David Henry, Chief, Eastern Affairs Division) to Department of State (6 December 1955), Desp. No. 374, confidential, in *Records of the U.S. Department of State relating to the Internal Affairs of East Germany, 1955–1959*, Decimal file 8628.413, p. 2.

388 Bernd Schäfer, "Staat und Katholische Kirche in der DDR bis 1961", in Hans-Jürgen Karp and Joachim Köhler (eds.), *Katholische Kirche unter nationalsozialistischer und kommunistischer Diktatur. Deutschland und Polen 1939–1989* (Cologne, Weimar and Vienna: Böhlau Verlag, 2001), p. 99.

389 As quoted in Paul Oestreicher, "Christian Pluralism in a Monolithic State: The Churches of East Germany 1945–1990", in *Religion in Communist Lands*, Vol. 21, No. 3–4 (1993), p. 272.

390 Constitution of the German Democratic Republic (7 October 1949), posted at www.cvce.eu/content/publication/1999/1/1/33cc8de2-3cff-4102-b524-c1648172a838/publishable_en.pdf [accessed on 6 June 2022].

391 Heike Trappe, *Emanzipation oder Zwang? Frauer in der DDR zwischen Beruf, Familie und Sozialpolitik* (Berlin: Akademia Verlag, 1995), pp. 41, 55.

392 Christel Sudau, "Women in the GDR", trans. from German by Biddy Martin, in *New German Critique*, No. 13 (Winter 1978), p. 75.

393 "Parlamentarische Entwicklungen in beiden deutschen Staaten", in *Bundeszentrale für politische Bildung* (12 December 2018), at www.bpb.de/geschichte/deutsche-geschichte/frauenwahlrecht/279358/parlamentarische-entwicklungen-in-beiden-deutschen-staaten [accessed on 17 August 2021]; David Childs, *The GDR: Moscow's German Ally*, 2nd ed. (London: Unwin Hyman, 1988), p. 250.

394 More than 70% in the early 1960s, 87% in 1977. – Childs, *The GDR*, p. 253.

395 Sudau, "Women in the GDR", p. 72.

396 Katrin Sieg, "Equality Decreed: Dramatizing Gender in East Germany", in *Women in German Yearbook*, Vol. 9 (1993), p. 118.

397 As quoted in Ionescu, *Communism in Rumania*, p. 157.

398 *Deutsche Tagespost* (18–19 December 1953), as cited in Emil Ciurea, "Religious Life", in Alexandru Cretzianu (ed.), *Captive Rumania* (London: Atlantic Press, 1956), p. 190.

399 Mihaela Şerban, "The Loss of Property Rights and the Construction of Legal Consciousness in Early Socialist Romania (1950–1965)", in *Law & Society Review*, Vol. 48, No. 4 (December 2014), pp. 773, 778, 780–783.

400 Deletant, *Communist Terror in Romania*, pp. 226–227.
401 G. I., "Rumania in 1952: A Political Analysis of the Economic Crisis", in *The World Today*, Vol. 8, No. 7 (July 1952), p. 298.
402 Gail Kligman and Katherine Verdery, *Peasants under Siege: The Collectivization of Romanian Agriculture, 1949–1962* (Princeton, NJ: Princeton University Press, 2011), p. 256.
403 *Ibid.*, p. 124. See also Robert Levy, *Ana Pauker: The Rise and Fall of a Jewish Communist* (Berkeley and Los Angeles: University of California Press, 2001), chap. 4.
404 *Scînteia* (3 June 1952), as quoted in G. I., "Rumania in 1952", p. 296, n1.
405 Dennis Deletant, "New Light on Gheorghiu-Dej's Struggle for Dominance in the Romanian Communist Party, 1944–49", in *The Slavonic and East European Review*, Vol. 73, No. 4 (October 1995), pp. 659–660; confirmed in Tismaneanu, *Stalinism for All Seasons*, p. 133.
406 Deletant, "New Light on Gheorghiu-Dej's Struggle", p. 673.
407 Lucian N. Leustean, "Constructing Communism in the Romanian People's Republic: Orthodoxy and State, 1948–49", in *Europe-Asia Studies*, Vol. 59, No. 2 (March 2007), p. 310. See also Levy, *Ana Pauker*, chap. 8.
408 Ionescu, *Communism in Rumania*, p. 217.
409 See Stefano Bottoni, *Stalin's Legacy in Romania: The Hungarian Autonomous Region, 1952–1960* (Lanham, MD: Lexington Books, 2018).
410 Stefano Bottoni, *Long Awaited West: Eastern Europe since 1944*, trans. by Sean Lambert (Bloomington and Indianapolis: Indiana University Press, 2017), p. 83.
411 Tismaneanu, *Stalinism for All Seasons*, p. 145.
412 *Ibid.*, pp. 140, 152, and 176.
413 Gabanyi, *Partei und Literatur in Rumänien*, p. 12.
414 *Ibid.*, p. 29.
415 Hugh Wood, "Music in Rumania", in *The Musical Times*, Vol. 109, No. 1510 (December 1968), p. 1117.
416 Nicolas Slonimsky, "Modern Composition in Rumania", in *The Musical Quarterly*, Vol. 51, No. 1 (January 1965), p. 239.
417 Robert R. King, *History of the Romanian Communist Party* (Stanford, CA: Hoover Institution Press, 1980), p. 55.
418 Deletant, *Communist Terror in Romania*, p. 90.
419 As quoted in Valentina Tănase, "The Status of Women in Romania During the Communist Regime: Legislative and Constitutional Rights of Women (1947–1989)", in *Romanian Journal of Historical Studies*, Vol. II, No. 1 (2019), p. 30.
420 *Ibid.*, pp. 32, 34.
421 Constitutia Republicii Populare Române din 1948, Articles 16, 18, 21.
422 *Ibid.*, Article 22.
423 *Ibid.*, Article 26.
424 Pedro Ramet, "The Soviet Factor in the Macedonian Dispute", in *Survey*, Vol. 24, No. 3 (Summer 1979), p. 128.
425 Nissan Oren, *Revolution Administered: Agrarianism and Communism in Bulgaria* (Baltimore and London: The Johns Hopkins University Press, 1973), p. 105; Crampton, *Concise History of Bulgaria*, p. 191.
426 *Le Figaro* (Paris), 5 October 1949, trans. into German under the title "Die Sowjetnote gegen Deutschland", in *Ost-Probleme*, 05/1949, in *The Central and Eastern European Online Library* (hereafter, CEEOL), p. 116.
427 *The Times* (London), 8 December 1949, trans. into German under the title "Kostow-Prozess", in *Ost-Probleme*, 15/1949, in CEEOL, p. 429.
428 As quoted in Bell, *The Bulgarian Communist Party*, p. 106.
429 Crampton, *Concise History of Bulgaria*, p. 189.
430 Brown, *Bulgaria Under Communist Rule*, pp. 27, 54.
431 *Ibid.*, p. 47.

432 Bell, *The Bulgarian Communist Party*, p. 115. See also Brown, *Bulgaria Under Communist Rule*, p. 66.

433 "Communism is Soviet Power+ Electrification of the Whole Country", in *Seventeen Moments in Soviet History*, at http://soviethistory.msu.edu/1921-2/electrification-cam paign/communism-is-soviet-power-electrification-of-the-whole-country/ [accessed on 6 August 2021].

434 "Access to electricity (% of population) – Bulgaria", *The World Bank – Data*, at https:// data.worldbank.org/indicator/EG.ELC.ACCS.ZS?end=2019&locations=BG&name_ desc=false&page=1&start=1990 [accessed on 7 August 2021].

435 *Water Supply and Sanitation in Bulgaria, the Czech Republic, Romania and the Slovak Republic* (The Hague: IRC International Water and Sanitation Centre, December 1994), at www.ircwash.org/sites/default/files/821-EUREAST94-14809.pdf [accessed on 7 August 2021], pp. 11, 12.

436 Piotr Wilczynski, *Environmental Management in Centrally-Planned Non-Market Economies of Eastern Europe*, Environment Working Paper No. 35 (Washington, DC: The World Bank, July 1990), at https://documents1.worldbank.org/curated/en/8074414933055 88896/pdf/Environmental-management-in-centrally-planned-non-market-econo mies-of-Eastern-Europe.pdf [acccessed on 6 August 2021], p. 7.

437 Mihai Gruev, "Collectivization and Social Change in Bulgaria, 1940s-1950s", in Constantin Iordachi and Arnd Bauerkämper (eds.), *The Collectivization of Agriculture in Communist Eastern Europe* (Budapest and New York: Central European University Press, 2014), p. 331.

438 *Ibid.*, p. 330.

439 Vladimir Migev, "The Bulgarian Peasants' Resistance to Collectivization (1948–1958)", in *Bulgarian Historical Review*, No. 1 (1997), p. 56.

440 *Ibid.*, pp. 56, 59.

441 *Ibid.*, pp. 56–57, 59, 60.

442 Bell, *The Bulgarian Communist Party*, p. 111.

443 Migev, "The Bulgarian Peasants' Resistance", pp. 62–63.

444 *Ibid.*, pp. 64–66; Gruev, "Collectivization and Social Change", pp. 354–355.

445 Migev, "The Bulgarian Peasants' Resistance", pp. 67–71.

446 Albena Tagareva, "Socialist Realism in the Bulgarian National Theatre's Stage Design: Processes, Influences, Concepts", in *Theatralia*, Vol. 21 (2018), No. 2, pp. 142–143.

447 As quoted in *Ibid.*, p. 156.

448 *Ibid.*, p. 148.

449 Stanimira Dermendzhieva, "The Politicization of Music During the Period of Totalitarian Rule in Bulgaria (1944–1989)", in *Muzykologiya/Musicology*, No. 25 (2018), p. 181.

450 *Ibid.*

451 *Ibid.*, p. 186.

452 Bell, *The Bulgarian Communist Party*, p. 114.

453 Donald D. Egbert, "Politics and the Arts in Communist Bulgaria", in *Slavic Review*, Vol. 26, No. 2 (June 1967), pp. 205–206.

454 As quoted in Raikin, "The Bulgarian Orthodox Church", p. 89.

455 Kalkandjeva, "The Bulgarian Orthodox Church", p. 84.

456 *Ibid.*, p. 84.

457 Spas T. Raikin, "Nationalism and the Bulgarian Orthodox Church", in Ramet (ed.), *Religion and Nationalism*, pp. 359–361.

458 Janice Broun, "Catholics in Bulgaria", in *Religion in Communist Lands*, Vol. 11, No. 3 (1983), p. 312.

459 Marin Pundeff, "Church-State Relations in Bulgaria under Communism", in Bohdan R. Bociurkiw and John W. Strong (eds.), *Religion and Atheism in the U.S.S.R. and Eastern Europe* (London: Macmillan, 1975), p. 340.

460 Broun, "Catholics in Bulgaria", pp. 312–313.

461 Paul Mojzes and N. Gerald Shenk, "Protestantism in Bulgaria and Yugoslavia since 1945", in Ramet (ed.), *Protestantism and Politics*, pp. 213–214.
462 Talip Küçükcan, "Re-claiming Identity: Ethnicity, Religion and Politics among Turkish-Muslims in Bulgaria and Greece", in *Journal of Muslim Minority Affairs*, Vol. 19, No. 1 (1999), pp. 55–56.
463 Nora Ananieva and Evka Razvigorova, "Women in State Administration in the People's Republic of Bulgaria", in *Women and Politics*, Vol. 11, No. 4 (1992), pp. 31–33.
464 Kristen Ghodsee, "Pressuring the Politburo: The Committee of the Bulgarian Women's Movement and State Socialist Feminism", in *Slavic Review*, Vol. 73, No. 3 (Fall 2014), p. 544.
465 Nikolina Ilieva, *The Bulgarian Woman* (Sofia: Sofia Press, 1970), p. 6.
466 Ghodsee, "Pressuring the Politburo", p. 560.

3

THE SOVIET BLOC, PART TWO

1956–1980

Economic trends, 1950–1975

By 1962, with the exception of Poland, the vast majority of arable land across the Soviet bloc had been collectivized and, with the sole exception of the German Democratic Republic, between 97% and 100% of industry was in the state sector. In the GDR, 88.4% of industry had been socialized by then, and the process of socialization of industry would continue.[1] During the first half of the 1950s, with the partial exception of Czechoslovakia, the countries of the bloc experienced robust economic growth, as reflected in industrial growth (see Table 3.1).

But by the start of the 1960s, growth in industrial production was slowing down in four of the six bloc states (see Table 3.2).

By 1963, Czechoslovakia faced an economic crisis. Ota Šik (1919–2004), a professor of economics, was put in charge of assessing the situation. After Šik completed his work, the Central Committee of the Czechoslovak Communist Party (KSČ[2]) met in January 1965 and agreed on guidelines to improve economic management. Specifically there was general agreement that the centralized system was not working as intended.[3] Abandoning central planning was not considered.

In Bulgaria, the regime became aware of economic difficulties by 1965 and, in December of that year, approved a set of draft theses for a New System of Planning and Management of the National Economy. The theses identified problems of over-centralization of planning, enterprise inefficiency, problems with workers' motivation, and arbitrary prices. In spite of this clear analysis, nothing was ever done to reduce centralized control and even the touted initiative to encourage planning from below was rendered largely meaningless when the April 1966 plenum of the CC demanded that enterprises satisfy state orders. Finally, in July 1968, the CC, meeting in a plenary session, adopted a resolution which effectively reaffirmed the centralized system, scuttling the proposed reform.[4]

DOI: 10.4324/9781003311515-3

TABLE 3.1 Annual Rates of Growth of Industrial Production, 1950–1956 in per cent

	1950	1951	1952	1953	1954	1955	1956
Bulgaria	15	19	16	15	11	8	15
Czechoslovakia	15	14	18	9	4	11	9
German Democratic Republic	26	23	16	12	10	8	6
Hungary	29	24	21	12	10	9	−10
Poland	28	22	19	17	11	11	9
Romania	—	24	17	15	6	14	11

Source: Z. M. Fallenbuchl, "The Communist Pattern of Industrialization", in *Soviet Studies*, Vol. 21, No. 4 (April 1970), p. 468.

TABLE 3.2 Annual Rates of Growth of Industrial Production, 1957–1964 in per cent

	1957	1958	1959	1960	1961	1962	1963	1964
Bulgaria	16	15	20	13	12	11	10	10
Czechoslovakia	10	11	11	12	9	6	−1	4
German Democratic Republic	8	12	12	8	6	6	4	6
Hungary	14	11	9	12	10	8	6	9
Poland	10	10	9	11	10	8	5	9
Romania	8	10	10	16	16	14	12	14

Source: Z. M. Fallenbuchl, "The Communist Pattern of Industrialization", in *Soviet Studies*, Vol. 21, No. 4 (April 1970), p. 468.

In East Germany, economists Friedrich Behrens and Arne Benary sounded the alarm as early as 1955, calling for a radical rethinking of the country's economic strategy. Specifically, they claimed that the East German economy would continue its downward spiral unless firms were granted greater autonomy in decision-making and unless profitability would be accepted as the main criterion for assessing the success of a firm.[5] It should be noted here that the country's economic difficulties were remedied in the short term once the Berlin Wall was erected in August 1961, sealing the GDR off from West Berlin and West Germany. But the radical ideas of Behrens and Benary came up against dogged resistance from conservatives and orthodox Marxist economists who would dominate economic policy until the start of 1962. Behrens was dismissed from his position as Director of the National Statistics Office, while Benary was demoted and reassigned to work as a member of the managerial staff at an obscure factory in Berlin.[6] Regarding the revival of the idea of economic reform in the first half of the 1960s, see below.

In Hungary, the Central Committee agreed in December 1964 to undertake a major reform and, within a year, accepted the idea that the reform needed to be market-oriented, which is to say to take supply, demand, and profit into account. But there continued to be fixed prices for energy and raw materials, while "staple products of mass consumption, and services . . . all remained subsidized."[7] Even in its limited scale, however, Hungary's economic reform stimulated the economy and the growth of a middle class at least in the short term.

TABLE 3.3 Annual Rates of Growth of Industrial Production, 1971–1979

	1966–70	1971–75	1976	1977	1978	1979
Bulgaria	11.8	9.2	7.1	7.2	6.9	6.6
Czechoslovakia	3.5#	6.7	5.5	5.6	3.7	4.5
German Democratic Republic	5.7	6.3	5.9	4.8	4.8	4.8
Hungary	7.0	6.4	4.6	6.6	4.9	2.8
Poland	7.7	10.5	9.3	6.7	4.7	2.8
Romania	12.1	12.9	11.4	12.2	9.1	8.0

= 1961–70

Source: "The Economics of the CMEA Countries and Yugoslavia at the end of the Decade (1979–1980)", Special issue of *Eastern European Economics*, Vol. 19, No. 4 (Summer 1981) – articles by Friedrich Levcik, Ilse Grosser & Paul Wiedemann, Gabriele Tuitz, Raimund Dietz, Benedykt Askanas, and Gabriel Kramarics; Benedykt Askanas, Halina Askanas, and Friedrich Levcik, "Economic Development of the COMECON Countries 1971 to 1975 and Their Plans until 1980", in *Eastern European Economics*, Vol. 15, No. 3 (Spring 1977), p. 35; Michel Vale, "The Economy of the CMEA Countries as the Second Half of the Seventies", in *Eastern European Economics*, Vol. 17, No. 3 (Spring 1979), p. 66; and Stanislaw Gomulka, "Industrialization and the Rate of Growth: Eastern Europe 1955–75", in *Journal of Post Keynesian Economics*, Vol. 5, No. 3 (Spring 1983), p. 391.

By the early 1970s, only Czechoslovakia recorded stronger rates of industrial growth than it had notched in the years 1962–1964, while industrial production in the GDR, Poland, Bulgaria, and Romania remained stable. But, over the course of the 1970s, the rate of industrial growth slowed in every bloc country, recording the lowest rate for 1979 in Poland and Hungary as shown in Table 3.3.

More troubling were the data recording the growth in imports from Western countries (see Table 3.4). The growth in such imports in the years 1971–75 was nothing short of remarkable. Poland tops the list with an average *annual* growth of 40.7% – all on credit – followed by Bulgaria (24.8%), the GDR (20.3%), and Romania (19.5%). Set in the context of the quadrupling of the price of oil in March 1974 and the fact that much of what was manufactured in the bloc could not compete in hard-currency markets, these figures set the stage for a forced but inconsistent belt-tightening across the bloc states. In Romania, the belt-tightening became all too consistent – and ruthless. What the communists understood all too well was that, as long as living standards and real wages improved – if only slightly – as long as the supermarkets had adequate stocks of basic foods, and as long as the most essential foods and other consumer goods could be obtained at very affordable (which is to say subsidized) prices, people would be unlikely to take to the streets in mass protests. The key to achieving this, as will be explained in greater depth both below and in the next chapter, was to take out large loans from Western banks (or import goods on credit) and to subsidize the basic foods and other goods on which the population depended. When these instruments became unsustainable, the communist system as it existed became likewise unsustainable.

There are two more measures of economic failure worth mentioning – real wages and poverty. Table 3.5 shows that the annual growth in real wages in the

TABLE 3.4 Annual Rates of Growth of Total Imports from Western Countries, in %

	1971–75	1976	1977	1978	1979
Bulgaria	24.8	−19.0	5.8	8.3	9.4
Czechoslovakia	13.9	11.7	6.6	6.3	15.3
German Democratic Republic	20.3	28.2	9.8	−1.9	20.6★
Hungary	16.2	−1.9	18.7	19.2	1.6★
Poland	40.7	9.7	6.7	1.9	0.5
Romania	19.5	−4.8	16.7	23.4	N/A

★ = estimate

Source: "The Economics of the CMEA Countries and Yugoslavia at the end of the Decade (1979–1980)", Special issue of *Eastern European Economics*, Vol. 19, No. 4 (Summer 1981) – articles by Friedrich Levcik, Ilse Grosser & Paul Wiedemann, Gabriele Tuitz, Raimund Dietz, Benedykt Askanas, and Gabriel Kramarics.

TABLE 3.5 Annual Rates of Growth of Real Wages & Salaries, 1971–1975

Average annual growth rate, in %

	1971–75	1976	1977	1978	1979
Bulgaria	2.9	0.8	0.4	0.4	
Czechoslovakia	3.4	1.9	1.8	1.4	0.5
German Democratic Republic	3.3	3.5	2.9	3.2	3.5
Hungary	3.3	0.1	3.8	3.1	
Poland	7.2	3.9	2.3	−2.7	1.8
Romania	3.7	5.8	5.5	9	2.1

Wages = nominal for the GDR; real for the other states.

Source: "The Economics of the CMEA Countries and Yugoslavia at the end of the Decade (1979–1980)", Special issue of *Eastern European Economics*, Vol. 19, No. 4 (Summer 1981) – articles by Friedrich Levcik, Ilse Grosser & Paul Wiedemann, Gabriele Tuitz, Raimund Dietz, Benedykt Askanas, and Gabriel Kramarics.

years 1976–1979 was less than 2% in Czechoslovakia and close to zero in Bulgaria, while wages actually shrank in Poland in 1978.

Finally, poverty was becoming a serious problem in Hungary, as well as in Yugoslavia, as shown in the figures in Table 3.6. Moreover, one should assume that at least as many as officially below the poverty line had to live frugally, with little money to spare on small luxuries.

The third phase, 1956–1971

One of the most striking features of the Stalinist era was the abuse of imprisonment and execution for political purposes. But far from delegitimating those who ended up behind bars, imprisonment could be a stepping stone toward leadership. Thus, in Poland, Władysław Gomułka was imprisoned from 1951 to 1954 only to be returned to power in October 1956. In Hungary, János Kádár, likewise spent the

TABLE 3.6 Poverty Levels in Soviet Bloc Countries & Yugoslavia, late 1980s

	% below the poverty line	*Year*
Bulgaria	2	1989
Czechoslovakia	7.3	1988
German Democratic Republic	few if any	1989
Hungary	14–16	1985–89
Poland	2.2	1987
Romania	6	1989
Yugoslavia	25	mid-1980s

Sources: Branko Milanović, "Poverty in Eastern Europe in the Years of Crisis, 1978 to 1987: Poland, Hungary, and Yugoslavia", in *The World Bank Economic Review*, Vol. 5, No. 2 (May 1991), p. 194; Jitka Bartošova and Tomáš Želinský, "The extent of poverty in the Czech & Slovak Republics 15 years after the split", in *Post-Communist Economics*, Vol. 25, No. 1 (2013), p. 120; Branko Milanović, *Income, Inequality, and Poverty during the Transition from Planned to Market Economy* (Washington D.C.: The World Bank, 1998), p. 68; and "Did poverty exist in East Germany (the GDR)", *Quora.com*, at www.quora.com/Did-poverty-exist-in-East-Germany-the-GDR [accessed on 9 January 2022].

years 1951–1954 in prison and, parallel to Gomułka, assumed the leadership post in the Hungarian communist party in October 1956. In Czechoslovakia, Gustáv Husák was sentenced to life imprisonment in 1950 but released from prison in 1960 and would rise to the pinnacle of power by spring 1969. What these cases show so dramatically is that, in the Stalinist years (and, for that matter, also in years to follow), the law was an instrument of power, not of justice. In essence, the system was corrupt at its very core. Corruption served the interests of those manipulating the system for their own purposes, but it corroded and eroded the system from within. If the system would not be reformed, it would inevitably collapse at some point in time. There were, of course, efforts at reform in almost all the countries of East Central Europe at one time or another, but these were focused on economics, not on the system of justice. This, in turn, is why the appearance of dissident voices already by the 1960s but growing in strength in the 1970s and 1980s was politically relevant. In a state characterized by the rule of law (even if not perfect), dissident voices only rarely have the power to reach beyond a small audience, let alone to effect meaningful change. In the United States in the 1960s and 1970s, folk singers Bob Dylan (b. 1941) and Joan Baez (b. 1941) sang protest songs focusing on social justice and on the Vietnam War, but they did not call the American system into question. In the communist world, by contrast, dissidents called the system itself into question.

The implosion of the Stalinist system in Hungary and Poland in 1956 and the consequent emergence of new leaders in those two states, as well as the change of leadership in Bulgaria that same year, were not the cause of the cultural and economic relaxation associated with the political upheaval. Rather, the political upheaval was a manifestation and, in its way, a consequence of the "thaw" which had begun in Bulgaria by 1953[8] and in Hungary in 1953 with the inception of Imre Nagy's first term as prime minister.

The cultural liberalization permitted in Poland at the end of 1956 and in Czechoslovakia belatedly in 1958[9] was not due to any sudden generosity or liberalism on the part of the communist leaders, however. It was the by-product of the weakness of the elites. Once leadership circles in Warsaw and Prague felt they had consolidated their power, they implemented policies of retrenchment. Weakness accounted for Gomułka's willingness in 1956 to accept all of Cardinal Wyszyński's demands, including that the Church would enjoy "complete freedom" for the enrollment of children in religious instruction in elementary and secondary schools, in those cases where parents so desired.[10] Weakness also accounted for the retreat from forced collectivization in Poland and Hungary and for Gomułka's toleration, for the interim, of the spontaneously formed workers' councils which were not beholden to communist authorities and which, in 1957, included an estimated 80,000 members elected by their respective enterprise workers.[11] The concession to the Church regarding religious instruction in the schools was later withdrawn, on the grounds that the content of religious instruction had been found to be in direct contradiction with the contents of classes in history and biology.[12] As for the workers' councils, they were never granted formal autonomy and were later quashed. On the other hand, after October 1956, Polish authorities scotched socialist realism at least temporarily.

In Hungary, in spite of a thaw in cultural policy and the abandonment of forced collectivization, authorities moved swiftly against those suspected of being implicated in the Revolution, investigating at least 35,000 persons, interning approximately 13,000, and executing 221 persons for their involvement in the events of October–November 1956.[13]

Gomułka's Poland

In Poland, October 1956 brought less radical change than in Hungary, when Gomułka returned to power. Now it was "springtime" for Poland, a honeymoon period with Poles in love with Gomułka. One of his first acts, as noted in the previous chapter, was to come to an agreement with Cardinal Stefan Wyszyński, the archbishop of Warsaw, who had been incarcerated in 1953. In elections to the Sejm on 20 January 1957, most of the exponents of Stalinism who had sat in the previous Sejm were not put up for reelection; indeed, of the more than 700 candidates for election (for 459 seats), only 83 had been members of that body in 1952–56.[14] In the economic sphere, there was toleration of limited private enterprise in the period of the Six-Year Plan and, by the end of 1957, the number of privately owned cafés, bars, and restaurants mushroomed. Real incomes grew by 10% during 1956–57 and the provision of basic foods improved. The regime also renounced socialist realism and ended forced collectivization. By mid-1957, more than 80% of the arable land which had been collectivized had returned to private ownership.[15] Workers' councils on the Yugoslav model appeared and were allowed to operate, and in November 1957 Poland's new First Secretary was in Moscow and gave an interview to the Moscow daily *Pravda*, in which he declared that Poland had to take its own separate path to socialism. But the honeymoon eventually came to an end. One important sign came in mid-April 1958, when the 18-month experiment with workers' councils was abruptly terminated. Subsequently, in March 1959, Gomułka removed his political foes from their party posts. Moreover, although he allowed farms to remain largely in private hands, he proved to be, in the main, a fairly orthodox communist. The lesson of the events of 1956, thus, was that the Kremlin would not tolerate any abandoning of communism. But it left open the prospect of reforming communism: the question was what were the permissible limits of reform. This question would be answered in Czechoslovakia in August 1968. Gomułka relaxed the controls in the cultural sphere. Thus, in literature, for example, the works of Western authors including John Steinbeck, William Faulkner, Norman Mailer, Agatha Christie, and T. S. Eliot now appeared in Polish translation. Polish playwrights such as Sławomir Mrożek, novelist Jerzy Andrzejewski, poet Zbigniew Herbert, and the later-famous film-maker Andrzej Wajda also benefited from the new liberalism in cultural policy. In early 1957, Gomułka dismissed the entire editorial board of the party news organ *Trybuna Ludu;* the student newspaper *Po Prostu* was suspended in June and shut down altogether in October 1957. About this time, approximately 200,000 persons were dropped from the party's membership rolls.[16]

Needless to say, Gomułka's liberalization in culture, agriculture, and religious policy was not welcomed by Stalinists. Indeed, Kazimierz Mijal and Wiktor Klosiewicz attacked Gomułka in 1957 for having given up on collectivization and for the rapprochement with the Catholic Church. Mijal and Klosiewicz would later flee to Albania where, in 1966, they set up a shadow Communist Party of Poland with a Maoist coloration.[17] In spite of his purge of Stalinists, by 1959 the First Secretary would restore some old Stalinists to grace and dismissed some of his early supporters from their positions, apparently seeking to construct a Gomułkaist "center".[18] But by the 1960s a new factional grouping was rising in importance, the so-called "Partisans" led by Generals Mieczysław Moczar and Grzegorz Korczyński. In March 1968, Moczar, who was the Minister of Internal Affairs at the time, made a bid for power, stirring up anti-Semitism and blaming the crimes of the Stalinist era on Jewish members of the elite, such as Jakub Berman. Although the campaign, accompanied by violence, started by attacking Jews, it soon expanded to include non-Jews. For a while, Moczar was riding high on the wave of anti-Semitism he had conjured and he was even elected to candidate membership in the Politburo. But as early as July 1968, he lost his post as Minister and, by September 1968, Gomułka was regaining his political strength, in part due to his support for the Soviet invasion of Czechoslovakia (described in more detail in the subsection on Czechoslovakia, below). Gomułka now hit back at those promoting hatred of the country's tiny Jewish minority (fewer than 30,000 Jews at the time). In the meantime, in late January 1968, a theatrical production of the nineteenth-century poet Adam Mickiewicz's saga, *Forefathers' Eve*, one of the great classics of Polish literature, was suppressed because of its animosity toward tsarist Russia. This set off protests by intellectuals and students, culminating in a mass meeting on 8 March, which was attacked by police and armed vigilantes.[19]

By this point, the huge popularity which Gomułka had enjoyed in October 1956 had evaporated, Poles' hopes for a better life had dimmed, and he was increasingly seen, not as a liberal communist, but as a staunch conservative. His rule came to an end in December 1970 after the Politburo decided, on 11 December, to raise the prices of sausages, other meat products, and other consumer goods by anywhere from 12% to 30%. On the following day, hundreds of party functionaries were dispatched to factories and other enterprises to read a letter from the Politburo announcing the price hikes and explaining the economic rationale for this measure. By 14 December, there were protest strikes in Gdańsk, spreading on the following day to Gdingen, Szczecin, and other cities. Workers demanded the retraction of the price hikes and, ominously, the establishment of "real" trade unions, among other things. Rather than listening to the strikers, Gomułka dispatched troops to shoot demonstrators in Gdańsk. Tanks and soldiers were sent onto the streets of a number of cities and, in the course of a week of violence, 45 persons were killed and another roughly 1,200 wounded or injured. The Soviets now demanded Gomułka's resignation and, on 20 December, the party's CC dismissed Gomułka and elected Edward Gierek (1913–2001), the erstwhile party chief in Upper Silesia, to take the reins as First Secretary of the Polish United Workers' Party (PZPR).[20]

Orchestral music, 1954–1971

Control of the cultural sphere was among the highest priorities for the communists wherever they took power. They understood that music, literature, and art always have the potential to be political and were certain that it would be absurd to believe that these cultural spheres can ever be entirely divorced from politics. For Theodor Adorno, the author of *Introduction to the Sociology of Music*,[21] "[m]usic is ideological" and has the power to engender "a false consciousness; transfiguring [us] so as to divert [us] from the banality of existence."[22] Music, art, and literature transport the consumer to another state of consciousness, in which certain values, even if hidden, are nonetheless present. Listening, for example, to Handel's Sarabande in D minor one is inclined to feel that the world is as it should be and that no action is necessary. The perspective and feeling conveyed by the terrifying first movement of Shostakovich's Symphony No. 7 ("Leningrad") is, of course, entirely different; here one hears danger, threat, the challenge to survival itself. The creator of musical works, as with art and literature, can affirm social reality or challenge it, induce emotional responses in listeners/viewers/readers or even, as with military marches, mobilize soldiers for combat. "[A]rt [as well as music and works of fiction] is for Adorno the social enterprise where the thought of freedom is [or has the potential to be] strongest, and therefore the enterprise in which society endangers its own authority."[23] The idea that composers could be allowed to create whatever music occurred to them, regardless of implicit or latent values, regardless of the emotions such music would evoke, without regard for the risks that such music might involve was not something the communists could accept. Music had to be controlled, channeled, and put to use.

In laying down the doctrine of socialist realism, communist authorities had in mind that cultural artifacts – whether musical compositions or works of fiction or painting, sculpture, or films – should be politically useful, supportive of the socialist project. But if conformity was the response for which the authorities hoped, there were also undesired side effects associated with the imposed doctrine – indeed, undesirable from the standpoint of the authorities. These included boredom with the prescribed formulae, apathy, and disgruntlement, sometimes manifesting itself in subtle or overt resistance. But there was an alternative involving neither conscious compliance nor some form of resistance, viz., (attempted) avoidance by choosing to work in a genre to which socialist realism might not seem applicable. This was the choice made by Witold Lutosławski (1913–1994) in the early 1950s. Although he composed some mass songs in the years 1950–52 in spite of himself, he soon set this service aside and, in the years up to 1954 and again in 1958–59, composed songs for children. These met with critical approval and, already on 9 December 1948, he was awarded the Music Prize of the City of Warsaw for some of his early children's songs. However, he could not entirely avoid catering to the authorities' expectations and in 1950 and 1951 received prizes for his mass songs. When, in 1954, he was awarded the Prime Minister's Prize for his children's music, the great composer scarcely knew what to make of this. Obviously, Lutosławski's attempt to avoid any connection with the political objectives of communist cultural policy had failed. In the "thoroughly penetrated" societies of the Soviet bloc of the 1950s, avoidance was at most a chimera.

Lutosławski's First Symphony (completed in 1947) had been suppressed in 1948, at which time he was dismissed from the executive committee of the Union of Polish Composers. His symphony was denounced as an example of "formalism", meaning that it was not politically useful.[24] But in 1959, in the relaxed post-October atmosphere, his symphony was revived and was played again in Warsaw. By then, the atonal and 12-tone technique of Anton Webern (1883–1945) was influencing Polish composers, including Lutosławski. Among his other early works were his *Musique Funèbre* from 1958 and his Second Symphony, composed in the years 1965–67. Not limited to concert music, Lutosławski also dabbled in popular music in the late 1950s and early 1960s, writing songs that became hits with the general public.[25]

Krzysztof Penderecki (1933–2020), 20 years younger than Lutosławski, burst onto the global music stage in 1960 with his *Threnody for the Victims of Hiroshima*. Like other early works of Penderecki's, *Threnody* reflects the influence of Luigi Nono, Pierre Boulez, Karlheinz Stockhausen, Iannis Xenakis, and above all the American composer John Cage (1912–1992). This was followed by *De Natura Sonoris I* (1966) and his *St. Luke's Passion* (also composed in 1966). Penderecki came onto the scene, thus, after socialist realism was largely defunct – at least in Poland.

Born the same year as Penderecki, Henryk Górecki (1933–2010) is best known for his Third Symphony, composed in 1976. Subtitled "Symphony of Lamentation

Songs", the piece was scored for soprano and orchestra. In 1992, American and British radio stations started playing the Elektra Nonesuch recording of the Third Symphony by the London Sinfonietta with American singer Dawn Upshaw. Soon Górecki's symphony succeeded in winning devotees not only among aficionados of classical music but also among people with no prior familiarity with concert music. Whatever else may be said about this work, it is clear that it touched and has continued to touch many listeners very deeply. Nonetheless, his earlier compositions, dating from the second half of the 1950s, reflected the influence above all of Webern, Stockhausen, and Olivier Messiaen. But, beginning in 1963, he began looking for simplicity in melodic lines and turning to medieval or religious themes for inspiration. Among his works from the years 1956–71, one may list: *Genesis I and II* (1962), *Old Polish Music* (1967–69), *Ad Matrem* (1971) for soprano, mixed choir, and orchestra, and *Two Sacred Songs* (also from 1971), for solo baritone and orchestra.

Novelists, 1954–1979

Among Polish writers of the second half of the twentieth century, perhaps the best known is Czesław Miłosz (1911–2004), whose book, *The Captive Mind*, completed in 1953, is a hybrid of fiction and sociology, offering a searing critique of the Stalinist system of that day and how it affected people.[26] That book was written while Miłosz was in France, as he had fled Poland after the communists had taken power in his native country. But *The Captive Mind* notwithstanding, Miłosz was best known in Poland as a poet and translator; his story and other accomplishments will not be recounted here. This section takes note of three novelists: Tadeusz Konwicki (1926–2015), Kazimierz Brandys (1916–2000), and Stanisław Lem (1921–2006).

Konwicki and Brandys both started their post-war careers at the cultural journal *Nowa Kultura:* Konwicki served as editor of the journal from 1950 to 1957, while Brandys was a member of the editorial staff. Konwicki tried to accommodate the requirement to respect the doctrine of socialist realism and his first novel to be published, *Władza* [Power], appearing in 1954, exemplified socialist realism. Over time he became alienated from that doctrine and stopped writing for nearly three years. When he once more took up his pen, he had freed himself from socialist realism. Convinced that the communist party was contributing to an erosion of moral values, he resigned his party membership in 1966.[27] Other writers – including Brandys, Adam Ważyk (1905–1982), and Jerzy Andrzejewski (1909–1983) – traveled the same path, initially supporting the communist order but later coming to view it as grounded in falsity. Konwicki's major work, *Mała Apokalypsa* [A Minor Apocalypse] was published in 1979. Rather than submit it to the censorship office for clearance, Konwicki published the novel in the émigré quarterly *Zapis*, from which it was translated into at least 13 languages. Konwicki was skilled at exposing the absurdities of communism, and his *Apocalypse* portrayed Polish people in the later years Edward Gierek was in charge as "cynical, confused, poverty-ridden, ailing, and opportunist."[28] In Konwicki's words, "There are no good or evil people . . . It is night. A night of indifference, apathy, chaos."[29]

Kazimierz Brandys's first major work, *Miasto niepokonana* [Invincible City] appeared in 1946 and won two literary prizes for its author. In subsequent writing, Brandys embraced socrealism, as it was sometimes abbreviated. In his 1951 novel, *Człowiek nie umiera* [Man Doesn't Die], he derided people who were hostile to communism.[30] His next novel, *Obywatele* [Citizens] was published in 1954 but, in spite of its ostensible adherence to socrealism, critics thought that it was lacking in positive proletarian figures, possibly tending also to sarcasm. By the mid-1950s, Brandys, like other aforementioned literati, was becoming alienated from the regime's cultural policy. Then, in January 1956, the journal *Twórczość* [Creativity] published a short story in which Brandys showed party stalwarts pushing a theatrical group to perform a piece of socialist realist rubbish, resulting in the group breaking up.[31] This was followed by *Matka Królów* [translated under the title, Sons and Comrades], published in 1957, considered by some to be his greatest work. The novel exposes the falsehood and hypocrisy of Poland's communists. The cultural thaw came to an end even before the end of 1957, as the party moved to suppress "revisionist" voices, purging 200,000 persons from the party.[32] In the course of 1959, there were even reaffirmations on the part of authorities of the continued validity of socialist realism.[33]

By contrast with Konwicki and Brandys, Stanisław Lem made his name (and his fortune) as a science-fiction writer. His best known work is *Solaris*,[34] published in 1961 and turned into a film by Andrei Tarkovsky in 1972. Given the proclivities of Stalinism, Lem's early sci-fi writings, like the sci-fi works of other Polish writers during 1948–56, were characterized by irrepressible optimism. Lem's novel, *Hospital of the Transfiguration*, completed in 1948 when he was only 27 years old, was written roughly in the spirit of socialist realism; it was published in 1956. After this, Lem had little use for socialist realism and would refer to the years 1948–56 as a time of "mild brainwashing" and, as he also put it, "devoid of any value."[35]

His 1959 novel, *Eden*, explored the possibility of human empathy with extraterrestrials and of people being able to understand their thoughts. Two years later saw the publication of *Solaris*, which tells the story of a mission to a distant planet inhabited only by a highly intelligent, giant ocean able to read the minds of the crew members. The ocean also conjures "Phi-creatures", who are effectively *Doppelgänger* of people from the past of the respective crew members, in each case provoking guilt.[36] Carl Tighe has suggested that

> Virtually all Lem's novels may be read as parables about what happens to society and people when channels of communication are blocked, about the difficulty of making a revolutionary society or fundamentally changing human nature by social and political engineering . . . As such, his novels are profoundly humanistic, [offering] a coded criticism of the kind of society that developed under Stalin and a plea for a socialism of gradual change.[37]

Science fiction was, in a sense, an ideal vehicle for political satire and insidious criticism of the system. Protected by the sheer scope of his fantasy, by the employment of extraterrestrials who are, after all, not human, and by his phenomenal popularity both inside and outside Poland, Lem was able to raise serious questions without risk of negative repercussions.

Women and gender equality, 1955–74

Although the Polish constitution of 1952 guaranteed equal rights to women in public life, in culture, in access to education, social security, rest and recreation, and established the principle of equal pay for equal work, in practice attaining something that might pass for substantive equality proved harder to realize. On the positive side, the proportion of women employed in industry rose from 30.2% in 1955 to 40.0% in 1974, and in construction, forestry, and transportation & communications from 12.4% to 17.6%, 6–4% to 18.7%, and 15.2% to 24.4% respectively. In addition, women dominated in the trade sector (51.4% in 1955, 73.1% in 1974), education, science, and culture (56.6%, 64.3%), health care and social services (76.7%, 81.2%), and financial institutions (57.0% in 1955, 79.7% in 1974).[38] Less impressive were the proportions of women in positions of authority; for example, in 1964 and again in 1968, women accounted for 0.5% of directors of industrial enterprises and less than 5% of deputy directors.[39] Moreover, in the years 1952–74, the proportion of women in the Sejm varied between 4% and 17%.[40]

Authorities were conflicted about the question of abortion. On the one hand, keeping abortion illegal was supportive of the regime's plans for a robust birthrate and was welcome to the Catholic Church. On the other hand, while large families had been promoted in the Stalinist years, by 1956 the authorities had come to the conclusion that the presence of a large number of children in a family contributed to poverty.[41] Under legislation passed in 1932, abortion had been available only when continuation of the pregnancy endangered the woman's health or when the pregnancy was due to incest or rape. In 1948, the Ministry of Health had started to demand that women seeking an abortion obtain permission from a state-appointed commission. The result was that women resorted to illegal abortions, thus circumventing the regulation; it has been estimated that there were no fewer than 300,000 illegal abortions per year prior to passage of the modest liberalization of access to abortion in 1956.[42] The law passed in April 1956 allowed women to obtain abortions when they faced "exceptionally difficult life conditions"; in practice, this wording was interpreted to limit access to the procedure to "mothers of many children who were already living in poverty."[43] Subsequently, in December 1959, the Ministry of Health deprived physicians of control over a woman's recourse to an abortion and assigned this right to women.

Marital instability was also a factor and authorities became worried when, in 1956, the rate of divorce rose to 50 per thousand. Domestic violence was a major problem for family life and underlying wife-beating was frequently male alcoholism.[44] Writing in 1978, Piotr Kryczka argued that "[a]lcoholism is without any doubt the Number One problem in Poland . . . What is typical is the relatively large intake of alcohol at one sitting; moreover, it is in most cases high-percentage alcohol (vodka), which leads to intoxication."[45] Moreover, rates of alcoholism rose in the 1960s and 1970s, as a result of rapid urbanization and the accompanying disruption of familial and social connections.

The Catholic Church

The release of Cardinal Wyszyński from detention in conjunction with the launch of Gomułka's revived leadership of the PZPR initiated a new era in Church-state relations in which the Church no longer had to fear the incarceration of her bishops and in which the bishops were able to be more outspoken on issues of concern to them. While still in detention, Wyszyński began to formulate a plan for a decade-long Great Novena of the Millennium to celebrate 1,000 years of Christianity in Poland, 966–1966. The Novena was launched in 1957, with a copy of the Black Madonna of Częstochowa being carried from parish to parish. As it arrived in each parish, there would be sermons, speeches, and celebrations. The Great Novena would culminate in a renewal, now by the Polish nation, of the vows originally made by King Jan Kazimierz in 1656.[46]

The dramatic demonstration of the loyalty of Poles to the Church in the course of the Novena as well as in well-attended pilgrimages was profoundly unsettling to the authorities, who did their best to obstruct the Novena, even confiscating the image of the Black Madonna at one point. In 1961, five years into the Novena, the regime backtracked on one of Gomułka's concessions to the Church, passing a law that banned religious instruction in the schools. This meant that, from that point forward, catechism had to be taught, if at all, after school hours. The following year, party officials warned, in a confidential report, that the Novena was undermining the party's effort to erode Catholicism.[47] In 1965, before the Great Novena had come to an end, Polish bishops attending the Second Vatican Council sent a conciliatory letter to the German Episcopate, extending an invitation to German bishops to come to Poland for the millennial celebrations the following year. The letter included a message of forgiveness for the suffering the Third Reich had inflicted on Poland (among other European countries) during the Second World War. The communist authorities were outraged, feeling that the Church had usurped the state's prerogative to forgive or not to forgive.[48] As for the Vatican's recognition of the new national borders, it was only in 1964 that the Holy See appointed a Pole (Edmund Nowicki) to head the archdiocese of Gdańsk upon the death of the previous incumbent, Karl Maria Splett, on 5 March 1964.[49] And it was only in June 1972 that the Vatican accepted that ecclesiastical administration in Poland's western and northern provinces should be entrusted to Polish clerics.[50]

In the meantime, Church-state relations deteriorated in the years of the Novena and, when Cardinal Wyszyński wanted to attend a Synod of Bishops in Rome, scheduled to start on 29 September 1967, the authorities refused to grant him a passport, as *Życie Warszawy* explained, "because of his unfriendly and disloyal attitude toward the Polish state."[51] In fact, the Cardinal had been banned from traveling outside Poland since 1965; the ban was lifted only in 1968, allowing Wyszyński to meet with the pope. The decade ended with Wyszyński revisiting the theme of the communists' confiscation of Church properties in the recovered territories (the land transferred from Germany to Poland at the end of World War Two). The authorities replied that the properties in question could be returned after West Germany signed a treaty with Poland, giving up any claim to those lands.[52]

Toward Czechoslovakia's liberal interlude

By the early 1960s, Novotný was increasingly confronted by problems in three areas: economic disarray; growing pressure for the rehabilitation of innocent persons condemned in the show trials of the early 1950s; and increasing restiveness among intellectuals specifically and Slovaks generally. The economy was, in some ways, the most urgent problem. After an overall doubling of the GNP between 1948 and 1957, economic growth started to decline. The heart of the problem was that economic planning had been based on the principles of emphasizing *extensive* growth, in blind imitation of the Soviet experience, whereas, given Czechoslovakia's level of development even as of 1945, a program balancing extensive and intensive growth would have been more suitable. In 1963, the Czechoslovak economy actually declined in absolute terms, forcing the political elite to agree to consider economic reform. Draft principles of economic reform were drawn up and made public in 1964; in early 1965, they were accepted by the party's Central Committee. But Nototný and his closest associates remained deeply hostile to some of the liberalizing elements in the New Economic Model, and therefore opted for a strategy of "selective implementation of less substantial remedies, not allowing for a thorough structural and functional transformation – without which the success of NEM was beyond reach."[53] By the end of 1967, the economy was in utter disarray and hostility to the system was being openly expressed.

The show trials of the early 1950s were another problem. The Slovaks, in particular, remained bitter about the decapitation of their party, and finally, under unrelenting pressure from Slovak communists, Novotný appointed a committee, in August 1962, to review all the trials conducted during the years 1949–54, including the trials of Gustáv Husák, Laco Novomeský, and (posthumously) Vladimír Clementis. Chaired by CC Secretary Drahomir Kolder, the commission submitted its preliminary report to the CC on 27 November 1962 and presented its final report on 3–4 April 1963. As with the preliminary report, the final report was reviewed by the Presidium of the CC before it was shared with the CC as a whole. The purpose of the review was to tone down some of the commission's findings. But even in its expurgated version, the report made it obvious that the purge trials of the 1950s had been conducted in the spirit of contempt for truth, morality, and legality. The report also identified those persons who were primarily responsible for the trials and called for them to be expelled from the Central Committee. This recommendation was ignored.[54] Shortly after the final report was delivered, even before the end of the month, the CC Presidium of the Slovak party convened and agreed to dismiss Karol Bacílek as First Secretary of the Slovak Communist Party (KSS). Alexander Dubček (1921–1992) was anointed as his successor.[55] Interestingly enough, Dubček had served on the Kolder Commission and was familiar with evidence implicating Novotný for his role in the trials of Slánský and others in the 1950s.[56] The commission's report came before the Supreme Court of Czechoslovakia which, on 22 August 1963, announced that it had completed its review of the political trials and that all of those convicted had been innocent![57] The following month, many veteran communists in the upper echelons of the party were dismissed. But Novotný stayed at the helm; he was reelected President of Czechoslovakia on 12 November 1964 and was reconfirmed as KSČ First Secretary at the Thirteenth Party Congress (31 May–4 June 1966).

In the meantime, there were political pressures, economic pressures, and new thinking in the cultural sphere. Politically, Soviet admissions of Stalin's tyranny at the 20th CPSU Congress in February 1956 stunned Czechoslovak leaders, as it did other Soviet bloc leaders.[58] In 1962, the monument to Stalin in downtown Prague was demolished and various streets, squares, and even a mountain named for him were renamed. Textbooks were reworked to remove praise for the deceased Soviet dictator. The economy represented a challenge in its own right; specifically, in 1963, the GNP recorded a decline of 2%. The idea was now put forward by Ota Šik and other economists to reintroduce elements of a free market in a limited way: Presidium members Oldřich Černik and Lubomir Štrougal declared themselves in favor of economic reform.[59] The problem, in a nutshell, was that adopting the Stalinist model for economic development had resulted in what Otto Ulč has called "the Great Leap Backward".[60] Šik proposed bold reform but conservatives were firmly opposed.

Sessions of the Central Committee at the end of October 1967, late December 1967, and early January 1968 provided the stage for vigorous battles between Novotný's opponents and adherents within the party. Already in October, Alexander Dubček, first secretary of the Slovak Communist Party since April 1963, delivered a comprehensive critique of party procedures under Novotný. Soviet General Secretary Leonid Brezhnev made a one-day visit to Prague on 8 December – a sure sign of the seriousness with which the Soviets viewed the intra-party dissension in Czechoslovakia. Finally, on 4 January 1968, Novotný was compelled to resign as First Secretary of the party, and Dubček was approved as his successor the following day.[61]

Novotný's resignation represented the victory of the reformers within the party – a diverse group which included communist veterans František Kriegel and František Vodsloň, economist Ota Šik, ideologist Václav Slavik, Moravian leader Josef Špaček, and intellectual Eduard Goldstücker. As early as February 1968, a party committee was appointed to hammer out a new party program. Subsequently, in March, there was a subtle, but all the same dramatic, shift in the political climate, as the reform movement ceased to be a purely internal party affair and began to engage large sectors of the public as well. By mid-March, censorship of the press had been virtually eliminated and prominent periodicals including the party news organ *Rudé právo*, the youth dailies *Mladá fronta* and *Smena*, the trade union newspaper *Práce*, and the theoretical journal *Nová mysl* were publishing articles reflecting a new freedom of expression.[62] On 22 March 1968, Novotný, who had still retained the post of President of the Republic, was eased out of this position as well, and the popular general, Ludvík Svoboda, became president.

On 5 April 1968, a plenary session of the Central Committee adopted an important document, entitled "The Action Program of the Communist Party of Czechoslovakia", drawn up by a commission chaired by Kolder. In a breach with normal protocol, the Action Program was not cleared in advance with the Soviets, although drafts found their way to the Kremlin, thanks to "helpful" conservatives in the Czechoslovak Communist Party.[63] The Soviets called a multilateral meeting for 23 March, to be held in Dresden. Romania, whose president, Ceaușescu, was showing sympathy for Prague's sudden independence, was pointedly not invited to attend. The Dresden meeting criticized Dubček's emerging policy and spoke of the need to strengthen the role of the political consultation committee of the Warsaw Treaty Organization (WTO), as a way of reining in wayward political tendencies.[64] With writers in Czechoslovakia already enjoying more liberty, CPSU General Secretary Brezhnev warned Dubček that the Hungarian "counterrevolution" in 1956 had started with small groups of writers.[65] Party secretaries from Soviet republics in the Western regions of the USSR, where the repercussions of the Prague Spring were already being felt, tended to favor military action; party secretaries from Central Asia, whose republics were unaffected by the new climate in Czechoslovakia, preferred to continue negotiations.[66] The Action Program called for an end to extralegal measures by the police, demanded the complete overhaul of the economic system to include pricing policies and the extension of operational autonomy to enterprises, and sought to limit the role of the government and party to setting general economic policy, formulating long-range plans, and protecting consumers' interests.[67] The Action Program called for more assistance to Czechoslovakia's small private sector in agriculture, and for a concerted strategy to correct Slovakia's economic lag behind the Czech lands.[68] The program confirmed Czechoslovakia's adherence to the Warsaw pact and reaffirmed the country's commitment to a socialist path (with the party trying to avoid the error committed by Imre Nagy in Hungary) but proposed to give industrial enterprises and agricultural cooperatives more freedom in choosing their markets. The program affirmed the right of travel abroad, the rights of national minorities, especially Slovaks, and the importance of free inquiry in the social sciences.[69]

As H. Gordon Skilling has pointed out, ". . . the Action Program did not envisage a system of free political competition among independent parties and other organizations but a kind of political partnership in which the primacy of the Communist Party would have to be recognized by all other participants."[70] At the same time, provisions in the program pledging to establish freedom of assembly, freedom of expression, and freedom to set up and take part in voluntary organizations made it obvious that the Czechoslovak model – sometimes called "socialism with a human face" – constituted a direct threat to the model of socialism propounded by the Soviet Union. Moreover, as Dubček recalled in his memoirs, "The program declared an end to dictatorial, sectarian, and bureaucratic ways [and] . . . proclaimed a return to freedom of the press."[71]

The Action Program sanctioned the expression of alternative opinions within the party as well as the advocacy of alternative policy initiatives – innovations daringly at variance with the Soviet model.[72] The Action Program further proposed to relieve trade unions of responsibility to implement economic directives of the party, but still expected them to educate workers and orient them "toward a positive solution of the problems of socialist construction."[73] About this time, the censorship mechanism ceased to function, thus permitting a much freer discussion of ideas in the press. The Action Program was published on 10 April 1968. A week later, Brezhnev denounced it, claiming that it aimed at restoring capitalism.[74]

A tentative repluralization now got underway, with various independent interest groups emerging. For example, by mid-June 1968, some 250,000 persons had joined a new and independent farmers' union. Demands were raised for the independence of the mass organizations. Within the youth organization, demands were heard for the restitution of civil freedoms, the reestablishment of the Constitutional Court, separation of powers, an inquest into the death of Jan Masaryk (1886–1948), the son of Tomáš Masaryk, whose dead body had been found in the courtyard of the Foreign Ministry below his bathroom window on 10 March 1948. New associations took shape, such as Club 231, a club for persons convicted under Article 231 of the penal code and dedicated to working for the rehabilitation of all purge victims, and the Club for Committed Non-Party Members, founded on 5 April by 144 persons (chiefly members of the Czechoslovak Academy of Sciences) and committed to the defense of individual sovereignty. Other groups also appeared, promoting free discussion, human rights, independence in creative writing, and so forth. Meanwhile, the censors continued to come to their offices, receive their pay, and read and cross out whatever they wished. But their crossings out were ignored; there continued to be, thus, a censorship office, but there was no censorship. In fact, on 26 June, the abolition of censorship was made official. The next day, four Czech newspapers published Ludvík Vaculík's "Two Thousand Words", which called on citizens to become directly involved in pushing democratization forward, establishing "watchdog" committees across Czechoslovakia.[75] In response, the communist party hastily convened to discuss Vaculík's text. The Soviets interpreted Vaculík's text as proof of "counterrevolutionary" tendencies. Then, on 1 July 1968, a network of workers' councils at the factory level came into being.

In any case, the Czechoslovak party leadership was aware that it was testing the limits of Soviet tolerance and thus reiterated several times that Czechoslovakia would remain communist and would remain a member of the Warsaw Pact, but this experiment with socialism started to be called "socialism with a human face" – a term which suggested that the form of socialism practised in the Soviet Union might be "socialism with an animal face". Dubček underlined his government's commitment to a socialist program and pointedly reassured Moscow about

Czechoslovakia's loyalty to the Warsaw Pact. Furthermore, as a token of good will, the Czechoslovak leadership even proposed in May that the next Warsaw Pact maneuvers be held on Czechoslovak soil.

Even so, the Kremlin became steadily more concerned about the developments in Czechoslovakia, which were quickly generating an alternative, and potentially infectious, political model. The main problem for the Soviets, thus, was that the Czechoslovak model of reform communism, which was already exciting a response in Ukraine, might destabilize the bloc, igniting – to borrow a famous phrase from Hegel – "a bacchanalian revel in which no member would be sober." In mid-July 1968, leaders of the USSR, the GDR, Poland, Hungary, and Bulgaria – but again not of Romania – met in Warsaw and issued a letter to the KSČ leadership, demanding an immediate reversal of the reform program. The Czechoslovak party leadership made some token gestures but neither those gestures nor direct negotiations between the Soviets and the Czechoslovaks at the border town of Čierna-nad-Tisou satisfied the Kremlin.

Eventually, in mid-August, a decision was taken to send in armed forces of the Warsaw Pact. Within Czechoslovakia, a small group of pro-Soviet communists began to plot to establish a "revolutionary" government with Soviet help. It was this group that asked the Soviets to schedule their planned invasion for the night of 20/21 August 1968, to follow on a KSČ Presidum meeting set for 20 August.[76] The conspirators planned to remove Dubček, Josef Smrkovský, František Kriegel, and others from their positions and recruit journalists at the party news organ *Rudé právo* as well as 20–30 broadcast journalists to endorse the conservative takeover. Meanwhile, the invasion went ahead and, in the night of 20/21 August 1968, 7,500 tanks and more than 1,000 aircraft poured into Czechoslovakia, with Soviet armed forces accompanied by small contingents from the GDR, Poland, Hungary, and Bulgaria. The conservative conspiracy collapsed, both because of dogged opposition in the Presidium to the proposed takeover and because, unknown to the conspirators, there was more than one radio station in Prague. Lacking a collaborationist government in place, the Soviets now kidnaped leading figures of the Czechoslovak Communist Party and brought them to the Soviet Union, where grueling negotiations started, under conditions of captivity. Finally, they were returned to Czechoslovakia, so that they could begin to dismantle their reforms. In April 1969, Dubček was replaced by Gustáv Husák (1913–1991), by then a high-ranking Slovak communist. Dubček was packed off to Turkey, where he served as Czechoslovak ambassador until 1970. With this, the reformist option was closed, not just in Czechoslovakia, but throughout the Soviet bloc.

The cultural sphere – films and art

Finally, in the cultural sphere there was what one may call – using the term rather loosely – a cultural renaissance centered in, but not limited to, Slovakia. Already in the second half of the 1950s, writers and pictorial artists were ignoring the strictures of socialist realism; in the art world, a major taboo was defied when some artists embraced abstract art. Western writings which had previously been banned now appeared in Slovak translation, and various famous people, including French philosopher Jean-Paul Sartre, American poet Allen Ginsberg, and French philosopher Roger Garaudy visited Bratislava in the years 1963–65. Moreover, by 1963, Slovak writers, intellectuals, activists in the youth organizations, and even party functionaries were becoming steadily more vocal, subjecting the entire system to severe criticism, demanding a more fair-minded representation of Tomáš Masaryk and writer Franz Kafka (1883–1924), bemoaning the lack of contact with the West, and demanding a lifting of state censorship.[77] Kafka's novel, *The Trial* – which had been proscribed since the days of Gottwald – was allowed to make a reappearance and an edition of 10,000 copies was sold out in Prague on the day it was published. One could speak of a Kafka revival now and this had a profound effect on the literary scene, especially in the prose of Fuks and Hrabal'. The Kafka revival also made a subtle contribution to the politics of reform, by establishing an ideal lying outside the framework of socialist realism.

The 1960s were also an exciting time in Czechoslovak film. One of the first films of this decade was the 1961 film *Witchhammer*, directed by Otakar Vávra. The plot is set in the late seventeenth century and shows religious zealots burning a supposed witch at the stake. The film could pass censorship because it portrayed Christian religion in a negative light. However, Lenka Řezníková has suggested that the director intended the film to serve as a metaphor for Czechoslovakia's political trials of the 1950s which, like the witch trials of the eighteenth century, involved denunciations of the innocent, forced confessions, and in some cases execution.[78] Among the best known films from this period outside the Czech Republic and Slovakia today are Karel Zeman's *The Fabulous Baron Munchausen* (1961) and Jiří Menzel's *Closely Watched Trains*, based on a novel by Bohumil Hrabal. Zeman combined animation, puppets, and actors to achieve his effects. *Baron Munchausen*, which recounts the tall tales of a noble of fine breeding and immense imagination who could ride a cannonball to inspect enemy fortifications, catching another cannonball to return back to give his report, and single-handedly defeat a Turkish army, won awards at Cannes and Locarno. Zeman's films are said to have influenced Terry Gilliam and Tim Burton.[79] *Closely Watched Trains* is the story of an innocent young apprentice railway worker who falls in love with the train's conductress. His hope for romance does not go well, but he redeems himself by blowing up a Nazi ammunition train. The film won an Oscar.[80]

While *Baron Munchausen* and *Closely Watched Trains* were not controversial, there were other films which did not make it past the censors. Among these were Miloš Forman's *The Firemen's Ball* (1967), Jan Němec's *The Party and the Guests* (1966), and Jan Švankmajer's films *The Flat* (1968) and *The Garden* (1968). Among Czechoslovak films from the 1960s which have been judged remarkable, perhaps significant, are two of Jaromil Jireš's films: *The Joke* (1968), an adaptation of Milan Kundera's novel of the same name, and the surrealist *Valerie and Her Week of Wonders* (1969).[81]

The mid-1950s also proved to be a turning point for pictorial art. Prior to 1948, the Czech art scene was noted for a style known as Cubo-Expressionism, a distinctly Czech blend of cubism and expressionism.[82] A few months after the February 1948 seizure of power, Gottwald met with artists to inform them of the guidelines they would be expected to follow. Avant-garde artists, such as those who had been painting in the Cubo-Expressionist style, found their creations branded as "formalist" and banned from public display. But in 1955, art historian Jaromír Neumann distanced himself from socialist realism, and was soon supported in this by Jiří Kotalík, a fellow art historian who had served in the early 1950s on the editorial board of the official art journal, *The Visual Arts*. That same year, *The Visual Arts* published more reproductions of Western art than of works by artists working in the bloc. "In 1957, for the first time since the Communist take-over of 1948, the works of the Czech Modernist avant-garde were publicly exhibited."[83] Obviously, in the late 1950s, the editors of *The Visual Arts* no longer endorsed socialist realism as the sole acceptable style.

The writers

In 1958, Josef Škvorecký's novel *Zbabělci* [The Cowards] appeared. Not only was the novel free of any traces of socialist realism, but the novel expressly violated a well-understood norm by offering a less than flattering account of the role of the Red Army in Czechoslovakia in 1945 and the activity of communist partisans during the war. The communist authorities punished both the author and the publisher, and confiscated all copies of the book. After some modifications, the book was allowed to reappear in 1963.[84]

Nor was Švorecký the only writer to give communist authorities headaches. In April 1963, the Slovak Writers' Union held a Congress. This was followed by a Congress of Slovak Journalists the following month. At the Writers' Congress, Laco Novomeský, by now politically rehabilitated, demanded the posthumous rehabilitation of his friend Vlado Clementis, while others condemned the damage inflicted on Slovak literature by baseless accusations of bourgeois nationalism which had been levied against Slovak writers such as Novomeský. Miro Hysko, a lecturer at the School of Journalism in Bratislava, addressed the Journalists' Congress, likewise responding to earlier charges of bourgeois nationalism which, he said, had been injurious to Czech-Slovak relations. Hysko went further, defending the right of journalists to criticize leading figures in the party. In the event, the party retreated: in December 1963, the Central Committee of the Czechoslovak Communist Party admitted that earlier charges of Slovak nationalism had no foundation and fully exonerated Novomeský and Husák.[85]

In September 1963, the cultural periodicals *Literární noviny, Plamen, Host do domu,* and *Kulturný život* took up the cause of cultural de-Stalinization. In 1964, Václav Havel brought out his first play, *The Garden Party*, in which he wanted to expose "the senselessness and inhumanity of life."[86] This was followed, two years later, by *The Memorandum*, which critiqued bureaucratic nonsense. Havel's third play, *The Increased Difficulty of Concentration* was premiered in April 1968. The play features a talking machine that throws out nonsensical questions such as "Which is your favorite tunnel?" and "How many times a year do you air the square?"[87]

In 1966, Ludvík Vaculík's novel *The Hatchet* was published, communicating the message that communist authorities could not understand rural people, let alone their hostility to Marxism-Leninism. Then came the publication, in 1967, of Milan Kundera's first novel, *The Joke*.[88] In this tale, a student and convinced communist sent a postcard to his girlfriend in which he jokingly wrote that he was a Trotskyite; the authorities did not appreciate the humor and packed the unwitting student off to an army penal unit. The (unintended) consequence of the authorities' harsh over-reaction was that the student was disabused of his earlier communist commitment.

It was about this time that the Fourth Congress of Writers was held (27–29 June 1967). Jiří Hendrych, member of the KSČ Secretariat, inflamed the writers in attendance, by accusing some of them of political mistakes and characterizing at least some of them as reactionaries. When Vaculík took the podium, he replied to Hendrych by accusing the communists of having failed to solve any of the country's problems – in essence, of having proven themselves useless. Hendrych had the last word at the Congress and used his time to denounce most of the speakers and, in the first place, Vaculík for trying to spread "views contrary to the interests of the people."[89] The party now set out to punish Vaculík, Havel, and two other writers, by ordering the cancelation of their election to the Central Committee of the Writers' Union. *Literární noviny*, the official organ of the Writers' Union, was prevented from printing any of the writers' speeches at the congress and was subsequently transferred from the control of the Writers' Union to the Ministry of Culture. On 22 February 1968, a new literary review, *Literární listy*, was launched. This was the periodical that published Vaculík's incendiary "Manifesto of Two Thousand Words" on 27 June 1968.

Gender equality

The Constitution passed on 11 July 1960 followed the model adopted throughout the Soviet bloc and was largely similar, in its provisions for women and the family, to its 1948 predecessor. There were, however, two differences. First, the stipulation in 1948 regarding "systematic measures in the interest of the increase of the population" had no counterpart in the 1960 Constitution. Second, the later document added a reference to women's "equal status . . . in public activity."[90] In fact, as Alena Heitlinger has noted, "after 1952, for a period of 15 years, women had no democratic representation in the political system of Czechoslovak society, because their organisation did not really exist."[91] Article 20 of the 1960 Constitution may have figured as a first step toward remedying this situation. But it was only in the course of November 1966-March 1967 that the Czechoslovak Union of Women (CUW) emerged, holding its national founding Congress on 5 July 1967. Meanwhile, women's share in the National Assembly rose from the 12% notched in 1948–54 to 22.66% in 1960–64, only to slip to 19.66% in the 1964–68 sessions.[92]

Shortly after seizing power, communist authorities set up an organization for women in order to mobilize women for specific goals determined by the regime, but the organization also served as an advocate on behalf of women to the authorities. One of the regime's central objectives, where women were concerned, was to encourage women to bear and raise children, although the regime also wanted more women to enter the labor force. After the authorities announced that the "woman question" in Czechoslovakia had been solved and dissolved the organization for women,[93] Marie Růžičková, Secretary of the Czech Trade Union Council, revisited this claim in 1974 and asserted that, on the contrary, "it cannot be assumed that the problems of women will be solved automatically with the development of socialist society."[94]

In terms of women's participation in the labor force and representation in positions of authority, Czechoslovakia again followed a common blueprint. Thus, although the proportion of women in the labor force rose steadily from 37.8% in 1948 to 41.8% in 1956, and to 47.0% in 1971, the number of women who were able to attain managerial positions in the economy remained modest. In 1966, only 1.6% of directors in industry, construction, and traffic were women, alongside 2.4% of technical specialists and 12.4% of managers in construction and civil engineering. Women did somewhat better in public administration and education, accounting for 30.1% of supervisors in communal administration, 27.8% of managers in media outlets, 11.9% of judges and public prosecutors, and 9.0% of members of the Academy of Sciences, professors, and assistant professors.[95]

The picture was much the same in the party-state apparatus. In 1949, women comprised 33% of the membership of the newly merged party but their proportion subsequently slipped and remained roughly stable at 27% during the 1950s and 1960s. In the years 1954–66, between 10.0% and 11.3% of full members of the party's Central Committee were women, dipping to 6.9% in 1971. In the National Assembly, women accounted for less than 20% of deputies in the early 1960s.[96] Finally, in the years 1959–70, Czechoslovak women earned almost exactly two-thirds of what men were earning.[97]

Shortly after the inception of the Prague Spring, the leadership of the CUW resigned (on 10–11 April 1968). Subsequently, at a plenary session held on 26–27 June 1968, the CUW Central Committee adopted its own Action Program, devoted to women's interests. Enthusiasm for this institution grew and, by January 1969, the CUW had 300,000 members, about twice as many as 12 months earlier. After the changing of the guard at the top of the party, the CUW claimed (in May 1969) to be an "independent organization"; this claim was condemned as "reactionary".[98]

The Catholic Church

The Catholic Church remained the largest single religious denomination in communist-ruled Czechoslovakia and, by that virtue, was targeted by the regime for infiltration by informers, subversion, and, to the extent possible, control and instrumentalization. The so-called Patriotic Priests, consisting of clergy prepared to adopt a friendly posture vis-à-vis the regime, was first called the Peace Committee of the Catholic Clergy in Czechoslovakia and then, in late 1966, the name was modified to the Peace Movement of the Catholic Clergy. It was headed by the defrocked ex-priest Josef Plojhar (1902–1981). Under the pressure of liberalizing trends, the movement was shut down during the Prague Spring.[99] In the religious sphere, the party authorized the relegalization on 13 June 1968 of the Greek Catholic Church and the Old Catholic Church, both of which had been banned after the February 1948 coup. This move came as a result of persistent agitation by Greek (or Eastern-Rite) Catholics, a spate of violence between March and June 1968 in which Greek Catholics seized 63 parish churches from the Orthodox Church and forcibly evicted seven Orthodox priests from their parish residences, and the public support for relegalization given by František Tomášek, apostolic administrator of the Roman Catholic archdiocese of Prague, in a letter dated 25 March 1968, as well as support from leading figures in the Lutheran Church.[100] Unlike some other major reforms enacted during spring and summer 1968, the reinstatement of the Greek Catholic Church survived the Soviet invasion and the subsequent removal of Dubček from power. The Catholic Church was now allowed to have contact with the Vatican, Protestants were allowed to reconstitute the YMCA and the YWCA, and the Eastern-Rite Catholic Church, suppressed in 1950, was allowed to operate legally and retrieve some property. The regime had hoped that some bishops might be prepared to sever ties with the Holy See and collaborate with the communists in setting up a Czechoslovak Catholic Church not beholden to the Vatican. However, by 1956, the authorities realized that there was no realistic prospect of this happening.[101] Archbishop Beran, released from prison in 1963, was allowed to leave Czechoslovakia for Rome in 1965.

Khrushchev's revelations at the Twentieth CPSU Congress in February 1956 shook up most of the communist parties of the Soviet bloc but made essentially no difference in religious policy in Czechoslovakia.[102] On the contrary, 20 diocesan bishops remained in prison in 1956 and six dioceses were left without bishops. Among monastic orders (for men), only those focused on charitable work were still permitted to exist after 1956, while the number of nuns grew steadily smaller. In spite of this, the pedagogical newspaper *Učitelské noviny* reported on 9 April 1959 that 81.3% of students enrolled at the medical faculty were members of one or another Church and that 48.7% were practising Christians. The paper reported that the statistics were similar at other faculties.[103] Indeed, while the communists had succeeded in weaning some Christians from their faith, in other cases, as the party organ *Rudé právo* admitted, administrative pressure had the opposite effect, provoking some believers to hold onto their faith and their Church more tightly than ever.[104] Under the circumstances, many Catholics were pleasantly surprised when three of Czechoslovakia's bishops were allowed to attend the Second Vatican Council (held 1962–65).

Kádárism in Hungary, Part One: 1956–68

On 4 November 1956, while the second Soviet intervention was still underway, János Kádár participated in the formation of a Revolutionary Workers' and Peasants' Government in Szolnok. Its first act was to nullify the Nagy government's declaration pulling Hungary out of the Warsaw Pact. Subsequently, the various alternative political parties which had emerged since October were suppressed. The Hungarian Workers' Party had had approximately 859,000 members in January 1956. After that party was shut down on 30 October, its successor, the Hungarian Socialist Workers' Party (HSWP) initially had just 103,000 members. Kádár was determined to build a party of the center and thus excluded both old Stalinists and reformers who wanted changes which he considered unrealistic. Strikingly, as Iván Berend has pointed out, members of the new ruling elite – Kádár, Gyula Kállay, György Marosán, György Aczél, and several others – "had spent years in jail during the early 1950s as the victims of the Rákosi [regime]."[105] By 1975, party ranks had grown to embrace 754,353 members.[106] The closure of internment- and forced labor camps was accomplished by the mid-1960s. About the same time, jamming of Western radio broadcasts was ended. Other steps taken in the early years of the new regime included authorizing a general increase in wages, while keeping prices stable, and resolving as early as December 1956 that raising the standard of living would be the party's highest priority in economic policy. In addition, Kádár allowed farmers who had reprivatized their farms in 1956 to keep their farms and gradually won them over to join the collective farms, by making the collectives attractive (e.g., by arranging for them to have superior farm equipment and by allowing the collectives to enjoy some real decision-making authority). And finally, he scaled back the cult of the personality and advised his comrades that they did not need to quote from his speeches when presenting their own.

Kádár wanted to build a consensus, if only a consensus based in large part on passive consent and resignation to the inevitable. Out of this came his famous declaration in 1961, "All those who are not against us are with us."[107] Of course, steady improvement in people's standard of living would be a critical ingredient for this formula to work. In token of the new climate, writers Tibor Déry and Gyula Háy were amnestied in March of the previous year, along with four others. Then, in 1962, it was decided that admission to university would no longer be limited to young people with proletarian or peasant backgrounds. Kádár ended the practice of having the secret police interfere in people's private lives and ended the earlier policy of having successful peasants liquidated. Instead, he welcomed them to join the revamped collective farms. With a combination of carrots and sticks, collectivization moved forward and, by 1962, three-quarters of all working peasants were in the socialist sector. Kádár's primary concern was not to establish anything that might be called "socialist legality". Rather, as Rudolf Tőkés has pointed out, his focus was on consolidating his own personal authority and, in this connection, an estimated 7,600 persons, mostly non-members of the party, were imprisoned in the years Kádár was in power.[108]

Applying legal standards to the Rákosi era was, of course, another matter and a three-man commission headed by Béla Biszku was appointed to review the record of the Rákosi regime's crimes between 1949 and 1952. In August 1962, the Biszku Commission presented its findings to the CC, which agreed to deprive two dozen high-ranking or formerly high-ranking officials, including the exiled Rákosi, of their party membership.[109] Central control of agriculture was relaxed in 1965. Thus, on 1 January 1968, Hungary's New Economic Mechanism came into force, scaling back central control of the economy.[110] The reform showed positive results in its first three years. But, by 1971, the balance of trade was showing negative numbers, due above all to an increase in imports of Western technology.[111] Needless to say, this reversal had not been foreseen and was most obviously unintended.

Cultural policy

There was also relaxation in the cultural sphere, with Endre Szervánszky (1911–1977), one of the most outstanding Hungarian composers since Bartok and Kodály, openly breaking with socialist realism. Indeed, his *Six Orchestral Pieces*, which he premiered in 1960, was inspired by the atonal and 12-tone methods of Austrian composer Anton Webern (1883–1945). The journal *Tempo* credited Szervánszky with musical innovations which were "very influential, important and effective in releasing Hungarian music from the constraints it had been suffering under during the preceding decade."[112] String Quartet, Opus 1, by György Kurtág (born 1926) was likewise praised as a "breakthrough" in its time.[113] Other prominent composers at this time included Sándor Balassa, Endre Szöllosi, and Zsolt Durko. The cultural thaw at the end of 1956 also made it possible for Hungarians to hear several works of Bartók which had been suppressed up to then. These included his *Miraculous Mandarin*, String Quartets 3 and 4, Piano Concertos 1 and 2, and his sonata for violin and piano.[114] These works reflected the influence of Schoenberg and Stravinsky.

Literature, film-making, and the pictorial arts also enjoyed greater freedom now and film-makers such as Miklós Jancsó, István Szabó, Pál Gábor, and Károly Makk offered fresh views of Hungary's early experiences with communism. The relaxation of controls in the cultural sphere encouraged Hungary's "engineers of human souls" to chart new courses and here the theatrical work and short novels of István Örkvény deserve mention. Among poets, Ferenc Juhász and László Nagy offered surrealistic images in their works.[115] But there continued to be pressures on Hungarian novelists to write works that were useful for the socialist project. Thus, in an article published in the journal *Kritika* in October 1963, László Illés demanded that literature support and promote socialism.[116] Two years later, addressing the ruling party's Central Committee, István Szírmai chastised unnamed intellectuals and students for "pessimistic" and "disillusioned" thinking. Indeed, Tibor Déry's utopian novel, *Mr. G. A. in X*, was said to be "full of dark foreboding, [and] grotesque senselessness."[117]

Among those testing the limits of the permissible was József Lengyel with his novel *Confrontation*, written in the late 1960s. The novel set the story in Hungary at the dawn of Stalinism. Although at least a decade and a half had passed since the time of the story, the text hit too close to home for authorities, who held up distribution of the book. Finally, there was the case of György Moldova's short story, "Hitler in Hungary", published in 1973. In this short work, the author invited readers to imagine how similar communist propaganda of the early 1970s was to Nazi propaganda.[118]

Hungarian art after 1956

In the years 1948–1956, the themes favored in pictorial art included factory workers, soldiers marching, docks and other engineering projects, and workers and peasants engaged in comradely cooperation, such as Endre Domanovszky's *Worker-Peasant Alliance* in 1955.[119] Zhdanov's doctrine of socialist realism could not be challenged as long as Stalin was alive – or even for a few years longer. Kádár's famous declaration, "Whoever is not against us is with us,"[120] had implications across all spheres of social life, including in the art world. Aesthetic surnaturalism gained a hold among Hungarian artists, as did also the not-so-socialist "magical realism" borrowed from the American art world and reflected for example in the paintings of Lászlé Gyémánt, such as his *Construction* of 1960 and his playfully surrealist *Carnival of Survivors* of 1963.[121] In the years 1964–69, Ferenc Kóka and György Korga, among others, offered ironic renderings of socialist realist iconography,[122] while László Lakner employed the dark colors one associates with Rembrandt's paintings and endeavored to fashion a new subgenre he called "historical Pop Art".[123] By the end of the 1960s, cubism and "Picasso-inspired post-cubism" had likewise found a place in Hungary's art world.[124] With this, Hungarian artists left socialist realism far behind.

Gender (in)equality, 1953–1975

Although Hungary, like other countries in the bloc, declared its commitment to attain and assure gender equality, in practice some communists betrayed an underlying contempt for any notion of equality between the sexes. As early as 1953, for instance, one of the members at a meeting of the Politburo complained that "[t]he proportion of women is too high in certain fields and in some positions. For example, 46 percent of all party instructors, 65 percent of all instructors in three- to six-month-long courses, and 40 percent of the employees at local party apparatuses are women."[125] Needless to say, much higher concentrations of men in various fields, and especially in leadership and managerial positions, were not considered problematic for gender equality. Thus, in 1960, women held only 7.4% of managerial positions in economic enterprises, 8.1% of leadership positions in public administration, 12.5% of leadership posts in city administration, and 21.0% of managerial positions in finance.[126] Where political offices were concerned, the Politburo set a target of 30% to be allocated to women.[127] This was clearly intended as a maximum for women. If an allocation of 30% maximum of political offices for women constituted equality, would an allocation of 30% for men and 70% for women also have qualified as equality? In the aftermath of the Hungarian Revolution, György Marosán, a member of the Politburo, spoke openly about the status of women, admitting, a bit sarcastically, "We were only interested in having the right number of women in folk costumes in Parliament."[128] Marosán added that women should make it a priority to smile as often as possible.[129]

The situation was much the same in the economy. As Éva Fodor has pointed out, the 1949 constitution guaranteed that women should be able to obtain "the *same* work under the same working conditions as men" while legislation passed before adoption of the constitution declared "that women should be allowed to fill any job."[130] Indeed, in the first years following the end of the Second World War, the dual imperatives of rebuilding the economic infrastructure after the damage inflicted in the war and rapid industrialization induced the party to prioritize the recruitment of women into the industrial labor force; thus, by the mid-1970s, almost all women of working age had full-time jobs.[131] But the authorities quickly qualified this ambition by considering "special ways" in which women could be recruited into the work force.[132] Moreover, women's wages were systematically lower than men's. In agricultural cooperatives, for example, women's wages in 1973 were on average 56% of those of men.[133] And yet, by 1970, the Politburo decided that the "woman question" had been solved.[134]

The Catholic and Lutheran Churches

The Catholic and Lutheran Churches were (and still are) the largest religious bodies in Hungary, with the former accounting for 67% of Hungary's 10 million inhabitants in 1949.[135] After 1956, the Catholic bishops, led by Archbishop József Grösz of Kalocsa, hoped to achieve something that might pass for "good relations" with the state and turn the page on the uncomfortable treatment meted out by the regime in earlier years.[136] Cardinal Mindszenty, enjoying the safety of asylum in the U.S. Embassy, was opposed to any accommodation with the communist regime, but his was a lone voice. In any event, the agreement reached in October 1964 was between the Vatican and the Hungarian government. Cardinal Agostino Casaroli (1914–1998), the Vatican Secretary of State, described the agreement as "neither a *modus vivendi* nor an accord," but merely a mechanism addressing "practical solutions in some matters."[137]

Indeed, some communists misunderstood the regime's intention in reaching this agreement. *Társadalmi Szemle* addressed this issue directly in its November 1964 issue, reminding communists that the party concluded the agreement with the Vatican for short-term reasons and remained committed to the eventual elimination of religion from Hungarian life.[138] In any event, this agreement could not have been concluded without the Kremlin's approval. The six states of the Soviet bloc operated within clear parameters, including where religious policy was concerned, and exceptions (as in the case of Poland's Catholic University of Lublin or the East German regime's funding of theology professors) had to be approved by the Kremlin.

Thus, representatives of the bloc religious affairs officers met in the Czech town of Karlovy Vary on 17–20 May 1961 to agree on a broadly common approach in the religious sphere in the light of guidelines provided in a Soviet "proposal" drafted two years earlier.[139]

In 1959, the Holy See had named four new bishops, only to see the regime decline to recognize their appointments at that time. Two years later, the regime imprisoned a number of Catholic priests and lay persons for having failed to respect the regime's restrictions on the practice of their faith.[140] Then, in 1962, in the wake of the conference at Karlovy Vary, the Budapest regime adopted a new approach in its effort to manage relations with the Churches: now, instead of imprisonment and other forms of persecution, authorities invited bishops to "friendly" conversations.[141] Needless to say, accommodation proved to be more comfortable than resistance. But there were limits to what the Church could accommodate and, by declining to accept the regime's suggestions for candidates to fill open episcopal vacancies, the Church faced a situation where, by the time the Second Vatican Council started its proceedings on 11 October 1962, only five of Hungary's 11 dioceses were headed by bishops.[142]

Meanwhile, Cardinal Mindszenty, sitting in internal exile in the U.S. Embassy in Budapest, was an awkward reminder of past Church-state tensions. In fact, Hungary's bishops told Pope Paul VI that Mindszenty's continued status as Primate of the Catholic Church in Hungary was detrimental to the Church. Mindszenty refused to step down voluntarily and, as a result, the pope simply deposed him in December 1973.[143]

Claiming more than 20% of Hungary's population, the Lutheran Church was likewise of interest to the communists, who wanted, among other things, to exercise a veto over the Church's personnel. Specifically, in the wake of the Hungarian Revolution, the regime called for the removal of certain pastors whom it accused of having nurtured "counter-revolutionary" sympathies. Bishop Lajos Ordass, the Presiding Bishop of Hungary's Lutheran Church, refused to dismiss the deputy bishop and others of whom the regime disapproved. Tensions between Ordass and the party-state continued into 1957 and 1958. Meanwhile, Zoltán Káldy (1919–1987), at the time the curate of Pécs, had presented a speech in summer 1955 in which he stated that "the Hungarian Lutheran of today cannot rebel against the state, because he who opposes the state authority in a rebellious way defies the order of God."[144] The regime deposed Ordass in June 1958, having lost patience with him. Later that summer, Káldy published an article comparing the situation of his Church at that time to "a car out of control that had finally landed in a ditch."[145] He summarized four paths each of which the Church should reject: (1) the Church as martyr; (2) the Church as total conformist to the state's wishes; (3) the Church focused solely on conversions and helping people to achieve salvation; and (4) the Church mixing Christianity and Marxism. In their place, he advocated a fifth path. Anticipating the formula adopted later by the Protestant Church in East Germany, he declared: "The Church should be a Church in socialism."[146]

A month and a half later, Káldy emerged as the sole contender to succeed Ordass to head the Church. The authorities gave their blessing to his election, which followed on 10 October 1958, and, on 4 November 1958, Káldy was formally installed as Presiding Bishop of the Lutheran Church in Hungary. He quickly accommodated the regime's wishes by removing the deputy bishop and several pastors, also deposing several deans at the same time. He also began to work out just what the phrase "Church in socialism" should entail. By 1964, on the occasion of being awarded an honorary doctorate from the Lutheran Theological Academy in Bratislava, he offered his thoughts on what he now called the Theology of Diakonia.[147] The word "diakonia" is Greek for *service* and the kind of service Káldy had in mind was service for the people in collaboration with the authorities and, since he explicitly endorsed the program of the Patriotic People's Front, one may say that his concept in practice embraced also service for the party-state.[148]

Romania – from Gheorghiu Dej to Ceaușescu

Nicolae Ceaușescu (1918–1989) became a full member of the RWP Central Committee and likewise of the Orgburo (later abolished) in May 1952, about the same time that Gheorghiu-Dej was removing his rivals from political office. A little over a year later, after the death of Soviet dictator Josef Stalin, the new Soviet leadership put pressure on parties in the bloc to introduce collective leadership and separate the offices of party leadership and head of the government; the reason for this was that Khrushchev and Malenkov, who occupied respectively the top party and governmental posts in the Soviet Union, each had his clients in the bloc states and each of them wanted to see his clients in positions of responsibility and influence. Before accommodating the Soviet demand, Gheorghiu-Dej had Pătrășcanu put on trial between 6 and 13 April 1954. Charged, falsely, with being a counter-revolutionary and a foreign spy, Pătrășcanu was executed during the night of 16–17 April. Two days later, on 19 April, Gheorghiu-Dej agreed to separate the party and government leadership posts. Instead of a single General Secretary, there would be, for the time being, a Secretariat consisting of Ceaușescu, Gheorghe Apostol (1913–2010), Mihai Dalea, and János Fazekas. Apostol became First Secretary of the RWP; Gheorghiu-Dej remained Chair of the Council of Ministers – in effect, Prime Minister. In September 1955, the collective Secretary was abolished, and Gheorghiu-Dej was once more General Secretary of the RWP.

Gheorghiu-Dej, Iosif Chișinevschi, Miron Constantinescu, and Petre Borila had attended the 20th Party Congress and were shell-shocked by Khrushchev's allegations in regard to Stalin. In the evenings, according to Tismaneanu, they sat around playing dominoes and discussing how to respond.[149] Constantinescu, however, was rather reticent, leading Gheorghiu-Dej to wonder if his taciturn comrade was perhaps nurturing notions of a bid for power. Indeed, there are reports that, with the encouragement of the Kremlin, Constantinescu and Chișnevschi had attempted to recruit fellow members of the Politburo in a conspiracy to remove Gheorghiu-Dej from the leadership. According to the same source, one of those whom they approached, Alexandru Moghioroş, revealed the plot to Gheorghiu-Dej. Constantinescu was moved from the chairmanship of the State Planning Commission to the office of Minister of Education and removed from the Politburo. Chişnevschi, likewise dismissed from the Politburo, was reassigned as a lecturer at the Institute for Specialized Teaching Staff – an enormous demotion.[150]

In the meantime, in the wake of the Hungarian Revolution, Romanian authorities took the precaution of forcing schools which had been teaching in Hungarian to merge with schools having Romanian as the language of instruction. Of particular interest was the forced merger of the Hungarian-language Bolyai University in Cluj with the Romanian-language Babeş University, likewise in Cluj. After that, Hungarian-language instruction slowly withered. Then, in 1960, the boundaries of the Hungarian Autonomous Region were changed, separating two districts with large Hungarian populations and adding territory with proportionately fewer Hungarians. With this, the percentage of the Region's population comprised by Hungarians dropped from 77% to 62%.[151] After Ceauşescu came to power in 1965, the Mures Autonomous Hungarian Region, as it had come to be called, was abolished.

The combination of the Hungarian Revolution and the contested return of Gomułka to power in Poland in October 1956 suggested to Gheorghiu-Dej that de-Stalinization could be destabilizing. As a preemptive measure, the RWP significantly increased spending on consumer goods during the years 1956–60.[152] It was about this time that Khrushchev hit on the idea of having the economies of the member-states of the bloc's Council for Mutual Economic Cooperation (COMECON) specialize in areas of comparative advantage. His idea was that Romania should deemphasize the development of heavy industry and place its stress on agriculture, food-processing industry, and petrochemical industry.[153] Gheorgiu-Dej disagreed, signalling the start of Romania's Stalinist deviation. Even so, this was a modulated Stalinism, allowing a new openness to cultural contact with Western countries. In token thereof, the jamming of Voice of America and Radio Free Europe was ended in August 1963. Gheorghiu-Dej's declaration of independence – if one may characterize it as such – followed in April 1964. This declaration boldly asserted that every communist party had the right to set its own path.[154] Gheorghe Gheorghiu-Dej died of lung cancer on 19 March 1965.

Gheorghe Apostol, who had served as President of the State Council from 21 March 1961, but who lost that post upon the death of Gheorghiu-Dej, might have seemed to be a potential successor to take the helm. But there were rival groupings within the RWP Politburo and Ceauşescu emerged as the compromise choice. He was sworn in as General Secretary of the RWP and, in December 1967, he assumed the presidency of the State Council as well, thus establishing himself as also head of state. In the meantime, in the run-up to the Ninth Congress of the party, held 19–24 July 1965, Ceauşescu had the party revert to its original name as the Romanian Communist Party. The Congress also provided an opportunity for the new General Secretary to confirm that Romania would continue to follow the economic course charted by his predecessor, which is to say to emphasize the continued development of heavy industry.[155] In the aftermath of the Ninth Congress, censorship was relaxed (temporarily, as it turned out) for newspapers and literature. The Congress had given Ceaușescu (again, only temporarily) the halo of a supposed reformer, even if he had stressed, on that occasion, the high value he placed on promoting the homogenization of the Romanian nation.[156]

Already at the Ninth Congress, Ceaușescu had mentioned his aspiration to achieve "active neutrality inside the world communist movement."[157] In a word, he wanted a special status on the world stage. In 1967, Romania and the Federal Republic of Germany established diplomatic ties; with that, the Federal Republic of Germany (FRG) had granted Romania a special exemption from its Hallstein Doctrine, under which no state could have diplomatic relations with both German states. Under Gheorghiu-Dej, Romania had declared its neutrality in the emerging rivalry between the Soviet Union and China and, under Ceaușescu, the regime stated categorically that the bloc should not condemn any communist state, meaning in this case China.[158] Ceaușescu's regime gave a further demonstration of its independent foreign policy in June 1967 when, in the context of the Six Day War pitting Israel against Egypt, Jordan, and Syria, Romania refused to join the rest of the Soviet bloc in breaking off diplomatic ties with Israel.[159]

Thus, as Soviet-Czech tensions heated up in the course of late spring and summer 1968, Ceaușescu saw that what was at stake was the right of every socialist state to chart its own course – in a word, not a right to full independence (which would have entailed the right to abandon socialism), but to autonomy. The Kremlin understood Ceaușescu's position from the start and therefore excluded Romania from the aforementioned Dresden meeting of six members of the Warsaw Pact on 23 March 1968. Later, after the Soviet bloc invasion of Czechoslovakia in August, Ceaușescu roundly condemned the intervention. In his public speech addressing the invasion, the Conducător added that, "the entire Romanian people will not allow anybody to violate the territory of our homeland . . . Be sure, comrades, be sure, citizens of Romania, that we shall never betray our homeland, we shall never betray the interests of our people."[160]

Abortion and inequality, 1957–1967

Access to abortion, or rather lack of access, would become one of the defining features of the Ceaușescu era (1965–89). But, in the wake of the Hungarian Revolution and the return of Gomułka to power in Poland, Romanian authorities decided to relax the policy on abortion in their country. Accordingly, on 25 September 1957, Decree No. 463 legalized abortion in Romania; subsequently, on 30 September 1957, a law was passed spelling out the conditions under which abortion would be available. Under the provisions of this law, pregnant women could obtain abortion on demand during the first trimester, meaning without having to obtain permission from a state commission. Abortion centers were set up in hospitals across the country, as well as in clinics attached to factories with large female labor forces. The decree had an immediate impact. Whereas, in 1957, there had been 407,819 live births and no legal abortions, by the following year the number of live births had declined to 390,500, alongside 112,068 legal abortions. In 1959, the number of live births skidded to 368,007, while the number of legal abortions jumped to 219,058. This trend continued, with younger couples increasingly preferring to have just one child. In terms of the birth rate, the number of live births per 1,000 persons sagged over time from 25.6 in 1955 to 14.3 in 1966.[161] In response, on 1 October 1966, the regime issued Decree No. 770, allowing abortions only under one of the following conditions: the woman seeking an abortion is older than 45; she has four children under her care; the continuation of the pregnancy would endanger the woman's life; and one of the sexual partners suffers from a serious, genetically transmittable disease.[162] Not surprisingly, a year after passage of the new law, the number of newborn children doubled, reaching 27.4 per 1,000 in 1967. But the law had the unintended effects of fostering or magnifying feelings of guilt among women who resorted to now-illegal abortions and increasing the incidence of death on the part of the women where conditions for abortion were not sanitary.[163]

Article 23 of the 1948 constitution proclaimed – much as other Soviet bloc constitutions had done – that "[i]n the SRR, women shall have equal rights with men. The state shall protect marriage and family and shall defend the interests of mother and child."[164] Article 18 proclaimed the principle of equal pay for equal work. But women were guided into lesser-paid positions in feminized sectors such as elementary education and textiles, where earnings were, on average, only about a third of what they were in male-dominated sectors such as mining and construction even as late as the 1980s.[165] But even in female-dominated sectors, women were rarely assigned managerial functions; these were reserved for men. Moreover, even though the 1954 civil code had declared that women and men enjoyed equal legal status, a principle reinforced by the 1965 constitution, neither wife-beating nor marital rape was illegal.[166] Underlying women's inequality in Romania was the demand that women marry and bear children so that the population could be expanded. After 1966, childbirth was seen as a couple's obligation to the state.

Music and literature

The post-war years saw a new generation of composers come to the fore. Among these were Laurentin Profeta and Tiberiu Olah, both of whom studied music composition in Moscow after the war ended. Andreas Porfetye tested the limits of socialist realism through his eclectic use of musical idioms, while Doru Popovici looked for inspiration to music that had been disparaged at the height of the *diktat* of socialist realism; indeed, he began his career by taking his cue from the music of Bartók, Hindemith, and Schoenberg.[167] As elsewhere in the bloc, the lifespan of socialist realism was relatively short. As early as 1958, Gheorghiu-Dej delivered a speech condemning socialist realism,[168] and, according to Lucian Grigorovici, at the end of the era of Gheorghiu-Dej, there were "practically no limitations" imposed on the country's composers.[169] The only Romanian composer ever brought before the court for a show trial was Mihai Andricu, placed on trial in 1959, not for his music but for criticizing the regime at an event at the Embassy of France. As a result of his indiscretion, he was stripped of all of his honors and expelled from both the Conservatory and the Romanian Academy. His music would not be performed for several years.[170] The music of Georges Enesco, who had died in Paris in 1955, continued to be prominent, while, in the 1960s, a new generation of young composers were looking, much as their counterparts elsewhere in the bloc were doing, to the erstwhile taboo music of Schoenberg, Webern, Berg, and Hindemith for inspiration.[171]

In the field of literature, the relaxation in cultural policy following 1953 allowed writers Ioan Alexandru (1941–2000), Ana Blandiana (b. 1942), Marin Sorescu (1936–1996), and Nichita Stănescu (1933–1983) to publish their works. The new cultural policy implemented by Leonte Răutu, opened the way for the publication also of books by Tudor Arghezi, George Bacovia, Lucian Blaga, Octavian Goga, Nicolae Iorga, Liviu Rebreanu, and Tudor Vianu which had previously been banned.[172] But in July 1958, the party news organ *Scînteia* published articles by Leonte Răutu (1910–1993) and Mihai Beniuc (1907–1988) warning against apolitical "neutralism", "negativism", and eclecticism. Two additional deviations were also listed: "obsequiousness" and "literary snobbery".[173] Addressing a regional party meeting two years later, Gheorgiu-Dej complained that writers were not paying sufficient attention to the tasks and accomplishments of socialism. Perhaps the most striking literary rehabilitation involved the works of Titu Maiorescu (1840–1917) in 1963. His championing of art for the sake of art and rejection of any notion that art should be socially useful signaled that Romanian literati were no longer bound strictly by socialist realism.[174] But that was still in the era of Gheorgiu-Dej. Two years later, Ceauşescu, by then General Secretary, presented a report to the Ninth Congress of the RCP on 19 July 1965, stressing the role of literature in "shaping the new man's Socialist consciousness" and declared that "deep-going Socialist Humanism should pervade literary and artistic creation."[175] Following on this, Paul Anghel wrote in *Gazeta literară* in spring 1968 that "the writer . . . has the duty to tell us what exactly reality is and not how it ought to be or how he would like it to be."[176]

That there was renewed relaxation in cultural policy in the late 1960s is clear from the fact that Sorescu's play *Iona* [Jonah] could be published in 1968 and performed until 1969. The play took the Biblical story of a seafarer who gets swallowed by a whale – a large fish, in Sorescu's retelling – and turned it into an allegory about the hopelessness of human existence. In the play, Jonah has a small knife and cuts his way out of the fish that swallowed him only to find that that fish had been swallowed by an even larger fish. Cutting his way through the flesh of that second fish, he finds himself within the belly of a still larger fish. At that point, Jonah gives up and commits suicide.[177] But even before the performances of *Jonah* had come to an end, there was a new chill in the literary scene. Specifically, a declaration published before the start of the Writers' Association conference in November 1968 held that "Marxism cannot accept the so-called independence or autonomy of art vis-à-vis society. It is the duty of literature to exercise a considerable influence on the intellectual, social, and moral life of the individual."[178] And needless to say, that influence needed to be "positive".

The Romanian Orthodox Church in the Era of Justinian

Justinian Marina (1901–1977) served as Patriarch of the Romanian Orthodox Church from his enthronement on 6 June 1948 until his death on 26 March 1977. He had witnessed the harsh treatment meted out to his fellow clerics in the years prior to his elevation to Patriarch and resolved to work for a modus vivendi with the regime, so that the Church could thrive. Justinian benefited from a personal bond he had formed with Gheorghiu-Dej during the Second World War when Justinian hid him and protected him after the future communist leader escaped from prison.[179] Accordingly, he gave his unqualified support to the regime. Neither the arrests of priests after the introduction of social reorientation programs in 1949 nor the renewed arrests of clergy and closures of various churches and monasteries in the years 1958–63 provoked any word of criticism from Justinian, even though approximately 4,000 monks and nuns were either incarcerated or secularized in the latter wave of repression. On the contrary, Justinian developed the theory of the "Social Apostolate", which held that the Church should be useful to the government, and pressed monks and nuns to learn "useful" trades.[180] He understood that his Church was operating from a position of weakness and had the horrific example of the Greek Catholic Church on which to reflect: in suppressing that body soon after taking power, the authorities had simply executed 400 Greek Catholic priests outright, putting the remaining approximately 200 in prisons from which they were never to emerge.[181] Justinian's collaboration paid off. The Church was able to conduct its activities without repression after 1963, though of course not without surveillance. Even as early as 1956, the Romanian Orthodox Church was publishing four theological journals, at least two of which were considered to be world-class journals.[182] The Romanian Orthodox Church also did better than most other Churches in the bloc in receiving financial support from the state to restore some old churches and to build approximately 30 new churches. In addition, the Orthodox clergy were paid salaries corresponding to the average earnings of Romanian citizens – better than what their Bulgarian counterparts were receiving.[183]

But it wasn't all milk and honey for the Church since, on 28 October 1959, the government decreed that men wishing to take monastic vows could not do so until they reached the age of 55, while women wanting to join a convent had to be at least 50 years old. Still, in the last half of Gheorghiu-Dej's rule, the Church increased its cooperation with the regime, among other ways by helping to promote better relations for the regime with Western countries and by supporting the regime's economic policies.[184] In recognition of his cooperative attitude, the regime awarded the patriarch the "Order of 23 August" medal, second class.[185]

After the death of Gheorghiu-Dej, the regime relaxed its stance vis-à-vis the Church and no longer closed monasteries or convents. Some imprisoned clergy were rehabilitated and support for the faculty of theology continued. From Ceauşescu's point of view, support from the Church could earn trust and confidence in Western capitals, in turn securing his relative autonomy from Moscow. In token of this transformation of Church-state relations, Ceauşescu praised the Church, in a 1968 speech, for the part it was playing in the development of Romania's sense of collective self.[186] Justinian is usually considered to have been successful in achieving his primary goal, which was to see his Church survive and flourish. As Alan Scarfe noted in his eulogy for Justinian, "He left behind him a thriving Church of 10,000 parishes with trained clergy to fill them all; two theological institutes of 1,400 students studying at undergraduate or graduate level and a reordered monastic life which has managed to preserve its spiritual vitality [at nearly 200 monasteries]."[187]

Bulgaria – from Chervenkov to Zhivkov

Even after having lost both the party leadership and the premiership, Chervenkov retained a certain amount of power in that he remained a member of the Politburo and now served as Deputy PM. Anton Yugov (1904–1991) succeeded Chervenkov as PM in April 1956. In September of that year, a commission chaired by Dimitur Ganev reported that the sentences handed down to Kostov's associates had been unjust; all but two of those convicted were restored to the ranks of the party. Meanwhile, Bulgaria's economic growth in the first decade of communist rule had been robust. Accordingly, in adopting the Third Five-Year Plan in June 1958, the Seventh BCP Congress set ambitious goals for increases in industrial and agricultural production. On 26 December 1958, *Otechestven Front*, citing an old slogan from Stalinist Russia, offered this message of intended inspiration to workers: "What is the meaning of the slogan, 'The Five-Year Plan in Three to Four Years'? It means to struggle for the fulfillment of the Five-Year Plan . . . in three to four years instead of in five."[188]

But, with the party's continued emphasis on heavy industry, agricultural production had been allowed to fall behind. Following an agreement with the Soviet Union, Czechoslovakia, and the GDR, Bulgaria was under obligation to increase, by considerable measure, its exports of certain agricultural products to the other partners to the agreement. In order to meet the targets for vegetable and fruit exports, Bulgaria had to reduce its production of wheat and cotton. Meanwhile, there were signs of tension between Yugov and Zhivkov. In November 1962, Yugov found himself accused of having ordered the arrest, during his years as Minister of Internal Affairs (1944–48), of innocent officials and of having disagreed with the party line, as well as of incompetence, vanity, rudeness, and dishonesty.[189] Yugov and his deputy, Georgi Tsankov, were dismissed from their posts and expelled from the CC. At the same time, Chervenkov was ejected from the party itself. The party journal *Novo vreme* justified Chervenkov's sacking by accusing the fallen leader of having presented himself as "the most important expert on each and every question" and of having conducted himself as "a veritable Zeus".[190]

Zhivkov had to withstand one more challenge to his political primacy. This came in the form of a 1965 conspiracy by a group of army generals to stage a coup to overthrow him. The conspiracy was discovered on 7 April. One conspirator committed suicide; nine others (five army officers and four civilians) were arrested, tried on the charge of high treason, and given prison sentences ranging from eight to fifteen years. After that, Zhivkov's leadership remained unchallenged until 1989. Twenty-five years later, on 15 June 1990, the nine convicted conspirators were rehabilitated.[191] Until 1971, Bulgaria was officially designated a "people's republic", but under the new constitution adopted that year Bulgaria was said to have completed the construction of socialism and hence redesignated a "socialist republic". From this point, there would be more emphasis on homogenizing Bulgarian society, in particular by eroding the distinctive and traditional culture of rural society.

Orchestral music

The post-war generation of Bulgarian orchestral composers was dominated by Pancho Vladigerov (1899–1978), Lyubomir Pipkov (190–1974), and Marin Goleminov (1908–2000). Vladigerov and Pipkov were among the founders of the Bulgarian Contemporary Music Society (in 1933), later renamed the Union of Bulgarian Composers. Among Vladigerov's works is his symphony the "Jewish Poem", composed in 1951. The following year, the Bulgarian government awarded him the Dimitrov Prize, the highest accolade bestowed on anyone working in the arts in Bulgaria at that time. His most beloved work is probably his patriotic Vardar Rhapsody, also performed under the title, Bulgarian Rhapsody. Pipkov served as chair of the Union of Bulgarian Composers from 1945 to 1954 and launched the magazine *Muzika*, later known as *Bŭlgarska muzika*, serving as its first editor. Pipkov had a low regard for communism, but he accepted the challenge to make his music intelligible to ordinary people and optimistic, as in his *Oratorio for Our Time* (1959). Although authorities disapproved of some of Pipkov's activities and removed him from these posts, he was later declared a Hero of Socialist Labor and a People's Artist of Bulgaria. Finally, Goleminov, whose works make use of traditional Bulgarian rhythms and melodies, served as Rector of the Sofia Opera from 1954 to 1956 and as Director of the same institution from 1965 to 1967.

Other orchestral composers of the post-war generation included Petko Staynov (1896–1977), Veselin Stoyanov (1902–1969), Parashkev Hadjiev (1912–1992), Trofin Silyanovski (1923–2005), Alexander Raichev (1922–2003), Lazar Nikolov (1922–2005), and Konstantin Iliev (1924–1988). As elsewhere in the Soviet bloc, there were pressures to compose music that was "optimistic" and inspired by socialist realism and, as well, to avoid complex tonalities that could bring accusations of formalism or, worst of all, atonalism. Silyanovski and Assen Ovcharov (1906–1972), who established the country's first classical jazz ensemble, both spent time in forced labor camps.[192] Within this political context, Vladigerov composed works in honor of the communist party (Symphony No. 2, "May", Opus 44, and "The

Ninth of September" overture, Opus 45) but, after these early works (both composed in 1949), Vladigerov tried to avoid politics.

Composers in the Soviet bloc were supposed to shun the (atonal) music of Austrian composers Arnold Schoenberg, Alban Berg, and Anton Webern, but as of the late 1950s, Bulgarian composers were increasingly tasting this forbidden fruit and even drawing inspiration from the atonal composers. Iliev and Nikolov in particular, members of the younger generation of composers, started writing atonal or 12-tone music. Conservative composers of the older generation and communist cultural watchdogs alike were scandalized and did their best to prevent atonal music from being performed.[193] In spite of the pall cast by the repression of the Hungarian Revolution across the bloc, Bulgarian composers increasingly took chances, even in the face of criticism for the curiously conceived sin of "European provincialism" (what, in an earlier era, would have been called cosmopolitanism).[194] Among chamber operas, Lazar Nikolov's *Prometheus Bound* is of particular interest. Inspired by the work of the ancient Greek dramatist Aeschylus, this opera, completed in 1969, developed the "theme of ethical stoicness [as] a symbol of artistic dissidence under government dictatorship."[195]

Writers

There were, as hinted in the previous chapter, some faint hints of relaxation in the cultural sector already in 1952/53. But cultural relaxation gained momentum with the Twentieth CPSU Congress in February 1956 and the republication in the Bulgarian news organ, *Rabotnichesko Delo*, on 29 March 1956 of an article originally appearing in the Moscow news organ *Pravda*, which criticized the leadership cult (specifically of Stalin). Insofar as Vulko Chervenkov had modeled himself on Stalin, the reappearance of the article in Bulgarian was clearly aimed at Bulgaria's "little Stalin". Indeed, it was less than three weeks later that Chervenkov was forced to relinquish the prime ministership. Now Dimitur Dimov's novel, *Tobacco*, which had been officially condemned shortly after its publication in 1951, was lauded as the best Bulgarian novel since Ivan Vazov's *Under the Yoke* (written in 1887–88). The reassessment of *Tobacco* was a straw in the wind, a token of an important policy shift which allowed pre-war authors to be rehabilitated and their writings republished.[196]

Bulgarian writers now turned their backs on socialist realism. Among the most prominent players in what Nissan Oren has termed the "writers' rebellion" were Emil Manov, Todor Genov, Liuben Stanev, Stoian Daskalov, and Liudmil Stoianov.[197] Manov's novel, *An Inauthentic Case*, turned a critical eye to life in the Stalinist era, as did Todor Genov's play *Fear*. Stanev's novel, *The Laskov Family*, exposed the opportunism in communist party ranks, and T. Nesnakomov's novel, *The Benefactor*, recounted how the wealthy exploited the poor in Bulgaria's communist society.[198] The literary journal *Plamŭk* (The Flame) was launched in January 1957 and promised to open its pages to young workers exploring new approaches.[199]

But the crushing of the Hungarian Revolution took its toll also on cultural expression throughout the bloc. In February 1957, Chervenkov was recalled to serve as Minister of Education and Culture, and set about to quash the radical aspirations of some intellectuals. A meeting of the Bulgarian Writers' Union took place in July 1957 and served as an occasion for attacks on "revisionism" and, more concretely, on the alleged "exaggeration" of errors committed in the Stalinist era.[200] Manov and Genov were singled out for criticism but defended themselves vigorously. Nonetheless, two months later, *Otechestven Front* warned that "the party is free to expel party members who use the party label to preach anti-party views."[201]

The attack on Manov and Genov was resumed in November 1957, when they were included with eight other prominent writers in a barrage of condemnation voiced at a meeting of the party organization of the Writers' Union: the ten were said to have adopted stances opposed to party policy. Then, in the course of 1958, eight writers were dropped from the editorial board of *Filosofska Misl* for the sins of "revisionism" and "non-Marxist" thinking. Among these were Manov and playwright Orlin Vassilev.[202] Especially striking in these months of conservative retrenchment was Manov's "mild and dignified apology" in 1957 for the storm that his *Inauthentic Case* had stirred up.[203] Chervenkov stepped down from the Ministry of Education and Culture following the Seventh BCP Congress in June 1958. But the frost continued and, by 1965, the last embers of liberal ideas in the cultural sector had been snuffed out.

Women's equality, 1960–72

One of the criteria for the communists in assessing progress toward gender equality was women's participation in the labor force. By this measure, there was tangible progress as women's share among industrial and office workers rose from 23.9% in 1948 to 43% by 1969. Indeed, by the latter year, women comprised 70.9% of the staff in public health, 64.5% of workers in education, culture, and the arts, and 47.3% of scientific workers.[204] Bulgarian women were also becoming steadily better educated, as the data from Table 3.7 (below) show.

Except in the case of secondary vocational-technical schools, women increased their presence in all educational institutions of Bulgaria, gaining a clear majority in college and universities. In 1960, 7% of working women had a bachelor's or master's degree; by 1975, 26% of women had such qualifications, and by 1988 the figure would rise to 51%.[205]

By comparison with Western democracies at that time, women's representation in the Bulgarian National Assembly was respectable, with women accounting for 18.7% of the deputies in the Assembly in 1971, alongside 25.65% of members of district-, town-, and village councils that same year.[206] Within the communist party itself, as of 1971, women comprised 25.7% of the membership and 19% of the membership of the Central Committee (27 among the Central Committee's 147 members).[207] As for equality within the family, Article 1 of the Family Code in force at the start of the 1970s specified that husband and wife should relate to each other on the basis of complete equality.[208] Based on this record, the party proudly

TABLE 3.7 Bulgarian Women Studying at Educational Institutions, as a % of total enrollment

	1965/66	1971/72
General educational polytechnic schools	49.9	50.0
Vocational-technical schools	30.5	33.6
Secondary vocational-technical schools	47.6	40.8
Technical colleges and art schools	40.7	44.8
Colleges	60.0	68.5
Universities	40.3	51.6
TOTAL	47.5	48.5

Source: Maria Dinkova, *The Social Progress of the Bulgarian Woman* (Sofia: Sofia Press, 1972), p. 12.

proclaimed in 1970 that Bulgaria had achieved "genuine social equality between man and woman."[209]

Religious communities in Bulgaria, 1958–1979

After the communists seized the Bulgarian Orthodox Church's charitable agencies, nationalized 65% of its arable land, took control of its candle industry, seized its bank deposits, and cut the state subsidy, the Church was in financial trouble. However, in 1948, the Ministry of Industry granted the Church permission to rent the Sofia candle factory and the subsequent sale of candles provided the Church with a certain income.[210] In 1958, the Bulgarian communist authorities called a halt to the harassment of Orthodox clergy and, by 1960, the last remaining clergy still in labor camps were released.[211]

Shorn of much of its wealth, the Bulgarian Orthodox Church was receptive to the offer of a state subsidy. In exchange for this contribution, the Church became active in support of the regime's peace propaganda and proposals for disarmament. The Church was allowed to publish a glossy, full-color magazine with photos of its churches for distribution abroad. The state's relations with the Church were organized in accordance with rules set forth by the Committee for Questions of the Bulgarian Orthodox Church and Religious Cults, a department of the Foreign Ministry.[212] In this way, the Church came to function in part as an agency of the Foreign Ministry. In spite of discrimination against believers, steady atheist propaganda, and surveillance of its bishops, the Orthodox religion showed signs of reviving by 1970, with increases in church weddings, baptisms, and funerals. Bishop Stepan, then First Secretary of the Holy Synod, estimated at the time that 70% of Bulgarians were members of the Orthodox Church (against a regime estimate of 40%).[213]

The second largest religious community in Bulgaria was (and still is) the Islamic community. In 1969, Wayne S. Vucinich estimated that there were just over a million Muslims living in Bulgaria, comprising 700,000 Turks, 180,000 Pomaks, 120,000 Roma (Gypsies), and 5,000 Tatars.[214] In the late 1950s, the regime stepped up its propaganda campaign against Muslims, characterizing Islam as a reactionary, alien religion constituting an impediment to the full integration of Bulgaria's Muslims into Bulgarian public life.[215] Like the Orthodox Church and the small Jewish community, the Islamic community received a subsidy from the state.

The Catholic Church did not fare well. Although the Greek-Rite Catholics were not suppressed, unlike their co-religionists in Czechoslovakia, Romania, and Ukraine, there were Catholic clergy in prison camps until 1964, when the regime declared an amnesty for those priests who were still alive.[216] Catholic seminaries remained closed and the religious instruction of children was forbidden. As of 1970, there were only 72 Catholic priests left in the country, and this number would shrink to 50 by the end of the 1970s, when there were about 70,000 Catholics in the country.[217] There were also Protestant communities, among which the largest, the Pentecostal Church, had some 10,000 members in 1975.[218]

The GDR under Ulbricht

Khrushchev's revelations at the CPSU Twentieth Party Congress electrified the SED elite as it did those in other bloc parties. Karl Schirdewan (1907–1998), a member of the Politburo, was particularly shocked by the Soviet leader's speech.[219] Indeed, the speech provoked demands in many sectors of East Germany for guaranteed freedom of speech and an end of SED interference in science. Within the Central Committee, opposition to Ulbricht was registered by Schirdewan, Ernst Wollweber (Minister of State Security), and Gerhard Ziller (CC Secretary for the Economy). They felt that de-Stalinization in the GDR had not gone far enough and were supported by Fred Oelssner (Poliburo member) and Fritz Selbmann (Deputy PM), who felt that Ulbricht's economic policy was wrongheaded. By October 1957, Ulbricht succeeded in removing Schirdewan and Oelssner from the Poliburo and sacking Wollweber. Ziller committed suicide. A few months later, in February 1958, Schirdewan and Wollweber once more raised the issue of de-Stalinization at an SED forum, this time also calling for Ulbricht's removal from office. They failed and both men were now expelled from the CC.[220] In the wake of this second confrontation, functionaries who had criticized Ulbricht were also relieved of their positions through new elections.

In the 1950s, the big challenge confronting the young East German state was the steady flight of its citizens across the open border in Berlin. Between September 1949 and mid-August 1961, a total of 2,691,270 East Germans fled to West Berlin.[221] This hemorrhaging of the population was having a negative effect on the economy. Finally, during the night of 12–13 August – after clearing this with the Soviets in advance – the SED regime authorized the construction of the Berlin Wall. With this, the East German economy was stabilized. Subsequently, in January 1963, a set of economic reforms was adopted under the rubric "the New Economic Mechanism" or NEM). However, that same year, the Soviets reduced exports, at special prices, of grain, meat, and steel to the GDR by 25–35%. Erich Apel, economic adviser to Ulbricht, was tasked with preparing a draft report; he submitted it in autumn 1965, demonstrating that Ulbricht's hope that the GDR could overtake West Germany in economic terms was entirely unrealistic. Ulbricht was displeased with this and, in December 1965, Apel shot himself.[222] Ulbricht, for his part, wanted to marry stronger control over enterprises with support for economic decentralization.

To finance his economic program, Ulbricht was accumulating debt in Western banks. As the debt mounted, it threatened to have consequences very different from what either Ulbricht or his successor Honecker intended. Even in the short run, Ulbricht's economic policies seemed misguided. True, there was steady growth in heavy industry between 1950 and 1970. But the planners proved unable to assure adequate stocks of consumer goods, provoking unrest in 1969–70 in parts of the country. In the Kremlin, Soviet leaders lost their patience with Ulbricht's arrogance and economic mismanagement and, on 28 July 1970, Brezhnev told Honecker that the Soviet Politburo wanted to see Ulbricht removed from office.[223] On 3 May 1971, it was announced that Ulbricht was stepping down as First Secretary, nominally for reasons of age. In his letter of resignation, Ulbricht proposed Honecker to succeed him.

Orchestral music, 1951–1975

In East Germany, two orchestral composers towered above all others – Hanns Eisler (1898–1962) and Paul Dessau (1894–1979). Born in Leipzig, Eisler was living in Berlin at the time of the Nazi *Machtergreifung*. Eisler left Germany soon after that and traveled around various countries until 1938, when he obtained a permanent visa to immigrate to the United States. In 1942, he moved to Los Angeles and wrote eight film scores, among them *Hangmen Also Die!* (1943), nominated for an Academy Award.[224] While in the USA, he got to know Aaron Copland, Roy Harris, Roger Sessions, Walter Piston, and other prominent American composers. However, Eisler, a convinced Marxist who had composed a Requiem for Lenin in 1935–37, ran into trouble when Senator Joseph McCarthy (1908–1957) launched a campaign against known and suspected communists.[225] Eisler left the USA in March 1948, initially moving to Prague, later settling in East Berlin. He is perhaps best known today for having composed the East German national anthem, for which he carried over a striking passage from his score for *Hangmen Also Die!* to use as the opening motif to celebrate the GDR.[226]

Paul Dessau, born in Hamburg, likewise left Germany in 1933 soon after the Nazi takeover and arrived in the United States in 1939, moving to Hollywood in 1943 where he wrote music for early Walt Disney films, among other scores. He returned to Germany in 1948, settling in East Berlin in what was then the Soviet zone of occupation. Like Eisler, Dessau was influenced by the twelve-tone method of composition, and especially by the music of Arnold Schoenberg, and, as with Eisler, this made for trouble with the GDR's musical commissars such as Ernst Hermann Meyer (1905–1988), the head of the German Composers' Union. As early as 1951, cultural authorities raised objections to the opera *The Trial of Lucullus*

[Das Verhör des Lukullus] for which Bertolt Brecht (1898–1956) had written the libretto and Dessau the music. Meyer and Egon Rentzsch (a representative of the Department of Culture) attended the rehearsals of *Lucullus* on 8 and 9 March and, three days later, delivered a report to the Central Committee, alleging that the music "contains all the elements of formalism, distinguishing itself by the pre-dominance of destructive, caustic dissonances and mechanical percussive music; the method of the triad and of tonality, if present at all, is mostly employed for the purpose of parody or of an archaic mysticism."[227] The opera was banned until Dessau carried out certain revisions to the score, as prescribed by the authorities. The opera was premiered on 12 October 1951, after some, but not all, of the desired revisions had been made.[228]

Two years later, a debate erupted over the libretto for Eisler's opera *Johann Faustus*. Since Eisler was committed to the principle that he was putting his work at the service of the party,[229] the pressure applied on Eisler may reflect, as Peter Davies has suggested, "that the SED perceived *Johann Faustus*" – for all of Eisler's professions of loyalty – "as a serious threat to the stability of its rule, and that the campaign against Eisler was an expression of weakness and desperation, rather than 'totalitar-ian' domination."[230] What Eisler offered was loyalty, but not obedience and hence, in December 1954, he presented a lecture in which he sang the praises of none other than his mentor Schoenberg, whose music the SED elite reviled. In that lecture, Eisler asserted that his mentor was the most important composer of the twentieth century up to then. Perhaps only Eisler, among East German composers, would have dared to speak out on behalf of Schoenberg. But against Eisler's strong defense of the twelve-tonalist, Karl Laux, a professor at the Dresden Academy of Music, accused Eisler of having "unleash[ed] a catastrophe with this lecture."[231] Two decades later – in 1975–22 years after his death, Schoenberg's opera *Moses and Aaron* was performed in Dresden and received critical approval.[232]

The aforementioned Ernst Hermann Meyer, though he never attained the worldwide recognition accorded to Eisler and Dessau, may be counted as East Ger-many's third most accomplished composer. Like Eisler and Dessau, he escaped from Nazi Germany (in 1933); unlike them, however, he chose exile in Great Britain, rather than in the United States. His doctoral dissertation, accepted at Heidelberg University in 1930, was published as a book in 1946.[233] His musical compositions included two symphonies, an opera, chamber music, and other works. As head of the German Composers' Union, Meyer, unlike Eisler and Dessau, was part of the cultural-political establishment and his works were treated as unproblematic. Not surprisingly, as Laura Silverberg has noted, "Meyer's *Mansfelder Oratorium* (1950) [was] lauded in the GDR as a textbook example of socialist realism."[234]

Celebrating past music, 1949–1977

The two Germanys were heirs to a rich musical tradition and the SED honored that tradition, *inter alia*, with commemorations of the tricentenary of the death of Johann Sebastian Bach in 1950 and the 125th anniversary of the birth of Beethoven in 1952. There was even consideration given to the construction of a mausoleum for Bach in Leipzig; this was finally resolved when Bach's last remains were disinterred from beneath the rubble of the Johanniskirche and reinterred in the Thomaskirche, where he had served as cantor.[235]

But when it came to Richard Wagner (1813–1883), there were serious reservations about performing some of his operas, although there were at least six Wagner operas staged in eastern Germany (the Soviet zone of occupation and the GDR) between 1947 and 1956, peaking at 19 performances in 1956.[236] In spite of that, Hitler's fascination with Wagner, the composer's well-known anti-Semitism, and the mysticism of some of his music all contributed to hesitation on the part of some in the cultural-political establishment. Some critics felt that Wagner's operas were beyond redemption and pointed, in particular, to the *Ring* cycle (1848–76) and *Parsifal* (1882). Dessau, for example, admitted that Wagner's music could have an "intoxicating" effect on its listener.[237] But there were repeated pleas on behalf of Wagner's operas, including from Heinz Bär who, in July 1958, suggested a selective approach, performing only those works of Wagner that were not contrary to socialist values.[238]

Ultimately, all of Wagner's operas were deemed acceptable or at least salvageable, provided that one could downplay the mystical and intoxicating aspects of his music (as suggested by Joachim Herz). Harry Kupfer rose to the ultimate challenge – to make *Parsifal*, that quasi-religious and most mystical of Wagner's operas, palatable for the cultural establishment. In 1977, he staged *Parsifal* at the Berlin Staatsoper. To make the opera suitable for his socialist audience, Kupfer changed the ending, among other things by having Parsifal leave his fellow knights behind and set forth on a new path and by giving the otherwise mystical opera an optimistic character.[239]

Writers, 1963–1968

The two most prominent East German novelists were Christa Wolf (1929–2011) and Anna Seghers (1900–1983), both committed communists and members of the SED. Born Christa Ihlenfeld, Wolf ignited her first debate in 1963 with the publication of her novel, *Der geteilte Himmel*, available in English translation under the title, *They Divided the Sky*.[240] The sky which is divided is, of course, the sky over Germany, divided at the end of World War Two. The novel recounts the breakup of a romantic couple living in the GDR when the male, Manfred, flees to West Germany just before the erection of the Berlin Wall in August 1961, leaving his partner, Rita, behind. The novel stirred interest because of its depiction of how political division can result in the severance of a romantic bond.[241]

Anna Seghers was born Netty Reiling in Mainz. Raised in an Orthodox Jewish family, she joined the communist party in 1928, formally exited the Jewish faith in 1932, and fled the Third Reich immediately after the torching of the *Reichstag* in February 1933. She fled abroad, finally ending up in Mexico City where she acquired Mexican citizenship. She returned to Europe after the war and settled in

East Berlin. Giving up her Mexican papers for GDR citizenship, she received the International Stalin Peace Prize in 1952 and was named president of the GDR Writers' Union, holding that office until 1978. Her novel, *Die Gefährden*, published in 1932, warned about the threat posed by Nazism. *The Seventh Cross* [Das siebte Kreuz, 1942] and *Transit* (published in English in 1944) are regarded as her most enduring works.[242] She rarely wrote about East Germany but, after Khrushchev's revelations in February 1956, she went to work on a critical reassessment of how justice was practised in the Soviet bloc; completed in 1964, it was published post-humously in 1990.

Looking at the East German literary scene more broadly, one may note that, by 1963–64, after the SED gave some signals that constructive criticism could be useful, some East German novelists were daring enough to cast light on certain unpleas-ant policies pursued by the SED in the years prior to 1956. Heiner Müller's novels were part of this wave, with his novel *The Construction* [Der Bau, 1965] figuring as an important element here.[243] But at the Eleventh Plenary Session of the SED Cen-tral Committee in December 1965, the leadership signaled that it was no longer willing to allow such criticism. Honecker, as a member of the SED Politburo, told the plenum that the party would not tolerate depictions of life in the GDR as "difficult".[244] Just how sensitive the SED was in Ulbricht's years was made clear with the huge controversy stirred up when the Berliner Ensemble prepared to stage *Seven Against Thebes*, written by the ancient Greek playwright Aeschylus in 467 BCE. The play was being debated just after the Soviets had invaded Czechoslovakia in August 1968. The controversy was only intensified by the fact that the theater group had prepared its own translation of the play, in which references to contem-porary developments were added. Critics believed that the ensemble's portrayal of the fratricide in the play was, or could be interpreted as, a reference to the invasion of Czechoslovakia, with Polynices symbolizing the Soviet Union and his brother Eteocles standing in for Alexander Dubček.

Gender equality

Alongside a promotion of ethical life in the family, the SED also pursued poli-cies which were standard throughout the communist world. Perhaps the SED's highest priority, especially in the first decade, was to bring more women into the work force. This policy was largely successful and, as of 30 September 1970, women comprised 42.5% of industrial workers, 45.8% of persons of working in agriculture and forestry, 68.8% of persons working in postal services and telecom-munications, and 69.2% of those employed in trade (with lower percentages in crafts, construction, and the transport sector).[245] The SED also sought to draw more women into political life. This endeavor was relatively successful in that, as of 1970, 30.4% of the GDR parliament was comprised of women – higher than the comparable figures for Poland, Romania, or Bulgaria.[246] Women made up 30% of the SED's membership at the time. On the other hand, of the 202 persons elected to membership in the SED Central Committee in 1976, only 24 were women. Moreover, during the years 1956–71, only two women were elected to candidate membership in the party's highest decision-making body, the Politburo: Edith Baumann, elected in 1958, and Margarete Müller, elected in 1963.[247] Yet, as early as 1961, the SED announced that, with "the victory of socialist relations of production in 1960/61 . . . the woman question . . . as a social question [has been] solved."[248] Five years earlier, the government passed a law on the family in 1965 which stipulated "the complete equality of the sexes as well as [the state's] protection of marriage and the family."[249] Furthermore, in connection with preparation of the Seven-Year Plan for 1959–65, it was noted that between 1955 and 1958, the number of women in the labor force had shrunk. To address this challenge, a campaign was set in motion at the beginning of the 1960s to improve the skills of the female work force.[250]

But even while wanting to bring more women into the work force, the SED was also concerned in the 1960s and 1970s with the declining birthrate, as women and men opted to raise fewer children than their parents had done. In 1963, the average number of children per family stood at 2.45; by 1974–75, the average number of children per family had sunk to approximately 1.5.[251] Although contraceptive products became available in the GDR in 1965, abortion was the main method of birth control in the 1960s. Under a law passed in 1950, abortion had been illegal except in cases of extreme medical emergency or high risk of a deformed child. But in November 1965, East German women were granted the right to legal abortions under certain specified conditions, among others in cases where the woman already had five or more children or was older than 40.[252] Within two years of passage of this law, the number of legal abortions doubled. For SED authorities, this was nothing short of a "national emergency", prompting them to harness the media to promote the benefits of bearing children.[253]

Toward Church-state rapprochement

The policy of the East German communists could only be different from the policies (themselves heterogeneous) of their fellow bloc communists for several reasons. First, at least in the early years, the SED understood that the Churches – or at least parts of the Churches – had proven to be a bulwark against Nazism.[254] Second, the presence of a large Protestant Church in West Germany and the accessibility of West German television in most of East Germany made it more complicated (than elsewhere in the bloc) to undertake any serious repression where the Churches were concerned. And third, the inter-German organizational unity of the Churches (not just of the mainline Protestant Church) meant that, for the first 20 years of the German Democratic Republic, the SED's religious policy would not be seen as a purely intra-GDR matter.

The first Churches to sever organizational ties with their Western counterparts were the Unity of Brethren (in 1945), the Federation of Free Evangelical

Communities (in 1950), and the Old Lutheran Church (in 1954). But the bishops of the mainline Protestant Church in the GDR held back for the time being from breaking organizational ties with their colleagues in the Federal Republic of Germany. In 1967, the SED increased pressure on the Protestant Church *(Evangelische Kirche)* to set up an organizational structure in the GDR independent of the Church in the FRG.[255] For the time being, the Protestant hierarchy maintained the position that, as a Church synod in April 1967 put it, "We Evangelical Christians in the GDR have no reason to destroy the community of the EKD [Evangelical Church of Germany]. We have good reasons to preserve it."[256]

However, in 1968, the regime adopted a new constitution which "specified that the Churches had to conduct their activities in conformity with the legislative and administrative parameters of the GDR."[257] Before the year was out, the district Churches of Saxony, Mecklenburg, and Thuringia broke links with the United Evangelical Lutheran Church in West Germany and, on 1 December, set up a new organization, restricted to East Germany. Finally, on 10 June 1969, the separation of the Protestant Church in East Germany from its sister Church in the West was completed with the establishment of the Federation of Protestant Churches in the GDR. The Quakers, Reformed Christians, and Methodists who had held back up to now, followed the mainline Protestant Church and, at this point, separated from their co-religionists in West Germany. Two years later, a gathering of Protestant Church leaders in Eisenach (in July 1971) embraced a formula associated with Bishop Albrecht Schönherr (1911–2009) that described the Protestant Church as a "Church in Socialism".[258] The point was that the Church was neither *for* socialism, nor *against* socialism; rather, it preserved its independence, adopting a stance which looked somewhat like loyal opposition. Although some other congregations, including the Baptist Federation and the Seventh Day Adventists, applauded the new formula, the Catholic Church rejected the formula, which seemed to suggest some form of accommodation to socialism.[259]

End of an era

As if to mark the end of an era, the leaders in the three countries of the northern tier were all removed within the two-year period beginning in spring 1969: Alexander Dubček in Czechoslovakia in April 1969, Władysław Gomułka in Poland in December 1970, and Walter Ulbricht in East Germany in May 1971. In the course of just 20 years, the communist states in the Soviet bloc had permanently transformed their societies through their policy of agricultural collectivization,[260] destroyed the pre-communist political elite, promoted the development of heavy industry, stripped the Catholic and Orthodox Churches of much of their wealth and power, and provided both positive and negative inducements to writers, pictorial artists, and composers to produce cultural artifacts the party considered useful. But in combination, Khrushchev's secret speech, the Hungarian Revolution, and the Prague Spring sent political tremors throughout the bloc, making it more than obvious that the old ways of doing business were not sustainable.

The fourth phase, 1971–1980: the failure of the reformist option

The Prague Spring was fundamentally different from the June 1953 uprising in East Germany and the Hungarian Revolution of 1956, even if, like those earlier episodes, it was suppressed by Soviet tanks. The difference lies in the fact that, in 1953 and 1956, people were rising up against communism and communist hegemony was directly attacked, whereas in 1968 it was the communists, declaring their loyalty to the Soviet Union, who were liberalizing the politics of their country. For that reason, the lessons drawn by people across the bloc after the invasion of Czechoslovakia were different, darker. I happened to be in Switzerland at the time of the Soviet bloc invasion of Czechoslovakia and came into conversation with a Czech tourist who, like myself, was taking in the views of the city of Zürich. She was shattered by the news of the invasion and, although she had intended her visit to Switzerland to be brief, a vacation thus, she was resolved not to return to her country. To her mind, she no longer had a country to which she could go back. In Bern, the capital of Switzerland and the next stop on my itinerary, I saw public walls covered with anti-Soviet graffiti. Europe was outraged – and perhaps more than had been the case in 1953 and 1956.

Václav Havel, the famous playwright, dissident, and eventually president of his country, put it this way:

> August 1968 was not merely a matter of replacing a comparatively liberal regime with a more repressive one. It was not just the usual freeze after a period of thaw – it was something more: the end of an era, the disintegration of a spiritual and social climate, a complete break with the past. The importance of the events which brought about this change and the depth of the experience which accompanied it fundamentally altered our whole view of the world. The carnival spirit of 1968 was crushed: not only that, but the entire world as we knew it, the world in which we were so cosily at home, in which we got along so well, the world which had, so to speak, reared us – the tranquil, somewhat comical, somewhat disjointed world of the '60s, so reminiscent of the early Victorian period – all this was destroyed.[261]

Reflecting a few years later on the dead-end which the communist states had reached, the Polish poet and scholar Stanisław Barańczak commented, in a passage cut from the Catholic journal *Więz:* "The existing criteria of value have been falsified and distorted. The force brought to bear against consciousness must, sooner or later, develop into physical force."[262] The disintegration and collapse of the entire communist world, thus, was only a matter of time.

'Normalization' in Czechoslovakia

The Husák era came to be identified with the buzzword "normalization". This embraced coercion (with the police force being increased from 50,000 to 95,000 by 1979), consumerism, and the staging of large events intended to distract people from their worries. In addition, when it came to foreign travel, citizens were divided into three classes: those allowed to travel out of the bloc with their families (the highest echelons); those allowed to travel out of the bloc with some members of their families, provided that a key member was left behind; and those not allowed to travel out of the bloc at all.[263] Leading reformists were expelled from the KSČ and assigned menial jobs, such as window washing. The Federal Assembly, the Czech National Council, the Slovak National Council, the Trade Union Council, the federal government, and the Union of Young People were all purged – in each case between three and six times in the period October 1969-March 1971.[264] Additional purges were carried out in the Ministry of Internal Affairs, the People's Militia, and the army, as well as of many regional and district chief secretaries. Then, in January 1972, police arrested approximately 200 members of the oppositionist Socialist Movement of Czechoslovak Citizens, which had been set up in October 1969, putting its leaders on trial.[265] Local wits, recalling Dubček's slogan, "socialism with a human face," now mocked Husák's policies and programs as amounting to "repression with a human face."[266]

At a CC meeting in January 1970, stealing a line from János Kádár, Husák declared: "He who is not against us is our potential ally. He is not an enemy, he must be cultivated, he must be won over."[267] Following the same formula applied in the other northern-tier bloc states, the Husák regime hoped to pacify the population by improving the availability of consumer goods, allowing Western films and soap operas to be shown on Czechoslovak television, and making it easier for Czechoslovaks to build weekend houses, the number of which increased from 128,000 in 1969 to 225,000 by 1981.[268] As in the case of other socialist bloc countries, heavy subsidization of food prices and basic services, such as bus tickets, was considered essential, even at the cost of mounting foreign debts.[269] But coercion was also part of Husák's toolkit and, in addition to the repressive measures already mentioned, those who refused to tow the line could be dismissed from their employment and the children of those identified as "dissidents" could be denied access to higher education. As for Havel, he was given a four-year prison term in May 1979. There were also political trials of other persons.[270]

As promised, the country was officially federalized on 1 January 1969 although federalization was rolled back just two years later when an amendment to the constitution restored federal authority over the economy and entrusted responsibility for state security to the federal Ministry of Internal Affairs.[271] In fact, the StB (the secret police) kept close tabs on the population. As Mary Heimann recounts, ". . . an ever increasing proportion of the population became aware of being watched, filmed or bugged, or actually had the experience of being called in by the StB for a 'little chat' (whether to be reprimanded, invited to collaborate, or both) . . ."[272]

Culture

Husák's idea of normalization included purging the Composers' Union, banning the publication of translations of Western novels, and suppressing theatrical works his regime considered problematic. Among those talented composers unable to present their works in "normalized" Czechoslovakia were Miroslav Kabeláč, Klement Slavický, Vladimir Sommer, Svatopluk Havelka, and Jan Klusák. The Union now became the domain of "mediocre and downright inept composers."[273] The theater journal *Divadlo*, which had displayed reformist inclinations was suppressed. Havel's plays were banned, as were also the works of Franz Kafka.[274] Publication of already completed translations of works by Ernest Hemingway, Jean-Paul Sartre, and F. Scott Fitzgerald, among other Western authors, was stopped while, among émigré Czech writers, Josef Škvorecký, A. J. Liehm, and Eduard Goldstücker were unable to publish their works in their native country.[275] Lest anyone be uncertain as to what the authorities wanted to see, *Svobodné slovo* [The Free Word] published a programmatic statement of the Czech Writers' Union in 1971, declaring that "Socialist literature, its artistic strength, should serve the people . . . [and] cultivate a feeling of pride on the part of citizens in the socialist homeland."[276] With that narrow focus, many ideas for the world of fiction could never be realized and, to take one example, it was only at the end of the 1970s that it became possible to publish science fiction.[277]

Nor was the film sector spared. The director of the Czechoslovak Film Export Company, Alois Poledňák, was arrested, accused of espionage, and finally released after he engaged in self-criticism. Later, the artistic staffs of the Czechoslovak film industry were purged. In consequence, a number of film directors, script writers, and camera operators emigrated.[278] Jiří Pick, writing in *Tvorba* in 1971, claimed that films made recently in Czechoslovakia exemplified the "degenerate" notion of "art for the sake of art," by which he meant ignoring the party's agenda for the cultural sector.[279] Reinforcing this position, M. Válek reported that speakers at the party's Fourteenth Congress (held in May 1971) had underlined "the necessity of waging a struggle to the finish against revisionist tendencies in the cultural sector."[280]

The story of the Jazz Section is unique in the Soviet bloc (though it had some equivalents in socialist Yugoslavia). What made it unique was the fact that it was established under the rubric of the Musicians' Union in 1971, which is to say that it was founded legally, only to be ordered to cease all activity in 1980 and dissolved in 1984. In the 11 years of its legal existence, the section launched a members-only *Jazzbulletin* that published 28 issues. The print run was 3,000 copies, matching the legal limit of 3,000 members. But as the bulletin was passed from hand to hand, it has been estimated that each issue was read by at least 100,000 persons.[281] In March 1974, authorities granted permission for the section to organize its first Prague Jazz Days festival. The second festival followed in March 1975, followed by the third already in October 1975. The festival became an annual event. But in 1980, the Jazz Section's Prague Jazz Days festival was banned "on the pretext that the event, for which some 15,000 fans had purchased tickets, might become the occasion for 'public disturbances'."[282]

In 1983, the regime decided to quash the Jazz Section, which numbered 7,000 members by then – 4,000 more than allowed. The Czech Musicians' Union was ordered to disband the Jazz Section; with neither the Union nor the Jazz Section in compliance with directives, the regime declared the dissolution of the entire Union in Fall 1984, thus including the Jazz Section.[283] Eventually, in September 1986, the authorities took five Section leaders into custody and put them on trial. They were convicted in March 1987 "of engaging in an 'unauthorized business venture'."[284] Two members received prison sentences of 16 months and 10 months respectively; the other three were handed suspended prison sentences.

Among the many talented rock bands in Czechoslovakia, the most famous is clearly Plastic People of the Universe. Formed by bassist Milan "Mejla" Hlavsa in 1968, less than a month after the Soviet invasion, the Plastic People took their name from a Frank Zappa song. The band, although highly nonconformist, was granted an official license to perform in public. But when it turned out that the Plastic People's concerts resembled "hippie happenings", the authorities became nervous and revoked the band's license. Oddly, the license was restored in 1972, only to be revoked for a second time after the authorities decided that the band's music was "morbid" and declared that it could have a "negative social impact".[285] But even without a license, they continued to perform privately at people's houses or at wedding parties. Their performances and texts were sometimes confusing as, for example, with their song "The Wonderful Mandarin", which they recorded attired in Roman-style togas.

When I met with two members of the Plastic People in Prague in 2018, they insisted that they had not intended to be political and that they had just wanted to play their music their way. But in 1976 they had released their album, *Egon Bondy's Happy Hearts Club Banned*, which included the obviously political song "One Hundred Points", with overtly anti-regime lyrics. The song included the lines:

> They are afraid of the old for their memory.
> They are afraid of the young for their innocence . . .
> They are afraid of the dead . . .
> They are afraid of party members.
> They are afraid of those who are not in the party.
> They are afraid of science.
> They are afraid of art.
> They are afraid of books and poems . . .
> They are afraid to let people out.
> They are afraid to let people in . . .
> They are afraid of their families.
> They are afraid of their relatives.
> They are afraid of their former friends and comrades.
> They are afraid of their present friends and comrades.
> They are afraid of each other . . .
> They are afraid of jokes.
> They are afraid of the upright.
> They are afraid of the honest.
> They are afraid of the educated . . .

They are afraid of Marx.
They are afraid of Lenin.
They are afraid of truth . . .
So why the hell are WE afraid of THEM?[286]

On 30 March 1976, police arrested the Plastic People, together with members of other unlicensed rock groups and their fans – totaling 27 persons. The Plastic People were put on trial and two of them – Ivan Jirous and Vratislav Brabenec – were found guilty of "organized disturbance of the peace"[287] and given prison sentences of 18 months and eight months respectively.

Another rock group at that time, DG307 was equally critical.[288] But the repression of the Husák era was not able to restrain the rockers, and the straight-laced authorities were outraged by the appearance of punk and by rock groups singing about sex or about the drab apartments in which they lived. In March 1983, a strident article signed by Jan Kryzl (a pseudonym) appeared in the publication *Tribuna*: in it, "Kryzl" alleged that ". . . rock music encouraged passivity and a retreat from reality into a dream world," adding that "[t]he aim is more than obvious – to . . . instill in young people's minds the philosophy of 'no future' and attitudes, conduct, and views that are alien to socialism."[289]

Gender inequality

Although the proportion of women serving in the Central Committee crept upwards from 8.7% in 1971 to 15% in 1976, women were less well represented in decision-making positions.[290] In conformity with standard practice throughout the bloc (with a modest exception in the GDR), in no representative or decision-making body did women account for more than 30% and, in the years 1971–1975, they made up just 24.7% of the representatives in the Chamber of Nations, although their representation in that body rose to 27.3% with the 1976 elections. This disproportion was mirrored in the economic sphere, where women accounted for about half of the work force but held only 4.8% of enterprise managerial positions in 1970.[291] This disparity may be due in part to socialization, judging from interviews conducted at 42 enterprises in the early 1970s, which showed that less than 10% of the women interviewed preferred to work under a female supervisor (compared with less than 3% of men), and that 44% of the women said that they were more comfortable working under male supervisors.[292]

The Catholic Church

After Husák took over as First Secretary of the party in April 1969, attacks on the Church in the party press intensified and party officials exerted pressure on parents to withdraw their children from religious instruction. In consequence, enrollments in religious instruction declined over the course of the 1970s.[293] Those children who nonetheless continued with religious instruction were denied university enrollment.[294] In the 1970s and into the 1980s, Catholic clergy had to endure harassment (including being administered extremely strict alcohol tests after drinking wine at Mass, if they were driving), intimidation, and confiscation of religious literature. Some clergy were even arrested.[295] Catholic activists fought back by launching the bulletin *Informace o církvi* [Information about the Church] and the theological journal, *Teologický sborník* (1977–79), followed by *Teologické texty*.

As a by-product of the Prague Spring, the pro-regime Peace Committee of Catholic Clergy had been shut down. But in August 1971, this association was resurrected under the new name, Pacem in Terris. Although Pacem in Terris was condemned by both the Holy See and Cardinal František Tomášek (1899–1992) of Prague, the regime insisted that only members of Pacem in Terris could be appointed to head dioceses. The result was that, in the years leading up to 1973, only one diocese (Prague) had a resident bishop (Tomášek); the remaining 12 were vacant. Then, in 1973, the Vatican agreed to the appointment of four members of Pacem in Terris to serve as bishops. There were no further episcopal appointments until 1988, when the Vatican was able to secure the appointment of three new bishops, among whom none were members of the regime's association for priests. Meanwhile, the number of ordinations was not keeping pace with need and, by 1981, one third of Catholic parishes lacked a priest.

Independent activism

The 1976 trial of the Plastic People of the Universe provided the spark for the launch of the Charter 77 human rights initiative. It was the members of the Plastic People of the Universe who contacted playwright Václav Havel to ask for his help. Havel and others who respected the band's right to perform became involved in the trial and, as early as December 1976, drafted a protest signed by 243 persons, including academics, journalists, former party functionaries, and writers, and made public on 6 January 1977. Havel, Pavel Landovský, and Ludvík Vaculík undertook to deliver a copy of the protest to the National Assembly. The protest merely asked the government to respect its own laws and the international covenants it had signed. However, the three were arrested before they could reach the Assembly. Nonetheless, the organizers of this initiative decided to continue to present reports and protests, focusing on human and civil rights, while insisting that Charter 77 was not an organization but rather "a free, informal, and open community of people of different convictions, different faiths, and different professions, united by the will to strive, individually and collectively, for the respect of civic and human rights."[296] The original declaration by Charter 77 was signed by 243 persons; by June 1980, more than a thousand persons had lent their names to the declaration.[297] In that declaration, the signatories offered the following account of their initiative:

> Charter 77 is not an organization; it has no rules, permanent bodies or formal membership. It embraces everyone who agrees with its ideas, participates in its work, and supports it. It does not form the basis for any oppositional

political activity . . . It does not aim, then, to set out its own programs for political or social reforms or changes, but within its own sphere of activity it wishes to conduct constructive dialogue with the political and state authorities, particularly by drawing attention to various individual cases where human and civil rights are violated.[298]

Charter 77 is discussed at greater length in the following chapter.

Not long after Charter 77 began to work, another human rights organization, the Committee for the Defense of the Unjustly Persecuted (better known under the acronym VONS) was formed on 24 April 1978. All of the members of VONS were Charter 77 signatories.[299] VONS began issuing reports on violations of people's most basic rights, including beatings and unwarranted house searches. Some of the leading activists in VONS were put on trial in 1979 and given prison sentences, but VONS continued to issue reports and protests. By mid-1986, VONS had prepared and issued more than 500 communiques and other materials concerning state repression in Czechoslovakia. There were other *samizdat* (underground) publications that emerged in Czechoslovakia in the late 1970s or the beginning of the 1980s, including the aforementioned *Informace o církvi* [Information about the Church], which came out on a monthly basis, beginning in 1980.

Poland – the Gierek formula

In Poland, Edward Gierek, the first secretary of the Katowice voivodship 1957–70, became First Secretary of the Polish United Workers' Party at the end of December 1970. He quickly developed a formula for rule, the "Gierek formula", which consisted of four elements: (1) populism (instead of democracy), meeting with ordinary factory workers to listen to their concerns, presenting himself as a 'man of the people', and presenting himself in short newsreels as a man concerned about people's problems; (2) raising wages; (3) keeping prices low (to be made possible by a combination of purchasing what Poland could in the GDR and borrowing from Western banks, then supposedly investing the funds in export-driven industries, so that the products could be sold abroad to pay off the debt); and (4) chopping up the voivodships into smaller administrative units in order to prevent a rival from copying his own route to power.

When Gierek came to power, Poland's indebtedness was low (US $1.2 billion in 1972) and initially Poland's standard of living improved in the 1970s. But the oil price hike hurt Poland (as well as Yugoslavia and other countries in the region) very hard, and borrowing got out of control. By 1980, Poland's foreign debt would rise to US $24 billion. In the meantime, on the one-year anniversary of his coming to power, Gierek projected confidence, telling delegates to the Sixth PZPR Congress in December 1971 that the party had overcome its past "errors and distortions" and projected that national income would increase by as much as 39% by 1975 and that industrial output would increase by 48–50% over the same period.[300] In the same report, Gierek called for increasing agricultural production and central planning and pledged that "Our supreme goal is the systematic improvement of the living standards of the work[ing] people."[301] In the short run, a Soviet credit in 1971 made it possible for the authorities to assure ample stocks of meat, grain, and lard. Wages grew by an average of 5.3% in 1971 and, over the next five years, wages rose by an average of 7.2% per year. Meanwhile, the cost of living rose by just 12.2% over the entire five-year period.[302] In the years 1970–75, the Polish GNP increased by 59% and industrial employment expanded by 14.8%. Moreover, thanks to a prolonged freeze on food prizes, real wages in 1975 were 40.9% greater than in 1970.[303] After a million apartments were constructed during the first five years under Gierek, the waiting time for an apartment was shorter than previously.[304] It looked like good times for Poles. But the oil price hike following the 1973 war in the Middle East sowed the seeds of future problems. Soon after the oil price hike was announced, taxi fares and the cost of bus tickets increased.

Moreover, the relative prosperity of the early 1970s, purchased with credits from Western banks, could not be sustained. Economic problems became apparent as early as mid-1974, with strikes and protests reflecting local discontent. Poland was, at that point, exporting meat; this resulted in shortages of meat which, in turn, provoked women in Warsaw to vent their anger by attacking several grocery stores. As Jan de Weydenthal has noted, "To some extent, [these economic difficulties] were brought on by a series of unintended consequences of Poland's reliance on foreign [credits] for stimulating domestic expansion."[305] In addition to meat shortages in many regions, there were also shortages of other consumer goods in Silesia.

Meanwhile, the ruling party increasingly felt that the heavy subsidization of food prices could not be sustained. Accordingly, on 24 June 1976, PM Piotr Jaroszewicz announced steep price increases in food prices, of 69% on average for meat and 50% for butter, while doubling the price of sugar.[306] Once again there were huge protests by industrial workers and, on 25 June, the government withdrew the price increases and continued with the massive subsidies needed to keep prices low. In the aftermath, authorities promised to consult with the public in the future before taking decisions affecting people's livelihood. In November, Moscow pledged to provide $1.3 billion worth of food, consumer goods, and raw materials on a credit basis. The PZPR understood that it would make sense to change its economic strategy; but aside from an insignificant increase in investments in light industry, economic mismanagement continued as before. Investments in heavy industry remained high and subsidies for food and consumer goods crept upwards. To manage all of this, the government increasingly relied on loans from Western banks. The mid-1980 debt to Western banks of $24 billion represented a sharp increase from $10 billion just four years prior.

In the meantime, on 16 October 1978, in a move that would add fresh impetus to the pressure on the communist system, the Catholic College of Cardinals elected Cardinal Karol Wojtyła, the Archbishop of Kraków (1920–2005), to the papacy. In honoring his three immediate predecessors, he took the name John Paul II. In a delayed reaction, Mieczysław Rakowski insisted, in March 1979, that Poland would "remain a lay state."[307] Just three months later, "the Polish pope", as

Poles proudly called him, made the first of seven visits to Poland, 2–10 June 1979. The visit was timed to be close to the 900th anniversary of the martyrdom of St. Stanisław, who had confronted the King over his immoral rule and who, as a consequence, had been put to death. As Cezar Ornatowski has noted,

> The Pope's first visit to Poland was a national awakening, a festival of reality, "nine days of freedom" that prepared the ground for everything that happened over the next twenty years. The crowds that attended the papal Masses went beyond anyone's expectations; the first public Mass in Warsaw's Victory Square was attended by 300,000 faithful . . . The Polish people began to see their strength in numbers and spirit. In spite of the communist façade, Poles discovered that most of them thought and felt alike.[308]

Meanwhile, already in July 1976, 14 intellectuals had formed a Committee for the Defense of Workers (KOR[309]), and began collecting information about participants in the strike. Among its founders were Jacek Kuroń, who had played a role in pushing for reform twenty years earlier, and novelist Jerzy Andrzejewski. In 1977, KOR launched the Flying University, under which lectures by specialists would be held in private homes. Then, on 29 September 1977, KOR took a new name, the Committee for Social Self-Defense-Committee for the Defense of Workers (KSS-KOR[310]). With that, the organization expanded its remit.[311] That same year, the Movement for the Defense of Human and Civil Rights (ROP-CiO) was formed and began issuing *samizdat* (underground) materials. KOR, ROPCiO, and other organizations brought out approximately 30 newspapers and other periodicals, printing some of these, mimeographing others. There were also *samizdat* publishers such as NOWa[312], headed by Miroslav Chojecki, as well as underground literary journals such as *Zapis* [Record], published in Łódź, and even underground political journals such as *Res Publica*.[313] Subsequently, in September 1979, journalist-historian Leszek Moczulski took the lead in founding the Confederation for an Independent Poland (KPN[314]) on the back of the underground newspaper, *Gazeta Polska*, which Moczulski had set up the previous February. The KPN was ideologically conservative and loyal to Catholic doctrine; it was the most clearly anti-communist of the underground organizations set up in the late 1970s.[315]

In mid-August 1980, strikes broke out at the Lenin Shipyard in Gdánsk, subsequently spreading to Warsaw and to mines in the south of Poland. On 16 August, representatives of 21 enterprises in and around Gdánsk, including from the shipyard, established an Interfactory Strike Committee led by electrician Lech Wałęsa.[316] The workers demanded the reinstatement of fellow workers who had been sacked, increases in pay, and a meeting with PM Jaroszewicz. The meeting with the PM focused on the workers' 21 demands, among which the key demand was recognition of the workers' right to establish independent trade unions. The government reluctantly conceded on this point, as well as on others, signing an agreement with representatives of the Interfactory Strike Committee at the end of August. On 22

September 1980, the Solidarity Independent Trade Union was formally established as a legal organization.

Andrzej Wajda

Looking over the list of twentieth-century filmmakers in East Central Europe, Andrzej Wajda (1926–2016) is clearly among the most accomplished. His best films include: *Ashes and Diamonds* (1958), which subtly subverted a pro-communist novel by Jerzy Andrzejewski; *Man of Marble* (1977), which tells the story of a television reporter who wanted to retell the story of the Stakhanovite campaign in the 1950s, in which a bricklayer (Mateusz Birkut, a fictional character) supposedly surpassed all previous records in bricklaying; *Danton* (1983), a Polish-French joint production starring Gerard Depardieu and ostensibly dealing with events associated with the French Revolution while, "between the lines", an observant viewer could discern that the real message was about Poland in the 1970s leading up to 1980; and *Katyn* (2007), which focused on the Katyn massacre of an estimated 15,000 Polish officers by the Soviets during World War Two. *Katyn* earned Wajda a nomination for Best Foreign Language Film, following a Lifetime Achievement Award from the Academy of Motion Picture Arts and Sciences in 2000.[317]

Wajda's *Man of Marble* is a film about propaganda and how it figured in the communist system. The image of the bricklayer-shock worker was a communist fabrication, even if film footage could be shot of his apparently celeritous work. The trick was to give the bricklayers to be filmed a special diet for several weeks, to build up their strength, to film the original bricklayer (and also the actor in the film) working at breakneck speed for, say, 30 minutes, and to allow viewers to imagine that he could work at that speed for the entire day. In fact, the routine in the Stakhanovite days was for the shock workers to be allowed to rest for most of the rest of the day after completing their display either for a live audience or for film.[318] The footage was also carefully edited to remove any negative features.[319]

Women and abortion

After the legalization of abortion in Poland in 1956, the Catholic Church mobilized for a long fight to reverse this legislation. In 1965 and again in 1971, clergy were given instructions on how to influence adults' thinking about family and children. In addition, the clergy were to emphasize that not only abortion but also artificial contraception and *coitus interruptus* were serious sins.[320] The Church's threats of supernatural punishment notwithstanding, the use of modern contraceptives increased six-fold between 1969 and 1979.[321] The only birth control method approved by the Church was the not entirely reliable rhythm method, involving abstinence during periods when the woman was fertile. The state backed the establishment of the Society for Conscious Motherhood (later renamed the Society for Family Development) which, with the benefit of state subsidies, set up a nationwide network of clinics/counseling centers. From the Church's point of view, the two-fold problem with state-supported counseling was that it endorsed contraceptives and did not condemn abortion. The Church competed with its own network of counseling centers which urged women to respect Church law. But, with the healthcare system covering 70% of the cost of contraceptives (when prescribed by a physician), the proportion of women making use of birth control pills increased during the 1970s.[322]

The Catholic Church in the 1970s

The decade opened with Gierek making several concessions to the Church; among these was permission for the construction of new churches, including in hitherto church-free Nowa Huta,[323] leading to a boom in church construction. There were three major events or episodes in the life of the Polish Church in the 1970s. The first involved the regime's proposed amendments to the constitution, announced in 1975. Among these amendments was a new constitutional guarantee of Poland's "unbreakable fraternal bond with the Soviet Union."[324] Both the Catholic hierarchy and a number of intellectuals protested but the regime made only a few innocuous modifications, and the amendments, largely intact, were ratified by the Sejm on 10 February 1976.

The other two major events – the election of Cardinal Wojtyła to the papacy and his first visit to Poland as pope – were already discussed above. What may be stressed here is that, as I wrote in 2017, with his election as pope, "the entire country pulsed with excitement or, where the communists were concerned, with consternation."[325] Where the pontiff's visit in 1979 is concerned, his call for official recognition of workers' right to form their own labor unions, greatly strengthened the resolve of workers to secure this right.[326]

Kádárism in Hungary, Part Two: 1968–1980

In the first years after the crushing of the Hungarian Revolution, Kádár was widely hated and generally seen as having betrayed Hungarian interests. Over time, however, by improving people's economic situation, allowing people a measure of freedom in their private lives, and declining to accept a cultic promotion of his leadership, Kádár was able to win a certain measure of popular acceptance. As Elemér Hankiss put it in 1990, under Kádár, "people renounced their rights to power and participation and, in exchange, they got (by Eastern European standards) a relatively tolerant administration . . . a kind of cultural pluralism, and the opportunity to build up for themselves a more and more comfortable Western-European-style material life."[327] In fact, soon after 1956, the regime relaxed its control of culture, granted more autonomy to news editors to decide on the coverage to be given to events, and pushed to improve and extend formal education.[328]

Hungary's New Economic Mechanism

By the early 1960s, the Hungarian economy was slowing down and, in December 1963, the Central Committee adopted a resolution commissioning an expert study of the country's economic situation. The commission was headed by Rezső Nyers (1923–2018). Following the commission's completion of its work, the Central Committee decided on a far-reaching economic reform known as the New Economic Mechanism (NEM). The first reforms were introduced in May 1966, but the launch of the NEM is typically associated with 1 January 1968, when a new system of pricing was introduced.[329] There was some loosening of central control, but the state kept prices of basic foods and raw materials stable.[330] Thanks to the NEM, Hungary maintained average annual growth rates of 6.8% in national product, 6.3% in growth industrial production, and 8.5% in gross capital investment during the years 1966–70.[331]

However, party conservatives objected to NEM's departure from economic orthodoxy and, by 1972, managed to bring the reform virtually to an end – at serious cost to the Hungarian economy. Conservatives insisted on making large capital investments at an average rate of 8.5% annually also in the years 1973–77. Since the Hungarian economy could not cover these investments, the economic planners turned to Western banks for hard-currency loans.[332] At the time that the New Economic Mechanism was launched, Hungary's foreign debt was modest, but, given the oil price "shock" of 1973–74 and the large capital investments pushed by party conservatives in spite of the hike in oil prices and other economic complications, the country looked increasingly to Western banks to cover deficits. Hungary's foreign debt increased by more than 500% in the years 1973–78, reaching an unsustainable $9 billion by 1980. Already by 1978, Hungary could meet its foreign debt service obligations only by taking out further loans.[333]

In 1978, the regime reversed course and revived the reforms initially introduced a decade earlier. It was also decided to allow a partial reprivatization in agriculture. NEM tolerated wide differentials in income, which did not benefit those at the lower end of the economic ladder. Indeed, as early as the early 1970s, the economic underclass comprised between 15 and 20% of the population.[334] In an interview in late 1982, economist Márton Tardos argued that the reforms which had been introduced up to then had not gone far enough. But the reforms which were needed to put the economy on stable footing, according to Tardos, "would inevitably entail negative side-effects on the living standards of 'certain social groups'."[335]

Cardinal Lekai's "small steps"

After the death of Cardinal Mindszenty in 1975 and the appointment of László Lekai (1910–1986) as his successor as Archbishop of Esztergom and Primate of Hungary in February 1976, a new chapter in relations between the Catholic Church and the Budapest regime opened. The Vatican chose Lekai precisely because it was confident that he would pursue a policy of compromise and accommodation with the communist state,[336] and Lekai lived up to expectations by adopting a strategy of making "small steps" to better the situation for the Church in Hungary. For its part, the regime allowed all episcopal vacancies to be filled that year; the following year, Kádár visited the Vatican, where he was received by Pope Paul VI.[337] Elevated to the College of Cardinals just over three months after his installation as Archbishop of Esztergom, Lekai pleased authorities in Budapest by condemning conscientious objectors to military service, calling those who argued for a social service alternative "destroyers of the Church".[338] While Lekai's willingness to compromise with the regime certainly contributed to a relaxation in Church-state relations, it also provoked the emergence of "small groups of close-knit communities of faithful patterned on the gatherings of early Christians."[339] Known as basis groups or base communities, they were led by Fr. György Bulanyi (1919–2010), a Piarist priest. Cardinal Lekai died on 1 July 1986 and was succeeded in the office of Primate and Archbishop of Esztergom by László Paskai (1927–2015), who had previously served as Bishop of Veszprém and as co-adjutor-Archbishop of Kalocsa. Archbishop Paskai would be elevated to the College of Cardinals in 1988.

The status of women

Hungarian women registered some improvement in terms of leadership positions in public administration and enterprises. In 1970, women accounted for 6.4% of enterprise managers, 11.8% of supervisors in public administration, 15.3% of supervisors in city administration, and 33.8% of financial managers and business executives; ten years later, the respective figures were 12.1%, 19.6%, 29.1%, and 40.9%.[340] Recall that, according to Marxist-Leninist doctrine, socialism should have afforded the best guarantee of the full equality of women with men. For that matter, in the years 1970–80, there were some 110 reports on the status and integration of women presented to the Politburo.[341] Meanwhile, throughout the 1970s, Hungarian women were overrepresented in unskilled and semiskilled jobs[342] – a sure sign that the party was lagging in its nominal aspiration to achieve full gender equality.

Where women were concerned, what absorbed the attention of Hungarian policy-makers the most was the birthrate. In 1953, a law had been passed banning abortions, regardless of the circumstances. But a new law was passed in the early 1960s, under which it was left up to each woman to decide if an abortion was indicated. This resulted in a steep decline in the number of births in the short run; indeed, immediately after this law was passed, the number of abortions almost matched the number of live births. Thus, in 1973, new restrictions on abortion were introduced, although these were not as severe as the regulations adopted 20 years earlier.[343]

However, there were unintended and most unfortunate consequences with the system under which Hungarian women could still obtain abortions after 1973. The first such consequence was that women seeking abortions were viewed as deviants and, given the circumstances, they were often shunted into overcrowded wards and not given the best treatment. This, in turn, had the further consequence of inducing "psychological stress, reinforc[ing] feelings of guilt and caus[ing] long-lasting problems for both women and their partners."[344]

Romanian exceptionalism

It was Romania which showed most clearly what were the limits of local auton-omy. Already in April 1954, Gheorghe Gheorghiu-Dej (1901–1965), General Sec-retary of the Romanian Communist Party, resisted Soviet pressure to share power along the lines of what Rákosi had been forced to do vis-à-vis Nagy. Subsequently, when, in 1962–63, Khrushchev advocated a division of labor among the Soviet bloc countries and wanted Romania to stress agriculture, Gheorghiu-Dej, backed by fellow Politburo member Nicolae Ceaușescu (1918–1989), refused and insisted on maintaining an emphasis on heavy industry, which is to say the Stalin model of economic development. In a confidential lecture to students at the party academy in 1964, Ceaușescu praised Stalin's theoretical legacy, especially his *Problems of Len-inism,* which he described as obligatory reading for anyone wishing to understand Marxism-Leninism.

After Gheorghiu-Dej passed away in March 1965; Ceaușescu took charge as General Secretary. Ceaușescu strengthened his control over party structures and, in November 1971, the Romanian Communist Party rehabilitated Stalinist aesthet-ics (socialist realism) and attacked "liberalism" within the party. In foreign policy, however, Ceaușescu was able to win a certain amount of freedom:

- he was the first among the bloc leaders to recognize the Federal Republic of Germany (1967);
- he refused to break relations with Israel in 1967;
- he purchased arms from Great Britain;
- he took Romania into the Nonaligned Movement, albeit as an observer;
- he was able to establish that there would be no Warsaw Pact exercises on Romanian soil and Romanian troops did not participate in Warsaw Pact exer-cises, being represented only by a few high officers;
- he supported Dubček in 1968.

The reason why the Soviets allowed Romanian deviation in foreign policy was that it did not present a threat to Soviet interests: to put it bluntly, Romania did not present an attractive alternative model (as Czechoslovakia did for a few months in 1968). On the contrary, controls in Romania were as severe as any in the bloc. Moroever, after the Romanian foreign debt reached a high level, Ceaușescu decided to pay it off – unlike other communist leaders facing similar situations. He did so by arranging to export most of what could be sold (including fine clothes and fine crystal) and by turning off the electricity in ordinary residences for all but three hours each evening. In restaurants, customers were handed a menu with a long list of choices; but in practice very few of the dishes listed were actually available.

Ceaușescu's rule was also characterized by an extreme form of nepotism and cro-nyism. His wife Elena was elected to the Central Committee in 1973, subsequently being admitted to the Permanent Bureau of the Political Executive Committee. His son Nicu became first secretary of the Union of Communist Youth in 1983. His brother Nicolae Andruta Ceauşescu (whom had N.C. forced to adopt a middle name) became Lt.-Gen. in the Ministry of the Interior. Another brother, Ion, became first vice chairman of the State Planning Commission in 1983. Yet another brother, Ilie, was appointed deputy minister of national defense and secretary of the Higher Political Council in 1983. Other family members with high office included adopted son Valentin, daughter Zoia Elena, older brother Marin, and Elena's brother Gheorghe Petrescu, who became deputy prime minister. In addition, Ceauşescu promoted a number of former neighbors from his home village of Scorniceşti.[345]

Ceauşescu looked to Romania's historical heroes to legitimate his rule and, accordingly, promoted the cult of Prince Stephen the Great of Moldavia (reigned 1457–1504) and the cult of Prince Michael the Brave of Wallachia (reigned 1593–1601). He and his wife even posed in ermine robes on at least one occasion and, when Elena failed to earn a Ph.D., her husband applied pressure so that she would be awarded the degree. The Ceauşescus took credit for successes but never took the blame for failures. Interestingly enough, Nicolae Ceauşescu was at one point named an honorary citizen of Disneyland!

Ceauşescu visited China in June 1971 and was enormously impressed with Mao's Cultural Revolution and the way it stamped out all expressions of individuality. The *Conducător*, as he liked to be called, was also impressed with the promotion of the cult of Mao Zedong. Back in Romania, Ceauşescu announced his July Theses on 6 July – a 17-point program for what amounted to a "little Cultural Revolution".[346] The term "cultural revolution" was not used in Romania. Rather, reference was made to "raising ideological consciousness in the many-sided developed socialist society."[347]

The beginnings of Ceauşescu's personality cult were evident as early as 1969, in the wake of his public criticism of the Soviet invasion of Czechoslovakia, but it was reinforced by his exposure to Maoism. Various epithets were conjured to refer to him, including "Titan of Titans", "The Fatherland's First Servant", "The Builder of Everything that is Good and Just", "the glorious oak from Scorniceşti", "the Guardian of the Kingdom of Romania", and "the Eternal Star in the Romanian Sky".[348] Other epithets applied to him included "the son of the sun", "the magic prince", "the morning star", and "the Jupiter of the Carpathians".[349] All levels of Romanian society took part in the cult, including children in kindergarten. Among other communist dictators, only Stalin and Hoxha had similarly extreme personality cults.

The cultural sector

In July 1971, Ceauşescu presented a report to the RCP's Executive Committee (equivalent of the Politburo), in which he called for renewed attention to Marxist-Leninist values in literature. Although he used the term "socialist humanism" to characterize what he had in mind, the gist of his remarks was that a restoration of socialist realism as the guidepost for literature would be beneficial.[350] Initially, literati and other cultural artists opposed this demand. But, after a short while, the regime was able to bring the writers into line.

In noncommunist countries, literature, art, and music need not be national; on the contrary, works in any of these genres can fantasize about people, places, and things and experiment with alternative methods of composition or art styles having no special connection with the home country. But in communist countries, the arts were supposed to be useful and, in this vein, the philosophical monthly *Revista Filozofie* carried an article in 1974 stating that ". . . art is national through its content, its value system [and] its traditions . . . and through the role it plays in society."[351] Indeed, the author was restating the concept spelled out in the party's 1974 program, which underlined that "Art develops in close connection with the social and national development of society in accord with the specific features of an epoch . . ."[352]

That meant, in turn, that works which were not relevant for Romania or useful to the Romanian CP did not need to reach the public. Thus, according to one Romanian novelist, in the world of theater, some of the best plays were not being staged.[353] The censors were ever vigilant for possible instances of "subversive ambiguity",[354] and viewed dramatists and novelists alike with deep suspicion, even hostility. From time to time, there were objections to renewed efforts to press writers into a common mold.[355] But there were rewards for compliance and penalties for opposition. Thus, after a few intellectuals dared to criticize the regime in 1977, they were quickly put behind bars.[356] Excellence in the creative arts was of little interest to the bureaucrats. Thus, not surprisingly, by the mid-1970s, there were new currents of conformity and dogmatism among writers.[357] And finally and predictably, Ceaușescu ordered his minions to obstruct translations of Western literature.

Gender inequality

As elsewhere in the bloc, women were viewed, in part, as baby machines and hence, when fertility and birth rates declined, abortion was either seriously restricted or simply banned. Romania under Ceaușescu did not differ in principle from the other bloc countries, but only in degree.[358] But, with Ceaușescu, extremes were the norm and thus the effort to suppress all abortions took on extreme dimensions. Of course, the controls were accompanied by maternity benefits considered sufficient to make it relatively simple, at least in theory, for women to carry babies to term. Policy-makers intended that women would not only give birth but also raise their children and, of course, teach them to love the Conducător. But wealthy women were able to obtain abortions for a "fee", some healthy babies were sold to Americans, and thousands of unwanted newborn babies were simply dumped at overcrowded state orphanages.[359]

As elsewhere in the bloc, women in Romania tended to be concentrated in jobs at the lower end of the pay scale. These jobs tended to require fewer skills than jobs held by men and, across the years of communist rule, Romanian women earned on average 72% of what men were earning.[360] Still, there was marked improvement in the direction of wage equality over time. By 1971–75, women's monthly wages stood had 84% of men's, rising to 91% by 1986–89.[361] Needless to say, women were also underrepresented in policy-making bodies. Even just within the communist party, women accounted for only 29.58% of the members in 1972 (albeit close to the apparent *de facto* limit of 30% throughout the bloc).[362]

Bulgaria

In 1973, Zhivkov mused that Bulgaria and the USSR could "act as [a] single body, breathing with the same lungs and nourished by the same bloodstream."[363] But this was no idle musing: Zhivkov wanted to see his country incorporated into the Soviet Union. He proposed this on two occasions – once to Khrushchev and once, in 1973, to Brezhnev – only to be turned down both times. But in the first half of the 1970s, the Bulgarian economy was doing very well. In the years 1961–75, Bulgaria had one of the fastest rates of economic growth in the Soviet bloc (in terms of real income per capita). In the years 1971–75 alone, real income per capita grew by 5.7%.[364]

At the same time, Bulgaria was building links with the West. Having visited General Charles de Gaulle in Paris in 1966, Zhivkov was able to establish full diplomatic relations with West Germany in December 1973 (six years after Romania's Ceauşescu had done likewise). Subsequently, in June 1975, Zhivkov paid a visit to Rome, where he had a private audience with Pope Paul VI.

Lyudmila Zhivkova, champion of Bulgarian culture

Lyudmila Zhivkova (1942–1981), the daughter of Bulgarian strongman Todor Zhivkov, had a truly extraordinary career. In 1966, she graduated from Sofia State University with a degree in history and subsequently undertook doctoral studies at the same university. In 1972, when she was just 30 years old, she assumed the post of deputy chair of the Committee for Art and Culture; three years later, she was put in charge of that committee. Then, in 1976, at the Eleventh Party Congress, she was elected to the BCP Central Committee as a full member, and in 1979 she was coopted into the Politburo as a full member. She may well have been the most intelligent member of that body. Certainly, she was already regarded by then as Bulgaria's chief authority in cultural policy. Increasingly, Zhivkova aspired to be the spiritual leader of Bulgarians and established a philosophical position independent of communist orthodoxy. She emphasized "humanistic values and individualistic ideals" and was influenced to a certain degree by Theosophy.[365]

An article which she wrote for the party daily, *Rabotnichesko Delo*, conveys a sense of her character and thought. Writing in 1979, she boldly asserted:

> We know that the banner of truth, scorched in the fire and soaked in the blood of all peoples and heroes, will fly in the air more freely if [hu]mankind

consciously moulds the world according to the laws of beauty . . . [B]rilliant crystals wrought out of the call of the will, will give the world new light, new paths of beauty and knowledge . . . [366]

In another context, championing the uncommunist notion of individualism, she told an audience at the opening of an Exhibition of Thracian Art:

> The right of man to develop and go on perfecting himself is a sacred right which every individual should defend through his self-realization in work, through concrete accomplishments . . . .. The awakening of individuality in each personality . . . will [allow each person to] live according to the laws of beauty.[367]

In the course of her short career, she energetically promoted Bulgarian culture, including prominently Bulgarian Orthodox culture from the distant past. She set up Bulgarian cultural centers abroad, organized a celebration of 1,300 years of Bulgarian statehood, and "initiated the building of a number of schools, reading rooms, and especially art galleries not just in Sofia but in the countryside as well."[368] She died on 21 July 1981 at the age of 39. She was loved by many Bulgarians, perhaps in part because she was completely different from other Politburo members. When she was to be interred, a huge number of mourners came to her funeral.

Bulgarian wayward cinema

In communist times, the fact that a film was made was no guarantee that it would be shown in cinemas – at least not until the passage of ten years or more. One film from 1968 will illustrate this point. Entitled *The Whale*, the film revealed the absurdity of the planned economy and bureaucratically determined production targets. In the film, certain fishermen were instructed to catch a certain number of fish. They managed to catch only a single sprat but, after some discussion, they reported that they had caught 30 kilograms of mackerel. The clerk who was supposed to relay this information to his superiors made a mistake and reported that the fishermen had caught 300 kilograms of belted bonito. In further transmissions, the haul next became a dolphin the size of a small whale and, finally, a whale from the Black Sea.[369] The director of the state fishery enterprise was so proud of these fishermen that he undertook to organize "a festival of whales" to celebrate this (supposed) event. But, as Velina Petrova relates, "during the preparations for the ceremonial welcoming of the bewildered fishermen, who have no idea that they are supposed to bring a whale, the lie unravels down the levels of the bureaucracy."[370]

Absurdism in Bulgarian theater

As the playwright who composed three absurdist plays, Slanislav Stratiev (1941–2000) occupies a unique niche in Bulgarian letters. His first play in this set was

Rimska bania [The Roman Bath], which premiered in February 1974. This was followed by *Sako ot velur* [The Suede Jacket] in December 1976 and *Reis* [The Bus Ride] in March 1980. The first two are the more famous and revolve around the troubles that befall one Ivan Antonov. *The Roman Bath* opens with the discovery of an ancient Roman bath in the middle of Antonov's living room. The discovery, of course, prompts archeological interest and Antonov quickly loses control over his own living room and ends up screaming at the workers on site to at least leave his kitchen alone. When he finds that a lifeguard has been posted in his living room, Antonov scarcely knows what to do.

If anything, *The Suede Jacket* carries absurdism to an ever greater extreme. It is, once again, the unfortunate Antonov, holding a master's degree and working as a research fellow, who is confronted by the impossible – in this case, a suede jacket that grows hair. He tries the local barber only to find that the barber refuses service because he does not shear *sheep!* After that setback, Antonov predictably takes the jacket to a sheepshearer, who points out that he does not give haircuts to *jackets!* In despair, he takes the jacket to the local administration for help; there, he is told that what he has is a sheep and that it must be allowed to graze. Thus, Antonov ends up "grazing" his jacket in his garden.[371]

One should be wary of reading anything political into Stratiev's plays. These are not political in any sense; they are simply brilliant examples of absurdism in literature.

The Honecker Era in the GDR

Erich Honecker was named First Secretary of the SED on 3 May 1971. But his economic program had been prefigured on 23 March when the majority of the Politburo endorsed prioritizing efforts to raise the living standard for ordinary East Germans and increasing labor productivity. Ulbricht gave this decision only a half-hearted nod.[372] Among other things, Honecker considered it vital to improve basic provisions and to keep them at a stable low price. But the economic problems that would eventually bankrupt the GDR were already detectable and, in November 1972, Gerhard Schürer (1921–2010), who served as chair of the State Planning Commission from 1966 to 1989, issued his first warning about the country's growing debts to Western banks.[373] In the short run, however, the early 1970s were a time of economic boom. Between 1971 and 1975, the living standard of people in East Germany improved steadily; industrial production rose by 30% between 1970 and 1974; and in the years 1971–75, half a million apartments were constructed or modernized.[374] In these same years, trade with the Soviet Union increased by 50%.

In diplomatic terms, the GDR came of age in December 1972 when East and West Germany signed a Basic Treaty under which the two states exchanged "permanent representatives" (the equivalent of ambassadors) and Bonn gave up its objection to international recognition of East Berlin.[375] Soon the GDR exchanged ambassadors with Austria, Switzerland, Sweden, Spain, Iran, and, in 1974, the United States. By 1978, the GDR had been recognized by 123 states.

But, by the mid-1970s, the country's economic difficulties were becoming obvious. One of the problems was that the heavy emphasis on social policy, with subsidies to keep food prices, rents, and the cost of public transportation low left little money for modernization of the industrial stock or for scientific-technological research. In April 1976, Schürer met with Honecker to try to convince him to reduce imports from the West. But Honecker refused; nor was he prepared to reduce or lift the subsidies.[376] The East German leader was haunted by memories of the June 1953 uprising in his country and also drew a lesson from how protests in Poland over an attempt to increase food prices in December 1970 had ended Gomułka's career as party leader. Schürer did not give up and tried once again soon after to convince Honecker of the need for belt-tightening. But Schürer was getting nowhere and, in April 1978, told Colonel-Lieutenant Horst Roigk of the State Security Service that Honecker, by then General Secretary, did not grasp the complexity of the country's economic situation; he also felt that Honecker was listening to bad advice.[377] As the balance-of-payments continued to worsen and the country's debt to Western banks continued to climb, Werner Kolilowski (b. 1928), a member of the SED Politburo, wrote to Soviet General Secretary Brezhnev on 24 October 1980 criticizing what he called Honecker's "consumer socialism" and warning that, insofar as it was built on credit and loans, it was likely to have disastrous consequences.[378]

The Biermann affair

Wolf Biermann (b. 1936) gained renown as the composer and performer of political songs. He had moved from West Germany in 1953, when he was 17 years old, out of enthusiasm for socialism as he understood it. He joined the SED but was expelled from the party in 1963 because, in his songs, he repeatedly went his own way, ignoring guidelines from the Ministry of Culture. In 1965, he performed his mournful "Song for My Comrades". In a key passage, he sang:

> Now I sing for all of my comrades
> the song of the betrayed revolution.
> For my betrayed comrades I sing
> and I sing [also] for my traitor comrades
> the great song of betrayal I sing.[379]

In December of that year, *Neues Deutschland* singled Biermann out for attack, claiming that he was championing bourgeois individualism, not, as he maintained, an alternative vision of socialism. But Biermann was too prominent and too widely loved to be put on trial or punished in some other way. Instead, in 1976, the authorities granted the singer permission to travel to West Germany. On 13 November, he performed in Cologne, where, in the course of his concert, he made some critical comments about the GDR. Four days later, the regime stripped Biermann of his GDR citizenship and told him that he would not be allowed to return to East Germany. This decision provoked a huge uproar, with 12 accomplished

East German writers, including Christa Wolf, Günter Kunert, Stephan Hermlin, Stefan Heym, and Heiner Müller, signing a protest and publishing it with *Agence France Presse*. After this, Heym and Wolf were stripped of their membership in the SED, while Kunert and a number of other East German writers left the GDR.[380]

Women and power

Although women and men were unequal in East Germany just as they were throughout the Soviet bloc and beyond, they were less unequal here than elsewhere in the bloc. The data in Table 3.8 (below) reveal that East German women were better represented in the GDR *Volkskammer* than women were in any of the legislatures of other bloc countries or Yugoslavia and even broke through the 30% barrier in 1976.

However, as of 1977/78, there were no women in the SED Politburo and only one woman for every 40 men in the government. Yet, as of 1977/78, 49.6% of the East German work force consisted of women.[381]

In 1971, the East German government passed additional laws establishing a full year of paid maternity leave, with the guaranteed right to return to their place of employment. Women were also granted one day of paid leave per month to devote to housework. These policies, adopted to promote childbirth, stoked jealousy among many East German men, who came to believe that the SED was privileging women. Thus, the unintended consequence of these policies was to promote male resentment of women.[382] In every year between 1952 and 1971, more than 10% of families had four or more children (more than 15% between 1957 and 1967); between 1975 and 1989, fewer than 5% of families had four or more children.[383]

The Protestant Church

The passage of the 1968 constitution and the subsequent agreement of the main Protestant Church to sunder organizational links with its co-religionists in West Germany marked the start of a new era in Church-state relations in the GDR. But

TABLE 3.8 Percentage of women in legislatures in East Central Europe, 1950–1976

	1950	*1965*	*1976*
Albania	14.0	16.7	14.0
Bulgaria	N/A	15.2	19.5
Czechoslovakia	10.1	20.0	28.6
German Democratic Republic	**27.5**	**30.6**	**33.5**
Hungary	17.4	20.0	28.6
Poland	N/A	12.4	20.6
Romania	12.4	14.2	14.0
Yugoslavia	6.5	17.3	17.2

Source: Renata Siemienska, "Women and Social Movements in Poland", in *Women & Politics*, Vol. 6, No. 4 (Winter 1986), p. 22.

there continued to be issues in contention between the two, among them: continued discrimination against young Christians who chose to fulfill their military
obligation by serving in the construction brigade, including their being excluded
from enrollment for university education; discrimination against believers in hiring
and promotion throughout the economy; and problems with obtaining permission
to construct new church facilities. But the formula "Church in socialism", declared
by Bishop Albrecht Schönherr, chair of the Federation of Evangelical [Protestant]
Churches, in 1971, communicated the message that the Church would remain
independent but would cooperate with the state where appropriate while offering
constructive criticism where appropriate.[384] Bishop Werner Krusche of Magdeburg
later explained that his Church sought to occupy "the narrow space between opposition and opportunism."[385]

In the meantime, in 1974, the SED redrafted the constitution, guaranteeing "for
all citizens, irrespective of belief, equal rights (and duties), freedom of belief and
religious observance, and the general rights of the Churches to manage their own
affairs 'in conformity with the Constitution and legal regulations of the GDR.'"[386]
Two years later, however, the Ninth SED Congress, meeting in May 1976, took up
the draft party program in which there was no reference to equal rights for all citizens regardless of religious belief or ideology; Church leaders protested volubly and
the guarantee found its way into the final text of the program. But this concession
was balanced by the addition of a clause affirming the importance that the SED
attached to seeing young people educated in the spirit of Marxism-Leninism.[387]
A few months later, on 18 August 1976, Pastor Oskar Brüsewitz poured gaso-
line over himself and lit a match, giving up his life to protest the flawed relations
between Church and state.

Back in 1967, the SED was already looking ahead to the commemoration of
the Luther quincentenary in 1983. Martin Luther (1483–1546) was no longer
to be regarded as a "spiritual ancestor of Hitler", as he had been cast in a 1947
publication[388]; on the contrary, by 1984, he was already being described as "one
of the greatest sons of the German people."[389] But the SED wanted to collaborate with the Church on this commemoration; to make this possible, a formal
rapprochement with the Church was essential. The result was a summit meeting
between SED General Secretary Honecker and Protestant Bishop Schönherr in
March 1978. The meeting was a success for both sides: the Church gained access to
radio and television, pensions for clergy over age 65, and permission to build new
church facilities in hitherto churchless cities; the SED hoped that a *modus vivendi*
with the Church would defuse any possible protests when the regime proceeded
with plans to introduce "pre-military" training in the ninth and tenth grades in
September 1978 and prepared to establish an official Martin Luther Committee for
the GDR, on 13 June 1980, headed by General Secretary Honecker.[390]

Alongside this new harmony between Church and state and their collaboration
in connection with the Luther quincentenary, the Church engaged itself to confront the regime not only over the pre-military training but also over other issues.
In 1980, the first "Peace Decade" was organized under the Church's sponsorship.

Over 10 days, Christians and non-Christians met for seminars and open discussions about peace, the arms race, environmental degradation, and other subjects. With these developments during 1978–80, it became clear just what one could expect under the formula "Church in socialism", as presented by Bishops Schönherr and Krusche.

Conclusion – A mismanaged system

The communists had a vision of the future, however vague and nebulous that vision was and they operated a planned society. Especially in the Stalinist years but also later (at least in some countries) they drew up plans not just for the economy but also for culture, for the sexual sphere (promoting gender equality and, at different times in different countries, controlling abortion), and also for the religious sphere, coopting some clergy into collaborative relations, drafting the statutes of most legal religious bodies, and banning some religious groups altogether. And yet there were problems.

Centralized economic management and the system of five-year (sometimes seven-year) plans had the unintended consequences of promoting inefficiency, holding back technological progress, and resulting in manufactures (such as television sets, radios, and cars) which were markedly inferior to their counterparts in the West. The result was technological dysfunction.

Efforts to ban the Catholic Church in Poland from the public sphere and to erode its base in faith had the unintended consequences of impelling that Church to defend itself in the public sphere and of reinforcing the loyalty of Poles to "their" Church. Efforts in Czechoslovakia to crush the Catholic Church had the unintended consequence of driving the Church to organize illegal channels of religious activity ("the underground Church"), to ordain women as priests, and to induce Slovak Catholics especially to keep their Church in their hearts. Since these results were unwelcome to the communist policy-makers, they were dysfunctional for the system the communists were trying to maintain.

Communist propaganda describing the industrial working class as the ruling class had the unintended effects of variously sowing deep cynicism among those workers who viewed themselves as powerless and, alternatively, evoking in some workers a sense of political entitlement. The emergence of the Solidarity Independent Trade Union at the end of phase 4 may have owed something to the communists' duplicitous and self-destructive propaganda and exposed to full view the total dysfunctionality of the system.

In Romania, the Ceauşescu regime's extensive prohibition of abortion had the unintended consequence of driving some pregnant women to seek illegal abortions, sometimes in less than sanitary conditions. The Hungarian regime's post-1973 policy on abortion also had unintended consequences, with those women who were able to obtain abortions being viewed as deviants, and developing feelings of guilt and long-lasting psychological problems. But the generous policy of the East German regime of Erich Honecker, granting women one day of paid vacation per month to devote to housework and providing for a year of maternity leave after each birth provoked resentment among some East German men. It seemed that whatever policy was adopted where childbirth and abortion were concerned, there was always a risk of unintended consequences.

Throughout the bloc, the efforts from the late 1940s until 1956 (and, in some cases, even longer) to impose socialist realism on writers, composers, and artists backfired, and to control and channel creative workers even after 1956 led to the unintended consequences that some writers, composers, and artists looked for ways around communist strictures and that some writers, such as Tadeusz Konwicki and Stefan Heym, published their works abroad. By the late 1980s, as the East German case showed, pictorial artists were producing abstract art and other works that ignored the old taboos.[391] And especially in Poland and Czechoslovakia, but also to a limited extent in Hungary,[392] the effort to control all publishing activity, censoring those publications they allowed to be distributed, ignited outrage and resistance, emerging in the form of *samizdat*.

There were, no doubt, other unintended consequences of the communist system. But those listed above are sufficient to pass judgment on communism, finding that, by 1980, it was a dysfunctional, failed system which could not survive given the presence, in East Central Europe and especially in the northern tier countries (the GDR, Poland, Czechoslovakia, and Hungary) of reasonably well-educated populations. Communism, as practised in the Soviet bloc, was a self-destructive system of political mismanagement.

Notes

1 Hermann Weber, *Geschichte der DDR,* Rev. & expanded ed. (Munich: Deutscher Taschenbuch Verlag, 2000), p. 215.
2 From the Czech: Komunistická strana Československa.
3 Ota Šik, "Czechoslovakia's New System of Economic Planning and Management", in *Eastern European Economics,* Vol. 4, No. 1 (Autumn 1965), p. 3.
4 L. A. D. Dellin, "Bulgarian Economic Reform – Advance and Retreat", in *Problems of Communism,* Vol. 19, No. 5 (September–October 1970), pp. 45, 48–50.
5 Paul Sanderson, "East German Economists and the Path to the 'New Economic System' in the German Democratic Republic", in *Canadian Slavonic Papers,* Vol. 23, No. 2 (June 1981), p. 169.
6 *Ibid.,* pp. 174–175.
7 Ivan T. Behrend, *Central and Eastern Europe 1944–1993: From the Periphery to the Periphery* (Cambridge: Cambridge University Press, 1996; reprinted 1998, 2001), p. 150.
8 According to Atanas Slavov, *The 'Thaw' in Bulgarian Literature* (Boulder, CO: East European Monographs, 1981), p. 6.
9 Miloš Jůzl, "Music and the Totalitarian Regime in Czechoslovakia", in *International Review of the Aesthetics and Sociology of Music,* Vol. 27, No. 1 (June 1996), p. 48.
10 "Komunikat komisji Wspólnej przedstawiciel i Rządu i Episkopatu", in *Trybuna Ludu* (Warsaw), 8 December 1956, trans. into German under the title "Beziehungen auf neuer Grundlage", in *Ost-Probleme,* 07/1957, p. 237, in *Central and East European Online Library* (CEEOL).
11 Włodzimierz Borodziej, *Geschichte Polens im 20. Jahrhundert* (Munich: C. H. Beck oHG, 2010), p. 302.

12 Mieczysław Maliński et al., "O sprawach młodzieży", in *Głos Nauczycielski* (Warsaw), no. 14 (1959), trans. into German under the title "Das Jugendproblem in polnischer Sicht", in *Ost-Probleme*, 14/1959, in CEEOL, p. 460.

13 János M. Rainer, "János Kádár (1912–1983). Der letzte Generalsekretär der ungarischen Kommunisten", trans. from Hungarian by Christian Mady, in Martin Sabrow and Susanne Schattenberg (eds.), *Die letzten Generalsekretäre. Kommunistische Herrschaft im Spätsozialismus* (Berlin: Ch. Links Verlag, 2018), p. 74.

14 Borodziej, *Geschichte Polens*, p. 303.

15 *Ibid.*, p. 305; Nicholas Bethell, *Gomułka, His Poland and His Communism* (London: Longmans, 1969), p. 233.

16 Jan B. de Weydenthal, *The Communists of Poland: An Historical Outline*, Rev. ed. (Stanford, CA: Hoover Institution Press, 1986), pp. 107–108.

17 *Ibid.*, pp. 96, 113.

18 Bethell, *Gomułka*, p. 244.

19 de Weydenthal, *The Communists of Poland*, p. 124.

20 Borodziej, *Geschichte Polens*, pp. 317–319. PZPR, from the Polish: Polska Zjednoczna Partia Robotnicza.

21 Theodor W. Adorno, *Introduction to the Sociology of Music* (New York: Seabury Press, 1975).

22 Theodor Adorno, "Sociology of Music", in John Shepherd and Kyle Devine (eds.), *The Routledge Reader on the Sociology of Music* (New York: Routledge, 2015), p. 69.

23 Donald B. Kuspit, "Critical Notes on Adorno's Sociology of Music and Art", in *The Journal of Aesthetics and Art Criteria*, Vol. 33, No. 3 (1975), p. 322.

24 Bernard Jacobson, *A Polish Renaissance* (London: Phaidon Press, 1996), pp. 79–80.

25 Tom Service, "A Guide to Witold Lutosławski's Music", in *The Guardian* (London), 15 January 2013, at www.theguardian.com/music/tomserviceblog/2013/jan/15/contemporary-music-guide-witold-lutoslawski [accessed on 20 October 2021], p. 2 of 5.

26 Czesław Miłosz, *The Captive Mind* (New York: Vintage Books, 1990).

27 Carl Tighe, "Tadeusz Konwicki's *a Minor Apocalypse*", in *The Modern Language Review*, Vol. 91, No. 1 (January 1996), p. 161.

28 *Ibid.*, p. 167.

29 Konwicki, *A Minor Apocalypse*, as quoted in *Ibid.*, p. 171.

30 Carl Tighe, "Kazimierz Brandys's *Warsaw Diaries*", in *Contemporary European History*, Vol. 7, No. 1 (March 1998), p. 87.

31 *Ibid.*, p. 89.

32 *Ibid.*, p. 90.

33 Zbigniew Folejewski, "Socialist Realism in Polish Literature and Criticism", in *Comparative Literature*, Vol. 13, No. 1 (Winter 1961), p. 79.

34 Published in English in a translation from French by Joanna Kilmartin and Steve Cox (San Diego, New York and London: Harcourt, 1970).

35 As quoted in Carl Tighe, "Stanisław Lem: Socio-Political Sci-Fi", in *The Modern Language Review*, Vol. 94, No. 3 (July 1999), p. 761.

36 Jerzy Jarzębski and Franz Rottensteiner, "Stanisław Lem, Rationalist and Visionary", in *Science Fiction Studies*, Vol. 4, No. 2 (July 1977), p. 116. See also Anthony Enns, "Mediality and Mourning in Stanisław Lem's *Solaris* and *His Master's Voice*", in *Science Fiction Studies*, Vol. 29, No. 1 (March 2002), p. 35.

37 Tighe, "Stanisław Lem", p. 758.

38 Renata Siemieńska, "Women and the Family in Poland", in Eugen Lupri (ed.), *The Changing Position of Women in Family and Society: A Cross-National Comparison* (Leiden: E. J. Brill, 1983), pp. 276, 281.

39 *Ibid.*, pp. 284–285.

40 *Ibid.*, p. 285.

41 Malgorzata Fidelis, *Women, Communism, and Industrialization in Postwar Poland* (Cambridge: Cambridge University Press, 2010), p. 193.

42 *Ibid.*, p. 192.
43 *Ibid.*, p. 191.
44 *Ibid.*, pp. 177–178, 196.
45 Piotr Kryczka, "Some Phenomena of Social Pathology in Poland", in *The Polish Sociological Bulletin*, No. 42 (1978), p. 102.
46 Jan Kubik, *The Power of Symbols Against the Symbols of Power: The Rise of Solidarity and the Fall of State Socialism in Poland* (University Park, PA: The Pennsylvania State University Press, 1994), pp. 110–117; Sabrina P. Ramet, *The Catholic Church in Polish History: From 966 to the Present* (London and New York: Palgrave Macmillan, 2017), p. 165; Robert E. Alvis, *White Eagle, Black Madonna: One Thousand Years of the Polish Catholic Tradition* (New York: Fordham University Press, 2016), p. 229.
47 Maryjane Osa, *Solidarity and Contention: Networks of Polish Opposition* (Minneapolis: University of Minnesota Press, 2003), pp. 72–73.
48 Vincent C. Chrypinski, "The Catholic Church in Poland, 1944–1989", in Pedro Ramet (ed.), *Catholicism and Politics in Communist Societies* (Durham, NC and London: Duke University Press, 1990), p. 122.
49 Splett had been appointed to head the Archdiocese of Danzig, as Gdańsk was then known, on 13 June 1938.
50 Vincent C. Chrypinski, "Church and Nationality in Postwar Poland", in Pedro Ramet (ed.), *Religion and Nationalism in Soviet and East European Politics*, rev. & expanded ed. (Durham, NC and London: Duke University Press, 1989), p. 246.
51 Ronald C. Monticone, *The Catholic Church in Communist Poland 1945–1985: Forty Years of Church-State Relations* (Boulder, CO: East European Monographs, 1986), p. 47.
52 *Ibid.*, pp. 49–50; Ramet, *The Catholic Church in Polish History,* p. 167.
53 Otto Ulč, "Czechoslovakia: The Great Leap Backward", in Charles Gati (ed.), *The Politics of Modernization in Eastern Europe: Testing the Soviet Model* (New York: Praeger, 1974), p. 101.
54 Zdeněk Suda, *Zealots and Rebels: A History of the Communist Party of Czechoslovakia* (Stanford, CA: Hoover Institution Press, 1980), p. 296.
55 *Ibid.*, pp. 296–298; Alexander Dubcek, *Hope Dies Last: The Autobiography of the Leader of the Prague Spring* (New York and Tokyo: Kodansha International, 1993), p. 87.
56 Mary Heimann, *Czechoslovakia: The State That Failed* (New Haven, CT: Yale University Press, 2011), p. 219.
57 Suda, *Zealots and Rebels*, p. 298.
58 See the discussion in J. F. A., "Caution in Prague: Reactions to the Khrushchev Report", in *The World Today,* Vol. 12, No. 8 (August 1956), pp. 339–348.
59 Heimann, *Czechoslovakia*, p. 220. See also in "Das neue System der Planung und Leitung", in *Probleme des Friedens und des Sozialismus* (Prag-Ostberlin), No. 8 (1965), reprinted under the title "Ota Šiks Argumente", in *Ost-Probleme,* No. 16 (1965), in CEEOL, pp. 495–501.
60 Ulč, "Czechoslovakia: The Great Leap Backward" [note 53].
61 This paragraph is based on H. Gordon Skilling, "The Fall of Novotný in Czechoslovakia", in *Canadian Slavonic Papers,* Vol. 12, No. 3 (Fall 1970).
62 Heimann, *Czechoslovakia*, p. 231; Harold Gordon Skilling, *Czechoslovakia's Interrupted Revolution* (Princeton, NJ: Princeton University Press, 1976), p. 199.
63 Kieran Williams, *The Prague Spring and the Aftermath: Czechoslovak Politics 1968–1970* (Cambridge: Cambridge University Press, 1997), p. 70.
64 Galia Golan, *Reform Rule in Czechoslovakia: The Dubček Era, 1968–1969* (Cambridge: Cambridge University Press, 1973), p. 204.
65 Williams, *The Prague Spring*, p. 72.
66 Jiri Valenta, *Soviet Intervention in Czechoslovakia, 1968* (Baltimore, MD: The Johns Hopkins University Press, 1979); Grey Hodnett and Peter J. Potychnyj, *Ukraine and the Czechoslovak Crisis* (Canberra: Department of Political Science, Australian National University, 1970).
67 Golan, *Reform Rule in Czechoslovakia*, pp. 27–30.

68 *Ibid.*, pp. 48–49.
69 A. H. Brown, "Political Change in Czechoslovakia", in *Government and Opposition*, Vol. 4, No. 2 (April 1969), p. 176.
70 Skilling, *Czechoslovkia's Interrupted Revolution*, p. 220.
71 Dubcek, *Hope Dies Last,* p. 148.
72 Suda, *Zealots and Rebels*, pp. 328–329.
73 As quoted in Golan, *Reform Rule in Czechoslovakia,* p. 62.
74 Williams, *The Prague Spring,* p. 73.
75 *Ibid.*, p. 90.
76 *Ibid.*, p. 122. See also Frank Cibulka, *Nationalism, Communism and Collaborationism: A Study of the Soviet-Led Invasion of Czechoslovakia and Its Aftermath*, Unpublished Ph.D. dissertation (The Pennsylvania State University, 1983), p. 218.
77 Detailed and discussed in Galia Golan, *The Czechoslovak Reform Movement: Communism in Crisis, 1962–1968* (Cambridge: Cambridge University Press, 1971).
78 Lenka Řezníková, "Beyond Ideology: Representations of the Baroque in Socialist Czechoslovakia as Seen Through the Media", in *Journal of Art Historiography,* No. 15 (December 2016), pp. 13–14.
79 Ruth Fraňková, "Karel Zeman – Wizard of the Big Screen", in *Radio Prague International* (3 April 2021), at https://english.radio.cz/masters-czech-animated-film-8710154/2 [accessed on 16 May 2021].
80 Peter Hames, "Czechoslovakia: After the Spring", in Daniel J. Goulding (ed.), *Post New Wave Cinema in the Soviet Union and Eastern Europe* (Bloomington and Indianapolis: Indiana University Press, 1989), p. 116; Roger Ebert, Review of *Closely Watched Trains* (29 May 1968), at www.rogerebert.com/reviews/closely-watched-train-1968 [accessed on 11 July 2021].
81 Hames, "Czechoslovakia", pp. 108, 112, 132.
82 Maruška Svašek, "The Politics of Artistic Identity: The Czech Art World in the 1950s and 1960s", in *Contemporary European History,* Vol. 6, No. 3 (November 1997), p. 384.
83 *Ibid.*, p. 398.
84 Hana Beneš, "Czech Literature in the 1968 Crisis", in *The Bulletin of the Midwest Modern Language Association,* Vol. 5, No. 2 (1972), p. 98.
85 H. Gordon Skilling, "Ferment Among Czechs and Slovaks", in *International Journal*, Vol. 19, No. 4 (Autumn 1964), pp. 502, 507–508, quoted extract at 512 n15.
86 Beneš, "Czech Literature", p. 100.
87 As quoted in Alan W. Sikes, "Politics and Pornography: Czech Performance in the International Arena", in *Theatre Journal,* Vol. 62, No. 3 (October 2010), p. 377.
88 Milan Kundera, *The Joke,* English translation by HarperCollins Publishers (London: Faber and Faber, 1992).
89 As quoted in Beneš, "Czech Literature", p. 105.
90 Constitution, 11 July 1960, at www.worldstatesmen.org/Czechoslovakia-Const1960. pdf [accessed on 10 July 2021], Article 20, Para. 3.
91 Alena Heitlinger, *Women and State Socialism: Sex Inequality in the Soviet Union and Czechoslovakia* (London and Basingstoke: Macmillan, 1979), p. 68.
92 J. L. Porket, "Czechoslovak Women Under Soviet-Type Socialism", in *The Slavonic and East European Review,* Vol. 59, No. 2 (April 1981), p. 257.
93 Sharon L. Wolchik, "Elite Strategy Toward Women in Czechoslovakia: Liberation or Mobilization?" in *Studies in Comparative Communism,* Vol. 14, Nos. 2–3 (Summer–Autumn 1981), pp. 133–134.
94 As quoted in Heitlinger, *Women and State Socialism,* p. 76.
95 Alena Köhler-Wagnerová, *Die Frau im Sozialismus – Beispiel ČSSR* (Hamburg: Hoffmann und Campe Verlag, 1974), pp. 34, 53.
96 Sharon L. Wolchik, "The Status of Women in a Socialist Order; Czechoslovakia, 1948–1978", in *Slavic Review,* Vol. 28, No. 4 (December 1979), pp. 593–594. See also Köhler-Wagnerová, *Die Frau im Sozialismus,* p. 54.
97 Wolchik, "The Status of Women", p. 589.

98 Heitlinger, *Women and State Socialism,* pp. 71–72.

99 See *Priestervereinigung "Pacem in terris" – Eine kritische Analyse* (Munich: Sozialwerk der Ackermann-Gemeinde, 1983).

100 Marty Manor Mullins, "A Remarkable Reversal: Communist Czechoslovakia's Reinstatement of Eastern Rite Catholicism During the Prague Spring", in *Journal of Church and State,* Vol. 58, No. 2 (2015), pp. 344, 349, 351; for background concerning the suppression of the Greek Catholic Church, see Jaroslav Coranič, "The Liquidation of the Greek Catholic Church in Communist Czechoslovakia, 1948–50", in *Journal of Ecclesiastical History,* Vol. 72, No. 3 (July 2021), pp. 590–610.

101 Karel Kaplan, "Church and State in Czechoslovakia from 1948 to 1956", Part 3, in *Religion in Communist Lands,* Vol. 14, No. 3 (Winter 1986), pp. 273–282.

102 Konstantin Urban, "Die Lage der Katholischen Kirche in der Tschechoslowakei", in *Osteuropa,* Vol. 13, Nos. 7–8 (July-August 1963), pp. 476–477; confirmed in Milan Reban, "The Catholic Church in Czechoslovakia", in Pedro Ramet (ed.), *Catholicism and Politics in Communist Societies* (Durham, NC and London: Duke University Press, 1990), p. 150.

103 Urban, "Die Lage der Katholischen Kirche", p. 477.

104 *Rudé právo* (27 February 1959), as cited in *Ibid.,* pp. 477–478, 481.

105 Iván T. Behrend, "Contemporary Hungary, 1956–1984", in Peter F. Sugar et al. (eds.), *A History of Hungary* (Bloomington and Indianapolis: Indiana University Press, 1994), p. 385.

106 Bennett Kovrig, *Communism in Hungary: From Kun to Kádár* (Stanford, CA: Hoover Institution Press, 1979), p. 379.

107 Kádár, as quoted in Behrend, "Contemporary Hungary", p. 386.

108 Rudolf L. Tőkés, *Hungary's Negotiated Revolution: Economic Reform, Social Change and Political Succession* (Cambridge: Cambridge University Press, 1996), p. 46.

109 *Ibid.,* p. 45.

110 Rudolf L. Tőkés, "Hungarian Reform Imperatives", in *Problems of Communism,* Vol. 33, No. 5 (September–October 1984), pp. 1–2.

111 Kovrig, *Communism in Hungary,* p. 390.

112 Ferenc Halmy, "Hungarian Composers Today: Endre Szervánszky", in *Tempo,* No. 88 (Spring 1969), p. 4.

113 László Kürti, "Hungary", in Sabrina P. Ramet (ed.), *Eastern Europe: Politics, Culture, and Society Since 1939* (Bloomington and Indianapolis: Indiana University Press, 1998), p. 77.

114 György Kroś, "New Hungarian Music", in *Notes,* Second Series, Vol. 39, No. 1 (September 1982), p. 44.

115 Behrend, "Contemporary Hungary", p. 396.

116 As quoted in Ann Demaitre, "The Hungarian Shores of Realism", in *Comparative Literature Studies,* Vol. 1, No. 4 (1964), p. 319.

117 Károly Nagy, "Literature as a Political Force in Hungary Today", in *Books Abroad,* Vol. 40, No. 1 (Winter 1966), p. 41.

118 George Schöpflin, "Hungarian Intellectuals Under Pressure", in *The World Today,* Vol. 30, No. 8 (February 1974), p. 79.

119 Color print in Edit Sasvári, Sándor Hornyik, and Hedvig Turai (eds.), *Art in Hungary 1956–1980: Doublespeak and Beyond* (London: Thomas and Hudson, 2018), pp. 30–31.

120 As quoted in Sándor Hornyik, "Reforming Socialist Realism: Encounters of Eastern Modernization and Western Modernism", in *Ibid.,* p. 113.

121 Both reproduced in color in Dávid Fehér, "(Dis)figuring Reality: New Forms of Figuration in Hungarian Painting, 1957–75", in Sasvári et al. (eds.), *Art in Hungary,* p. 142.

122 *Ibid.,* p. 143.

123 *Ibid.,* p. 148.

124 See the color reproductions of Jenö Barcsay's *Szentendre Mosare* (1970) and Gyula Hincz's *Science* (1967), in Hornyik, "Reforming Socialist Realism", pp. 116–117.

125 As quoted in Éva Fodor, "Smiling Women and Fighting Men: The Gender of the Communist Subject in State Socialist Hungary", in *Gender and Society*, Vol. 16, No. 2 (April 2002), p. 259.

126 Chris Corrin, *Magyar Women: Hungarian Women's Lives, 1960s-1990s* (New York: St. Martin's Press, 1994), p. 60.

127 Fodor, "Smiling Women", p. 258.

128 As quoted in *Ibid.*, p. 250.

129 *Ibid.*, p. 258.

130 Éva Fodor, *Working Difference: Women's Working Lives in Hungary and Austria, 1945–1995* (Durham, NC and London: Duke University Press, 2003), p. 114 (Fodor's emphasis).

131 Fodor, "Smiling Faces", p. 245.

132 Fodor, *Working Difference*, p. 115.

133 Corrin, *Magyar Women*, p. 65.

134 Fodor, "Smiling Women", p. 246.

135 András Fejérdy, *Pressed by a Double Loyalty: Hungarian Attendance at the Second Vatican Council, 1959–1965* (Budapest and New York: Central European University Press, 2017), p. 70.

136 Steven Polgar, "A Summary of the Situation of the Hungarian Catholic Church", in *Religion in Communist Lands*, Vol. 12, No. 1 (1984), p. 17; see also Leslie László, "The Catholic Church in Hungary", in Ramet (ed.), *Catholicism and Politics in Communist Societies*, p. 159.

137 As quoted in Polgar, "A Summary of the Situation", p. 19.

138 László, "The Catholic Church in Hungary", p. 163.

139 Fejérdy, *Pressed by a Double Loyalty*, p. 47.

140 Árpád von Klimó, "Vatican II and Hungary", in Piotr H. Kosicki (ed.), *Vatican II Behind the Iron Curtain* (Washington, DC: Catholic University of America Press, 2017), p. 58.

141 *Ibid.*, p. 60.

142 Fejdéry, *Pressed by a Double Loyalty*, p. 71.

143 Árpád von Klimó, "Anticommunism and Détente: Cardinal Mindszenty in the USA, 1973/74", in *Catholic Historical Review*, Vol. 107, No. 2 (2021), p. 241.

144 As quoted in J. V. Eibner, "Zoltán Káldy: A New Way for the Church in Socialism?" in *Religion in Communist Lands*, Vol. 13, No. 1 (1985), p. 37.

145 As quoted in *Ibid.*, p. 39.

146 As quoted in *Ibid.*

147 *Ibid.*, p. 40.

148 See *Ibid.*, p. 41.

149 Vladimir Tismaneanu, *Stalinism for All Seasons: A Political History of Romanian Communism* (Berkeley and Los Angeles: University of California Press, 2003), p. 144.

150 Mary Ellen Fischer, *Nicolae Ceauşescu: A Study in Political Leadership* (Boulder, CO: Lynne Rienner Publishers, 1989), p. 57; Tismaneanu, *Stalinism for All Seasons*, pp. 155, 157, 160, 162.

151 Tismaneanu, *Stalinism for All Seasons*, p. 131.

152 Dragoş Petrescu, "Community-Building and Identity in Gheorghe-Dej's Romania, 1956–64", in Tismaneanu (ed.), *Stalinism Revisited: The Establishment of Communist Regimes in East-Central Europe* (Budapest and New York: Central European University Press, 2009), p. 415.

153 Fischer, *Nicolae Ceauşescu*, p. 61.

154 Petrescu, "Community-Building and Identity", p. 420.

155 Fischer, *Nicolae Ceauşescu*, pp. 85–87.

156 Tismaneanu, *Stalinism for All Seasons*, p. 197.

157 *Ibid.*, p. 197.

158 Cezar Stanciu, "Autonomy and Ideology: Brezhnev, Ceauşescu and the World Communist Movement", in *Contemporary European History*, Vol. 23, No. 1 (February 2014), pp. 115–134, especially pp. 116–119.

159 For discussion, see Cezar Stanciu, "Romania and the Six Day War", in *Middle Eastern Studies,* Vol. 50, No. 5 (2014), pp. 775–795.

160 As quoted in Fischer, *Nicolae Ceauşescu,* p. 144.

161 Henry P. David and Nicholas H. Wright, "Abortion Legislation: The Romanian Experience", in *Studies in Family Planning,* Vol. 2, No. 10 (October 1971), p. 205; Karl Heinz Mehlan, "Legal Abortions in Roumania", in *The Journal of Sex Research,* Vol. 1, No. 1 (March 1965), p. 32; Gail Kligman, *The Politics of Duplicity: Controlling Reproduction in Ceauşescu's Romania* (Berkeley and Los Angeles: University of California Press, 1998), pp. 23, 48.

162 Kligman, *The Politics of Duplicity,* pp. 54–56; Andreea Andrei and Alina Branda, "Abortion Policy and Social Suffering: The Objectification of Romanian Women's Bodies Under Communism (1966–1989)", in *Women's History Review,* Vol. 24, No. 6 (2015), p. 883; David and Wright, "Abortion Legislation", p. 206.

163 Gail Kligman, "The Politics of Reproduction in Ceauşescu's Romania: A Case Study in Political Culture", in *East European Politics and Societies,* Vol. 6, No. 3 (Fall 1992), p. 376; see also Andrei and Branda, "Abortion Policy", pp. 881, 884.

164 As quoted in Kligman, "The Politics of Reproduction", p. 373.

165 Maria Bucur and Mihaela Miroiu, *Birth of Democratic Citizenship: Women and Power in Modern Romania* (Bloomington and Indianapolis: Indiana University Press, 2018), p. 31; Mihaela Miroiu, "'Not the Right Moment!' Women and the Politics of Endless Delay in Romania", in *Women's History Review,* Vol. 19, No. 4 (September 2010), p. 583.

166 Miroiu, "Not the Right Moment", p. 584.

167 Nicolas Slonimsky, "Modern Composition in Rumania", in *The Musical Quarterly,* Vol. 51, No. 1 (January 1965), pp. 241, 242; Lucian Grigorovici, "Younger Rumanian Composers", in *Perspectives of New Music,* Vol. 7, No. 2 (Spring–Summer 1969), pp. 182–183.

168 Horia Mihai-Coman, "Socialist Content in National Form: A Guiding Principle of the 'Communist Project' in Romanian Architecture", in *Periodica Polytechnica Architecture,* Vol. 51, No. 1 (2020), p. 95.

169 Lucian Grigorovici, "Younger Rumanian Composers", in *Perspectives of New Music,* Vol. 7, No. 2 (Spring–Summer 1969), p. 182.

170 Joel Crotty, "A Preliminary Investigation of Music, Socialist Realism, and the Romanian Experience, 1948–1959: (Re)reading, (Re)listening, and (Re)writing Music History for a Different Audience", in *Journal of Musicological Research,* Vol. 26, Nos. 2–3 (2007), p. 166.

171 Grigorovici, "Younger Rumanian Composers", p. 182.

172 Tismaneanu, *Stalinism for All Seasons,* p. 183.

173 Ghiţa Ionescu, *Communism in Rumania, 1944–1962* (London and New York: Oxford University Press, 1964), pp. 310–311.

174 Dennis Deletant, "Cheating the Censor: Romanian Writers Under Communism", in *Central Europe,* Vol. 6, No. 2 (November 2008), p. 132.

175 As quoted in *Ibid.,* p. 134.

176 As quoted in *Ibid.,* p. 136.

177 Marin Sorescu, "Jonah", in *The Thirst of the Salt Mountain: A Trilogy of Plays by Marin Sorescu,* trans. from Romanian by Andrea Deletant and Brenda Walker (London and Boston: Forest Books, 1985).

178 As quoted in Deletant, "Cheating the Censor", p. 139.

179 Alan Scarfe, "The Romanian Orthodox Church", in Pedro Ramet (ed.), *Eastern Christianity and Politics in the Twentieth Century* (Durham, NC and London: Duke University Press, 1988), p. 220.

180 Olivier Gillet, *Religion et Nationalisme: L'Ideologie de l'Eglise Orthodoxe Roumaine sous le Regime Comunista* (Bruxelles: Editions d'Universite de Bruxelles, 1997), pp. 18–24; Lavinia Stan and Lucian Turcescu, "The Romanian Orthodox Church and

Post-Communist Democratisation", in *Europe-Asia Studies,* Vol. 52, No. 8 (December 2000), p. 1468. See also Alan Scarfe, "Patriarch Justinian of Romania: His Early Social Thought", in *Religion in Communist Lands,* Vol. 5, No. 3 (1977), p. 164.

181 Scarfe, "The Romanian Orthodox Church", p. 218.

182 Lucian N. Leustean, "Religious Diplomacy and Socialism: The Romanian Orthodox Church and the Church of England, 1956–1959", in *East European Politics and Societies,* Vol. 22, No. 1 (2008), p. 13.

183 Lucian N. Leustean, "The Romanian Orthodox Church", in Lucian N. Leustean (ed.), *Eastern Christianity and the Cold War, 1945–91* (London and New York: Routledge, 2010), p. 47.

184 *Ibid.,* pp. 48–50.

185 Leustean, "Religious Diplomacy", p. 36.

186 Lavinia Stan and Lucian Turcescu, "The Romanian Orthodox Church: From Nation-Building Actor to State Partner", in *Kirchliche Zeitgeschichte,* Vol. 25, No. 2 (2012), p. 409.

187 Scarfe, "Patriarch Justinian of Romania", p. 165.

188 As quoted in J. F. Brown, *Bulgaria Under Communist Rule* (New York: Praeger, 1970), p. 84.

189 *Ibid.,* pp. 135–137.

190 Nikolaj Iribadshakov, "Dogmatizŭm i tvorčeski marksizŭm", in *Novo vreme* (Sofia), 1962, no. 1, trans. into German under the title "Bulgarischer Theoretiker analysiert den Personenkult", in CEEOL, *Ost-Probleme,* 08/1962, p. 253.

191 J. F. Brown, "The Bulgarian Plot", in *The World Today,* Vol. 21, No. 6 (June 1965), pp. 261–263; Hearing before the Subcommittee on Inter-American Affairs, *House of Representatives, Eighty-Ninth Congress, Second Session* (Washington, DC: U.S. Government Printing Office, 1966), pp. 296–297.

192 Stanimira Dermendzhieva, "The Politicization of Music During the Period of Totalitarian Rule in Bulgaria (1944–1989)", in *Muzikologiya / Musicology,* Vol. 25 (2018), p. 182, n7 and n9.

193 *Ibid.,* pp. 185–186; Edward Greenfield, "Bulgarian Impressions", in *The Musical Times,* Vol. 102, No. 1425 (November 1961), p. 692.

194 Dermendzhieva, "The Politicization of Music", p. 187.

195 Maria Kostakieva, "Bulgaria (Opera)", in S. Sadie (ed.), *The New Great Dictionary of Opera* (London: Macmillan, 1992), p. 638, as quoted in Dermendzhieva, "The Politicization of Music", p. 188.

196 J. F. Brown, "Frost and Thaw in Bulgarian Culture", in *Studies in Comparative Communism,* Vol. 2 (July–October 1969), pp. 98–99.

197 Nissan Oren, *Revolution Administered: Agrarianism and communism in Bulgaria* (Baltimore and London: The Johns Hopkins University Press, 1973), p. 137.

198 *Ibid.,* pp. 137–138.

199 John D. Bell, *The Bulgarian Communist Party from Blagoev to Zhivkov* (Stanford, CA: Hoover Institution Press, 1986), p. 116.

200 Brown, "Frost and Thaw", p. 101.

201 *Otechestven Front* (17 October 1957), as quoted in Brown, "Frost and Thaw", p. 101.

202 Brown, "Frost and Thaw", pp. 101–102.

203 *Ibid.,* p. 102.

204 Nikolina Ilieva, *The Bulgarian Woman* (Sofia: Sofia Press, 1970), pp. 10–11.

205 Miglena Sternadori, "Heroines Under Control: Unexpected Portrayals of Women in the Organ of the Bulgarian Communist Party, 1944–1989", in *Women's Studies in Communication,* Vol. 36 (2013), p. 145.

206 Maria Dinkova, *The Social Progress of the Bulgarian Woman* (Sofia: Sofia Press, 1972), p. 38.

207 *Ibid.,* p. 39.

208 *Ibid.,* p. 42.

209 Ilieva, *Bulgarian Woman,* p. 3.

210 Daniel Kalkandjieva, "The Economic Development of the Bulgarian Orthodox Church Since the Liberation of Bulgaria (1878)", in *Archives de Sciences Sociales des Religions,* No. 185 (January–March 2019), pp. 133–134.

211 Daniela Kalkandjeva, "Martyrs and Confessors in the Bulgarian Orthodox Church Under Communism", Paper presented at a conference at the Monastery of Bose, Italy (N.D.), typescript, p. 7.

212 *Country Reports on Human Rights Practices for 1983,* Report submitted to the Committee on Foreign Affairs, U. S. House of Representatives and the Committee on Foreign Relations, U. S. Senate, by the Department of State (Washington, DC: U. S. Printing Office, February 1984), p. 038.

213 "For Bulgaria's Orthodox Church, a Renaissance", in *New York Times* (1 August 1970), p. 6.

214 As cited in Petya Nitzova, "Islam in Bulgaria: A Historical Reappraisal", in *Religion, State and Society,* Vol. 22, No. 1 (1994), p. 101 n1.

215 *Ibid.,* p. 101.

216 Janice Broun, "Catholics in Bulgaria", in *Religion in Communist Lands,* Vol. 11, No. 3 (1983), pp. 313–314.

217 *Ibid.,* pp. 310, 314.

218 Lindsey Davies, "Pentecostals in Bulgaria", in *Religion in Communist Lands,* Vol. 8, No. 4 (1980), p. 299.

219 Weber, *Geschichte der DDR,* p. 190.

220 Karl Wilhelm Fricke, *Opposition und Widerstand in der DDR. Ein politischer Report* (Köln: Verlag Wissenschaft und Politik, 1984), pp. 114–115.

221 Weber, *Geschchte der DDR,* p. 220.

222 See Jeffrey Kopstein, "Ulbricht Embattled: The Quest for Socialist Modernity in the Light of New Sources", in *Europe-Asia Studies,* Vol. 46, No. 4 (1994), pp. 600, 604–605.

223 *Ibid.,* p. 611; Andreas Malycha, *Die SED in der Ära Honecker. Machtstrukturen, Entscheidungsmechanismen und Konfliktfelder in der Staatspartei 1971 bis 1989* (Göttingen: De Gruyter-Oldenbourg, 2014), pp. 51ff.

224 See Sally Bick, "A Double Life in Hollywood: Hanns Eisler's Score for the Film *Hangmen also Die* and the Covert Expressions of a Marxist Composer", in *The Musical Quarterly,* Vol. 93, No. 1 (Spring 2010), pp. 90–143.

225 See Albrecht Betz, *Hanns Eisler – Political Musician,* trans. from German by Bill Hopkins (Cambridge: Cambridge University Press, 1982), pp. 203–204.

226 Sally Bick, "Political Ironies: Hanns Eisler in Hollywood and Behind the Iron Curtain", in *Acta Musicologica,* Vol. 75, No. 1 (2003), p. 65.

227 Joy Callico, "The Trial, the Condemnation, the Cover-Up: Behind the Scenes of Brecht/Dessau's *Lucullus* Opera(s)", in *Cambridge Opera Journal,* Vol. 14, No. 3 (November 2002), p. 320.

228 *Ibid.,* p. 321; Margaret Setje-Eilers, " 'Wochenend und Sonnenschein': In the Blind Spots of Censorship at the GDR's Cultural Authorities and the Berliner Ensemble", in *Theatre Journal,* Vol. 61, No. 3 (October 2009), pp. 364–365. See also Joachim Lucchesi (ed.), *Das Verhör in der Oper. Die Debatte um Brecht/Dessau's "Lukullus" 1951* (Berlin: BasisDruck, 1993); Mattias Tischner, *Komponieren für und wider den Staat. Paul Dessau in der DDR* (Vienna and Cologne: Böhlau Verlag, 2009).

229 Eisler is said to have declared, at one point: "in this time of great struggles between people and people for a new world, musicians can no longer be deserters." – As quoted in Julian Silverman, "Only a Composer's Reflections on the Eisler Centenary", in *Tempo,* New Series, No. 206 (September 1998), p. 25.

230 Peter Davies, "Hanns Eisler's 'Faustus' Libretto and the Problem of East German National Identity", in *Music & Letters,* Vol. 81, No. 4 (November 2000), p. 586.

231 Wes Blomster, "The Reception of Arnold Schoenberg in the German Democratic Republic", in *Perspectives of New Music,* Vol. 21, Nos. 1–2 (Autumn 1982–Summer 1983), p. 122.

232 See *Ibid.*, p. 127.
233 "Obituary: Ernst Hermann Meyer", in *The Musical Times,* Vol. 130, No. 1752 (February 1989), p. 95.
234 Laura Silverbeg, "Between Dissonance and Dissidence: Socialist Modernism in the German Democratic Republic", in *The Journal of Musicology,* Vol. 26, No. 1 (Winter 2009), p. 50.
235 Andrew Demshuk, "A Mausoleum for Bach? Holy Relics and Urban Planning in Early Communist Leipzig, 1945–1950", in *History and Memory,* Vol. 28, No. 2 (Fall/Winter 2016), p. 75.
236 Peter Kupfer, "*Ehrt euren Deutschen Meister:* Reproducing Wagner in the GDR", in Kyle Frackman and Larson Powell (eds.), *Classical Music in the German Democratic Republic: Production and Reception* (Rochester, NY: Camden House, 2015), p. 77.
237 *Ibid.*, p. 82.
238 Joy Haslam Calico, *The Politics of Opera in the German Democratic Republic, 1945–1961,* Unpublished Ph.D. dissertation (Duke University, 1999), p. 303.
239 Kupfer, "*Ehrt euren Deutschen*", p. 86.
240 Christa Wolf, *They Divided the Sky,* trans. from German by Luise von Flotow (Ottawa: University of Orrawa Press, 2013).
241 See Julia Hell, "Christa Wolf's *Divided Heaven* and the Collapse of (Socialist) Realism", in *Rethinking Marxism,* Vol. 7, No. 3 (1994), pp. 62–79.
242 Christiane Zehl Romero, "Anna Seghers", in *Jewish Women's Archive,* last updated on 5 July 2021, at https://jwa.org/encyclopedia/article/seghers-anna [accessed on 5 November 2021], pp. 5 and 7 of 13.
243 Dennis Tate, *The East German Novel: Identity, Community, Continuity* (New York: St. Martin's Press, 1984), pp. 104, 130–132.
244 *Ibid.*, p. 133.
245 *Statistical Pocket Book of the German Democratic Republic 1986* (Berlin: Staatsverlag der Deutschen Demokratischen Republik, 1986), p. 37.
246 David Childs, *The GDR: Moscow's German Ally,* 2nd ed. (London: Unwin Hyman, 1988), p. 251.
247 *Ibid.*, p. 25.
248 As quoted in Heike Trappe, *Emanzipation oder Zwang? Frauen in der DDR zwischen Beruf, Familie und Sozialpolitik* (Berlin: Akademie Verlag, 1995), p. 62.
249 *Ibid.*, p. 63.
250 *Ibid.*, p. 58.
251 *Ibid.*, p. 67.
252 Katharina von Ankum, "Political Bodies: Women and Re/Production in the GDR", in *Women in German Yearbook,* Vol. 9 (1993), pp. 130, 134.
253 *Ibid.*, pp. 136–138.
254 On this point, see Sabrina P. Ramet, *Nonconformity, Dissent, Opposition, and Resistance in Germany, 1933–1990: The Freedom to Conform* (London: Palgrave Macmillan, 2020), chapters 2–3.
255 Peter Fischer, *Kirche und Christen in der DDR* (Berlin: Verlag Gebr. Holzapfel, 1978), p. 28.
256 As quoted in *Ibid.*, p. 89.
257 Sabrina Petra Ramet, "Protestantism in East Germany, 1949–1989: A Summing Up", in Sabrina Petra Ramet (ed.), *Protestantism and Politics in Eastern Europe and Russia: The Communist and Post-Communist Eras* (Durham, NC and London: Duke University Press, 1992), p. 56.
258 See *Kirche als Lerngemeinschaft. Dokumente aus der Arbeit des Bundes der Evangelischen Kirchen in der DDR* (Berlin: Evangelische Verlagsanstalt, 1981), pp. 161–162.
259 See Robert F. Goeckel, "The Catholic Church in East Germany", in Pedro Ramet (ed.), *Catholicism and Politics in Communist Societies* (Durham, NC and London: Duke University Press, 1990), pp. 93–116, especially pp. 103–104.
260 On this point, Jowitt, "Stalinist Revolutionary Breakthroughs", p. 20.

261 As quoted in Alexander Tomsky, "*Spectrum:* A Journal from the Czech Cultural Hinterland", in *Religion in Communist Lands*, Vol. 8, No. 3 (1980), p. 181.

262 As quoted in Tighe, "Stanisław Lem", p. 758. The passage was recorded in the Censorship Department's internal journal, *Bulletin on Themes of Materials Censored* (Second Quarter, 1974).

263 See Otto Ulč, "The 'Normalization' of Post-Invasion Czechoslovakia", in *Survey*, Vol. 24, No. 3 (Summer 1979).

264 Heimann, *Czechoslovakia*, p. 275.

265 Cibulka, *Nationalism, Communism and Collaborationism*, p. 250.

266 Ulč, "Normalization", p. 204.

267 As quoted in Vladimir V. Kusin, "Husák's Czechoslovakia and Economic Stagnation", in *Problems of Communism*, Vol. 31, No. 3 (May–June 1982), p. 29.

268 Ulč, "Normalization", p. 205; Kusin, "Husák's Czechoslovakia", p. 28.

269 Gustáv Husák, "Political Report of the Central Committee of the Communist Party of Czechoslovakia to the 17th Party Congress, March 1986", in G. Husák (ed.), *Speeches and Writings* (Oxford: Pergamon Press, 1986), p. 211.

270 Michal Pullmann, "Gustáv Husák (1913–1991). ČSSR: Der Herr mit Vergangenheit", in Sabrow and Schattenberg (eds.), *Die letzten Generalsekretäre*, p. 160.

271 Cibulka, *Nationalism, Communism, and Collaborationism*, p. 281.

272 Heimann, *Czechoslovakia*, p. 281.

273 Miloš Jůzl, "Music and the Totalitarian Regime in Czechoslovakia", in *International Review of the Aesthetics and Sociology of Music*, Vol. 27, No. 1 (June 1996), p. 47.

274 Sikes, "Politics and Pornography", p. 378.

275 "'Normalisierte' Kulturpolitik in der Tschechoslowakei", in *Osteuropa*, Vol. 22, No. 5 (May 1972), p. A328.

276 As quoted in *Ibid.*, p. 342.

277 Eva Hauser, "Science Fiction in the Czech Republic and the Former Czechoslovakia: The Pleasures and Disappointments of the New Cosmopolitanism", in *Science Fiction Studies*, Vol. 21, No. 2 (July 1994), p. 134.

278 "'Normalisierte' Kulturpolitik", p. A332.

279 *Tvorba*, no. 37 (1971), as quoted in *Ibid.*, p. A333.

280 *Pravda* (Bratislava), 9 November 1971, p. 3, in "'Normalisierte' Tschechoslowakei", p. A335.

281 Josef Škorecký, "Hipness at Noon", in *New Republic* (17 December 1984), p. 28.

282 Sabrina Petra Ramet, *Social Currents in Eastern Europe: The Sources and Consequences of the Great Transformation*, 2nd ed. (Durham, NC and London: Duke University Press, 1995), p. 128.

283 Kenneth Roth, "Prague and the Perils of Jazz", in *Commonweal* (5 June 1987), p. 352.

284 Ramet, *Social Currents in Eastern Europe*, p. 129.

285 As quoted in Jon Pareles, "Czechoslovak Band That Suffered for its Art", in *New York Times* (24 April 1989), p. 13.

286 Lyrics by Plastic People of the Universe, as quoted in Sabrina Petra Ramet, "Rock Music in Czechoslovakia", in Sabrina Petra Ramet (ed.), *Rocking the State: Rock Music and Politics in Eastern Europe and Russia* (Boulder, CO: Westview Press, 1994), pp. 62–63, citing "One Hundred Points", by the Plastic People of the Universe, as given in *Across Frontiers* (Spring 1986).

287 As quoted in Pareles, "Czechoslovakia Band".

288 Ramet, "Rock Music in Czechoslovakia", pp. 60–61.

289 *Tribuna* (23 March 1983), p. 5, trans. in *Joint Publications Research Service*, no. 83438 (10 May 1983), pp. 21, 22. For further discussion of the Czechoslovak rock scene, see Sabrina P. Ramet and Vladimir Đorđević, "The Three Phases of Rock Music in the Czech Lands", in *Communist and Post-Communist Studies*, Vol. 52, No. 1 (March 2019), pp. 59–70.

290 Wolchik, "The Status of Women", p. 594.

291 *Women in Parliaments 1945–1995* (Geneva: Inter-Parliamentary Union, July 1995), at http://archive.ipu.org/PDF/publications/women45-95_en.pdf [accessed on 13 January 2022], p. 104.

292 Wolchik, "The Status of Women", p. 591.

293 See Alexander Tomsky, "*Modus Moriendi* of the Catholic Church in Czechoslovakia", in *Religion in Communist Lands*, Vol. 10, No. 1 (1982), pp. 23–53, especially p. 29.

294 Sabrina P. Ramet, "The Czechoslovak Church Under Pressure", in *The World Today*, Vol. 38, No. 9 (September 1982), pp. 355–356.

295 A. Hlinka, "Katholiken in der Slowakei", in *Kirche in Not*, no. 23 (1975), pp. 106–107.

296 As quoted in Janus Bugajski, *Czechoslovakia: Charter 77's Decade of Dissent*, Washington Papers No. 125 (New York: Praeger, 1987), p. 12. See also H. Gordon Skilling, "Socialism and Human Rights: Charter 77 and the Prague Spring", in *Canadian Slavonic Papers*, Vol. 20, No. 2 (June 1978), p. 159.

297 H. Gordon Skilling, *Samizdat and an Independent Society in Central and Eastern Europe* (Columbus: Ohio State University Press, 1989), p. 44.

298 As quoted in Catherine Fitzpatrick and Janet Fleischman, *From Below: Independent Peace and Environmental Movements in Eastern Europe and the USSR* (New York and Washington, DC: Helsinki Watch, October 1987), p. 6.

299 Skilling, *Samizdat and an Independent Society*, p. 27; Ramet, *Social Currents in Eastern Europe*, p. 127.

300 Edward Gierek, *Party's Tasks in the Further Socialist Development of the Polish People's Republic: Programme Report of the Political Bureau for the 6th PUWP Congress*, Delivered by First Secretary of the Central Committee Edward Gierek (December 6th, 1971), trans. & published by the Polish Interpress Agency (1971), pp. 4, 11.

301 *Ibid.*, p. 15.

302 Marcin Zaremba, "Edward Gierek (1913–2001). Der Erfinder des 'Bigos-Sozialismus' in Polen", in Sabrow and Schattenberg (eds.), *Die letzten Generalsekretäre*, p. 195.

303 de Weydenthal, *The Communists of Poland*, p. 153.

304 Borodziej, *Geschichte Polens*, p. 345.

305 de Weydenthal, *The Communists of Poland*, p. 160.

306 *Ibid.*, p. 162.

307 *Polityka* (25 March 1979), as quoted in de Weydenthal, *The Communists of Poland*, p. 174.

308 Cezar M. Ornatowski, "'Let Thy Spirit Renew This Earth': The Rhetoric of Pope John Paul II and the Political Transformation in Poland, 1979–1989", in *Journal for the Study of Religion*, Vol. 14, No. 1 (2001), p. 79. For a review of the religious aspects of the pope's 1979 visit, see James Ramon Felak, *The Pope in Poland: The Pilgrimages of John Paul II, 1979–1991* (Pittsburgh: University of Pittsburgh Press, 2020), *passim*.

309 From the Polish: Komitet Obrony Robotników.

310 KSS from the Polish: Komitet Samoobrony Społecznej.

311 See Jan Zielonka, "Die Bewegung der gesellschaftlichen Selbstverteidigung in Polen (KSS-KOR)", in *Osteuropa*, Vol. 35, No. 2 (February 1985), especially pp. 87, 90–91.

312 Niecenzurowana Oficyna Wydawnicza [Uncensored Publishing House].

313 Skilling, *Samizdat and an Independent Society*, pp. 13–14.

314 From the Polish: Konfederacja Polski Niepodleglej.

315 For more on the KPN, see Ramet, *Social Currents in Eastern Europe*, pp. 102–103.

316 See Adam Bromke, "Poland's Upheaval – An Interim Report", in *The World Today*, Vol. 37, No. 6 (June 1981), pp. 211–218.

317 Michał Oleszczyk, "Andrzej Wajda's Ten Best Films", in *RogerEbert.com* (16 October 2016), at www.rogerebert.com/far-flung-correspondents/andrzej-wajdas-ten-best-films [accessed on 20 December 2021]; Anna Krakus, "The Abuses, and Uses, of Film Censorship: An Interview with Andrzej Wajda", in *Cineaste* (Summer 2014), p. 3.

318 Elżbieta Ostrowska, "Andrzej Wajda: How to Be Loved and Serve One's Country?" in *Studies in Eastern European Cinema*, Vol. 8, No. 1 (2017), p. 80.

319 See Gordana P. Crnković, *Literature and Film from East Europe's Forgotten "Second World"* (New York and London: Bloomsbury Academic, 2021), pp. 57–59.
320 Sylvia Kuźma-Markowska and Agata Ignaciuk, "Family Planning Advice in State-Socialist Poland, 1950s-80s: Local and Transnational Exchanges", in *Medical History*, Vol. 64, No. 2 (2020), p. 259.
321 Joanna K. Mishtal, "How the Church Became the State: The Catholic Regime and Reproductive Rights in State Socialist Poland", in Shana Penn and Jill Massino (eds.), *Gender Politics and Everyday Life in State Socialist Eastern and Central Europe* (New York: Palgrave Macmillan, 2009), p. 137.
322 *Ibid.*, p. 138.
323 Regarding other concessions, see Ramet, *The Catholic Church in Polish History*, p. 169.
324 As quoted in Jan Siedlarz, *Kirche und Staat im kommunistischen Polen 1945–1989* (Paderborn: Ferdinand Schöningh, 1996), p. 166.
325 Ramet, *The Catholic Church in Polish History*, p. 171.
326 See J. B. de Weydenthal, "The Pope's Pilgrimage to Poland", in *Religion in Communist Lands*, Vol. 12, No. 1 (1984), p. 73.
327 Elemér Hankiss, *East European Alternatives* (Oxford: Clarendon Press, 1990), p. 35, as quoted in Joseph J. Arpad, "The Question of Hungarian Popular Culture", in *Journal of Popular Culture*, Vol. 29, No. 2 (Fall 1995), p. 23.
328 Arpad, "The Question of Hungarian Popular Culture", pp. 13, 15; Tőkés, *Hungary's negotiated revolution*, pp. 122–123.
329 Behrend, "Contemporary Hungary", pp. 391–392.
330 *Ibid.*, pp. 392–393.
331 Benedykt Askanas, Halina Askanas, and Friedrich Levcik, "Economic Development of the COMECON Countries 1971 to 1975 and Their Plans Until 1980", in *Eastern European Economics*, Vol. 15, No. 3 (Spring 1977), pp. 5, 6, 19.
332 Tőkés, "Hungarian Reform Imperatives", p. 2.
333 Hana Istvanffy Lorinc, "Foreign Debt, Debt Management Policy and Implications for Hungary's Development", in *Soviet Studies*, Vol. 44, No. 6 (1992), pp. 997–998.
334 Tőkés, "Hungarian Reform Imperatives", pp. 5–6.
335 *Ibid.*, p. 9.
336 Steven Polgar, "A Summary of the Situation of the Hungarian Catholic Church", in *Religion in Communist Lands*, Vol. 12, No. 1 (1984), p. 24.
337 Dennis J. Dunn, "The Vatican's Ostpolitik: Past and Present", in *Journal of International Affairs*, Vol. 36, No. 2 (Fall/Winter 1982/83), p. 251.
338 As quoted in János Wildmann, "Hungary: From the Ruling Church to the 'Church of the People'", in *Religion in Communist Lands*, Vol. 14, No. 2 (1986), p. 166.
339 Polgar, "A Summary", p. 12.
340 Corrin, *Magyar Women*, p. 60.
341 Fodor, "Smiling Women and Fighting Men", p. 251.
342 Julia Szalai, "Some Aspects of the Changing Situation of Women in Hungary", in *Signs*, Vol. 17, No. 1 (Autumn 1991), p. 158.
343 Julia Szalai, "Abortion in Hungary", in *Feminist Review*, No. 29 (Summer 1988), pp. 98–99.
344 *Ibid.*, p. 100.
345 René de Flers, "Socialism in One Family", in *Survey*, Vol. 28, No. 4 (Winter 1984).
346 Thomas Kunze, *Nicolae Ceaușescu. Eine Biographie*, 4th ed. (Berlin: Christoph Links Verlag, 2017), p. 188. See also Trond Gilberg, "Ceaușescus kleine Kulturrevolution", in *Osteuropa*, Vol. 22, No. 10 (October 1972).
347 Kunze, *Nicolae Ceaușescu*, p. 196.
348 *Ibid.*, p. 235. The last epithet in the list comes from an old Radio Free Europe report.
349 Kunze, *Nicolae Ceaușescu*, p. 236.
350 Deletant, "Cheating the Censor", p. 141.
351 As quoted in Anneli Ute Gabanyi, "Ceaușescus national-dogmatische Kulturpolitik – Ein dritter Weg?" in *Osteuropa*, Vol. 26, No. 3 (March 1976), p. 195. The author was Dionisie Petcu.

352 As quoted in *Ibid.*, p. 194.
353 Ion Coja, "Rumänien: Schriftsteller kritisiert die Zensur", in *Osteuropa,* Vol. 29, No. 4 (April 1979), p. A254. The article was trans. from *Viaţa Românească,* no. 7–8 (1978).
354 *Ibid.*, p. A255.
355 Anneli Ute Gabanyi, *Partei und Literatur in Rumänien seit 1945* (Munich: R. Oldenbourg, 1975), p. 181.
356 Mary Ellen Fischer, *Nicolae Ceauşescu: A Study in Political Leadership* (Boulder, CO: Lynne Rienner, 1989), p. 239.
357 *Ibid.*, p. 191.
358 On this point, see Kligman, "The Politics of Reproduction in Ceauşescu's Romania", p. 376.
359 Amy Mackinnon, "What Actually Happens When a Country Bans Abortion", in *Foreign Policy* (16 May 2019), at https://foreignpolicy.com/2019/05/16/what-actually-happens-when-a-country-bans-abortion-romania-alabama/ [accessed on 14 January 2022].
360 Daniela Andrén and Thomas Andrén, "Gender and Occupational Wage Gaps in Romania: From Planned Equality to Market Inequality?" in *Journal of European Labor Studies,* Vol. 4, No. 10 (2015), pp. 1–2, 14.
361 *Ibid.*, p. 6.
362 Trond Gilberg, *Modernization in Romania Since World War II* (New York: Praeger, 1975), p. 37.
363 As quoted in R. J. Crampton, *A Concise History of Bulgaria,* 2nd ed. (Cambridge: Cambridge University Press, 2005), p. 195.
364 Kristen Ghodsee, "Red Nostalgia? Communism, Women's Emancipation, and Economic Transformation in Bulgaria", in *L'Homme,* Vol. 15, No. 1 (2004), p. 40.
365 Ivanka Nedeva Atanasova, "Lyudmila Zhivkova and the Paradox of Ideology and Identity in Communist Bulgaria", in *East European Politics and Societies,* Vol. 18, No. 2 (2004), p. 291.
366 Ludmila Zhivkova, "Join Hands, Friends All Over the World", trans. from an article in *Rabotnichesko Delo* (15 August 1979), in L. Zhivkova, *Her many Worlds – New Culture & Beauty – Concepts & Action* (Oxford and New York: Pergamon Press, 1982), p. 191.
367 *Ibid.*, p. 75.
368 Atanasova, "Lyudmila Zhivkova", p. 296.
369 Velina P. Petrova, "Are We Going to Have a Race of Angels? Post-Communist Interpretations of Bulgarian Dissident Cinema", in *Berkeley Journal of Sociology,* Vol. 47 (2003), p. 34.
370 *Ibid.*, p. 34.
371 E. J. Czerwinski, "Bulgaria's Stanislav Stratiev: Racing with the Lion", in *World Literature Today,* Vol. 60, No. 3 (Summer 1986), pp. 396–397.
372 Malycha, *Die SED in der Ära Honecker,* p. 59.
373 Andreas Malycha, "Ungeschminkte Wahrheiten", in *Vierteljahrshefte für Zeitgeschichte,* Vol. 59, No. 2 (2011), p. 286.
374 Weber, *Geschichte der DDR,* p. 289.
375 *Ibid.*, pp. 292–293.
376 Malycha, "Ungeschminkte Wahrheiten", pp. 288, 290, 295.
377 *Ibid.*, p. 301.
378 *Ibid.*, p. 294.
379 As quoted in G. Ann Stamp Miller, *The Cultural Politics of the German Democratic Republic: The Voices of Wolf Biermann, Christa Wolf, and Heiner Müller* (Irvine, CA: Brown Walker Press, 2004), p. 77.
380 Ines Geipel and Joachim Walther, *Gesperrte Ablage. Unterdrückte Literaturgeschichte in Ostdeutschland 1945–1989* (Düsseldorf: Lilienfeld Verlag, 2015), pp. 181, 232.
381 Josie McLellan, *Love in the Time of Communism: Intimacy and Sexuality in the GDR* (Cambridge: Cambridge University Press, 2011), p. 57.
382 See Susanna Kranz, "Women's Role in the German Democratic Republic and the State's Policy Toward Women", in *Journal of International Women's Studies,* Vol. 7, No. 1 (November 2005), pp. 78, 80.

383 Trappe, *Emanzipatien oder Zwang?* p. 68.

384 See Robert F. Goeckel, *The Lutheran Church and the East German State: Political Conflict and Change Under Ulbricht and Honecker* (Ithaca, NY: Cornell University Press, 1990), *passim.*

385 As quoted in Gisela Helwig, "Zwischen Opposition und Opportunismus. Zur Lage der Kirche in der DDR", in *Deutschland Archiv*, Vol. 9, No. 6 (June 1976), p. 578.

386 Caroline Ward, "Church and State in East Germany", in *Religion in Communist Lands*, Vol. 6, No. 2 (1978), p. 92.

387 See *Ibid.*

388 Wolfram von Hanstein, *Von Luther bis Hitler* (Dresden: Voco-Verlag, 1947), pp. 22–23, as cited in Stephen P. Hoffmann, "The GDR, Luther, and the German Question", in *Review of Politics,* Vol. 48, No. 2 (Spring 1986), p. 250.

389 As quoted in Robert F. Goeckel, "The Luther Anniversary in East Germany", in *World Politics*, Vol. 37, No. 1 (October 1984), p. 121.

390 Albrecht Schönherr, "Nach zehn Jahren: Zum Staat-Kirche-Gespräch am 6. März 1978", in *Kirche in Deutschland,* Vol. 14, No. 1 (February 1988), p. 5; Harald Wessel, "Martin-Luther-Komitee der DDR in Berlin konstituiert", in *Neues Deutschland* (14/15 June 1980), p. 1.

391 See Martin Damus, *Malerei der DDR. Funktionen der bildenden Kunst im Realen Sozialismus* (Reinbek bei Hamburg: Rowohlt, 1991).

392 See Skilling, *Samizdat and an Independent Society*, p. 35.

4

THE SOVIET BLOC, PART THREE

1980–1989

When communism finally collapsed in much of East Central Europe in Autumn 1989, it seemed to some observers rather sudden. But the collapse was only the last act in a long drama, with the seeds of the ultimate collapse planted already when the communist systems were established, and the weaknesses of the system were repeatedly being reinforced by the unintended consequences of misconceived policies, as summarized at the end of the previous chapter. Even so, the appearance of the Independent Trade Union Solidarity in Poland made a powerful contribution to the by-then inevitable collapse of communism; after summer 1980, the clock was ticking. Among observers of communist East Central Europe through the 1970s and most of the 1980s, there were two rival opinion groups. On the one hand, self-proclaimed "realists" and inveterate skeptics tended to write off Solidarity and its underground reincarnation, as well as Charter 77, the East German peace movement, and the myriad of dissident and protest movements and groups as politically irrelevant, not recognizing them as epiphenomena of a deeper malaise that was eating away at the foundations of the system. Many realists were led astray by the highly influential volume, *Political Order in Changing Societies*, by Samuel P. Huntington. Huntington opened his book with the bold challenge:

> The most important distinction among countries concerns not their form of government but their degree of government . . . Communist totalitarian states and Western liberal states both belong generally in the category of effective rather than debile political systems. The United States, Great Britain, and the Soviet Union have different forms of government, but in all three systems the government governs. Each country is a political community with an overwhelming consensus among the people on the legitimacy of the political system.[1]

DOI: 10.4324/9781003311515-4

Huntington may have mistaken apathy and resignation for positive embrace of the system and, in any event, he tied legitimacy both directly and indirectly (via Marxist-Leninist ideology) to authority and coercive power, rather than to values and political culture.[2] This in turn led Huntington to conclude that "Communist states . . . demonstrate high levels of political stability"[3] – which is to say that they should not have been vulnerable to collapse or disintegration.

Another analyst, citing Huntington's book, claimed in 1986 that the Leninist (i.e., Soviet-style) system introduced by the Soviets in some of its client states in the Middle East and Africa had proven stable and immune to coups.[4] Again, echoing the realist paradigm, sociologist Zygmunt Bauman claimed, in 1971, that the East Central European communist systems were "immune" to revolution because of the "ability and readiness of the government to deal with the basic social and economic issues" which confronted them.[5] Consistent with this point of view, "Bauman wrote off the intellectuals as an isolated caste, commenting on 'the [at best] apathetic response which the intellectuals' manifestos win in the other strata of the nation' and on the impossibility of an effective alliance between intellectuals and workers"[6] such as would emerge in Poland in the mid-1970s.

In his essay, "The Power of the Powerless", Václav Havel offered an insight that may serve as a preliminary reply to Huntington and Bauman. Havel cites the example of the local greengrocer who hangs a sign, "Workers of the World Unite", on his shop window. For Havel, this does not reflect, to cite Huntington's words, "an overwhelming consensus among the people on the legitimacy of the political system." Rather, what the greengrocer wanted to communicate was his resignation to things as they were, his effective impotence – thus, a declaration that he was not a political troublemaker. In Havel's words,

> . . . the greengrocer . . . does not put the slogan in his window from any personal desire to acquaint the public with the ideal it expresses . . . The slogan is really a *sign*, and as such it contains a subliminal but very definite message. Verbally, it might be expressed this way: "I, the greengrocer XY, live here and I know what I must do. I behave in the manner expected of me. I can be depended upon and am beyond reproach. I am obedient and therefore I have the right to be left in peace."[7]

But, to repeat, this is not about the legitimacy of the system; it is about fear and caution. In contrast to the realists' stress on coercive power, Havel, the archetypal idealist, emphasized precisely those things which realists left to the side: values, moral principles, and "living in truth", as he called integrity. Idealists such as H. Gordon Skilling and Vladimir Tismaneanu, precisely because of their focus on values and moral principles, saw change coming. In his *Charter 77* (1981) and *Samizdat and an Independent Society* (1989), Skilling highlighted the centrality of human rights – a focus of idealists – and noted that an unintended consequence of the Czechoslovak regime's repeated attacks on Charter 77, both in the media and via police harassment, was to give it high visibility, a dysfunctional result from the regime's standpoint.[8] Moreover, in the latter work, writing in 1988, Skilling understood that the communist system was in serious trouble – a fact denied or ignored by most, if not all, "realists" to the bitter end. Where Tismaneanu is concerned, his edited volume, *In Search of Civil Society*, completed before the crash in Autumn 1989, reflected his conviction that communist rule in East Central Europe was in its last days.[9] For Tismaneanu, as also for all idealists, not only are values important in themselves but they also affect politics and play a role, in Tismaneanu's words, "in shaping political strategies."[10] Political decision-makers should work for the common good, Tismaneanu stresses, but, as he wrote in his *Fantasies of Salvation*, "As the Leninist authoritarian order collapsed, societies have tended to be atomized and deprived of a political center able to articulate coherent visions of a common good."[11] Not surprisingly, his *Stalinism for All Seasons* bristles with outrage at Ceauşescu's moral turpitude and posturing as the "helmsman of national destiny" and as "a brilliant political thinker and revolutionary leader."[12] Idealists view politics as the arena in which societies and states can pool their resources in order to achieve common goals and maximize gains for all players. Idealists are, to underline the point, convinced of the importance of ideals and principles, such as those championed by Solidarity (the right to form labor unions), Charter 77 (human rights), the East German peace movement of the 1980s, and various other groups championing freedom of speech, of assembly, of religion, of choice of sexual partner, etc.; idealists believe (as Havel did) that defending such ideals, such principles, can be a source of power ("the power of the powerless" as Havel called it) and that, in the long run, the power of ideals is stronger than the power of armed force.

Functionalists take note of dysfunctions in a system and argue that serious dysfunctions render a system unsustainable. As Robert K. Merton noted in his *Social Theory and Social Structure*, "dysfunctions . . . lessen the [capacity for] adaptation or adjustment of the system."[13] Serious dysfunctions create "strains [which] may be . . . instrumental in leading to changes in that system. In any case, they exert pressure for change."[14] In many cases, dysfunctions were the unintended consequences of certain policy choices. Writing in 1987, in an implicitly functionalist mode, Ivan Volgyes forecast that Hungary would soon be hit by a political storm. The reasons he gave were that the communist party was "in disarray and the state apparatus was unable to effect any changes," setting in motion a "process of disintegration."[15] In other words, the communist system was dysfunctional. Idealists and functionalists looked below the surface and believed that the social consensus that there was no available alternative to communism was breaking down; accordingly, they came to believe that the accumulated unintended consequences, dysfunctions, and strains on the system rendered the collapse of communism only a matter of time. Nor should one forget Zbigniew Brzezinski's aptly titled volume, *The Grand Failure: The Birth and Death of Communism in the Twentieth Century*, published on 1 March 1989.[16] And, of course, one can be an idealist and a functionalist at the same time.

In history, there are always actors and, while the ultimate collapse of the communist order came about as the result of decisions and activity on the part of a large number of persons, there were certain actors whose actions and activity made the most difference. Here I will highlight six key players: the Czech playwright and eventual president Havel, for his initiative and central role in Charter 77; the Polish labor leader and eventual president Wałęsa, for his initiative and leadership role in Solidarity; Pope John Paul II for inspiring Polish and Slovak Catholics especially but also for giving encouragement to oppositionist currents across the northern tier; Soviet leader Gorbachev, for ending any claim to Soviet hegemony in East Central Europe and for establishing in his country a model for reform in the region; and Polish First Secretary Gierek and East German General Secretary Honecker for running their respective countries on credit, driving their countries into bankruptcy.

The fifth phase, 1980–1989/90: the decay of the communist system

By the end of the 1970s, the economy was a problem throughout East Central Europe, indebtedness was high everywhere except for Albania, and disillusionment had set in, with the failure of the communist parties to deliver on their promises. Three events mark the end of the consumer/coercion phase and the inception of a phase of system disintegration and decay: (1) 16 October 1978, the election of Karol Cardinal Wojtyła, the Archbishop of Kraków, as Pope John Paul II; (2) 4 May 1980, the death of Yugoslav President Josip Broz Tito; and (3) August 1980, the outbreak of strikes at the Lenin Shipyards in Gdańsk. This new phase was marked by five patterns which, according to an influential theory developed by Crane Brinton,[17] marked this phase as *prerevolutionary:* financial failure, characterized among other things by rising indebtedness, with East Germany, Poland, and Hungary especially impacted; "the desertion of the regime by intellectuals,"[18] as manifested in the proliferation in the northern tier of dissidents and protest groups such as the East German peace movement and the Czechoslovak Charter 77 movement; the politicization of new strata and the growing confidence of sectors of the public to defy the authorities and a readiness to organize (manifested most obviously in the Polish and East German cases); a corresponding loss of confidence on the part of the political elite (manifested in Poland, during Kania's term in office, in the replacement of the propaganda of success with the propaganda of failure, with the political elite claiming the right to rule on the basis of understanding their own ineptitude and mistakes best); and a political unraveling as the old structures proved unable to meet the new challenges arising in this phase (again, Poland provides an obvious example, with the declaration of martial law in December 1981 effectively sidelining the communist party). In addition, there were two further factors which became prominent in the 1980s. The first was the growing frustrations expressed by citizens of these countries with problems that affected their everyday lives. In all of the bloc countries, scarcity of some goods and the low quality of such goods as were available were sources of constant irritation. In such cases, such as East Germany and Hungary, people wanting to buy a Trabant car (the obvious choice in both of these countries) had to wait for years before a new one could become available (with the result that a used Trabant, which one could purchase without having to wait, was typically more expensive than a new one). Moreover, when I visited four cities in the German Democratic Republic in summer 1988, I heard a lot of complaints about the restrictions on their travel, with my conversation partners expressing a desire to see London, Paris, and Rome especially. The second factor was resentment among religious believers at communist religious policy, however diverse it was.

The repluralization of Poland

From summer 1980 to December 1981, Poland experienced a massive repluralization, involving the appearance of the Independent Trade Union Solidarity (legally registered on 10 November 1980) as well as of other independent organizations such as Rural Solidarity, Fighting Solidarity, and an independent student union, while the Democratic Party (DS) and the United Peasant Party (ZSL), which had been functioning as transmission belts of the ruling PZPR, suddenly began acting independently. The Soviets were not pleased. From the beginning of September 1980, the SED was arguing that the West, meaning in the first place the USA, was behind the "counterrevolution" in Poland. By mid-October, SED General Secretary Honecker had reached the conclusion that only decisive military force could bring an end to the Polish "crisis", as the bloc leaders viewed the situation, and made it known that he was prepared to commit East German troops to a bloc invasion of Poland.[19] Honecker believed that the emergence of Solidarity posed an existential threat to SED hegemony in eastern Germany and, thus, to the very survival of the GDR. Accordingly, on 26 November 1980, Honecker sent an urgent letter to CPSU General Secretary Brezhnev, urging that Warsaw Pact troops be sent into Poland and requesting a meeting of all leaders of Warsaw Pact states.[20] But Honecker's was the only voice calling for intervention, although Brezhnev let it be known that he believed that what was happening in Poland threatened the interests of the entire socialist commonwealth. Polish developments certainly sparked interest elsewhere in the bloc. In Hungary, for example, the first issue of the *samizdat* journal *Beszélő*, appearing in November 1981, was clearly influenced in part by the political transformation in Poland since summer 1980,[21] while, in Czechoslovakia, activists associated with Charter 77 were following events in Poland closely and would issue two statements concerning the situation in Poland in the course of 1982.[22] Meanwhile, at the end of November 1980, the 11 members of the Soviet Politburo met to discuss the option of invading Poland; the Politburo rejected invasion by a vote of six to five, with Brezhnev casting the deciding vote.[23] Meanwhile, the legalization of Solidarity was followed by the emergence of Rural Solidarity as its counterpart in the countryside and by an Independent Student Union. The PZPR's fraternal parties – the United Peasant Party and the Democratic Party – were starting to behave like independent parties rather than as transmission belts for the PZPR.[24] There was also a new atmosphere of freedom in the cultural sector. The Soviets were getting fed up.

But instead of organizing an invasion, the Soviets sent Marshal Viktor Kulikov, commander-in-chief of Warsaw Pact forces, to Warsaw in January and March 1981 to monitor Polish plans to deal with the "counterrevolution".[25] In fact, as Barbara Falk has revealed, the Polish regime mulled over the possibility of declaring martial law as early as Spring 1981, following the installation of General Jaruzelski (1923–2014) as PM in February.[26] A few months later, on 14 August, Kania and Jaruzelski traveled to Crimea to meet with Brezhnev. What was obvious to the two Poles was that Brezhnev's patience was running thin.[27] In the meantime, Stanisław Kania (1927–2020), whom Brezhnev personally had chosen to take over after the removal of Gierek as First Secretary,[28] launched a media campaign against Solidarity and tried, but failed, to stop the spontaneous formation of self-managing workers' councils at Polish factories.[29] In fact, Kania appeared to be powerless to restore anything that the Soviets would recognize as order. On 11 September 1981, Brezhnev spoke with Kania by phone and expressed his concern that Solidarity was having a dangerous impact on other states in the region.[30] In mid-September 1981, the CPSU Central Committee issued a public statement, warning of anti-Soviet trends in Poland and demanding that the PZPR leadership "take determined and radical steps in order to cut short the malicious anti-Soviet propaganda."[31]

In September 1981, General Jaruzelski had a long conversation with Marshal Dimitry F. Ustinov, the Soviet defense minister, during military exercises; the two men sat in a helicopter on the ground, talking for several hours, as Ustinov impressed upon Jaruzelski the urgency of the situation).[32] The fact that Marshal Ustinov met with Prime Minister Jaruzelski, rather than with party First Secretary Kania, is telling. Indeed, with Kania failing to deliver the results the Soviets demanded, the Kremlin forced Kania to resign and installed General Jaruzelski as First Secretary of the PZPR on 18 October 1981; Jaruzelski retained the prime ministerhip. But, in the weeks following his appointment, hundreds of thousands of people resigned from membership in the PZPR,[33] even as Solidarity's public rhetoric became more radical. The transcript of a CPSU Politburo meeting held on 17 September reveals the extent of Soviet anxiety concerning developments in Poland. While they agreed that steps needed to be taken urgently to end the euphoria, the consensus among Politburo members – as expressed by both Andropov and Ustinov – was that it would not be possible to deploy Soviet troops to quash Solidarity because, as Ustinov put it euphemistically, "They, the Poles, are not ready to receive our troops."[34] The alternative, broached in the Politburo already in April 1981,[35] was for Polish authorities to impose martial law.

The PZPR Central Committee met on 27–28 November 1981 and adopted a statement indicating that it was empowering the government to adopt whatever measures were necessary to restore "law and order, and public security."[36] On 6 December, the Warsaw district leadership of Solidarity decided to organize a mass demonstration in the city center to commemorate the events of December 1970. In his memoirs, Jaruzelski recounts that, upon being informed of this, he felt numb. He decided he needed to preempt the demonstration and, accordingly, resolved to declare martial law before the planned demonstration could take place.[37] He and his closest confidants decided on the night of 12/13 December as the date when they would impose martial law. But, in a reflection of some nervousness, Polish leaders phoned the Kremlin several times in the intervening days to inquire about the availability of Soviet military assistance in the event that the plan to impose martial law ran into trouble; the Soviets informed Warsaw that they were bogged down in Afghanistan and could not spare any troops for Poland.[38]

Jaruzelski "crossed the Rubicon" during the night of 12/13 December when he declared martial law, sending tanks onto the streets of Poland's major cities, cutting telephone lines, shutting down all of Solidarity's periodicals, and detaining thousands of persons, including Solidarity leaders and activists, among them Wałęsa, but not Bujak.[39] A new body was set up – the Military Council of National Salvation – to operate as the *de facto* authority in the country and generals were appointed to head the Ministry of Internal Affairs and the Ministry of Local Administration. Jaruzelski appeared on television to offer this justification of his decision:

> Today I address myself to you as a soldier and as the head of the Polish government. I address you concerning extraordinarily important questions. Our homeland is at the edge of an abyss. The achievements of many generations and the Polish home that has been built up from the dust are about to turn into ruins. State structures are ceasing to function. Each day delivers new blows to the waning economy.

He concluded his talk by pledging to work to restore "legal balance . . . [and] to create guarantees that give a chance to restore order and discipline" and offered that his intention in declaring martial law was to "save the country from collapse."[40]

Underground solidarity and underground society in Poland

Solidarity activists had anticipated that something was brewing but did not know what. They had hidden weapons in secret locations, but the locations were betrayed to the communist authorities. Thus, when the Committee for the Defense of the Country (KOK) imposed a curfew, the weapons were quickly confiscated by the authorities, Solidarity activists were rounded up and incarcerated, schools and universities were temporarily closed, and soon the ZSL and DS were brought back in line. Rather than giving up, Solidarity activists who remained free decided on a new strategy. Wiktor Kulerski, a Solidarity activist, explained this strategy in 1982: "This movement should create a situation in which the authorities will control empty stores but not the market, the employment of workers but not their livelihood, the official media but not the circulation of information, printing plants but not the publishing movement, the mail and telephones but not communications, and the school system but not education."[41]

Martial law failed to serve its intended functions. On the contrary, the repluralization of society, including in the cultural sector, could not be reversed; but, deprived of the possibility to act openly, independent activism went underground.

This seemed to signal an end to any possibility of a compromise between the regime and what was now an emergent parallel society. In a word, martial law quickly proved to be a completely dysfunctional tactical choice. Of course, until the house of cards collapsed in the course of 1988–89, independent activists were at a clear disadvantage. Yet, the parallel society which developed included independent funding for scientific research, underground plays, suitcase art (involving unofficial art which guests would bring in suitcases to evening parties), underground publishing of books, newspapers, and bulletins, and the emergence of underground political organizations committed to Polish independence and repluralization. As of summer 1985, there were an estimated 50,000 to 70,000 Poles who were either writing for the underground press or engaged in its publication, with another 200,000–250,000 helping in other ways, such as by distributing the underground press.[42]

Solidarity and the more radical Fighting Solidarity thus continued their work underground. But there were also other clandestine organizations, including (among others): Niepodległość (Independence), which was committed to reestablishing political pluralism in Poland; the Committee of Social Resistance (KOS), which demanded independence of the Soviet Union and pluralist democracy; Freedom-Justice-Independence (WSN), which likewise advocated independence and the overthrow of the communist organizational monopoly, calling for the establishment of an underground state; Wyzwolenie (Liberation), founded in 1984, which favored a mixed economy, but otherwise worked for the same basic goals as the aforementioned organizations; and the Confederation for an Independent Poland (KPN), founded in 1979 by Leszek Moczulski, who likewise demanded independence and pluralism for Poland and who was arrested in September 1980 on charges of slandering the Polish republic, because he had told the German magazine *Der Spiegel* that he expected the authorities to ban Solidarity in due course.[43]

Solidarity remained in a legal limbo from December 1981 until October 1982, when the regime issued a new law on trade unionism, stripping Solidarity of its legal status, leaving only the official trade union recognized under law.[44] Solidarity's legal status would be restored only in April 1989, at the same time that the hitherto banned Independent Student Union and Rural Solidarity also regained their legal status. In the meantime, although martial law was technically lifted in July 1983, some of its stipulations were incorporated into law; among those organizations that were banned, in addition to those mentioned above, were the Journalists' Association and the Writers' Union.[45] In the short term (in September 1982), five leading members of Solidarity already in detention, among them Jacek Kuroń and Adam Michnik, "were formally 'arrested' on charges of trying to overthrow the state by force. Three months later, as the last of the internees were being released, the government announced the 'arrest' of seven more, interned activists on similar charges of treason."[46]

In April 1982, Solidarity activists in Gdańsk, Mazowsze, Lower Silesia, and Małopolska set up the Interim Coordinating Committee (TKK); those signing the founding declaration were Bujak, Władysław Frasnyniuk, Władysław Hardek, and Bogdan Lis. (Wałęsa was in detention at the time and would be released only in November 1982.) In July, TKK Solidarity approached the regime with a five-point proposal for reconciliation. The regime ignored the proposal. Meanwhile, the security service fought Solidarity with bogus broadcasts which purported to represent Solidarity's views, infiltrated underground Solidarity cells, and hired a Wałęsa-lookalike who was filmed behaving in an obnoxious way.[47] The regime also tried to buy Wałęsa's support with a combination of flattery and offers of positions in the Patriotic Movement for National Renewal and in the advisory council for trade union affairs.[48] By spring 1984, Solidarity activists felt increasingly confident and, on 1 May, Wałęsa, together with a large group of supporters, infiltrated "the official May Day parade in Gdańsk. Wałęsa and his adherents paraded defiantly, passing within ten feet of the stand where party officials were seated. As they passed, Wałęsa turned to the party barons and flashed a V-for-victory sign."[49] An amnesty was proclaimed that year, although many of those amnestied at the time were rearrested soon after. A second, albeit limited, amnesty was announced on 17 July 1986. Subsequently, on 11 September 1986, Czesław Kiszczak, the Minister of Internal Affairs, announced the unconditional release of 225 political prisoners. Among these were all former Solidarity leaders still in detention, including Bujak, who had been picked up only two months earlier.

In addition to those underground organizations already mentioned earlier in this section, there were several other underground organizations of varying importance: the Polish Socialist Labor Party (formed in September 1981 with headquarters in Szczecin), the independent peace movement Freedom and Peace (which came into being in April 1985), the Polish Socialist Party (apparently a revival of an earlier party operating under that name), and *13 Grudnia* [13 December], named for the date on which martial law had been declared. Based in Kraków, *13 Grudnia* advocated a free-market economy and underlined the importance of individual freedom. In addition to these, there was also a satirical group, the Orange Alternative, led by Waldemar Frydrych, aka "the Major", which, among its various antics, assembled about a thousand young people equipped with horns and trumpets in June 1988 and elected Jaruzelski "King of Poland".[50]

Prices had been "adjusted" in 1982 but, in January 1988, the regime attempted to implement increases in food prices averaging 40%. This immediately sparked a demonstration by 3,000 persons in Gdańsk, followed by disturbances in Kraków and other cities. When the official trade union halted bus and tram service in Bydgoszcz in protest of the price increases, strikes spread quickly to Nowa Huta, Gdańsk, Warsaw, and elsewhere, and even the Manifesto mine in Jastrzębie in mid-August 1988. Most of these strikes were settled when the government agreed to significant pay hikes (e.g., 63% in Bydgoszcz). The strike at the Manifesto coal mine cost the regime 148,000 tons of coal in just nine days, worth an estimated $7.4 million.[51] A new generation of workers, who had not participated in the strikes of 1980, walked off their jobs in August. On 18 August, Jaruzelski declared that he was prepared to meet with strikers in Szczecin. By the end of the month, the Central Committee had agreed in principle to hold Round Table talks with the opposition. It took until February 1989 to work out the organization and agenda for these talks, which took place from 6 February to 5 April 1989.

Charter 77

Make no mistake about it: Charter 77 was the single most important human rights initiative in East Central Europe in the years 1977–89. In the 12 years of its existence, Charter 77 issued 572 documents – some of them informational in character, others being appeals to the authorities to undo one or another injustice.[52] Charter spokespersons pointed to Article 29 of the Czechoslovakia constitution, which proclaimed the right of citizens "to submit their proposals, suggestions and complaints" to the government.[53] Charter 77 underlined this point in document no. 2 (8 January 1977), in declaring that the Charter "does not in the slightest degree violate Czechoslovak laws but on the contrary is defending them."[54] Although the Chartists were convinced, thus, that everything they were doing was in conformity with the laws and, in token thereof, signed their names to all their documents, the authorities had a different view. For his part, Husák derided ". . . the Chartists as the most rabid enemies of the regime who no longer dare to preach the return of factories to the capitalists and therefore . . . [have] resorted to the Trojan horse tactics of calling for an 'improvement of socialism'."[55] Accordingly, the regime treated the Chartists as political criminals. Already in January 1977, Havel was arrested under section 98 of the constitution, which covered "serious crimes against the basic principles of the Republic."[56] Jan Patočka (1907–1977), a professional philosopher who had played a key role in organizing Charter 77, was hauled in for interrogation by the secret police after he received a visit from the Dutch foreign minister. He was subjected to a series of interrogations, with the final one on 12 March 1977, lasting for 10 hours, at which point Patočka collapsed; the next day he died of a brain hemorrhage.[57] Other signatories were also taken to police headquarters for questioning and badgering or had their houses searched. Some lost their jobs, being typically restricted after that to working in menial jobs for low pay.[58]

The range of Charter documents is impressive, with scrupulously researched and documented reports, among other subjects, on political criteria for admission to university (January 1977), freedom of religion (April 1977), discrimination in literature (June 1977), and the right to history (May 1984).[59] The last of these was a key document in that it struck at a central pillar of the communist party's claim to legitimacy. This document argued that

> It is typical of the totalitarian manipulation of history that it eventually must lead to history's gradual eradication, because the eradication of [competitive] politics, public opinion, morals, and other social values cannot be consistently undertaken without the elimination of the historical dimension . . . [T]his 'process of forgetting', which the state authorities find so desirable must be actively opposed. None of us ought to allow the death within himself or

herself of the memory of justice and injustice, truth and falsehood, good and evil, the memory of reality altogether.[60]

In addition to issuing communiques, letters, appeals, and reports, Charter 77 also promoted private (i.e., unofficial) concerts, theatrical performances, lectures in private apartments, and art exhibitions. In 1988, Charter 77 even dared to suggest that a monument to the victims of Stalinism be erected.

Finally, as I wrote in 1995,

> Charter 77 aspired to be the social conscience of Czechoslovak society . . . Charter 77 was an important political phenomenon in at least two respects. First, it addressed issues which were of wide interest to the population, from environmental deterioration to discrimination in education and hiring to religious freedom; and it contributed to the sustenance of a lively underground publishing scene and an equally lively underground culture. Second, it signaled the defection of at least part of the intelligentsia, and this, [as noted in Crane Brinton's classic *Anatomy of Revolution*,] . . . is one of the central ingredients not only in political decay but in any emergent revolutionary situation, regardless of its final outcome.[61]

Independent activism elsewhere in the bloc, 1977–89

Ceaușescu distanced **Romania** from the Warsaw Pact. But the conditions for independent activism in Romania were far harsher than those Poland, Hungary, and the GDR. Tismaneanu characterized communist Romania as guided by *national Stalinism*, as opposed to *national communism*, which he rightly associated with Dubček's Czechoslovakia and Tito's Yugoslavia. This put Romania in the same set with Hoxha's Albania, Kim il Sung's North Korea, and Husák's Czechoslovakia.[62] In this Stalinist enclave, Ceaușescu's leadership cult continued and even escalated, with the Thirteenth RCP Congress (in 1984) acclaiming the Romanian leader for his "clear-sightedness", "creative spirit", "revolutionary devotion and fervent patriotism", adding that his "boundless devotion serves the supreme interests of all our people" and that under his "wise leadership the Romanian people have registered the richest accomplishments – in their entire history – in the past 20 years."[63] His wife Elena was lauded (in 1985) for her "tremendous scientific achievements" and "warm generosity", while their son Nicu, whom the *Conducător* was grooming to be his successor, was said to be a "scientist of international reputation."[64] In token of his purported "boundless devotion" to his people, this self-declared "genius of the Carpathians" undertook a massive program at the start of the 1980s to transform the cityscape of Bucharest, clearing 20% of old Bucharest to make space for a huge Palace of the Republic. Between 30,000 and 50,000 residents of the old city were forced out of their apartments and almost a dozen historic churches, including the sixteenth-century Mihai Vodă Monastery, would have been demolished but for the intervention of civil engineer Eugeniu Iordăchescu, who devised a plan to put the churches on wide metal tracks, similar to railway tracks, and move them to safety. Then, in 1988, Ceaușescu unveiled his plan to bulldoze circa 8,000 villages and move their erstwhile inhabitants into more than 6,000 concrete apartment blocks. This "systematization" campaign, as Romania's propagandists called it, was intended to promote changes in the mental outlook of the peasants being moved into apartment blocks, thereby advancing the emergence of a homogeneous society.[65]

In Ceaușescu's madhouse, it was more challenging than elsewhere in the bloc to raise one's voice in protest. Even so, in 1977, inspired by the example set by Charter 77, the famous writer Paul Goma (1935–2020), together with several colleagues, tried to put together a committee to advocate for human rights in Romania. For their trouble, Goma and others were arrested on 1 April 1977. Goma was released on 6 May 1977 after pressure from abroad was brought to bear. He moved to Paris with his wife and son in November 1977.[66]

In spite of Ceaușescu's despotic rule, there were diverse sources of opposition to his regime from the beginning and, over time, it became harder for the regime to contain such opposition as emerged.[67] There were occasional expressions of opposition in the theater and in films and, according to Trond Gilberg, also in music.[68] In 1980, eight members of the School of Architecture set up Form-Trans-Inform to promote avant-garde concepts in architecture. They staged their first exhibition that same year with about 80 persons attending. Between January 1981 and March 1982, Form-Trans-Inform organized a series of meetings at the rate of one per month. These meetings, which the group called "actions", often took place in forests outside Bucharest or in demolished parts of the city where they could feel safe from surveillance. They also felt that working amid ruins was a learning experience.[69]

A Hungarian-language *samizdat* journal called *Ellenpontok* [Counterpoints] made its appearance in 1981 and published 10 issues before being shut down in 1983. During the two years it was in existence, those associated with it were subjected to repeated police harassment and arrest, and pressured to emigrate. Another *samizdat* periodical, the *Hungarian Press of Transylvania*, was launched in May 1983 and focused on the discriminatory treatment of members of the Hungarian minority by the regime.[70] But, of all the stories of harassment and persecution, the strangest has to do with yoga and transcendental meditation (TM).

In the 1970s, some Romanians started to promote yoga and even offered instruction in that art. Then, in 1977, the Central Committee approved an experimental program in TM, with the idea that it could sharpen the mind and strengthen a person's immune system. Later, in 1981, officials at the Ministry of Education and Research investigated the program and determined that it had assumed characteristics of a religious sect and counted TM as inharmonious with communism. Yoga was now condemned as an "oriental-inspired ritual" and, on 27 August 1982, yoga, karate, and budō were all condemned by the authorities. In defiance of this proscription, some Romanians continued to practise yoga, karate, etc.[71] The reason why the authorities decided to clamp down on yoga especially was that they feared that "yoga promoted self-control, concentration, tranquility, creativity, and the connection between mind and body, a recipe for strong women with a propensity for questioning authority."[72] Although these initiatives reflected some measure of resistance to the communist regime in Bucharest, what was missing was any organized initiative able to last more than two years. In this, Romania was strikingly different from the GDR, Poland, Czechoslovakia, and Hungary.

In **Hungary,** dissident activity in the 1980s included the publication and distribution of *samizdat* journals. The best known and most influential of these journals was *Beszélő* [The Talker], launched in 1981. In 1987, *Beszélő* brought out a special issue featuring a political program under the title "Social Contract". The program called for the restoration of private enterprise, a reduction of censorship, better protection for human rights, and opening Hungary's economy to the world market.[73] Other *samizdat* journals in Hungary included: *Kisúgo* [The Outsider], launched in 1981 and more radical than *Beszélő; ABC Hírmondő* [The Courier], launched in 1983 and focusing on human rights and democratic values; and *Demokrata,* a monthly launched in January 1987 and dedicated to promoting the democratization of Hungary.[74] The emergence of these journals may be traced back to 1980, when Gábor Demszky and László Rajk, Jr., the son of the minister of internal affairs executed in 1949, visited Poland in order to inform themselves about the operation of independent publishing in that country. Soon after their return to Hungary, Rajk opened a *"samizdat* boutique" in his apartment. When police found out about this shop, they ejected him from his apartment and confiscated a large amount of *samizdat.* Rajk found a new apartment and resumed selling *samizdat* there. As for Demszky, upon his return to Hungary, he set to work to create *Hírmondő;* in 1983, police pulled him over for an allegedly routine traffic stop and beat him up.

There was marked ideological diversity among oppositionists, with Tamás Bauer, for example, suggesting in 1982 that Hungary should follow Yugoslavia's path, i.e., fashion a liberalized one-party state, while Pál Szalai favored a multi-party socialist system and Erzsébet Szalai hoped for a "liberal alternative".[75] But, for all of their differences, intellectuals who made up Hungary's opposition were united in their respect for sociologist István Bibó (1911–1979), who, in urging fellow oppositionists to seek common ground and collaborate in identifying solutions to Hungary's crisis,[76] may be identified as a paradigmatic idealist. While those in critical opposition may have nurtured rival visions for the future political system, they came together on issues of environmental protection. In June 1986, Hungary saw the launch of *Vizjel* [Watermark], the first independent periodical in East Central Europe dedicated to questions of environmental protection. There were also independent environmental groups, among which the most prominent were the Danube Circle, focusing on water pollution, and the Blues, focusing primarily on air pollution – founded in 1984 and 1985 respectively. Both of these groups became involved in protests against the planned Gabčíkovo-Nagymaros Dam project. In addition to the foregoing, independent activism also included: a Peace Group for Dialogue, formed in September 1982 by university students and recent graduates; a "Flying Kindergarten", offering lectures and even seminars in private homes; an independent Foundation for the Support of the Poor; private art groups and independent theaters; and Demszky's AB Publishing House, which published both the works of Hungarian authors and translations of works originally appearing in other languages, including George Orwell's *1984*, Teresa Toranska's *Them*, and Milan Kundera's *The Unbearable Lightness of Being*.

In **East Germany**, the most prominent dissidents in the 1970s were: Robert Havemann, a professor chemistry at Humboldt University, who lost his job after he began championing freedom of speech; Wolf Biermann, a song writer and performer, who was expelled from the SED in 1963 for his nonconformist lyrics; and Rudolf Bahro, who was banned from publishing in 1966 but who, in defiance of that ban, brought out his book, *The Alternative*, spelling out a communist (or socialist) alternative to the SED-managed system and publishing it with a West German publishing house. Havemann died in 1982; as previously mentioned, Biermann was granted permission to perform in Cologne in 1976 and then, once in West Germany, stripped of his GDR citizenship and denied permission to return to East Germany; and Bahro was escorted to the border with West Germany in 1979 and "encouraged" to leave the GDR.[77]

From the start of the 1980s, the main vehicle for critical opposition in the GDR was the independent peace movement associated with the Scriptural words "Swords into Plowshares". The Protestant Church made space available to the pacifists to meet, and the movement numbered an estimated 2,000 to 5,000 activists as of 1983, with an additional 30,000–50,000 supporters – a huge number for a communist country.[78] That same year, SED authorities expelled 20 independent pacifists from the GDR and arrested several persons demonstrating for peace in (East) Berlin. By January 1984, eight more independent pacifists, all of them from Weimar, found themselves behind bars.[79] Obviously, the SED did not object to the championing of peace; indeed, the SED had its official GDR Peace Council and also approved of the unofficial Christian Peace Conference. What bothered the SED was the independence of the Swords into Plowshares movement, as well as the contacts of its adherents with the Protestant Church.

Finally, where **Bulgaria** is concerned, there was little to report until the late 1980s. But, by March 1989, there were nine independent associations in Bulgaria.[80] Among these were: an association devoted to ending authorities' interference in the Churches; a Green Party set up in the town of Burgas; the Eco-Glasnost Movement, formed in March 1989; and an independent trade union known as Support, founded in February 1989 but claiming only 60 members as late as August 1989.[81]

Apocalypse culture – Rock, Punk, & Hip-Hop

When the political system in a society with well-educated and socially conscious citizens begins to unravel, it is quite common to find an increasingly active dissident scene with independent activism, searching for and advocating new solutions and new visions, as explored above. It is also common to find highly innovative and creative cultural manifestations, whether in music, theater, painting, fiction, or the other arts. This syndrome, which I call *apocalypse culture*, played out in Vienna in the waning years of the Austro-Hungarian Empire. This same syndrome also played out throughout the Soviet bloc – more strongly in the northern tier (the GDR, Poland, Czechoslovakia, and Hungary) but faintly also in Romania and Bulgaria.

In the years prior to 1980, orchestral music was a focus of controversy and, especially in the years leading up to 1956 (though also later in Czechoslovakia and Romania), communist cultural tsars were keen on corralling composers, as also writers and visual artists, into socialist realist (or, in Ceaușescu's Romania, socialist humanist) marching formation. But, beginning gradually in the 1950s and gathering steam over the years, rock bands changed the calculus, becoming a greater headache for communist authorities than orchestral composers and, in any event, there could be no thought of infiltrating any version of socialist realism into rock. Not all rock bands criticized local communist elites and their policies, but some did. In the Soviet Union, the Happy Guys band provided an example of a group willing to sing lyrics that were positive about the Soviet Union. But there were not many such groups in East Central Europe. Moreover, even when rock bands steered clear of politics, their attire, long hair for men, and songs about love and sex were troubling for some straightlaced communists.

In undertaking research into Poland's rock scene, I made two trips to the country, in order to conduct interviews with appropriate persons: in October 2013, to visit Kraków and Łódź, and in October 2015 to visit Warsaw and Gdańsk/Sopot. While in Kraków, I had a long conversation with a local musician who was highly knowledgeable about the rock scene and rock musicians in Poland. As we sat at the Hard Rock Café, just off Mariacki Square, enjoying a late breakfast, he told me about Polish rock, past and present. While he continued to find the rock scene stimulating, he recalled the 1980s as the golden age of Polish rock since it was then, as it was also elsewhere in the bloc as well as in Yugoslavia, that rock bands took up political themes and, at times, challenged the regimes. It was then that rock bands addressed social issues, mocked the communists, and even attacked the communists directly.

Rock music (or rock 'n' roll, as it was called initially) reached the region in the mid-1950s, followed by punk toward the end of the 1970s. Hip-hop reached the GDR, Romania, and Bulgaria in the early 1980s and came to Poland only toward the end of the 1980s, with recordings by American rappers offering locals their first exposure to the new genre.[82] It was only after the collapse of communism in late 1989 that hip-hop came to Czechoslovakia and later to Hungary.

Of course, many rock and punk songs from the 1980s were not political; in many cases, the rock musicians sought rather to put on a good show and to be inventive and interesting. As it turns out, in Czechoslovakia, rock performers Vladimir Merta and Vladimír Mišík were taken to task by the authorities in 1984 precisely for music and lyrics that were judged to be "too inventive and interesting."[83] In fact, rock music was generally unwelcome to authorities in the Soviet bloc. Thus, that same year, Georgi Dzhagarov, deputy chair of the Council of State and chair of the Standing Commission on Spiritual Values, charged that "the whole country has been disquieted by the muddy stream of music trends sweeping away all the true values of music."[84]

But there were also bands in every bloc state prepared to take up political themes. Some did so indirectly, by implication, as in the Bulgarian group Crickets' 1980 song, "Wedding Day", nominally mourning the bride's loss of freedom as she took her wedding vows. But, significantly, the Crickets borrowed the music of the Beatles' song "Back in the USSR" for their lamentation of the loss of freedom.[85] Others were more explicit, such as the Hungarian Coitus Punk Group (CPG) who sang, in implicit reference to Kádár:

> We have a puppet for a king,
> His legs and arms jerk on a string,
> We're the people, we bow and scrape,
> We're really humble.[86]

Not satisfied with that broadside, the CPG returned with an even more scathing song in 1984, entitled "Standing Youth" and including the nonsensical phrase "Duli-dul-balalaika":

> In the meadow a young shock worker is standing.
> He had just come from a Communist Saturday meeting
> Duli-dul-balalajka, duli-dul-balalajka.
> Statues, pictures – you schem[ing] bandit,
> The workers' hero has to play along with it.
> Duli-dul-balalajka, duli-dul-balalajka.
> Rotten stinking communist gang –
> Why has nobody hanged them yet?[87]

After this ostentatious outrage, punctuated by the tearing up of a live chicken on stage, the authorities arrested the four band members and sentenced them to prison terms ranging from 18 months to two years.

Other groups reflected on life under communism, such as the Hungarian band URH, which sang:

> Too many cops, too many informers,
> Not enough pimps, not enough whores,
> Not enough cops, not enough informers,
> Too many pimps, too many whores.[88]

Then again, there was the East German group Pankow which, in its 1988 song "Langeweile", sang:

> Seen the same country too long
> Heard the same language too long

Waited too long, hoped too long
Honored the old men too long,
I ran around
ran around so much
ran around so much
and nothing happened anyway.[89]

Or again, taking up the theme of mass conformity, the Polish punk band WC sang in 1984:

Posers, fetishists – destroy them all!
A generation of conformists – destroy them all!
Your ideals – destroy them all![90]

The sentencing of members of CPG to prison terms after they called for hanging communist leaders was the exception; by and large, communist authorities restricted themselves to verbal attacks on rock bands in the party-controlled press.

Few, if any rock musicians suffered from the illusion that their songs and performances could contribute to the collapse of the communist political order. What they could do was to give voice to the growing outrage among ordinary citizens and hold fast to some form of integrity – to "live in truth" as Havel put it. They could also highlight certain civilizational values at a time, as Tadeusz Konwicki put it in his novel, *A Minor Apocalypse*, of "unease at the prospect of the collapse of all values, all morality, into cultureless, timeless barbarism clothed in the invisible perfection of the Soviet Empire's clothes."[91]

Gender equality and incipient feminism

The status of women changed in the Soviet bloc over the course of the years of communist rule. The following are the chief results of the approximately four decades of bloc-style socialism. First, the proportion of women with at least university education if not also a higher degree rose steadily over the four decades of communist rule. Second, the principle of equal pay for equal work was generally respected, but women were concentrated in lower-paid jobs, with the result that the average salary of women remained lower than that of men. Third, at the same time, there was a new emphasis on women having careers, and there were increasing numbers of professional women not content to do nothing in life but raise children and take care of their husbands. Fourth, access to abortion became easier in most of the bloc states, but harder to obtain in Romania; after the fall of communism, abortion became harder to obtain the newly unified Germany and Poland, but considerably easier in Romania. Fifth, in terms of numbers, there was improved representation of women in political bodies, including in national parliaments but especially at local levels, but women rarely held positions at the upper levels. And sixth, in spite of pro-equality rhetoric from the authorities, the patriarchal family continued largely unaffected, with women doing the bulk of the housework and cooking and men enjoying the privilege of resting at home after finishing their salaried work. Feminism was late in coming to East Central Europe and, as of the 1980s, only East Germany was experiencing the first glimmers of feminism.[92] Elsewhere among countries of the Soviet bloc, in the region, such as in Slovakia, "feminism" was often considered a dirty word and used only in a disparaging way.[93]

The churches: collaboration, opposition, opportunism, or constructive criticism?

The largest religious bodies in the Soviet bloc were the Catholic Church (the Roman rite in Poland, Czechoslovakia, and Hungary; the Greek rite in Romania), the Orthodox Church (in Romania and Bulgaria, with small pockets elsewhere), and the Lutheran Church (mainly in the GDR and Hungary, but also a small community in Slovakia). The Reformed Church in Hungary was smaller than either the Catholic or the Lutheran Church, while, in the GDR, the Lutheran and Reformed Churches had been merged in 1817 to form the *Evangelische Kirche* or Protestant Church, as I am calling it in this book.

These three religious bodies were treated somewhat differently by their respective regimes and, in turn, developed their own styles. What sets the Catholic Church apart from all other Christian Churches is the papacy, with its headquarters in Rome. In communist times, this made a difference for communist policies. Once the communists realized that they were not going to succeed in persuading local archbishops to break with the Holy See, they had to confront the reality that the Catholic Church remained unified. The Catholic and Orthodox Churches both nurtured national culture, both are socially conservative, and both have been convinced that they needed to combat changes in sexual mores, especially as regards homosexuality, divorce, and abortion. Where the Orthodox Churches of Romania and Bulgaria differed from the Catholic and Protestant Churches alike was their cooptation by their respective regimes, under conditions explained earlier in this volume. The Orthodox Church press in these two countries was likewise coopted, meaning that their texts were written fully in line with regime directives; this was reflected, for instance, in the praise for Ceaușescu which the Romanian Church press lavished on the *Conducător*. By contrast, in Poland, the Catholic press was not coopted but was subjected to prepublication censorship.

The Protestant Church in the GDR and the Lutheran Church in Hungary were less nationalistic than the Catholic Church in Poland or either of the large Orthodox Churches in the bloc. Moreover, each of them reached a certain accommodation with the respective regime. In the case of the Protestant Church in the GDR, itself less conservative when it came to sexual mores, the summit meeting between Honecker and Bishop Albrecht Schönherr in March 1978 prepared the ground for a collaboration between the Church and the SED in celebrating the quincentenary of Martin Luther's birth in 1983, even if each side emphasized different aspects of Luther's role in history. The SED regime's treatment of the Protestant Church press differed from the treatment meted out to the Catholic and Orthodox presses elsewhere in the bloc. Thus, instead of a coopted press or a press subjected to prepublication censorship, the Church press in East Germany was subjected to post-publication censorship. What this meant in practice was that entire issues of a Church newspaper could be confiscated and banned after being printed; this happened, as already mentioned, to the Berlin regional newspaper *Die Kirche* in 1988.

If the Protestant Church tried to walk a fine line "between opposition and opportunism," as Bishop Werner Krusche put it, opting thereby for a posture that could be equated with loyal opposition, the Lutheran Church in Hungary, by embracing a theology of diakonia (service) chose a posture of unmitigated loyalty. As Joseph Pungur explained in a 1992 publication, the "practical consequence [of the Church's embrace of the theology of diakonia] was that the Church offer[ed] full and unconditional support to the building of socialism and to the state's sovereign policy objectives."[94]

The two most important events in religious life in the bloc in the 1980s both took place in 1983. For the Catholic Church, this signal event was the second papal visit by John Paul II to his homeland, 16–23 June 1983. The visit was timed to coincide with the 600th anniversary of the Black Madonna of Częstochowa. In his first speech after his arrival in Poland, the pope called on the authorities to respond positively to Solidarity's demand for relegalization.[95] In his first meeting with Jaruzelski (on 17 June), the pope extracted a promise from the party leader to lift martial law and suggested also that a wide-ranging amnesty should be announced. Jaruzelski agreed to the pope's requests, lifting martial law on 22 July 1983 and declaring the first of two amnesties on 21 July 1984.[96] Although the regime was gratified to hear the pope's implicit recognition of Poland's western frontier, authorities were displeased with the pope's repeated affirmations of the right of workers to form independent trade unions.

The pope's visit was both exultant and poignant, coming just a little more than two years after the 13 May 1981 attempt on his life.[97] John Paul II recovered and later had a meeting with his would-be assassin, forgiving him. However, on 19 October 1984, the charismatic Catholic priest, Fr. Jerzy Popiełuszko was kidnapped and murdered by two security police officers. Popiełuszko had been saying weekly Masses for Solidarity and was deeply loved. It is striking that, in his last public words, spoken less than an hour before he was kidnapped, Popiełuszko told those in attendance at his Mass: "In order to defeat evil with good, in order to preserve the dignity of man, one must not use violence. It is the person who has failed to win on the strength of his heart and his reason, who tries to win by force . . . Let us pray that we be free from fear and intimidation, but above all from the lusts for revenge and violence."[98]

The other major religious event of 1983 was the Luther Quincentenary, already mentioned in the previous chapter. It was both more elaborate and less complicated than the papal visit. It was more elaborate in that it involved specially commissioned biographies of Luther, concerts in his honor, speeches, and, with funding from the state, the restoration of various churches and objects of historical significance. It was less complicated because of the spirit of collaboration between Church and state, with, for example, Church representatives taking part in the work of the official Martin Luther Committee of the GDR. And for the regime, it was an opportunity to claim the Protestant reformer as "one of the greatest sons of the German people."[99]

Finally, as would be revealed after the pertinent archives were opened following the collapse of communist rule, Catholic and Protestant clergy alike functioned as informers for the State Security Service (secret police) in the bloc countries, as did Orthodox clergy in Romania and Bulgaria.[100] There were some prominent Catholic informers, such as Archbishop Ján Sokol of Trnava, Slovakia, and Archbishop Stanisław Wielgus of Plock, Poland; the latter had reportedly collaborated with the secret police from 1967 to 1987. The situation was similar where Bulgarian and Romanian Orthodox clergy were concerned. Lavinia Stan and Lucian Turcescu report that the Bulgarian Committee for State Security (secret police) succeeded in recruiting about half of all Orthodox priests and theology students to collaborate as informers.[101] "[B]y January 2012, 11 of Bulgaria's 15 metropolitan bishops had been exposed as former collaborators with the communist security service," together with the Islamic mufti and the head of the Catholic Church in Bulgaria.[102] In Romania, Orthodox clergy are said to have "passed along information obtained in the confessional" to the Securitate; thousands of regular priests may have served as informers, alongside at least six members of the Holy Synod.[103] All in all, as the era of communist party rule came to a close, the record of the Christian clergy was mixed. There were heroes, such as Popiełuszko, loved by many, but there were also informers for the police, some of whom were, no doubt, motivated by the desire to simplify their lives.

The unraveling of the bloc economies

With the exception of Romania, net debt in convertible currency increased throughout the bloc between 1970 and 1989, as shown in Table 4.1.

The situation was the most serious in East Germany, Hungary, and Poland, as debt increased from less than $1 billion in each case to between $19 billion and $38.5 billion. Although total debt was highest in Poland, on a per capita basis the most indebted countries in the bloc were Hungary ($1,839 debt per capita), East Germany ($1,464), and Bulgaria ($1,055), with Poland close behind ($1,015 per capita) – see Table 4.2. By comparison with the foregoing, Czechoslovakia's per capita debt in 1989 – $370 – seems relatively modest.

The economies of the East Central European countries were in serious trouble by the end of the 1980s, as shown in Table 4.3. Bulgaria's robust GDP growth rate of 6.1% in 1987 shrank in the following year and went into negative numbers in 1989–90. Czechoslovakia maintained modest rates of GDP growth in 1986–89 but slid into the red in 1990. Hungary's GDP scarcely grew at all during 1988–89 and then shrank by 6.5%, while Poland, with GDP likewise stagnant in 1988–89, registered a contraction of 12% in 1990, matching that of Bulgaria.

TABLE 4.1 Net Debt in Convertible Currency in Billions of USD, 1970–1989 by country

	1970	1975	1980	1985	1987	1988	1989
Bulgaria	0.7	2.3	4.1	2.0	6.3	7.3	9.5
Czechoslovakia		−0.7	5.0	3.8	5.3	5.7	5.8
East Germany	0.9	3.6	11.6	7.3	10.1	10.7	23.5
Hungary	0.8	3.0	7.7	11.8	18.0	18.2	19.1
Poland	0.9	7.8	24.0	28.4	37.7	37.1	38.5
Romania	1.0	2.3	9.2	6.4	4.3	1.1	−1.2

Source: Judit Kiss, "Debt Management in Eastern Europe", in *Eastern European Economics*, Vol. 32, No.3 (May-June 1994), p. 55.

TABLE 4.2 Per Capita Net Debt in Convertible Currency in Billions of Dollars, 1989, among the five indebted countries of the Soviet bloc, in declining order of debt per capita

	Debt per capita
Hungary	$1,839
German Democratic Republic	$1,464
Bulgaria	$1,055
Poland	$1,015
Czechoslovakia	$370

Source: Calculated from the data in Table 4.2.

TABLE 4.3 GDP Growth in Selected East Central European Countries, 1985–1990 in per cent

	1986	1987	1988	1989	1990
Bulgaria	4.2	6.1	2.6	1.9	12.0
Czechoslovakia#	2.6	2.1	2.3	1.9	−3.5
Hungary	1.5	3.4	0.1	0.5	−6.5
Poland	1.5	3.4	0.1	0.1	−12.0

\# = Net Material Product

Source: Andrés Solimano, "The Economies of Central and Eastern Europe: An Historical and International Perspective", in Vittorio Corbo, Fabrizio Coricelli, and Jan Bossak (eds.), *Reforming Central and Eastern European Economies: Initial Results and Challenges* (Washington D.C.: The World Bank, 1991), p. 19.

The Romanian economy also deteriorated in the 1980s – the unintended consequence of sloppy construction in industrial projects and poor urban infrastructure, huge investments in projects (often of a ceremonial nature) that were never brought to completion, and the razing of "traditional villages . . . [which were] replaced by rural housing projects that lacked electricity or running water."[104] After the country's external hard currency debt reached $9.2 billion in 1980, Ceauşescu decided to repay the debt in full. By combining virtual self-sufficiency in all sectors of production with strict limits on imports, a policy of stepping up exports of luxury goods such as fine crystal, and limiting electric power to three hours a day (except for the districts where the elite lived), Ceauşescu succeeded in paying off the debt by 1989 and even running a current account surplus of $1.2 billion.

Poverty was also a growing problem in several bloc states, as the indicative data for Poland, Hungary, and Yugoslavia (in Table 3.6) already suggested. I will comment below on the three countries with the largest hard currency debts at the time – Hungary, East Germany, and Poland.

Hungary

The Hungarian state's hard currency debt continued to rise in the 1980s, from an unstainable $7.7 billion in 1980 to a crippling $19.1 billion in hard currency debt by 1989 (see Table 4.1). Like all other socialist countries, Hungary suffered from chronic shortages of goods.[105] In addition to the problems already mentioned in the previous chapter, there were also miscalculations and mismanagement where investment strategy was concerned.[106] The troubles in the Hungarian economy can be traced back to 1976, but it took another eight years before problems became acute. János Kádár spoke candidly about the situation when he addressed the Central Committee on 17 April 1984, conceding that Hungarians were living beyond the means of their country. He even stated that "we cannot offer hope and a way out [of our difficulties]. The party and the regime have been unable to show new perspectives."[107]

Like East Germany's Honecker (see below), Kádár was convinced that social peace (in a one-party state) required stable prices. That meant that prices had to be subsidized. But the money to subsidize prices and wages and to fund new investments could only come, in sufficient measure, from further Western loans. The Hungarian authorities understood this. In fact, CC Secretary Ferenc Havasi, responsible for the Office of National Planning, and PM György Lázár argued strenuously against taking out any more foreign loans, but Kádár insisted on taking more loans and had his way.[108] So Hungary took out additional loans from Western banks in the mid-1980s and Hungary's foreign debt climbed further. In 1986, Kádár met with Soviet General Secretary Gorbachev, who admitted that he was "deeply concerned" about the state of the Hungarian economy.[109] Later, at a meeting of the CC on 18–19 November 1986, Kádár told those in attendance baldly, "The country has consumed more than it has produced."[110] On that same occasion, the CC took the unprecedented step of transferring responsibility for managing the economy from the party to the government, while continuing to maintain its own apparatus for economic policy. The appointment of 38-year-old Miklós Németh to take charge of the CC's Department of Economic Policy was accompanied by the recruitment of new, often younger people into policy-planning posts. However, these changes came too late to save the HSWP. In fact, as of late 1988, there were 21 recently formed political associations in Hungary challenging the policies of the ruling party.

The German Democratic Republic

The GDR's hard currency debt likewise swelled in the course of the 1980s, doubling from an already large debt of $11.6 billion in 1980 to $23.5 billion in 1989. There were a number of factors contributing to bringing the East Germany economy to the edge of an abyss, including increases in the wages of industrial workers,[111] the guaranteed right to work, with protection against being laid off, together with the aspiration to assure full employment, and the two oil price shocks of 1973–74 and 1979–80. In addition, the East German economy became less competitive on the global market, even as foreign and domestic debts increased. In fact, "the country's economy stagnated or shrank in 1980, 1982, 1986, and 1987 according to West German calculations."[112] But, according to Martin Schmidt, what brought the East German state to the brink of bankruptcy was the SED's ambitious and broadly conceived social policy which embraced: significant subsidies for basic food items, certain industrial goods, infant and children's clothing, children's shoes, school materials (including textbooks), and fuel; artificially low prices for drinking water and public transport; generous family assistance; the subsidization of rents; and generous provisions for healthcare.[113] In 1980, price subsidies alone consumed 11.6% of the state budget; this rose to 20.1% in 1989.[114] The GDR, like Hungary and Poland, was living beyond its means.

In the 1971–75 Five Year Plan, about 1.4 billion East German Marks were allocated for pay raises and price relief; by the end of the plan period, 5 billion Marks had been spent for these purposes.[115] To finance all of what was involved here, the country's economic managers authorized a step-by-step reduction in investments in industry, a reduction about which Willi Stoph (1914–1999), Chair of the Council of Ministers, expressed his concern as early as October 1972. To finance the price subsidies and generous social safety net, and to import consumer goods from the West, the GDR relied on credits and loans from Western banks. As noted in chapter 3, Gerhard Schürer (1921–2010), Chair of the State Planning Commission, issued his first warning as early as November 1972 that the country's debt to Western banks was reaching alarming proportions. The Politburo discussed the situation in January 1973 and believed that improvements to the export capacity of industry and a reduction in imports from the West could, in theory, reduce the country's foreign debt.[116] But the Honecker regime was unwilling to authorize the investments which were needed in industry to make the GDR's industrial products competitive on the world market. As already noted, Honecker was haunted by memories of the nationwide tumult in June 1953 and by the lesson he drew from Gomułka's failed effort to raise food prices in Poland in December 1970. Indeed, Honecker feared that any "drastic erosion in the quality of life of the population" would result in "political instability, social unrest, and a strengthening of the domestic opposition."[117] For Honecker, thus, price stability became dogma and credits from Western banks seemed to be the only way to finance his consumer-oriented economic and social policy. In the years Honecker was at the helm, 1971–1989, prices for meat, butter, milk, bread, heating, electricity, postage, and other staples were completely stable; yet, between 1970 and 1989, wages rose by an average of 205%.[118] At the same time, because of Honecker's misconceived investment policy, the country was unable to keep up with international standards in natural science and medicine.

Throughout Honecker's years in power, Schürer repeatedly spoke out against the huge subsidies being paid to keep prices and rents low[119] – but to no avail. He and others in the Politburo argued further that it was necessary to make cuts to the budget for the country's social benefits[120] – again to no avail. A report presented to the Politburo on 31 October 1989 confirmed that, since 1971, consumption had risen faster than economic growth – an unsustainable formula.[121] Adding to the GDR's economic worries was the Kremlin's decision in 1980 to reduce discounted sales of oil to East Germany from 19 million tons a year to just over 17 million tons. The announcement of this reduction made Honecker frantic and he wrote two letters to Brezhnev, pleading with the Soviet General Secretary to reverse this decision. Instead of accommodating this plea, Brezhnev sent CC Secretary Konstantin Russakov to Berlin to explain to Honecker that this was the best that the USSR could afford.[122] By the end of the 1980s, the GDR was on the brink of economic disaster.

On 31 October 1989, the Politburo received a report prepared by Schürer. The report, commissioned by then-SED General Secretary Egon Krenz, warned ominously that "Capping the debt alone" – which is to say not undertaking to reduce it – "would require a 25–30% reduction in the living standard in 1990 and would make the GDR ungovernable."[123] Although Schürer may have overestimated the size of the GDRs external hard currency debt, it was clear that Honecker and his team had "colossally overestimated the resilience of the economy and society."[124] In this context, German reunification offered the prospect of saving East Germany from its self-made economic quandary.

Poland

As Poland entered the 1980s, both the system and society were in deep crisis. Table 4.1 shows Poland sinking ever deeper into debt from 1970 to 1989 and with the proportion of persons living below the poverty line more than doubling between 1978 and 1987. Even in 1971–75, when the economy seemed to be flourishing, with an average annual rate of 9.8% growth in national product, there were troubling signs, in particular the fact that the expansion of the economy in those years was funded for the most part by Western credits and the fact that earnings from exports to the West covered the costs of only 54% of imports from Western countries.[125] Poland's hard currency debt had risen to a staggering $24 billion by 1980, by far the highest figure among the Soviet Union's six bloc states. Blame for the economic crisis was pinned on Prime Minister Piotr Jaroszewicz, who was forced to resign his office. His replacement, who took office on 18 February 1980, was Edward Babiuch (1927–2021), who had served as one of four deputy prime ministers since 1976 and whom Zwass and Vale characterized as "an excellent apparatchik" but not an economist.[126] Babiuch moved slowly and by August he too would be fired, serving as a convenient scapegoat for Poland's continued morass. (In May 1981, Babiuch would be suspended from the PZPR and placed under investigation that he had engaged in fraud during the seven months he had served as prime minister.[127])

But the following years, with nearly a year and a half of repluralization (from August 1980 to December 1981), followed by martial law, and subsequently the development of an extensive political and cultural underground[128] were challenging. In 1983, Poland's economic planners thought that the economy was back on track.[129] In fact, the government led by General Wojciech Jaruzelski (1923–2014), which had declared martial law on 13 December 1981, promised to implement only partial reforms and the economic crisis was, if anything, only getting worse.[130] In terms of national income, the country had registered only a marginal increase of 1.6% as an average annual rate during the years 1976–80 and had shrunk dramatically by 13.0% in 1981 and by a further 5.5% in 1982. Although the country registered a respectable 6.0% growth of national income in 1983, the rate of growth would shrink with each of the following four consecutive years. Industrial output also contracted at the start of the 1980s – by 19% in 1981 and by 0.2% in 1982. After that, the pattern of initial recovery followed by gradual decline closely matched the pattern of decline of rates of growth of national income.[131] And just as Poland's hard currency debt rose from $24 billion in 1980 to $38.5 billion in 1989, Poland had a negative trade balance with other COMECON countries every year but one during the years 1977–86, weighing Poland down with the largest intra-bloc debt of the seven states (including the Soviet Union).[132] As for ordinary citizens, they had seen their real incomes decline to the point that, in 1989, the cost of food alone accounted for 55% of the average family's budget.[133]

The collapse of communism

Although it was obvious by summer 1980, if not earlier, that there were tectonic shifts in the political landscape in East Central Europe, it was only in April 1988, with the spread of strikes across Poland, that it seemed completely obvious to many observers that communism's days were numbered. Although those strikes were settled, there were further strikes in August of that year, leading to the aforementioned Round Table talks from 6 February 1989 to 5 April 1989 in which Polish authorities agreed to hold semi-free elections that year: semi-free elections for the lower house of the parliament, but with some seats reserved for the PZPR and its supposed allies; and completely free elections for the upper house. The June elections gave Solidarity control of 99 of the 100 seats in the Senate, with the remaining seat won by an independent candidate; in the lower house, the Sejm, the PZPR lost its advantage when its supposed allies, the DS and the ZSL, broke ranks and began to cooperate with Solidarity. By August 1989, Tadeusz Mazowiecki, a Catholic journalist, was sworn in as prime minister of Poland. There were major amendments to the Polish constitution in 1989 and 1990, followed by a "small constitution" in 1992, intended as an interim measure until a more proper constitution could be adopted (as it was in 1997). Jaruzelski assumed the presidency in July, but was forced to resign from office by the end of 1990. At that point, Wałęsa was elected president of Poland.

Round Table talks were subsequently held in all the remaining bloc states except Romania. Hungary was the next state to hold such talks. Here János Kádár had been forced to step down on 22 May 1988; his successor, Károly Grósz, was in office when Round Table talks started in Hungary, running from 13 June to 18 September 1989. Grósz resigned on 7 October 1989. Eleven days later a new constitution was adopted, entering into force on 23 October 1989. Whereas "section 3 of the pre-1989 Constitution [had] stated that 'the Marxist-Leninist Party of the working class is the leading force in society,'"[134] the new constitutional document removed any reference to the Marxist-Leninist party and, instead, declared Hungary to be "a state founded on the rule of law."[135] Section 8, para. 1, of the document recognized "inalienable and inviolable human rights," while section 60, para. 1, guaranteed "the right to freedom of thought, conscience, and religion."[136]

The next country to hold Round Table talks was Czechoslovakia. Unlike Poland and Hungary, where the Round Table talks produced agreements to dismantle their respective communist systems, in Czechoslovakia the communist leaders resigned on 24 November 1989, after 23 days of protests on the streets of Prague. Only then were Round Table talks organized. The election of dissident playwright Václav Havel as President on 29 December signalled the opening of a new chapter in the history of Czechs and Slovaks. But democratic Czechoslovakia did not last long since differences between the Czech and Slovak governments over economic policy led to a gentleman's agreement to divide the country in two, effective 1 January 1993. Because it was bloodless, this came to be known as the Velvet Divorce; (the resignation of the communist leaders and transition to democracy had already been dubbed the Velvet Revolution). Havel was now elected President of the Czech Republic on 2 February 1993.

Meanwhile, in May 1989, the GDR authorities gave out fraudulent results after local elections. Since independent activists had conducted exit polls, the ruse was exposed, severely undermining the credibility of the regime. That same month, the Hungarian government opened its border with Austria. Immediately, tens of thousands of East Germans, knowing that if they could make it to West Germany they would be treated as West German citizens, fled through Hungary to Austria, and onward to West Germany. In September, more than 2,000 East Germans took refuge in the West German embassy in Prague, with about the same number fleeing to the West German embassy in Warsaw. An agreement was reached and, on 1 October, the roughly 4,000 refugees were allowed to travel by train to West Germany. Meanwhile, weekly protests in Leipzig, the GDR's second largest city, began, initially, on 11 September, involving only a few hundred participants. But this grew to a thousand a week later and to more than 5,000 standing in front of Leipzig's Nikolai church on 25 September. The number of protesters continued to grow until 300,000 people assembled on Leipzig's streets on 23 October.[137] In the meantime, Honecker had stepped down as General Secretary and Egon Krenz (b. 1937) had assumed that function on 18 October 1989.

On 9 November 1989, the Berlin Wall was breached and began to be torn down. By 3 December, Krenz had likewise been forced to resign and Gregor Gysi was appointed as a "caretaker" for the party, serving in that capacity for only eight days. Round Table talks started on 7 December, running to early 1990. The SED disbanded on 16 December 1989, leaving Hans Modrow (b. 1928), who had been elected PM on 13 November 1989, to oversee the country's politics. In January 1990, Modrow called for elections to the Volkskammer (the GDR parliament) to be held on 18 March. The CDU/East, German Social Union, and a new party calling itself the Democratic Awakening formed the Alliance for Germany, a coalition promising to establish a monetary union with West Germany. Honecker's ill-conceived economic strategy was now exerting real pressure on the country: as Schürer had told a small group of SED leaders the previous May, "the GDR's debt to the West was increasing by 500 million Valutamarks (VM) [the equivalent of 500 million DM] a month, and . . . , if things continued along these lines, the GDR would be insolvent by 1991."[138] But many Germans just wanted to end the political division of their nation. With a voter turnout of more than 90% in the elections, the Alliance for Germany swept to victory, garnering more than 50% of the vote. Lothar de Maizière of the CDU/East now became PM and negotiations for the reunification of the two halves of Germany got underway. Reunification was achieved on 3 October and the GDR Volkskammer was dissolved on the same day. On 30 November 1990, the Ministry of Justice of reunified Germany issued an arrest warrant for Honecker, holding him responsible for ordering the shooting of East Germans who had tried to escape over the Berlin Wall. Rather than stand trial, Honecker and his wife Margot fled to a Soviet military airstrip and were flown from there to Moscow. Since the Kremlin was coming under pressure from the Federal Republic of Germany to extradite the Honeckers, they now took refuge in the Chilean embassy in Moscow. Margot was soon able to flee to Chile but the FRG eventually secured Erich Honecker's extradition to Berlin in July 1992. He and four co-defendants went on trial on 12 November, "charged with 68 counts of manslaughter and attempted manslaughter at the inner-German border."[139] However, given his declining health, the court ended the trial on 12 January 1993 and allowed the former SED leader to fly to Chile the next day, to join his wife and daughter. He died in Santiago, Chile, on 29 May 1994.

The last bloc state to hold Round Table talks was Bulgaria. These ran from January to May 1990. Prior to that, Bulgaria's long-serving General Secretary, Todor Zhivkov, had been ousted on 10 November. His replacement, Petar Mladenov (1936–2000), had served as Foreign Minister for 28 years and quickly swept most of the old guard out of the Politburo. Zhivkov was expelled from the Bulgarian Communist Party on 13 December and an investigation was launched into corruption on the part of high-ranking officials, including Zhivkov. On 9 January 1990, officials announced that they had uncovered sufficient evidence to proceed with criminal proceedings against the former Bulgarian leader. Arrested on

19 January 1990, Zhivkov was charged with having misappropriated state property and with having abused the power of his position. By 2 February 1990, Mladenov had to resign from office and, on 3 April 1990, the Bulgarian Communist Party dissolved itself, while Round Table talks were still in progress. On 1 August 1990, the Bulgarian parliament put its seal on the death of communism in Bulgaria by electing 59-year-old Zhelyu Zhelev of the Union of Democratic Forces President. Zhivkov's trial began on 25 February 1991; his trial ended in September with his conviction of embezzlement. He was sentenced to seven years in prison but died on 5 August 1998, just before the expiration of that term. In the meantime, the Grand National Assembly of Bulgaria adopted a new constitution on 13 July 1991. In a key provision (Article 11), it was declared that "(1) Political activity in the Republic of Bulgaria shall be founded on the principle of political pluralism. (2) No political party or ideology shall be proclaimed or affirmed as a party or ideology of the State."[140]

Finally, Romania was the only bloc state in which violence contributed to the collapse of the old order. In mid-December 1989, agents of the security service arrived in Timişoara to arrest the popular Reformed clergyman Rev. László Tőkés, who had been involved in championing the rights of Hungarians living in Transylvania. Local Hungarians circled his church to protect him, with local Romanians joining, to give their support to the Hungarians. Security forces then opened fire and charged the crowd with fixed bayonets. This only provoked more locals to enter the fray and soon there were thousands of people around the church. By 19 December, demonstrators were shouting, "Down with the communists!" and "Death to the dictator!"[141] and, by 20 December, the protesters controlled the streets of Timişoara. The following day, Ceauşescu attempted to present an open-air speech in downtown Bucharest, in which he tried to pin the blame for the unrest on "fascist agitators".[142] When the crowd started to jeer at him, Ceauşescu responded with a promise to raise wages. But the crowd was not appeased. By then, the army had turned against the *Conducător* and was battling with security forces. Nicolae and Elena Ceauşescu boarded a helicopter and tried to flee, but the army forced the helicopter to land. The Ceauşescus were captured on 23 December and executed on 25 December. The Red Cross estimated that approximately 5,000 people had been killed in the fighting.[143] At this point, a group of former communists led by Ion Iliescu, who had served as Minister for Youth between 1967 and 1971, declared the formation of a National Salvation Front as a *de facto* government and established their control in Romania. The new authorities immediately halted the destruction of villages, and soon published a program calling for a multiparty system, free elections by April 1990, a free enterprise system, and guarantees for freedom of religion.

Why did communism crumble? The immediate trigger was the insolvency of these states, which had funded their programs by taking out huge loans and credits which finally broke the backs of the bloc regimes. Legitimate states can survive economic disaster, as the U.S. experience with the 1929 stock market crash and subsequent depression demonstrated. But the states of the Soviet bloc were not legitimate political formations and this was the underlying problem. The political systems in the bloc were illegitimate for at least five reasons: first and foremost, they were not independent states but subordinates to the Soviet Union, with the national satraps having to clear any decisions of consequence either with the Soviet ambassador or with the Kremlin directly; other factors included the lack of pluralism, people's contempt for the controlled media, and the failure of the communists to deliver on their promises of equality. This was compounded by a fifth factor – the economic inefficiency of the system, as manifested in perennial shortages of some goods; East Europeans also complained about restrictions on travel to non-communist countries, about the unavailability of Western goods such as televisions, stereos, and clothing, and about the policy of promoting atheism in the schools and elsewhere. The satraps had pursued policies having unintended consequences, presiding over a fundamentally dysfunctional system.

Notes

1 Samuel P. Huntington, *Political Order in Changing Societies* (New Haven, CT and London: Yale University Press, 1968), p. 1.
2 *Ibid.*, p. 8.
3 *Ibid.*, p. 336.
4 Steven R. David, "Soviet Involvement in Third World Coups", in *International Security*, Vol. 11, No. 1 (Summer 1986), pp. 8, 29, 35.
5 Zygmunt Bauman, "Social Dissent in the East European Political System", in *Archives Européenes de Sociologie,* Vol. 12, No. 1 (1971), p. 50.
6 Sabrina P. Ramet, *Social Currents in Eastern Europe: The Sources and Consequences of the Great Transformation*, 2nd ed. (Durham, NC and London: Duke University Press, 1995), p. 30, quoting from Bauman, "Social Dissent", p. 49.
7 Václav Havel, "The Power of the Powerless", in *Václav Havel – Living in Truth,* ed. by Jan Vladislav (London and Boston: Faber and Faber, 1987), pp. 41–42.
8 H. Gordon Skilling, *Samizdat and an Independent Society in Central and Eastern Europe* (Columbus: Ohio State University Press, 1989), p. 50.
9 Vladimir Tismaneanu (ed.), *In Search of Civil Society: Independent Peace Movements in the Soviet Bloc* (London and New York: Routledge, 1990).
10 Vladimir Tismaneanu, "Understanding National Stalinism: Reflections on Ceauşescu's Socialism", in *Communist and Post-Communist Studies,* Vol. 32 (1999), p. 170; see also p. 166.
11 Vladimir Tismaneanu, *Fantasies of Salvation: Democracy, Nationalism and Myth in Post-Communist Societies* (Princeton, NJ: Princeton University Press, 1998), p. 14.
12 A sycophant, as quoted in Vladimir Tismaneanu, *Stalinism for All Seasons: A Political History of Romanian Communism* (Berkeley and Los Angeles: University of California Press, 2003), p. 212.
13 Robert K. Merton, *Social Theory and Social Structure*, Enlarged ed. (New York and London: Free Press & Collier Macmillan, 1968), p. 105.
14 *Ibid.*, p. 176.
15 Ivan Volgyes, "Hungary: Before the Storm", in *Current History*, Vol. 86, No. 523 (November 1987), p. 373.
16 Published by Prentice Hall.
17 Crane Brinton, *The Anatomy of Revolution*, rev. & expanded ed. (New York: Vintage, 1965).

18 Ramet, *Social Currents in Eastern Europe*, p. 31.
19 Fred Oldenburg, "Die DDR und die polnische Krise", in *Osteuropa*, Vol. 32, No. 12 (December 1982), pp. 1005–1007; Reinhardt Gutsche, "Das Erschrecken Jaruzel-skis", in *der Freitag* (14 December 2020), at Freitag.de/autoren/reinhardt-gutsche/das-erschrecken-jaruzelskis [accessed on 19 February 2022], p. 4 of 6.
20 Nils Werner, "Vom Umgang mit der polnischen Solidarność-Bewegung in der DDR", in MDR.DE (22 December 2021), at www.mdr.de/geschichte/polen-ddr-solidarnosc-honecker-100.html [accessed on 19 February 2022], pp. 4–5 of 8.
21 András Bozóki, "Die Politik der Opposition in Ungarn der achtziger Jahre. Debatten des Samizdats 'Beszélő'", in Aron Buzogany and Ralf Frankenberger (eds.), *Osteuropa. Politik, Wirtschaft und Gesellschaft* (Baden-Baden: Nomos Verlag, 2007), p. 262.
22 These documents are published in translation in: Commission on Security and Coop-eration in Europe, Congress of the United States, *Human Rights in Czechoslovakia: The Documents of Charter 77, 1977–1982* (Washington, DC: U.S. Government Printing Office, July 1982), pp. 200, 210.
23 See Ramet, *Social Currents in Eastern Europe*, p. 87.
24 See Pedro Ramet, "Poland's 'Other' Parties", in *The World Today*, Vol. 37, No. 9 (Sep-tember 1981), pp. 332–338.
25 Jan de Weydenthal, *The Communists of Poland: An Historical Outline*, rev. ed. (Stanford, CA: Hoover Institution Press, 1987), p. 2.
26 Barbara J. Falk, *The Dilemmas of Dissidence in East-Central Europe: Citizen Intellectuals and Philosopher Kings* (Budapest and New York: Central European University Press, 2003), p. 51.
27 Wojciech Jaruzelski, *Mein Leben für Polen. Erinnerungen* (Munich and Zurich: Piper, 1993), p. 268.
28 Marek Jeziński, "Wojciech Jaruzelski (1923–2014), Polen: Zwischen Pragmatismus und Opportunismus", in Martin Sabrow and Susanne Schattenberg (eds.), *Die letzten General-sekretäre. Kommunistische Herrschaft im Spätsozialismus* (Berlin: Ch. Links Verlag, 2018), p. 239.
29 Alain Touraine, François Dubet, Michel Wievorka, and Jan Strzelecki, *Solidarity: The Analysis of a Social Movement: Poland 1980–1981*, trans. from French by David Denby (Cambridge and Paris: Cambridge University Press & Editions de la Maison des Sci-ences de l'Homme, 1983), p. 85; de Weydenthal, *The Communists of Poland*, p. 202.
30 "Information about Cde. L. I. Brezhnev's Telephone Conversation with Cde. S. Kania", Top Secret, Document No. 18, in *Soviet Deliberations during the Polish Crisis, 1980–1981*, ed., trans., annotated, & introduced by Mark Kramer (Washington, DC: Woodrow Wil-son International Center for Scholars, Special Working Paper No. 1, April 1998), p. 142.
31 As quoted in de Weydenthal, *The Communists of Poland*, p. 203.
32 Ramet, *Social Currents in Eastern Europe*, p. 87.
33 Touraine, *Solidarity*, p. 152.
34 "Session of the CPSU CC Politburo, 29 October 1981", Top Secret, Document No. 20, in *Soviet Deliberations during the Polish Crisis*, ed. by Mark Kramer, p. 152.
35 "Session of the CPSU CC Politburo, 9 April 1981, Top Secret, Document No. 2, in *Ibid.*, p. 105.
36 As quoted in de Weydenthal, *The Communists of Poland*, p. 203.
37 Jaruzelski, *Mein Leben für Polen*, pp. 286–287.
38 Klara Kemp-Welch, *Antipolitics in Central European Art: Reticence as Dissidence Under Post-Totalitarian Rule 1956–1989* (London and New York: I. B. Tauris, 2014; paperback ed., 2017), p. 254.
39 See the account in Lech Wałęsa, *A Way of Hope: Lech Walesa, An Autobiography*, trans. from Polish by Marete B. Zeleski et al. (New York: Henry Holt, 1987).
40 As quoted in Katarzyna Ścieránska, "The Introduction of Martial Law in Poland", in ENRS (no date), at https:// https://enrs.eu/article/the-introduction-of-martial-law-in-poland [accessed on 23 February 2022], p. 2 of 3.

41 As quoted in *Reinventing Civil Society: Poland's Quiet Revolution 1982–1986* (New York: Helsinki Watch, 1986), p. 7.

42 Ramet, *Social Currents in Eastern Europe,* p. 86, citing to Roman Dumas, "Poland's 'Independent Society'", in *Poland Watch,* No. 8 (1986), p. 65.

43 Details concerning these organizations are given in Ramet, *Social Currents in Eastern Europe,* pp. 98–103.

44 David Ost, *Solidarity and the Politics of Anti-Politics: Opposition and Reform in Poland Since 1968* (Philadelphia: Temple University Press, 1990), p. 153.

45 Catherine Fitzpatrick and Janet Fleischman, *From Below: Independent Peace and Environmental Movements in Eastern Europe and the USSR* (New York and Washington, DC: Helsinki Watch, October 1987), p. 73.

46 Ost, *Solidarity and the Politics,* p. 154.

47 Janusz Bugajski, "Polish Security Service Operations Against the Solidarity Underground", in *Radio Free Europe Report* (10 April 1984), pp. 4, 6–7; Roman Dumas, "Poland's 'Independent Society'", in *Poland Watch,* No. 8 (1986), p. 69.

48 Wałęsa, *A Way of Hope,* p. 237.

49 Ramet, *Social Currents in Eastern Europe,* pp. 93–94.

50 For more on the Orange Alternative, see *Ibid.,* pp. 105–106.

51 *Ibid.,* pp. 115–117.

52 Falk, *The Dilemmas of Dissidence in East-Central Europe,* p. 251.

53 As quoted in H. Gordon Skilling, *Charter 77 and Human Rights in Czechoslovakia* (London: George Allen & Unwin, 1981), p. 64.

54 As quoted in *Ibid.,* p. 64.

55 As quoted in Vladimir V. Kusin, *From Dubček to Charter 77: A study of 'normalisation' in Czechoslovakia, 1968–1978* (Edinburgh: Q Press, 1978), p. 314.

56 As quoted in Mary Heimann, *Czechoslovakia: The State that Failed* (New Haven, CT and London: Yale University Press, 2009; first paperback ed., 2011), p. 287.

57 *Ibid.,* p. 288.

58 Skilling, *Charter 77,* p. 137.

59 Vilém Prečan, "An Annotated List of Charter 77 Documents (1977–1986)", in *Radio Free Europe Research* (6 August 1987), pp. 2–3. Document 12 on "Discrimination in Literature" (30 June 1977) is translated in *Human Rights in Czechoslovakia,* pp. 71–72.

60 "The Right to History", Charter Document No. 11/1984 (20 May 1984), as excerpted in *Radio Free Europe Research* (29 August 1984), p. 11.

61 Ramet, *Social Currents in Eastern Europe,* p. 127.

62 Tismaneanu, "Understanding National Stalinism", pp. 168–169.

63 As quoted in Tismaneanu, *Stalinism for All Seasons,* p. 210.

64 As quoted in *Ibid.,* pp. 219, 220.

65 Dinu C. Giurescu, *The Razing of Romania's Past* (Bath: The Bath Press, 1990), p. 42, as cited in Helen Stratford, "Enclaves of Expression: Resistance by Young Architects to the Physical and Psychological Control of Expression in Romania During the 1980s", in *Journal of Architectural Education,* Vol. 54, No. 4 (May 2001), p. 219.

66 Skilling, *Samizdat and an Independent Society,* p. 192; Tismaneanu, *Stalinism for All Seasons,* pp. 210–211.

67 Anneli Ute Gabanyi, *Die unvollendete Revolution. Rumänien zwischen Diktatur und Demokratie* (Munich: R. Piper GmbH, 1990), p. 48.

68 Trond Gilberg, *Nationalism and Communism in Romania* (Boulder, CO: Westview Press, 1990), p. 195.

69 Stratford, "Enclaves of Expression", pp. 221–222.

70 Skilling, *Samizdat and an Independent Society,* pp. 194–195.

71 Simona Petracovschi and Jessica W. Chin, "Sports, Physical Practice, and the Female Body, 1980–1989: Women's Emancipation in Romania Under Communism", in *Critical Studies in Media Communication,* Vol. 36, No. 1 (2019), p. 41.

72 *Ibid.,* p. 42.

73 Skilling, *Samizdat and an Independent Society,* p. 186; Falk, *The Dilemmas of Dissidence,* p. 132.
74 Skilling, *Samizdat and an Independent Society,* p. 186.
75 András Bozóki, "Die Politik der Opposition im Ungarn der achtziger Jahre. Debatten des Samizdats 'Beszélő'", in Aron Buzogany and Ralf Frankenberger (eds.), *Osteuropa. Politik, Wirtschaft und Gesellschaft* (Baden-Baden: Nomos Verlag, 2007), p. 265.
76 See Falk, *The Dilemmas of Dissidence,* pp. 261, 266.
77 For further discussion by and of these dissident figures, see: Robert Havemann, *An Alienated Man,* English translation of *Fragen, Antworten, Fragen* (1970), by Derek Masters (London: Davis-Poynter, 1973); Rudolf Bahro, *Die Alternative. Zur Kritik des real exist- ierenden Sozialismus* (Köln: Europäische Verlagsanstalt, 1979); Ines Weber, *Sozialismus in der DDR. Alternative Gesellschaftskonzepte von Robert Havemann und Rudolf Bahro* (Berlin: Ch. Links Verlag, 2015); Peter Thompson, "Wolf Biermann: Die Heimat ist weit", in David Robb (ed.), *Protest Song in East and West Germany Since the 1960s* (Rochester, NY: Camden House, 2007). See also Werner Volkmer, "East Germany: Dissenting Views During the Last Decade", in Rudolf L. Tőkés (ed.), *Opposition in Eastern Europe* (London and Basingstoke: Macmillan Press, 1979), pp. 113–141.
78 Pedro Ramet, "Church and Peace in the GDR", in *Problems of Communism,* Vol. 33, No. 4 (July–August 1984), p. 51. See also Klaus Ehring and Martin Dallwitz, *Schwerter zu Pflugscharen* (Hamburg: Rowohlt Taschenbuch Verlag, 1982).
79 Ramet, "Church and Peace", p. 54.
80 Bulgaria Situation Report, *Radio Free Europe Research* (9 March 1989), p. 17.
81 Ramet, *Social Currents in Eastern Europe,* p. 282.
82 Artur Szarecki, "The Making of Polish Hip-Hop: Music, Nationality, and the Limits of Hegemony", in Patryk Galuszka (ed.), *Made in Poland: Studies in Popular Culture* (New York and London: Routledge, 2020), p. 155.
83 *Gegenstimmen* (Vienna), Winter 1983, trans. in *Joint Publications Research Service* (JPRS), no. EPS-84–023 (10 February 1984), p. 2.
84 *Narodna Kultura* (24 February 1984), as quoted in Bulgaria Situation Report, *Radio Free Europe Research* (30 March 1984), p. 12.
85 Ramet, *Social Currents in Eastern Europe,* p. 254.
86 As quoted in László Kürti, " 'How Can I Be a Human Being?' Culture, Youth, and Musical Opposition in Hungary", in Sabrina P. Ramet (ed.), *Rocking the State: Rock Music and Politics in Eastern Europe and Russia* (Boulder, CO: Westview Press, 1994), p. 82.
87 As quoted in Zsolt Krokvay, "Politics and Punk [in Hungary]", in *Index on Censorship,* Vol. 14, No. 2 (April 1985), p. 20.
88 As quoted in *Ibid.,* p. 82.
89 As quoted in Olaf Leitner, "Rock Music in the GDR: An Epitaph", trans. from German by Margaret A. Brown, in Ramet (ed.), *Rocking the State,* p. 37.
90 As quoted in *Der Spiegel* (Hamburg), 28 May 1984, p. 171, in Ramet, *Social Currents in Eastern Europe,* p. 241.
91 As quoted in Donald Pirie, "Literature", in Donald Pirie, Jekaterina Young, and Chris- topher Carrell (eds.), *Polish Realities: The Arts in Poland 1980–1989* (Glasgow: Third Eye Centre, 1990), p. 36.
92 See Myra Marx Ferree, "The Rise and Fall of 'Mommy Politics': Feminism and Unifi- cation in (East) Germany", in *Feminist Studies,* Vol. 19, No. 1 (Spring 1993), pp. 89–115.
93 See Michal Groch, "Feminism in Slovakia – Finally Escaping the Clichés?" *Radio Prague International* (12 July 2007), at https://english.radio.cz/feminism-slovakia-finally-escap ing-cliches-8601304; Romy Caverlé and Marijn Butter, "No Place for the Modern Feminist in Traditional Slovakia", in *The International Angle* (28 May 2019), at https:// theinternationalangle.com/index.php/2019/05/28/no-place-for-the-modern-femi nist-in-traditional-slovakia/ – both [accessed on 1 March 2022].
94 Joseph Pungur, "Protestantism in Hungary: The Communist Era", in Sabrina Petra Ramet (ed.), *Protestantism and Politics in Eastern Europe and Russia* (Durham, NC and London: Duke University Press, 1992), p. 137.

95 Cezar M. Ornatowski, "'Let Thy Spirit Renew This Earth': The Rhetoric of Pope John Paul II and the Political Transformation in Poland, 1979–1989", in *Journal for the Study of Religion*, Vol. 14, No. 1 (2001), p. 81.

96 Karl Hartmann, "Politische Bilanz des zweiten Papstbesuches in Polen", in *Osteuropa*, Vol. 33, No. 11/12 (November–December 1983), p. 895; Ost, *Solidarity and the Politics of Anti-Politics*, p. 154; Bogdan Turek, "Poland Declared a Conditional Amnesty for All Jailed . . .", UPI (21 July 1984), at www.upi.com/Archives/1984/07/21/Poland-declared-a-conditional-amnesty-today-for-all-jailed/6847459230400/ [accessed on 2 March 2022].

97 See Paul B. Henze, *The Plot to Kill the Pope* (New York: Scribner, 1983).

98 As quoted in "Blessed Jerzy Popieluszko", in *Roman Catholic Saints* (2011), at www.roman-catholic-saints.com/blessed-jerzy-popieluszko.html [accessed on 2 March 2022], p. 3 of 3. See also John Moody and Roger Boyes, *The Priest and the Policeman: The Courageous Life and Cruel Murder of Father Jerzy Popiełuszko* (New York: Summit Books, 1987).

99 As quoted in Robert F. Goeckel, "The Luther Anniversary in East Germany", in *World Politics*, Vol. 37, No. 1 (October 1984), p. 121.

100 See Sabrina P. Ramet, "Religious Organizations in Post-Communist Central and Southeastern Europe: An Introduction" and "The Catholic Church in Post-Communist Poland: Polarization, Privatization, and Decline in Influence" – both in Sabrina P. Ramet (ed.), *Religion and Politics in Post-Socialist Central and Southeastern Europe: Challenges Since 1989* (Basingstoke: Palgrave Macmillan, 2014).

101 Lavinia Stan and Lucian Turcescu, "The Orthodox Churches and Democratization in Romania and Bulgaria", in Ramet (ed.), *Religion and Politics,* p. 272.

102 Ramet, "Religious Organizations", p. 10.

103 *Ibid.* See also Lucian Turcescu and Lavinia Stan, "The Romanian Orthodox Church", in Lucian N. Leustean (ed.), *Eastern Christianity and Politics in Twenty-First Century* (London and New York: Routledge, 2017).

104 Clifford Poirot, "Macroeconomic Policy in a Transitional Environment: Romania, 1989–1994", in *Journal of Economic Issues,* Vol. 30, No. 4 (December 1996), p. 1061.

105 This sentence is closely paraphrased from Henryk Flakierski, *Economic Reform & Income Distribution: A Case Study of Hungary and Poland* (Armonk, NY: M. E. Sharpe, 1986), p. 132.

106 *Ibid.*, p. 3.

107 As quoted in Rudolf L. Tőkés, *Hungary's Negotiated Revolution: Economic Reform, Social Change and Political Succession* (Cambridge: Cambridge University Press, 1996), p. 273.

108 *Ibid.*

109 As quoted in *Ibid.*, p. 274.

110 As quoted in *Ibid.*, pp. 274–275.

111 Irwin L. Collier, Jr., "GDR Economic Policy During the Honecker Era", in *Eastern European Economics*, Vol. 29, No. 1 (Fall 1990), p. 21.

112 Martin G. Schmidt, "Social Policy in the German Democratic Republic", in Manfred G. Schmidt and Gerhard A. Ritter (eds.), *The Rise and Fall of a Socialist Welfare State: The German Democratic Republic (1949–1990) and German Unification (1989–1994),* trans. from German by David R: Antal and Ben Veghte (Heidelberg: Springer, 2013), p. 77.

113 *Ibid.*, pp. 42, 46, 70, and 108.

114 *Ibid.*, p. 92.

115 Andreas Malycha, *Die SED in der Ära Honecker. Machtstrukturen, Entscheidungsmechanismen und Konfliktfelder in der Staatspartei 1971 bis 1989* (Göttingen: De Gruyter-Oldenbourg, 2014), p. 182.

116 *Ibid.*, p. 183.

117 *Ibid.*, p. 207; see also p. 178.

118 *Ibid.*, p. 393.

119 *Ibid.*, p. 344.

120 Andreas Malycha, "Ungeschminkte Wahrheiten", in *Vierteljahrshefte für Zeitgeschichte*, Vol. 59, No. 2 (2011), p. 294.

121 Malycha, *Die SED in der Ära Honecker,* p. 368.

122 *Ibid.,* pp. 252–253.

123 As quoted in Schmidt, "Social Policy", p. 110.

124 *Ibid.,* p. 115.

125 Adam Zwass and Michel Vale, "The Economic Situation in Poland in Light of the Eighth Party Congress", in *Eastern European Economics,* Vol. 20 No. 1 (Autumn 1981), pp. 6–7.

126 *Ibid.,* p. 19.

127 "A Former Premier of Poland is Being Investigated", in *New York Times* (24 May 1981), p. 11.

128 See Ramet, *Social Currents in Eastern Europe,* chapter 4.

129 See Zbigniew Messner, "Some Problems of Poland's Economic Policy in 1986–1990", in *Soviet and Eastern European Foreign Trade,* Vol. 23, No.3 (Fall 1987), p. 87.

130 Marjorie Castle, *Triggering Communism's Collapse: Perceptions and Power in Poland's Transition* (Lanham, MD: Rowman & Littlefield, 2003), pp. 34–35.

131 Ramet, *Social Currents in Eastern Europe,* pp. 33–34.

132 Jan Lisowski, "Problems of Poland's Foreign Debt", in *Economic and Political Weekly* (12 August 1989), p. 1827.

133 Stanislaw Wellisz, "Poland Under 'Solidarity' Rule", in *Journal of Economic Perspectives,* Vol. 5, No. 4 (Fall 1991), p. 211.

134 Istvan Pogany, "Constitutional Reform in Central and Eastern Europe: Hungary's Transition to Democracy", in *The International and Comparative Law Quarterly,* Vol. 42, No. 3 (April 1993), p. 335.

135 *Ibid.,* p. 341.

136 Both as quoted in *Ibid.,* p. 346.

137 Sabrina P. Ramet, *Nonconformity, Dissent, Opposition, and Resistance in Germany, 1933–1990: The Freedom to Conform* (Cham: Palgrave Macmillan, 2020), p. 197. See also Detlev Pollack, "Der Zusammenbruch der DDR als Verkettung getrennter Handlungslinien", in Konrad H. Jarausch and Martin Sabrow (eds.), *Weg in den Untergang. Der innere Zerfall der DDR* (Göttingen: Vandenhoeck & Ruprecht, 1999), p. 44.

138 Hans-Hermann Hertle, "The Fall of the Wall: The Unintended Self-Dissolution of East Germany's Ruling Regime", in *Cold War International History Project Bulletin,* No. 12 (Winter/Spring 2001), p. 133.

139 "Ex-East Germany Leader Erich Honecker's Arrest: 25 Years on", in *Deutsche Welle* (29 July 2017), at www.dw.com/en/ex-east-germany-leader-erich-honeckers-arrest-25-years-on/a-39886159 [accessed on 7 March 2022], p. 3 of 4.

140 Constitution of the Republic of Bulgaria (adopted on 13 July 1991), at www.ilo.org/dyn/natlex/docs/ELECTRONIC/26650/72971/F7039954/BGR26650%20En%20 2007.pdf [accessed on 7 March 2022].

141 Ramet, *Social Currents in Eastern Europe,* p. 361.

142 As quoted in Stephen McGrath, "Executing a Dictator: Open Wounds of Romania's Christmas Revolution", in *BBC News* (25 December 2019), p. 4 of 16.

143 See also other estimates in Ramet, *Social Currents in Eastern Europe,* p. 362. For further discussion, see Peter Siani-Davies, *The Romanian Revolution of December 1989* (Ithaca, NY: Cornell University Press, 2007).

5

SOCIALIST MAVERICKS

Yugoslavia and Albania, 1943–1991

In 1990, Elez Biberaj published a book entitled *Albania: A Socialist Maverick*.[1] The book was aptly titled, as Albania went its own way, to a significant extent, in the post-war era. Socialist Yugoslavia was likewise a maverick and shared some features in common with Socialist Albania. To begin with, Yugoslavia was expelled from the socialist camp in 1948 and, thus, was excluded from the Soviet-run Council of Mutual Economic Relations (COMECON) when it was founded in February 1949, although the country signed an agreement in 1964 for cooperation with COMECON members; Albania joined the organization at its founding but ceased to take an active part in COMECON by the end of 1961. Similarly, while Yugoslavia was never a member of the Warsaw Pact, the Soviet-led military alliance, Albania, which joined the pact at its founding in May 1955, ceased to play any role in it from 1961 and announced its formal withdrawal from the pact in September 1968. Yugoslavia and Albania shared some features in common with other socialist states in East Central Europe, including de facto one party rule, party control of the media (but with the communist party organizations in the individual constituent republics supervising the media in Yugoslavia beginning in the 1960s), an anti-religious policy (gradually liberalized in Yugoslavia, while escalated in Albania), a planned economy (but, in Yugoslavia, with repeated replanning in the middle of a plan), and agricultural collectivization (abandoned in Yugoslavia in the 1950s). But, unlike the states of the Soviet bloc, the Yugoslav and Albanian regimes did not clear their policy decisions with the Kremlin and did not take orders from Moscow. By the 1970s, Socialist Yugoslavia had developed the most liberal system among the East Central European countries run by communist parties, with small private enterprises, such as restaurants, able to operate after the economic reform of 1965; thus, as of 1972, there were 7,500 private businesses in Belgrade alone, not counting cafés, and 85% of farmland was in private hands.[2] Yugoslavia also introduced a system known as workers' self-management between 1950 and 1952, authorizing

DOI: 10.4324/9781003311515-5

the establishment of workers' councils allowed to make some decisions (eventually extending, at least nominally, to questions related to production) in the country's enterprises; after this the Yugoslav communists called their system "self-managing socialism" (*samoupravni socijalizam*). In Albania, by contrast, private concerns had been nationalized without compensation in 1944–45 and state and collective farms accounted for 86.9% of sown land by 1960.[3] Enver Hoxha's dictatorship was the most extreme in the region, as reflected in the fact that, at one point, Albanians with Christian forenames were ordered to adopt new non-Christian names.

There is one more, very striking feature about these two socialist states, viz., that their leaders – Josip Broz Tito in Yugoslavia and Enver Hoxha in Albania – stood at the apex of their respective political hierarchies for longer than any of the Soviet satraps elsewhere in the region. Hoxha headed the Albanian Party of Labor (known until 1948 as the Communist Party of Albania) from March 1943 to his death in April 1985, thus for 42 years. Tito was head of the Communist Party of Yugoslavia (which changed its name in 1952 to the League of Communists in Yugoslavia) from August 1937 to his death of May 1980, for almost 43 years, although he was in a coma most of the time from March 1980 onward. No other communist leader in East Central Europe exceeded 40 years in office; the Bulgarian leader, Todor Zhivkov, was the third-longest reigning party chief, maintaining his position from March 1954 until November 1989, for a total of 35 years; the only other East Central European communist to lead his party for more than 30 years was János Kádár, who occupied the top position in the Hungarian hierarchy from October 1956 until May 1988. The shortest reigning party chiefs in the region were Egon Krenz, who took over as General Secretary of the East German SED on 18 October 1989 only to be forced to resign that post less than seven weeks later on 3 December, and Ernő Gerő, who served as First Secretary of the Hungarian Workers' Party from 18 July 1956 until 25 October 1956.

The communists of Yugoslavia

The communist state that would rule Yugoslavia after 1944 grew out of the anti-Axis Partisan movement headed by Josip Broz Tito (1892–1980), since 1937 head of the Communist Party of Yugoslavia (CPY); the Partisans had been formed to fight against German Nazi and Italian Fascist occupation of the country. Half Croat and half Slovene (but declaring himself as Croat), Broz had joined the communist party in 1919 and, by 1928, he was head of the Zagreb party organization. He used various aliases during his years in the political underground, including "Walter". In 1934, he adopted the *nom de guerre* "Tito" and the name stuck. In November 1942, 68 delegates selected by the CPY met in Bihać in northwestern Bosnia and declared the formation of the Anti-Fascist Council of the People's Liberation of Yugoslavia (AVNOJ[4]). The council was intended to serve as the formal political executive of the Partisan movement and elected a Supreme Staff consisting of 10 communists. The inner circle of the Partisans' Supreme Staff (*Vrhovni štab*) consisted of Tito, Edvard Kardelj (1910–1979), Aleksandar Ranković (1909–1982), and

Milovan Djilas (1911–1995). At this first session, AVNOJ made several important decisions regarding the future federal components of Yugoslavia and their boundaries. Even before AVNOJ convened for its first session (in November 1942), the Partisan leadership had agreed that Bosnia-Herzegovina should be established as its own federal unit.[5] Then, at the first session of AVNOJ there was still some debate about whether it should be a republic equivalent in status and autonomy to Serbia, Croatia, or Slovenia, or whether it should be a province attached to one or another republic and within what boundaries. These issues were resolved in November 1943, when it was decided to grant Bosnia-Herzegovina status as a republic within its historic boundaries. The Sandžak was to remain divided between Serbia and Montenegro, Eastern Srem, which had historically been part of Croatia, was assigned to Vojvodina, a province within the republic of Serbia, Croatia lost an additional sliver of territory to Montenegro, and Kosovo was established as an autonomous region within Serbia. Those Albanians who were prepared to be loyal to Belgrade had demanded full republic status for Kosovo, while most Serbian leaders demanded that Kosovo be incorporated fully into Serbia. The decision taken was, thus, a compromise which, however, satisfied neither side.

AVNOJ held its second session in Jajce in liberated territory in central Bosnia on 29–30 November 1943. One hundred and forty-two out of 268 selected delegates attended this second session. Although AVNOJ included noncommunists as well as communists, the latter were in control. The second session proclaimed that post-war Yugoslavia would be organized as a federation and confirmed that the future Yugoslav state would consist of six equal constituent republics, in alphabetical order: Bosnia-Herzegovina, Croatia, Macedonia, Montenegro, Serbia, and Slovenia.[6] On the first day of the session, AVNOJ elected a nine-member National Committee of Liberation (among whom five were communists) as a *de facto* provisional government.[7] AVNOJ did not make any further provision for the future political order and, at this point in time, Tito took pains to deny that he had any intention of introducing communism in Yugoslavia.

The Partisans waged their war against German and Italian occupation forces (and also against Bulgarian forces occupying Macedonia and a significant part of Nedić's Serbia[8] as well as against Hungarian occupation forces in certain regions in the north of the country), as well as against forces of the quisling governments of Milan Nedić (1877–1946) in rump Serbia and Ante Pavelić (1889–1959) in Axis Croatia. The Chetniks, a Serbian fighting force headed by Colonel Draža Mihailović (1893–1946), aspired to create an expanded Serbian state from which most non-Serbs would be expelled.[9] The tide turned in September 1943, when Italy, led up to now by Benito Mussolini (1883–1945), surrendered unconditionally to the Allies. On 23 September 1943, a Slovenian Homeguard *(Domobranci)* was established. The *Domobranci*, numbering around 13,000 troops, collaborated with the Germans against the Partisans.[10]

After the winter of 1942–43, when the German *Wehrmacht* failed to capture Stalingrad, German military might was clearly in decline and, by early 1944, the eventual collapse of the Third Reich was obvious to anyone who was paying attention. In May 1944, British Prime Minister Winston Churchill (1874–1965) hosted Ivan Šubašić (1892–1955), the former Ban (Governor) of Croatia, for consultations about a potential agreement with Tito. Stalin advised Tito not to decline a meeting with Šubašić and arrangements were made for the former Croatian Ban to meet Tito on the Dalmatian island of Vis in the Adriatic on 14 June 1944. Šubašić's idea was that the Partisans should recognize the King and join in creating a joint, representative government. Šubašić even allowed himself to imagine that Tito might be satisfied with being named Minister of War in the future government.[11] The Tito-Šubašić Agreement was signed eventually on 1 November 1944, after Tito's forces had entered Belgrade, and laid the groundwork, if only implicitly, for the end of the royal monarchy which had ruled Yugoslavia in the interwar years. In March 1945, the composition of the provisional government was announced: Šubašić was named Foreign Minister; Milan Grol (1876–1952), leader of the Serbian Democratic Party, would serve as Deputy Prime Minister; and Tito was confirmed as Prime Minister. By then, Tito commanded a Partisan army of more than 800,000 officers and enlisted.[12] It was the fourth largest army in Europe.[13] When the war in Europe ended on 8 May 1945, with the surrender by the German High Command, between 50 and 55 million people in Europe had been killed, counting both combatants and civilians.[14] Croatian demographer Vladimir Žerjavić estimated that the number of people in Yugoslavia who lost their lives due to combat or war crimes totalled approximately 1,027,000. More than half of these – some 530,000 – were Serbs; among the total were also 192,000 Croats.[15]

The birth of the second Yugoslavia, 1944–50

By the beginning of October 1944, the Partisans, benefitting from steady supplies of arms from Great Britain and the United States, which had begun in 1943[16] and from the Soviet Union beginning in late 1944,[17] had cleared most of Yugoslavia of foreign occupation forces and their domestic collaborators. On 20 October, the Partisans, backed by the Red Army, entered Belgrade in triumph. The following day, Tito went to the balcony of National Theater and addressed the people of Yugoslavia.[18] A new era was dawning.

In addition to Šubašić and Grol, several other prominent noncommunists were also included in the cabinet: Juraj Šutej and Frane Frol (both members of the Croatian Peasant Party); Sava Kosanović (Independent Democratic Party); and Jaša Prodanović (Republican Party). Edvard Kocbek, a Slovenian poet and Christian Socialist, was named Minister for Slovenia in the provisional government.[19] But controversy soon erupted over the draft election law, which Grol considered undemocratic. When the election campaign got underway, Grol challenged the communists. The latter campaigned under the slogan "Ballots for Tito, bullets for Grol!"[20] Unidentified hooligans burned down the offices of Grol's newspaper, *Demokratija*. By August 1945, Grol was fed up and resigned from the government. Two months later, Šubašić and Šutej tendered their resignations, citing Tito's betrayal of the agreement he had signed with the former. When the election was finally held on 11 November, official results gave the communist-controlled Popular Front 81.53% of the vote, while the opposition was credited with having attracted just 18.7% of the vote.[21] Dragoljub Jovanović, General Secretary of the People's Agrarian Party, spoke out to denounce communist practices in the assembly; because of this, he was expelled from that body in July 1946.[22] The following year, Jovanović was arrested, charged with trying to overthrow the government, and sentenced to nine years at hard labor. In 1955 or 1956, he was assigned to a road gang near Belgrade.[23]

Political trials of various opposition figures continued into 1948. Independent newspapers were gradually strangled. After *Narodni glas*, the next to go was *Demokratija*, Milan Grol's paper. *Republika* continued to appear until 1956 and *Slobodni dom* (of the HRSS) until 1963, long after the demise of their supposed sponsoring organizations and after losing their character as independent newspapers. Fresh elections were held on 26 March 1950, with a single list but permitting "no" votes and there were high percentages of "no" votes registered in some rural areas of Serbia, Croatia, Slovenia, and Vojvodina – as much as 35% in some locations. In Vojvodina as a whole, 13.1% of ballots were marked "no", alongside 6.2% in Kosovo, 7.7% in the rest of Serbia, and 4.0% in Slovenia. The percentage of "no" votes the following year dropped everywhere except in Slovenia, where the proportion rose to 7.6%.

For the time being, there continued to be skirmishes and small-scale operations in various parts of the country, with *Križari* (Crusaders, former members of the armed forces of the fascist state of Croatia) and Chetniks holding out. There was also resistance by Albanian forces of the anti-communist *Balli Kombëtar* to the reincorporation of Kosovo into a reborn Yugoslavia, but by July 1945 the Albanian resistance had been crushed. In March 1946, Draža Mihailović was taken into custody and the remnants of the Chetniks forced had been scattered. The Chetnik leader was put on trial in June-July 1946 together with 23 other persons (13 in custody like Mihailović, with the remaining 10 being tried *in absentia*). The accused were ultimately found guilty of collaboration with the Germans, the Italians, and the marionette government of Milan Nedić; Mihailović and 10 others were sentenced to death, with the remaining three given prison sentences ranging from 18 months to 20 years. Mihailović was executed on 17 July 1946.[24] Nonetheless, as late as January 1951, there were reportedly still four to five Chetnik brigades in the backwoods of Yugoslavia, with each brigade numbering about 400 men.[25]

Taking control of the religious sphere

The CPY, like communist parties elsewhere in the region, placed a high priority on gaining control of the religious sphere, targeting the country's three major religious organizations above all: the Catholic Church (mainly Roman rite, but with a small presence of Greek-rite Catholics in Croatia); the Serbian Orthodox Church; and the Islamic community. One of the first actions taken against the religious organizations was to suppress their publications, either by denying them access to newsprint or by confiscating their presses. The printing presses of the Islamic Religious Community (Islamska Vjerska Zajednica, or IVZ) were likewise confiscated without compensation.[26] The land reform, adopted in May 1945, severely reduced the landholdings of the two large Christian Churches. Under the terms of the reform bill, churches, monasteries, and convents could, in each case, occupy a maximum of 10 hectares of land, although Church properties with special artistic or historical significance were allowed to keep up to 30 hectares of farmland plus 30 hectares of forest. With this, the two largest Christian Churches were deprived of 85% of their previous holdings.[27] Both Churches were troubled by the land reform. However, Metropolitan Josif of the Serbian Orthodox Church asked only that land being confiscated from the Orthodox Church be divided among Orthodox believers living in the community; this was granted. Catholic Archbishop of Zagreb Alojzije Stepinac (1898–1960) took a different stand and, in a letter on 10 July 1945 to Vladimir Bakarić, head of the CP in Croatia, rejected the land reform altogether.[28] When Stepinac saw that his letter to Bakarić failed of its purpose, he wrote to Tito on 17 August 1945, calling the proposed land reform an unfriendly act against the Church.[29] Like his previous letter to Bakarić, Stepinac's letter to Tito failed to sway him from his declared policy. The IVZ lost more than 1,900 hectares of land, including forests, in connection with the 1945 land reform. In 1948, the regime seized hospitals, other medical facilities, public baths, and other objects from the Islamic community. Sharia courts, set up during Ottoman times and allowed to continue to function during the Habsburg era as well as by the interwar Kingdom, were shut down in 1946. They had handled inter-Muslim disputes in accordance with Islamic law and, thus, operated outside the secular law system.[30] The communists offended Islamic tradition by allowing the marriage of Muslims and non-Muslims, whereas many Muslims viewed the marriage of a daughter to a non-Muslim as a stain on the family's honor. The communists also launched a mass unveiling campaign and, in August 1947, the new High Vakuf Assembly of the IVZ *(vrhovni vakufski sabor)* declared its support for the unveiling of Muslim women. After September 1950, a woman wearing a veil in public could be punished with a prison sentence of up to three months and a fine of up to 20,000 dinars; anyone putting pressure on a woman to wear a veil could be punished with a sentence of up to two years at forced labor and a fine of up to 50,000 dinars. There was some resistance to these measures and it was necessary for the regime to bring massive pressure to bear in order to effect the unveiling of Muslim women.[31]

A third policy which affected the religious organizations was the regime's decision "to abolish all private high schools, following the completion of the 1945–1946 school year, and . . . to eliminate religious instruction from the curriculum of state elementary schools."[32] The Islamic school of theology was forced to close its doors in 1945 and six *madrassas* (Islamic schools or colleges) for young people and a *madrassa* for women in Sarajevo were likewise soon liquidated. In 1946, all Islamic religious instruction in schools was suppressed (although, in 1953, it became possible for Muslim children to be instructed in the Koran provided that such instruction took place in the mosques). The *mektebs* (Islamic primary schools) were forced to close in 1952. After that, the Gazi Husrevbeg Madrassa in Sarajevo was the only Islamic educational institution left in all of Yugoslavia.[33] The communists also seized the property of the Catholic charity Caritas, made civil marriage mandatory for couples wishing to live together, and promoted the establishment of "progressive" priests' associations that would be friendly toward the regime and lie beyond the authority of the bishops. Members of the priests' associations received health insurance from the state, subsidies (for approved publications, for example), and, of course, easier access to the bureaucracy. The Serbian priests' association was able to launch a periodical, *Vesnik*, in March 1949. In spite of a letter from the Catholic Episcopal Council on 26 April 1950 declaring the priests' associations "inexpedient",[34] the ranks of the Catholic priests' associations gradually grew, as did those of the Orthodox associations. Among Catholic clergy across Yugoslavia as a whole, only 27% were members of the Catholic priests' association in 1955. By contrast, that same year, 77% of Orthodox priests were members of their corresponding progressive priests' association.[35]

But, in some ways, the most painful blows suffered by the three largest religious organizations involved the trials of and verdicts handed down to leading Islamic functionaries, two Catholic bishops and two Orthodox hierarchs. In fact, immediately after war's end, the communists put some high-ranking members of the ulema, such as Ali Aganović and Muhamed Pandža, on trial. Eight more high-ranking Islamic functionaries were put on trial in the months leading up to the end of 1946. They were accused of having collaborated with German occupation authorities during the war and of having set up an illegal organization after war's end, for the purpose of overthrowing the newly installed government. The accused were given sentences at hard labor; in addition, they were deprived of their civil rights and their property was confiscated. On 5 August 1947, the Executive Committee of the High Vakuf Assembly, cowed into subservience, officially declared its readiness to cooperate with the new regime.[36]

Turning now to the two Christian Churches, two Catholic bishops – Archbishop Stepinac and Bishop Petar Čule of Mostar (1898–1985) – were accused of collaboration with the wartime fascist regime in Croatia and arrested respectively in September 1945 and April 1948; Bishop Čule was also accused of hiding a "renegade" and of attributing the massacre of about 15,000 Polish officers in the Katyn woods to the Soviets – whose NKVD (secret police) did in fact carry out the massacre.[37] He was sentenced to 11 ½ years in prison, developed tuberculosis in prison, and was released in October 1955. Stepinac's fate is discussed below. The Orthodox hierarchs – Assistant Bishop of Sarajevo Varnava Nastić and Metropolitan Arsenije Bradvarović of the Montenegrin littoral – were arrested respectively in 1948 and July 1954. The Orthodox hierarchs were not accused of collaboration with the Nedić regime but rather of a more serious offense, viz., of plotting counterrevolution – and this allegedly in collaboration with émigré circles. Bishop Varnava received an 11-year prison sentence, while Metropolitan Arsenije was given an 11 ½-year prison term. The bishop was released from prison in 1960 and was canonized by the Serbian Orthodox Church in 2005. On appeal, the metropolitan's sentence was reduced to 5 ½ years; when his asthma worsened, he was released in August 1956.[38] In addition, according to Klaus Buchenau, roughly 150 Orthodox priests were executed between 9 May 1945 and May 1946, with or without judicial process.[39]

But, by far, the trial which excited the strongest emotions both domestically and abroad was the trial, on fabricated charges, of the Archbishop of Zagreb, Alojzije Stepinac. Ivan Šarić (1871–1960), who had served as Archbishop of Sarajevo from 1922 until his death in 1960, had been openly pro-Ustaša (pro-fascist) and evidence could have been found to put him on trial, even though he had left the country, taking refuge in the Episcopal Palace in Klagenfurt, Austria, if the regime had wanted to try him *in absentia*. But Šarić was not the senior Catholic clergyman in Yugoslavia; that was Stepinac. And there were two problems with Stepinac from the regime's point of view. First, Tito had wanted Stepinac to have more "independence" (Tito's word) of the Holy See and adopt a more cooperative posture with his regime. Thus, on 2 June 1945, Tito held a meeting with Bishops Franjo Salis-Seewis and Josip Lach and told them:

> I would say that our Church needs to be national [*nacionalna*], that it be more responsive to the [Croatian] nation . . . I would like to see that the Catholic Church in Croatia now, when we have all the preconditions there, would have more independence . . . That is the basic question . . . and all other questions are secondary questions which will be easy to work out.[40]

Two days later, Tito and Vladimir Bakarić received Stepinac for a discussion, hoping to persuade the prelate to sever ties with the Holy See. Instead of showing any receptivity to this suggestion, however, Stepinac used the occasion to register various complaints.

The second problem was that Stepinac was repeatedly speaking out against communist policies. The archbishop's remonstration against the land reform has already been mentioned above. But he also wrote to Tito to ask that the prosecution of collaborators stop because, he wrote, the continuation of investigations and indictments would make it "necessary . . . to imprison ordinary worker, peasants," among others.[41] Tito ignored the archbishop's request and, between June 1945 and mid-1946, approximately 65,000 war criminals, traitors, and alleged "enemies of the people" were identified.[42]

Eventually, Stepinac was arrested on 18 September 1945 and added to a trial of 15 other persons which was already in progress – by any normal jurisprudential standards not merely highly unusual but also contrary to law. On 30 September the charges against the archbishop were read in court, accusing him of collaboration with the fascist regime which he had repeatedly criticized and denounced in his sermons.[43] The trial ended on 11 October 1946, with the archbishop sentenced to 16 years at hard labor; however, the sentence was never carried out and was commuted to incarceration in a double-cell, which included a private chapel. In 1951, he was transferred to house arrest in his hometown of Krašic.[44] Communist thugs continued to bully and beat up priests for the first few years; this ended only in 1952, when Tito gave a speech calling for this to end.

Building a new society, 1945–48

For Britain, France, and Germany, the Second World War ended on 8 May 1945. Later that month about 60,000 Chetniks, Croatian troops, Slovenian *Domobranci*, and their families fled into Austria and reached British lines. They tried to surrender to the British but the British had sent them back to Partisan lines. Tito's troops massacred these would-be refugees at Bleiburg, Kočevje, and elsewhere.[45] Other collaborators were forced to march to designated concentration camps which had been quickly set up. Many of them died on the march before they could reach the camps.[46] For Tito's Partisans, these actions marked the end of their engagement in the war. (In this connection, it is worth recalling that, on 14 May 1945, Tito had sent a telegram to the main HQ of the Slovenian Partisans, prohibiting the execution of POWs and directing that persons suspected of war crimes be transferred to a military court.[47])

The communists set about building a new society – not yet a "communist" society, which they thought of as a project for the distant future, but a *socialist* society as they understood the concept. They set up mass organizations, such as a Pioneer organization for young children, organized volunteer labor brigades to help with reconstruction, built up the party press, and on 29 November 1945, on the second anniversary of the second session of AVNOJ, abolished the monarchy. A new constitution was adopted on 31 January 1946; the text was virtually identical to the Soviet constitution of 1936. Economic reconstruction was launched but many people survived only thanks to food shipments by the United Nations Relief and Rehabilitation Administration (UNRRA). According to a story I heard in Yugoslavia, the Americans contributed large quantities of peanut butter, but when locals opened the jars some of them were convinced that this unfamiliar substance was unfit for human consumption and fed it to their farm animals.

An AVNOJ decree dated 21 December 1944 had previously authorized "the confiscation of the property of the Third Reich and its citizens, along with the assets of war criminals, collaborators, and traitors."[48] Two years later, on 5 December 1946, the communists declared the nationalization of banks, shops, transport companies, and other businesses; as of 1947, about 90% of all production was in the hands of the state. The authorities moved quickly with setting a Five-Year Plan for 1947–51 in motion and forecast wildly enormous growth rates in industrial and agricultural production. The targets could not have been reached even under better circumstances. But between the Yugoslavs' poor investment choices and the break with the Soviet Union in 1948, the Plan eventually had to be scrapped.[49]

In addition to fantasies about economic growth, Tito also nurtured dreams of expanding his newly gained empire. He tried through diplomatic means to gain portions of Austria and Italy and sent his troops to occupy Trieste, Gorizia, and Klagenfurt. He worked with Koçi Xoxe, the second highest-ranking communist leader in Albania (about whom, more later in this chapter) to try to bring about the incorporation of that country into Yugoslavia. And he engaged in ultimately abortive negotiations with Georgi Dimitrov, the Bulgarian leader, about setting up a federation of their two countries.[50] Nothing came of any of these fantasies.

Meanwhile, the communists continued to suppress opposition politicians and their revived political parties and newspapers. Among those noncommunists who were put on trial and sentenced on various charges between 1946 and 1948 were: Franjo Gaži, a member of the Croatian Peasant Party (CPP), included in the trial of Dragoljub Jovanović and sentenced to five years at hard labor; Tomi Jančiković, a prominent member of the CPP and, during the Second World War an opponent of the Croatian fascists, tried in 1948 and sentenced to 10 years in prison for having allegedly participated in a plot to assassinate leading communist officials (he died in prison in 1951 under suspicious circumstances); and Dr. Ivo Tartaglia, a committed anti-fascist, tried in June 1948 on the absurd charge of having displayed pro-Mussolini sentiments and sentenced to seven years at hard labor.[51]

If the Yugoslav communists thought that the Soviets would be impressed, they were mistaken. To begin with, Stalin was irritated at the speed with which the Yugoslavs achieved these results, at a time when he was still hoping to minimize tensions with Great Britain and the United States and, even moreso, by the fact that the Yugoslavs had not been coordinating their moves with him. Stalin was especially irritated by the apparently headlong speed with which Tito and Dimitrov seemed to be coming to a meaningful agreement. In fact, following the meeting between the two southeast European leaders in Bled, Dimitrov informed Stalin about these discussions. Jože Pirjevec records that Stalin was furious at this news. Dimitrov tried to calm Stalin by claiming that nothing would be (or would have been) finalized without the Soviet General Secretary's approval.[52]

The Soviet-Yugoslav rift

As early as 27 May 1945, Tito gave a speech in Ljubljana, in which he declared: "Our goal is that every man [should] be the master in his own house. We are not going to pay the balance on others' accounts, we are not going to serve as pocket money in anyone's currency exchange, we are not going to allow ourselves to become entangled in political spheres of interest. Why should it be held against our peoples that they want to be completely independent?"[53] Moscow immediately protested the speech, handing a note to Kardelj, calling it an "unfriendly attack on the Soviet Union."[54]

Soviet-Yugoslav frictions may be traced to 1941, but they became more serious in 1947–48; indeed, in September 1947, Cavendish W. Cannon, assigned to the U.S. Embassy in Belgrade, informed the U.S. Department of State that the Tito regime "may well some day [come into] conflict with Soviet purpose."[55] For that matter, the Soviet ambassador to Belgrade was sending dispatches to the Kremlin confirming that Tito was intent on being his own man. One communication from the ambassador reported that "Tito and the other leaders of the CPY do not mention Comrade Stalin in their declarations as the most important theorist of our times – a worthy successor to Marx, Engels, and Lenin."[56]

By the beginning of 1948, the frictions between the Soviet Union and Yugoslavia were becoming more and more obvious. The chief problem, from Stalin's viewpoint, was Tito's refusal to be subservient, including the Marshal's intention to send troops into southern Albania, while, from Tito's standpoint, perhaps the biggest problem involved Soviet efforts to recruit agents within the Yugoslav party, government, army officer corps, and secret police (efforts blocked, to a considerable extent, by Ranković's secret police).[57] But there were other sources of friction, including Yugoslav meddling in the Greek Civil War (which Stalin opposed), the joint enterprises in which the Soviets benefited in excess of their contribution, arguments about how significant Red Army assistance in 1944 had been, and Soviet refusal to back Yugoslav claims to Carinthia and for concessions in Venezia Giulia and Gorizia. All of this was compounded by Yugoslav communist claims that the construction of socialism in their country was tangibly farther advanced than it was elsewhere in the newly communist-run countries of the region.

Stalin was getting fed up with Tito and his crew and summoned Tito to Moscow in early 1948. Defiantly, Tito declined Stalin's "invitation", pleading illness, and instead sent Kardelj, Djilas, and Bakarić to be browbeaten at the Kremlin in February. Again, Stalin was not pleased.[58] The following month, Stalin recalled all of his military advisers and civilian experts from Yugoslavia. About this time, the Soviets hoped that their friends in Belgrade – Andrija Hebrang (1899–1949), who had served as chair of the Federal Planning Commission from 13 June 1946 to 8 January 1948, and Sreten Žujović (1899–1976), a member of the Politburo – might help to change the dynamics in Belgrade. The Kremlin let it be known that it fancied Žujović to replace Tito as General Secretary of the CPY and Hebrang to replace Tito in the office of prime minister.[59] However, the two were expelled from the Central Committee in May 1948; they were arrested the same month.

Then came the Cominform meeting on 28 June 1948 – the date having been selected by Stalin in order to add emotional force to the event since that was the date in 1389 when a Christian army led by Serbian Prince Lazar met an Ottoman army led by Sultan Murad I on the field of battle in Kosovo (and also the date, in 1921, when the constitution for the Kingdom of Serbs, Croats, and Slovenes was adopted). There, the assembled bloc delegates, led by the Soviets, accused Tito and his comrades of having lapsed into Trotskyism, among other things. Some Soviet sympathizers from Yugoslavia fled to Hungary, Romania, or Bulgaria. Yugoslavia was expelled from the Cominform and an economic blockade was imposed on the country.

For Tito and his circle, the question arose, how to respond to this development. The decision taken, in the short run, was to deny that there was any real problem and claim that Stalin was simply receiving erroneous information. As late as July 1948, in his speech to the Fifth Congress of the CPY, Tito underlined his party's loyalty to the USSR and, at the end of the speech, there were orchestrated chants "Tito! Stalin!".[60] Tito's regime also decided to step up agricultural collectivization, by way of "proving" to Stalin that the Yugoslavs were good communists. By the fourth quarter of 1949, 6,625 cooperatives had been established; by 1950, this number had grown to 6,968 and involved 418,659 households.[61] As had been the case in the Soviet Union and elsewhere, peasants resisted. Communist officials were murdered, sheep were slaughtered (some 50,000 sheep in Trebinje alone), and there was an armed insurrection in the Cazin region (in northwest Bosnia-Herzegovina) involving more than 700 insurrectionists in May 1950. The insurrection was eventually suppressed and its leaders were shot.[62] But even in June 1951, 2.5 million peasant households had still not been collectivized. Bad harvests and peasant discontent provided powerful disincentives and the regime eventually abandoned the program. By September 1953, only about 2,000 agricultural cooperatives remained in the country.

In the meantime, some 11,128 persons had been punished "by summary administrative procedure" for alleged Cominformism, according to figures supplied by Ranković.[63] Radovan Radonjić has provided higher figures, citing 55,663 certified Cominformists, of whom 16,288 were arrested and/or sentenced. Of the 16,288, 7,235 were Serbs, 3,439 were Montenegrins, and only 436 were Albanians. Among the 55,663, 28,661 (or 51.49%) were living in Serbia, according to Radonjić, while Serbs predominated among Cominformists in Bosnia-Herzegovina, Vojvodina, and Kosovo.[64] The most likely reason is that at least some of these were probably Chetniks, who had crossed over to Partisans late in the war out of opportunism, taking Stalin's side out of continued hostility toward Tito.

The Soviets now formed armed units of disgruntled Yugoslavs, training them in the USSR and then smuggling them back into Yugoslavia. In Bucharest, 200 defectors from Yugoslavia were trained in espionage and sabotage, beginning in 1949; they were then parachuted back into Yugoslavia. The rapid build-up of the Hungarian, Romanian, and Bulgarian armed forces and the conduct of military maneuvers close to the Yugoslav border during the first six months of 1950 were but the prelude to an intended invasion of Yugoslavia. Because of the threat of a Soviet bloc invasion, Yugoslavia increased its expenditure for defense from 6.4% of national income in 1948 to 21.4% in 1952. By 1960, however, the budget for defense had been rolled back to 8% of national income.[65] Meanwhile, after the firm US response on 25 June 1950 to the North Korean offensive, Stalin called off the invasion. Stalin still thought in terms of having Tito assassinated. In one scenario, Iosif Romualdovich Grigulevich, a Kremlin agent known as "Max", was to shoot Tito or infect him with lethal bacteria or give him a poisoned jewel box. The plan, code-named "Scavenger", had not been finalized, when Stalin died.[66]

Census data from 1948 and 1961

The first three post-war censuses were conducted in 1948, 1953, and 1961. The data for 1948 and 1961 are presented in Table 5.1, in order of declining numbers for 1961.

TABLE 5.1 Population of Yugoslavia by nationality group (1948, 1961)

	1948	1961
Serbs	6,547,117	7,806,213
Croats	3,784,353	4,293,850
Slovenes	1,415,432	1,589,192
Macedonians	810,126	1,045,530
Ethnic Muslims	808,921	972,954
Albanians	750,431	914,760
Montenegrins	425,703	513,833
Hungarians	496,492	504,368
Yugoslavs, undetermined	N/A	317,125
Turks	97,954	182,964
Slovaks	83,626	86,433
Bulgarians	61,140	62,624
Romanians	64,095	60,862
Czechs	39,015	30,331
Italians	79,575	25,615
TOTAL	15,772,098	18,549,291

Source: Paul Shoup, *Communism and the Yugoslav National Question* (New York & London: Columbia University Press, 1968), pp. 266–268.

Several things are worth noting here. First, although Albanians outnumbered Montenegrins, the latter were included among the *narodi* (peoples) of the country and therefore entitled to their own republic, while the Albanians were not; the Yugoslav communists offered the explanation that the constituent republics were considered sovereign subjects and that, since the Albanians already had a sovereign state (Albania), they could not (or should not) have a second one. Second, in the results for 1953, not shown here, 998,698 persons declared themselves "Yugoslavs, undetermined" while there was no entry for "ethnic Muslims". It is a safe assumption that the latter predominated among those declaring themselves Yugoslavs in that census. Third, all of the national groups noted here increased in number between 1948 and 1961 except for Romanians, Czechs, Germans, and Italians. It is likely that the members of these four national groups moved to their respective national homelands. Finally, although the largest group, the Serbs, were in a numerical minority, they outnumbered the next three largest groups (Croats, Slovenes, and Macedonians) in combination.

The failure of collectivization

In addition to the loss of life, the deliberate policies of the occupation forces, together with the civil war which raged across Yugoslavia between Partisans on the one side and Chetniks, the forces of the marionette regimes in Belgrade and Zagreb, and other Axis collaborators on the other side during the Second World War, resulted in significant property damage. A total of 6,690 public buildings were destroyed (including churches); in addition, 3,438 factories, 6,573 bridges, 372,660 farm houses, and 59,810 houses or apartments in cities were destroyed. Nor did losses stop there. An estimated 67% of horses and 57% of cattle were killed in the course of the fighting, and 25% of fruit trees and vineyards were destroyed.[67] The war had reduced many people to poverty and there was a risk of starvation in large parts of the country. Shipments of food from the UNRRA saved people from starvation. In all, UNRRA distributed approximately two million tons of food, draft animals, farm machinery, and trucks in Yugoslavia. Thanks to this massive aid, the country had 15 million acres under cultivation within a year of war's end.[68]

Following the Marxist-Leninist playbook, the Yugoslav communists launched an effort to bring as much of the country's agricultural sector as possible into state farms and agricultural cooperatives (collective farms). Peasants did not want to give up their private farms and engaged in both passive and active resistance to pressure from the authorities. As a result, by 1951, after six years of efforts to collectivize farming, the socialist sector of agriculture accounted for just 39% of arable land.[69] Even these cooperatives did not survive, as a result of incompetent mismanagement, insufficient agricultural machinery, and the resistance offered by the peasants, manifested among other ways in low morale and poor work on the cooperatives. By early 1951, many peasants simply left the cooperatives and, in November of that year, the CPY Central Committee accepted this result, admitting that collectivization had failed and legitimating the return of collectivized land to their original owners, albeit within the aforementioned 10-hectare limit. From a height of 7,012 cooperatives in 1951, only 896 were left by 1954.[70] At that point, 91% of tilled land was in private farms.[71] In May 1957, Tito told an audience in Skopje, "We openly admit that in the past we attempted to socialize village life by making use of administrative methods and forcing the peasants to join the co-operatives although they did not always want to do so . . . Where the peasants were forcibly driven into the co-operatives, they sabotaged everything."[72] For the interim, the authorities levied compulsory deliveries of farm produce at prices which they fixed but, after 1952, compulsory deliveries were abolished and price controls on fruit and vegetables were lifted.[73] But even with the abandonment of most cooperatives, agricultural production never met the planned targets, as the figures in Table 5.2 show.

TABLE 5.2 Average Annual Rates of Growth of Agricultural Production in Yugoslavia, 1961–85 – in %

	Planned	*Actual*	*Plan fulfilment*
1961–65	7.5	1.4	19
1966–70	4.6	3.0	65
1971–75	3.5	2.8	80
1976–80	4.0	2.2	55
1981–85	4.5	2.2	49

Source: Ivan Lončarević, "Prices and Private Agriculture in Yugoslavia", in *Soviet Studies*, Vol. 39, No. 4 (October 1987), p. 630.

The cultural fallout from the Tito-Stalin rift

An unintended consequence of the Soviet-Yugoslav rift was, after a short while, the abandonment of socialist realism as the official dogma for the arts and, over time, the liberalization of the cultural sector, allowing for the development or new styles or, in music, the use of twelve-tone and atonal techniques banned in the bloc, and, in the case of naïve art, the revival of an earlier style of painting but reimagined in an original way.[74] Not all writers adapted very well to the new situation created by the country's break with the homeland of Lenin and Stalin. Some writers, who had felt quite comfortable churning out optimistic works of socialist realism, responded by writing about trivia, while others were still struggling to find their literary way in the early 1960s. Still others, according to Sveta Lukić, dazed by the sudden unpredictability in culture, had trouble getting much done.[75]

The story of culture in post-rift Yugoslavia may be said to have begun with the first exhibition mounted by the Yugoslav Association of Fine Arts in Belgrade in 1949. The idea was to showcase works created in the spirit of socialist realism. But, in fact, many of the paintings on display were not works of socialist realism at all, but represented a diversity of styles and schools.[76] Nonetheless, it was still too early to shout "Let freedom ring!", since, as a result of pressure from Stalinist critics, about three-quarters of the paintings submitted for display in another exhibition that year – in this case, in Croatia – were rejected because their content or style did not conform to politically dictated aesthetic standards.[77]

The first volley fired at socialist realism was Oskar Davičo's essay "Poezija i otpori", which he read at the 1949 session of the Serbian Writers' Association. At the time, this seminal essay encountered little response. But, upon its publication in *Mladost* two years later, it catalyzed a lively debate in literary and artistic circles and stimulated new thinking. Then, in 1952, Miroslav Krleža (1893–1981), the author of a huge historical novel, *Zastave* [Banners], of which five volumes were completed,[78] and, by general agreement, Croatia's greatest writer of the twentieth century, launched a frontal attack (with the prior approval of Tito and Djilas) on the doctrine of socialist realism in his address to the Congress of Yugoslav Writers.[79] As Anthony Mlikotin has underlined, "in a Communist state radical changes of an ideological nature in one discipline always reflect[ed and stimulated] equally radical changes in other disciplines as well."[80]

Change in literary policy was undertaken quite deliberately, though reflecting processes already underway. Thus, in 1953, writers attending a special plenum of the Association of Yugoslav Writers voted unanimously in favor of major changes in literary policy. Marko Ristić, a member of the Association, felt that every writer was entitled to express his or her views on any subject and even to adopt the posture of a rebel.[81] Josip Vidmar and Zoran Mišić told the plenum that there had been too much stress even up to then on producing realistic work and that this had resulted in an impoverishment of literature in which "the magical, the fantastic, and the unusual" were scarcely visible, if at all.[82] Many non-Marxists felt that dialectical materialism could be married to styles and concepts very different from anything one might find in Marxism. An unintended consequence of a parallel effort to expand and broaden Marxist analysis was to open the gates to non-Marxist thinking.[83] Non-Marxist writers retained some basic terms from Marxism, but interpreted them each in his own way; Boris Ziherl, an orthodox Marxist, responded, writing that what had resulted amounted to "ideological disorder".[84] Ziherl also dismissed the works of French existentialist Jean-Paul Sartre as worthless; this provoked a sharp rejoinder the following year.[85] By the end of 1955, the clash between cultural realists, still adhering to something akin to socialist realism and in any event demanding that art be politically relevant, and modernists demanding literary freedom and dismissing the idea that art should be at all politically involved was coming into the open and spread to Macedonia, where realists Dimitar Mitrev, Dimitar Solev, and Georgi Stardelov were challenged by modernists Milan Djurčinov and Aleksandar Spasov. The same camps were in contention in poetry and in painting, where some modernists championed abstract art.[86] In poetry, the dominant style prior to 1944 had been "primitive folklorism, [mixed] with naïve patriotic pedagogy."[87] This style was now abandoned. Around 1955, the League of Communists of Yugoslavia (as the CPY had renamed itself) adopted a *laissez faire* posture as regards novels and poems, except in those rare instances when it was feared that a certain work seemed likely to impact foreign policy interests negatively.[88]

In 1945, the world renowned novelist, Ivo Andrić (1892–1975) published his novel, *Na Drini ćuprija* [The Bridge on the Drina], for which he received the 1961 Nobel Prize for Literature. *Na Drini ćuprija* is an innovative novel, offering a reflection on Bosnia-Herzegovina's history through a series of short stories linked by the bridge.[89] The writing is subtle, but, even so, it has sometimes been read (by Serbs) as a tableau of Serbian suffering though it is better understood as a plea for bridge-building and overcoming of historical trauma.[90]

Orchestral music proved to be less controversial than either literature or pictorial art and, for that matter, also than orchestral music in the GDR, Poland, and other Soviet bloc states.[91] Indeed, expressionism, twelve-tone music, and atonalism – taboo in the Soviet bloc – were all adopted by some Yugoslav composers. There was pressure on composers until 1948 to produce music reflective of socialist realism; but after Yugoslavia went its own way, strictures melted away. Among other things, this entailed moving away from citations to folk music – another idiom favored in Moscow at the time and one reflected in the early post-war compositions of Jakov Gotovac, Stevan Hristić, and Mihailo Vukdragović.[92] None of the foregoing composers worked in a socialist realist style or bore political themes in mind.

Ljubica Marić has been described as Yugoslavia's most important composer in the decades following World War Two. Her compositions are marked by twelve-tone and quarter-tone elements. In fact, twelve-tone and serial techniques reached Yugoslavia soon after 1948, as reflected also in the compositions of Krešimir Fribec, whose works include *Metamorphoses* for chamber orchestra (1953) and the opera

Blood Wedding (1957). Over time, interest in twelve-tone and serial techniques increased among local composers, who looked above all to Schoenberg, Berg, and Webern for inspiration.[93]

Yugoslav dynamics, 1950–68

From post-Stalin rapprochement to a second Soviet-Yugoslav rift

After Yugoslavia's expulsion from the Cominform, the Yugoslavs began to gravitate toward the West, signing the Balkan Pact with Greece and Turkey in June 1954 and applying for the Socialist Alliance of Working People of Yugoslavia (a communist-controlled organization intended to draw non-party members into cooperation with the regime) to be admitted to the Socialist International, a Social Democratic organization. To the Yugoslavs' disappointment, their Socialist Alliance was denied membership due to the fact that it did not recognize a right to strike.[94] As for the Balkan Pact, it never amounted to much and would be scuttled by 1960.[95] This left Yugoslavia neither of the East nor of the West. But Tito was already building bridges with various Third World countries, forming personal friendships with India's Jawaharlal Nehru (1889–1964), Egypt's Gamal abd al-Nasser (1918–1970), and Indonesia's (Kusno Sosrodihardjo) Sukarno (1901–1970). The governments of Burma, India, Indonesia, Pakistan, and Sri Lanka co-sponsored the famous Bandung Conference of April 1955, where the foundation of the later Nonaligned Movement was laid. (The Nonaligned Movement would be formally constituted in Belgrade in 1961, on Tito's initiative.) The conference censured both Western and Soviet colonialism, adopting a 10-point declaration in which the principles of respect for other nations' territorial integrity and sovereignty, nonaggression, and noninterference in the internal affairs of other countries were established. China pressed for a second conference of nonaligned states at which, Beijing hoped, certain Asian, African, and Latin American states would adopt strongly anti-Western positions. To head off this attempt to divert the nonaligned states into some form of alignment with the Soviet bloc, Yugoslavia and the United Arab Republic (Egypt) organized their own conferences of nonaligned states, defending the original principles spelled out in Bandung.

Nikita Khrushchev, who had become First Secretary of the Communist Party of the Soviet Union (CPSU) in September 1953, wanted to develop relations with Third World countries and looked to Tito to introduce him to Third World leaders. In addition, Khrushchev considered the notion of an intra-communist rift undesirable. For both reasons, he wanted to repair the damaged relations with Belgrade and traveled to Belgrade in May 1955, where he read a speech in which he blamed the problems between the two regimes on "Beria, Abakumov and others – recently exposed enemies of the people."[96] Khrushchev declared Soviet acceptance of Yugoslavia's right to chart its own path to socialism and to friendly relations with Western states. This was followed quickly by a declaration of friendship and cooperation, signed on 2 June 1955, in which the signatories affirmed their respect for the sovereignty of all socialist states, their respect for the principle of noninterference in each other's internal affairs, and acceptance of the principle of peaceful coexistence between the two blocs.

In June 1956, four months after Khrushchev's secret speech, Tito and his wife Jovanka visited Moscow and, for a brief period, there was a kind of honeymoon. By September 1956, however, there were differences between Moscow and Belgrade over how much latitude the Polish communists should enjoy; and, with the publication in March 1958 of the CPY's new draft program, there were renewed tensions. The program, published in advance of the Seventh CPY Congress, to be held in Ljubljana, held up Yugoslav "self-managing socialism" as a model for the world and as the "best" system which had been devised, i.e., a system better than what the Soviets had.[97] The Soviets were not pleased. Soviet-Yugoslav relations soured in the wake of the Seventh Congress and, by 1961, Khrushchev was alleging that the Yugoslav leaders "plainly suffer from national narrow-mindedness [and] have turned from the straight Marxist-Leninist road on to a winding path that has landed them in the bog of revisionism."[98]

The Djilas affair

Between November 1953 and January 1954, Milovan Djilas published a series of articles in *Borba*, accusing Yugoslav communists of monopolizing power and building not socialism but bureaucratic despotism, and demanded that greater democracy be permitted.[99] I have discussed the Djilas affair at some length in my *Three Yugoslavias*[100]; what is relevant here is to highlight the difference between the way Djilas was treated after launching frontal attacks on the communist party in the daily press and the way Slánský, Rajk, and Kostov had been treated in Czechoslovakia, Hungary, and Bulgaria respectively. Whereas they had been executed without their having committed any offenses, Djilas, who had committed the egregious offense of using the party press to attack the communist party, was treated much more leniently. Although he was ousted from his political posts, the only other punishment he received at that time was an 18-month suspended prison sentence. It was only after he wrote an article for an American magazine, in which he supported the Hungarian Revolution, that he received his first prison sentence. The difference between the treatment of Slánský, Rajk, and Kostov in the bloc states and the treatment of Djilas in non-bloc Yugoslavia is important in at least two regards. First, it provides yet another confirmation that, after the break with the Soviet Union, Yugoslavia became more liberal. Second, it shows that Tito felt sufficiently confident of his power that he did not feel existentially threatened by Djilas' articles.

Yugoslavia and the Hungarian Revolution of 1956

From Tito's perspective, the positive value of the Hungarian Revolution in potentially weakening Soviet power was more than offset by the encouragement it might give to Yugoslav discontents.[101] Initially, during October, the Yugoslav party news-organ *Borba* was generally neutral, while nonetheless urging that the uprising was "not a counter-revolution". By 1 November, however, *Borba* had adjusted its perspective and now warned of "right-wing elements" present in Hungary.[102] On 2 November, Khrushchev and Malenkov came to Brioni to discuss Hungarian developments with Tito, Ranković, Kardelj, and Veljko Mićunović, the Yugoslav ambassador to Moscow; their conversation lasted from 7 p.m. on 2 November until 5 a.m. the next day. Khrushchev had by then decided on a military intervention in Hungary and favored János Kádár to replace Gerő as Hungarian party leader. Tito agreed with Khrushchev on the need to intervene and also favored Kádár for the post of General Secretary of the Hungarian party. Tito would allegedly tell a visiting Soviet military delegation later that, if the Soviets had not suppressed the insurrection, Yugoslav troops would have been sent into Hungary for that purpose.[103] On 3 November, Khrushchev informed Tito that he planned to send in troops to crush the Hungarian uprising; the Soviet invasion began the following day.

The Yugoslavs telephoned Nagy at 1 a.m. on 4 November, just as the invasion was being put into action, and offered him refuge in the Yugoslav Embassy. Nagy, together with several of his colleagues, then fled to the embassy. As Johanna Granville has pointed out, this served two contradictory ends for Tito: on the one hand, it effectively incarcerated Nagy, preventing him from rallying Hungarians to resist the Soviets; on the other hand, it allowed Tito to present himself to the West as protecting Nagy from the Soviets while also presenting his country as "a responsible, sovereign state . . . honour[ing] the principles of international law."[104] Subsequently, the Soviets colluded with Kádár to persuade Nagy and his colleagues that they could play a role in the new post-revolutionary government, as noted in chapter 2. What is important here is that Tito felt betrayed by the subsequent kidnaping of Nagy and his entourage and, in a letter to the CPSU Central Committee on 24 November, Tito wrote that "The Yugoslav government cannot accept the version that Nagy and the others voluntarily went to Romania, since it was known . . . – while they were still here in the Yugoslav embassy – that they wanted to stay in their own country."[105] The Soviets' double-cross of Tito set the stage for a second falling out between Belgrade and Moscow, which would come to full bloom when the Yugoslavs published the draft program for their Seventh LCY Congress.

From workers' councils to the Reform package of 1965

The Yugoslav leaders' initial reaction to the Cominform Resolution of 28 June 1948 was stunned disbelief – in spite of the steadily escalating tensions between Moscow and Belgrade over the preceding months. At first, as previously mentioned, they convinced themselves that Stalin had to be misinformed and believed that, by pushing forward with ambitious programs of industrialization and agricultural collectivization, they could persuade "Comrade Stalin" that they were good communists and establish the kind of relationship with him that they desired – a relationship of equals. But by 1950, the Yugoslavs had been forced to recognize the folly of their thinking. They also told themselves that, given how Stalin was behaving toward them, there had to be something fundamentally wrong with the Soviet Union. Three years before Djilas' critical articles in *Borba*, he and Kardelj returned to the Marxist classics. Here, Djilas was struck by a reference, in volume 2 of Marx's *Kapital*, to "a future 'association of primary producers' as a form of transition to communism."[106] Marx envisioned a system in which workers themselves would be in charge of the factories where they worked. It occurred to Djilas that returning to Marx's vision of councils of workers running the factories looked truer to the spirit of Marx and Engels than having the economy run by an elaborate state bureaucracy with planning from above. One rainy day, Djilas, Kardelj, and Boris Kidrič (1912–1953), the chief economic thinker in the early days of post-war Yugoslavia, had driven to Djilas' villa. Waiting for the rain to let up, they remained in the car talking. Djilas mentioned the notion of using workers' councils to give workers a role in managing their enterprises. At first, Kardelj and Kidrič were skeptical but then came around to believing that the idea was brilliant – a perfect riposte to the Soviets' accusations and potentially the foundation for a claim to be constructing a uniquely democratic system. As Boris Kidrič related later, they were also inspired specifically and above all by the example of the Paris Commune of 1871, as described by Marx in his *Civil War in France*.[107] They passed this idea along to Tito who, after thinking in silence for a few moments, exclaimed, "But this is Marxist – factories to the workers!"[108] By June 1950, Tito was telling the delegates to the People's Assembly that setting up workers' councils was "the only right road" to bring about "the withering away of state functions in the economy"[109] – a supposed goal of the communist party.

In 1950, workers' councils were introduced on an experimental basis in some parts of Yugoslavia, with the idea that they would give workers a say in the operation of their respective work places. Two years later, the system of workers' councils – known as self-management – was adopted more officially. In 1953, a Basic Law was passed, which deleted passages of the 1946 constitution. In combination, these measures signaled that Yugoslavia was charting its own political path.

By the end of the 1950s, there were further pressures for change. There were demands for the devolution of administrative responsibility to local party organizations. There were demands for more a coherent codification of constitutional principles. There was pressure for the reform of the economic system. And it was noticed that the priority given to building up industry had drawn some of its labor force from the countryside, resulting in shortages of agricultural workers.[110]

At the dawn of the 1960s, Yugoslavia was run by a small circle of functionaries:

- Josip Broz Tito, president since January 1953 and General Secretary of the party
- Aleksandar Ranković, a conservative Serb, General Secretary of the Socialist Alliance of Working People of Yugoslavia since 1960, minister of internal affairs until 1963, vice president of the SFRY beginning in 1963
- Edvard Kardelj, a liberal Slovene, vice chair of the Federal Executive Council and president of the Committee for Legislation and the Building of People's Power

- Mijalko Todorović (1913–1999), a liberal Serb, exercising the leading authority in the economic sphere beginning in 1958
- Svetozar Vukmanović-Tempo (1912–2000), a Montenegrin and president of the Yugoslav labor union
- Ivan Gošnjak (1909–1980), a Croat, state secretary for people's defense
- Koča Popović (1908–1992), a Serb and foreign minister from 1953 to 1965 (and also a surrealist poet).

Other important figures included:

- Vladimir Bakarić (1912–1983), a Croat and secretary of the League of Communists of Croatia
- Petar Stambolić (1912–2007), a Serb and a senior figure in the Serbian party apparatus.

They presented a united front to the outside world, but actually, as already noted, there were serious differences of opinion between them. The major antagonists were Kardelj and Ranković. Kardelj was pro-reform and held to an organicist view of the nations comprising the population, meaning that he believed that Slovenes, Croats, Serbs, Macedonians, Bosniaks, and Montenegrins could and should all preserve their individual, respective cultures, languages, and traditions and could, at the same time, be loyal to socialist Yugoslavia. Ranković, by contrast, was against the reforms Kardelj was preaching and held to an integralist program for Yugoslavia's composite nations, meaning that he wanted them to meld together around a common culture, language, and set of traditions. In this, he is known to have been an admirer of Soviet nationalities practices.

In a word, Kardelj wanted, among other things, to see the constitution offer some measure of assurance for the sundry peoples of Yugoslavia to preserve their languages and cultures and protect their interests, while Ranković focused on the interests of Yugoslavia as a whole and did not consider the preservation of, for example, the Slovenian and Macedonian languages to be a high priority. The figures given in Table 5.1 make clear just how complex Yugoslavia's ethnic make-up was. And thus, framing a new constitution would inevitably take a position on how the country's nationality groups should be treated.

Work began on a new constitution, which was supposed to be ready by 1962. Kardelj prepared the draft for a new constitution together with some colleagues, finishing it in early 1962. When Ranković read it, he became very upset, because the draft constitution was granting the republics real powers. Ranković contacted Tito to complain and it was agreed to convene a secret session of the Executive Committee (Politburo) of the LCY on 14 and 16 March 1962. At this session, Ranković and other proponents of centralized power crossed swords with Kardelj and other exponents of the grant of meaningful powers and prerogatives to the republics. Ranković even wanted to scale back self-management, which had become one of the central pillars of legitimation for the regime. In the event, the final text of the constitution reflected a compromise between the conservative and liberal conceptions, with the constituent republics gaining some additional prerogatives. To compensate Ranković for what he considered a palpable setback, he was named Vice President of the Republic, thus assuming an office which was created for his benefit. To many observers, this seemed to anoint Ranković as Tito's heir apparent. The new constitution, which came into effect on 7 April 1963, changed the name of the country from the Federative People's Republic of Yugoslavia *(Federativna Narodna Republika Jugoslavija)* to the Socialist Federative Republic of Yugoslavia *(Socijalistička Federativna Republika Jugoslavija)*, pointedly retaining the word "federativna" in order to signal that the republics were already sovereign when they decided to federate to create their Yugoslav state, rather than the more common "federalna", which does not carry this connotation. By including the word "socijalistička" in the new name of the republic, Yugoslavia's leaders were signaling that the country had completed the construction of socialism.[111] Already the 1963 constitution made two concessions to Kardelj's point of view, declaring the right of the republics to leave the federation (albeit in agreement with the other republics) and elevating Kosovo from a "region" to a "province" on a par with Vojvodina. In addition, the new constitution established that all laws would be published in four official languages: Serbo-Croatian, Croato-Serbian, Slovenian, and Macedonian.

Then came the Eighth Congress of the League of Communists in December 1964, which saw the first open clash between the two main wings in the party. Croats and Slovenes also used the occasion to voice their demands for investment decisions to be based on profitability, and questioned the wisdom of some of the investments made in the southern regions of the country which, they alleged, had been politically motivated. The Eighth Congress proved to be the first occasion for an open debate about the national question, specifically about whether LCY policy should be directed toward developing a unified Yugoslav culture in which the sundry peoples of the country could share (as Ranković favored) or whether, on the contrary, Serbian, Croatian, Slovenian, Macedonian, and all the other national groups that made up socialist Yugoslavia should be allowed and even encouraged to preserve their distinct cultures and national identities (as Kardelj and Bakarić wanted). Tito had been hesitating to make a choice between these two competing visions but he now decided in favor of the liberal vision championed by Kardelj and Bakarić. Thus, addressing the delegates to the Eighth Congress, Tito declared: "Certain people, even communists . . . confuse the idea of unity between our peoples with the elimination of nationalities and the creation of something new and artificial, that is a single Yugoslav nation, bearing resemblance to assimilation and bureaucratic centralism, unitarism, and hegemony."[112] The LCY did aspire to bring Yugoslavia's various peoples together (under the rubric of Yugoslav socialist patriotism), Tito continued, but the party was building "a new type of social community, where all the nationalities find common interests."[113]

Social product had grown by 9.79% in the ten-year period, 1954–65, but was slowing down by the end of this decade. In addition, unemployment, which was not supposed to be present in a country governed by a communist party, was also becoming noticeable.[114] The Slovenian and Croatian party leaderships had already been pressing for reform in the economic sector, when a recession during 1961–62 gave added force to their demands and between 1964 and 1965 a series of decisions came into force, known collectively as "the Reform". These included: the transfer of considerable responsibility for the management of the economy from the federal government to the republics; the adoption of a more realistic rate of exchange; a complete revision of price ratios, including steep hikes in the prices of raw materials and agricultural goods; the enhancement of the authority and role of banks and economic enterprises, at the expense of the federal government; and the abolition of the General Investment Fund, which had controlled investment decisions. Ranković and his lieutenants in Serbia, Bosnia-Herzegovina, and Montenegro continued to oppose these measures, however, and did their best to obstruct the operationalization of the reform. In response, Kardelj and his allies prepared the ground for a battle against Ranković. In early 1965, Vojin Lukić, a key ally of Ranković, was moved from his post as federal secretary for internal affairs, to a less sensitive job within the Serbian party. Then, on 16 June 1966, a special commission was set up to prepare a case against Ranković. The commission was headed by Krste Crvenkovski of Macedonia. Other members of the commission included Miko Tripalo from Croatia, France Popit from Slovenia, and Djuro Pucar a Serb from Bosnia-Herzegovina. But the real players, who were not on the committee, were Kardelj, Bakarić, and Stambolić.

Ranković was left in the dark until the eve of the plenary meeting to be held on 1 July 1966 on the main Brioni island about the agenda for the meeting.[115] Once all the Central Committee members had assembled, the commission's report was read to them, charging that, under Ranković's leadership, the work of the state security service had been characterized by "weaknesses, deformations, and serious abuses."[116] In addition, Tito accused Ranković of having deviated from party policy as early as 1964, of having authorized wiretaps on his (Tito's) phone as well as on the phones of other leading communists, such as Kardelj, and of obstruction "in carrying out the decisions of the Eighth Congress – in fact, they have as much as completely forgotten about the decisions altogether."[117] Although the discussion was lively, not a single delegate came to Ranković's defense.[118] The commission recommended that Ranković be dismissed from office – a recommendation endorsed by unanimous vote.[119] Accordingly, Ranković was stripped of his posts and expelled from the Central Committee; subsequently, on 10 April 1967, he was expelled from the LCY.

At this point, one could speak of the ascendancy of a liberal coalition embracing leading figures in the Slovenian, Croatian, and Macedonian parties, and later also the Serbian party. The leading liberals were:

- Stane Kavčič (1919–87), chair of the executive council of Slovenia 1967–72
- Miko Tripalo (1926–95), Secretary of the LC Croatia until December 1971
- Savka Dabčević-Kučar (1923–2009), president of the LC Croatia and prime minister of Croatia 1967-December 1971

- Krste Crvenkovski (1921–2001), Secretary of the LC Macedonia 1963-March 1969
- Latinka Perović (b. 1933), Secretary of the LC Serbia 1968–1972
- Marko Nikezić (1921–91), president of the CC of the LC Serbia 1968–1972.

Yugoslav policies regarding Gender Equality

For Marx, Engels, and their successors, "the woman question" *(žensko pitanje)*, as they called the problem of gender inequality, was a class question. By that, they meant that the issue of gender inequality could not be tackled autonomously but could be solved only within the framework of the construction of a socialist society. Gender equality, thus, would be achieved as a by-product of the construction of socialism and, it followed, any undertaking to focus on gender inequality as a task in and of its own right could only draw focus away from carrying on with socialist revolutionary processes. Western-style feminism, thus, was counterrevolutionary. That did not mean, of course, that Yugoslavia's communists downplayed the problem. On the contrary, as early as 7 August 1945, the People's Front of Yugoslavia (which would later be recast as the Socialist Alliance of Working People of Yugoslavia) had adopted a program asserting that the equality of women had already been achieved, while adding, in the spirit of self-contradiction, that "the further consolidation [of that equality] and the complete participation of women in all areas of political and social life must be one of the basic assignments of every adherent of the Front."[120] A few months later, the People's Assembly adopted the country's first post-war constitution. Article 24 of this document affirmed that

> Women enjoy equal rights with men in all spheres of state economic and social life. Women are entitled to a salary equal to that of men for the same work, and enjoy special protection in the labour relationship. The state particularly protects the welfare of mother and child by the establishment of maternity hospitals, children's homes and day nurseries, and by ensuring the right to paid leave before and after [childbirth].[121]

Later, access to abortion was liberalized, as were the regulations governing divorce. Indeed, legislation accompanying the 1974 constitution allowed for abortions to be available on the demand of the pregnant woman during the first 10 weeks of pregnancy.[122] Not surprisingly, given the unavailability of contraceptives and the lack of knowledge about them, this resulted in a rise in the number of legal abortions across Yugoslavia.

The communist strategy to promote the equality of women entailed (1) increasing the rate of literacy among women, (2) women's advancement in education, (3) the inclusion of women in the labor force and the promotion of the most capable to positions of managerial authority, and (4) the inclusion of women in decision-making and other political bodies. Where the first of these criteria is concerned, real progress was notched: in 1931, 54.4% of females over age 10 were illiterate. By

1961, this figure had been reduced to 28.8%. Again, women accounted for 19% of those enrolled in higher education in 1939 while, during the years 1945–77, women accounted for 36.5% of those graduating from institutions of higher education.[123] Further, whereas women made up just 18% of the labor force in 1940, by 1953 this figure had risen to 22.8%, crossing the 30% threshold by 1968 and reaching 36.0% in 1981.[124] On the face of it, one might conclude that, with this, the LCY was recording real progress in three of the four policy areas listed above. However, when it came to inclusion in the labor force, although the principle of equal pay for equal work was by and large honored, inequality persisted for two reasons. The first was that women often did not enjoy access to better paying work. The result was that, in 1981, women earned an average of 16% less than men.[125] The second, related factor was that women tended to be concentrated in lower-paying sectors.

Table 5.3 provides only a part of the picture. Although textiles, hotels, and tourism, for example, were lesser-paying sectors, another problem, possibly the main problem, lay with the jobs available to women *within* these sectors (as mentioned above). Thus, for example, women were typically excluded from managerial positions, regardless of their experience and credentials (although, for some women, family obligations made them disinterested in such positions). Thus, across

TABLE 5.3 Women as a proportion of the Yugoslav labor force in certain sectors of the economy, 1970–1980 – in %

	1970	1975	1980
Social services	71.0	74.5	79.4
Healthcare	68.0	71.1	73.7
Textiles	66.3	68.4	78.4
Finance & insurance	61.5	65.5	N/A
Social insurance	58.4	64.5	N/A
Leather industry	52.6	59.4	69.9
Hotels	56.6	47.8★	60.4
Tourism	47.0		54.7
Schools	52.8	54.8	56.6
Cultural institutions	51.4	53.2	N/A
Tobacco industry	49.7	48.0	49.7
Foreign trade	45.5	48.2	52.8
Graphics	46.2	45.2	44.8
Science	43.0★★	43.8	44.0
Retail trade	41.4	46.3	53.2
Wholesale trade	37.7	40.9	32.2
AVERAGE	31.1	34.0	35.5

★ = Hotels & tourism
★★ = 1973

Sources: Olivera Burić, "Položaj žene u sistemu društvene moći u Jugoslaviji", in *Sociologija*, Vol. 14, No. 1 (1972), p. 64; *Statistički bilten*, no. 980 (Belgrade: Savezni zavod za Statistiku, October 1976), p. 21; and *Statistički Godišnjak Jugoslavije 1981* (Belgrade: Savezni zavod za Statistiku, August 1981), pp. 128–129.

Yugoslavia as a whole, even in enterprises where women were well represented or for that matter constituted the majority, men predominated in positions of authority, including in educational institutions. In 1980, for example, in the Rud-nik fashionwear enterprise in Gornji Milanovac, "97% of the employees [were] women. Yet of the nine members of the self-managing secretariat, only six [were] women."[126] In fact, in economic enterprises in general, women made up 1.2% of directors in 1962, 0.8% in 1964, 0.6% in 1968, and 0.9% in 1972.[127] The same pattern was repeated in self-management organs, as the figures in Table 5.4 make clear.

Thus, in terms of the third leg of the communist strategy for promoting women's equality – inclusion and advancement in the labor force – the communists fell short.

The fourth leg of the communist strategy entailed the advancement of women in politics. Among the relevant measures would be party membership, representation in the Federal Assembly, and inclusion among high-ranking federal functionaries. On these criteria, Yugoslavia did not measure up to its own criteria. In 1945, 25% of party members were women, but by 1979 this figure had shrunk to 20%. The representation of women in the Federal Assembly fell from 15.2% in 1963 to 6.3% in 1969; during the same time, female representation in the assemblies of the republics slid from 16.1% to 7.5%. And, in 1975, among the 792 highest-ranking federal functionaries, only 41 (5.2%) were women.[128] This problem of gender inequality in leadership bodies would persist into the post-Tito era. Thus, in 1985, while women accounted for 27.0% of members of the LCY, they comprised barely over half that proportion – 14.1% – of members of the Central Committee.[129] That same year, there were no women in the LCY's highest executive organ and only one woman in the Federal Executive Council, the government's highest decision-making body.[130]

Although the record of the LCY's program to advance the equality of women looks mixed, when measured against the LCY's own standards and goals, it is worth stressing that the provision of paid maternity leave and the establishment of

TABLE 5.4 Representation of women in the labor force and in positions of authority, in selected sectors (1972) – in %

	Employees	Members of workers' councils	Presidents of workers' councils
Economic enterprises	27.3	16.8	5.5
Elementary & middle schools	52.9	38.9	18.7
Academic institutions	62.9	22.3	5.2
Scientific institutes	41.9	29.2	17.0
Cultural, educational, & artistic Institutions	34.8	35.5	26.7
Healthcare	67.9	43.0	28.1
Social institutions	69.7	68.1	54.4

Source: Olivera Burić, "Izmena strukturę društvene moć: Uslov za društvenu ravnopravnost žene", in *Sociologija*, Vol. 17, No. 2 (1975), pp. 209–210.

nurseries, free universal health care, subsidized sport opportunities for children, and good local public schools all helped working mothers and were markedly ahead of what is available even today across East Central Europe and, for that matter, the USA.

Feminist-minded scholars and other professionals organized in the mid-1970s, forming groups at the Universities of Zagreb and Ljubljana as well as at the student cultural centers in Belgrade and Ljubljana. In particular, the Student Cultural Center in Belgrade, under its director, Dunja Blažević, was the most important center for feminism in Yugoslavia, organizing the country's first feminist conference in 1978.[131] Subsequently, further feminist conferences were organized in the 1980s. Among the most prominent feminist scholars at the time were Žarana Papić, Rada Iveković, Slavenka Drakulić-Ilić, Lydia Sklevický, Nada Ler Sofronić, and Lepa Mlađenović.

Meanwhile, although spokespersons for the LCY continued, from time to time, to intone the Marxist mantra that "the solution of all questions of the social position of women in essence demands a class approach,"[132] the delegates to the Eleventh Congress of the LCY (Belgrade, 20–23 June 1978) adopted a programmatic statement blaming the persistence of inequality between the sexes on "primitivism, religious beliefs and other conservative prejudices"[133] – in a word, on patriarchal culture. With this, the LCY admitted that the "woman question", in the party's terminology, could *not* be reduced to a class question.

A Church for Macedonia

Among Macedonian clergy, there had been some desire for a while to enjoy a measure of self-administration: this, of course, could mean either *autonomy*, thus still respecting the authority of the Serbian Patriarch, or *autocephaly*, meaning that it would not recognize any ecclesiastical authority above its own metropolitan. In fact, at the end of the Second World War, Macedonian clergy let it be known that they wished to have their own autocephalous Church. However, at the time there was no support for that among Macedonian communist leaders.[134] The Macedonian clergy recalled that they had had an Archbishopric of Ohrid until it was suppressed by the Ottoman Sultan in 1767 and argued that this constituted an institutional precedent for the establishment – or, in their view, reestablishment – of a Macedonian Orthodox Church. With the Holy Synod of the Serbian Church delaying any action, the Macedonian clergy convoked a meeting in Ohrid on 5 October 1958, attended by 290 persons, both clergy and laity. This assembly now declared the reestablishment of the Archbishopric of Ohrid and elected Auxiliary Bishop Dositej (Stojković) Metropolitan of Ohrid. This was now set up as an autonomous body and the assembly published a constitution for the newly declared Church. For his part, Tito had a political interest in seeing the emergence of a Macedonian Church, as it would strengthen the CPY's claim that the Macedonian nation was distinct from the Bulgarian nation – a claim disputed by the Bulgarian regime.[135] He therefore asked Serbian Patriarch German to accept the Macedonian

TABLE 5.5 Membership in the Main Christian Churches of Yugoslavia, 1953, 1973

	1953	1973
Catholics	5,370,760	6,537,348
Orthodox	6,984,686	6,692,541
	of which, Macedonian Orthodox: 600,000	

Source: Stella Alexander, *Church and State in Yugoslavia since 1945* (Cambridge: Cambridge University Press, 1979), p. 297.

fait accompli. German did so and, upon visiting Ohrid shortly thereafter, he was welcomed by a representative of the Macedonian government, in token of the high interest this had also for local politicians.[136]

The Macedonian clergy intended this as a first step toward autocephaly but, when the Macedonian Church hierarchy approached the Serbian Sabor in May 1966 with a request that its status be raised to that of autocephaly, the Serbian Sabor refused to forward this request to sister Orthodox Churches, effectively killing it. In this, the Serbian Church enjoyed the support and protection of Aleksandar Ranković.[137] But when Ranković was dismissed from his positions in July 1966, the Macedonian Church saw its opportunity and, before the end of the year, "sent the Sabor a formal demand for autocephaly, [and] repeated its [earlier] threat to act unilaterally if this was not granted."[138] The Serbian Sabor took more than five months to respond, finally refusing the Macedonians' demand on 24 May 1967.

In response, the Assembly of the Macedonian Orthodox Church convened in Ohrid on 17–19 July 1967 and unilaterally declared its autocephaly, on the 200th anniversary of the Ottomans' abolition of the Archbishopric of Ohrid. The Macedonian party welcomed the proclamation of autocephaly and, on 20 September 1967, the party organ *Nova Makedonija* ran an article both heralding the proclamation of autocephaly and criticizing the Serbian Church for refusing to accept this result. As the figures in Table 5.5 show, Macedonian Orthodox believers accounted for just over 10% of those counted as Orthodox.

Self-managing socialism and its demise, August 1968–June 1988

The Soviet invasion of Czechoslovakia in August 1968 marked a watershed in the history of socialist Yugoslavia. In April 1968, Tito traveled to Moscow for talks with Soviet General Secretary Brezhnev about developments in Czechoslovakia. Tito urged the Soviet leader to desist from any resort to armed force to crush the liberal currents in that country. Brezhnev assured his Yugoslav counterpart that he and his Politburo were not considering invasion.[139] When Brezhnev mentioned the presence of "enemy elements" in Dubček's Czechoslovakia, Tito conceded the point but stressed that the country was headed by a strong communist party and had an army that was a loyal partner in the Warsaw Pact.[140] On 9 August, Tito visited Prague to affirm his full support for the democratization underway in Czechoslovakia. But none of this made any difference for Soviet calculations. In the wake of the Soviet invasion of that country, Yugoslavia concluded military agreements with Italy, Greece, and Turkey. Then, on 11 February 1969, a law was passed setting up a territorial defense force. This force was entrusted with responsibility to organize guerrilla resistance in the event of hostile (Soviet) military action. The government also increased its military budget, which soon reached between 5% and 6% of the country's GDP.[141]

In Yugoslavia, 1968 was also the year when Belgrade was struck by student demonstrations (in June), the year when "Albanians who had been convicted in the Prizren trial of 1956 were rehabilitated on the grounds that the security apparatus under Ranković had rigged the proceedings, fabricated evidence, and bribed witnesses,"[142] and the year in which (in November) a new Serbian party leadership was elected, elevating Latinka Perović, a young liberal intellectual, to the post of Secretary of the LC Serbia, and Marko Nikezić, erstwhile FM, to the presidency of the LC Serbia. Meanwhile, in Croatia, anti-Serb sentiments were percolating to the surface and grew in intensity after the Zagreb newspaper *Telegram* published a protest, in its 17 March 1971 issue, of a newly published dictionary for Serbo-Croatian or Croato-Serbian, in which Serbian usages were consistently presented as the standard variant, while Croatian usages were portrayed as a special regional variant, in other words a dialect.[143]

The Croatian mass movement

In the wake of the fall of Ranković, Croats in particular became more outspoken about their complaints. In December 1954, prominent linguists and literary figures from Serbia, Croatia, and Montenegro met in Novi Sad and declared that Serbian, Croatian, and Montenegrin were a single language, existing in two variants: ijekavski (which they called Croato-Serbian) and ekavski (which they called Serbo-Croatian). They also signed an agreement, agreeing to collaborate on the creation of a common orthography and a dictionary for the common language. By 1967, they had succeeded in publishing the first two volumes of the dictionary. But now in March 1967, the Zagreb literary weekly *Telegram* published a "Declaration on the Name and Position of the Croatian Literary Language," repudiating the Novi Sad Agreement and demanding that all laws and treaties be published in four languages, instead of three (hence, Serbian, Croatian, Slovenian, and Macedonian). The LCC Central Committee, at its Seventh Plenum, accused the authors of the Declaration of having prepared a document "directed against the brotherhood and unity of the peoples and nationalities of the SFRY" and characterized all the signatories as "politically immature".[144]

Equally disturbing both to Croats and, in a different way, to the higher echelons of the party were claims made by Šime Djodan (1927–2007) and Marko Veselica (1936–2017), both of them economists at the University of Zagreb, that Croatia was being discriminated against in economic policy and that Serbia was being disproportionately favored. For example, Djodan reported that, while Croats had accounted for 23.15% of the population of Yugoslavia in the 1961 census, Croatia had been the beneficiary of only 18.05% of investment funds during the years 1956–70; by contrast, while that same census recorded that Serbs comprised 42.08% of the population in 1961, Serbia had been allocated 62.14% of investment funds during those same years.[145] If one recalls that some Serbs lived in Croatia, then the disproportion appears to be even greater. *Hrvatski tjednik*, the weekly newspaper of the Croatian cultural society *Matica Hrvatska*, claimed that Belgrade's banks were monopolizing credit along Croatia's Dalmatian coast, squeezing out Croatian banks, and that Serbs were being brought from Serbia to work in the Croatian hotel industry.[146] This was related to the question of demographic displacement, with Croats accounting for the largest number of Yugoslav *Gastarbeiter* working in Germany and Serbs constituting the largest number of labor migrants to Croatia. There were also fears about a possible campaign to separate Dalmatia from Croatia; this was fueled by pamphlets distributed during 1971, calling for the immediate organization of autonomous Serb provinces in Dalmatia and elsewhere in Croatia, and their subsequent removal from Croatia. And finally, there were allegations that inclusion in Yugoslavia had had a negative impact on Croatia's banking sector in general and that Croatia was being economically exploited.

From March 1967 to December 1971 there was a strong assertion of the Croatian spirit, with the weekly newspaper *Hrvatski tjednik* and the bimonthly journal *Kolo* playing prominent roles in this regard, but supported also by the periodicals *Kritika, Vidik*, and *Dubrovnik*. Among other things, there were demands that only Croatian linguistic conventions be used in Croatian publications and that Stjepan Radić (1871–1928), leader of the Croatian Peasant Party in the 1920s, and Ban Josip Jelačić (1801–1859), a Field Marshal in the Habsburg Army who defended the empire against Hungarian rebels in 1848–49, be reclaimed. The cultural association Matica Hrvatska expanded rapidly, and started to politicize cultural questions. The LC Croatia was also showing new colors and, at the Tenth Plenum of the Central Committee of LC Croatia (15–17 January 1970), Dabčević-Kučar stated that stress should be placed on fighting "unitarism" (conservative centralism) rather than on resisting demands for liberalization.[147] She also argued that the chief threat to Yugoslav stability came from Serbian nationalism. Another issue, according to Ante Čuvalo,[148] was that textbooks in use in Croatian schools in 1966–72 devoted more space to literature produced by writers from other nations than to Croatian literature. Moreover, Vlatko Pavletić, writing for the newspaper *Hrvatski tjednik*, claimed that important artifacts of Croatia's cultural heritage were being represented in textbooks as the work of Serbs.

In Serbia too, there was a change in the political atmosphere in November 1968, when Nikezić and Perović assumed the offices of president and secretary, respectively, of the LC Serbia. Turning a new page in Serbian politics, they adopted the principle of noninterference in the internal affairs of the other republics and defended the Croatian party leadership from conservative critics. What Perović and Nikezić wanted was to see Yugoslavia develop a market economy – something to which Tito was opposed.[149] Within Serbia, Draža Marković (1920–2005), president of the Serbian Assembly from 1969 to 1974 and a leading conservative within the Serbian party, had opposed the election of Nikezić and Perović and was constantly feeding Tito information that Perović and Nikezić were against him. Among other things, Marković and his associates became convinced that Perović and Nikezić should have interfered in political matters in Croatia and that they favored a democratization of Serbia, which would have the effect of downgrading Tito's authority.[150] Meanwhile, the liberals brought about the adoption of 19 amendments to the federal constitution during 1967–68 and a further 23 amendments on 30 June 1971. These amendments enhanced the powers of the republics and provinces at the expense of the federal government and granted the provinces near parity with the republics. Economic questions of general interest were to be resolved in consultation among representatives of the republics. There was deep resentment in some circles in Serbia at the upgrading of the prerogatives of the autonomous provinces. One of the loudest critics protesting the amendments was Mihailo Đurić, an influential Serbian philosopher who took part in a public discussion of the 1971 amendments at the Law Faculty soon after they were published. In his speech on that occasion, later published together with other speeches in the journal *Anali Pravnog Fakulteta u Beogradu*, Đurić asserted that

> It is obvious that the borders of the present Socialist Republic of Serbia are neither national nor the historic borders of the Serbian nation . . ..The Serbian nation lives in four of the five other republics, but not in one of these republics can it live its own life.[151]

The offending issue of the journal was quickly banned, the most outspoken professors were dismissed from their posts, and Đurić was sent to prison, where he served nine months of a two-year prison sentence for having allegedly undermined the harmony of Yugoslavia's peoples.

In the course of 1971, there were also polemics in the press, with various "incidents", some of which were probably blown up by the press.[152] As time passed, party conservatives, especially in the Serbian party, placed increasing pressure on Tito to curb the liberals. Tito, in fact, visited Zagreb in July 1971; the visit only reinforced Tito's fears that Croatia was pulling the country into fratricidal civil war.[153] The Croatian party was not united, however, and there was internal in-fighting within the party between liberals and conservatives, while Croatian nationalists (outside the party) claimed that there was discrimination against Croats in Bosnia–Herzegovina. Various demands were voiced now. On 5 November 1971, for example, Dabčević-Kučar demanded that Croatia be allowed to retain a greater share of its foreign currency earnings than had been the case up to then. There were also demands, from various quarters: that the Croatian Sabor become the highest organ of power in Croatia (meaning not the local communist party); that a separate Croatian currency be created; that the Croatian district of the Yugoslav People's Army (JNA) become in effect a Croatian Army (with Croatian recruits to serve under Croatian generals); that Croatia issue its own postage stamps; that

Croatia be represented in the UN; that Croatia pass its own legal code on an autonomous basis, even that Croatia be enlarged by being allowed to annex land from Herzegovina and Montenegro.[154] Collectively, these demands amounted to a demand for independence and by December 1971, Tito had had enough. Tens of thousands of members were expelled from the League of Communists of Croatia; at higher echelons, 741 persons were stripped of their posts, including Dabčević-Kučar, Tripalo, Pero Pirker, Marko Koprtla, and Dragutin Haramija.[155] Some intellectuals, such as Šime Djodan, Ivan Zvonimir Čičak, Marko Veselica, and Franjo Tudjman were sent to prison. Fourteen periodical publications in Croatia were shut down, as was *Matica Hrvatska*. Dabčević-Kučar and Tripalo were subsequently expelled from the party (on 8 May 1972). Liberals were purged also from the Slovenian, Macedonian, and Serbian parties.

The underdeveloped regions

Communism was driven by the commitment to overcome huge inequalities of wealth and income and establish a situation of relative equality. This commitment extended not merely to individual citizens but also to regions and entire federal units of Yugoslavia. At the time the federation was launched, the communists were aware that some parts of the country were seriously less developed than other parts. Initially, the regime allocated subsidies to the less developed areas through a General Investment Fund but, as of 1963, national income per worker ranged from a high of 122% of the Yugoslav average in Slovenia to a low among republics of 76% in Macedonia and 77% in Montenegro.[156] These two republics plus Kosovo benefited from federal economic subsidies from the beginning (1947), although parts of Bosnia-Herzegovina were added later. But discontent with the existing system of subsidizing the less developed areas was growing. Finally, the 1963 constitution established the principle that a more concerted effort be made to assist the less developed regions and confirmed that a federal fund should be set up for this purpose.[157] In terms of living standards, the poorest of the eight federal units was Kosovo. Of course, in multiethnic Yugoslavia, economic inequality between federal units was understood as entailing also interethnic inequality.

To address this challenge, the Federal Assembly passed a bill in February 1965, setting up a Fund for the Accelerated Development of the Underdeveloped Republics and the Province of Kosovo, funding it with a 1.85% tax on the social product of every unit, including the beneficiaries of the fund. Bosnia-Herzegovina, Macedonia, Montenegro, and Kosovo were designated underdeveloped for purposes of funding. In spite of this special funding, however, economic growth in the four units receiving subsidies from the fund remained lower than growth in the more developed republics during 1966–70 and only began to outpace growth in the more developed republics by a small margin during 1971–75.[158] Even so, more troubling was the fact that, between 1965, the first year when funding was channeled through the federal fund, and 1971, national income per worker sank in Montenegro from 80% of the Yugoslav average to 73%, in Bosnia-Herzegovina from 91% to 84%, and in Kosovo from 79% to 70%. Among the four federal units designated as underdeveloped, only Macedonia registered improvement by this measure in this period, as national income per worker in that republic increased from 81% of the Yugoslav average in 1965 to 93% in 1971.[159] In Kosovo, investment tended to be concentrated in capital intensive rather than labor intensive industry. As a result, there was no easing of the problem with unemployment in that province.

But the nature of local investments does not tell the whole story. Illiteracy rates were also holding back the less developed parts of the country. What is immediately clear from the data in Table 5.6 is that there is an almost perfect inverse correlation between level of literacy and national income per capita.

Moreover, as a *proportion* of the Yugoslav average, per capita social product in Kosovo declined from 49.3% in 1947 to 34.1% in 1970, shrinking further to 32.2% of the Yugoslav average by 1976.[160] Moreover, in 1972, with 7% of the Yugoslav population, Kosovo had only 4.9% of vocational-technical schools, 2.7% of the country's cinemas, one Albanian-language daily newspaper, and two radio stations (out of 174 in all of Yugoslavia). Illiteracy was also a problem, with 36% of Kosovar Albanians admitting to being illiterate in 1971.

Back in 1945, as already noted, Kosovar Albanians who were loyal to Tito wanted to have a republic for Kosovo.[161] Although the denial of that request provoked some resentment, a more serious problem was the discrimination against Albanians in hiring for the police, the security service, and the administrative apparatus. For example, Serbs accounted for 23.5% of Kosovo's population in 1956, but 58.3% of the region's security forces and 60.8% of the police; Albanians accounted for 64.9% of the population of Kosovo, but only 13.3% of security police and 31.3% of regular police.[162] There were serious tensions between Serbs and Albanians in Kosovo in the 1950s. In particular, during the winter of 1955–56, UDBa confiscated about 9,000 firearms from Albanians; some Albanians resisted and between 37 and 70 Albanians were killed in the process, according to official figures released during 1966–67. Then, in July 1956 several Albanians were put on

TABLE 5.6 Percentage of Illiterates in Yugoslavia, by federal unit (1971)

	%
Kosovo	**31.6**
Bosnia-Herzegovina	**23.2**
Macedonia	**18.1**
Serbia-proper	**17.6**
Montenegro	**16.7**
Vojvodina	**9.1**
Croatia	**9.0**
Slovenia	**1.2**

Source: Demographic Research Center, *The Population of Yugoslavia* (Belgrade: Institute of Social Sciences, 1974), p. 37.

trial in Prizren on charges of subversion and espionage for Albania. They received prison terms ranging from three to 12 years but, strangely, soon after the trial, all evidentiary materials and documentation related to the trial were destroyed. Twelve years later, as already mentioned, those who had been convicted were exonerated and it was now admitted that the "evidence"against them had been fabricated. Albania smuggled an estimated 675 agents into Kosovo between 1948 and 1961, hoping to destabilize Yugoslav rule in the province, according to official Yugoslav data. In the years 1957–61, 115 Albanian citizens were arrested inside Kosovo and sent to prison for having crossed into Yugoslavia illegally. Illegal activity continued throughout the 1950s, as Kosovar Albanians resented having been denied the right of self-determination.[163] The over-representation of Serbs and Montenegrins in the security organs in Kosovo in 1966 and corresponding underrepresentation of Albanians are shown in Table 5.7.

Between March 1961 and March 1962, approximately 300 Kosovar Albanians were put on trial on charges of espionage, subversion, irredentism, and gun-running. Six years later, in October 1968, there were anti-Serb protests in Suva Reka, Prizren, and Peć, followed by violent demonstrations across Kosovo on 27 November 1968.[164] The November demonstrations left 37 injured (including 13 police) and one dead. In the wake of these events, Kosovo and Vojvodina were granted some additional prerogatives and the official name of the former was changed from Kosovo-Metohija to simply Kosovo, dropping the traditional Serbian portion of the name. Locals were also allowed to fly the Albanian flag below the Yugoslav one, and more Albanians were promoted to positions of responsibility. It was at this time that an independent University of Priština was established.

There was a new mood in Kosovo as Albanians started to display their hostility toward their Serbian neighbors openly, and, by March 1969, thousands of Serbs and Montenegrins had moved out of Kosovo, most of them professionals and specialists with higher education. Some Serbs now expressed concerns that Serbia was losing Kosovo. By the end of 1974, 58.2% of those employed in the social sector were Albanians, and by 1978 this figure had risen to 83%, at which point Serbs accounted for just 9.3% of those employed in the social sector.[165]

In 1973, Albanian nationalists started to disseminate separatist propaganda; behind this was the underground Revolutionary Movement of United Albania,

TABLE 5.7 Representation of Nationality Groups in the Security Organs in Kosovo, in comparison to the local population (1966) – *in %*

	State security	*Anti-crime dept.*	*Regular police*	*Population*
Serbs	58.33	50.34	60.80	23.5
Montenegrins	28.34	26.22	7.86	3.9
Albanians	13.33	23.44	31.29	64.9
Others			0.50	7.7

Source: Isabel Ströhle, *Aus den Ruinen der alten erschaffen wir die neue Welt! Herrschaftspraxis und Loyalitäten in Kosovo 1944–1974* (Munich: De Gruyter Oldenbourg, 2016), p. 206.

led by Adem Demaqi (1936–2018), who would spend 29 years behind bars for his activity on behalf of Kosovar Albanian self-determination. Various other secessionist groups were also operating during the 1970s. Student demonstrations in Priština in December 1974 resulted in the arrest of more than 100 Albanians. There were further demonstrations in March–April 1981, spreading across the entire province; the regime rushed in tanks and armoured personnel carriers and imposed a curfew. In the resulting clashes, as many as 1,000 persons were killed and about 1,000 injured.[166] Resistance continued for more than two weeks, and included the derailing of trains and arson at the local power station at Kosovo Polje. The riots contributed to a fresh exodus of Serbs and Montenegrins.

The golden age

In a 1998 publication, I highlighted the years 1974–80 as a brief "Golden Age" in Yugoslavia and indicated that it was especially pronounced in the cities of Belgrade, Zagreb, and Ljubljana. These were years of economic boom, in spite of the OPEC price hike in the wake of the October 1973 Arab-Israeli war. "Purchases of cars and televisions soared, telephones became customary, and young people started spending serious money on fashions."[167] Single young people in their twenties and thirties often continued to live with their parents, thus saving money for the commodities they wanted and other forms of self-gratification. This was an era of political and economic stability and may be dated from passage of the country's fourth constitution to the death of Tito in early May 1980.

Patrick Patterson employs the term "the Yugoslav Dream" to refer to that era and, by narrowing his focus to economics, sees this "dream" beginning in the 1960s.[168] Yet this consumer society which was emerging in socialist Yugoslavia had its limits. As I saw for myself during 1979–80, normal coffee could not be found in the shops of Belgrade (though it was available in the hotels and restaurants), oranges were available only in a small shop near the Ministry of Internal Affairs – its location there was surely a coincidence – bananas could not be found anywhere until one day when a shop near Vračar district suddenly obtained a supply, resulting in customers holding bags of bananas, streaming out in all directions, 50-watt, 75-watt, and 100-watt light bulbs were available only along the Croatian coast (where tourists visited) and probably Slovenia, and no cabbage could be found anywhere in town until the harvest came in, at which point there were huge piles of cabbage lying in the street in front of every shop. People living in Slovenia and northwest Croatia could drive to the Italian border town of Trieste to purchase coffee; not surprisingly, many shops (especially shops selling coffee) in Trieste had signs in both Slovenian and Croatian. The "Golden Age" was, thus, a time marked by shortages – though never of cigarettes, alcohol, and chocolate, which were always available in ample quantities; there were even shops selling little besides these three key items. More problematic than the persistent shortages of various staples, however, was the fact that this "good life", as Patterson calls it, "was inherently transient, since it was purchased with uncontrolled borrowing, which sent the Yugoslav foreign debt spiraling upwards."[169]

After Tito, Tito

Yugoslavia's fourth post-war constitution was passed in 1974, and was quasi-confederal in concept.[170] The Yugoslavs boasted that this constitution, drafted by Kardelj, was the longest constitution in the world and that it contained guarantees of the rights of citizens, among other things, to a clean environment. By now, the (partial) legitimation obtained through the Partisan struggle against Axis occupation was fading, as the old Partisan generation passed away. The claim to political legitimacy was, thus, increasingly based on the triadic concept: self-management, nonalignment, brotherhood and unity. The last of these referred to the harmony which was supposed to prevail among Yugoslavia's diverse peoples and was tied to the so-called "ethnic key", in practice a system of ethnic quotas throughout the political system.

More important was the aura of Tito, a man larger than life who was sometimes described as the country's only "Yugoslav" (although, actually, the 1981 census recorded the presence of 1,216,463 self-declared "Yugoslavs", many of them the offspring of ethnically mixed marriages). In an effort to protect the system after he would pass away, Tito put in place (in the late 1970s), mechanisms of collective leadership and rotation of cadres. After he died on 4 May 1980, the rotation at the center continued to function for another 10 years. The problem was that that was not where power lay: significant power had been devolved to the republics.

Tito's passing left Yugoslavia without a helmsman and his successors promoted the slogan "After Tito, Tito", as if he was somehow still present. For the first months after his death, the country's major newspapers regularly published photos of Tito meeting world leaders, consulting with his comrades, visiting ordinary citizens, giving speeches. From the newspapers, one might well imagine that Yugoslavia's "president without limitation of mandate" was still alive. With weakness at the center, there was a new freedom in the country – a freedom not founded on legal guarantees or even on well-established customs, but rather on the sudden weakness of the center. This weakness also benefited the republics, for better or worse.

There was a general recognition that both the economic system and the political system were dysfunctional. In response, the party appointed a commission chaired by Sergej Kraigher (1914–2001) to study the economic system and a commission chaired by Tihomir Vlaškalić (1923–1993) to study the political system. The Kraigher commission presented its report in April 1982, offering extensive recommendations for reform; the report was ignored – a clear sign of the weakness of the center and ability of the republics to ignore reports issued from the center. The Vlaškalić commission presented its report in December 1985, again with extensive and detailed recommendations for reform, this time in the political sphere; this too was ignored by the republic leaderships. Meanwhile, in October 1984, the Serbian party presented a draft reform program, calling for a strengthening of the federal government and curtailment of the powers of the republics and provinces. Croatia, Slovenia, Kosovo, and Vojvodina were all opposed. In fact, the federal institutions were remarkably weak. Between June 1986 and June 1988, the SFRY presidency adopted 322 acts and resolutions on specific policy matters; most of these were never carried out or respected. Only the resolutions dealing with the military and with security affairs were ever carried out.

Excluding Comrade Dolanc

In June 1978, Stane Dolanc (1925–1999), a conservative Slovene who had been elected to the Executive Committee of the LCY in 1968, was selected for a new post: Secretary of the Presidium (as the Executive Committee was now called). In July 1978, just one month later, Dolanc sought to reduce the 47-member Presidium by half (presumably to purge members who were less conservative than he was) and to establish a seven-member Political Bureau to be headed by himself and above the Presidium. As Pirjevec recounts, Vladimir Bakarić quickly rallied the old guard to block Dolanc and told the ambitious Slovene "that party elders knew perfectly well how Stalin had come to power [in the Soviet Union] after Lenin's death."[171] Apparently under pressure from Tito, Dolanc resigned his Secretaryship on 15 May 1979 but continued to wield enough influence that rumors persisted that, in spite of his resignation, he still aspired to become Tito's eventual successor. I was living in Belgrade from October 1979 to August 1980 and I can remember very clearly seeing open-air stalls set up downtown, piled high with copies of a Serbo-Croatian translation of Isaac Deutscher's *Stalin: A Political Biography*. It was common knowledge that this was intended as a warning about Dolanc, arranged by his political foes. But Dolanc was not a spent force and, by 1982, he had been installed as Minister of Internal Affairs until he was elected to the Yugoslav collective presidency in 1984, remaining there until his retirement in 1989.

Clamping down on opposition ideas

After Tito died, free-thinking intellectuals giving interviews to foreign journalists and circulating manuscripts not to the regime's fancy were put on trial and imprisoned. The first prominent intellectual to be arrested was Franjo Tudjman, a former Partisan colonel turned historian, who had previously spent a year in prison in 1972–73 for his criticism of the communist authorities and most likely also for his revision of the number of Serbs who lost their lives in fascist Croatia during the Second World War; indeed, during the Croatian Spring of 1970–71 Tudjman had published articles which Tito found offensive.[172] Now, in 1980, he was taken into custody once again, as were Marko Veselica and Vlado Gotovac, also known for defending Croatian interests as they perceived them, between 1980 and 1981. In Gotovac's case, an interview he had given to Swedish Television, in which he potrayed the situation in Croatia in unfavorable terms was considered punishable.[173] In 1980, Tudjman had given interviews to West German television and French radio – interviews in which he was highly critical of the Belgrade regime; Veselica was also giving interviews to foreign journalists. All three were tried, found guilty of hostile propaganda, and imprisoned; Tudjman served two years of a three-year prison sentence.[174]

In Serbia, the first publication to anger the post-Tito regime was a collection of poetry written by Gojko Djogo entitled *Vunena vremena* [Woolly Times]. Although it was clear enough that Djogo was satirizing dictatorship, the editors at the publishing house did not at first notice any reference to Yugoslavia. But there was a line in one of his poems referring to "the old rat from Dedinje." Once the editors at his publisher, Prosveta, belatedly noticed this line, they became alarmed, since Dedinje was the Belgrade suburb where Tito had lived. The book was withdrawn from distribution and Djogo was arrested, tried, and put in prison.[175]

Much better known, however, is the case of Vojislav Šešelj (b. 1954), who was teaching political science at the University of Sarajevo; Šešelj criticized Brano Miljuš, a colleague at the department, accusing him of having plagiarized about 40 pages of his master's thesis. Miljuš had powerful friends, who saw to it that Šešelj lost his job and was expelled from the League of Communists. Šešelj was later reinstated but demoted. He was arrested in mid-May 1984 after Stane Dolanc gave an interview to TV Belgrade, in which he criticized Šešelj's advocacy of the abolition of two of Yugoslavia's four republics (Montenegro and Bosnia-Herzegovina) and the withdrawal of recognition from allegedly artificial national groups (Bosnia's ethnic Muslims and Montenegrins). He received an eight-year prison sentence on 9 July 1984 to be served in Bosnia, and was adopted as a "prisoner of conscience" by Amnesty International; he was released only in March 1986.

In Bosnia-Herzegovina, the *cause célèbre* of the 1980s was the arrest of Alija Izetbegović (1925–2003) and 12 other persons in March 1983, culminating in an initially 14-year prison sentence for Izetbegović, of which he served just five years (1983–88). Like Tudjman, Izetbegović had spent time in prison previously – in his case in 1946–49 for his contribution to the journal *El-Hidaje* and on the charge of affiliation with the Young Muslim organization.[176] This time, on the strength of his *Islamic Declaration*,[177] finished in 1970 but not published in Yugoslavia, he and his co-defendants were put on trial for having "created a group for carrying out criminal acts [thereby presenting] a counterrevolutionary threat to [Yugoslavia's] social order and sending Yugoslavia's citizens beyond its borders to carry out hostile activity."[178] He was also accused of having sought to create a religiously homogeneous Bosnia-Herzegovina, a charge which implied a desire on his part either to exterminate non-Muslims or to expel them from Bosnia (unless, of course, they could be converted to Islam).

Izetbegović rejected the charges against him, denied that the purported group had ever existed, noted that he had never met five of his alleged co-conspirators, and pointed out that the original Bosnian-language version of his declaration existed in only six typed copies – a clear sign that it was not intended for a Yugoslav readership.[179] His hope was to see it published in Arabic, English, Turkish, and German translations; indeed, it had already been published in Kuwait in an Arabic translation with a print run of 100,000 copies, as well as in Pakistan, Malaysia, and Algeria. The importance of this trial lay in the fact that it gave Izetbegović a prominence which he might otherwise not yet have attained.

What the regime saw in these three intellectuals was that they were finding an audience for ideas which were either anti-Yugoslav (as in the cases of Tudjman and Šešelj) or implicitly anti-atheist (as in the case of Izetbegović's *Islamic Declaration*). The communists could not know, of course, that Tudjman and Izetbegović would later lead their respective republics or that Šešelj would set up a neo-Chetnik political party in 1989 and run for president of Serbia. But that was not the end of the political trials in the post-Tito transition. On the contrary, on 20 April 1984, police entered a private apartment in Belgrade, where 27 people had arrived to hear Milovan Djilas present a talk on problems of nationalism. The police seized books and manuscripts, arrested all 28 persons (thus, including Djilas), and beat several of them while they were in custody.[180] Six of them were ultimately put on trial with writer Miodrag Milić given a one-year sentence. Even though those put on trial were unknown outside Serbia, the Western press nonetheless reacted.

Three years earlier, following the provincial-wide protests across Kosovo, 232 Albanians, mainly teachers and students, were put on trial. By September 1981, all of them had been given prison sentences ranging from one to 15 years.[181] In 1982, Amnesty International published a list of nine Yugoslav writers, journalists, and academics who had been sent to prison on political charges. Among these was the aforementioned Adem Demaqi, author of a historical novel and an advocate of human rights, who had already spent 17 years in prison by 1982. As of September 1984, there were an estimated 500 persons in Yugoslav prisons because of their views; most of these were Croats and Albanians, typically accused of wanting to separate their ethnic homelands from the Yugoslav federation.[182]

The last high-profile political trial of the 1980s took place in Ljubljana in 1988 – but controversially the trial was held in Serbo-Croatian, instead of Slovenian, the official language of Slovenia. Four young Slovenes were brought to trial: Janez Janša (b. 1958), a journalist for the weekly magazine *Mladina;* David Tasić, another *Mladina* journalist; Franci Zavrl, *Mladina's* editor; and Sergeant Major Ivan Borštner. The reason for the trial was that Borštner had secretly taped a meeting on 29 March 1988 at which high-ranking representatives of the army met with certain members of the LCY Central Committee and urged that prominent Slovenian liberals be arrested and put on trial. It should be stressed that Milan Kučan (b. 1941), at that time Chairman of the League of Communists of Slovenia, protested vigorously against the army's proposal. At any rate, Borštner took the tape to *Mladina*, which published an article exposing the cabal. This led directly to the arrest of Janša and Borštner on 31 May, of Tasić on 4 June, and of Zavrl somewhat later. Their trial electrified the Slovenian public, which gathered on public squares waving the Slovenian flag. Although all four were found guilty on 27 June 1988, their sentences were relatively light, especially by communist standards: four years for Borštner, 18 months for Janša and Zavrl, and five months for Tasić.[183] Janša went on to become Slovenia's Minister of Defense and later PM for three nonconsecutive terms (2004–08, 2012–13, and 2020–22).

Meanwhile, Dobrica Ćosić (1921–2014), one of the most influential Serbian writers of his generation, had completed his four-part novel about Serbian suffering during World War One; entitled *Vreme smrti* [A Time of Death], it was published between 1972 and 1979 and would become, in the 1980s, a testament for the Serbian national reawakening. Between 1978 and 1983, it was published in four volumes by Harcourt Brace Jovanovich in an English translation prepared by Muriel Heppell. The spirit of Ćosić's great saga may be discerned already in volume 1, where he suggests that people would do many things for love (e.g., of country) but would be more highly motivated by hatred and ready to undertake *anything* when the opportunity arose to punish enemies who have hurt us.[184] There are striking portrayals of Serbs and Serbia in *Vreme smrti*, for example when Ćosić has the French envoy declare to Vukašin Katić, a Serbian liberal: "You are a people living not in space but in time and in spirit . . . In your spirit there is something eternal. You outlive your defeats."[185] Then there is the advice that the Russian envoy, Prince Trubetskoy, offered to Serbian PM Nikola Pašić (in Ćosić's account) in hopes of persuading him to agree to allow Bulgaria to annex Macedonia. "You have to choose between Macedonia and the interests of all Southern Slavs," Ćosić has the Russian prince tell Pašić, to which the latter replies, "In that case, we shall choose Macedonia."[186] And throughout the novel, there is the theme that Serbia faced the Central Powers (Germany, Austria-Hungary, Bulgaria, and Turkey) alone and that England and France were nothing more than nominal allies: "The English are our open enemies," he has Katić complain.[187]

In 1968, Ćosić burned his bridges with the Titoist regime, resigning his membership in the LCY in July of that year. He was, as Nicholas Miller recounts, "a true believer"– just not in Tito's vision – and "an idealist". Having resigned previously from the Serbian Writers' Union, Ćosić chose the path of nonconformity, even dissent.[188] Yet, in spite of his open break with Titoism, unlike Djogo, he was not put on trial or sent to prison. Although his prestige and personal connections in high places certainly provide part of the explanation, more important were the fact that the nationalist temper was rising in Serbia and the fact that he was situated to become a leading figure in the ensuing Serbian national movement.[189]

Dysfunctions in the system

Within less than three years of Tito's death, various senior politicians were expressing concern that Yugoslavia was in deep crisis. For example, Stipe Šuvar, a high-ranking Croatian functionary, offered his diagnosis of Yugoslavia's multiple ailments, suggesting that the country had sunk into a multifaceted political, economic, cultural, and moral crisis.[190] The following year, in October 1983, Slovenian historian Dušan Biber "told a group of historians meeting in Zagreb that if current trends continue[d], 'we will turn into a second Lebanon.'"[191] Then, on 10 November 1984, on the initiative of Dobrica Ćosić, a Committee for the Defense of Freedom of Thought and Expression was formed in Belgrade. Later, on 25 November 1987, twenty prominent public figures – among them, Kosta Čavoški, Ljubomir Tadić, Mihailo Marković, Vojislav Koštunica, Matija Bečković, and of course Dobrica Ćosić – signed a public petition addressed to the Federal Assembly as well as to the SFRY public. In this petition, the signatories charged that the system was marked by "the absence of elementary political democracy" leading to "frequent failures in the capacity of the legal system to function effectively, [to] lack of respect for human and civil rights, . . . and to a general collapse of public morality."[192] The petition included several demands, including for the introduction of direct and secret elections to all representative bodies at all levels, abolition of the LCY's power monopoly, constitutional guarantees for press freedom, recognition of the right to establish independent labor unions (with the right to go on strike), and an independent judiciary.[193]

Meanwhile, the Yugoslav economy was in serious trouble, with the country's foreign debt to the West exceeding $20 billion by 1983, foreign currency reserves largely depleted, and 860,000 persons jobless in 1982, according to OECD figures.[194] By the later 1980s, 25% of Yugoslavs were living below the povery line and, as of 1991, 15% of Yugoslavs were unemployed.[195] There were also shortages and, in one instance, involving Titograd, local would-be shoppers went on a looting spree when sundry staples were in short supply or simply unavailable. Moreover, by the early 1980s, party officials openly admitted that self-management had never really functioned as it was supposed to and, after the Soviet invasion of Afghanistan – a member-state of the Nonaligned Movement – at the end of December 1979, some Yugoslavs questioned the utility of nonalignment. Finally, as for brotherhood and unity – that too was shredding.

Then there was the "national question" *(nacionalno pitanje)*, as the communists called the persistent interethnic resentments, fears, and sometimes hatreds afflicting this country in which every nationality group was in a numerical minority. The statistics for the ethnic composition as recorded in socialist Yugoslavia's last census are shown in Table 5.8.

There were tensions between Serbs and Slovenes, between Serbs and Croats in Croatia, between Serbs and Albanians in Kosovo, and between all three nationality groups in Bosnia-Herzegovina, though above all between Serbs and non-Serbs and latent tensions between Macedonians and Albanians in Macedonia. In 1970–71, the prospect had opened for the country to evolve in a different direction from that in which it ultimately moved. Liberal politicians were in charge of the party organizations in Serbia, Croatia, Slovenia, and Macedonia and offered a liberal, albeit non-Titoist vision of the future. Tito decided to remove the liberals and, with this, as I warned in 1984,

> . . . the party condemned a unique reform experiment and cut off the system's best chance for self-correction. The immediate result was a deepened alienation from the party [on the part] of the people, especially in Croatia, Bosnia, and Kosovo, and a deepening of distrust between Serbs and

TABLE 5.8 Population of Yugoslavia by National Group (1981)

National group	Number	Per cent
Serbs	8,136,578	36.3
Croats	4,428,135	19.7
Ethnic Muslims	2,000,034	8.9
Slovenes	1,753,605	7.8
Albanians	1,731,252	7.7
Macedonians	1,341,420	6.0
"Yugoslavs"	1,216,463	5.4
Montenegrins	577,298	2.6
Hungarians	426,865	1.9
TOTAL (including other categories not listed above):	22,418,331	100.00

Source: *Statistički calendar Jugoslavije 1982* (Belgrade : Savezni zavod za statistiku, February 1982), p. 37.

non-Serbs, especially Croats and Albanians. As a result of the party's short-sightedness in that crisis, it is probably only a matter of time before another bloodbath occurs between Serbs and Croats.[196]

Popular culture/subculture in the 1980s (and beyond) – mainstream, teen-, & subcultural

From the standpoint of the communists, distinctions between hard rock, heavy metal, punk, and New Wave were unimportant. The communists thought in terms of whether a band was *problematic* (such as the Slovenian industrial band Laibach or, at times, the Sarajevo band Zabranjeno pušenje – Smoking Forbidden[197]), *friendly*, best illustrated by the pro-Tito song "Yugoslavia" sung by the Sarajevo group Indexi (Indeksi) and Kornell Kovach's early song "People's Government",[198] or *politically irrelevant*, such as the Sarajevo bands Crvena jabuka (Red Apple) and Plavi orkestar (Blue Orchestra).

From the standpoint of the musicians and the audiences, however, different categories make more sense. Here we can distinguish between: *mainstream* groups such as the Sarajevo group Bijelo dugme (White Button), sometimes called "the Beatles of Yugoslavia"[199] and the Macedonian group Leb i Sol (Bread and Salt); *teen-oriented* bands such as the aforementioned Crvena jabuka and Plavi orkestar; *New Wave* bands such as the legendary band Azra of Zagreb or the *progressive rock* band Indeksi; and *punk* bands, such as Pankrti (Bastards) of Ljubljana and Termiti (Termites) of Rijeka.

New Wave and punk may be considered *subcultures*, in the sense that the fans listened to distinctive music and exhibited "a set of behaviours and beliefs, [and] culture, which . . . differentiate[d] them from the larger culture to which they belong[ed]."[200] Insofar as subcultures serve to set off certain groups from the rest of society and may be distinguished by characteristic clothing, hair styles, and make-up one may say that the stronger the subculture, the greater the functional tension it will generate with mainstream culture and, as Merton has noted, "Functional tensions . . . constitute a strong driving force for change."[201]

Benjamin Perasović distinguishes among three forms of subculture: the criminal underground; the subculture of withdrawal, typically associated with the use of illegal drugs; and conflict subculture – or, as I prefer to cal lit, dissident subculture – challenging the political and social establishment.[202] Obviously, Yugoslav youth in the 1980s were to some extent associated with the third type of subculture. But it should immediately be underlined that their dissidence was rarely political; it consisted primarily in choice of music and in distinctive attire, ornaments (such as metal rings in their lips), style of makeup (such as black fingernail polish), special slang, even posture, gestures, and facial expressions.[203] Even so, when I met with Bijelo dugme's Goran Bregović in September 1989, he offered his view that the rock scene

> . . . in communist countries has much more importance than rock 'n' roll in the West. We can't have any alternative parties or any alternative organized politics. So there are not too many places where you can gather large groups of people and communicate ideas which are not official. Rock 'n' roll is one of the most important vehicles for helping people in communist countries to think in a different way.[204]

A subculture is defined primarily by the medium through which its members associate with each other and realize their collective identity. In this section, my concern is above all with the music subculture, though I will have something to say toward the end of this section also about the graffiti subculture and the subculture that grew primarily but not solely in Serbia in the 1980s around clairvoyance, faith healing, and other forms of what may be called magic. Where music was concerned, the three most important subcultures (as already indicated) were those associated with heavy metal, New Wave, and punk. But by the 1980s, heavy metal was in decline among young people, who were increasingly drawn to the New Wave and punk milieux. Research conducted in Pula found that parents did not like their adolescents to gravitate to punk, but often had no problem with their attending heavy metal concerts, since heavy metal was a "language" at least some of the parents could understand.[205]

The most popular New Wave bands in Yugoslavia were: the Belgrade bands Idoli, Šarlo akrobata, and Električni Orgazam; and the Zagreb bands Prljavo kazalište, Azra, Film, and Haustor. New Wave was, in the first place, an urban phenomenon; although Belgrade, Zagreb, and Sarajevo were the main centers for New Wave rock, there were also New Wave bands performing in other cities, notably: the Novi Sad bands Luna and La Strada; the Slovenian bands Buldožer and Borghesia (both from Ljubljana) and Lačni Franz (from Maribor); as well as Laki pingvini (Belgrade) and Boa (Zagreb). Jelena Božilović includes the Slovenian band Laibach among New Wave bands, but I prefer to think of this industrial-art rock-satirical-pop fascist-later experimental electronic musical ensemble as *sui generis* (although early Laibach bears a certain resemblance to the German band Rammstein).[206] Božilović has suggested that New Wave may be understood "as a subcultural and urban phenomenon which openly confronted the parental and socialist culture. New Wave represent[ed] a phenomenon through whose music style the whole generation of young people [strove] to create their own identity."[207] In other words, New Wave was politically not entirely irrelevant. Indeed, rock critic Petar Popović believed that "With their songs and acumen, Indexi gathered the power to change people's affinities and habits."[208] On this point, Prljavo kazalište's song, "Modern Girl", hints at social change: "She works in a factory, doesn't dream the same as other women/She dreams of a new world . . ."[209]

Bijelo dugme, in its day arguably the most influential rock band in Yugoslavia, emerged out of New Wave. Based in Sarajevo, Bijelo dugme fashioned its own hard rock style (while innovating what has been called "pastirski rok" (shepherd's rock) early in its career) and proved to be one of the more politically conscious groups in socialist Yugoslavia, singing a love song in Albanian following the riots by Kosovar Albanians in spring 1981: it was Bijelo dugme's message of empathy and solidarity. Later, in 1986, the band brought out the song "Spit and Sing, My Yugoslavia", with its warning that the country risked heading to a sanguinary break-up.[210]

In the first half of the 1980s, active punk bands included: the Ljubljana bands Pankrti (led by Peter Lovšin), Lublanski psi (Ljubljana dogs), Otroci socializma (Children of Communism), and Niet (No); Belgrade bands Totalna destrucija, Berliner Strasse (also known as Urbana Gerila), and Radnička kontrola (Workers' Control); the Rijeka bands Paraf and Termiti; and the Pula bands Problemi and KUD Idijoti – among others.[211] In terms of messaging, Yugoslav punk bands were diverse, but found a common voice in anti-fascism, anti-authoritarianism, and opposition to war. As Vesna Zaimović has noted, the New Primitives, consisting of Zabranjeno pušenje, led by Nele Karajlić (to use his stage name) and Elvis J. Kurtović and the Meteors were "a Sarajevo version of the punk movement, which was not primarily an attack on the establishment but rather a self-ironic response to the artistic pretentiousness of new wave, and the condescending way in which Sarajevan and Bosnian culture was sometimes perceived and interpreted in Yugoslavia's culture at large."[212] Where fans of punk were concerned, Ines Prica distinguishes between real punks, who shared a common hostility to government and politics, and "fashion punks" who liked to dress up in punk style and go to punk concerts, but did not share the beliefs and values of "real punks".[213]

Inevitably, there were also bands that crossed boundaries, such as the Belgrade bands Bajaga i instruktori, formed in 1984, and Partibrejkers, formed in 1982, as well as the Novi Sad band Pekinška patka (Peking Duck), playing both New Wave and punk. And there were hard rock bands such as Riblja čorba (Fish Stew), a Belgrade band led by Bora Đorđević. In any event, the rock musicians' and rock fans' first love was music – whether New Wave, punk rock, industrial rock, or classic hard rock. And yet, there were messages – some conveyed by the musicians' clothing, long hair, and presentation, and some indeed by their lyrics. Years later, sociologist and former member of Pankrti Gregor Tomc recalled: "We played rock music that had certain subversive connotations – above all because the authorities were politically paranoid."[214]

Laibach, an avant-garde group formed in the Slovenian mining town of Trbovlje in 1980, was and is in a class by itself, not only because its fascist-style outfits (sometimes adorned with the Malevich cross) and, in the early years, usually strident performances misled some people into supposing that the band was committed to some form of neo-Nazism, but also because it is the only band to emerge from socialist Yugoslavia to have enjoyed considerable commercial success outside the region which once composed Yugoslavia. Fans, critics, and innocent by-standers could be excused for misunderstanding the intentions of Laibach's members. Laibach was and is an art group working across genres and, especially in the early years, playing with fascist motifs not as politics but as an art form and, if anything, to expose the dead-end nature of that ideology. In 1983, Laibach issued a 10-point manifesto, of which excerpts follow:

1. Laibach works as a team (the collective spirit), according to the model of industrial production and totalitarianism, which means that the individual does not speak; the organization does. Our work is industrial, our language political . . ..
4. . . . Laibach adopts the organizational system of industrial production and the identification with ideology as its work method. In accordance with this, each member personally rejects his individuality . . ..
7. Laibach excludes any evolution of [an] original idea . . ..
8. Laibach practises provocation on the revolted state of the alienated consciousness (which must necessarily find itself an enemy) and unites warriors and opponents into an expression of a static totalitarian scream. *It acts as a creative illusion of strict institutionalism, as a social theatre of popular culture, and communicates only through non-communication* . . ..
10. Laibach is the knowledge of the universality of the moment . . .[215]

Of course, by admitting, even stressing, that what Laibach was presenting on stage and in its recordings was "a creative illusion . . . as a social theatre of popular culture," Laibach gave the game away. And further, if Laibach "communicates only through non-communication," then it follows that the texts of Laibach songs are not to be treated as communication. Moreover, after Laibach had established itself, the band's intentions, its motives were, if anything, commercially motivated and certainly not pro-fascist.

But Merton warned, in his classic work, *Social Theory and Social Structure*, that functions should not be identified with motives or effects with intentions.[216] What, then, were the functions of the rock subcultures in 1980s Yugoslavia? The principal manifest functions, as is obvious, was to bring enchantment into young people's daily lives, providing venues for them to have a good time and allowing them, as Ines Prica has suggested, to imagine "magical solutions" to personal and social problems.[217] Other manifest functions included allowing messages that, by means of hints, allegories, metaphors, and cloaked meaning, could expand the possibilities for freedom of expression. And, of course, rock concerts afforded an opportunity for young people to meet their friends in a pleasurable atmosphere.

Were there any latent functions? Certainly, though it is in the nature of latent functions that they are not as obvious as manifest, intended functions, at least where the participants are concerned. But here I suggest that Petar Popović's insight into the effects of Indexi concerts may be generalized to suggest that the rock subcultures of socialist Yugoslavia had the latent effect of "chang[ing] people's affinities and habits" and thus, in some ways, also their values, their hopes, and, at least for some, their expectations.

I mentioned at the outset of this section, that I would have a few words also about graffiti and the paranormal in the Yugoslav context. Graffiti has a long tradition, with examples having been found in ancient Greece, on the ruins of Pompeii,[218] and on the external walls of medieval cathedrals, among other places. Graffiti, which involves written messages or symbols sometimes associated with a specific gang or group of persons, should be distinguished from street art, in which often huge paintings are committed to public walls. While the former is typically an individual creation, and in any event not art, the latter is clearly an art form and can include members of the local community, directly or indirectly, in a joint project. In some countries, such as the United States and Australia, laws have been passed declaring graffiti to be illegal and mandating that graffiti be erased or covered over as quickly as practical, thus imposing "landscape control and surveillance."[219] But, as Gill Valentine and his collaborators have pointed out,

> the space of the street is often the only autonomous space that young people are able to carve out for themselves and . . . hanging around, larking about, on the streets, in parks and shopping malls, is one form of youth resistance (conscious and unconscious) to adult power.[220]

To the extent that young people want to send a message – in the spirit of agitation (short messages) rather than propaganda (calculated argument), to use vocabulary drawn from communist jargon – public walls are the perfect choice: they are free, they are easily accessible to the graffiti writer, they are highly visible, and they are anonymous (unless, of course, they are signed). But, from the standpoint of the authorities, whether in parliamentary democracies or in authoritarian systems, "Graffiti art disrupts the coherence of common-sense aesthetics. It violates the urban habitus."[221] Graffiti may even strike observers as a form of aggression, an invasion of the public space.

In the Yugoslav region (I use this expression because my memories of graffiti date from the 1990s), there were broadly speaking four kinds of graffiti: personal statements, including declarations of love; sports-related graffiti; rock-related graffiti; and political graffiti. The first of these need not detain us but, for the second, I recall both in the 1990s and in the early 2000s repeatedly seeing the inscription "BBB" on public walls in Zagreb. The acronym refers to the Bad Blue

Boys, as fans of the local football team refer to themselves (in English). Favorite rock bands are also frequently celebrated on public walls and I can recall seeing graffiti in downtown Ljubljana years ago celebrating the Leningrad Cowboys, a Finnish rock group known for performing covers on such songs as "American Woman" and "Those were the days". Finally, there are political graffiti and, from what I have seen, it appears that young persons resorting to graffiti do so, often, to express or reject extremist views, rather than to espouse anodyne views such as "Let's fight pollution together!" or "Let's get rid of street crime!" I recall that, in 1997, driving along part of the Croatian coast, we came to a town with the letters "NDH" scrawled in full view, referring to the Nezavisna Država Hrvatska ("Independent State of Croatia" but not independent but a satellite of the Third Reich during its brief existence, 1941–45). Since this was two years after the end of Croatia's war for survival (the Domovinski Rat, or Homeland War, as the Croats called it), it seems clear that the war provoked deep hatred of Serbs among some Croats, hatred which was not dying down quickly. Nonetheless, some of these graffiti had appeared as early as 1990, as Serb-Croat tensions heated up. And finally, visiting Belgrade at some point after 2003, I came across a wall somewhere downtown with two rival messages. The first message, written in Cyrillic, affirmed simply "Šešelj – junak" [Šešelj – hero]. This was crossed out and a second message, written in Serbia's Latin alphabet, affirmed, on the contrary, "Šešelj – zločinac" [Šešelj – criminal]. The graffiti cited here were not intended to change anyone's mind about the topics that inspired them. "BBB" would not have been expected to recruit more football fans; nor would emblazoning "Leningrad cowboys" in downtown Ljubljana be likely to increase attendance at that band's wildly popular concerts. Rather, these figure merely as explanations of the writer's tastes. The same holds true for political graffiti.

Finally, a few words about the paranormal in Milošević's Serbia. Folk beliefs about magic and the paranormal have a long history in the lands of the South Slavs but, according to Srdjan Garčević, belief in magic and the paranormal escalated rapidly after the death of Tito in 1980 and, more particularly – where Serbia was concerned – in the years 1987–2000 when Milošević was at the helm of power. In connection with this, Garčević mentions the alleged regular appearance to a group of children in the Herzegovinan town of Medjugorje beginning in 1981.[222] When I visited Medjugorje in 2007, I saw the main street festooned with Croatian flags – a clear sign that the apparition was not only a Catholic phenomenon but also a Croatian one. It soon turned out that Serbia was the epicenter of the paranormal. In the late 1980s and into the early 1990s, there was a proliferation of clairvoyants, seers, and healers turning up in Serbia, such as Allan Chumak, a Russian faith-healer, and Vangeliya Dimitrova (better known as Baba Vanga), the blind Bulgarian prophet.[223] It was also now, at the height of Milošević's power, that a transvestite called Kleopatra, who had started her career as a folk singer, began telling fortunes, calling herself the "queen of clairvoyants".[224] Then, once Milošević was removed from power, most of the magic mania evaporated and interest in the paranormal subsided.

What was it about Milošević's reign that was conducive to sparking interest in the paranormal? Why was it precisely there, in Serbia, where nationalism was first spiking, that some Serbs found magic alluring or, to put it differently, that they hoped for magical solutions? What researchers into reported apparitions of the Virgin Mary – whether at Fatima or Guadalupe or Marpingen or Medjugorje or Ukraine in the 1950s – have discovered is that, when a society experiences severe stress and when hope in mundane solutions disappears, the Virgin Mary appears – or is reported to appear – to save people from despair, to give them hope. Or again, when intense nationalism winds a society up so that people believe that they are threatened by enemies (whether the threat is real or not) and the culture becomes pocked with paranoid memes, once again magic and the paranormal can offer solace and reassurance – hope revived. The paranormal, thus, figures as the ultimate form of escapism.

What the people of Serbia (and, for that matter, of Socialist Yugoslavia) had hoped for was to survive the country's years of crisis and break through the borders of the limits of what had been possible up to then and to build a new world, entering new time. For a long time, Yugoslavs had placed their hopes in the successful construction of what Armin Medosch called "dreamworlds of cybernetic socialism".[225] Based on their study of cultural transformations in Ljubljana in the 1980s, Aleš Erjavec and Marina Gržinić concluded that "[w]hat the alternative scene brought about was precisely the fight for a new type of state – instead of the fight 'against the state'."[226] The Slovene rock group Buldožer may have been glimpsing this vision with the song "New Time":

Comrades! (the group sang)
Our work assignment
in the future transition:
We guard the borders of possibility.

Comrades and lady comrades!
Our mutual wish
[is] to take a step forward
in a new light

[into] new, new, new time
in gradual growth
in years of crisis
We will again prove [ourselves]
if that is necessary.[227]

The rise of Milošević and the end of socialist Yugoslavia

In September 1986, Yugoslavia was shaken by a political earthquake when the Belgrade daily *Večernje novosti* published extracts from a leaked and supposedly unfinished Memorandum (always capitalized) drawn up by writers associated with the Serbian Academy of Sciences and Art. Although more than a dozen writers collaborated in the preparation of this document, the main authors were novelist Antonije Isaković, historian Vasilje Krestić, economist Kosta Mihajlović, and former *Praxis* collaborator Mihailo Marković. What they crafted was a litany of complaints and accusations, alleging, among other things: that Serbs in Kosovo were victims of an ongoing genocide at the hands of local Albanian civilians; that the region which should have belonged to Serbia was divided after World War Two to create the allegedly artificial republics of Macedonia and Montenegro; that the Serbs in Croatia were in great danger, reminiscent of the darkest days of the Second World War; that the establishment of Kosovo first as an autonomous region and later as a province was a blow against Serbian sovereignty; and that Serbs were underrepresented in the LCY Central Committee. Near the end of this Memorandum, the authors seemed to be quivering with fear and profound resentment as they charged:

> Under the influence of the ruling ideology, the cultural heritage of the Serbian people is being alienated, usurped, invalidated, neglected, or wasted; their language is being suppressed and the Cyrillic alphabet is vanishing . . .. No other Yugoslav nation has been so rudely denied its cultural and spiritual integrity as the Serbian people. No literary and artistic heritage has been so routed, pillaged, and plundered as the Serbian one.[228]

Overnight, this inflammatory document, which betrayed nothing but scorn for the Tito-era principle of brotherhood and unity, changed the entire political landscape. Soon self-pitying songs were being performed, a perfume was manufactured in a bottle shaped by a grenade, and conversations in the local *kafane* found little time for anything besides lamentations about alleged Serbian suffering. No matter that the Memorandum's claims were both blatantly false and classically paranoid, political figures now felt the need to either condemn the Memorandum (as Milošević, Serbia's future president, did at the time[229]) or embrace its message as a program for a campaign of revenge against non-Serbs.

In the wake of the publication of this self-pitying manifesto, paranoia raged in the Serbian press, with claims: that, at the time the country was threatened by Soviet invasion, factories were moved from the plains of Serbia to areas protected by mountains in other republics not to keep them from being seized by the Soviets but to weaken Serbia; that Serbian children in Bosnia-Herzegovina were being poisoned by Muslim physicians; and that more than a million persons, mostly Serbs, had died at the Jasenovac camps during the Second World War (whereas, as already noted, the total number of dead of all nationalities as a result of the war and extermination came to a little over one million).[230] It was under the influence of this frenzy that Milošević, an opportunist at heart, picked up the nationalist banner and initiated preparations for war.

Slobodan Milošević (born on 29 August 1941 in Požarevac, eastern Serbia) entered politics in 1984 as head of the Belgrade city committee, after earning a law degree at the University of Belgrade and serving as general director of Tehnogas and as president of Beobanka, a large banking concern.[231] In May 1986, his friend Ivan Stambolić (1936–2000) vacated his seat as chair of the CC LC Serbia to become president of Serbia; he proposed Milošević to inherit his seat as CC chair. Not quite a year later – on 24 April 1987 – Milošević visited Kosovo, meeting with about 300 restless Serbs. Some 15,000 Serbs and Montenegrins showed up and tried to get into the hall. Police blocked their way and started to beat them. Then, in a dramatic gesture which would be cited and discussed for years thereafter, Milošević raised his hand to direct the police to stop and then told the Serbs, "No one will ever beat you again!"[232] The Serbs and Montenegrins now were allowed in – as many as there was room for – and Milošević stayed there through the night, listening to their complaints and talking with them for 14 hours. He heard allegations that Albanian men had been raping Serbian women, that they were injuring Serb-owned cattle, and that Albanians were driving Serbs out of Kosovo. With this, Milošević had gained the spotlight, and emerged from that meeting energized.

Five months later, at the Eighth Plenum of the CC LC Serbia (23–24 September 1987), Milošević orchestrated the stripping of his erstwhile friend Stambolić of power, leaving him in office as a lame duck until his eventual dismissal from office three months later. Milošević, however, would not assume the post of president of Serbia until May 1989. What happened at the Eighth Plenum of the Serbian party was a *putsch*, and contrary to party rules (in other words, it was illegal). Branko Mamula, the SFRY Minister of Defense from May 1982 to May 1988, was troubled and contacted the leaderships in Slovenia, Croatia, and Bosnia-Herzegovina to see if they wanted to take any steps to rein in Milošević, or even to remove him from office. But these leaderships were too self-absorbed and did not consider the matter sufficiently important to be worthy of their time.

Milošević hoped ideally to be a new Tito and to bring all of Yugoslavia under his authority. In pursuit of that goal, he relied on mobs organized by the Committee for the Protection of Kosovar Serbs and Montenegrins, headed by Miroslav Šolević. In July 1988, there were mass rallies of Serbs in Kosovo, demanding the abrogation of the autonomy of Kosovo and Vojvodina. This was followed, in October, by demonstrations on the streets of Novi Sad, the capital of Vojvodina. An estimated 100,000 persons took part in those demonstrations, carrying portraits of Milošević, Tito, Soviet leader Lenin, and Ivo Lola Ribar, a Yugoslav communist who had been killed during World War Two. The leadership of Vojvodina felt intimidated and resigned, allowing Milošević to install his own people.

There was renewed pressure in Kosovo the following month. This brought about the resignation of the popular Azem Vllasi (born in 1948) from the provincial leadership; Milošević now installed Rahman Morina as his viceroy in Kosovo. On 11 January 1989, there was an outbreak of renewed, orchestrated unrest in Podgorica, the capital of Montenegro (after demonstrations the previous year). Starting with 15,000 demonstrations, the protest swelled to 50,000 the following day and, as had happened in Vojvodina and Kosovo, the entire leadership resigned. Again, Milošević installed his own people in power. With this, Milošević controlled four of the eight federal units of Yugoslavia. Back in Kosovo, Albanian miners engaged in a protest strike at the Trepča mine; 15,000 JNA troops were sent to the province in response. At this point, the Slovenian Writers' Association took up Kosovo's cause and protested Serbian policy in Kosovo. In response, protest meetings were held across Serbia and Montenegro, objecting to the Slovenes' protest. On 28 February 1989, the Serbian Writers' Association broke off relations with its Slovenian counterpart. This conflict between the writers' associations quickly escalated to the level of the republic leaderships of Slovenia and Serbia.

In February 1989, the Serbian Assembly adopted a series of amendments to its constitution to curtail the autonomy of the two provinces. The Assembly of Kosovo was obliged to endorse the amendments; the police met with the members of that body individually before the vote, in order to put pressure on them to vote "correctly". On 23 March 1989, the Kosovar Assembly endorsed the amendments, by a vote of 168 to 10, with two abstentions. After this, the entire province was engulfed in mass protests of up to 10,000 people at a time. Paramilitary forces were rushed into Kosovo, tanks patrolled the streets in several towns, and violent clashes took place between local Albanians and Serbian security forces throughout the rest of 1989 and most of 1990.

28 June 1989 was, of course, the 600th anniversary of the Battle of Kosovo, which Serb myth-makers had turned into a metaphor for the crucifixion of Serbia. With pressure and encouragement from the Serbian regime as well as from the Patriarch of the Serbian Orthodox Church, Serbian society rallied, as if returning to the battle itself. Special songs were composed, with one of them, "Vidovdan" [St. Vitus Day], composed by Milutin Popović-Zahar, attaining something like a status as "the second Serbian anthem."[233] The song celebrated the centrality of Kosovo to Serbia's sense of identity and spiritual well-being. Then there was the ambitious film *The Battle of Kosovo* [Boj na Kosovu], directed by Zdravko Šotra. In spite of various glitches, including a red Coca-Cola truck being visible in the background behind the staged battle and some of the extras who were lying as if dead, wearing tracksuits and jeans, the film nonetheless contributed to evoking Serb nationalist emotions.[234]

The climax of the commemorations came on 28 June 1989, when between 600,000 and two million persons assembled at Gazimestan, the memorial site near the field where the battle took place, some of them arriving on horseback or in horse-drawn carriages, while many were bused to the location. Leading representatives of the Serbian Church (including Patriarch German), the Yugoslav People's Army, and of course the LCY were seated near the stage when a helicopter appeared overhead, bearing Milošević, the new knez, who landed from the sky like a god. Once safely on the ground Milošević spoke to those who had come to think about what the battle meant for Serbs and what it meant to be a Serb. In a provocative passage, Milošević told them,

> Six centuries ago, Serbia heroically defended itself in the Kosovo Field, but it also defended Europe. At that time, Serbia was the bastion that defended

European culture, religion, and European society in general. Six centuries later, we are now once again . . . engaged in battles . . . They are not armed battles, although such things cannot yet be ruled out.[235]

With this implied threat, Milošević announced that he was already foreseeing a war between Serbia and unnamed other Yugoslav republics. Croatia and Bosnia-Herzegovina were most obviously potential targets.

Three months later, in September 1989 the Assembly of the Republic of Slovenia published a series of draft amendments to the Slovenian constitution, asserting Slovenia's right of secession, declaring that only the Slovenian Assembly could introduce a state of emergency in Slovenia, and proscribing the deployment of military forces in Slovenia except with the express consent and authorization of the Slovenian Assembly.[236] Serbian newspapers criticized the amendments, calling them "destabilizing". Šolević's committee now declared its intention to bring between 30,000 and 40,000 Serbs and Montenegrins to Ljubljana for a protest rally on 1 December 1989, in order to explain the "real" situation in Kosovo to Slovenes. The Slovenian government decided that this would constitute an act of war[237] ; first, the Slovenian government asked the SFRY presidency to ban the proposed meeting, but Milošević controlled four of the eight votes on the presidency and so there was no ban. The flaw in Šolević's plan was that he intended to bring his protesters to Ljubljana by train. So, when the Slovenian and Croatian railway unions stopped the trains carrying the protesters and turned them back, the plan was foiled. The Socialist Alliance of Working People of Serbia now cut its ties with its Slovenian counterpart and called on Serbian enterprises to cut all cooperative links with Slovenia. Within two weeks, Serbian enterprises had canceled contracts with 98 Slovenian enterprises; in economic terms, this was an act of war.

Then came the Fourteenth "Extraordinary" Congress of the LCY 20–22 January 1990, which collapsed in disarray when the Slovenian and Croatian delegations walked out. Twelve days later, the LC Slovenia pulled out of the LCY and renamed itself the Party of Democratic Renewal.[238] Subsequently, the Slovenian Assembly announced that it was terminating payments to the fund to support the underdeveloped republics and the province of Kosovo, and reduced its contribution to the federal budget by 15%. Spring 1990 saw free elections in Slovenia and Croatia. The anti-communist DEMOS coalition won in Slovenia in April, and Lojze Peterle (a Christian Democrat) became prime minister, remaining in office until April 1992. In Croatia, the Croatian Democratic Union (HDZ) formed by Franjo Tudjman won the election in May, and Tudjman became president of Croatia. Between May 1990 and June 1991, the country slid toward war. In a preliminary move, the JNA confiscated the weapons of the territorial militias in Croatia and Bosnia-Herzegovina, and about 70% of the weaponry which had been assigned to the territorial militia in Slovenia[239] ; to compensate for this illegal confiscation, Slovenia and Croatia began to smuggle in weapons from abroad (in the Croatian case, from Hungary). Meanwhile, the JNA delivered weapons, illegally, to newly established Serb militias in Croatia and Bosnia-Herzegovina, training the Serb militiamen.[240]

In July 1990, Croatian Serbs set up a Serbian National Council (again, an illegal move) and, during August-September 1990, conducted an illegal referendum, on the basis of which they declared autonomy. This action preceded Croatia's declaration of independence and therefore cannot be considered a response to Croatia's declaration of independence. That same month – specifically, on 28 September 1990 – the Serbian Assembly passed a new constitution, declaring the Serbian president (Milošević) commander-in-chief of the armed forces: this was contrary to the provisions of the federal constitution and therefore signified, in strictly legal terms, the secession of Serbia from Yugoslavia (nine months before Slovenia and Croatia would leave the federation).

During these months, the JNA retired a number of Slovenian and Croatian senior officers, promoting Serbs to take their place.[241] The JNA also dismantled a number of arms factories in Bosnia-Herzegovina, moving the parts out of the republic and reassembling them in Serbia. All of this suggested that war was imminent. Then, in November 1990, Slovenia, Vojvodina, Croatia, and Kosovo announced that they would make no further tax payments to the federation.[242] The following month, Milošević arranged for the Bank of Yugoslavia to grant Serbia a "loan" of $1.8 billion, effectively breaking the budget. In reply, the Slovenian and Croatian governments announced that they would not recognize any further debts incurred by the federal government. By this point, the federal government was functioning in the red and had to let 2,700 federal officials go.[243]

A series of summit meetings involving the leaders of the six republics during the early months of 1991 got nowhere and, by March 1991, Slovenia, Croatia, and Serbia had all organized military units not under federal command, although those in Croatia were technically police units. In late 1990, a referendum on independence held in Slovenia produced the result that 88% of Slovenes voted for independence. A parallel referendum held in Croatia the following May showed that 94.3% of Croats favored independence. It was also in May that the supposedly agreed scheme for rotating the chairmanship of the SFRY collective presidency broke down. Borisav Jović, the Serbian representative on that body, was supposed to relinquish the chairmanship on 15 May so that Stipe Mesić, the Croatian delegate, could assume that role. Instead, Jović conspired with the Montenegrin, Vojvodinan, and Kosovar delegates – all controlled by Milošević by then – to block the rotation.[244]

The summit meetings ran aground as four of the republics held to fixed positions. Serbia and Montenegro demanded centralization of power under a strong federal government; Slovenia and Croatia had proposed a confederal solution in October 1990 (possibly, as Dejan Jović has argued, as a first step toward gaining independence for their republics[245]) and continued to press for that outcome, if they were to retain any form of association with the other republics; only Macedonia and Bosnia-Herzegovina were flexible, just wanting to find a way to keep Yugoslavia together in some form or another. The confederal proposal was rejected in the state presidency by a vote of six to two. On 25 June 1991, Slovenia and Croatia declared their "disassociation" from Yugoslavia, followed by Macedonia on 8 September and Bosnia-Herzegovina on 3 March 1992. By 11

August 1992, Slovenia had been recognized by more than 40 states, including the United Kingdom, Germany, Italy, Norway, the United States, and Russia, and Slovenia and Croatia recognized each other's independence. It was only on 18 June 1993 that the United States recognized Bosnia-Herzegovina, as the 40th state to do so. As of that date, only seven states had recognized the Republic of Macedonia, as it was called at the time; among these were Slovenia, Croatia, and Bosnia-Herzegovina. The United States extended diplomatic recognition to Macedonia on 13 Septmber 1995.

In the meantime, war had broken out on 27 June 1991 – first between the JNA and Slovenia, later between Serbian insurgents supported by Serbia and the forces under the command of both Croatia and Bosnia-Herzegovina. By the time the fighting ended in November 1995, between 97,207 and 110,000 persons lay dead, according to a tally prepared by Sarajevo's Research and Documentation Center, 2.7 million people had been displaced from their homes, and the cost of the war just to Bosnia-Herzegovina's economy came to an estimated $115 billion. As of 1996, 60% of Bosnia's inhabitants were living below the poverty line and many residents of Croatia, Bosnia-Herzegovina, and Serbia were suffering from post-traumatic stress disorder and other psychological ailments. Croatia regained the territory it lost temporarily during the war, while Bosnia-Herzegovina was divided into two autonomous parts in a peace accord signed at Dayton, Ohio, in November 1995. Who benefited from more than four years of savagery? Not the peoples as a whole, nor their states, nor even all of those who steered the country to war, as Milošević, for example, ended his days in incarceration in The Hague. The only real beneficiaries, as Paolo Rumiz has documented, were the looters who stole household goods from civilians driven from their homes and squatters who took over possession of abandoned homes.[246] How did Yugoslavia plunge into tragedy? The evidence shows quite clearly that the breakup and the war were the direct result of policies adopted by Slobodan Milošević, who carefully prepared for war by importing arms from the Soviet Union, having the JNA confiscate arms from Slovenia, Croatia, and Bosnia-Herzegovina, arming and training Serb irregulars in Croatia, and having arms factories moved out of Bosnia.

The communists of Albania

Enver Hoxha may well have been the cruelest communist dictator of East Central Europe. Quite apart from arranging for the execution of his first Minister of Internal Affairs and Organizational Secretary, Koçi Xoxe (1911–1949), in 1949 and the probable murder of his longtime prime minister, Mehmet Shehu (1913–1981), in 1981, he displayed a ruthlessness for which Soviet General Secretary Stalin provides the only parallel in the European communist world. Clergy of Albania's four major religious groups – Sunni Muslims, Bektashi Muslims, Eastern Orthodox, and Roman Catholics – were all treated roughly but the Catholic clergy were treated especially brutally, with the foreign clergy expelled immediately, some native clergy murdered, and still others put on trial on charges of collaboration with Axis forces and executed. As Bernhard Tönnes noted, "By the end of 1946, a total of 20 Catholic priests had been executed and over 40 had been imprisoned."[247] Orthodox clerics and Islamic religious leaders were also persecuted (details to follow). Communists themselves, if they voiced opinions that differed from Hoxha's views could be accused of being "enemies of the people" and liquidated.[248] Writers and artists who showed an inclination to think for themselves could be rounded up and taken to industrial sites or collective farms to live and work there for two to six months – so that they could learn from "the people".[249] Those were the lucky ones. Edison Gjergo, a painter, was arrested in January 1975 and charged with including cubist elements in his paintings; charges of agitation and propaganda were added and, in April 1975, he was sent to work in a mine for eight years. Another painter, Maks Velo, received a 10-year prison sentence (in 1979) for having painted in an abstract style. Dhimiter Xhuvani, a writer, was likewise put in prison; the offensive material in his case was his novel, *The Tunnel*. Harsher sentences were also meted out: thus, Vilson Blloshmi met his end by firing squad because Hoxha was displeased by his novel, *Sahara*, and Genc Leka, a young poet, was likewise brought before a firing squad – in his case because his verse was thought to reflect Western fashions in poetry.[250] One wonders if Hoxha or others in the party elite were really following trends in Western poetry. Like other communist leaders in the region, Hoxha talked of creating a new society, in which men and women would change their ways of thinking and behaving, becoming, as the socialist terminology had it, New Socialist Men and New Socialist Women. In his vision, there would be no room for religion beyond the short term, no room for patriarchal values, no room for experimentation in art and literature, and no room for opinions or interpretations that differed from his.

Hoxha learned French during the time he lived in France, while benefiting from a scholarship awarded by the government of King Zog. Upon his return to Albania in 1936, he initially taught French, first in Tirana and later in Korçë. He read widely, including the works of Balzac, Shakespeare, Montaigne, and Molière, and is said to have had some ability in Russian, English, Italian, and Serbo-Croatian.[251] He is also credited with having written 80 volumes of political reflections, published between 1968 and 1989.

The birth of communist Albania

Fascist Italy occupied Albania in April 1939 and enlarged it in May 1941 by adding Kosovo and parts of Montenegro to occupied Albania. In September 1943, after Italy surrendered to the Allies, German troops moved into Albania. Resistance to first Italian and then German occupation began early in the war. Hoxha's rise to power began during World War Two, when the rival communist groups from Shkodër, Korçë, and Tirana met in October and November 1941, with emissaries from the Communist Party of Yugoslavia present (Miladin Popović and Dušan Mugoša), and agreed to unite to form the Albanian Communist Party, electing a collective leadership. In July 1942, the ACP decided to try to bring all anti-fascist groups in Albania under one umbrella; two months later, an agreement was reached with leaders of some non-communist resistance groups to form a united organization – the National Liberation Movement (NLM). However, some non-communists realized that the communists intended to dominate the NLM and kept their distance. Among them were liberals Midhat Frashëri and Ali Klissura who, in late October 1942, set up a rival resistance force, the *Balli Kombëtar* (National Front, or BK). The BK wanted to see a parliamentary system established after the war, as well as retention of Kosovo within the borders of the post-war Albanian state.[252] On 17 March 1943, the ACP convened its first national conference, at which it was decided to create an Army of National Liberation. A Central Committee consisting of 11 members and six candidates was elected at the time; Hoxha was elected First Secretary. The Army of National Liberation took shape on 10 July 1943, under the command of Spiro Moisiu (1900–1981), a member of the ACP; Hoxha was appointed political commissar to the army.

The British Military Mission wanted to see Albanian anti-fascists focused on fighting Axis forces rather than each other and, under British pressure, delegates of the NLM and the BK met in the village of Mukaj on 2 August 1943. They agreed to coordinate their combat operations and to collaborate in administering liberated areas, and also to allow a post-war plebiscite to decide to which country Kosovo would be attached.[253] This solution was, however, unacceptable to leading figures in the Communist Party of Yugoslavia and Svetozar Vukmanović-Tempo, by then the senior Yugoslav communist in Albania, demanded that the ACP repudiate the Mukaj Agreement without delay. The Albanian communists did so immediately, circulating a letter to this effect to local party organizations on 8 August 1943. This made it clear that the ACP was effectively subordinated to the Yugoslav communist party.[254] In addition to the army of the NLM and the *Balli Kombëtar*, there was a third, albeit weaker, resistance group – the *Legaliteti* (Legality), seeking to restore King Zog to power, as well as a fourth, politically marginal Trotskyist Left group.[255]

The communist era, 1944–91

In May 1944, Hoxha was appointed Supreme Commander of the Army of National Liberation and, by October, three-quarters of Albania had been cleared of German forces. That same month, the communists set up a provisional government, with Hoxha as PM. The following month, the National Liberation Front (as the NLM had renamed itself) took control of Tirana and, by early December 1944, the last German forces left Albania. In December, the ACP nationalized the country's factories and soon after seized control of banks, the transportation network, foreign trade, wholesale trade, and all land, including mineral deposits. A decree issued in January authorized the seizure of the property of persons designated "enemies of the people". There was resistance to these measures; for example, rather than surrender their motor vehicles to the state, some people damaged them beyond repair or hid them.[256] On 26 January 1945, a Special People's Court was established, under the supervision of Koçi Xoxe, the Minister of Internal Affairs and member of the Politburo, and at the time, the second most powerful man in Albania.

In the immediate post-war period, there were three factions or groupings within the ACP: those surrounding Hoxha, who wanted to see Albania pursuing a strictly communist course, with the acceleration of agricultural collectivization and party control of all facets of society, including the arts, as well as the maintenance of Albania's territorial integrity; a grouping around Sejfulla Malëshova (1900–1971), a minor poet and member of the Politburo who had been appointed Minister of Culture and Propaganda in 1945 and who wanted to see a liberal policy in the arts, including literature, a postponement of collectivization, and the maintenance of friendly relations with both the socialist camp and the Western states; and a faction loyal to Xoxe, who collaborated with Yugoslav agents and wanted to see Albania annexed to Yugoslavia, as that country's seventh constituent republic. The key difference between Malëshova and Xoxe is that the former was advocating certain programs for domestic and foreign policy, while the latter wanted power – albeit in a constituent republic within the Yugoslav federation. Malëshova had no powerful supporter or protector and, on 21 February 1946, the Sixth Plenum of the ACP Central Committee condemned his views and removed him from both the Central Committee and *ipso facto* also from the Politburo, and dismissed him as Minister of Culture. The Plenum called for an acceleration of the nationalization of industry. Agricultural collectivization was also stepped up with about 150 collective farms being set up between 1946 and 1955. Some peasants resisted collectivization and preferred to slaughter their livestock rather than turn over their animals to the collective farms. The result was a sharp drop in livestock and food production. The communists treated those resisting collectivization as class enemies and increased the pressure on them. By late 1959, fully 83% of Albania's arable land had been collectivized.[257] As for Malëshova, he survived by taking a low-status job and refusing to talk to any adults.

For a while, Xoxe seemed to be ascendant; indeed, after Yugoslav PM Tito criticized Nako Spiru, who had met with Yugoslav officials to discuss a joint Five-Year Plan (proposed by the Yugoslavs), Xoxe's faction bore down on Spiru. Feeling isolated and finding no obvious support from any quarter, Spiru committed suicide in November 1947.[258] Meanwhile, the Albanian regime, which had signed a Treaty of Friendship, Cooperation and Mutual Aid with Belgrade in July 1946, now signed a similar treaty with Sofia in December 1947,[259] in a show of independence that could only have been unwelcome to the Yugoslav regime. The Eighth Plenum of the ACP Central Committee (26 February–8 March 1948) marked the zenith of Xoxe's power. He was able to bring about the expulsion from the party of various prominent people – among them Liri Belishova, Spiru's widow – and to orchestrate the dismissal of Mehmet Shehu from his position as Chief of the General Staff of the Army and the cancelation of his candidate membership in the CC. Shehu had been a vocal critic of Xoxe's plan to merge Albania into Yugoslavia. To fend off volleys fired in his direction, Hoxha engaged in calculated self-criticism and, with that, was able to keep his post as party General Secretary (as the leadership post had been renamed). In a striking but transient victory for Xoxe, the Plenum gave its approval to Xoxe's plan to merge the Albanian and Yugoslav armies and economies!

By then, Xoxe was laying the groundwork for a series of political trials through which he hoped to get rid of Hoxha and other leading figures in the anti-Yugoslav faction.[260] Xoxe, still only second-in-command, presumed to convene a meeting of the Politburo in April 1948, planning to persuade the members of that body to request that Albania be admitted into the Yugoslav federation. But Hoxha's people were in the majority in the Politburo and killed Xoxe's plan. Hoxha now attacked the Belgrade regime and, in mid-June 1948, ordered the closure of the Yugoslav information center in Tirana and banned further sales of the Yugoslav newspaper *Borba*. When the Soviets kicked Yugoslavia out of the Cominform on 28 June 1948, Hoxha seized the opportunity this presented and immediately took a stand with Stalin and against Tito, thereby channeling Soviet support for his position against Tito's preferred Albanian, Xoxe. On 1 July 1948, the Albanian regime denounced all economic agreements which had been reached with Belgrade and ordered all Yugoslav advisers and specialists out of Albania. In September, Moscow signed an agreement with Tirana, compensating Albania for the loss of economic and technical assistance from Yugoslavia.

That same month, the Eleventh Plenum of the CC was convoked. Now, Shehu, Belishova and other party members who had been purged from their functions by Xoxe were rehabilitated and restored to their former positions. At the same time, Xoxe was stripped of his position as Organizational Secretary, though he continued for the time being to sit in the Politburo. It was also on this occasion that the Albanian Communist Party redesignated itself as the Albanian Party of Labor (APL).[261] Then, in October 1948, in a dramatic demotion, Xoxe lost his post as Minister of Internal Affairs, assuming responsibility now as Minister of Industry because of "grave errors".[262] Shehu took over as Minister of Internal Affairs. Xoxe held his new post for just over seven weeks, being expelled from the party, together with his associate Pandi Kristo, in late November.

Xoxe and his closest collaborators were arrested in December 1948 on charges of Trotskyism (code for pro-Yugoslav sympathies) and treason.[263] At a secret trial held in May 1949, Xoxe and his co-defendants were found guilty.[264] Xoxe was executed on 11 June 1949; his co-defendants were sent to prison. After this, there were trials of alleged Titoists in Tirana, Durrës, and Kukës, continuing into 1950. From December 1948 until early 1952, Hoxha purged about 4,000 people (8%) from the ranks of the party. After this, there were no serious challenges to Hoxha's primacy.

The Philby affair

The British and Americans also attempted to remove Hoxha from power in the early years after Albania's break with Tito. The most serious effort was undertaken in October 1949 under the patronage of Britain's Secret Intelligence Service (SIS) unit MI6. A key actor in the operation was H. A. R. "Kim" Philby (1912–1988), who was assigned to work with the British Office for Policy Coordination, which was tasked with conducting sabotage and subversion in communist states in East Central Europe. The hitch was that Philby, a senior British agent who was sent to Washington D.C. as the SIS liaison officer with the CIA was passing along information to the Soviets. He had access, thus, to high-level discussions and privileged information regarding anti-communist operations. He knew, thus, that the British were training anti-communist Albanians in techniques of warfare developed by the British during the war years. SIS and the CIA agreed to smuggle nine of these Albanians by sea into Albania. Philby was appointed joint commander of the operation in September 1949 and met with his Soviet handler that same month, passing along details about the operation, including details concerning the planned landing at Karaburun peninsula. Nine British-trained Albanian guerrillas landed on Albanian territory in October and immediately split into two groups. The smaller group, consisting of four armed men, was ambushed by Albanian forces, who killed three of their number; the fourth man disappeared. The other group made some contact with Albanian villagers, who could not understand why the guerrillas had not brought significant supplies of firearms and ammunition for an uprising. Toward the end of October, this group of five decided to retreat to Greece. Again, the group split up, with two of them reaching Greece safely; the other three clashed with communist forces, suffering one casualty and the other two managing to escape to Greece. In the final tally, of the nine guerrillas smuggled into Albania, four were killed, one disappeared, and four escaped to Greece.[265] The Americans did not like the idea of landing guerrillas by sea, as the British favored, and set up their own Albanian insurgency force in 1950, having them parachute into Albanian territory in early 1952; these agents were quickly apprehended and "forced to radio the 'all clear' signal to their base on Cyprus. Subsequently, between seven and twelve additional Albanians were dispatched to their demise."[266] The Americans continued to have Albanian agents parachute into Albania and Philby continued to pass along relevant information to the Soviets who, in turn, passed this along to the Albanian regime. Altogether about 60 anti-communist Albanian agents were air-dropped into Albania by the Americans; almost all of them were surrounded by security troops soon after they landed. Most were killed on the spot, one or two escaped to Greece, and in April 1954 the Albanian regime put a few surviving agents on trial and exposed the whole Western plot.[267]

Economic planning, 1951–70

At the start of the post-war era, Albania had a very poor road and railroad network, and thus assigned a certain priority to this sector after the war's end, with the Yugoslavs initially providing rails and steam locomotives. After 1948, Poland and Czechoslovakia stepped into the breach, with the latter supplying locomotives powered by diesel engines.[268] The first Five-Year Plan was launched in 1951, with ambitious goals; two years into the plan, the party had to revise its targets downward. From the beginning, as the data in Table 5.1 make clear, the regime assigned the highest priority to building up the country's industry. In the first plan period, especially high rates of growth were achieved in chromium and coal mining and, during the Second Five-Year Plan, Albania outperformed the rest of the world in *per capita* extraction of chromium ore[269] (see Tables 5.9 and 5.10). Agriculture continued to occupy the second highest priority during the first five plan periods. During the Third Five-Year Plan, food production increased by 51% over levels achieved previously, though this was not enough for Albania to achieve self-sufficiency in food production.[270]

In January 1957, the Soviet Union extended a new credit of $18.5 million and in April 1957 canceled Albanian earlier debts totaling $105 million. The Soviets extended a further credit of $40 million in November 1957, followed by a credit of $75 million in January 1959. In the years ending in 1961, 4,500 Albanian students studied in the Soviet Union and elsewhere in the Soviet bloc. China began to extend economic assistance to Albania as early as 1954, with a modest grant of $2.5 million and a loan of $12.5 million. This was followed by a loan of $13.75 million in January 1959 and an agreement on 2 February 1961 for a loan of $125 million to pay for construction of 25 industrial projects during the Third Five-Year Plan. In addition, during 1960–63, Albania received 430,200 tons of wheat and corn from China. In 1961, 54% of Albania's foreign trade was still with the Soviet Union and only 7% with China. This would change dramatically in the following years.[271]

TABLE 5.9 Distribution of Investments in Albania by Five-Year Plan (in %)

	1951–55	*1956–60*	*1961–65*	*1966–70*
Industry	52	44	49	46.6
Agriculture	12	18	15	16.0
Transportation & communication	13	13	11	11.4
Housing	8	8	8	6.9
Education, health, & culture	6	5	4	5.4
Other	9	12	13	13.7

Source: Peter R. Prifti, *Socialist Albania since 1944 : Domestic and Foreign Developments* (Cambridge, Mass.: MIT Press, 1978), p. 63.

TABLE 5.10 Average Growth Rates in Industrial Production in Albania, 1951–70 (in %)

	1951–55	*1956–60*	*1961–65*	*1966–70*
Oil	7.4	33.1	4.7	15.2
Chromium	18.5	19.1	1.4	9.3
Coal	36.5	7.8	6.2	11.9
Copper	3.2	13.8	38.7	25.1
All industry	22.6	16.9	6.8	12.9

Source: Peter R. Prifti, *Socialist Albania since 1944 : Domestic and Foreign Deveopments* (Cambridge, Mass.: MIT Press, 1978), P. 62.

Relations with the Soviet Union and China

Khrushchev undertook two initiatives in 1955–56 that gave Hoxha a serious jolt. The first was the Soviet First Secretary's visit to Belgrade in May 1955, which provided the occasion for a reconciliation between Moscow and Belgrade and issuance of the aforementioned Belgrade Declaration. Hoxha viewed the Yugoslav regime as revisionist, which is to say not truly socialist; the Soviet-Yugoslav rapprochement signified, in Hoxha's eyes, thus, nothing less than the Soviet legitimation of the mortal sin of revisionism. Worse yet, after his reconciliation with Tito, Khrushchev sent chief party ideologue Mikhail Suslov and CC member Pyotr Pospelov to Tirana to ask the Albanian leader to rehabilitate Xoxe posthumously. Hoxha considered this an affront and refused to accommodate this request.[272] The second initiative by Khrushchev which proved deeply troubling to Hoxha was the Soviet leader's secret speech in February 1956, described earlier in this book. After this speech, there was renewed pressure on the Albanian leader, both from domestic and from foreign (chiefly Soviet) actors to change his course. Hoxha replied defiantly, telling a plenary session of the APL Central Committee on 13 February 1957, "In spite of all [his] mistakes, Stalin remains a great Marxist-Leninist. Stalin was never mistaken in such questions as the protection of the interests of the working class and Marxist-Leninist theory, the fight against imperialism and other enemies of socialism. He was and remains an exemplary figure."[273] According to his own account, Hoxha had expected that Vyacheslav Molotov (1890–1986), Foreign Minister under Stalin, would inherit the leadership mantle of the CPSU after Stalin's death and viewed Khrushchev, by contrast, as a buffoon.[274] Hoxha, Shehu, and Gogo Nushi attended the Twentieth CPSU Congress. In the volume of his memoirs devoted to Khrushchev, Hoxha recalled, "We returned to Albania heart-broken over what we had seen and heard in the homeland of Lenin and Stalin."[275] Hoxha denied that Stalin had unleashed *any* terror in the USSR, calling this a Khrushchevite fabrication, adding that, "[I]f there were some excesses in the course of [the Soviet Union's] just and titanic struggle, it was not Stalin who committed them, but Khrushchev, Beria and company."[276]

In spite of the sharpness of Hoxha's rhetoric, the Kremlin tried at first to woo the Albanian regime. When this proved to be a nonstarter, the Soviets encouraged those members of the Albanian leadership with whom they were on speaking terms to overthrow Hoxha.[277] The rift between the Khrushchev and Hoxha regimes became obvious in June 1960, when the Albanian delegation to the Congress of the Romanian Communist Party in Bucharest endorsed China's views against those of the Soviet leadership after a severe criticism of the Chinese party by Khrushchev.[278] Following the Bucharest Congress, the Soviets made severe cuts to their aid to Albania, just as Albania was facing a serious drought and shortage of grain. China was suffering from a famine at the time but nonetheless came to Albania's rescue by using some of its hard currency reserves to purchase wheat from France and have it shipped directly to Albania.

Soviet-Albanian relations reached the breaking point in April 1961, when the Soviets informed the Albanians that Soviet specialists would be withdrawn forthwith, because of Albania's "unfriendly attitude".[279] Fifty Soviet specialists were withdrawn the next day. The Albanians stole six Soviet submarines before the Soviets could pull the rest of their submarine fleet out of Albanian waters. The Soviets accused the Albanians of piracy and terminated all economic assistance. By May, East Europeans stopped coming to Albania as tourists. Finally, in December 1961, the Soviet Union severed diplomatic relations with Albania. For the time being, Albania remained a nominal, if inactive, member of the Warsaw Pact. A trade agreement between Beijing and Tirana was signed the same month as Moscow terminated assistance; as part of this agreement, the Chinese provided Albania with almost as much in credits as had been promised by the Soviets.[280] During the following 17 years, China loomed large for Albania, providing economic and technical assistance and validating Hoxha's defense of Stalin.

The Soviet invasion of Czechoslovakia in August 1968 proved to be a watershed, not only for member states of the Soviet bloc but also for Albania and, as we have seen above, Yugoslavia. After the Soviet invasion of Czechoslovakia, Albania formally withdrew from the Warsaw Pact, strengthened its military and defense capability, offered to come to the aid of Yugoslavia and Romania in the event of a Soviet attack, and increased economic and cultural ties with Western countries.[281] Albania also normalized ties with Yugoslavia and Greece. The introduction of television about this time had the unintended consequence of exposing Albanians to what the regime called "bourgeois" life styles.[282]

The assault on religion

For nearly 40 years, the data from the 1938 census were cited for the distribution of religious belief in Albania, thus ignoring the results of the 1945 census carried out by the communist authorities. Yet the differences between the results in 1938 and those reported in 1945 do not seem significant. In 1976, Gjon Sinishta offered updated estimates (see Table 5.11), suggesting that the proportion of Muslims in Albania was almost exactly the same in 1976 as it has been in 1938, while the proportion of Roman Catholics edged upwards from 10% in 1938 to 13% in 1976, with the proportion of Orthodox declining slightly. There were an estimated 200 Jews living in Albania in 1938; by the end of the war, the number of Jews in the country had risen to 300.

In the early post-war years, the regime initially adopted a cautious policy vis-à-vis the country's Muslims and Orthodox, but beginning in 1948 policies toughened. The first religious community targeted by the regime was the Catholic Church, followed by the Islamic community.[283] With the land reform of 1945, all three religious associations were deprived of some of their facilities, including monasteries, seminaries, and libraries. The regime imposed restrictions on religious instruction, beginning with the Islamic community. Islamic religious leaders who were either incarcerated or executed in the wake of the land reform included: Mustafa effendi Varoshi, mufti of Durrës; Hafëz Ibrahim Djibra, at one time grand mufti of Albania; and Sheh Xhemal Pazari of Tirana.[284]

TABLE 5.11 Religious distribution in Albania, 1938, 1945, 1976 in %

	1938	1945	1976
Muslims	69	72.8	68
Orthodox Christians	21	17.1	19
Roman Catholics	10	10.1	13

Sources: 1938 data, as cited in Bernhard Tönnes, "Religious persecution in Albania", trans. from German by G. M. Ablitt and Anne Atkinson in *Religion in Communist Lands*, Vol. 10, No. 3 (1982), p. 243; 1945 census, as cited in Peter R. Prifti, *Socialist Albania since 1944: Domestic and Foreign Developments* (Cambridge, Mass.: MIT Press, 1978), p. 150; and estimates by Gjon Sinishta in G. Sinishta, *The Fulfilled Promise: A Documentary Account of Religious Persecution in Albania* (Santa Clara, Calif.: H&F Composing Service, 1976), p. 1.

The Albanian Orthodox Church had been subordinated to the Ecumenical Patriarch, but the regime wanted to see it subordinated to the Moscow Patriarchate. Archbishop Kristofer Kisi opposed this transfer and was deposed on 28 August 1949, for the alleged crime of "plotting to detach the Church from the Eastern Orthodox Faith and surrender it to the Vatican."[285] The charge was, of course, false, but even if it had been true there would have been no legal foundation for treating an initiative to embrace Catholicism as a crime. The regime wanted a quiescent Orthodox Church and therefore replaced independent-minded bishops with more compliant hierarchs. Among those Orthodox put in prison not long after the consolidation of communist power were: Bishop Agathangjel of Berat; Bishop Irenei, deputy metropolitan of Korcë and Gjirokastër; and Archbishop Kisi, who was tortured to death.[286]

As already noted, 20 Catholic priests had been executed by 1946. At the start of the communist era, the Franciscans operated a monastery in Lezha, a novitiate, a school of philosophy and theology, an elementary school, and a printing press and had their main center in Shkodër in the north of the country. The Jesuits were also present in Shkodër, where they operated St. Xavier College. The Jesuits also operated an elementary school, an apostolic school, and a large printing press. There were also nuns from the Salesian, Servite, and White Charity Orders and were involved, like the Franciscans, in cultural, social, and educational work.[287] The authorities moved swiftly against the Church's infrastructure; as early as 1946, the authorities ordered all Jesuit institutions in Shkodër and Tirana to close; the Jesuits were thereupon outlawed and all property of the Order was confiscated. At the start of the following year, secret police in Shkodër planted guns and ammunition in the Franciscan church of Gjuhadol; later, the police "discovered" the weapons and bullets and arrested many Franciscans. Subsequently, the regime suppressed all Franciscan institutions and confiscated the Order's property.[288] Sinishta records that

[b]esides the Jesuits and the Franciscans, all the sisters of different orders were thrown into the streets and their property, including their personal belongings, [was] confiscated. Their habits were taken from them and they

were prohibited to wear them any longer. A great number of the sisters who resisted the police raid[s] were arrested, tortured and sent to the prison camps while others were ridiculed and a few were forced to walk through the streets naked.[289]

Then, in July 1951, the government annulled the Catholic Church's link with the Vatican and declared the establishment of a "national" Church under the supervision of the state.[290] For Enver Hoxha, religion was something foreign, something that did not belong in Albania. In his words:

> All the religious sects existing in our country were brought into Albania by foreign invaders, and served them and the ruling classes of the country. Under the cloak of religion, god, and the prophets, there operated the brutal law of the invaders and their domestic lackeys.[291]

The struggle over gender equality

In 1945, 92% of females were said to be illiterate.[292] In the south of Albania (in the Tosk areas), at the dawn of the communist era, one could still find brides being sold to the highest bidders. There was also discrimination on the basis of sex.[293] Against the traditional patriarchy deeply rooted in Albanian culture, Hoxha presented himself as a champion of female equality, telling an audience in a speech in 1942 that, in his view, "there must not be a single forum without women."[294] The Albanian Union of Women was established in September 1943 to serve as an institutional engine to fight against patriarchal traditions and elevate the status of women. The following year the National Liberation Council released a statement to the effect that women enjoyed "equal rights with men, and the right to participate in the political and social life of the country."[295] This principle was incorporated into Albania's 1946 constitution, while a law passed in 1948 dictated that marriage partners had equal rights in their relationship.[296]

Gradually, women's status improved. In the years 1947–55, the number of girls who could read and write increased by 66.8% and, in April 1956, the APL announced that illiteracy among members of both sexes below the age of 40 had been totally eradicated. Female illiteracy was reduced to just 8% by 1989.[297] Albanian women obtained the right to vote in September 1945. In 1946, women constituted just 3.6% of the deputies to the People's Assembly but their representation in that body rose steadily, reaching 16.6% by 1966 and 27.3% as of 1970. By the early 1980s, women comprised approximately 33% of deputies in the People's Assembly. In 1967, across councils at all levels, 36.7% of members were women; three years later (after the conclusion of the Cultural Revolution) the figure had risen to 45.8%. Women enrolled in increasing numbers in secondary schools (42.5% of enrolled students in 1984) as well as in vocational-secondary schools (47.8% of those enrolled as of 1985).[298]

The cultural sector

After the war had ended, the communists set about creating a cultural infrastructure. Thus, they established a network of museums across Albania, founded the Albanian Institute of Folklore in 1960, and authorized archeological excavations at Durrës, Pojan, and Butrint, where ancient Illyrian settlements had been located. They also promoted drama; not surprisingly, most theatrical plays after 1944 dealt with the National Liberation War and the construction of socialism. Theater was supposed to be useful to the party and, thus, was entirely politicized. Female emancipation was also a legitimate theme for plays and *"Quiet" Line*, written by Arsinoi Bino, one of Albania's foremost female playwrights, showcased an erstwhile submissive wife's successful rebellion against her patriarchal husband.[299]

The Albanian public was also given the opportunity to see plays by Shakespeare, Molière, Gogol, Brecht, and Arthur Miller, among others. In 1950, the first puppet theater for children was opened, albeit offering heavily politicized fare. An opera, *Spring*, by Tish Daija, took the National Liberation War as its theme. Another opera, by Pjetër Gaçi, presented mine workers as socialist heroes. There was also a ballet entitled *The Partisan*, with the score composed by Kozma Lara.[300] A Gallery of Fine Art opened in Tirana in 1954, displaying paintings and sculptures by Albanians. In line with socialist realism, Albanian painters, sculptors, writers, and composers were expected to create works suffused with optimism about the present and future.

A few words should be written here about Ismail Kadare (b. 1936), Albania's greatest and most famous novelist. In the course of his long career, Kadare produced works that revisit important periods and episodes of Albanian history. Throughout his novels, Kadare painted a picture of Albania as a heroic nation, alone and courageously resisting all onslaughts, with the Turks occupying a special historical niche.[301] One of Kadare's best known novels is *The General of a Dead Army*, first published in 1963 and subsequently translated into 15 languages, including English, German, French, and Russian.[302] Kadare achieved an international reputation and, because of this, was allowed to travel abroad in Hoxha's time and even to express some critical views. No other cultural figure, let alone ordinary citizen, was allowed such liberties.

The Cultural Revolution

The Albanian Cultural Revolution, concentrated in the years 1966–69, was a concerted effort to change people's thinking, to strip people of their religious beliefs, of patriarchal attitudes, of any hint of individualism and self-seeking, and of course of anything the regime might interpret as bourgeois values. Stripped of those beliefs, attitudes, and values, what would be left, Hoxha hoped, would be the New Socialist Man and New Socialist Woman. Hoxha's focus on changing people's thinking was obvious from his declaration, in November 1966, that

> [s]o long as the complete victory of the socialist revolution in the fields of ideology and culture has not been assured, neither can there be any security

or guarantee of the gains of the socialist revolution in the political and economic fields. That is why the struggle on the ideological front, for the complete destruction of the bourgeois and revisionist ideology, at bottom concerns the question: can socialism and communism be constructed and the restoration of capitalism . . . avoided?[303]

The Cultural Revolution may be said to have started on 27 January 1966 with the publication in the party daily *Zëri i Popullit* of a letter signed by 91 writers and artists, in which they indicated their intention to go to the countryside in order to live among the peasants and join in the farm work. This was the signal for the "rectification" of intellectuals to begin. Too many intellectuals, Hoxha thought, were developing original ideas and failing to pay close attention to party dicta. A poem published during the Cultural Revolution was intended to inspire what the Soviets called *partiinost* [party mindedness].

The Party – it is my first and last love,
The red rose of peace over the graves of the fallen,
The golden promise of future triumphs . . ..
The Party – it is the warmth of our handshake, . . .
Every good thing I have or shall ever have
[I owe to the Party],
The Party – it is my first and last song.[304]

In February 1966, the anti-bureaucratic campaign was set in motion, running through November of that year. During these months, the number of ministries was reduced from 19 to 13, 15,000 persons were dismissed from employment in the ministries or elsewhere in the bureaucracy, and military ranks were abolished.[305] The equality of women was also given extra emphasis now, with a CC plenum in June 1967 calling for a focus on eradicating patriarchal prejudices, customs, and views. The APL gave high priority to the recruitment of women into its ranks and the proportion of women in the party rose from 12.5% in 1966 to 22.5% in 1971.[306] The highpoint of the Cultural Revolution came in September 1967 when authorities announced that all 2,169 churches, mosques, monasteries, and other religious buildings were being shut down. These were now converted into warehouses, offices, cinemas, or other secular facilities or simply demolished.

Ever since his break with the Kremlin, Hoxha had been wary of Moscow-trained technicians and managers. In 1966, under the cover of combating "a privileged class of party and state bureaucrats, economic directors, artists, scientists, and cultural figures, who [are] earning the most and enjoying a higher lifestyle [than] the workers,"[307] Hoxha targeted those technicians and managers who had been trained by Soviet specialists. Subsequently, the regime ordered the formation of workers' committees in factories and other enterprises, assigning them certain responsibilities in an effort to limit the authority of the managers. Then, in December 1969, the APL Central Committee introduced measures to encourage ordinary workers to attack Soviet-trained managers and technicians; with time, all the Soviet-era functionaries were removed.[308] At the same time, the regime pressured workers to "volunteer" to take part in work brigades on public projects such as the Rrogozhina-Fier railway or the Malësia e Madhe highway. In harmony with this thinking, an education reform bill was adopted in 1969, stipulating that Albanian schooling was to combine three major and complementary components – academic study, productive work, and physical and military training.

From friendship with China to isolationism (August 1968-December 1990)

Hoxha clearly felt conflicted about the Prague Spring and the Soviet invasion in August 1968. On the one hand, the rapid liberalization of Czechoslovak politics within the span of a few months was unsettling to him and he would declare, "I call on the party and the working class to view these events with deep concern and not to think they are only happening in revisionist countries and therefore have nothing to do with us."[309] On the other hand, the Soviet Union's proclamation of its *duty* to intervene wherever and whenever it felt socialism was threatened was deeply unnerving and resulted, as already mentioned, in Albania building bridges with Yugoslavia and Romania, among other initiatives.

Sino-Albanian relations remained close until the death of Chairman Mao Zedong in September 1976. Two factions contended for the succession in China: a radical faction headed by Mao's widow, and a moderate faction led by Hua Guofeng. Inevitably, Hoxha backed the radicals, but it was the moderate faction that prevailed. By June 1977, Deng Xiaoping, who had been dismissed from the post of party Vice Chairman in April 1976 and whom Hoxha had publicly denounced, was rising in the party hierarchy. This was followed by an invitation to Yugoslav President Tito to visit China (which he did in 1977); Hoxha experienced this as a personal insult.[310] When Tirana started to bombard the new Chinese authorities with hostile propaganda, the once friendly Sino-Albanian relationship turned frosty. Beijing terminated its assistance to Albania as of July 1978, withdrew its technical advisers, and cut off all trade.

Hoxha turned 71 in 1980 and the question of succession was on the minds of party members, at least in the higher echelons. But as of 1980, foreign observers believed that PM Shehu, who ranked second in the party hierarchy, was the most likely to assume the leadership of the party once Hoxha would pass away. But on the eve of the November 1981 Eighth APL Congress, the two comrades clashed over economic priorities, with Shehu calling for an increase in investments in consumer goods industries at the expense of heavy industry and Hoxha taking the opposite view. Biberaj has suggested that "Shehu's advanced age, ill health, and lack of political finesse" probably also counted against him.[311] Hoxha had, by then, decided that he did not want Shehu to succeed him and therefore tried to persuade him to retire gracefully. In this spirit, Hoxha authorized the publication of volume 1 of Shehu's collected works. When Shehu continued to refuse to step down, Hoxha organized a verbal lynching of the PM at a Politburo meeting on 17 December 1981. The next day it was announced that Shehu had committed suicide. In Belgrade, local wits asked, "What were Shehu's last words before he committed suicide?" Their answer was: "Enver, don't shoot!" In fact, some foreign observers considered it unlikely that Shehu had taken his own life and, indeed, Yugoslav press reports held that "Shehu was killed during a meeting of the Central Committee."[312] U.S. government officials also suggested that the PM had been killed, rather than committing suicide.[313] Finally, in March 1985, a month before Hoxha's death, *Zëri i Popullit* belatedly conceded that Shehu had been liquidated and repeated Hoxha's earlier claim that Shehu had served at various times as a spy for the USA, the Soviet Union, and Yugoslavia.[314] Ramiz Alia (1925–2011), a northerner (Gheg) who had joined the CC in 1948 and the Politburo as a candidate member in 1956 and had become a full member in 1961, was now the heir apparent.

In the years after breaking with China, Hoxha's regime touted the country's self-reliance and struggled to keep the society afloat. When the communist system ended in 1991, the country was debt-free, having refused to contract loans, but impoverished.[315] Hoxha left Albania a mixed legacy. On the positive side, illiteracy, once widespread, was all but eradicated, women had made great strides and, by 1985, accounted for 50.1% of economists, 48.5% of physicians and other healthcare workers, 43.4% of teachers, and 20.8% of engineers,[316] and occupied a third of the seats in the Assembly. The road and railway networks as well as the electrical grid had all been expanded. In addition, among the various institutions founded after 1945, it is worth mentioning that the University of Tirana was founded in 1957.

On the negative side of the ledger, Hoxha's cruelty and ruthlessness were unparalleled among communist leaders in East Central Europe, he had clergy of all three major faiths imprisoned and/or killed, eventually suppressing all religious institutions in 1967; he suffocated initiative and creativity in literature and the other arts; he forced professionals and students to "volunteer" for stints at industrial sites or collective farms; and soon after coming to power set up forced labor camps at Tirana, Valias, Burrel, Kavajë, Berat, Porto Palermo, Tepelenë, and Vloçisht. By January 1976, there were an estimated 18 labor camps for political prisoners in operation, as estimated by Amnesty International.[317] Moreover, although by 1978 the production of cereal grains was enough for the needs of the country, food supplies were never entirely adequate.

The end of communism in Albania

As late as January 1990, Ramiz Alia declared that Albania would not succumb to the "revisionist" winds blowing out of Moscow. Subsequently, in July and again in December 1990, in an effort to win popular acquiescence in his continued rule, Alia removed some top functionaries in the party, in order to unblock his plan to open doors to the West. Parts of his strategy involved making concessions to the practice of religion, allowing small-scale private enterprise, and introducing freedom to travel. But for most Albanians, as also for the European Union and the CSCE, these concessions were insufficient.[318] Beginning in 1990, reformers within the APL tried to change the country's course and the new party program in spring 1991 offered half-hearted recognition of the rule of law and market economics. In the meantime, a Democratic Party was founded at the University of Tirana on 11 December 1990. Multi-party elections were now held, in two rounds, on 31 March 1991 and 7 April 1991. With a 98.92% turnout, the APL captured 56.17% of the vote and 169 of the 250 seats in the parliament.

A new constitution had been passed as a prerequisite for the elections. Now, on the basis of the new constitution, the parliament elected Ramiz Alia on 29 April 1991 to serve as President of the Republic, with 172 votes in favor (with three opposition deputies joining the APL deputies in his favor), against two negative votes and 71 invalid ballots. As a requirement for assuming the presidency, Alia had to resign from leadership of the APL; his successor in that office was Xhelil Gjoni. After the 1991 elections, reformer Fatos Nano was named PM. Nano established a coalition government, involving the APL, the Democratic Party, and three parties not represented in the parliament: the Social Democrats, the Peasant Party, and the Republican Party. With that, the era of one-party rule by the communist party came to a definitive end. Shortly thereafter, in June 1991, the APL publicly repudiated its past Stalinism.[319]

Dysfunctionality in the Western Balkans

Both Yugoslavia and Albania were manifestly dysfunctional throughout the era of rule by communists. To begin with, Yugoslavia was set up on a federative basis and devolved more power to the republics in 1963 and even more in 1974, in order to dampen inter-ethnic tensions and bind all component nationality groups to Yugoslavia on the basis of tolerance and mutual respect. Instead, the consequence of decentralization and devolution was that the republics came to function as the defenders and even fortresses of their titular nationalities (with the obvious exception of Bosnia-Herzegovina), laying the foundation for inter-ethnic frictions to be expressed as inter-republican frictions. The ultimate breakup of federated Yugoslavia was due, in part, to this dual strategy. A second problem was the strategy of seeking legitimation through Tito's charisma and from the triad, self-management, brotherhood and unity, and nonalignment. Tito would inevitably die, self-management was never realized as intended and sometimes amounted to little more than a time-wasting bureaucratic hurdle, brotherhood and unity in combination offered a glorious vision but were never achieved, and the nonaligned movement itself lost some of its luster when the members of the Nonaligned Movement found that they could make no meaningful response to the Soviet invasion of Afghanistan in December 1979. The upshot was that the claimed legitimacy of self-managing socialism hinged on transitory factors and even the memories of the courageous resistance by the Partisans to Axis occupation ceased to stir the younger generations as it had the Partisan generation.

But there were also unintended consequences and manifestations of dysfunctionality in the economic sector. For example, after the great economic Reform (typically spelled with a capital "R" in Serbo-Croatian/Croato-Serbian), the policies and programs of that Reform were repeatedly undermined and obstructed by Aleksandar Ranković and comrades loyal to him. Locals were not oblivious to the problems. For example, in 1982, Mihailo V. Popović published an insightful summary of the unintended consequences and dysfunctions in Yugoslav economic policy. He referred, for example, to the "excessive investment without adequate financial resources" – a result, at least in part, of the desire on the part of each republic to have its own college, if possible its own airline, and other facilities and services already offered in other republics – and wrote that this was leading to "economic and social instability" and was, furthermore, associated with an "inflationary style of behavior."[320] He identified dysfunction manifesting itself

> . . . even in the highest political forums [where] the discrepancy between 'professed political goals and political behavior has reached alarming proportions . . . Immoderate social and economic goals also manifest themselves as the deviation of words from deeds.[321]

In 1971, Tito came to the conclusion that the leeway he had granted the liberal Croatian troika was having undesirable consequences and, for that matter, that liberal policies elsewhere in the federation were having consequences which he at least had not intended and did not welcome. In his view, the Croatian party in 1971 had come to resemble a runaway train. This is why he removed the leadership of the Croatian party and carried out an extensive purge across four republics. But after Tito's death, there was, to some extent, a power vacuum at the top, at least initially. The result was that it became increasingly possible for special interests of one or another republic to pursue policies and adopt programs which were not in harmony with the interests of the country as a whole.[322] As a result, "not infrequently social contracts and self-management agreements remain dead letters on paper or are violated without any consequence for those who do not honor them."[323] The unintended result of tendencies for "particular interests often [to] prevail over general social interests" was "the impermissibly high structural and functional incoherence of the Yugoslav social system as a whole."[324] Add to that Yugoslavia's increasing foreign indebtedness, growing rates of poverty,[325] unresolved problems of unemployment,[326] and the inability of the leaders of the six constituent republics in their summit meetings in the first half of 1991 to agree on anything that might pass for a common vision or consensus on how to move forward to meet the political and economic challenges they were confronting, against the background that, as a one-party state, the Yugoslav federation was, at bottom, politically illegitimate, and it is obvious that dysfunction was sewn into the very political-constitutional fabric of the state.

Where Albania is concerned, Hoxha's policies were hamstrung by various unintended consequences. To begin with, the unintended consequences of the planning system, the clogged bureaucracy, and restrictions on scientific research were inefficiency in production and difficulty in keeping up with technological developments.[327] The dogged peasant resistance to collectivization, extending to the slaughter of cattle and sheep, was clearly another unintended consequence of his policies, as was the sabotage by Albanians of their automobiles. The *de facto* forced recruitment of "volunteers" to work for fixed periods at industrial sites or collective farms likely aggravated the permanent workers in those sectors and, in any event, would not have provided highly motivated and effective labor. Nor did the closure of places of worship achieve its purpose; rather, it resulted in families praying and venerating saints within the privacy of their homes. And again, the severe intolerance of criticism or even complaints deprived policy-makers of potentially useful feedback, contributing to the failure to reassess policies producing problematic results and thus to "long-standing defects and weaknesses in the country's economic system."[328] Late-communist Albania may not have been burdened by massively heavy debts, as was the case with East Germany and Poland, but the system was dysfunctional and Hoxha's ruthlessness traumatized many Albanians, leaving psychological scars among family members of his victims.

Final thoughts

As already mentioned, during the 1979–1980 academic year, I lived in Belgrade, having been granted a Fulbright Fellowship for that period so that I might research my dissertation. On 3 May 1980 I took an overnight train to Dubrovnik, arriving the next day to see black flags hung on all public buildings. Tito had died during the time I was taking the train from Belgrade. A couple of days later, by which time we found ourselves in Split, Tito was given a funeral fit for a king, attended by leaders from around the world. Locals crowded into bars, restaurants, and hotel lobbies to watch the funeral on television in the company of fellow mourners. We joined them and it seemed that the death of the country's longtime president had brought the country together. Indeed, in the following weeks, young people gathered at railway stations, bus stations, and other public places to sing "Druže Tito, mi ti se kunemo, da sa tvoga puta ne skrenemo" [Comrade Tito, we pledge to you that we shall not deviate from your path] as well as another patriotic song, "Jugoslavijo". I happened to be back in Croatia about six weeks later, this time visiting Zagreb. While I was there, a platform was erected on the Square of the Republic and speakers and singers ascended the platform to address the large crowd which had gathered and to perform for us. The slogan of the day was "Poslije Tita, Tito!" – After Tito, Tito! This was not merely a pledge not to deviate from the deceased leader's path. It was something more: an expression of the realization that the country had no suitably charismatic leader who might be seen as more Yugoslav than Serb or Croat and who might take Tito's place. It was also an appeal to preserve the unity which had flared as Tito left the scene and an effort to reassure people that there would be no drastic changes in the country's politics.

It was similar in Albania when Enver Hoxha passed away. Thus, in the national newspaper *Zëri i Popullit*, a poem in Hoxha's honor was printed:

> Enver Hoxha died.
> He was . . .
> No, He is!
> . . .
> He died, He was . . .
> No, He is, He is . . .[329]

Albanians also recalled a poem first published in 1971, brimming with (mandated) enthusiasm for Hoxha:

> I first heard those five dear letters at the dawn of my life.
> Ever since, your name became as dear to me as my paternal home,
> As precious as socialism,
> As lofty as the mountains,
> As vital as light . . ..
> We shout ENVER!
> And the sky seems to us loftier than ever,
> The space around us vaster,
> The sun bigger,
> And our perspectives ever more magnificent.
> We shout ENVER!
> And our days take on color and meaning
> As they fall in like soldiers
> Into the great ranks of the revolution.[330]

By contrast with Yugoslavia, Albania declined to accept foreign delegations to show their respect at Hoxha's funeral. Radio Tirana broadcast that a number of foreign states had suggested sending delegations but explained that the funeral committee felt that "it is not the practice in our country that such events should be attended by foreign state delegations."[331] Even without foreign delegations present, the funeral was imposing, with the leader's last remains first lying in state, then taken to Tirana's Martyrs of the Homeland cemetery, with hundreds of thousands of Albanian citizens in attendance, Ramiz Alia paying tribute to Hoxha, and large choirs singing dirges.[332]

The eras of Tito and Hoxha ended with apparent triumph, but their passing marked the end to the system which had existed in each country up to then. Tito had tried to preserve something of his legacy by setting in place a rotating collective presidency; this functioned for a while, but proved unable to stem the tide of expansionist nationalism coming from Serbia or to heal the wounds which some, if not many, Croats felt after the quashing of the Croatian Spring at the end of 1971. Hoxha had tried to assure continuity by anointing Ramiz Alia as his successor even knowing that Alia was the most liberal figure in his entourage. Alia, however, was faced with a double challenge – to find remedies for the country's serious economic plight, extending to food shortages, and to address Albanian people's hunger for political change. Today, Tito is still remembered with nostalgia in some parts of the lands that once constituted Yugoslavia[333]; Hoxha, by contrast, is widely reviled.

Notes

1 I am debted to Elez Biberaj for the inspiration for the title of this chapter.
2 *New York Times* (29 October 1972), Section F, p. 5.
3 Peter R. Prifti, *Socialist Albania Since 1944; Domestic and Foreign Developments* (Cambridge, MA: MIT Press, 1978), p. 66.
4 From the Serbo-Croatian: Antifašističko Vijeće Narodnog Oslobodjenja Jugoslavije.
5 Mehmedalija Bojić, *Historija Bosne i Bošnjaka (vii-xx vijek)* (Sarajevo: TKD Šahinpašić, 2001), pp. 222–223.
6 Xavier Bougarel, *Islam and Nationhood in Bosnia-Herzegovina: Surviving Empires*, trans. from French by Christopher Mobley (London and New York: Bloomsbury Academic, 2018), p. 68.
7 Ivo Goldstein and Slavko Goldstein, *Tito* (Novi Sad: Akademska knjiga, 2018), p. 299; Jože Pirjevec, *Tito and His Comrades* (Madison, WI: The University of Wisconsin Press, 2018), p. 113; and CIA, *National Intelligence Survey*, Section 53, Chap. V, NIS 21: "Yugoslavia – Political Dynamics", 1 August 1960, vol. 17, C, decl. 22 November 2000, under the authority of NND 011144 by SDT/SL, p. 10, on deposit at the National Archives (NA) at College Park, Maryland.
8 Sabrina P. Ramet and Sladjana Lazić, "The Collaborationist Regime of Milan Nedić", in Sabrina P. Ramet and Ola Listhaug (eds.), *Serbia and the Serbs in World War Two* (Basingstoke: Palgrave Macmillan, 2011), 24. See also Dimitrije Kulić, *Bugarska okupacija 1941–1944*, vol. 1 (Niš: Prosveta, 1970).
9 Branko Petranović, *Srbija u Drugom svetskom ratu 1939–1945* (Belgrade: Vojnoizdavački i novinski centar, 1992), p. 214.
10 Tone Ferenc, "Die Kollaboration in Slowenien", in Werner Röhr (ed.), *Okkupation und Kollaboration (1938–1945): Beiträge zu Konzeption und Praxis der Kollaboration in der deutschen Okkupationspolitik* (Berlin and Heidelberg: Hüthig Verlagsgemeinschaft, 1994), p. 343.
11 Pirjevec, *Tito and His Comrades*, p. 127.
12 Vlado Strugar, *Der jugoslawische Volksbefreiungskrieg 1941 bis 1945*, trans. from Serbo-Croatian by Martin Zöller (Berlin: Deutscher Militärverlag, 1969), pp. 298–300; confirmed in Srećko M. Džaja, *Die politische Realität des Jugoslawiens (1918–1991). Mit besonderer Berücksichtigung Bosnien-Herzegowinas* (Munich: R. Oldenbourg Verlag, 2002), p. 88.
13 Pirjevec, *Tito and His Comrades*, p. 142.
14 Walter Rauscher, *Hitler und Mussolini. Macht, Krieg und Terror* (Darmstadt: Wissenschaftliche Buchgesellschaft, 2001), p. 602; confirmed in Peter Hoffmann, *German Resistance to Hitler* (Cambridge, MA: Harvard University Press, 1988), p. 130.
15 Vladimir Žerjavić, *Gubici stanovništva Jugoslavije u drugom svetskom ratu* (Zagreb: Jugoslavensko viktimološko društvo, 1989), pp. 61–66.
16 Sabrina P. Ramet, *The Three Yugoslavias: State-Building and Legitimation, 1918–2005* (Washington, DC and Bloomington: The Wilson Center Press & Indiana University Press, 2006), p. 157.
17 Adam Ulam, "The Background of the Soviet-Yugoslav Dispute", in *The Review of Politics*, Vol. 13, No. 1 (January 1951), p. 43.

18 Jasper Ridley, *Tito: A Biography* (London: Constable, 1994), p. 248.
19 Regarding Kocbek, see John Taylor, "Poetry Today", in *The Antioch Review*, Vol. 63, No. 1 (Winter 2005), pp. 185–188.
20 Ramet, *The Three Yugoslavias*, p. 168.
21 Telegram (13 November 1945), Richard C. Patterson, Jr., Ambassador/Belgrade to Department of State, in U.S. Department of State, *Records Relating to the Internal Affairs of Yugoslavia, 1945–1949*, Decimal file 860h, at NA, Reel 1 (files 00/1–245 to 00/4–246).
22 Vojislav Koštunica and Kosta Čavoški, *Party Pluralism or Monism: Social Movements and the Political System in Yugoslavia, 1944–1949* (Boulder, CO: East European Monographs, 1985), p. 117.
23 DS76 (22 October 1956), C, Niles W. Bond, Counselor/R to State, 768.00/10–2256 HBS, in *Records of the U.S. Department of State Relating to the Internal Affairs of Yugoslavia, 1955–1959*, Decimal file 768 (RG59, C0034), Reel 1 (files .00/9–2756 to -00/1–2758), at National Archives, College Park, Maryland (hereafter, NA).
24 Dispatch 389 (18 June 1946), S, Harold Shantz/B to State, in *Records 1945–1949*, Reel 2 (files 00/4–346 to 00/10–1046); Telegram (15 June 1946), S, Shantz/B to State via War, in *Records 1945–1949*, Reel 2; Jozo Tomašević, *War and Revolution in Yugoslavia, 1941–1945: The Chetniks* (Stanford, CA: Stanford University Press, 1975), pp. 458–460; and *The Trial of Dragoljub-Draža Mihailović*, Stenographic Record and Documents from the Trial of Dragoljub-Draža Mihailović (Salisbury, NC: Documentary Publications, 1977; reprint of Belgrade, 1946), pp. 17–19, 24, 27–28, 34, 41–44, 47, 50, 54–59, 136.
25 Report from Ronald J. Wenner, S/A, 66th CIC Det., Reg VII, 12 January 1951, Ref. VVJ-2790, C, decl. 16 January 1998, in *Records of the Army Staff*, ROACS, G-2, Intelligence File, *Security Classified Intelligence and Investigative Dossiers, 1939–1976*, RC 319, Stack Area 270, Row A, Box 107 – *Ustaše*, at NA.
26 The first sentence here is closely paraphrased from Stella Alexander, *Church and State in Yugoslavia Since 1945* (Cambridge: Cambridge University Press, 1979), pp. 62–63. For the Islamic part, see Armina Omerika, *Islam in Bosnien-Herzegowina und die Netzwerke der Jungmuslime (1918–1983)* (Wiesbaden: Harrassowitz Verlag, 2014), p. 156.
27 Klaus Buchenau, *Orthodoxie und Katholizismus in Jugoslawien 1945–1991. Ein Serbisch-Kroatische Vergleich* (Wiesbaden: Harrassowitz Verlag, 2004), p. 105.
28 *Ibid.*, pp. 112–113.
29 *Ibid.*, p. 50.
30 Omerika, *Islam in Bosnia-Herzegowina*, pp. 156–157.
31 *Ibid.*, pp. 158, 161, 163, 165.
32 Sabrina P. Ramet, *Balkan Babel: The Disintegration of Yugoslavia from the Death of Tito to the Fall of Milošević*, 4th ed. (Boulder, CO: Westview Press, 2002), p. 85.
33 Omerika, *Islam in Bosnien-Herzegowina*, p. 154.
34 Alexander, *Church and State*, p. 125.
35 Buchenau, *Orthodoxie und Katholizismus*, pp. 190, 198.
36 Omerika, *Islam in Bosnien-Herzegowina*, pp. 150–151.
37 George Sanford, "The Katyn Massacre and Polish-Soviet Relations, 1941–43", in *Journal of Contemporary History*, Vol. 41, No. 1 (January 2006), p. 95.
38 Alexander, *Church and State*, pp. 252–253; Buchenau, *Orthodoxie und Katholizismus*, p. 129.
39 Buchenau, *Orthodoxie und Katholizismus*, p. 151.
40 As quoted in O. Aleksa Benigar, *Alojzije Stepinac, Hrvatski Kardinal* (Rome: Žiral, 1974), pp. 502–503.
41 Ramet, *Balkan Babel*, p. 85.
42 Buchenau, *Orthodoxie und Katholizismus*, p. 107.
43 See, *inter alia*, Ivo Goldstein, *Hrvatska 1918–2008* (Zagreb: EPH Liber, 2008), p. 232.
44 Miroslav Akmadža, *Katolička crkva u komunističkoj Hrvatskoj 1945–1980* (Zagreb and Slavonski Brod: Hrvatska Povijest, 2013), pp. 65–85. An edited version of portions of the official transcript of the trial was published in Jakov Blažević, *Mač a ne mir. Za pravnu*

sigurnost gradjana [Vol. 3 of Memoirs, 4 vols.] (Zagreb/Belgrade/Sarajevo: Mladost/Prosveta/Svjetlost, 1980).

45 Ramet, *The Three Yugoslavias*, p. 160. See also Pål Kolstø, "Bleiburg: The Creation of a National Martyrology", in *Europe-Asia Studies*, Vol. 62, No. 7 (September 2010), pp. 1153–1174.

46 Pirjevec, *Tito and His Comrades*, p. 151.

47 "Tito je jedina svjetska ličnost medju hrvatskim političarima" (An interview with historian Zorica Stipetić), in *Nacional* (Zagreb), No. 425 (6 January 2004), p. 52.

48 Pirjevec, *Tito and His Comrades*, p. 165.

49 Goldstein and Goldstein, *Tito*, pp. 428–429.

50 See Slobodan Nešovič, *Bledski sporazumi: Tito-Dimitrov (1947)* (Zagreb: Globus & Školska knjiga, 1979); Georgi Dimitrov, *Georgi Dimitrov, Dnevnik 1933–1949*, ed. by Dimitûr Sirkov (Sofia: Universitetsko Izdatelstvo "Sv. Kliment Ohridski", 1997).

51 D576 (22 October 1956), C, Niles W. Bond, Counselor / R to State, 768.00/10–2256 HBS in *Records of the U.S. Department of State Relating to the Internal Affairs of Yugoslavia, 1955–1959*, Decimal file 768 (RG59, C0034), at NA, Reel 2 (files .00/9–2756 to .00/1–2758); *The Times* (London), 24 February 1948, p. 3; *Vjesnik* (Zagreb), 25 June 1948, trans. in ED91 (30 June 1948), S, Consul Theodore J. Hohenthal / Z to State, in U.S. Department of State, *Records Relating to the Internal Affairs of Yugoslavia 1945–1949*, Decimal file 860h at SL, Reel 5.

52 Pirjevec, *Tito and His Comrades*, pp. 170–171. See also Ridley, *Tito*, pp. 284–285.

53 As quoted in Milovan Djilas, *The Fall of the New Class: A History of Communism's Self-Destruction*, trans. from Serbo-Croatian by John Loud, ed. by Vasilije Kalezić (New York: Alfred A. Knopf, 1998), p. 64.

54 As quoted in *Ibid.*, p. 65.

55 Dispatch 1017, 7 September 1947, R, Cavendish W. Cannon to State, in *Records of the U.S. Department of State Relating to the Internal Affairs of Yugoslavia, 1945–1949*, Reel 4.

56 As quoted in Pirjevec, *Tito and His Comrades*, pp. 171–172, from the Russian State Archive of Social and Political History.

57 Ulam, "The Background of the Soviet-Yugoslav Dispute", p. 51.

58 Goldstein and Goldstein, *Tito*, p. 451.

59 Stjepan Đureković, *Ja, Josip Broz Tito* (Zagreb: International Books-USA, 1982), pp. 35–39; Vladimir Dedijer, *The Battle Stalin Lost: Memoirs of Yugoslavia, 1948–1953* (New York: Viking Press, 1971), p. 141.

60 Duncan Wilson, *Tito's Yugoslavia* (Cambridge: Cambridge University Press, 1979), pp. 61–62.

61 Robert Lee Wolff, *The Balkans in Our Time* (Cambridge, MA: Harvard University Press, 1956), pp. 430–431.

62 Goldstein and Goldstein, *Tito*, p. 518; Bojić, *Historija Bosne i Bošnjaka*, p. 240. See also Vera Kržišnik-Bukić, *Cazinska buna 1950* (Sarajevo: Svijetlost, 1991).

63 "Yugoslavia – Political Dynamics" (1 August 1960), C, decl. 22 November 2000 under the Freedom of Information Act, by the authority of NND 0011144, by SDI/SL, vol. 17, in Central Intelligence Agency (CIA), *National Intelligence Survey*, section 53, chap. V, NIS #21, RG 273, Box 92, on deposit at NA.

64 Ivo Banac, *With Stalin Against Tito: Cominformist Splits in Yugoslav Communism* (Ithaca, NY: Cornell University Pres, 1988), pp. 148–149, 150–151.

65 Closely paraphrased from Ljubo Sirc, *The Yugoslav Economy Under Self-Management* (London and Basingstoke: Macmillan, 1979), p. 3.

66 Béla K. Király, "The Aborted Soviet Military Plans Against Tito's Yugoslavia", in Wayne S. Vucinich (ed.), *At the Brink of War and Peace: The Tito-Stalin Split in a Historic Perspective* (New York: Brooklyn College Press, 1982), pp. 274–275, 278–279, 285–286; see also *Agence France-Presse* (AFP), 11 June 1993, in *Lexis-Nexis Academic Universe*.

67 Gerald G. Govorchin, "Reconstruction in New Yugoslavia", in *Social Science*, Vol. 23, No. 2 (April 1948), p. 114.

68 *Ibid.*, p. 115.
69 V. M., "Collectivization in Yugoslav Agriculture", in *The World Today*, Vol. 14, No. 2 (February 1958), p. 81.
70 *Ibid.*, pp. 82–83.
71 Ivan Lončarević, "Prices and Private Agriculture in Yugoslavia", in *Soviet Studies*, Vol. 39, No. 4 (October 1987), p. 628.
72 As quoted in V. M., "Collectivization in Yugoslav Agriculture", p. 84.
73 Lončarević, "Prices and Private Agriculture", p. 629; V. M., "Collectivization in Yugoslav Agriculture", p. 85.
74 See Tanja Zimmermann, "Oto Bihalji-Merin and the Concept of the 'Naïve' in the 1950s", in *Acta Historiae Artis Slovenica*, Vol. 23, No. 1 (2018), esp. pp. 189–196.
75 Sveta Lukić, *Contemporary Yugoslav Literature: A Sociopolitical Approach*, ed. by Gertrude Joch Robinson; trans. by Pola Triandis (Urbana: University of Illinois Press, 1972), p. 68.
76 Bojana Videkanić, "Yugoslav Postwar Art and Socialist Realism: An Uncomfortable Relationship", in *ARTMargins*, Vol. 5, No. 2 (2016), p. 4.
77 Reuben Fowkes, "Croatia/Hungary: Socialist Realist Art Criticism at the Crossroads in the 1950s", in *Third Text*, Vol. 20, No. 2 (March 2006), p. 202.
78 See Dubravka Juraga, "Miroslav Krleža's *Zastave*: Socialism, Yugoslavia, and the Historical Novel", in *South Atlantic Review*, Vol. 62, No. 4 (Autumn 1997), pp. 32–56.
79 Videkanić, "Yugoslav Postwar Art", p. 20.
80 Anthony M. Mlikotin, "Yugoslav Revision of Marxist Aesthetics: A Review Article", in *The Slavic and East European Journal*, Vol. 11, No. 3 (Autumn 1967), p. 324.
81 *Ibid.*, p. 325, citing Marko Ristić, "O funkciji književnosti i o društvenoj odgovornosti književnika", in *Izvanredni plenum književnika Jugoslavije* (Belgrade: Savez Književnika Jugoslavije, 1955), pp. 56, 58.
82 Mlikotin, "Yugoslav Revision", p. 325.
83 *Ibid.*, pp. 325–327.
84 *Ibid.*, citing Boris Ziherl, "Još jednom o našoj kritici", in *Književnost i društvo*, 2 vols. (Sarajevo: Svjetlost, 1958), vol. 1, p. 48.
85 Lukić, *Contemporary Yugoslav Literature*, p. 15.
86 *Ibid.*, p. 16.
87 *Ibid.*, p. 27.
88 *Ibid.*, p. 107.
89 Milimir Drazić, "Ivo Andrić, the Bard of Bosnia", in *Books Abroad*, Vol. 36, No. 1 (Winter 1962), pp. 25–26; Thomas Eekman, "The Later Stories of Ivo Andrić", in *The Slavonic and East European Review*, Vol. 48, No. 112 (July 1970), pp. 341–356 at 341; Alba della Fazia, "Nobel Prize, 1962, and 'The Bridge on the Drina' Revisited", in *Books Abroad*, Vol. 57, No. 1 (Winter 1963), pp. 24–26.
90 Marina Antić, "Ivo Andrić: Against National Mythopoesis", in *Slavic Review*, Vol. 77, No. 3 (Fall 2018), pp. 704–725, at 705–707.
91 These two paragraphs are based on Everett Helm, "Music in Yugoslavia", in *The Musical Quarterly*, Vol. 51, No. 1 (January 1965), pp. 215–224.
92 *Ibid.*, pp. 217, 220.
93 *Ibid.*, pp. 219, 222.
94 Pirjevec, *Tito and His Comrades*, p. 264.
95 C. M. Woodhouse, *Modern Greece: A Short History*, 5th ed. (London and Boston: Faber & Faber, 1997), p. 281.
96 Robert Bass and Elizabeth Marbury (eds.), *The Soviet-Yugoslav Controversy, 1948–58: A Documentary Record* (New York: Prospect Books, 1959), p. 53. See also Pirjevec, *Tito and His Comrades*, p. 264.
97 See *Yugoslavia's Way: The Program of the League of Communists of Yugoslavia (adopted by the Seventh Congress)*, trans. by Stoyan Pribichevich (New York: All Nations Press, 1958). See also Goldstein and Goldstein, *Tito*, p. 601.
98 As quoted in William E. Griffith, *Albania and the Sino-Soviet Rift* (Cambridge, MA: MIT Press, 1963), p. 97.

99 Thomas Taylor Hammond, "The Djilas Afffair and Jugoslav Communism", in *Foreign Affairs*, Vol. 33, No. 2 (January 1955), p. 30.

100 On pages 190–194.

101 Johanna Granville, "Josip Broz Tito's Role in the 1956 'Nagy Affair'", in *The Slavonic and East European Review*, Vol. 76, No. 4 (October 1998), p. 682.

102 As quoted in *Ibid.*, p. 682.

103 Johanna Granville, "Hungary 1956: The Yugoslav Connection", in *Europe-Asia Studies*, Vol. 50, No. 3 (May 1998), p. 498.

104 Granville, "Josip Broz Tito's Role", pp. 694–695, extract on p. 694.

105 As quoted in *Ibid.*, p. 698.

106 Djilas, *Fall of the New Class*, p. 116.

107 Boris Kidrič, *Sabrana dela* [Collected Works] (Belgrade: Kultura, 1961), as summarized in Jakov Sirotković, "Influence of the Self-Management System on the Development of the Yugoslav Economy", in *Eastern European Economics*, Vol. 20, No. 2 (Winter 1981–1982), p. 58.

108 As quoted in Djilas, *Fall of the New Class*, p. 117.

109 *Borba* (27 June 1950), as quoted in Fred Warner Neal, "The Reforms in Yugoslavia", in *The American Slavic and East European Review*, Vol. 13, No. 2 (April 1954), p. 230.

110 Sirc, *The Yugoslav Economy*, p. 14.

111 Pirjevec, *Tito and His Comrades*, pp. 314–315; Goldstein and Goldstein, *Tito*, pp. 608–609.

112 Josip Broz Tito, *Osmi kongres Saveza komunista Jugoslavije* (Belgrade: Komunist, 1964), p. 36, as quoted in Hilde Katrine Haug, *Creating a Socialist Yugoslavia: Tito, Communist Leadership and the National Question* (London and New York: I. B. Tauris, 2012), p. 184.

113 Tito, as quoted in Haug, *Creating a Socialist Yugoslavia*, p. 184.

114 Branko Petranović, *Istorija Jugoslavije 1918–1988, Vol. 3: Socijalistička Jugoslavija 1945–1988* (Belgrade: Nolit, 1988), p. 382.

115 Vojin Lukić, *Sećanja i saznanja* (Titograd: N. Jovović, 1989), p. 25.

116 *Borba* (Belgrade ed.), 2 July 1966, p. 1.

117 J. B. Tito, *Govori i članci*, as quoted in Othmar Nikola Haberl, *Parteiorganisation und nationale Frage in Jugoslawien* (Berlin: Otto Harrassawitz, 1976), p. 32.

118 Goldstein and Goldstein, *Tito*, p. 616.

119 *Borba* (3 July 1966), p. 1.

120 As quoted in Dušan Bilandžić, "Kongresi SKJ o društvenom položaju žene", in *Žena*, Vol. 39, No. 3 (1981), p. 32.

121 As quoted in Suzana Djurić and Gordana Dragičević, *Women in Yugoslav Society and Economy* (Belgrade: Medjunarodna Politika, 1965), p. 6.

122 Aleksandra Beluhan, "Sociološki aspekti prekida trudnoće", in *Žena*, Vol. 42, No. 4 (1984), p. 55; Sabrina P. Ramet, "In Tito's Time", in Sabrina P. Ramet (ed.), *Gender Politics in the Western Balkans: Women and Society in Yugoslavia and the Yugoslav Successor States* (University Park, PA: The Pennsylvania State University Press, 1999), p. 96.

123 Ramet, "In Tito's Time", pp. 95–96; Obrad Kesić, "Women and Revolution in Yugoslavia (1945–1989)", in Mary Ann Tetreault (ed.), *Women and Revolution in Africa, Asia, and the New World* (Columbia: University of South Carolina Press, 1994), p. 238; Vida Tomšič, *Women in the Development of Socialist Self-Managing Yugoslavia* (Belgrade: Jugoslovenska stvarnost, 1980), p. 114.

124 Pedro Ramet, "Women, Work and Self-Management in Yugoslavia", in *East European Quarterly*, Vol. 17, No. 4 (January 1984), p. 460.

125 Lydia Sklevický, "Reluctant Feminists: The 'Woman Question' – A New Approach in Yugoslavia", unpublished paper (1987).

126 Ramet, "Women, Work and Self-Management", p. 466.

127 *Ibid.*, p. 467.

128 Sabrina P. Ramet, "Feminism in Yugoslavia" – chap. 9 in *Social Currents in Eastern Europe: The Sources and Consequences of the Great Transformation*, 2nd ed. (Durham, NC and London: Duke University Press, 1995), pp. 220–221.

129 Jasna A. Petrović, "Žene u SK danas", in *Žena*, Vol. 44, No. 4 (1986), p. 7.
130 Barbara Jancar, "The New Feminism in Yugoslavia", in Pedro Ramet (ed.), *Yugoslavia in the 1980s* (Boulder, CO: Westview Press, 1985), p. 204.
131 Zsófia Lóránd, *The Feminist Challenge to the Socialist State in Yugoslavia* (Cham: Palgrave Macmillan, 2018), p. 4.
132 Report by Nadežda Gerasimovska-Hristova, in *Trinaesti kongres Saveza Komunista Jugoslavije, Beograd 25–28 jun 1986. Magnetofonske beleške*, vol. 2 (Belgrade: Izdavački centar Komunist, 1988), p. 188.
133 As quoted in Ramet, "In Tito's Time", p. 101.
134 Petranović, *Istorija Jugoslavije*, vol. 3, p. 64.
135 See Pedro Ramet, "The Soviet Factor in the Macedonian Dispute", in *Survey*, Vol. 24, No. 3 (Summer 1979), pp. 128–134.
136 Alexander, *Church and State in Yugoslavia*, p. 266.
137 Zachary T. Irwin, "The Macedonian Orthodox Church in the New Millennium", in Sabrina P. Ramet (ed.), *Orthodox Churches and Politics in Southeastern Europe: Nationalism, Conservatism, and Intolerance* (Cham: Palgrave Macmillan, 2019), p. 171.
138 Alexander, *Church and State in Yugoslavia*, p. 282.
139 Ridley, *Tito*, p. 385.
140 Goldstein and Goldstein, *Tito*, p. 648.
141 Pirjevec, *Tito and His Comrades*, pp. 351–353.
142 Ramet, *The Three Yugoslavias*, p. 295, citing Radio Belgrade (10 February 1968).
143 For more details, see *Ibid.*, pp. 230–231.
144 As quoted in Goldstein, *Hrvatska*, p. 533.
145 Zdenko Radelić, *Hrvatska u Jugoslaviji 1945–1991. od zajedništva do razlaza* (Zagreb: Školska knjiga, 2006), p. 417. See also Goldstein, *Hrvatska*, p. 546.
146 *Hrvatski tjednik* [HT] (25 November 1971), p. 7; and HT (12 November 1971), p. 7.
147 Radelić, *Hrvatska u Jugoslaviji*, p. 408.
148 Ante Čuvalo, *The Croatian National Movement, 1966–1972* (Boulder, CO: East European Monographs, 1990), pp. 105, 106.
149 See Jože Pirjevec, *Il giorno di San Vito: Jugoslavia 1918–1992 – Storia di una tragedia* (Torino: Nuova Eri Edizioni, 1993), pp. 375, 396.
150 Pirjevec, *Tito and His Comrades*, p. 386.
151 Mihailo Đurić, "Smišljene smutnje", in *Anali Pravnog Fakulteta u Beogradu*, No. 3 (1971), p. 231, as quoted in Dejan Guzina, "Socialist Serbia's Narrative from Yugoslavia to a Greater Serbia", in *International Journal of Politics, Culture, and Society*, Vol. 17, No. 1 (Fall 2003), p. 97.
152 Ramet, *The Three Yugoslavias*, pp. 250–251.
153 Savez Komunista Hrvatske, Centralni komitet, *Izvještaj o stanju u Savezu komunista Hrvatske u odnosu na prodor nacionalizma u njegove redove* (Zagreb: Informativna služba CK SKH, 1972), pp. 83, 84.
154 Ramet, *The Three Yugoslavias*, p. 254. See also Radelić, *Hrvatska u Jugoslaviji*, p. 386.
155 *Izještaj o stanju u Savezu komunista Hrvatske*, pp. 127–128. See also Radelić, *Hrvatska u Jugoslaviji*, pp. 455–462; Goldstein, *Hrvatska*, p. 550.
156 Stephen R. Sacks, "Regional Inequality in Yugoslav Industry", in *The Journal of Developing Areas*, Vol. 11, No. 1 (October 1976), p. 67.
157 Ksente Bogoev, "The Policy of More Rapid Development of the Underdeveloped Republics and Province", in *Eastern European Economics*, Vol. 10, No. 4 (Summer 1972), pp. 397–398.
158 Milivoje Vujačić, "Investment, 1966–1975", in *Yugoslav Survey*, Vol. 18, No. 2 (May 1977), pp. 61–62.
159 Sacks, "Regional Inequality", p. 67.
160 Dušan Ristić, "Kosovo i Savez Komunista Kosova izmedju dva kongresa i dve konferencije", in *Obeležja*, Vol. 9, No. 5 (September–October 1979), p. 41.
161 See Miloš Mišović, *Ko je tražio republiku: Kosovo 1945–1985* (Belgrade: Narodna knjiga, 1987).

162 Branko Horvat, *Kosovsko pitanje* (Zagreb: Globus, 1988), p. 62.
163 Isabel Ströhle, *Aus den Ruinen der alten erschaffen wir die neue Welt! Herrschaftspraxis und Loyalitäten in Kosovo, 1944–1974* (Munich: De Gruyter Oldenbourg, 2016), pp. 223–225.
164 Ramet, *The Three Yugoslavias*, p. 296.
165 *Bilten pokrajinskog zavoda za statisticku SAPK* (1975), as cited by Nebi Gaši, "Nacionalna ravnopravnost na Kosovu i politika zapošljavanja", in *Udruženi rad i medjunacionalni odnosi* (Belgrade: Komunist, 1978), p. 158.
166 *The Times* (London), 4 April 1981, p. 4; *New York Times* (7 April 1981), p. A3; and *Frankfurter Allgemeine* (27 April 1981), p. 3.
167 Sabrina P. Ramet, "Yugoslavia", in Sabrina P. Ramet (ed.), *Eastern Europe: Politics, Culture, and Society Since 1939* (Bloomington: Indiana University Press, 1998), p. 169.
168 Patrick Hyder Patterson, *Bought and Sold: Living and Losing the Good Life in Socialist Yugoslavia* (Ithaca, NY: Cornell University Press, 2011).
169 Ramet, "Yugoslavia", p. 170.
170 For discussion, see Radelić, *Hrvatska u Jugoslaviji*, pp. 472–484.
171 Pirjevec, *Tito and His Comrades*, p. 403.
172 Haug, *Creating a Socialist Yugoslavia*, p. 242.
173 Goldstein, *Hrvatska*, p. 613.
174 Ramet, *The Three Yugoslavias*, p. 309.
175 Biljana Šljivić-Šimšić, Review of *Vunena vremena* by Gojko Djogo in *World Literature Today*, Vol. 56, No. 4 (Autumn 1982), p. 724.
176 Anto Knežević, "Alija Izetbegović's *Islamic Declaration:* Its Substance and its Western Reception", in *Islamic Studies*, Vol. 36, Nos. 2–3 (Summer/Autumn 1997), p. 497.
177 A 1990 revision of the *Islamic Declaration* is posted here: www.angelfire.com/dc/mbooks/Alija-Izetbegovic-Islamic-Declaration-1990-Azam-dot-com.pdf [accessed on 2 May 2022].
178 From the indictment, as quoted in Knežević, "Alija Izetbegović's *Islamic Declaration*", p. 498.
179 *Ibid.*, p. 499.
180 *New York Times* (16 July 1984), p. 23.
181 Anton Logoreci, "Riots and Trials in Kosovo", in *Index on Censorship*, No. 2 (1982), p. 24.
182 *New York Times* (28 September 1984), p. 10.
183 Ramet, *The Three Yugoslavias*, pp. 314–316.
184 Dobrica Ćosić, *Into the Battle* [vol. 1 of the English translation) (San Diego: Harvest/HBJ, 1983).
185 As quoted from vol. 4 in Vasa D. Mihailovich, "Aspects of Nationalism in Dobrica Ćosić's Novel *A Time of Death:* Chauvinism or Sincere Patriotism?" in *World Literature Today*, Vol. 60, No. 3 (Summer 1986), p. 416.
186 As quoted in *Ibid.*, p. 414.
187 *Ibid.*
188 Nicholas J. Miller, "The Nonconformists: Dobrica Ćosić and Mića Popović Envision Serbia", in *Slavic Review*, Vol. 58, No. 3 (Autumn 1999), pp. 516, 522.
189 See Jasna Dragović-Soso, *Saviours of the Nation: Serbia's Intellectual Opposition and the Revival of Nationalism* (Montreal: McGill-Queen's University Press, 2002); Florian Bieber, *Nationalismus in Serbien vom Tode Titos zum Ende der Ära Milošević* (Vienna: LIT Verlag, 2005).
190 *Vjesnik* (Zagreb), 27–30 November 1982, p. 6.
191 Pedro Ramet, "Yugoslavia and the Threat of Internal and External Discontents", in *Orbis*, Vol. 28, No. 1 (Spring 1984), p. 109.
192 Mladen Srbinović, signing, "Committee for the Defence of Freedom of Thought and Expression" (Belgrade, 25 November 1987), in *Index on Censorship* (1988), No. 5, p. 35.
193 *Ibid.*, p. 36.

Ramet

194 *Economic Surveys: Yugoslavia* (Paris: Organisation for Economic Co-operation and Development, July 1982), p. 14; *Ibid.*, May 1983, p. 15.
195 Sabrina P. Ramet, *The Liberal Project and the Transformation of Democracy: The Case of East Central Europe* (College Station: Texas A&M University Press, 2007), pp. 24, 25.
196 Ramet, "Yugoslavia and the Threat", p. 114.
197 Regarding Zabranjeno pušenje, see Sabrina Petra Ramet, "Shake, Rattle, and Self-Management: Making the Scene in Yugoslavia", in Sabrina Petra Ramet (ed.), *Rocking the State: Rock Music and Politics in Eastern Europe and Russia* (Boulder, CO: Westview Press, 1994), pp. 111–112.
198 Details in Ramet, *Balkan Babel*, p. 131.
199 See Darko Glavan and Dražen Vrdoljak, *Ništa mudro – Bijelo dugme: Autorizirana biografija* (Zagreb: Polet Rock, 1981).
200 "Subculture", in *The Art and Popular Culture Encyclopedia*, at www.artandpopular culture.com/Subculture [accessed on 7 May 2022].
201 Merton, as summarized in Peter Sohlberg, *Functionalist Construction Work in Social Science: The Lost Heritage* (London and New York: Routledge, 2021), p. 209.
202 Benjamin Perasović, "Sociologija subkultura i hrvatski kontekst", in *Društvena istraživanja*, Vol. 11, Nos. 2–3 (58–59) (2002), p. 487.
203 Nikola Božilović, "Youth Subcultures and Subversive Identities", in *Facta Universitatis – Philosophy, Sociology, Psychology and History* [hereafter, *Facta Universitatis*], Vol. 9, No. 1 (2010), p. 49.
204 Goran Bregović, in interview with Sabrina Ramet, Sarajevo, 14 September 1989. The entire interview is published in Ramet (ed.), *Rocking the State*, pp. 133–139 – quoted extract on p. 135.
205 Joshua Kalčić, "Subkulture mladih u Puli: od *Punka* do rasapa alternativne scene", in *Narodna umjetnost*, Vol. 49, No. 2 (2012), p. 86.
206 See Jelena N. Božilović, "New Wave in Yugoslavia: Socio-Political Concept", in *Facta Universitatis*, Vol. 12, No. 1 (2013), pp. 69–70; Gregor Tomc, "'Comrades, We Don't Believe You!' Or Do We Just Want to Dance with You? The Slovenian Punk Subculture in Socialist Yugoslavia", in Danijela S. Beard and Ljerka V. Rasmussen (eds.), *Made in Yugoslavia: Studies in Popular Music* (New York and London: Routledge, 2020), p. 198.
207 Božilović, "New Wave in Yugoslavia", p. 70.
208 As quoted in Vesna Andree Zaimović, "The Sarajevo Pop-Rock Scene: Music from the Yugoslav Crossroads", trans. by Danijela Beard in Beard and Rasmussen (eds.), *Made in Yugoslavia*, p. 40.
209 As quoted in David Albahari (ed.), *Drugom stranom: Almanah novog talasa u SFRJ* (Belgrade: Istraživačko-izdavački centar SSO, 1983), p. 74.
210 Ana Petrov, "Bijelo Dugme: The Politics of Remembrance Within the Post-Yugoslav Popular Music Scene", in Beard and Rasmussen (eds.), *Made in Yugoslavia*, p. 114.
211 Vladan Jeremić, "Politike vizuelnih reprezentacija i interpretacija arhiva jugoslovenskog panka i novog talasa", in Đorđe Tomić and Petar Atanacković (eds.), *Novi društveni pokreti u Jugoslaviji od 1968. do danas* (Novi Sad: Cenzura, 2009), p. 103; Tomc, "Comrades, We Don't Believe in You!" p. 198.
212 Zaimović, "The Sarajevo Pop-Rock Scene", p. 44.
213 Ines Prica, *Omladinska potkultura u Beogradu: simbolička praksa* (Belgrade: Etnografski Institut SANU, 1991), pp. 50, 65.
214 As quoted in Natalja Kyaw, "*Računajte na nas.* Pank i Novi Talas / Novi Val u Socijalističkoj Jugoslaviji", in Tomić and Atanacković (eds.), *Novi društveni pokreti*, p. 98.
215 "Laibach: 10 Items of the Covenant", written by the group members in 1982 and first published in *Nova revija* in 1983; English translation posted at https://garagemca.org/en/exhibition/nsk-from-kapital-to-capital/materials/laibach-desyat-statey-zaveta-laibach-10-items-of-the-covenant [accessed on 7 May 2022], my emphasis.

216 Robert K. Merton, *Social Theory and Social Structure*, Enlarged ed. (New York and London: Free Press & Collier Macmillan, 1968), pp. 114–115.

217 Prica, *Omladinska potkultura u Beogradu*, p. 9.

218 Regarding ancient Greece and Pompeii, see J. A. Baird and Claire Taylor, "Ancient Graffiti", in Jeffrey Ian Ross (ed.), *Routledge Handbook of Graffiti and Street Art* (London and New York: Routledge, 2016), pp. 17–26, especially pp. 17–21.

219 Terri Moreau and Derek H. Alderman, "Graffiti Hurts and the Eradication of Alternative Landscape Expression", in *Geographical Review*, Vol. 101, No. 1 (January 2011), p. 107.

220 Gill Valentine, Tracey Skelton, and Deborah Chambers, "Cool Places: An Introduction to Youth and Youth Culture", in Skelton and Valentine (eds.), *Cool Places: Geographies of Youth Cultures* (London: Routledge, 1998), p. 7, as quoted in Ricardo Campos, "Youth, Graffiti, and the Aestheticization of Transgression", in *Social Analysis: The International Journal of Anthropology*, Vol. 59, No. 3 (Autumn 2015), p. 20.

221 Joe Austin, "More to See Than a Canvas in a White Cube: For an Art in the Streets", in *City*, Vol. 14, Nos. 1–2 (2010), p. 44, as quoted in Campos, "Youth, Graffiti", p. 22.

222 For further discussion, see Sabrina P. Ramet, "The Miracle at Medjugorje – A Functionalist Approach", in *South Slav Journal*, Vol. 8 (1991), pp. 12–20.

223 Srdjan Garčević, "Magic in the Twilight of Yugoslavia", in *The Nutshell Times* (31 October 2018), at https://thenutshelltimes.com/2018/10/31/magic-during-the-twilight-of-yugoslavia/ [accessed on 8 May 2022], pp. 2–3 of 7.

224 *Ibid.*, p. 3 of 7.

225 As quoted in Ivana Bago, "Yugoslavia as World History: The Political Economy of Self-Managed Art", in *ARTMargins*, Vol. 8, No. 1 (February 2019), p. 81.

226 Aleš Erjavec and Marina Gržinić, *Ljubljana, Ljubljana: The Eighties in Slovene Art and Culture*, trans. from Slovenian by Mojca Majcen and Milan Mlačnik (Ljubljana: Založba Mladinska knjiga, 1991), p. 12.

227 From Albahari, *Drugom stranom*, p. 10.

228 *Memorandum of the Serbian Academy of Sciences and Art* (1986), trans. by Dennison Rusinow with Aleksandar and Sarah Nikolić and printed as an appendix to Dennison Rusinow, "The Yugoslav Peoples", in Peter F. Sugar (ed.), *Eastern European Nationalism in the Twentieth Century* (Washington, DC: American University Press, 1995), p. 342.

229 Tim Judah, *The Serbs: History, Myth and the Destruction of Yugoslavia* (New Haven, CT: Yale University Press, 1997), p. 160.

230 See the discussion in Ramet, *Balkan Babel*, pp. 52–53; also Sonja Biserko, "Nacija protiv pojedinca", in *Helsinška povelja* (Belgrade), Vol. 10, Nos. 81–82 (March–April 2005), p. 19.

231 Regarding Milošević, see: Adam Lebor, *Milošević: A Biography* (Polmont, Stirlingshire: Bloomsbury, 2002); Louis Sell, *Slobodan Milošević and the Destruction of Yugoslavia* (Durham, NC: Duke University Press, 2002); Massimo Nara, *Milosevic: La tragedia di un popolo* (Milan: Rizzoli, 1999); Vidosav Stevanović, *Milošević, jedan epitaf* (Belgrade: Montana, 2002).

232 As quoted in Louis Sell, "The (Un)Making of Milosevic", in *The Wilson Quarterly*, Vol. 23, No. 3 (Summer 1999), p. 22.

233 Radina Vučetić, "Kosovo 1989: The (Ab)use of the Kosovo Myth in Media and Popular Culture", in *Comparative Southeast European Studies*, Vol. 69, Nos. 2–3 (2021), p. 230.

234 *Ibid.*, p. 233.

235 As quoted in *Ibid.*, p. 237.

236 *Svet* (Belgrade), September 1989, special edition, p. 7.

237 *Delo* (Ljubljana), 21 November 1989, p. 5.

238 See Radelić, *Hrvatska u Jugoslaviji*, p. 590.

239 Viktor Meier, *Wie Jugoslawien verspielt wurde*, 2nd ed. (Munich: C. H. Beck, 1996), pp. 265–266.

240 For details and documentation, see Ramet, *Balkan Babel*, p. 60; Branka Magaš, *The Destruction of Yugoslavia: Tracking the Break-Up, 1980–92* (London: Verso, 1993), p. 311. See also Davor Marijan and Nikica Barić, *The Fall of Yugoslavia and the Creation of the Croatian State* (Zagreb: Hrvatski Institut za Povijest, 2019), p. 81.

241 Meier, *Wie Jugoslawien verspielt wurde*, pp. 266, 268.

242 *Oslobodjenje* (Sarajevo), 12 November 1990, p. 1, trans. in FBIS, *Daily Report* (Eastern Europe), 29 November 1990, p. 74.

243 *Borba* (Belgrade), 26 December 1990, p. 3; and Tanjug (3 March 1991), trans. in FBIS, *Daily Report* (Eastern Europe), 4 March 1991, p. 41.

244 For further discussion, see Stipe Mesić, *Kako je srušena Jugoslavija: Politički memoari*, 2nd ed. (Zagreb: Mislav Press, 1994).

245 Dejan Jović, "The Slovenian-Croatian Confederal Proposal: A Tactical Move or an Ultimate Solution?" in Lenard J. Cohen and Jasna Dragović-Soso (eds.), *State Collapse in South-Eastern Europe: New Perspectives on Yugoslavia's Disintegration* (West Lafayette, IN: Purdue University Press, 2008), pp. 251–252.

246 See Paolo Rumiz, *Masken für ein Massaker. Der manipulierte Krieg; Spurensuche auf dem Balkan*, trans. from Italian by Friederike Hausmann and Gesa Schröder (Munich: Verlag Antje Kunstmann, 2000).

247 Bernhard Tönnes, "Religious Persecution in Albania", trans. from German by G. M. Ablith and Anne Atkinson, in *Religion in Communist Lands*, Vol. 10, No. 3 (1982), p. 251.

248 Anton Logoreci, *The Albanians: Europe's Forgotten Survivors* (London: Victor Gollancz, 1977), p. 104.

249 Prifti, *Socialist Albania Since 1944* [note 3], p. 188.

250 These cases are all derived from Fjoralba Satka Mata, "Albanian Alternative Artists vs. Official Art Under Communism", in *History of Communism in Europe*, Vol. 2 (2011), pp. 81–83.

251 Prifti, *Socialist Albania Since 1944*, pp. 33–34.

252 Nicholas C. Pano, *The People's Republic of Albania* (Baltimore: The Johns Hopkins Press, 1968), pp. 41–49.

253 See Miranda Vickers, *The Albanians: A Modern History* (London and New York: I. B. Tauris, 1995; reprinted 2006), pp. 151, 153, 168.

254 Pano, *The People's Republic*, pp. 51–53.

255 Prifti, *Socialist Albania Since 1944*, p. 11.

256 *Ibid.*, pp. 53–54.

257 Logoreci, *The Albanians*, p. 117.

258 Prifti, *Socialist Albania Since 1944*, p. 79.

259 Logoreci, *The Albanians*, pp. 11–12.

260 Pano, *The People's Republic*, p. 82.

261 *Ibid.*, p. 85.

262 Agence-France Presse and *Albanian Information Bulletin* (both: 29 October 1948), as summarized in Dispatch A-627, sent on 29 October 1948 from Cavendish W. Cannon / U.S. Embassy, Belgrade; received on 4 November 1948 by the U.S. Secretary of State, in U.S. Department of State, *Records Relating to the Internal Affairs of Albania 1945–1949*, Decimal file 875, Reel 2 (files .00/3–2546 to .01/6–2945).

263 Enclosure to Dispatch 189 (27 May 1949), from U.S. Embassy, Belgrade to Secretary of State, in *Records 1945–1949*, Reel 2.

264 Summary of the Belgrade press regarding the Xoxe trial, in Dispatch (27 May 1949), from R. Borden Reams, Counselor at the U.S. Embassy Belgrade, to Secretary of State, in *Records 1945–1949*, Reel 2; Pano, *The People's Republic of Albania*, p. 92.

265 Nicholas Bethell, *The Great Betrayal* (London: Hodder and Stoughton, 1994), pp. 3–5, 82–87; Michael W. Dravis, "Storming Fortress Albania: American Covert Operations in Microcosm, 1949–54", in *Intelligence and National Security*, Vol. 7, No. 4 (1992), pp. 428–432.

266 Dravis, "Storming Fortress Albania", p. 433.

267 *Ibid.*

268 Derek R. Hall, "Albania's Growing Railway Network", in *Geography*, Vol. 69, No. 3 (June 1984), p. 264.

269 Prifti, *Socialist Albania Since 1944*, p. 57.

270 *Ibid.*, p. 69.

271 *Ibid.*, pp. 78–81.

272 Logoreci, *The Albanians*, p. 121.

273 As quoted in Stavro Skendi, "Albania and the Sino-Soviet Conflict", in *Foreign Affairs*, Vol. 40, No. 3 (April 1962), pp. 472–473.

274 Enver Hoxha, *The Khrushchevites* (Scottsdale, AZ: Prism Key Press, 2011), pp. 10, 15.

275 *Ibid.*, p. 131.

276 *Ibid.*, p. 17.

277 Biberaj, *Albania: A Socialist Maverick*, p. 23.

278 Griffith, *Albania and the Sino-Soviet Rift*, p. 41.

279 As quoted in *Ibid.*, p. 77.

280 *Ibid.*, pp. 78–79.

281 Peter R. Prifti, "Albania and the Sino-Soviet Conflict", in *Studies in Comparative Communism*, Vol. 6, No. 3 (Autumn 1973), pp. 249–250.

282 *Ibid.*, p. 262.

283 Logoreci, *The Albanians*, p. 154.

284 Prifti, *Socialist Albania Since 1944*, p. 152.

285 *Ibid.*, p. 152.

286 *Ibid.*; Bernhard Tönnes, "Religious Persecution in Albania", trans. from German by G. M. Ablitt and Anne Atkinson, in *Religion in Communist Lands*, Vol. 10, No. 3 (1982), p. 249.

287 Gjon Sinishta, *The Fulfilled Promise: A Documentary Account of Religious Persecution in Albania* (Santa Clara, CA: H&F Composing Service, 1976), pp. 39, 42–44.

288 *Ibid.*, pp. 42–52.

289 *Ibid.*, p. 54.

290 Logoreci, *The Albanians*, p. 154.

291 As quoted in Prifti, *Socialist Albania Since 1944*, pp. 157–158.

292 Klejd Këlliçi and Emira Danaj, "Promoting Equality, Perpetuating Inequality: Gender Propaganda in Communist Albania", in *History of Communism in Europe*, Vol. 7 (2016), p. 42.

293 *Ibid.*, p. 48; confirmed in Esilda Luku and Elvin Luku, "Emancipation Policy or Propaganda? The Position of Albanian Women under State Socialism", in *Hiperboraca*, Vol. 7, No. 1 (2020), p. 67.

294 As quoted in Këlliçi and Danaj, "Promoting Equality", p. 49.

295 As quoted in Prifti, *Socialist Albania Since 1944*, p. 97.

296 Këlliçi and Danaj, "Promoting Equality", p. 41.

297 Luku and Luku, "Emancipation Policy", p. 61; Këlliçi and Danaj, "Promoting Equality", p. 42.

298 Luku and Luku, "Emancipation Policy", pp. 59, 61–62.

299 Prifti, *Socialist Albania Since 1944*, pp. 114, 121–122.

300 *Ibid.*, pp. 123–126.

301 See Enis Sulstarova, "Constructing Albanian Communist Identity Through Literature: Nationalism and Orientalism in the Works of Ismail Kadare", in *History of Communism in Europe*, Vol. 3 (2012), pp. 131–146.

302 Paul Lendvai, *Das einsame Albanien. Reportage aus dem Land der Skipetaren* (Zürich and Osnabrück: Edition Interform & Verlag A. Fromm, 1985), p. 88.

303 As quoted in Prifti, *Socialist Albania Since 1944*, p. 143.

304 As quoted in *Ibid.*, p. 181.

305 Pano, "The Albanian Cultural Revolution", p. 51.

306 *Ibid.*, p. 54.
307 *Zëri i Popullit* (6 March 1966), as quoted in Isa Blumi, "Hoxha's Class War: The Cultural Revolution and State Reformation, 1961–1971", in *East European Quarterly*, Vol. 33, No. 3 (September 1999), p. 316.
308 Blumi, "Hoxha's Class War", p. 320.
309 As quoted in Logoreci, *The Albanians*, p. 161.
310 Biberaj, *Albania*, p. 28.
311 *Ibid.*, p. 36.
312 *New York Times* (3 January 1982), p. 15.
313 *Ibid.*
314 *New York Times* (5 March 1985), p. 4.
315 See Berit Backer, "Self-Reliance under Socialism: The Case of Albania", in *Journal of Peace Research*, Vol. 19, No. 4 (1982), pp. 355, 356.
316 Biberaj, *Albania*, p. 31.
317 As cited in Logoreci, *The Albanians*, pp. 195–198.
318 Hans-Joachim Hoppe, "Demokratischer Machtwechsel in Albanien", in *Osteuropa*, Vol. 42, No. 7 (July 1992), p. 612.
319 *Ibid.*, pp. 615–617.
320 Mihailo V. Popović, "Uzroci ekonomske i društveno-političke nestabilnosti u Jugoslaviji", in *Sociologija*, Vol. 24, No. 2–3 (1982), published in English translation by Helen M. Kramer under the title "Causes of Economic and Sociopolitical Instability in Yugoslavia", in *Eastern European Economics*, Vol. 23, No. 1 (Autumn 1984), p. 16.
321 *Ibid.*, p. 14.
322 *Ibid.*, p. 9.
323 *Ibid.*, p. 10.
324 *Ibid.*, p. 7.
325 See Branko Milanović, "Poverty in Eastern Europe in the Years of Crisis, 1978 to 1987: Poland, Hungary, and Yugoslavia", in *The World Bank Economic Review*, Vol. 5, No. 2 (May 1991), pp. 187–205.
326 See Susan Woodward, *Socialist Unemployment: The Political Economy of Yugoslavia, 1945–1990* (Princeton, NJ: Princeton University Press, 1995); Janez Malačić and Aleš Vahčić, "Yugoslav Economists on Unemployment in Yugoslavia", in *Eastern European Economics*, Vol. 15, No. 4 (Summer 1977), pp. 60–72; Janez Malačić, "Unemployment in Yugoslavia from 1952 to 1975", in *Eastern European Economics*, Vol. 17, No. 4 (Summer 1979), pp. 85–109; Emil Primorac and Mate Babić, "Systematic Changes and Unemployment Growth in Yugoslavia, 1965–1984", in *Slavic Review*, Vol. 48, No. 2 (Summer 1989), pp. 195–213.
327 See Prifti, *Socialist Albania Since 1944*, p. 83.
328 *Ibid.*, p. 87.
329 *Zëri i Popullit* (13 April 1985), as quoted in Pauline Hodges, "Albania After Hoxha's Death", in *Religion in Communist Lands*, Vol. 14, No. 3 (Winter 1986), p. 266.
330 Sulejman Mato, "Enver" (excerpts), *Nëndori*, Vol. 18, No. 12 (December 1971), p. 117, as quoted in Prifti, *Socialist Albania Since 1944*, p. 182.
331 "Albanian Says Foreign Representatives not Invited to Hoxha Funeral", in *AP News* (13 April 1985), at https://apnews.com/article/294c2b5a3d7c14bdff4cef342407b8ab [accessed on 21 March 2022].
332 Tony Paterson, "Albanian Leader Enver Hoxha Buried", in *UPI Archives* (15 April 1985), at www.upi.com/Archives/1985/04/15/Albanian-leader-Enver-Hoxha-buried/8546482389200/ [accessed on 21 March 2022].
333 See Mitja Velikonja, *Titostalgia: A Study of Nostalgia for Josip Broz* (Ljubljana: The Peace Institute, 2008), at www.mirovni-institut.si/wp-content/uploads/2014/08/Titostalgia.pdf [accessed on 21 March 2022].

6

EPITAPH

A functionalist interpretation

History is littered with examples of unintended consequences of policies gone awry. Moreover, even policies that accomplish what they are designed to do can have unintended consequences and, as the record of communist rule in East Central Europe demonstrates, unintended consequences, whether latent functions or side effects, can have greater weight than even the most successfully realized results (manifest functions) of policies. The communist leaders of East Central Europe, whether satraps operating within limits set by the Soviet Union or independent potentates as Tito and Hoxha were, wanted to create new societies, or one might say even a new society, since the blueprint was similar from one country to the next. They wanted to reshape people's thinking and behavior, creating what they called the New Socialist Man and New Socialist Woman, to steer religion into oblivion or, as Trotsky would say, into the dustbin of history, and to see social organizations such as organizations for women and young people, trade unions, and religious organizations, for as long as the last of these continued to exist, operate as transmission belts, carrying out tasks assigned by the respective communist party and feeding information upward to higher party echelons. For a short while, in the Stalinist era, running in the Soviet bloc from roughly 1948 until Khrushchev exorcised Stalinism in 1956, it seemed, both to the outside world and to many local cadres, that the communists were realizing their ambition. But cracks soon appeared – in 1952 when the Yugoslav communists introduced workers' councils in the factories, following this up by adopting the Basic Law the following year; in 1953, when workers took to the streets in East Germany and Czechoslovakia; and in 1956, when there were changes at the top not only in Hungary and Poland but also in Bulgaria.[1] It is not unusual for societies to have to deal with crises, but the crises in the communist states first rattled their foundations and then later

DOI: 10.4324/9781003311515-6

shook them, eventually causing them to crumble. With the appearance of the Independent Trade Union Solidarity in Poland in summer 1980, communism's days were numbered, as some Western observers quickly understood. The chief problems which brought down communism throughout the bloc as well as in Yugoslavia were (1) the huge debts accumulated through policies undertaken on the basis of wishful thinking, (2) the severe limits to private enterprise, to cultural expression, to access to independent media (except in East Germany, where locals had access to West German television), and, to varying degrees from country to country, to religious freedom, (3) the Soviet veto of both alternative political parties (as the Hungarian example showed) and even programs to relax communist controls over the media and public life (as the Czechoslovak example showed), and (4) the underlying lack of legitimacy of communism, rooted in the fact that the communists did not come to power through free elections and could not convince people that they alone should hold the reins of power. The debts were accumulated as an unintended consequence of programs which could be funded only by foreign loans. The limits imposed in culture, media, and religion had the unintended consequence of feeding disaffection[2] and fueling dissent and opposition.[3] And the prevention of the emergence of alternative political parties had the unintended consequence of depriving the communist parties of the possibility of attracting support in competition with other parties, thereby freezing the illegitimacy with which the communists had come to power. The communists themselves could not have preserved their personal power without fundamental changes to their policies and ambitions – in other words, without ceasing to be communists.

Mikhail Gorbachev. who was elected General Secretary of the Communist Party of the Soviet Union in March 1985, realized that communism was in trouble but tried to deal with the symptoms rather than with the underlying problems. He saw that, because of an obsession with secrecy even about such ordinary matters as mineral deposits and the location of mountains, access to useful information was problematic; among other things, airline pilots were routinely issued maps with mountains, cities, and other features shifted out of place and had to correct their maps by pen and ink. Gorbachev's policy of *Glasnost'* (usually translated as openness) was designed to improve access to useful information. He saw that the highly centralized economic system with five-year plans drawn up without adequate information about either supply or demand, was not working and launched what he called *Perestroika* (restructuring). There was also a problem with how the law was understood. Among the many examples which could be cited, one may suffice here. There was a publicly available law specifying what criteria a group of religious believers needed to satisfy in order to obtain legal registration of a newly founded religious organization; but there was also a secret law, not available to the public, which spelled out that certain religious groups should not be granted registration, even if they met the legal requirements. Gorbachev wanted to see uniformity and evenhandedness in the law; his program here was promoted under the rubric of *Zakonitost* (lawfulness). And finally, he was convinced that the Soviet Union's foreign relations, including with the states of the Soviet bloc, needed a new think-ing (*Novoe Myshlenie*). One result of this new thinking was the decision to allow the leaders of the communist bloc states to make their own decisions, without coordinating with the Kremlin. The point to be emphasized here is that the first three problems were endemic throughout communist East Central Europe, though not always to the same degree, and that, just as in the Soviet case, the East Central European satraps hoped to save their system by addressing symptoms, rather than the underlying problems.

In an article for *The American Sociological Review*, Robert K. Merton noted that the problem of "unanticipated consequences" has been addressed by such prominent past writers as Niccolò Machiavelli, Giambattista Vico, Adam Smith, Karl Marx and Friedrich Engels, Vilfredo Pareto, Graham Wallas, Charles Horton Cooley, Pitirim Sorokin, F. Stuart Chapin, and Alexander von Schelting, among others.[4] I have preferred to employ the term "unintended consequences" since there can be problems also with consequences which are anticipated but not intended or chosen. In the same article, Merton cautioned against the casual supposition "that purposive action implies 'rationality' of human action (that persons always use the objectively most adequate means for the attainment of their end[s]."[5] In the context of East Central Europe, thus, there is no reason to assume that the show trials of Slánský, Rajk, or Kostov were "rational", in the sense of being "the objectively most adequate means" to secure the dominance of one party faction over another not just in the short term but over a longer period. Political actors may exercise good judgment on some occasions and dreadful judgment on other occasions, they may choose wise courses of action or make serious and costly mistakes. Moreover, as Andrew Ira Friedson has noted, "Legislation that is aimed at addressing one issue in society may have effects elsewhere that dampen or even reverse the gains the policy sought to acquire in the first place."[6]

Throughout this volume, I have been interested in policies and in their stated purposes and actual functions, including in economic policy, religious policy, pol-icy regarding gender equality, and cultural policy. What the historical record shows is that none of these policies played out exactly as planned; there were always instances of deviance (as in gender policy), resistance (as in the religious and cul-tural spheres), subversion (again, in the cultural sphere), and a mix of incompe-tence, corruption, and lack of information (in the economic sphere).

To be interested in communism is to be interested in the policies it generated and that, in turn, is to be interested in the functions such policies were intended to fulfill as well as in latent functions, side-effects, and dysfunctions. It follows that to take communism seriously is to be a functionalist theorist.

The typical and the heterogeneous

The communist systems of East Central Europe had a number of typical features. These included the single-party system, party control of the mass media, five-year economic plans, party-sponsored organizations for women and young people, pro-regime priests' organizations, controls in the cultural sector (especially in but not limited to the Stalinist era), and collective farms. Institutions are established to carry out certain specified functions; the fact that more or less the same institutions were typical throughout the communist region tells us that the same functions needed to be fulfilled in several, if not all, the bloc states. But there were differences in conditions across the region, which dictated some variation also in institutions. The most obvious examples come from Poland where the strong Catholic Church and the intensity of peasant resistance to collectivization, combined with Gomułka's conviction that private farming was better suited to Poland, produced a more liberal approach in religious policy and the abandonment of agricultural collectivization. In brief, in Polish conditions, the pre–October 1956 policies in these sectors had proven dysfunctional and therefore had to be abandoned. There were also variations in terms of the political establishment itself, with some party-states making use of pro-regime sister parties (Poland, East Germany, Czechoslovakia, and Bulgaria) and others doing without such transmission belts (Yugoslavia, Albania, Hungary, and Romania). Again, while a cult of the leader was typical across the region, it reached absurd, gargantuan proportions arguably only in Romania, in the era of Nicolae Ceauşescu, while it was totally abandoned in Hungary by János Kádár. And while all of the parties professed to be adhering to Marxism-Leninism, Ceauşescu and Albania's Enver Hoxha adopted some ideas from Mao Zedong's Great Proletarian Cultural Revolution, while the Yugoslavs, after a while, started describing their ideology as "self-managing socialism", highlighting the role that workers' councils were supposedly playing in their country.

There were also ritual phrases and slogans that recurred from one country to the next. Perhaps the most striking was the assertion "religion is the private affair of the individual" – a sentence not enunciated in Albania, for obvious reasons. But in the other seven countries, what the assertion meant was that religion should not be brought into the public sphere and that Churches should stay out of public debates. The communists were able to enforce this stricture prior to 1956 but, once the limited thaw set in, Churches in East Germany and especially Poland increasingly entered into public debates, including, in Poland in the mid-1970s, concerning the draft constitution being discussed at the time.

Opaque propaganda was also a feature of the communist states. It was opaque in the sense that people exposed to it would ordinarily not reflect on its literal meaning. When locals would hear references to the state being a workers' state, few of them would think about what one might usefully mean by that claim. Propaganda figured, in some ways, thus, as "verbal noise, a stream of words and phrases whose meaning [was] irrelevant," according to Jan Kubik,

> but which prevent[ed] people from communicating and clearly articulating their own views, ideas, convictions, or beliefs. Thus even when [the] language of propaganda [was] not effective in realizing its other functions, it [could] still be highly efficient in obstructing social communication.[7]

The proliferation of slogans pasted on walls and billboards contributed to the dulling of the mind. In Bulgaria, for example, public signs in the communist era included "Expose the violators of cleanliness," "Criticism and self-criticism are an objective necessity for each labour collective," and the ironic "Verbal waste is inadmissible."[8] The constant bombardment with communist formulations, slogans, and propaganda also entailed a "furious assault on non-ideological cognition,"[9] and, in the presence of feelings of powerlessness, had the potential to induce alienation and promote political apathy. While apathy was not one of the communists' original goals, they could live with it, as reflected in Kádár's famous slogan, "Whoever is not against us is with us."

Positive and negative features of communism

It is easy to find literature pointing at negative features of communism. Apart from the authoritarian character of the East Central European regimes of the communist era and the direct subservience of the six bloc states to the Kremlin, one can also mention the economic inefficiency of the communist systems, the limits to religious and cultural freedom which they imposed, the extensive surveillance in at least some of these societies (Romania as an extreme example), and the abuse of legal and extra-legal mechanisms to control society and to punish or even liquidate so-called "enemies of the people". Add to that the control of the media and limits to foreign travel and you have the picture of closed societies. Indeed, in certain countries of the region, citizens could be punished for any contacts with foreigners.

But communism, as practised in East Central Europe between the late 1940s and the end of the 1980s, was not without some benefits for citizens. To begin with, the necessities of life such as basic foods, fuel, rent, and public transport were heavily subsidized, thus keeping prices low. Second, medical care was provided free of charge. Third, novelists, composers, and artists who were prepared to create works that were pleasing to the authorities were richly rewarded, with high salaries, high prestige, and other perks. Fourth, although these regimes fell far short of achieving gender equality whether in political representation or salaries or home life, they did somewhat better than their Western counterparts when it came to political representation and salaries.[10] By and large, the communists honored the principle of equal pay for equal work. Inequality crept in when women proved unable to obtain or retain certain positions and found the doors open to work in lesser-paid jobs in hospitality or textiles, for example. Fifth, for those wanting to attend public concerts or drama, the prices were so heavily subsidized that attendance was all but free (as I recall from the time I enjoyed a front-row seat at a concert in Budapest in 1968). And sixth, higher education was available at no cost or low cost to any who were not politically compromised.

Yet communism could be grey – in the most literal sense of the word. Traveling by U-Bahn between East and West Berlin in summer 1988, I was struck by how drab the buildings of East Berlin were, as contrasted with the gaily colored buildings of West Berlin. Also – at that time – the only restaurants in East Berlin were

320 Sabrina P. Ramet

those offering the cuisines of the bloc countries: here a Czech restaurant, there a Russian restaurant, and so forth. When I inquired about an Italian or Mexican restaurant, I was told that these cuisines were not found in the German Democratic Republic's capital city (although these cuisines were increasingly present in socialist Yugoslavia). This reveals two things about the communism of the bloc: first, that these were not rich countries but, on the contrary, countries having to focus on sufficiency, rather than luxury for any but the elite; and second, that, in the absence of private enterprise, there was no need to attract attention to one brand over others – indeed, in many cases, whatever the labels might suggest, there was only one brand.[11]

There was something else which struck me during the year I spent in Belgrade, October 1979-August 1980, and in subsequent visits to that city as well as to other cities in socialist Yugoslavia, which is that, in the check-out queues in supermarkets, before one reached the cashier, there were always political books on sale – especially, in the "old days", the works of Tito and Kardelj. Needless to say, since I was writing about the politics of socialist Yugoslavia, I was pleased to be able to take advantage of these offerings, even if I could find a greater variety of political writings at the local "Komunist" bookshop.

I have stressed elsewhere, including herein and also in the foregoing chapters, why communism crumbled and imploded.[12] But, where Yugoslavia was concerned, there was also the extreme federalization of the system, beginning in 1967 and culminating in the constitution of 1974 with its fissiparous dynamic. In addition, throughout East Central Europe there was the example of the West, often misunderstood or fancifully imagined, but by that virtue all the more powerful. I shared a train compartment with some working class Yugoslavs in Autumn 1979. I remember them being excited to learn that I lived at the time in the United States. Their reaction was to express envy at the "fact" that "everyone" in America was rich. When I told them that I was a working class kid and not rich, they would not believe me. "You live in America," they replied. "Obviously, you are rich." There were, of course, blind spots about the West – including how some profit-driven companies treat their employees, how certain political parties may serve the interests of the rich and not those of the general public, and how certain religious organizations may transgress individual rights, especially, in the Reagan era and since 2016, where access to abortion is concerned. But these and other illusions and blind spots about the West likewise contributed to the speed with which communism was abandoned in 1989–1990. They spied a planet from afar and mistook it for a star.

Notes

1 In Bulgaria, Chervenkov, who was stripped of his prime ministership in April 1956, had lost the party leadership two years earlier.
2 See my definition of *disaffection* in my article, "Disaffection and Dissent in East Germany", in *World Politics,* Vol. 37, No. 1 (October 1984).

3 See my definitions of the terms *dissent* and *opposition* in my book, *Nonconformity, Dissent, Opposition, and Resistance in Germany, 1933–1990* (London and New York: Palgrave Macmillan, 2020).

4 Robert K. Merton, "The Unanticipated Consequences of Purposive Social Action", in *American Sociological Review*, Vol. 1, No. 6 (December 1936), p. 894, n1.

5 *Ibid.*, p. 896.

6 Amdrew Ira Friedson, *The Essays on Unintended Consequences of Public Policy,* Syracuse University: Economics Dissertations 91 (2012), p. 1, at https://surface.syr.edu/cgi/viewcontent.cgi?article=1090&context=ecn_etd [accessed on 28 November 2021].

7 Jan Kubik, *The Power of Symbols Against the Symbols of Power: The Rise of Solidarity and the Fall of State Socialism in Poland* (University Park: The Pennsylvania State University Press, 1994), p. 48.

8 Dimana Trankova, Anthony Georgieff, Georgi Lozanov, and Mihail Gruev, *A Guide to Communist Bulgaria, Vol. 3: Signs of the Times,* trans. by Ivan Sokolov, consultancy and advice by Mihail Gruev, ed. by Anthon Georgieff (London: Free Speech International Foundation, 2018), pp. 196, 203, 207.

9 Maurice Bloch (1985), as quoted in Kubik, *The Power of Symbols*, p. 147.

10 Sharon Wolchik, "Ideology and Equality: The Status of Women in Eastern and Western Europe", in *Comparative Political Studies*, Vol. 13, No. 4 (January 1981), pp. 445–476.

11 This is not unknown in the United States. When I was in high school in Anaheim, California, in the 1960s, I spent one summer working at the local Kraft Foods factory where we packed the same mayonnaise into jars with labels from three or four different brands.

12 See, for example, my *Social Currents in Eastern Europe: The Sources and Consequences of the Great Transformation*, 2nd ed. (Durham, NC and London: Duke University Press, 1995), especially chap. 1–2.

FURTHER READING

This section includes mainly works written in English, but also a few written in German. I list six works in each section, and have included at least some of the most basic literature. However, I have also included some lesser known works which I believe should not be forgotten.

General & regional

Behrend, Ivan T. *Central and Eastern Europe 1944–1993: Detour from the Periphery to the Periphery* (Cambridge: Cambridge University Press, 1996)

Crampton, R. J. *Eastern Europe in the Twentieth Century and After*, 2nd ed. (London and New York: Routledge, 1997)

Falk, Barbara J. *The Dilemmas of Dissidence in East-Central Europe: Citizen Intellectuals and Philosopher Kings* (Budapest and New York: Central European University Press, 2003)

Fejtö, François. *A History of the People's Democracies Since Stalin* (Harmondsworth: Penguin Books, 1974)

Ramet, Sabrina P. *Social Currents in Eastern Europe: The Sources and Consequences of the Great Transformation*, 2nd ed. (Durham, NC and London: Duke University Press, 1995)

Skilling, H. Gordon. *Samizdat and an Independent Society in Central and Eastern Europe* (Columbus: Ohio State University Press, 1989)

Albania

Biberaj, Elez. *Albania: A Socialist Maverick* (Boulder: Westview Press, 1990)

Dravis, Michael W. "Storming Fortress Albania: American Covert Operations in Microcosm, 1949–54", in *Intelligence and National Security*, Vol. 7, No. 4 (1992): 425–442

Griffith, William E. *Albania and the Sino-Soviet Rift* (Cambridge, MA: MIT Press, 1963)

Logoreci, Anton. *The Albanians: Europe's Forgotten Survivors* (London: Victor Gollancz, 1977)

Prifti, Peter R. *Socialist Albania Since 1944: Domestic and Foreign Developments* (Cambridge, MA: MIT Press, 1978)

Schnytzer, Adi. *Stalinist Economic Strategy in Practice: The Case of Albania* (Oxford: Oxford University Press, 1982)

Bulgaria

Atanasova, Ivanka Nedeva. "Lyudmila Zhivkova and the Paradox of Ideology and Identity in Communist Bulgaria", in *East European Politics and Societies*, Vol. 18, No. 2 (2004): 278–315

Bell, John D. *The Bulgarian Communist Party from Blagoev to Zhivkov* (Stanford, CA: Hoover Institution Press, 1986)

Brown, J. F. *Bulgaria Under Communist Rule* (New York: Praeger Publishers, 1970)

Crampton, R. J. *A Concise History of Bulgaria*, 2nd ed. (Cambridge: Cambridge University Press, 2005)

Doynov, Plamen. "The Sovietization of Bulgarian Literature and the 'Bulgarization' of Socialist Realism", in *Studia Litteraria Universitatis Iagellonicae Cracoviensis*, Vol. 10, No. 4 (2015): 333–345

Oren, Nissan. *Revolution Administered: Agrarianism and Communism in Bulgaria* (Baltimore and London: The Johns Hopkins University Press, 1973)

Czechoslovakia

Heimann, Mary. *Czechoslovakia: The State That Failed* (New Haven, CT: Yale University Press, 2009)

Köhler-Wagnerová, Alena. *Die Frau im Sozialismus – Beispiel ČSSR* (Hamburg: Hoffmann und Campe Verlag, 1974)

Lukes, Igor. "The Rudolf Slánský Affair: New Evidence", in *Slavic Review*, Vol. 58, No. 1 (Spring 1999): 160–187

Skilling, H. Gordon. "Independent Currents in Czechoslovakia", in *Problems of Communism*, Vol. 34, No. 1 (January–February 1985): 32–49

Suda, Zdenek. *Zealots and Rebels: A History of the Ruling Communist Party of Czechoslovakia* (Stanford, CA: Hoover Institution Press, 1980)

Williams, Kieran. *The Prague Spring and Its Aftermath: Czechoslovak Politics 1968–1970* (Cambridge: Cambridge University Press, 1997)

German democratic republic

Childs, David. *The GDR: Moscow's German Ally*, 2nd ed. (London: Unwin Hyman, 1988)

Fricke, Karl Wilhelm. *Opposition und Widerstand in der DDR. Ein politischer Report* (Cologne: Verlag Wissenschaft und Politik, 1984)

Fulbrook, Mary. *Anatomy of a Dictatorship: Inside the GDR 1949–1989* (Oxford: Oxford University Press, 1995)

Goeckel, Robert F. *The Lutheran Church and the East German State: Political Conflict and Change Under Ulbricht and Honecker* (Ithaca, NY: Cornell University Press, 1990)

Malycha, Andreas. *Die SED in der Ära Honecker: Machtstrukturen, Entscheidungsmechanismen und Konfliktfelder in der Staatspartei 1971 bis 1989* (Göttingen: De Gruyter-Oldenbourg, 2014)

Weber, Hermann. *Geschichte der DDR*, rev. and expanded ed. (Munich: Deutscher Taschenbuch Verlag GmbH, 2000)

Hungary

Behrend, Iván T. "Contemporary Hungary, 1956–1984", in Peter Sugar et al., eds. *A History of Hungary* (Bloomington and Indianapolis: Indiana University Press, 1990)

Demaitre, Ann. "The Hungarian Shores of Realism", in *Comparative Literature Studies*, Vol. 1, No. 4 (1964): 311–323

Kovrig, Bennett. *Communism in Hungary: From Kun to Kádár* (Stanford, CA: Hoover Institution Press, 1979)

Molnár, Miklós. *A Concise History of Hungary* (Cambridge: Cambridge University Press, 2001)

Sasvári, Edit, Sándor Hornyik, and Hedvig Turai, eds. *Art in Hungary 1956–1980: Doublespeak and Beyond* (London: Thomas and Hudson, 2018)

Tőkés, Rudolf L. *Hungary's Negotiated Revolution: Economic Reform, Social Change and Political Succession* (Cambridge: Cambridge University Press, 1996)

Poland

Borodziej, Włodzimierz. *Geschichte Polens im 20. Jahrhundert* (Munich: C. H. Beck oHG, 2010)

Bylander, Cindy. "Responses to Adversity: The Polish Composers Union and Musical Life in the 1970s and 1980s", in *The Musical Quarterly*, Vol. 95, No. 4 (Winter 2012): 459–509

de Weydenthal, Jan B. *The Communists of Poland: An Historical Outline*, rev. ed. (Stanford, CA: Hoover Institution Press, 1986)

Lukowski, Jerzy, and Hubert Zawadzski. *A Concise History of Poland*, 3rd ed. (Cambridge: Cambridge University Press, 2019)

Ornatowski, Cezar M. "'Let Thy Spirit Renew This Earth': The Rhetoric of Pope John Paul II and the Political Transformation in Poland, 1979–1989", in *Journal for the Study of Religion*, Vol. 14, No. 1 (2001): 67–88

Pirie, Donald, Jekaterina Young, and Christopher Carroll, eds. *Polish Realities: The Arts in Poland 1980–1989* (Glasgow: Third Eye Centre, 1990)

Romania

Deletant, Dennis. "Cheating the Censor: Romanian Writers Under Communism", in *Central Europe*, Vol. 6, No. 2 (November 2008): 122–171

Ionescu, Ghita. *Communism in Rumania, 1944–1962* (Oxford: Oxford University Press, 1964)

King, Robert R. *History of the Romanian Communist Party* (Stanford, CA: Hoover Institution Press, 1980)

Kunze, Thomas. *Nicolae Ceaușescu. Eine Biographie*, 4th ed. (Berlin: Christoph Links Verlag, 2017)

Stan, Lavinia, and Lucian Turcescu. "The Devil's Confessors: Priests, Communists, Spies, and Informers", in *East European Politics and Societies*, Vol. 19, No. 4 (2005): 655–685

Tismaneanu, Vladimir. *Stalinism for All Seasons: A Political History of Romanian Communism* (Berkeley and Los Angeles: University of California Press, 2003)

Yugoslavia

Buchenau, Klaus. *Orthodoxie und Katholizismus in Jugoslawien 1945–1991* (Wiesbaden: Harrassowitz Verlag, 2004)

Erjavec, Aleš, and Marina Gržinić. *Ljubljana, Ljubljana: The Eighties in Slovene Art and Culture* (Ljubljana: Založba Mladinska knjiga, 1991)

Pirjevec, Jože. *Tito and His Comrades* (Madison, WI: University of Wisconsin Press, 2018)

Ramet, Sabrina P. *Balkan Babel: The Disintegration of Yugoslavia from the Death of Tito to the Fall of Milošević*, 4th ed. (Boulder, CO: Westview Press, 2002)

———. *The Three Yugoslavias: State-Building and Legitimation, 1918–2005* (Washington, DC and Bloomington: The Woodrow Wilson Center Press & Indiana University Press, 2006)

Wachtel, Andrew Baruch. *Making a Nation, Breaking a Nation: Literature and Cultural Politics in Yugoslavia* (Stanford: Stanford University Press, 1998)

ABOUT THE AUTHOR

Sabrina P. Ramet is a Professor Emerita at the Norwegian University of Science & Technology (NTNU). She earned her Ph.D. in Political Science at UCLA in 1981. She has conducted more than 400 research interviews in Germany, Austria, Hungary, Italy, Norway, Poland, the Czech Republic, Slovenia, Croatia, Bosnia-Herzegovina, Serbia, Macedonia, and the United States. She is the author of 15 previous scholarly books, including *Alternatives to Democracy in Twentieth-Century Europe: Collectivist Visions of Modernity* (Central European University Press, 2019) and *Nonconformity, Dissent, Opposition, and Resistance in Germany, 1933–1990: The Freedom to Conform* (Palgrave Macmillan, 2020). She is also editor or co-editor of 40 books – most recently *Anti-fascism in European History: from the 1920s to Today,* co-edited with Jože Pirjevec and Egon Pelikan (Central European University Press, in production).

INDEX